INTERNATIONAL BACCALAUREATE

Business Management

FOURTH EDITION

Paul Hoang

Copyright ©IBID Press, Victoria, Australia.

www.ibid.com.au

First published in 2018 by IBID Press, Victoria, Australia.

Library Catalogue:

Hoang P.

1. Business Management 4th Edition

2. International Baccalaureate.

Series Title: International Baccalaureate in Detail

ISBN: 978-1-921917-90-5

Cover design by Key-Strokes.

Published by IBID Press, 36 Quail Crescent, Melton, 3337, Australia.

Printed in China through Red Planet Print Management.

Dedication

About the author

Paul Hoang is Vice Principal and IB Coordinator at Sha Tin College, part of the English Schools Foundation in Hong Kong. Sha Tin College was the first ESF School to introduce the IB Diploma Programme in Hong Kong and has over 350 IB Diploma Programme students in the Senior School. In the past, Paul has also taught Mathematics, ICT, TOK and Physical Education. Previously he taught at Hasmonean High School in London and Wallington Grammar School in Surrey, both in the UK.

Paul is a highly experienced teacher trainer and internationally recognized author. He has been teaching both IB Business Management and IB Economics since 2001. He has experience as an IB examiner and is a Workshop Leader for the IB Diploma Programme in Business Management and Economics. Paul is also the Group 3 associate editor for IB Review, published by Hodder Education, and lead-author of Extended Essay: Skills for Success, also published by Hodder Education. He is author of the annual Case Study Pack resource for the pre-seen Paper 1 Business Management exams, available from Level7 Education. Paul has also been an educational consultant at his alma mater, The Institute of Education, University of London, UK.

Aside from work, Paul is a practicing 2nd Dan Taekwondo instructor and likes to play football on a regular basis; being a Londoner, he is a passionate follower of Arsenal Football Club. Most important though, Paul enjoys spending time with his wife and two sons.

Paul Hoang

E: paulhoang88@gmail.com

T: paulhoang88 #IBBusinessManagement

Paul Hoang with some of his Business Management students

Author's acknowledgements

I would like to thank Roz and Richard Paisey, Ian and Pauline Ashworth, Margo Goodchild, Pastor Harry Lucenay, Sangu Ngan and Lisa Hoang. You have all shaped me in more ways than you will ever know. I am forever grateful for all the things that you have done for me and the family.

I would also like to thank the publishers and editors at IBID Press: Rory McAuliffe who believed in me and gave me the opportunity to undertake this project back in 2007 when we published the first edition textbook; Fabio Cirrito for his guidance and trust in my approach; and to Millicent Henry and Jodie Henry for their endless hours of proof-reading and editing the fourth edition. I could not have completed this project without their on-going advice and support. It has been a pleasure and priviledge to have worked with you all for over 10 years.

Paul Hoang

Acknowledgements

The publisher and author would like to thank the following individuals and organizations for their kind permission to reproduce personal and copyright material:

Pages: 18 Flowers by Cam: Cam Tran; 19 EXP The Chinese Experience: Keith and Tonina Hoang; 31 Adidas logo: Adidas Group; 44 Kidzplap Bouncy Castles; 56 Skoda logo: Skoda Auto; 57 Shell logo: Royal Dutch Shell; 86 Hoang Ahn; 88 A.S. Watson Group logo: A.S. Watson Group; 100 Carlsberg Group logo: Carlsberg Group; 159 Ferrari; 175 Vinayak Textiles; 215 The Body Shop Internation plc; 226 Deutsche Telekom logo: Deutsche Telekom; 227 The Association of Teachers and Lecturers logo: ATL; 238 diamonds: Wiki Commons GFL; 250 Goff's Fruit & Veg.: courtesy Ian Goff, USA; 252 Apple store frontage Apple Inc.; 260 © Photo courtesy of Katia Torralba Jewellery Ltd.; 261 TMR Day-Care Centre: courtesy CentreThuy and Mark Rees, Hong Kong; 266 Airbus: © AIRBUS – Central Entity; 284 Platform 9 3/4: Wiki Commons GFL; 288 Holden utility: GMH Australia; 308 ACS Playframes; 329 Chelsea FC: Wiki Commons GFL; 362 FC Barcelona: Wiki Commons GFL; 381 Oasis photo: Oasis Hong Kong Airlines; 382 Photgraph courtesy of Victor Chine; 383 Photo courtesy of Andrea Winders and Tina Dutton, www.pinkladiesmembers. co.uk; 388 Photograph courtesy of Laura Brown; 411 EBEA logo: EBEA magazine www.ebea.org.uk; 410 Zafran Craftphoria, courtesy Wahida Mostfa; 433 French Connection logo: French Connection Group plc; 438 FCUK, Festival Walk branch, Hong Kong: French Connection Group plc; 447 Virgin Blue logo: Virgin Group Ltd.; 454 Yoda postage stamp: © 2007 USPS. All Rights Reserved.; 456 WWF logo: World Wildlife Fund; 460 Ferrari F430 Spider (Paris Motor Show 2011): © Sébastien Morliere; 463 Kim Do Yi logo: Kim Do Yi Ltd.; 465 YouTube logo: TM YouTube; 473 Costco logo: Costco Wholesale Corporation; 485 Wallington High School for Girls emblem: Wallington High School for Girls; 505 Amazon delivery van: Wiki Commons GFL; 524 Bristol Cars logo: Bristol Cars Ltd. www.bristolcars.co.uk; 529 'Bristol Fighter': Bristol Cars Ltd., www.bristolcars.co.uk; 534 Subway, www. subway.com; 545 Mercedes-Benz AMG: Mercedes-Benz; 548 BSI Kitemark: British Standards Institution; 559 Volkswagen; 568 DS Cafe, Brisbane, Australia; 587 Johnson & Johnson logo: Johnson & Johnson; 589 Steve Jobs: Wiki Commons GFL; 639 MLA logo: Modern Language Teachers Association.

About this book

This is the fourth edition of Paul Hoang's bestselling textbook, covering the IB Diploma specifications in Business Management (first exams May 2016).

The text is presented in full colour. The content has been revised throughout to match the fourth edition of the Guide to the course (updated May 2017, with the latest Guide released in October 2017). There are 225 exam-style questions. Over 700 key terms have been identified and defined. There are review questions for every Unit. Each Unit ends with a section on the six conceptual themes in Business Management: change, culture, ethics, globalization, innovation and strategy (CUEGIS). These concepts help students to think about Business Management in a more critical and holistic way. A total of 125 examination tips and over 200 Theory of Knowledge questions are integrated throughout the book, along with 70 IB Learner Profile connections. Another new feature of the 4th edition textbook is the inclusion of over 40 Common Mistakes to avoid in the exams and 70 CUEGIS essay questions for students to attempt. Over 130 short case studies have also be included to encourage students to apply their learning to the context of real world business organizations.

An accompany Answer Book and Student Workbook, both written by Paul Hoang, are available from IBID Press (http://www.ibid.com.au/business-management/). The Student Workbook also comes complete with suggested answers to all questions.

Testimonials

"This textbook is, unquestionably, the standard to which all other books attempt to measure up." Marc Brothers, Indonesia

"Thank you very much for this textbook – I really, truly appreciate this! From everything that I have seen and read, Paul Hoang is a leader within the IB Business Management field." Pam Monte Zosa, Uruguay

"I am very impressed! I can see from your textbook the enormous time and effort you have dedicated to education. I need to congratulate Sha Tin College for being able to hire such a top class educator. Maureen Tam, Hong Kong

"Let me please reiterate my thanks for your wonderful book. My students and I are enjoying it immensely - it reads and flows so well." Bettina Hoar, USA

"Sincere thanks to Paul as this textbook makes the students' lives (and ours too!!) so much easier, being so well tailored to the IB requirements, with excellent recent and relevant examples." Roxie Burnes, United Kingdom

"Simply the best textbook for the IB Business Management course – my students love the book!" Matt Temp, Canada

"If you are teaching this subject at an IB school, there is no other choice - buy Paul Hoang's textbook, you will not regret it. I cannot recommend his work enough, it is now in the 4th edition, and better than ever. His workbook also helped me out tremendously." Fabrice Vanegas, Thailand

"Your book is my absolute favourite for IB Business! Honestly, I wouldn't be without it. It adds so much extra than the typical course textbook - thank-you!" Helen Staniland, UAE

"I would like to offer my gratitude to you for your amazing book, which has helped me to understand the many aspects of Business Management. Your case studies really make the understanding of everything much easier. We have been using your textbook from Day 1 and honestly surviving IB BM would have been impossible without it!" Yatharth Dhoot, Tamil Nadu, India (IB student)

TEACHER SUPPORT PACK

Solutions to the exercises can be purchased as a pdf.

Full details about these solutions can be found at our website:

www.ibid.com.au

Contents

1.1 Introduction to business management

SL/HL content	Assessment objective
The role of businesses in combining human, physical and financial resources to create goods and services	AO2
The main business functions and their roles: • human resources • finance and accounts • marketing • operations	AO2
Primary, secondary, tertiary and quaternary sectors	AO2
The nature of business activity in each sector and the impact of sectoral change on business activity	AO2
The role of entrepreneurship (and entrepreneur) and intrapreneurship (and intrapreneur) in overall business activity	AO3
Reasons for starting up a business or an enterprise	AO2
Common steps in the process of starting up a business or an enterprise	AO2
Problems that a new business or enterprise may face	AO2
The elements of a business plan	AO2

© IBO, 2017

Business organization and environment

CORE

The role of businesses

The role of businesses in combining human, physical and financial resources to create goods and services. AO2
© IBO, 2017

A **business** is a decision-making organization involved in the process of using inputs to produce goods and/or to provide services (see Figure 1.1.a). *Inputs* are the resources that a business uses in the production process, e.g. labour and raw materials. This process generates *outputs* (also known as products). The term **product** can refer to both goods and services. **Goods** are physical products, e.g. cars, computers, books and food. **Services** are intangible products, e.g. haircuts, bus rides, education and health care. Businesses can also provide goods and services to other organizations, such as freight transportation and distribution.

Management guru Peter Drucker famously said that the only purpose of a business is to create customers, i.e. the role of businesses is to combine human, physical and financial resources to create goods and services in order to satisfy the needs and wants of people, organizations and governments.

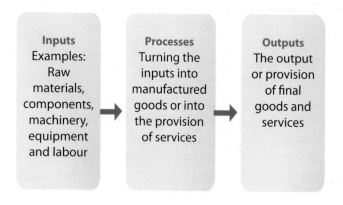

Figure 1.1.a The production process

1

Needs are the basic necessities that a person must have to survive, e.g. food, water, warmth, shelter and clothing. **Wants** are people's desires, i.e. the things they would like to have, e.g. a cake, a larger home, a new smartphone or to go on an overseas holiday.

Figure 1.1.b Cakes are a desire, not a need

Common mistake

The terms **customer** and **consumer** and are often used interchangeably by candidates, although they have different meanings. Make sure you can distinguish between the two concepts and use them in the right context – *customers* are the people or organizations that buy a product whereas *consumers* are the ones who actually use the product. These may be the same entity (e.g. someone who buys and eats a meal), but not necessarily such as parents (customers) paying for their children's (consumers) birthday presents.

Box 1.1.a Types of products

- **Consumer goods** are products sold to the general public, rather than to other businesses. They can be further split into *consumer durables* (products that last a long time and can be used repeatedly, e.g. electronic gadgets, cars, jewellery, clothes and home furniture), or *non-durables* (those that need to be consumed shortly after their purchase as they do not last or cannot be reused, e.g. fresh food, beverages, medicines and newspapers.
- **Capital goods** (or **producer goods**) are physical products bought by businesses to produce other goods and/or services. Examples include buildings (premises), computers, machinery, tools and specialist equipment.
- **Services** are intangible products provided by businesses. The service is not tangible, but the results are, e.g. health care, transportation, dining, sports (recreation) centres, legal advice, financial advice and education.

The main functions of business

The main business functions and their roles: human resources, finance and accounts, marketing and operations. AO2
© IBO, 2017

For a business to operate effectively, tasks must be carried out by functional areas (or departments). These interdependent functional areas are: human resources, finance and accounts, marketing and operations management. The main business functional areas must work together in order to achieve the organization's goals.

Human resources – The human resources (HR) department is responsible for managing the personnel of the organization. In managing people, the HR department is likely to deal with the following issues: workforce planning, recruitment, training, appraisal, dismissals and redundancies, and outsourcing human resource strategies (see Unit 2.1).

Finance and accounts – The finance and accounts department is in charge of managing the organization's money. The finance and accounts director must ensure that accurate recording and reporting of financial documentation takes place. This is to comply with legal requirements (e.g. to prevent deliberate understating of profits to avoid corporate taxes) and to inform those interested in the financial position of the business (such as shareholders and potential investors). Finance and accounts topics are covered in Units 3.1–3.9.

Marketing – The marketing department is responsible for identifying and satisfying the needs and wants of customers. It is ultimately in charge of ensuring that the firm's products sell. This is done through a series of activities such as market research, test marketing, advertising and branding. Functions of the marketing department can be summed up as the traditional four Ps of marketing (see Unit 4.5):

- **Product** – ensuring that goods and services meet the customer's requirements, such as a product's various sizes, colours, packaging and core functions. Other roles related to the product include product differentiation and product position mapping (see Unit 4.2).

- **Price** – using various pricing strategies to sell the products of a business. Numerous pricing strategies (see Unit 4.5) can be used, depending on factors such as the level of demand, the costs of producing the good or service, and the number of substitute products available.

- **Promotion** – making sure that customers know about the firm's products. This is often done through the mass media, e.g. television and newspaper advertising. Alternatively, cheaper methods include the use of sales promotions, social networking and guerrilla marketing (see Unit 4.5).

- **Place** – ensuring that goods and services are available in convenient places for consumers to buy. Marketing managers must ensure that they select appropriate ways to distribute products to the marketplace, e.g. online purchases, retail outlets, vending machines.

Operations – Also known as **operations management** or **production**, this functional area of an organization is responsible for the process of converting raw materials and components into finished goods, ready for sale and delivery to customers. Examples of production include the extraction of crude oil, car manufacturing and the construction of roads. Operations also applies to the process of providing services to customers as in the case of hotels, restaurants, beauty salons and financial institutions. Operations topics are covered in Units 5.1–5.7.

A large organization is able to allocate resources to each of the four functional areas, making their roles easily identifiable. In a small business owned by just one person, each function would need to be carried out by the same person. In practice, the four functional areas of a business are highly interrelated, e.g. the production department relies on the talents of effective marketing staff to sell their products. Equally, marketers can only do their jobs if they have a decent product to sell and the necessary financial resources to do so.

Question 1.1.1   The business of education

Education is big business. Schools can earn **revenue** from numerous sources, such as tuition fees (for fee-paying schools), grants from the government and fund-raising events. They might also lease out their facilities (such as classrooms, sports hall, drama studios and swimming pool) during weekends and school holidays. Schools use the revenues to finance their **costs of production**, such as staff salaries and the maintenance of the buildings. Parents might also have to pay for items such as school uniform, textbooks, stationery, sports equipment and food.

(a) Distinguish between **revenue** and **costs of production**.　　　　　*[4 marks]*

(b) Examine how business functions operate in an organization such as a school.　　　*[6 marks]*

Business sectors

Primary, secondary, tertiary and quaternary sectors. AO2
The nature of business activity in each sector and the impact of sectoral change on business activity. AO2
© IBO, 2017

Businesses can be classified according to the stage of production that they are engaged in.

Primary sector

Businesses operating in the primary sector are involved with the extraction, harvesting and conversion of natural resources, e.g. agriculture, fishing, mining, forestry and oil extraction. Primary sector activities tend to account for a large percentage of output and employment in *less economically developed countries* (LEDCs). Businesses operating in the primary sector in *more economically developed countries* (MEDCs) use mechanisation and automation, such as combine harvesters and automatic watering systems.

Figure 1.1.c Agriculture is part of the primary sector

Business organization and environment

CORE

3

As economies develop, there is less reliance on the primary sector in terms of employment and national output, partly because there is little **value added** in primary production (the difference between the value of inputs (the costs of production) and the value of outputs (the revenue received for the goods sold). For example, LEDCs can only sell tea leaves and coffee beans at relatively low prices.

Secondary sector

Businesses that operate in the secondary sector are involved in the manufacturing or construction of products, e.g. clothes manufacturers, publishing firms, breweries and bottlers, construction firms, electronics manufacturers and energy production companies. The output is then sold to customers, be they other businesses, governments, foreign buyers or domestic customers.

Economically developing countries tend to have a dominant secondary sector that accounts for a relatively large proportion of the country's national output. Economists argue that the secondary sector is the wealth-creating sector because manufactured goods can be exported worldwide to earn income for the country. Value is added to the natural resources used during the production process, e.g. the mass production and export of motor vehicles and consumer electronics have helped countries such as Taiwan and South Korea to prosper.

Fiigure 1.1.d Construction is part of the secondary sector

Tertiary sector

Businesses in the tertiary sector specialise in providing services to the general population. Examples of industries in the tertiary sector include: retailing, transportation and distribution, banking, finance, insurance, health care, leisure and tourism, and entertainment.

Note that goods can be transformed in the process of providing a service. This happens in a restaurant when the chef prepares a meal with fresh ingredients. The focus is, nevertheless, on the people who are providing the service – the chef and the waiting staff who serve the diners.

In MEDCs such as Canada and Germany, the tertiary sector tends to be the most substantial sector in terms of both employment and as a percentage of *gross domestic product* (the value of the country's output each year). For example, in the USA and UK, around 80% of the labour force work in the tertiary sector. The decline of the manufacturing sector in MEDCs also signifies their growing reliance on the tertiary sector.

Figure 1.1.e Public transportation is part of the tertiary sector

Quaternary sector

A subcategory of the tertiary sector, businesses in the quaternary sector are involved in intellectual, knowledge-based activities that generate and share information. Examples include information communication technology (ICT), research and development (R&D), consultancy services, and scientific research. For example, pharmaceutical companies invest heavily in R&D to create innovative products, develop new production methods, improve efficiency, and to tap into markets. The quaternary sector exists mainly in MEDCs as it requires a highly educated workforce. It is also the sector in which businesses invest for further growth and evolution.

Figure 1.1.f ICT is part of the quaternary sector

The four business sectors are linked through the **chain of production** which tracks the stages of an item's production, from the extraction of raw materials used to make the product all the way through to it being delivered to the consumer (see Figure 1.1.g).

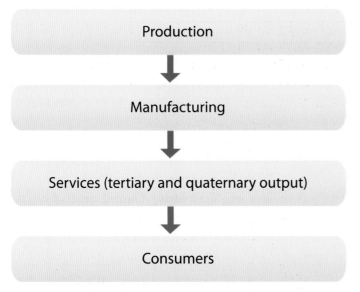

Figure1.1.g The chain of production

All four business sectors are *interdependent* because each sector relies on the others to remain in existence. For example, raw materials such as crude oil, would not be extracted if there was no need for oil refinery whilst there would not be any need for oil refiners if there were no customers of the oil, such as motorists and airline companies in the tertiary sector. Likewise, firms in the secondary sector rely on their suppliers for stocks to ensure that their production targets are met. Businesses are also interdependent as they all need energy, ICT, manufactured producer goods, financial services and management consultants.

Sectoral change refers to a shift in the relative share of national output and employment that is attributed to each business sector over time. Typically, countries develop by shifting the majority of national output being contributed by the primary sector (such as agriculture, fishing and mining) to manufacturing and then eventually to the tertiary and quaternary sectors.

Primary sector production tends to yield low added value. In order to develop economically, there must be a shift in business activity to the manufacturing and service sectors which have higher added value. This process is known as industrialisation. Nevertheless, some countries are still able to exploit their natural advantage and specialisation in the supply of agricultural and primary products. For example, even though only 2% of the French population work in the primary sector, the country benefits immensely from its agricultural exports sold all around the world.

Automation and mechanisation in modern societies have caused decline in the secondary (manufacturing) sector in terms of employment.

More economically developed countries are able to exploit the tertiary and quaternary sectors as the main contributors to national output and employment. Businesses such as Apple and Samsung see themselves as operating in the services sector (they outsource production of their smartphones and computer hardware to manufacturers such as Foxconn). Apple realises that there is more added value in the tertiary sector – rather than receiving one-off payments from selling manufactured equipment, it can receive a flow of revenue from offering after-sales services such as maintenance and support services.

The sectoral change in MEDCs has been due to changes in several factors, including the ones below. These changes have created huge opportunities for the tertiary and quaternary sectors.

- Higher household incomes – The demand for services is positively correlated to changes in income levels. As a country develops, consumers demand more services such as dining out at restaurants, visits to the hairdresser and seeking advice on financial planning.

- More leisure time – A feature of higher standards of living is the increase in leisure time. As nations develop, people tend to have more time for leisure and recreation (such as sporting activities, visits to the theatre, and going on holiday).

- Greater focus on customer services – Firms have realised that good customer service before, during and after a sale can be an important source of competitive advantage.

- Increasing reliance on support services – Businesses need ever more sophisticated support services. Firms are increasingly relying on the services of other businesses, such as: subcontractors, advertising agencies, market research analysts, technicians and management consultants. As businesses grow internationally, they will also increasingly rely on the services of financiers, accountants and lawyers.

Business organization and environment

CORE

Question 1.1.2 Production sectors

Study the data below and answer the questions that follow. A, B and C represent three countries: France, Bangladesh and the Philippines (although not necessarily in that order).

Structure of employment (%)

	A	B	C
Agriculture	29	3	41
Manufacturing	18	24	30
Services	53	73	29

(a) Identify the countries A, B and C.   *[3 marks]*

(b) With reference to the data above, explain your answer to Question 1.1.2 (a).   *[6 marks]*

The role of entrepreneurship and intrapreneurship

The role of entrepreneurship (and entrepreneur) and intrapreneurship (and intrapreneur) in overall business activity.

AO3

© IBO, 2017

An entrepreneur is an individual who plans, organizes and manages a business, taking on financial risks in doing so. The term was coined by Richard Cantillon (1680–1734) an Irish–French economist. Entrepreneurship describes the trait of business leaders who tend to be distinctive in their temperament, attitude and outlook who drive the business. French economist and businessman Jean-Baptiste Say (1767–1832) described an entrepreneur as an individual who combines the other three factors of production (see Box 1.1.b) to produce a good or service. By selling the good or service produced, the entrepreneur pays rent for land, wages to labour and interest on capital – what remains is then the profit for risk taking.

Entrepreneurs have the skills needed to oversee the whole production process, whilst having the ability and willingness to take potentially high risks. Successful entrepreneurs tend to be creative, innovative and passionate. They search for and exploit business opportunities by forecasting and/or responding to changes in the marketplace.

Intrapreneurship is the act of being an entrepreneur but as an employee within a large organization. The term was coined by American entrepreneurs Gifford and Elizabeth Pinchot (1978), co-founders of the Bainbridge Graduate Institute in the USA. They described an **intrapreneur** as an employee who thinks and acts as an entrepreneur within a section of the organization. The intrapreneur is independent, proactive, creative, and generates new ideas and innovations to the organization. Hence, the intrapreneur takes direct responsibility and risks for turning a project or idea into a profitable finished product for the organization. As the intrapreneur thinks like an entrepreneur looking for business opportunities to increase profits, it is in the best interest of an organization to encourage intrapreneurship.

An example would be a project manager of a large company who is given the authority to exercise independent entrepreneurial initiatives to develop and launch a new product for the organization, or to lead a subsidiary of the organization. Companies such as 3M and Google are well known for promoting intrapreneurship. These companies encourage and fund intrapreneurs to create and oversee projects of their own choice.

Case study

Arthur Fry (born 1931) is credited for inventing and commercialising the Post-it note in 1980 whilst working as a new product development researcher at 3M. Post-it notes are now sold in over 100 countries around the world.

Case study

Paul Buchheit, an employee of Google, is credited as the creator of Gmail. In 2001, he programmed the first working version of Gmail in just one day(!), and was the lead developer. He left Google in 2006, and worked at Facebook until 2010. In 2011, Buchheit won The Economist Innovation Award for the computing and telecommunications field.

Case study

Steve Jobs (1955–2011), the co-founder of Apple, did not graduate from university because his adoptive parents could not afford the tuition fees. Instead, he took the risk of. setting up Apple with two friends (Steve Wozniak and Ronald Wayne) in 1976. However, Ronald Wayne sold his share of the company within a couple of weeks for (just) $2,300.

Jobs went on to reinvent computing, music and mobile phones, making Apple the highest valued company in the world, just two months before he died. *Forbes* estimated the wealth of Jobs to be more than $8.3 billion.

Box 1.1.b Factors of production

Factors of production are the four types of inputs or resources necessary for the production process.

- **Land** – natural resources used for production, e.g. wood, water, fish, crude oil, minerals, metal ores and physical land itself.
- **Labour** – the physical and mental efforts of people in the production of a good or service.
- **Capital** – all non-natural (manufactured) resources used in the production of other products, e.g. tools, machinery, buildings, equipment and vehicles.
- **Entrepreneurship** – the management, organization and planning of the other factors of production. The success or failure of a business rests on the talents and decisions of the entrepreneur.

Box 1.1.c Differences between entrepreneurs and intrapreneurs

Entrepreneurs
- Owners and/or operator of organization
- Takes substantial risks
- Visionary
- Rewarded with profit
- Responsibility for workforce (labour)
- Failure incurs personal costs.

Intrapreneurs
- Employees of organization
- Takes medium to high risks
- Innovative
- Rewarded with pay and remuneration
- Accountability to the owner / operator
- Failure is absorbed by the organization.

Reasons for starting up a business

Reasons for starting up a business or an enterprise. AO2

© IBO, 2017

There are several reasons why people decide to set up a business or an enterprise. These reasons can be remembered by the mnemonic GET CASH©:

Growth   Entrepreneurs such as Wang Jianlin, the wealthiest real estate tycoon in the world, who have their own businesses, benefit personally when there is an appreciation in the value of their assets, such as property and land which tend to increase in value over time. This is called capital growth. It is quite common for the capital growth of a business to be worth more than the value of the owners' salaries. Bill Gates, the world's second wealthiest man, made his fortunes mainly from the capital growth of Microsoft, the world's largest software-maker.

Earnings   The Chinese have a saying that "*You can never get rich earning money from working for someone else.*" That is because the potential returns from setting up your own business can easily outweigh the costs, even though the risks are high. It is common that entrepreneurs earn far in excess of salaries from any other occupation that they might otherwise pursue. Tim Cook, CEO of Apple, is reported to have an annual remuneration package of around $378 million!

Transference and inheritance   In many societies it is the cultural norm to pass on assets, including businesses, to the next generation. Many self-employed entrepreneurs view their business as something that they can pass on (transference) to their children (inheritance) to give them a sense of security that might not be possible if they chose to work for someone

Business organization and environment

CORE

else. The Walton family (the richest family in the world with an estimated wealth of over $150 billion) own over 50% of the shares in Walmart, the world's largest retailer.

Challenge   Some people might view setting up and running a business as a challenge. It is this challenge that drives them to perform and what gives them personal satisfaction. Being successful in business boosts self-esteem. This is perhaps one reason why billionaires such as Warren Buffet, Carlos Slim and Li Ka-shing continued to work past the official retirement age.

Autonomy   Working for someone else means exactly that. Employees have to follow the instructions and rules set by the organization that they work for, such as the conditions of employment, working hours, benefits and holiday entitlement. Conversely, being self-employed means that there is autonomy (independence, freedom of choice and flexibility) in how things are done within the organization.

Security   Similarly, there is usually more job security for someone who is their own boss. By contrast, employees can be dismissed, made redundant, or even replaced by technology. Although the risks are great, being self-employed also makes it potentially easier to accumulate personal wealth (financial security) to provide higher funds for (early) retirement.

Hobbies   Some people might want to pursue their passion or to turn their hobby into a business. Successful entrepreneurs have a passion for what they do and this is made easier if the nature of the work is directly related to their interests. Top selling author, J.K. Rowling is an example. Jamie Oliver, the television celebrity and chef who has set up several of his own restaurants is another example. Internet entrepreneur Mark Zuckerberg, who co-founded Facebook, became the world's youngest billionaire when he was just 23 years old.

Theory of knowledge

Look at the reasons for starting up a business. How do *reason* and *emotion* interact to affect the decision-making process? Is *emotion* or *reason* more important in this process?

Steps in the process of starting up a business

Common steps in the process of starting up a business or an enterprise. AO2
© IBO, 2017

The steps in the process of starting up a business or an enterprise will vary from one country to another. The OCED reports that it takes an average of 13.4 days to set up a business in economically developed countries, whereas it takes 41 days in China and 119 days in Brazil! Nevertheless, the common steps in the process of starting up a business include:

1. **Write a business plan.**   Once the entrepreneur has a feasible business idea, this is officially formulated in a business plan. This document will include the goals and objectives for the new business with an outline plan of how these targets are to be accomplished.

2. **Obtain start-up capital.**   Starting a business requires money. Quite often, small business owners will use their own savings and/or obtain loans to finance their start-up. The loan process can take several months to complete, with the lender usually requesting a completed business plan before any funds are approved.

3. **Obtain business registration.**   Before a business can trade or hire workers, it must satisfy registration and licensing requirements. The owner(s) must also register the legal status of the business, i.e. the type of business organization, such as a partnership or limited liability company (see Unit 1.2).

4. **Open a business bank account.**   To facilitate the financial operations of the new business, the owner(s) need to set up a business bank account. This allows the business to pay for its costs of operation and to receive payments from customers (whether through bank deposits of cash, bank account transfers or credit card payments). Almost all business bank accounts have online banking facilities too.

5. **Marketing.**   Potential customers need to know about the business and its products. This is done through the marketing activities of the new business, such as advertising and other promotional materials. For many businesses, this will also include establishing a presence on the Internet. Having an effective website is essential to capture business opportunities with new customers and to establish credibility.

Starting a new business is highly risky because the owners and investors are taking a step into the unknown, even if risks are calculated. Most new business ideas fail, mainly due to mismanagement. For example, the owners might have underestimated the challenges faced when setting up a business or being self-employed. The level of demand for the firm's products might not be sufficient for it to recoup its start-up costs (see Box 1.1.d), let alone to earn any profit. Nevertheless, the pursuit of profit remains a key incentive for entrepreneurs to take such risks. Careful consideration of various factors (see Table 1.1.a) in the business plan can also reduce the risks of setting up a new business.

Box 1.1.d Examples of start-up costs for a new business

- **Buildings,** e.g. alterations, fixtures and fittings and insurance costs.
- **Capital equipment,** e.g. office furniture, telephones, computers, machinery, tools, and motor vehicles.
- **Human resources,** e.g. recruitment, induction and training costs.
- **Legal and professional fees,** e.g. costs of solicitors, licenses, permits and copyright permission.
- **Marketing costs,** e.g. market research, advertising and promotional campaigns.
- **Premises,** e.g. purchase costs, mortgage deposit payment or rental deposit costs.

Business organization and environment

CORE

Table 1.1.a Factors to consider when setting up a business

Factor	Description
Business idea	A feasible business idea is needed. This might be done by identifying and filling a *niche* (unfilled gap) in a market or by providing products that have a *unique selling point*. Amazon.com (online book retailing), Dell (custom-made computers) and Dyson (bag-less vacuum cleaners) are examples of successful businesses based on innovative ideas at the time. It is also possible to enter existing markets although these may be saturated so the chances of success might be lower.
Finance	Finance is needed to fund business activities, such as manufacturing and marketing of the firm's products. However, finance is usually the key barrier to setting up a new business. Record keeping of financial accounts (see Unit 3.4) also needs to be done. Many firms hire accountants to help them do this.
Human resources	Human resources are needed at all stages of business activity, from the design and development of a product to delivering it to the consumer. Entrepreneurs have to consider the need for hiring, training, retaining and motivating their staff.
Enterprise	Entrepreneurial skills are required to successfully plan, organize and manage the business. Effective leadership and negotiation skills are required to deal with different *stakeholder groups* (see Unit 1.4) such as employees, suppliers and the government. Entrepreneurs must also have self-confidence and a passion for what they do.
Fixed assets	Fixed assets are needed, such as premises and capital equipment. The location decision (see Unit 5.4) is also a crucial but a problematic one; a popular location improves the chances of attracting customers, but the cost of land and property is much greater.
Suppliers	Suppliers are needed to provide the business with its raw materials, finished stock of products and support services. Negotiations over issues such as prices and delivery times also need to be undertaken.
Customers	Customers need to be attracted because without them the business will fail. This might be done by using market research to create products that are desirable, available at the right prices and sold in the right places.
Marketing	Marketing is essential, irrespective of how good a business idea might be. Many investors turned down Anita Roddick's idea of The Body Shop and J.K. Rowling's Harry Potter books. Marketing is needed to convince lenders and buyers that the product is a winner.
Legal issues	Legalities (legal issues) also need to be considered, e.g. consumer protection laws, copyright and patent legislation, and employment rights. Infringement of legal issues can present huge problems for a business, e.g. if a restaurant breaks food hygiene laws, it might be required to cease all operations.

Problems that a new business may face

Problems that a new business or enterprise may face. AO2
© IBO, 2017

Results from around the world consistently show that around 20 to 25 per cent of new businesses fail in their first year. A new business is likely to face problems that must be dealt with immediately to prevent them from escalating and threatening its survival. Such problems include:

- **Lack of finance** All businesses need finance for the purchase of *fixed assets*, such as premises, buildings, machinery and equipment. However, most owners of new or small businesses do not have the credentials to secure external funding without major difficulties. Even if entrepreneurs are able to borrow money, the funds may be insufficient or the relatively high interest charges might seriously affect the cash flow position of the firm (see Unit 3.7). Hence, new business owners often have to remortgage their own homes to raise the finance needed, thereby offering the lender more *collateral* (financial security in case borrowers fail to repay the loan).

- **Cash flow problems** Financing working capital (the money available for the daily running of a business) is also a major problem for many new businesses. A business might have a lot of stock, such as raw materials or semi-finished output, which cannot be easily turned into cash. Customers might demand a lengthy credit period (buy now pay later schemes), i.e. the business will not receive the cash payment until the credit period is over (usually between 30 to 60 days). However, businesses still need to pay for their ongoing costs such as wages, rent, utility bills, taxes and interest payments on bank loans. A lack of working capital is the single largest cause of business failure. Hence, it is common for a new business to produce a cash flow forecast in the business plan so that provisions can be made to cover any shortfalls.

- **Marketing problems** Marketing problems arise when businesses fail to meet customer needs, thereby resulting in poor sales. Supplying the right products at the right price is especially crucial for new businesses. However, small and new businesses might lack the know-how to do this. Quite often, the key to small business success is to identify a *niche* (or gap) in the market and then fill it. For example, Amazon identified huge opportunities of using the Internet as a channel of distribution for books and other products. European airlines such as easyJet and Ryanair identified early on the niche for no-frills (budget) air travel.

- **Unestablished customer base** A major problem facing new businesses is attracting customers, i.e. building a customer base. The problem is intensified when there are well established rivals that already operate in the market. Customer loyalty is built over a long period of time, which may require marketing know-how and large amounts of money.

Fig 1.1.g A sole trader business in Morocco

- **People management problems** New businesses may lack experience in hiring the right staff with all the necessary skills. This can lead to poor levels of customer service and the need to retrain staff or to rehire people, all of which can be very expensive. Moreover, new businesses might not know the ideal *organizational structure* (see Unit 2.2) that best suits their needs.

- **Legalities** It is necessary for businesses to comply with all necessary legislation, e.g. business registration procedures, insurance cover for staff and buildings, consumer protection laws and copyright rules. The paperwork and legal requirements of setting up a new business can be tedious, confusing, time consuming and expensive. Any oversight could result in the business having to pay compensation or penalty fees. This would obviously damage the already vulnerable cash flow position of new businesses.

- **Production problems** It can be difficult for new businesses to accurately forecast levels of demand so they are more likely to either over produce or under produce. Overproduction tends to lead to stockpiling, wastage and increased costs (see Unit 5.5). By contrast, underproduction leads to dissatisfied customers and a loss of potential sales.

- **High production costs** New businesses are likely to experience high production costs due to the large amount of money needed to pay for the cost of equipment, machinery, stocks (inventory), rent, advertising, insurance and so forth. Smaller businesses will also be at a cost disadvantage as they cannot benefit from *economies of scale* (see Unit 1.6). By contrast, economies of scale allow larger and more established businesses to benefit from lower average costs of production due to their scale of operations, such as being able to get discounts from their suppliers for bulk purchases or being able to borrow money at a lower interest rate because of their larger size.

- **Poor location** Businesses face a dilemma in the location decision: busy areas offer the highest potential number of customers, but the premises in these areas will also cost the most. Fixed costs, such as rent or mortgage payments, form a large percentage of total costs for many businesses. An aim for any new business is to break-even as soon as possible, by keeping fixed costs down. This is one reason why many entrepreneurs set up small businesses that operate initially from their own homes (which also has some tax advantages). Jeff Bezo, the founder of Amazon. com, started his online business in his garage. Of course, this option is not ideal for all businesses where location (see Unit 5.4) plays a key factor in business survival.

- **External influences** All businesses, irrespective of size or how long they have been in operation, are prone to exogenous shocks that create a difficult trading environment, such as an oil crisis or economic recession (see Unit 1.5). However, more established firms tend to be better resourced to handle these external influences. Hence, new businesses are more vulnerable to external shocks so the potential for business failure is greater.

In summary, people set up their own businesses to satisfy their personal desires such as to be their own boss, to fulfil a personal vision, to have the opportunity to achieve success or simply to live a more extravagant lifestyle (if and when the business is successful). However, a significant number of new businesses fail to survive. There are three interrelated reasons for this: a lack of cash in the business, poor cost control and management incompetence.

Common mistake

Candidates often claim that businesses should not pursue a particular project because of the risks involved. However, all business decisions carry an element of risk. Mark Zuckerberg, co-founder of Facebook, said that the biggest risk for entrepreneurs is not taking any risks, especially in a rapidly changing business world.

Theory of knowledge

To what extent is luck an essential part of being successful in business? How does this impact the knowledge needed to succeed as an entrepreneur?

The elements of a business plan

The elements of a business plan. AO2

© IBO, 2017

A **business plan** is a report detailing how a business sets out to achieve its goals and objectives. It is a useful planning tool as it requires the owner(s) to consider the marketing, financial and human resources of the business.

The business plan also helps to reassure financial lenders, such as banks and venture capitalists (see Unit 3.1), that the entrepreneur has comprehensively researched the business idea and has given reasons to support the venture. Investors will assess both opportunities and risks that may be reflected in a business plan before making any decisions. They will also look for potential problems with the venture, even if these are not outlined in the business plan. Therefore, it helps financiers to make a more objective judgement regarding the firm's likely success and hence its ability to repay the loans. The business plan can also be used by other stakeholders such as shareholders to assess the potential gains from their investment in the business.

Although there is no universally accepted format for writing a business plan, the contents of a typical business plan will include information shown in Table 1.1.b on page 12.

Many business plans have sections devoted to a *SWOT analysis* (see Unit 1.3) and a *contingency plan* (see Unit 5.7) outlining what the entrepreneur will do if things do not go as planned. Finally, any appropriate supporting evidence (such as statistics, charts and other reference material) should appear in an appendix at the back of the business plan.

Business organization and environment

CORE

As bank managers are busy people, a business plan is often no more than 5 to 6 pages long. If this is not possible, such as in the case of an international joint venture, then an *executive summary* is written and placed at the front of the business plan. This summarises the information given in the main report of the business plan, highlighting the key points and conclusions. The executive summary can be read within a few minutes to get an overview of the business plan and the bank manager can then decide whether or not to read the rest of the document.

> ## IB Learner Profile – Be an inquirer
>
> Learn more about how to write a business plan by using online tools from websites such as www.bplans.com, www.myownbusiness.org and www.businessballs.com.

Table 1.1.b Contents of a typical business plan

Element	Description
The business	• Name and address of the proposed business (for new businesses) • Cost of premises and other start-up costs (for new businesses) • Details of the owner(s) and past business experience • The type of business organization, e.g. sole trader or partnership • Quantifiable goals and objectives of the proposed business or project
The product	• Details of the good(s) and/or service(s) being offered • Supporting evidence showing why customers will pay for the product(s) • Where and how production will take place, e.g. the equipment that is needed • Details of the suppliers of resources such as raw materials or components • Costs of production, i.e. the expected costs of operating the business • Pricing strategies to be used
The market	• The expected number of customers or the forecast level of sales • The nature of the market such as customer profiles and market segmentation • The expected growth of the market in the foreseeable future • Competitor analysis, e.g. market share, strengths and weaknesses
The finance	• Proposed sources of finance, i.e. how the business or project will be funded • Break-even analysis (see Unit 3.3) • Security (financial guarantees) in case the borrower defaults on the loan • Cash flow forecast and steps to deal with cash flow problems (see Unit 3.7) • Forecast profit and loss account (see Unit 3.4) for the first year of trading • Forecast balance sheet (see Unit 3.4) showing the firm's financial health • A forecast rate of return for investors of the business venture
The personnel	• The number and job roles of the workers likely to be employed • Organizational structure of human resources (see Unit 2.2) • Details of payment systems, e.g. remuneration such as wage rates
The marketing	• Market research and test marketing (see Unit 4.4) • The distribution plan, detailing where the products will be sold • Details of the promotional mix used to target customers • Any unique or distinctive selling point to differentiate itself from rivals.

Introduction to Business Management and the CUEGIS concepts

Concept-based learning is a three-dimensional model that structures **facts** (content) and **skills** with **concepts** of a particular discipline. In the Business Management course, these concepts are known as the CUEGIS concepts – **c**hange, **c**ulture, **e**thics, **g**lobalization, **i**nnovation and **s**trategy. They provide six *conceptual lenses* through which students (and teachers) investigate, analyse and evaluate factual content to create a deeper understanding of Business Management.

Business activity is the process of turning inputs (land, labour, capital and enterprise) into outputs (goods and services) in order to meet the needs and wants of different customers. Irrespective of the culture, all businesses strive to add value in the production and provision of goods and services as part of their business strategy.

Essentially, the purpose of business activity is to satisfy the needs and desires of customers whilst fulfilling the organization's own objectives (see Unit 1.3), such as profit maximisation. In the long run, all businesses must generate profit or surplus in order to survive, although there will be similarities and differences in how for-profit and not-for-profit organizations go about doing this. Complexities in the global corporate world mean that change, culture, ethics, globalization, innovation and strategy are central to Business Management.

Read more about concept-based learning and the CUEGIS concepts in Business Management, in Chapter 6.1, pages 609-622

Fig 1.1.h The CUEGIS concepts affect all aspects of a business

REVIEW QUESTIONS

1. What is a business?

2. Distinguish between goods and services.

3. Distinguish between customers and consumers of a business.

4. What are the four functional areas of a business?

5. Describe the four business sectors of the economy.

6. What is meant by the chain of production?

7. What is meant by sectoral change?

8. Differentiate between entrepreneurs and intrapreneurs.

9. What are the main reasons for starting up a business?

10. What are the main steps in starting up a business?

11. What are the problems that new businesses may face?

12. What is a business plan and what are the main elements that go into a business plan?

CUEGIS ESSAY

With reference to an organization of your choice, examine the impact of **change** and **ethics** on the organization.   *[20 marks]*

Business organization and environment

CORE

KEY TERMS

Adding value is the practice of producing a good or service that is worth more than the cost of the resources used in the production process.

Business plan refers to the document that sets out the business idea, its goals and objectives and other details of how the business will operate (such as its marketing, operations and finance). It is often a crucial part of an attempt to raise external sources of finance.

Businesses are organizations involved in the production of goods and/or the provision of services.

Consumers are the people or organizations who actually use a product.

Customers are the people or organizations that buy the product.

Entrepreneurs are owners or operators of an organization who manage, organize and plan the other three factors of production. They are risk takers who exploit business opportunities in return for profits.

Entrepreneurship refers to the collective knowledge, skills and experiences of entrepreneurs.

Factors of production are the resources needed in the production process, i.e. land, labour, capital and entrepreneurship.

Goods are physical products produced and sold to customers, e.g. laptops, contact lenses, perfume, and toys.

Intrapreneurship is the act of behaving as an entrepreneur but as an employee within a large business organization. Intrapreneurs work in an entrepreneurial capacity, with authority to create innovative products or new processes for the organization.

Needs are the basic necessities that a person must have to survive, e.g. food, water, warmth, shelter and clothing.

Primary sector refers to businesses involved in the cultivation or extraction of natural resources, e.g. farming, mining, quarrying, fishing, oil exploration and forestry.

Product can refer to both goods and services. Goods are physical products, e.g. cars, books and food. Services are intangible products, e.g. haircuts, bus rides, education and health care.

Production is the process of creating goods and/or services, using factors of production to add value.

Quaternary sector is a subcategory of the tertiary sector, where businesses are involved in intellectual, knowledge-based activities that generate and share information, e.g. information communications technology and research organizations.

Secondary sector is the section of the economy where business activity is concerned with the construction and manufacturing of products.

Sectoral change refers to a shift in the relative share of gross domestic product (or national output) and employment that is attributed to each business sector.

Services are intangible products sold to customers, e.g. air flights, restaurants, cinemas, finance, health spas, public transportation, consultancy and education.

Tertiary sector refers to the section of the economy where business activity is concerned with the provision of services to customers.

Wants are people's desires, i.e. the things they would like to have, e.g. a larger home, a new smartphone or to go on an overseas holiday.

Business organization and environment

CORE

1.2 Types of organizations

"To open a business is very easy; to keep it open is very difficult." - Chinese proverb

SL/HL content	Assessment objective
Distinction between the private and public sectors	AO2
The main features of the following types of for-profit (commercial) organizations: • sole traders • partnerships • companies/corporations	AO3
The main features of the following types of for-profit social enterprises: • cooperatives • microfinance providers • public–private partnerships (PPP)	AO3
The main features of the following types of non-profit social enterprises: • non-governmental organizations (NGOs) • charities	AO3

© IBO, 2017

The private and public sectors

Distinction between the private and the public sectors. AO2

© IBO, 2017

Organizations that operate in the **private sector** are owned and controlled by private individuals and businesses, rather than by the government. They differ in size, ranging from those owned and run by just one person, to large multinational companies that operate around the world. The main aim of most, although not all, private sector organizations is to make **profit**, i.e. the positive difference between a firm's **sales revenue** (the money earned from selling its products) and its **costs** (production expenditure such as wages and rent).

Organizations that operate in the **public sector** are under the ownership and control of the government. Traditionally, they provide essential goods and services that would be underprovided or inefficiently provided by the private sector, e.g. health care, education and emergency services. Organizations that are wholly owned by the government are called **state-owned enterprises**, e.g. the UK's Transport for London, Hong Kong's Airport Authority, Singapore Airlines, and Canada Post (postal services).

Figure 1.2.a Emergency services are provided by the public sector

Business organization and environment

CORE

Case study

Australia Post (www.auspost.com.au), established in 1809, is a state-owned enterprise providing postal services. It employs over 32,700 people across its network of over 4,400 retail outlets, enjoying revenues in excess of AUD6.8bn (USD5.3bn).

Case study

China Mobile is the world's largest mobile phone operator with over 880 million subscribers. Founded in 1997, China Mobile is a state-owned enterprise. The company is listed on both the New York Stock Exchange and the Hong Kong Stock Exchange, although the government of the People's Republic of China holds over 74% of the publically traded shares. It has around 70% market share in the Chinese mobile phone industry.

Box 1.2.a   Reasons for public sector business activity

- Ensures that everyone has access to basic services such as education, health care, museums, museums ,public parks and public libraries.
- To avoid wasteful competition as the government is able to achieve huge economies of scale (cost savings from operating on a large magnitude) in the provision of certain services, such as postal services or national defence.
- To protect citizens and businesses through institutions such as the police or the courts that govern the law and order system.
- To create employment, e.g. governments tend to be a large employer of teachers, doctors and nurses.
- To stabilise the economy, e.g. many private sector banks were nationalised (bought by the government) during the global credit crisis of 2008, to prevent further financial turmoil.

Question 1.2.1   Provision of basic services

Education, housing and health-care services can be provided by both private-sector firms and the public sector.

(a) Distinguish between the aims of organizations operating in the public sector and the private sector.   *[4 marks]*

(b) Examine how housing provided by a housing cooperative might differ from that provided by a private-sector firm.   *[6 marks]*

Profit-based organizations

The main features of the following types of for-profit (commercial) organizations: sole traders, partnerships and companies/corporations. AO3

© IBO, 2017

Most businesses that operate in the private sector aim to make profit. After all, a business can only survive in the long term if it is profitable. Profit-based organizations differ in terms of *ownership* and *control* (you do not have to run a business simply because you own it), how they raise finance, and how the profits are distributed. The three main types of profit-based organizations are sole traders, partnerships and limited liability companies.

Sole traders

A **sole trader** (or **sole proprietor**) is an individual who runs and owns a personal business. The owner is held responsible for its success or failure. It is the most common type of business ownership. Examples include self-employed decorators, plumbers, mechanics, restaurateurs and freelance photographers. Sole traders may work alone or they might employ other people to help run the business. Sole proprietorships are often small family-run businesses and can be set up with relatively little capital. Start-up capital is usually obtained from personal savings and borrowing.

Figure 1.2.b A sole trader business in China

Many well-known companies started as sole traders. For example, Chanel (The House of Chanel) was started by Coco Chanel in 1910 and has a huge global presence today. Marks & Spencer was set up in 1904 by partners Michael Marks and Thomas Spencer (who originally operated as sole traders). Multinational retailer Tesco was started in 1919 as a sole proprietorship by Jack Cohen.

Some advantages and disadvantages of sole proprietorship are listed in Table 1.2.a.

An important legal point about sole traders is that the business is **unincorporated**. This means the owner is the same legal entity as the business. Since there is no legal difference between the business and the owner, the sole trader bears full responsibility for all losses/liabilities if the business collapses (as the owner is personally responsible for all the debts of the business).

Case study

The eBay concept was created in 1995 by entrepreneur Pierre Omidyar in response to difficulties his fiancée encountered when she was trying to sell collectibles such as PEZ candy dispensers. Omidyar started a sole proprietorship, using a prototype called Auction Web, to sell these and other goods to a growing online community. Three years later, eBay become a public limited company in 1998, making Omidyar a billionaire at the age of 31.

Table 1.2.a Advantages and disadvantages of sole proprietorships

Advantages	Disadvantages
Few legal formalities Sole traders are quite easy to set up and start-up costs are usually much lower in comparison to starting other types of business organizations.	**Unlimited liability** As an unincorporated business, there is no limit to the amount of debts that a sole trader is legally responsible for if the business fails.
Profit taking The sole trader is the only owner and therefore receives all of any profits made by the business. This gives the sole trader an incentive to work hard and to become successful.	**Limited sources of finance** Sole traders often find it difficult to secure any funds beyond their personal savings. Trying to expand can also be problematic due to the lack of sources of finance available to sole traders.
Being your own boss Sole traders do not take orders from anyone, have flexibility in decision-making (such as dictating their own working hours), and self-esteem from being successful. Decisions are also made quicker.	**High risks** Statistically, sole proprietorships have the largest risk of failure. The presence of larger and more established firms creates a huge threat to the profits and survival of smaller businesses.
Personalised service Sole traders can provide a personalised service to customers. Larger firms might not have the time to get to know all their customers so their services often become impersonal.	**Workload and stress** Owners often have to do their own accounts, marketing and human resource management. The sole trader is unlikely to be equally effective in these different roles, so there is added workload and stress.
Privacy Unlike other types of business ownership, sole traders enjoy privacy as they do not have to make their financial records available to the public, i.e. the owner enjoys confidentiality (although the accounts can be scrutinised by the tax authorities).	**Limited economies of scale** A sole trader is not able to exploit the benefits of large scale production, so their prices might be less competitive compared with those of larger rivals. This tends to reduce the competitiveness and profits for the business.
	Lack of continuity The running of a business can be jeopardised if the owner is not present. If the owner decides to go on holiday, or becomes ill, or dies, then the business might have problems in continuing.

Business organization and environment

CORE

Question 1.2.2 Flowers by Cam

Cam Tran is a **sole trader** who operates a small florist shop in Forest Hill, London (UK). Cam arranges and delivers flowers to local hospitals, hotels and schools in the local area. At times, she receives large orders for weddings. She has three school-aged children.

(a) Define the term **sole trader**. *[2 marks]*

(b) Examine the costs and benefits to Cam Tran in operating as a sole trader. *[6 marks]*

Source: photo courtesy of Cam Tran, owner of Flowers by Cam

Partnerships

A **partnership** is a profit-seeking business owned by two or more persons. For **ordinary partnerships**, the maximum number of owners is 20 (although this can vary from one country to another). The few exceptions to this rule include professions such as solicitors and accountants where issuing shares is prohibited.

Like sole traders, partnerships are financed mainly from the personal funds of each owner. However, partners can pool their funds together to raise more finance than sole traders. They can also raise money from owners who do not actively take part in the running of the partnership but have a financial stake in it. These investors are called **silent partners** (or **sleeping partners**) and are eligible for a portion of the profits. At least one owner must have unlimited liability, as partnerships are unincorporated businesses, but typically all partners share the liability.

Although it is not a legal requirement, most partnerships formulate a legal agreement between each of the partners.

Without a contract, profits or losses must be shared equally amongst the partners and all partners have the same rights in the running of the business. If a legal contract is drawn up, known as a **deed of partnership** (or **partnership deed**), then it is likely to include:

- the amount of finance contributed by each partner

- the roles, obligations and responsibilities of each partner

- how profits or losses will be shared among the partners

- conditions for introducing new partners

- clauses for the withdrawal of a partner

- procedures for ending the partnership.

Some advantages and disadvantages of partnerships are shown in Table 1.2.b on page 19.

Figure 1.2.c Partnerships consist of two or more owners

Exam tip !

Unlimited liability exists to prevent sole traders and partners from making careless decisions in managing their businesses. It makes private individuals accountable for their actions and decisions. However, the risk of loss of private property can influence some entrepreneurs, causing them to make safe decisions instead of taking risks.

Table 1.2.b Advantages and disadvantages of partnerships

Advantages	Disadvantages
Financial strength Partnerships have more financial strength than sole proprietorships as there are more owners who can invest in the business, yet they are still fairly easy to set up. In general, it is also easier to secure external sources of finance in partnerships than sole proprietorships due to the lower risks.	**Unlimited liability** Legally, partnerships are responsible for their debts 'wholly or severally' meaning the debts can be repaid by either one partner (wholly) or shared among the partners (severally). The rare exception is with limited liability partners who have been elected to have limited liability.
Specialisation and division of labour Unlike sole traders, partners can benefit from shared expertise, shared workload and moral support. For example, a law firm might have partners who specialise in corporate law, divorce law and criminal law. As a result, its client base is likely to be much larger.	**A lack of continuity** Problems might still exist if a partner dies or leaves the firm as the partnership deed becomes invalid, i.e. it has to be set up again. It is possible to accommodate some changes in a partnership deed, although solicitors will spend time (and money) on drafting the new contract.
Financial privacy Like sole proprietorships, partnerships do not have to publicise their financial records. Therefore they can enjoy a fair degree of financial privacy.	**Prolonged decision-making** In comparison to sole traders, decision-making is likely to take longer as there are more owners involved. Disagreements and conflict might also occur.
Cost-effective Partnerships can be more cost-effective than sole traders as each partner specialises in certain aspects of their business, thus raising productivity.	**Lack of harmony** Disagreements and conflict within partnerships is common, but there must also be mutual trust. Each partner is legally and financially answerable to the others, so a mistake made by one person can reduce the profits for all other partners.

Question 1.2.3   EXP: The Chinese Experience

EXP is a small Chinese restaurant with take-away service located in London. It was established in 2006 by partners Keith and Tonina Hoang. *EXP* is run as an **ordinary partnership** with each partner having 50% of the stake in the business. They have a workforce of 12 people, including chefs and delivery staff. *EXP* relies heavily on local customers but faces competition from nearby pizza outlets and Indian restaurants.

EXP's popularity has grown with a loyal customer base. Keith and Tonina had to discontinue with the distribution of take-away menus in the local area as *EXP* was already operating near full capacity. Keith and Tonina thought it best to maintain the quality of their food and the punctuality of their home deliveries to maintain the image that they had established.

(a) Define the term **ordinary partnership**.   *[2 marks]*

(b) Explain **two** advantages of running *EXP* as a partnership.   *[4 marks]*

(c) Discuss the costs and benefits of *EXP* remaining as a small business.   *[10 marks]*

Companies (corporations)

Companies are businesses owned by their shareholders. Shareholders are individuals or other businesses that have invested money to provide capital for a company. Corporations are sometimes called **joint-stock companies** because the shares of the business (or 'stock') are jointly held by numerous entities.

Companies are *incorporated* businesses, i.e. there is a legal difference between the owners of the company (the shareholders) and the business itself. The company, being a separate entity, has its own legal rights and duties. For example, the company, rather than the owners, would take those who infringe copyright and patent laws to court. It also means that companies have **limited liability** – shareholders do not stand to lose personal belongings if the company goes into debts. The maximum shareholders can lose is the value of their investment in the company. This is to safeguard investors - imagine an ordinary individual, as a shareholder, having to share the debts of a large multinational company that s/he had invested in!

Setting up a company can be complicated and expensive, e.g. there are rules and regulations that must be obeyed for shares to be sold on the Stock Exchange. One reason for such legislation is to protect investors who buy shares in businesses that they do not run or control. A **board of directors** (BOD) is elected by shareholders to run the company on their behalf. Directors are elected because of their skills and expertise and because shareholders do not necessarily want to get involved in the daily running of the company. The BOD is held responsible for the running of the company but is held accountable to the shareholders. In most cases, each share held equals one vote, so the more shares held by an investor the more voting power they have. In reality, individual shareholders tend to have very little say as it is the large institutional investors and directors who hold the majority of the shares.

There are two types of limited liability companies – private and public limited companies.

A **private limited company** is a company that cannot raise share capital from the general public. Instead, shares are sold to private family members and friends. The shares cannot be traded without the prior agreement from the BOD, so that the directors can maintain overall control of the company. For this reason, many private limited companies are run as family businesses. The business will usually have the word "Limited" or the letters 'Ltd.' after its name. However, this practice varies from one country to another (see Box 1.2.b).

By contrast, a **public limited company** is able to advertise and sell its shares to the general public via a stock exchange. It often carries the letters 'PLC' after its name, but again this varies between countries (see Box 1.2.b). Table 1.2.c shows examples of limited liability companies.

Box 1.2.b Abbreviations for public limited companies

- Australia – Pty. Ltd. (short for 'proprietary limited company')
- Gremany – AG (short for 'AktienGesellschaft' meaning 'shareholder corporation')
- Hong Kong – Ltd. is used by both private and public limited companies
- Sweden – AB (short for 'Aktie Bolag' meaning 'limited liability company')
- USA – Inc. or Corp. (short for 'incorporated' or 'corporation').

Table 1.2.c Examples of private and public limited companies

Private Limited Companies	Public limited companies
Chanel – fashion and Cosmetics (France)	Apple - Technology (USA)
Ernst & Young - Accounting (USA)	Coca-Cola Company - Soft drinks (USA)
IKEA - Home furnishing (Sweden)	HSBC - Banking (UK and Hong Kong)
LEGO - Toys (Denmark)	Mercedes-Benz - Automobiles (Germany)
Level7 Education - Online education (Hong Kong)	Michelin - Tyre manufacturer (France)
Mars Inc. - Confectionary (USA)	Nike, Inc. - Sportswear and sports equipment (USA)
Rolex - Prestigious wristwatches (Switzerland)	Philips - Electronics conglomerate (Netherlands)
PriceWaterhouse Coopers - Accounting (USA)	Samsung - Electronics (South Korea)
Virgin Group - Global conglomerate (UK)	Vodafone - Telecommunications (UK)

Before companies can begin trading, two documents must be produced and submitted to the appropriate authorities:

- **Memorandum of Association** – a relatively brief document outlining the fundamental details of the company, e.g. its name, its main purpose, the registered address and the amount of share capital invested.

- **Articles of Association** (or **Articles of Incorporation**) – the longer of the two documents, stipulating the internal regulations and procedures of the company, e.g. the rights, roles and power of the BOD and shareholders. Administrative issues are also covered, such as procedures of the Annual General Meeting (AGM), the processes for the appointment of directors and how profits will be distributed.

Once the authorities are satisfied with the above documents and an application fee has been paid, a **Certificate of Incorporation** is issued to the company. This licence recognises the business as a separate legal entity from its owners and allows the business to start trading as a limited liability company.

Figure 1.2.d Companies House in central London, UK

Flotation occurs when a business first sells all or part of its business to external investors (shareholders), a process known as an **initial public offering** (IPO). The IPO makes the company *listed* on a stock exchange. Flotation helps to generate additional sources of finance, e.g. the Agricultural Bank of China raised $22.1 billion from its IPO in 2010.

The largest shareholders of companies tend to be institutional and commercial investors, i.e. companies have shares in other companies. For example, Porsche is the majority shareholder of Germany automaker Volkswagen, which in turn owns a majority of the shares in Audi, Bentley, Bugatti, Lamborghini, SEAT and Skoda.

Nevertheless, shareholders face potential risks, despite their liability being limited. Unprofitable companies that are unsuccessful cannot distribute any dividends. The share price is likely to fall as a result, causing negative capital growth. Shareholders also place their trust in the management team to run the company on their behalf, although the interests of managers and shareholders might conflict with each other (see Unit 1.4). For example, managers and directors might decide to improve pay and conditions but this could reduce the amount available for dividends to the shareholders. Advantages and disadvantages of a company structure are given in Table 1.2.d.

All companies must hold an **Annual General Meeting** (AGM) to allow the owners to have a say (or vote) in the running of the business. There are three main processes at a typical AGM:

- Shareholders vote on (promises or declarations) and the re-election (or sometimes election) of the board of directors.

- Shareholders ask questions of the chief executive officer, directors and chairperson about various aspects of the company.

- Shareholders approve the previous year's financial accounts after the directors present the annual report containing information about the company's performance.

Table 1.2.d Advantages and disadvantages of companies/corporations

Advantages	Disadvantages
Raising finance Companies can raise large amounts of capital by selling shares. There are no interest charges and shareholders are paid only if the company makes a profit.	**Communication problems** Quite often, as a company becomes larger, services and relationships can become more impersonal to both customers and employees.
Limited liability As all companies have this, it is easier to attract investors as the risks are relatively low for investors.	**Added complexities** Running a sole-proprietorship or partnership is cheaper and less bureaucratic than running a corporation.
Continuity Unlike partnerships and sole traders, the legal difference between the company and its owners means it can continue to operate as a separate entity, even with a change of owners.	**Compliance costs** For public limited companies, the high costs of complying with the rules and regulations of the stock exchange adds to their running costs.
Economies of scale Due to their larger size, companies can benefit from economies of scale (lower unit costs of production as the firms enlarges). For example, it is usually cheaper for a company to borrow money than it is for sole traders or partnerships as limited companies are less of a financial risk.	**Disclosure of information** Financial data must be provided to all shareholders. This can be a time consuming and expensive task as auditors have to be paid and annual reports have to be published and distributed. Privacy no longer exists, in comparison to that enjoyed by sole traders and partners.
Productivity Companies can hire specialist directors and managers to run the firm as there is no need for the owners to be directly involved in the daily running of the business. They are also more likely to employ specialist staff such as marketers, lawyers and accountants. Therefore, the output and productivity levels of limited companies are generally higher than found in sole proprietorships and partnerships.	**Bureaucracy** There is far more bureaucracy involved in setting up and running a company, e.g. in the Republic of Ireland, a minimum of €38,000 ($51,600) must be issued as share capital, with at least 25% being paid into the company account for business use. Solicitors must be hired to ensure that all documentation is legally accurate. Advertising and promoting the company's IPO adds to the costs. Hosting the AGM is also a huge and expensive task.
Tax benefits Sole traders and partnerships pay income tax on their profits. By contrast, companies pay corporate tax on their profits. The highest income tax rate tends to be greater than the rate for corporate tax. Companies also benefit from a wider range of allowances and tax-deductible costs.	**Loss of control** Whilst sole traders and partnerships retain control of their businesses, public limited companies face the potential threat of a takeover by a rival company that purchases a majority stake in the business (as shares are openly available for purchase on the stock exchange).

Question 1.2.4 Mars Inc.

Mars is a global confectionery and food processing manufacturer with annual sales in excess of $30 billion. Perhaps more surprisingly, and unusual for a business of this size, *Mars* is entirely owned by the Mars family, as a **private limited** company - making it one of the largest family-owned businesses in the world.

It all started with Franklin Clarence Mars (1883–1934) back in 1911 when he and his wife Ethel started making and selling a variety of butter-cream candies in their home in Washington, USA. In 1920, Frank and his son Forrest Edward Mars produced the Milky Way bar, known in Europe and other parts of the world as the 'Mars bar'. It was an immediate success. Today, the portfolio of *Mars* brands includes Snickers, Wrigley, M&M's and Twix. Having diversified into pet foods, its brands also include Pedigree, Whiskas, Cesar and Sheba. Mars brands are recognised and used in almost every country.

Source: adapted from Mars website (www.mars.com)

(a) Define the term **private limited company**.   *[2 marks]*

(b) Discuss the decision of the Mars family to keep their business as a private limited company.   *[10 marks]*

For-profit social enterprises

The main features of the following types of for-profit social enterprises: cooperatives, microfinance providers and public-private partnerships (PPP). AO3

© IBO, 2017

Social enterprises are revenue-generating businesses with social objectives at the core of their operations. Whilst commercial for-profit businesses strive to return a profit for their owners, social enterprises strive to return a surplus for social gain. Social enterprises can be operated as a non-profit organization or as a for-profit company. Either way, all social enterprises have two main goals: to achieve social objectives and to earn revenue in excess of costs. After all, social entrepreneurs (those who use businesses to solve social issues) cannot deliver the social good they desire if they do not manage the financial health of their business. Their success in helping others depends on their ability to operate as a sustainable business, i.e. without a surplus or profit, there is no business.

There are three main types of for-profit social enterprises: cooperatives, microfinance providers and public–private partnerships (PPP).

Case study

Television celebrity chef Jamie Oliver campaigns to improve children's diets in schools. Since 2002, he has trained disadvantaged young people, many of whom were expelled from school or unemployed, to become chefs at his social enterprise called *Fifteen*, a chain of restaurants that operates in London and Cornwall (UK), Melbourne (Australia) and Amsterdam (Netherlands). *Fifteen* uses all profits for giving young people greater opportunities to have a better future.

Cooperatives

Cooperatives are for-profit social enterprises owned and run by their members, such as employees or customers, with the common goal of creating value for their members by operating in a socially responsible way. All employees (member of the cooperative) have a vote, thus contribute to decision-making. Cooperatives share any profits earned between their members.

Cooperatives operate in various industries, including retailing, financial services, child-care services, housing associations and agriculture (see Box 1.2.c). Canada, for example, has more than 9,000 cooperatives with more than 18 million members. The

UK's Cooperative Group is the world's largest consumer-owned business with more than 4.5 million members.

There are three main types of cooperatives, all of which are democratically owned and controlled:

- **Consumer cooperatives** are owned by the customers who buy the goods and/or services for personal use. Examples include food, credit unions (financial services), child care, housing, and health-care cooperatives. In most cases, members get access to goods and services at lower prices than those charged by traditional commercial businesses.

- **Worker cooperatives** are set up, owned and organized by their employee members. Examples include cooperatives involved in production and manufacturing, cafés, printers and tourism and communications. By operating as an enterprise, members are provided with work.

- **Producer cooperatives** are cooperatives that join and support each other to process or market their products. For example, a farmer cooperative might unite to buy equipment, fertilizers and seeds collectively, by pooling their funds, thus benefiting from bulk-purchase discounts. Farmer cooperatives are the most common example of producer cooperatives.

Some advantages and disadvantages of a cooperative structure are given in Table 1.2.e.

Box 1.2.c   Examples of cooperatives

- Associated Press – a non-profit multinational news agency headquartered in the USA
- Aurora Wine Cooperative – a producer cooperative in Brazil
- Cooperative Bank – a British commercial bank, founded in 1872, with assets of £23 billion ($15.9bn)
- Crédit Agricole Group – France's largest bank and credit union
- Mondragon Corporation – a Spanish worker-cooperative that produces food and industrial products
- Ocean Spray – a farmer-based cooperative of the popular cranberry and grapefruit juice drinks
- Sunkist – US farmer-based producer cooperative that makes the famous Sunkist brand of fruit juices
- Xinjiang Quanliang – a dairy farmers' cooperative in China , founded in 1980.

Business organization and environment

CORE

Table 1.2.e Advantages and disadvantages of cooperatives

Advantages	Disadvantages
Incentives to work Employees have a key stake in the cooperative so are more interested in how it performs. This can enhance staff motivation and labour productivity.	**Disincentive effects** There might be inefficient managers and employees as cooperatives do not pay high salaries and bonuses as incentives to work.
Decision-making power Employees also have a say in how the business is run. There is a democratic system of members having equal voting rights. This can also improve the members' commitment and motivation.	**Limited sources of finance** Cooperatives might suffer from a lack of finance as most of them cannot raise funds through a stock exchange. Sources of finance can be limited to the amount contributed by their members.
Social benefits Cooperatives are run on socially responsible principles, leading to gain for other members of society rather than for the owners. Thus, cooperatives create social gains that can be enjoyed by the wider community.	**Slower decision-making** Decisions are likely to be slowed down (delayed) as all members of the cooperative work in a democratic way and are involved in the decision-making process.
Public support A key advantage of social enterprises such as cooperatives is that there tends to be public support, i.e. people (including customers) want to help them succeed because they believe in the cause.	**Limited promotional opportunities** Cooperatives tend to have flatter organizational structures (see Unit 2.2), so there are fewer opportunities for employees to progress in their professional careers.

Microfinance providers

Microfinance is a type of financial service aimed at entrepreneurs of small businesses, especially females and those on low incomes. As a social enterprise, microfinance providers enable the disadvantaged members of society to gain access to essential financial services to help eradicate poverty. Access to banking and insurance services may be very limited for small businesses; quite often, finance is only available from unofficial money lenders at extremely high costs to the borrower. The funds are approved for microenterprise development. According to the World Bank, more than 500 million individuals have directly benefited from access to microfinance. The World Bank also claims that nearly 3 billion people in LEDCs have little or no access to official financial services to help them increase their incomes and standards of living.

Some advantages and disadvantages of microfinance providers are given in Table 1.2.f on page 25.

IB Learner Profile – Be an inquirer

Cooperatives operate under the guidelines and principles of the International Cooperative Alliance (ICA), founded in 1895. Investigate the role of the ICA (http://ica.coop/) and how it supports the cooperative movement around the world.

Figure 1.2.e Microfinance has helped women in Vietnam who make and sell bamboo products

Case study

Formerly known as the Bangladesh Rural Advancement Committee, BRAC is the largest microfinance provider in Bangladesh. Founded in 1972, its headquarters are in Dhaka, Bangladesh. According to its website (http://www.brac.net/) BRAC has over 100,000 staff, most of whom are women, and has helped more than 126 million people with its services in 14 different countries.

Table 1.2.f Advantages and disadvantages of microfinance providers

Advantages	Disadvantages
Accessibility Microfinance helps those in poverty to become financially independent, whereas banks do not typically lend such small amounts and to this particular market segment.	**Immorality** Critics claim that microfinance is an unethical operation of lenders as the providers are for-profit organizations, so profit from the poor and the unemployed.
Job creation The effective use of microfinance can help create new job opportunities, with beneficial effects on society as a whole.	**Limited finance** Microfinance schemes only offer small amounts of money to borrowers given the high risk of default (failure to repay loans).
Social wellbeing Successful applicants who receive microfinance are less likely to take their children out of school. It also allows recipients better access to health-care services for their families.	**Limited eligibility** Not all poor individuals qualify for microfinance. As a for-profit organization, microfinance providers have to minimise their own risks by ensuring borrowers have the ability to repay their loans.

Public–private partnerships

Public–private partnerships (PPP) occur when the government works together with the private sector to jointly provide certain goods or services. Hence, they are also known as **public–private enterprises**. The Japanese refer to such social enterprise businesses as operating in the Daisan sector (or the third sector), as they are hybrid organizations of both the private and public sector. For example, in some countries the private sector runs public sector hospitals and schools, without the services being actually privatised.

Public-private partnership can benefit from the dynamics, finances and efficiencies of the private sector alongside the benefits of public sector funding and support. Examples of such projects include London's Olympic Stadium, the Sydney Harbour Tunnel, New York's Central Park, the World Health Organization (WHO) and Hong Kong Disneyland (see Question 1.2.5).

Figure 1.2.f The Sydney Harbour Bridge, Australia, was built using private–public funding

Question 1.2.5   Hong Kong Disneyland

Hong Kong Disneyland (HKDL) is a theme park with three on-site hotels. The theme park is jointly owned by the Hong Kong government (the majority **shareholder**) and the Walt Disney Company. HKDL opened on 12th September 2005, having created 36,000 jobs. The company did not earn a profit until 2012, declaring a **net profit** of HK$109m ($13.97m). The government estimated that the theme park would generate HK$148bn ($19bn) in net benefits to the economy over a 40-year period.

(a)   (i) Define the term **shareholder**.   *[2 marks]*

(a)   (ii) Define the term **net profit**.   *[2 marks]*

(b)   Examine the benefits of the HKDL public-private partnership to the Hong Kong economy.   *[6 marks]*

(c)   Discuss whether a government should use tax revenues to fund public-private partnerships.   *[10 marks]*

Non-profit social enterprises

The main features of the following types of non-profit social enterprises: non-governmental organizations (NGOs) and charities. AO3

© IBO, 2017

Non-profit social enterprises are businesses run in a commercial-like manner but without profit being the main goal. Instead, non-profit organizations (NPOs) use their surplus revenues to achieve their social goals rather than distributing the surplus as dividends to shareholders. Examples include public libraries, state schools, museums, government hospitals and social services. Well-known non-profit social enterprises include Amnesty International, Habitat for Humanity, Oxfam, the Red Cross, and the World Wide Fund for Nature.

The term 'non-profit organization' does not mean that the business does not strive to earn a profit or surplus but that this must be retained in the business for its self-preservation and growth. Profit is the reward that is distributed to the owners or investors of a business in return for risking their money in the business. By contrast, NPOs retain this surplus in the business. For example, many private fee-paying schools are NPOs because any surplus that they make is reinvested into the schools to enhance their facilities and expansion plans. The two main types of non-profit social enterprises are non-governmental organizations (NGOs) and charities.

Case study

The Bill & Melinda Gates Foundation was set up in 2000 to enhance health care and reduce extreme poverty around the world. It is the largest private foundation in the world – such non-profit social organizations do not solicit funds from the general public, unlike charities. The Foundation is controlled by its three trustees (the people at the top of the organization): Bill Gates, Melinda Gates and Warren Buffett – the three most generous philanthropists in the USA. According to CNBC, Bill and Melinda Gates had donated over $50bn to the Foundation between 1997 and 2017.

Non-governmental organizations (NGOs)

A **non-governmental organization** (NGO) is non-profit social enterprise that operates in the *private sector*, i.e. it is not owned or controlled by the government. However, unlike most private sector businesses, NGOs do not aim primarily to make a profit. Instead, NGOs (also known as **private voluntary organizations** or PVOs), are set up and run for the benefit of others in society. The United Nations (UN) defines NGOs as "private organizations that pursue activities to relieve suffering, promote the interests of the poor, protect the environment, provide basic social services or undertake community development". Examples of NGOs include: Friends of the Earth (environmental protection), Amnesty International (human rights) and UNICEF (children's welfare). There are two types of NGOs:

- **Operational NGOs** are established from a given objective or purpose. These NGOs tend to be involved in relief-based and community projects, e.g. Oxfam and UNICEF.

- **Advocacy NGOs** take a more aggressive approach to promote or defend a cause, striving to raise awareness through direct action (such as lobbying, public relations and mass demonstrations), e.g. Greenpeace and Amnesty International.

Charities

A charity is a non-profit social enterprise that provides voluntary support for good causes (from society's point of view), such as the protection of children, animals and the natural environment. Its key function is raising funds from individuals and organizations to support a cause that is beneficial to society. Since charities do not necessarily 'sell' anything to customers, they must use refined marketing strategies to catch the attention of donors, e.g. the use of celebrity endorsements, holding special charity events or promoting their cause in the mass media.

Some charities are very large organizations, such as Oxfam and The World Wide Fund for Nature. They are run by a group of managers and trustees, similar to a limited company's board of directors. Depending on the organization itself, some managers and employees of charities are paid for their services, whilst others operate on a voluntary basis. The USA has the largest number of charities, with over one million registered charitable organizations.

Table 1.2.g Advantages and disadvantages of charities

Advantages	Disadvantages
Social benefits Charities provide financial support for the welfare of society, whether domestically (such as Age Concern) or internationally (such as Friends of the Earth). Many charities help to raise funds for medical research and other worthy causes including the protection of children and the prevention of cruelty to animals.	**Bureaucracy** Charities must be registered before they can operate. In Australia, for example, charities are registered with the Taxation Office (wwww.ato.gov.au/nonprofit). UK charities must register with the Charity Commission (www.charity-commission.gov.uk). These governing bodies also place restrictions on what charities can and cannot do.
Tax exemptions for NPOs As non-profit organizations, charities are exempt from corporate tax. There are also concessions for other taxes such as business rates, stamp duty (land taxes), capital gains tax and inheritance tax on gifts made in a will.	**Disincentive effects** The lack of a profit motive can cause problems, e.g. most volunteers cannot offer their services for extended periods of time. Even salaried workers are likely to be paid far less than what they could earn in for-profit organizations.
Tax incentives for donors Donors, be they private individuals or organizations, can get income tax allowances on the funds that are donated to charity. This raises the incentive for donors to give money to charities.	**Charity fraud** Financial activities must be recorded and reported to a governing body. This is to protect the interest of donors and to prevent charity fraud (the misuse of charitable donations.
Limited liability Charities can register to be limited companies to protect the interest of employees and managers who have limited liability.	**Inefficiencies** Although limited liability charities offer protection to the owners, it also means that those who run the charity are not personally held liable for any debts incurred.
Public recognition and trust Once registered with the authorities as a charity, the social enterprise can raise funds for its cause(s), with the general public and corporate donors being more confident in donating money to the charity.	**Limited sources of finance** Most charities survive solely on one source of finance – donations. With the huge number of rival charities and limited funds from donors, especially during an economic downturn, they have to constantly compete for donations.

Exam tip !

Although charities are not-for-profit social enterprises, this does not mean that they do not strive to make a surplus. The surplus is not classed as 'profit' because it does not get distributed to the owners or taxed by the government, but is reinvested in the charity.

Theory of knowledge

Can we 'know' if for-profit organizations do not care about society as much as non-profit social enterprises?

Types of organizations and the CUEGIS concepts

The reasons for setting up a business can vary from one country and culture to another. For example, only a few legal procedures are needed to establish a business in Singapore, Hong Kong and New Zealand, thus promoting an entrepreneurial spirit where creative and innovative businesses can thrive. In other countries, such as Chad, Libya and Myanmar, a risk-taking entrepreneurial culture is not so apparent.

There are various factors that affect the strategic choice of business organization, including:

- **Amount of finance** Sole traders need less capital than a public limited company to set up. A change in the legal status of a firm will usually require more finance.

- **Size** The larger the business operation, the more likely it is to be a company (corporation). Sole traders, for instance, find it unnecessary or unaffordable to hire lots of workers.

Business organization and environment

CORE

- **Limited liability**   The desire to have limited liability, in order to protect the personal possessions of the owners, can affect the choice of legal status of a business.

- **Degree of ownership and control**   Those who wish to retain control and ownership of a business may prefer to stay as sole traders or even as private limited companies.

- **The nature of business activity**   The type and scale of business activity can influence the legal status of a firm, e.g. mainstream aircraft and motor vehicle manufacturers rely on external sources of finance (see Unit 3.1), so are likely to be formed as public limited companies.

- **Change**   As a business grows and evolves (see Unit 1.6), it may need additional sources of finance and human resources. Thus, the type of organization is likely to change.

Fig 1.2g - Some businesses choose to remain small

CUEGIS ESSAY

With reference to an organization of your choice, examine how **change** has influenced business **strategy**.

[20 marks]

REVIEW QUESTIONS

1. Distinguish between the private sector and the public sector.

2. Compare and contrast the benefits of a partnership with those of a sole trader.

3. Why is the concept of limited liability important for investors?

4. What is the difference between a private limited company and a public limited company?

5. Distinguish between non-profit organizations and non-governmental organizations.

6. What are social enterprises?

7. Distinguish between cooperatives, microfinance providers and public–private partnerships.

8. Outline the benefits of social enterprises from society's point of view.

9. Distinguish between non-governmental organizations (NGOs) and charities.

10. What is the difference between an operational NGO and an advocacy NGO?

Fig 1.2.h The NYSE is on Wall Street, Lower Manhattan in New York City

KEY TERMS

Charities are non-profit social enterprises that provide voluntary support for good causes (from society's point of view), such as protection of children, animals and the natural environment.

Cooperatives are for-profit social enterprises set up, owned and run by their members, who might be employees and/or customers.

A **company** (or **corporation**) refers to a business that is owned by shareholders. A certificate of incorporation gives the company a separate legal identity from its owners.

Deed of partnership is the legal contract signed by the owners of a partnership. The formal deeds specify the name and responsibilities of each partner and their share of any profits or losses.

Incorporation means that there is a legal difference between the owners of a company and the business itself. This ensures that the owners are protected by limited liability.

An **initial public offering (IPO)** occurs when a business sells all or part of its business to shareholders on a stock exchange for the first time.

Limited liability is a restriction on the amount of money that owners can lose if their business goes bankrupt, i.e. shareholders cannot lose more than they invested in the company.

Microfinance is a type of financial service aimed at entrepreneurs of small businesses, especially females and those on low incomes.

Non-governmental organizations (NGO) are private sector not-for-profit social enterprises that operate for the benefit of others rather than primarily aiming to make a profit, e.g. Oxfam and Friends of the Earth.

Partnerships are a type of private sector business owned by 2-20 people (known as partners). They share the responsibilities and burdens of running and owning the business.

A **private limited company** is a business owned by shareholders with limited liability but whose shares cannot be bought by or sold to the general public.

The **private sector** is the part of the economy run by private individuals and businesses, rather than by the government, e.g. sole traders, partnerships, companies and cooperatives.

A **public limited company** is an incorporated business that allows the public to buy and sell shares in the company via a stock exchange. All shareholders enjoy limited liability.

Public–private partnerships occur when the government works together with the private sector to jointly provide certain goods or services.

The **public sector** is the part of the economy controlled by the government. Examples include state health and education services, the emergency services and national defence.

A **sole trader** is a self-employed person who runs and controls the business and is the sole person held responsible for its success (profits) or failure (unlimited liability).

Social enterprises are revenue-generating business with social objectives at the core of their operations. They can be for-profit or non-profit businesses, but all profits or surpluses are reinvested for that social purpose rather than being distributed to shareholders and owners.

State-owned enterprises are organizations wholly owned by the government.

A **stock exchange** is a market place for trading stocks and shares of public limited companies. Examples include the London Stock Exchange (LSE) and the New York Stock Exchange (NYSE).

Unlimited liability is a feature of sole traders and ordinary partnerships who are legally liable for all monies owed to their creditors, even if this means that they have to sell their personal possessions to pay for their debts.

Business organization and environment

CORE

1.3 Organizational objectives

"To accomplish great things, we must not only act, but also dream, not only plan, but also believe." -
Anatole France (1844–1924), Nobel Prize winner for Literature, 1921

SL/HL content	Assessment objective
Vision statement and mission statement	AO2
Aims, objectives, strategies and tactics, and their relationships	AO3
The need for organizations to change objectives and innovate in response to changes in internal and external environments	AO3
Ethical objectives and corporate social responsibility (CSR)	AO1
The reasons why organizations set ethical objectives and the impact of implementing them	AO3
The evolving role and nature of CSR	AO3
SWOT analysis of a given organization	AO3, AO4
Ansoff matrix for different growth strategies of a given organization	AO3, AO4

© IBO, 2017

Vision statements and mission statements

Vision statement and mission statement. AO2

© IBO, 2017

Having *vision* means to have an *image* of an ideal situation in the future. A **vision statement** therefore outlines an organization's aspirations (where it wants to be) in the distant future. For example, "To be the leading sports brand in the world" is the vision of Adidas, the German sportswear and sports equipment giant (Figure 1.3.a). Vision statements also tend to relate to the attainment of success, i.e. visualisation of what success would look like. Martin Luther King Junior's famous "I have a Dream" speech shows how having a clear vision can bring about radical change.

Having a *mission* means to have a clear purpose. A **mission statement** tends to be a simple declaration of the underlying purpose of an organization's existence and its core values. For example, a school might set its mission as 'provision of wide opportunities and achievement for all'. Unlike objectives, the mission statement does not have a distinct time frame and tends to be qualitative rather than quantitative. A well-produced mission statement is clearly defined and realistically achievable. It provides a sense of direction, guides decision-making and unifies all people and corporate cultures within the organization in an attempt to achieve the overall vision.

Although vision and mission statements are quite often confused, they do serve complementary purposes. The main differences are:

- The vision statement addresses the question 'what do we want to become?' whereas the mission statement deals with the question 'what is our business?'

- Vision statements are focused on the very long term, whereas mission statements can focus on the medium or long term.

- Hence, mission statements are updated more frequently than vision statements.

Figure 1.3.a The Adidas logo

31

- Vision statements do not have to be actual targets that must be achieved (this is the purpose of setting mission statements). Instead, vision statements allow people to see what could be.

- The mission statement tends to outline the values of the business, i.e. its beliefs and guiding principles that set the framework for how managers and employees operate on a daily basis.

Despite the advantages of vision and mission statements, there are some limitations. Critics argue that such statements are no more than a public relations stunt. After all, the ultimate purpose of most businesses, they argue, is to maximise profits. Constructing vision and mission statements can also be very time consuming; it is very difficult to draft a statement that caters for all the dynamics of a business. Even the best thought-out statements might not be supported by all stakeholders, such as employees on part-time or temporary contracts. In such cases, it can be a lengthy process to convert people's beliefs and behaviour.

Box 1.3.a Steps in setting mission statements

1. Defines the organization, i.e. what it is
2. Outlines what the organization aspires to be (in line with its vision statement)
3. Limited enough to exclude certain ventures
4. Broad enough to allow for growth in a creative or innovative way
5. Distinguishes the organization from others
6. Serves to evaluate current business activities
7. Phrased clearly so that it is understood by all.

IB Learner Profile – Be reflective and a be a thinker

The IBO Mission states that: "The International Baccalaureate aims to develop inquiring, knowledgeable and caring young people who help to create a better and more peaceful world through intercultural understanding and respect." Think and reflect on the extent to which Business Management addresses the IB mission statement.

IB Learner Profile – Be an inquirer

Visit Franklin Covey's mission statement builder website (www.franklincovey.com/msb/) and investigate the mission statements of famous leaders such as Benjamin Franklin, Mahatma Gandhi, Martin Luther King Jr. and Ludwig van Beethoven. Then think about your own values to build your personal mission statement.

IB Learner Profile – Be reflective

Reflect on your own school's vision or mission statement. To what extent is it valid to all stakeholder groups of the school? To what evident is the vision or mission statement evident in the daily operations of your school?

Question 1.3.1 Vision and mission statements

- To be the most successful premium manufacturer in the industry – BMW
- The company exists to benefit and refresh everyone it touches – Coca-Cola
- To organize the world's information and make it universally accessible and useful – Google
- Creating the finest ice cream – Häagen-Dazs
- To solve unsolved problems innovatively – Mary Kay Cosmetics
- To help people and businesses throughout the world realise their full potential – Microsoft
- A just world without poverty – Oxfam
- To make people happy – Walt Disney Company.

Source: Company websites

(a) Define the term **mission statement**. [2 marks]

(b) With reference to the the above examples, examine the role of vision and mission statements in business organizations. [6 marks]

Aims, objectives, strategies and tactics

Aims, objectives, strategies and tactics, and their relationships.
AO3
© IBO, 2017

Aims are the general and long-term goals of an organization. They are broadly expressed as vague and unquantifiable statements, e.g. 'to provide high quality education to all' or 'to promote social and environmental integrity'. Aims serve to give a general purpose and direction for an organization and are often expressed in a mission statement. Aims are usually set by the senior directors of the organization.

Objectives are the short-to-medium-term and specific targets an organization sets in order to achieve its aims. They are more specific and quantifiable (measurable). For example, a school's objective could be 'to achieve a 95% pass rate within two years' or 'to encourage the use of ICT to enhance teaching and learning'. Objectives must be consistent with the firm's aims. They can be set by managers and their subordinates (Table 1.3.a).

Without having clear aims and objectives, organizations have no sense of direction or purpose. It is rather like getting into a taxi and not knowing where you want to go! Organizational aims and objectives are important for three reasons:

- *To measure and control* – Aims and objectives help to control a firm's plans as they set the boundaries for business activity. They provide the basis for measuring and controlling the performance of the business as a whole.

- *To motivate* – Aims and objectives can help to inspire managers and employees to reach a common goal, thus helping to unify and motivate the workforce. They also encourage managers to think strategically and plan for the long term.

- *To direct* – Aims and objectives provide an agreed clear focus (or sense of purpose) for all individuals and departments of an organization. They are the foundation for decision-making and are used to devise business strategies.

Common mistake

Students often misuse the terms 'aims' and 'objectives' treating them as synonyms, i.e. using the terms interchangeably. This reveals a lack of understanding and application of these terms.

Strategies are the medium to long-term plans of action to achieve the strategic objectives of an organization. **Tactics** are short-term methods used to achieve an organization's *tactical objectives*. Both strategy and tactics serve matching purposes, i.e. how a business plans to get to where it wants to be. Once a business has decided on its short and long term goals, it can then decide on the most suitable methods to achieve these targets. There are several levels of business strategy:

- *Operational strategies* are the day-to-day methods used to improve the efficiency of an organization. These are aimed at trying to achieve the tactical objectives of a business, e.g. a restaurant might investigate how to reduce customer waiting time without compromising the quality of its service.

- *Generic strategies* are those that affect the business as a whole. These generic strategies look at ways in which a business can gain a competitive advantage in order to meet its goals.

- *Corporate strategies* are targeted at the long term goals of a business, i.e. they are used to achieve the strategic objectives of an organization. For example, a firm might aim for market dominance through mergers and takeovers of rivals in the industry.

Table 1.3.a Summary of differences between aims and objectives

Aims	Objectives
What the business wants to achieve	What the business has to do to achieve the aims
Not necessarily time-bound	Time-bound
Vague or abstract goal	Specific and measurable target
What a business wants to happen	What a business needs to happen
Set by senior leaders	Set by managers or their subordinates

Business organization and esnvironment

CORE

Tactical objectives are short-term goals that affect a section of the organization. They are specific goals that guide the daily functioning of certain departments or operations, e.g. to raise sales by $10 million within the next year or to keep staff turnover below 10%. Tactical objectives tend to refer to targets set for up to 12 months, such as:

- *Survival* – New and unestablished businesses are likely to encounter a number of problems (see Unit 1.2) such as limited recognition from customers and/or intense competition from existing firms. Hence, survival becomes a key priority. Survival can also be important for more established organizations, e.g. an economic *recession* (see Unit 1.5) can quite easily threaten the survival of many businesses. Alternatively, if a business becomes a takeover target (see Unit 1.6), then its survival as it currently exists could easily become the key tactical objective.

- *Sales revenue maximisation* – New businesses strive to maximise their sales revenue to establish themselves in the marketplace. Sales staff and agents, such as those selling insurance or real estate, favour this tactical objective as their earnings are linked to the level of sales. However, sales revenue is not *profit* (the surplus that remains after all costs are paid). In the long run, a firm with high sales but low or no profit will struggle to survive.

Strategic objectives are the longer-term goals of a business. Some examples are outlined below (but note that these vary between businesses, based on their own circumstances and priorities):

- **Profit maximisation**   Traditionally, the main strategic objective of most private sector businesses is to maximise profits. Profit provides an incentive for entrepreneurs to take risks in setting up and running a business. For incorporated businesses (Unit 1.2), a proportion of the profits (known as **dividends**) is distributed to their shareholders. Without profit, owners and investors find it difficult to justify the existence of the business.

- **Growth**   The growth of a business is usually measured by an increase in sales revenues or by market share (the percentage of the industry's sales made by the business). Growth is essential for business survival, especially with the exposure of businesses to mergers and takeovers (see Unit 1.6). The failure to grow may result in declining competitiveness.

Figure 1.3.b Growth is essential for business survival

- **Market standing** - This refers to the extent to which a business has presence in the industry. For example, Microsoft has high market standing as the market leader in the computer software industry. Walmart has high market standing for being the world's largest retailer. Toyota gained higher market standing when it overtook General Motors as the world's largest car producer in 2012. Apple has high market standing due to its innovative products and designs. The Body Shop has high market standing for being a socially responsible business.

- **Image and reputation**   Businesses may strive to enhance their image and reputation. A bad image, perhaps portrayed by the media, can turn customers against a firm's products and services and tarnish the corporate image of the business. Increasingly, businesses strive to deliver improved levels of customer service, better facilities and superior after-sales care. Employees are more likely to be motivated and proud if the business has a positive corporate image. This helps to attract high-calibre staff during recruitment. Suppliers also prefer to do business with organizations that are reputable and reliable.

Theory of knowledge

Some people argue that by targeting children, especially in an era of growing child obesity in many parts of the world, parents face unnecessary pressure to buy their children fast-food products. Do you consider McDonald's marketing of its 'Happy Meal' as unethical? Justify your answer.

In practice, businesses have a combination of the aforementioned strategic objectives. These objectives will also change from time to time, such as survival being a key objective if a firm is threatened by a takeover. The organizational culture and whether a business operates in the private or public sector are also factors that affect the aims and objectives it sets.

Exam tip!

Ensure that you understand the differences and links between aims, objectives, strategies and tactics (OATS):

- **Objectives** specify what an organization needs to achieve in order to get what it wants, e.g. survival or increased market share.
- **Aims** state what an organization wants, e.g. to become the market leader in the industry.
- **Tactics** are short-term actions used to achieve an organization's tactical objectives, e.g. improved market research.
- **Strategies** are the actions that enable an organization to meet its goals, e.g. expanding into new markets.

Question 1.3.2   Lenovo

Chinese multinational technology firm *Lenovo* acquired the personal computers division of IBM in 2005. *Lenovo's* aim was to establish itself outside of the Asian market by owning IBM's globally recognised brands such as ThinkPad laptops. *Lenovo* is committed to four key values:

- Customer service - serving customers
- Trust and integrity
- Teamwork across cultures
- Innovation and entrepreneurial spirit.

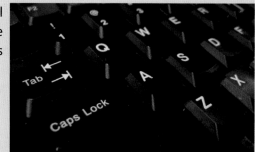

Lenovo has tried to increase its market presence by sponsoring key sporting events and teams, such as McLaren, the British Formula One (Grand Prix) Team, the Williams Formula One racing team, the National Basketball Association (NBA), and the 2008 Beijing Olympic Games. In 2012, *Lenovo* became the official sponsor of the National Football League (NFL), its largest sponsorship in America. Its **strategy** has helped the company to gain **market share** around the world.

Source: adapted from www.lenovo.com

(a) (i) Define the term **strategy**.   *[2 marks]*

(a) (ii) Define the term **market share**.   *[2 marks]*

(b) Explain why is it important for Lenovo to specify its organizational objectives.   *[4 marks]*

(c) Examine the barriers that might prevent Lenovo meeting its objectives.   *[6 marks]*

CORE

The need for changing objectives

The need for organizations to change objectives and innovate in response to changes in internal and external environments. AO3
© IBO, 2017

There are various factors that can cause the aims and objectives of an organization to change, requiring innovative responses to these factors. Some of the internal factors (those within the control of the organization) include:

- *Corporate culture* (the accepted norms and customs of a business) – Firms with a flexible and adaptable organizational culture are more likely to have innovative objectives over time.

- *Type and size of organization* (see Unit 1.2) – Any change in the legal structure of a business is likely to cause a change in its objectives. With a separation of ownership and control, such as in public limited companies, various stakeholder objectives need to be considered, including managerial objectives (e.g. higher bonuses) and shareholder objectives (e.g. higher profits).

- *Private versus public sector organizations* – Unlike most private sector firms, public sector organizations do not strive for profit maximisation but to provide a service to the general public.

- *Age of the business* – Newly established firms tend to have break-even and survival as their key objectives. Established firms might strive for growth and higher market share.

- *Finance* – The amount of available finance will determine the scale of a firm's objectives. For example, a huge sum of money is needed if the objective is to expand into overseas markets.

- *Risk profile* – If managers and owners have a relatively high willingness and ability to take risks, then more ambitious objectives are likely to be set, such as the pursuit of new innovations.

- *Crisis management* – Businesses may face internal crises such as unexpectedly high rates of staff absenteeism and staff turnover, falling productivity and motivation problems, liquidity problems (see Unit 3.7), or issues about quality standards.

Case study

In early 2014, General Motors recalled 1.46 million cars from China due to a safety issue with the fuel pumps in its Buick and Chevrolet cars. Ford also recalled 81,000 of its Kuga cars due to steering problems. In late 2013, Volkswagen recalled over 640,300 vehicles due to oil problems. In 2018, Tesla recalled 123,000 Model S cars worldwide due to steering problems.

External factors (those beyond the control of the organization) can change the objectives of a business. These factors include:

- *State of the economy* – The state of the economy (see Unit 1.5) can change organizational objectives, e.g. booms (when national income and employment are high) provide opportunities whereas slumps (when unemployment is high and consumption is low) cause threats.

- *Government constraints* – Some government rules and regulations (see Unit 1.5) can limit what a business might strive to achieve. For example, environmental protection laws can limit the ability of firms to maximise profit due to the higher costs of compliance.

- *The presence and power of pressure groups* – Pressure groups (see Unit 1.4) can force a business to review its approach to ethics through their lobbying. Pressure

groups may harm a firm's image if it is not adopting a socially responsible approach to conducting business.

- *New technologies* – New technologies and innovations (Figure 1.3.c) can create many new business opportunities, thus change organizational objectives. Innovative firms such as Samsung were able to exploit digital technologies to dominate the smartphone and smart TV industries. The use of e-commerce (see Unit 4.8) has also revolutionised how most businesses operate.

Figure 1.3.c Self check-in technology provide cost-saving benefits to airlines

Exam tip !

Whist there is little, if anything, that a business can do about changes in the external environment, successful businesses alter their practices and operations to adapt to such changes. Also, remember that positive changes can occur from the external environment, thus creating business opportunities.

It should be noted that objectives have the potential to conflict. For example, employees may demand better pay and working conditions which may subsequently reduce profits, at least in the short term. Nevertheless, in the pursuit of success, managers must base their strategy on achieving the organizational objectives. As US media mogul William Randolph Hearst (1863–1951) said, "*You must keep your mind on the objective, not on the obstacle.*"

Ethical objectives

Ethical objectives and corporate social responsibility (CSR). AO1

The reasons why organizations set ethical objectives and the impact of implementing them. AO3

The evolving role and nature of CSR. AO3

© IBO, 2017

Ethics are the moral principles that guide decision-making and strategy. Morals are concerned with what is considered to be right or wrong, from society's point of view, e.g. the use of direct marketing techniques aimed at children is banned in many countries. Health and Safety at Work legislation (such as regular rest breaks and a safe working environment) helps to prevent exploitation of employees. **Business ethics** are therefore the actions of people and organizations that are considered to be morally correct. An ethical and socially responsible business acts morally towards workers, customers, shareholders and the natural environment (see Figure 1.3.d, and Boxes 1.3.b and c).

Figure 1.3.d Littering is considered to be an unethical act in most societies

Pressures to act ethically might come from within the business, e.g. employees might demand better opportunities for training, development and promotion. Ethical behaviour might also be imposed upon a business by external factors. Customers, for instance, do not want to be associated with businesses that earn profit through illegal, immoral or irresponsible actions.

Box 1.3.b Examples of ethical objectives

- Reducing pollution by using more environmentally friendly production processes
- Disposal of waste in an environmental manner
- Increased recycling of waste materials
- Offering staff sufficient rest breaks during work
- Fairer conditions of trade with less economically developed countries (LEDCs).

Box 1.3.c Examples of unethical behaviour

- *Financial dishonesty* occurs if a business mismanages its finances, e.g. deliberate misrepresentation of its financial accounts (which is also illegal). There might also be moral issues, such as extravagant business expenses incurred by the directors (unethical but not illegal).
- *Environmental neglect* and damage often occur as business activity can create harmful consequences to the natural environment, e.g. pollution and the depletion of non-renewable resources.
- *Exploitation of the workforce* occurs if employers mistreat staff through the deliberate neglect of employee welfare. Many multinational companies have been criticised for the poor pay and working conditions offered to staff in LEDCs.
- *Exploitation of suppliers* happens when large businesses take advantage of their suppliers, forcing them to cut prices. This is controversial, especially when the business is exploiting suppliers in LEDCs or when the savings are not passed onto consumers in terms of lower prices.
- *Exploitation of consumers* happens if firms knowingly sell products that have harmful side-effects, e.g. tobacco, alcohol and gambling services. Large firms with few, if any, competitors might abuse their market power by charging excessively high prices.

Case study

In 2006, Indian Airlines (now merged with Air India) was heavily criticised by the mass media for grounding female flight attendants for being 'too fat' to travel. They were told to lose weight or risk losing their jobs.

In 2010, female workers at Hooters, the American fast food chain known, file law suits against the company of claims of weight discrimination, with at least one worker being placed on weight probation.

Business organization and esnvironment

CORE

Case study

Faced with negative exposure in best-sellers like Fast Food Nation and movies such as Super-size Me (https://goo.gl/mvGa2h), McDonald's responded to public demand for improvements by broadening its product range to include fresh salads and other healthier alternatives.

Socially responsible businesses are those that act morally towards their stakeholders (see Unit 1.4), such as their employees and the local community. These obligations are known as **corporate social responsibilities** (CSR). For example, McDonald's staff regularly go on litter patrol to collect rubbish (including trash not generated by McDonald's customers) in the vicinity of their restaurants. Lenovo, China's largest computer-maker, commits 1% of its pre-tax income to good causes as part of its CSR policy. There are three broad views and attitudes towards the role of businesses in delivering CSR:

- *The self-interest (non-compliance) attitude* The role of businesses is to generate profits for their owners. Governments, not businesses, are responsible for sorting out social problems. In pursuing the profit motive, firms become more efficient and prosperous, thereby helping society indirectly (through employment, wealth creation and corporation tax payments).

- *The altruistic attitude* Humanitarian and unselfish behaviour, i.e. altruistic businesses do what they can to improve society such as willingly donating money to charity or investing in local community projects, regardless of whether their actions help to increase profits.

- *The strategic attitude* This view argues that businesses ought to be socially responsible only if such actions help them to become more profitable. Such firms see CSR as a method of long-term growth.

To achieve their ethical objectives, an increasing number of businesses have adopted an ethical **code of practice** and publish this in their annual report. The code of conduct refers to the documented beliefs and philosophies of the business. It is important because people need to know what is considered acceptable or not acceptable within an organization, e.g. guidelines and expectations on employee behaviour, such as having personal integrity and consideration for others. These values might differ from one individual to another and from one business to another. Hence, a code of ethics can provide a framework for consistency and uniformity.

IB Learner Profile – Being principled

Scenario: You see a teacher drop her wallet in the school corridor, but the teacher doesn't realise she's done so. There are no other people around. What should you do?

The answer will depend upon the values or moral principles that you feel are important. These could be determined by numerous factors such as:

- Integrity – how honest you are.
- Sympathy – how you feel about the teacher losing her wallet.
- Empathy – if you have experienced losing your own valuables, you will have a better understanding of the feelings that the teacher has.
- Loyalty – the teacher could be your favourite teacher or someone you really respect.
- Conscience – whether the student has any concerns or feelings of guilt.
- Justice – you might think the teacher is rather careless and should learn the hard way!

Theory of knowledge

In reality, is it possible to determine whether CSR is genuine altruism or selfish acts used to improve a firm's corporate image? Does this even matter?

Table 1.3.b Advantages and limitations of ethical behaviour

Advantages	Limitations
Improved corporate image Improved corporate image - Acting ethically and in a socially responsible way can help to enhance the corporate image and reputation of a business. Conversely, the media will report unethical business behaviour which could seriously damage the firm's corporate image.	**Compliance costs** The costs of being socially responsible are potentially very high, e.g. organic agricultural products are far more expensive to harvest than genetically modified crops due to the additional time and money involved.
Increased customer loyalty Customers are more likely to be loyal to a business that does not act immorally. For example, The Body Shop has established a large customer base worldwide based on its ethical policy of not testing its products on animals.	**Lower profits** If compliance costs cannot be passed onto consumers in the form of higher prices, profitability is likely to fall. An *ethical dilemma* for the business exists when ethical decision-making involves adopting a less profitable course of action.
Cost cutting Ethical behaviour can help to cut certain costs, e.g. being environmentally friendly can reduce the amount of (excess) packaging. Socially responsible businesses can benefit from avoiding litigation costs (expenses associated with legal action taken against a business) due to unethical and irresponsible business activities.	**Stakeholder conflict** Not all stakeholders are keen on the business adopting CSR, especially if this conflicts with other objectives such as profit maximisation. Speculative shareholders and financial investors are more concerned with short term profits than its long term ethical stance. So, managers may be pressured into pursuing goals other than ethical ones.
Improved staff morale and motivation Ethical and socially responsible behaviour can help a business to attract and retain highly motivated staff. People are more likely to be proud of the business they work for if it acts ethically and within the law. Thus, it is a driving force for improved productivity and employee loyalty.	**Ethics and CSR are subjective** Views about what is considered right or wrong depend on the beliefs and principles held by individuals and society. Legislation can help to provide guidelines about what is socially accepted.

Case study

In 1991, McDonald's became the world's first company to voluntarily phase out the use of chlorofluorocarbons (CFCs) in the production of foam packaging. CFCs were associated with ozone depletion, so their withdrawal by the world's largest restaurant chain helped to reduce the harmful effects on the ozone layer. In 2018, the company announced it would phase out the use of plastic straws.

Theory of knowledge

Using any two Ways of Knowing, discuss how it is possible to 'know' what is right for managers to do.

The evolving role and nature of corporate social responsibility (CSR)

Attitudes towards CSR may change over time. What was once considered acceptable by society, such as smacking or caning disruptive students in school, may no longer be the case. Environmental protection was not a major issue prior to the 1980s. Some countries do not think it is necessary to impose a national minimum wage, whilst others feel that this should prevent some businesses from paying unethically low wages to their employees. The advertising of tobacco products is considered socially immoral in many parts of the world (where advertising of tobacco products is banned), but this is not the case in other countries. The nature of CSR is rather subjective – what is considered 'right' or 'wrong' is largely based on public opinion, which tends to change over time.

Changes in societal norms mean that businesses need to review their CSR policies and practices from time to time. For instance, objectives and strategies have changed in recent times due to a more positive attitude towards the hiring and promotion of female staff. Through education, there has also been a greater tolerance and acceptance of multiculturalism and this has directly affected employment practices (see Unit 2.1). Media exposure in many countries has meant that large multinational companies are expected to donate part of their profits to charity. Customers are more careful about spending money on products from socially irresponsible firms. Investors are more wary of placing their money with unethical firms, such as those that employ child labour.

Through pressure group action and educational awareness, an increasing number of businesses are actively trying to do their part for the environment. Climate change and environmental damage are huge concerns of governments and citizens around the world, so businesses are changing their objectives to reflect

Business organization and esnvironment

CORE

their part in the preservation of the planet. Businesses that continue to pollute and damage the environment are likely to earn themselves a poor corporate image with devastating consequences. Hence, society's changing perception of what is considered socially moral will directly affect an organization's view of its own corporate social responsibilities.

CSR is further complicated when businesses operate in different countries. What is considered acceptable in one country may be totally undesirable in others. For example, Serbia and Russia are huge consumers of tobacco, so cigarette advertising is less stringent than in other countries such as the UK or Singapore. Australia and Canada judge environmental concern as a key indicator of CSR, whereas India and China place less emphasis on environmental protection.

Finally, some analysts argue that it is not the role of managers to decide what is right or wrong. This is because managers do not use or risk their own money when making decisions about what they personally believe to be socially responsible. Instead, managers are employed to run a business on behalf of the owners who seek profit, rather than using money in socially responsible ways such as donating money to charity. Moreover, it can be difficult to measure or monitor the extent to which a business is socially responsible due to the subjective and evolving nature of CSR. Nevertheless, the potential benefits of being socially responsible suggest that managers have a role in promoting and encouraging CSR in the workplace (see Box 1.3.d).

The evolving role and nature of CSR means that businesses must adapt to meet their social responsibilities. There are numerous ways they might do this, such as by:

- Providing accurate information and labelling – This can help consumers to make better informed decisions, e.g. food manufacturers might provide truthful nutritional information.

- Adhering to fair employment practices – Firms can fulfil their social responsibilities to their employees by providing

decent working conditions, fair remuneration and training opportunities. Conversely, some multinational companies have been criticised for exploitation of child labour by hiring under-aged workers in less economically developed countries.

- Having consideration for the environment – Firms may seek to use more recycled materials in the production process, recycle a greater proportion of their waste materials and aim to reduce any pollution caused by their operations.

- Active community work – This includes voluntary and charity work, helping to give something back to society, e.g. sponsoring and participating in local community events.

Figure 1.3.e Many businesses support local community events such as charity runs

Businesses have long realised that a good reputation (how others view the organization) can give them an important competitive edge. According to *Fortune* magazine, the top 500 American firms donate over 2% of their post-tax profits to charity. This might be due to their goal or desire to act in a socially responsible way, or it could be due to the fear of negative publicity caused by non-compliance. Acting responsibly can help to improve a firm's reputation, but the compliance costs will add to its expenses. For staff to help the organization meet its ethical objectives, they must be convinced that CSR is in their best interest too.

Box 1.3.d   Encouraging corporate social responsibility
- The media, e.g. encouragement, exposure or pressure from the media (mass, press and social media)
- Ethical codes of practice, e.g. provide guidelines and parameters for the workforce
- Training, e.g. updating employee skills in delivering CSR, such as good customer care
- Government assistance, e.g. subsidising the purchase of energy-efficient equipment and machinery
- Government legislation, e.g. minimum wage laws, pollution fines or littering charges
- Competitors' actions, e.g. pressure from rival businesses to adopt CSR policies.

Question 1.3.3 McDonald's versus Burger King

Ronald McDonald House Charities (RMHC) is a non-profit organization, created by McDonald's. The charity's mission statement is to "directly improve the health and well-being of children". Operating in 42 countries, RMHC has helped to make a difference to millions of seriously ill children and their families.

Source: www.rmhc.org

Burger King, the world's second largest fast-food chain and the largest rival of McDonald's, has used humanely-sourced meat and eggs since 2007. This means Burger King gives priority and better deals to suppliers that provide cage-free chickens and free-range pigs. Burger King operates two national charitable organizations: the Have It Your Way Foundation (which focuses on hunger alleviation, disease prevention and community education) and the McLamore Foundation (providing scholarships to students since 2000).

Source: www.bkmclamorefoundation.org

(a) In the context of the above case studies, describe the meaning of ethical business behaviour.   *[2 marks]*

(b) Discuss whether acting ethically ultimately provides McDonald's and Burger King with competitive advantages.

[10 marks]

Despite the driving forces for setting ethical objectives, whether a business acts in a socially responsible way depends on several interrelated factors:

- The involvement, influence and power of various stakeholders, such as pressure groups

- Corporate culture and attitudes towards CSR

- Societal expectations, i.e. the general public's awareness of concerns for CSR issues

- Exposure and pressure from the media

- Experience – quite often it takes a crisis or bad experience to precipitate attention to CSR

- Compliance costs, i.e. the human and financial resources needed to implement CSR policies

- Laws and regulations, i.e. legislation that govern how firms conduct themselves responsibly.

Theory of knowledge

Does the awareness and knowledge of ethics bring about an obligation for businesses to behave morally?

Theory of knowledge

Does the study of Business Management tend to steer people towards ethical or self-centred decision-making? Does this matter?

Question 1.3.4   Walmart

Walmart is the world's largest retailer and largest private sector employer in the USA. The company has, on numerous occasions, been fined millions of dollars by the US government for violating air and water pollution legislation. This obviously harmed the image of the global retailer, with the media alleging that 8% of customers had stopped shopping at *Walmart* as a result of its neglect of the environment.

Labour unions have criticised *Walmart's* unethical business practices which have caused staff turnover rates of around 70% in some stores. *Walmart* has also been taken to court for not paying employees for overtime, forcing them to work without proper rest breaks, and discriminating against female workers for pay and promotion.

(a) State two possible barriers to socially responsible business behaviour.   *[2 marks]*

(b) Discuss whether it is morally correct for businesses such as *Walmart* to put profits before the environment and the welfare of their employees.   *[10 marks]*

SWOT analysis

SWOT analysis of a given organization. AO3 and AO4

© IBO, 2017

SWOT analysis is a simple yet very useful decision-making tool. SWOT is an acronym for **S**trengths, **W**eaknesses, **O**pportunities and **T**hreats. It can be used to assess the current situation of a business organization. SWOT analysis considers both internal factors (strengths and weaknesses) and external factors (opportunities and threats) that are relevant to the organization under investigation.

- **Strengths** are internal factors that are favourable compared with competitors, e.g. strong brand loyalty, a good corporate image or highly skilled workers. Strengths help the business to better achieve its objectives. Hence, strengths need to be developed and protected.

- **Weaknesses** are internal factors that are unfavourable when compared with rivals, i.e. they create competitive disadvantages. Weaknesses are therefore likely to prevent or delay the business from achieving its goals. Hence, to remain competitive, the business needs to reduce or remove its weaknesses.

- **Opportunities** are the external possibilities (prospects) for future development, i.e. changes in the external environment that create favourable conditions for a business. For example, India and China present many business opportunities, such as a huge customer base and rapid economic growth. Hence, SWOT analysis can help firms to formulate their business strategy.

- **Threats** are the external factors that hinder the prospects for an organization, i.e. they cause problems for the business. Examples include: technological breakdowns, product recalls, changes in fashion, price wars, oil crises, recessions, natural disasters, and the outbreak of infectious diseases.

SWOT analysis can be an extremely useful tool for investigating all sorts of business situations. It can, for example, be used to provide a framework for:

- *Competitor analysis*, e.g. the threats posed by a rival or the strengths of a competitor.

- *Assessing opportunities*, e.g. the development and growth of the organization.

- *Risk assessment*, e.g. the probable effects of investing in a certain project or location.

- *Reviewing corporate strategy*, e.g. the market position or direction of the business.

- *Strategic planning*, e.g. the decision to diversify or expand overseas.

Note: SWOT analysis should not be a list of advantages and disadvantages of a decision or issue. Instead, it is a situational analysis in relation to the external and internal factors that relate to an organization.

Table 1.3.c Advantages and disadvantages of SWOT analysis

Advantages	Disadvantages
Completing a SWOT analysis can be quite simple and quick.	It is rather simplistic and does not demand detailed analysis.
It has a wide range of applications, e.g. reacting to the threat of rivals entering the market.	The model is static whereas the business environment is always changing, so the shelf life of a SWOT analysis is rather limited.
SWOT analysis helps to determine the organization's position in the market and therefore aids the formulation of business strategy for its long-term survival.	The analysis is only useful if decision-makers are open about the weaknesses and willing to act upon them, i.e. devoting time, people and money to tackling weaknesses and threats.
It encourages foresight and proactive thinking in the decision-making process.	SWOT analysis is not typically used in isolation. Better decisions are made if more information is available, so other strategic tools are also used.
It can help reduce the risks of decision-making by demanding objective and logical thought processes.	

Case study

The outbreak of SARS (severe acute respiratory syndrome) in 2003 meant that tourists stayed away from Southeast Asia. Airline companies suffered hugely as did travel agents and hotels. The *South China Morning Post* reported that Ocean Park (a popular Hong Kong theme park) lost HK$15 million ($2 million) a month due to the SARS outbreak. The cost to the global economy was estimated to be HK$40bn ($5.16bn).

Exam tip !

When carrying out a SWOT analysis, remember that strengths and weaknesses are the *internal* factors that an organization *currently* faces. Opportunities and threats are the *external* factors that the organization is *likely* to face in the near future.

Exam tip !

A common exam question will require you to examine the position of a business by using a SWOT analysis framework. Therefore, be sure to learn how to use a SWOT analysis properly. Remember that the strengths and weaknesses refer to the current and internal position of the firm. The opportunities and threats should stem from a STEEPLE analysis of the external environment (see Unit 1.5).

Exam tip !

When using a SWOT analysis in the exam, do not present the SWOT in tabular form. Using such a format can encourage candidates to squeeze their answers to fit inside the table (drawn by the student). Instead, examiners prefer written explanations and justifications. It is acceptable to write in bullet point format under each SWOT heading so long as the examiner can understand the reasoning behind your arguments.

Business organization and esnvironment

CORE

Table 1.3.d SWOT analysis template (illustrative example)*

Strengths	Weaknesses
• Unique selling point • Brand awareness and brand loyalty • Experience, knowledge and skills • Market share / market dominance • Corporate image and reputation • Accreditation, endorsement or official support • Core competencies, e.g. product quality • Geographical location • Value for money (price in relation to quality)	• Limited revenue streams • Escalating costs of production • Poor cash flow / liquidity problems • Higher prices than competitors • Demotivated and/or unproductive workforce • Limited sources of finance • Lack of spare capacity • Restricted product range • Poor location
Opportunities	Threats
• Economic growth / upswing in trade cycle • Trade liberalisation • Weakening exchange rate • Technological developments / innovations • Market growth • New markets and locations • Demographic and social lifestyle changes • Government spending programmes • Mergers and acquisitions of rival firms	• New entrants in the market place • Economic downturn (recession) • Inflation (causing higher production costs) • Pressure group action, e.g. protests • Social, environmental and legal constraints • Negative media coverage and publicity • Unfavourable changes in seasons and weather • Adverse changes in fashion and tastes • Crises, e.g. natural disaster or power shortage

* Note: what might be strengths for one firm, such as its brand reputation and human capital, might actually be weaknesses for another business. Equally, some threats, such as a change in weather, might also be considered as opportunities for other businesses.

Question 1.3.5 Kidzplay Bouncy Castles

Kidzplay Bouncy Castles is a private business that caters for children's parties and events in London, UK.

Outline whether each of the following scenarios represents a strength, weakness, opportunity or threat to Kidzplay Bouncy Castles.

(a) Limited competition in a niche market. *[2 marks]*

(b) Limited marketing on its new website *[2 marks]*

(c) Issues of recruiting and retaining staff. *[2 marks]*

(d) Demand in the winter months is low. *[2 marks]*

(e) Large profit margins could attract new competitors. *[2 marks]*

The Ansoff matrix

Ansoff matrix for different growth strategies of a given organization.

AO3 and AO4

© IBO, 2017

The **Ansoff matrix** (1957) is an analytical tool that helps managers to choose and devise various product and market growth strategies. Professor Igor Ansoff (1918–2002) showed the different growth strategies a firm can take depending on whether it wants to sell new or existing products in either new or existing markets (see Figure 1.3.f). The four product–market growth strategies, or growth options, are explained below.

		Products	
		Existing	*New*
Markets	*Existing*	Market penetration	Product development
	New	Market development	Diversification

Figure 1.3.f The Ansoff matrix

Market penetration

This is a low-risk growth strategy as businesses choose to focus on *selling existing products in existing markets*, i.e. to increase their market share of current products. This might be achieved by offering more competitive prices or by improved advertising to enhance the desirability of the product. In addition to attracting more customers, firms might attempt to entice existing customers to buy more frequently, perhaps by offering customer loyalty schemes. Brands might also be repositioned (see Unit 4.2) to achieve market penetration.

An advantage of market penetration is that the business focuses on markets and products that it is familiar with. Hence, market research expenditure (see Unit 4.4) can be minimised. It is also the safest of the four growth strategies. A limitation is that competitors, especially stronger rivals, will retaliate to firms trying to take away their customers and market share. This can lead to aggressive reactions, such as price wars, thereby harming profits (in the short run at least). Also, once existing markets become saturated, alternative strategies are required if the business is to continue its growth.

Product development

This is a medium-risk growth strategy that involves *selling new products in existing markets*. Apple's launch of the iPhone revolutionised the mobile phone industry. McDonald's often frequently adds new products to its menu. Car manufacturers introduce new models and occasionally limited editions of their cars.

Product development tends to rely heavily on **product extension strategies** to prolong the demand for goods and services that have reached the saturation or decline stage of their product life cycle (see Unit 4.5). Product development is also reliant on **brand development** (see Unit 4.5) to appeal to the existing market. For example, well-established firms such as Sony or Nike can use their brands to launch new products to the market as there are fewer risks of introducing a new product under a well-known brand name. Product development is also a reason for acquiring other companies. For example, Tata Motor's acquisition of Jaguar Land Rover in 2008 meant it could cater for different types of customers without the huge costs and risks of starting a new company.

Case study

Tata Motors (www.tatamotors.com) was founded in 1945 and has become India's largest automaker, with a product range that includes cars, vans, trucks, buses, coaches, and military vehicles. In 2004, it acquired South Korean truck manufacturer Daewoo Commercial Vehicles Company. In 2008, it purchased UK luxury brands Jaguar and Land Rover. It also produces the Tata Nano, the world's cheapest mass-produced car.

Market development

Market development is a medium risk growth strategy that involves *selling existing products in new markets*, i.e. an established product is marketed to a new set of customers. This might be done through new distribution channels such as selling the existing product overseas (although this could be quite risky if the business is unfamiliar with local market conditions and cultures). Alternatively, promotional strategies could be tweaked to make the product more appealing to the new audience. Prices could also be changed to attract different market segments. A key advantage of this growth strategy is that the firm is familiar with the product being marketed.

Business organization and esnvironment

CORE

Examples of developing new markets for existing products are sportswear manufacturers Nike and Adidas successfully marketing their clothing products for leisure rather than specifically for sport. Nokia uses market development to sell its mass produced mobile phones that have a short product life cycle in economically developed countries (where customers frequently upgrade their phones) by selling these in lower income countries such as India, Sri Lanka, Indonesia and Nigeria. However, the success of a product in one market does not necessarily guarantee its success in other markets. For example, French retailing giant Carrefour pulled out of Thailand, Malaysia and Singapore in late 2010 after failing to establish a market presence. Google also struggled to establish itself in China, where local firm Baidu maintains about 70% market share.

Diversification

Diversification is a high-risk growth strategy that involves *selling new products in new markets*. For example, The Virgin Group is a diversified company with its various strategic business units such as Virgin Atlantic, Virgin Mobile, Virgin Trains, Virgin Cola, Virgin Hotels and Virgin Books. In addition to gaining market share in established markets, a key driving force for diversification is to spread risks by having a well-balanced product portfolio (see Unit 4.3). Diversification is also suitable for firms that have reached saturation and are seeking new opportunities for growth.

One way to diversify is to become a **holding company**. This is a business that owns a controlling interest in other diverse companies, i.e. it owns enough shares to be able to take control of other businesses. Holding companies (or **parent companies**) can benefit from having a presence in a range of markets in different regions of the world. An example is Time Warner, the parent company of **subsidiaries** (firms owned by a holding company) such as Warner Brothers, CNN, HBO and Cartoon Network.

There are two categories of diversification. **Related diversification** occurs when a business caters for new customers within the broader confines of the same industry. For example, large commercial banks have diversified to offer insurance services. Toyota, Nissan and Honda have strategic business units (Lexus, Infiniti and Acura, respectively) that cater for higher income customers.

By contrast, **unrelated diversification** refers to growth by selling completely new products in untapped markets. An example is Samsung, with operations in consumer electronics, shipbuilding, construction, retail, chemicals and insurance. Related diversification is less risky as it builds on the product and market knowledge of the business.

Nevertheless, diversification remains the riskiest of the four growth options as the business is not on familiar territory when launching new products in markets it has little, if any, experience of. For example, UK clothing retailer Next failed to establish itself in the tablet computer market in 2010. New distribution channels also need to be established and this could be time consuming and costly. Such distractions can mean an organization loses focus of its core business, with serious consequences.

Case study   Virgin Group

Virgin Group Ltd. is a UK multinational conglomerate, co-founded by Sir Richard Branson and Nik Powell in 1970. Virgin is a truly diversified business, with operations in industries as diverse as healthcare, travel, media, entertainment, hospitality, high-speed rail, retail, communications, banking, motorsport, cruise line, charity, and even aerospace.

Table 1.3.e Summary of the Ansoff matrix

Market penetration	Product development	Market development	Diversification
Same products for existing customers	New products for existing customers	New customers for existing products	New products for new customers
Minimal risk	Moderate risk	Moderate risk	High risk
Seek to maintain or increase market share	Innovation to replace existing products	Entering overseas markets	Spreading risks
Intense competition	Product improvements	New distribution channels	Use of subsidiaries and strategic business units

Question 1.3.6   The Ansoff matrix

Use the Ansoff Matrix to explain the growth strategies in the following cases:

(a) Cadbury, the chocolate manufacturer, launches new products under the names of *Crème Eggs, Flake, Crunchie* and *Heroes* in order to compete with existing rivals.   *[4 marks]*

(b) Toyota, the world's largest car manufacturer, launches a new line of upmarket cars under the *Lexus* brand to cater for wealthier customers.   *[4 marks]*

(c) Tesco, the world's second largest retailer, expands to provide petrol and financial services to its customers.   *[4 marks]*

Organizational objectives and the CUEGIS concepts

Management experts Peter Drucker (1909–2005) and Tom Peters (born 1942) argue that successful businesses have a clear vision of their aspirations and a mission that outlines their ultimate purpose. These serve to provide a clear focus and a shared sense of purpose for business strategy. The use of organizational objectives is the starting point to achieving the vision and mission of a business. Businesses must be able to assess the effectiveness of their objectives. One way to do this, put forward by Peter Drucker, is to set **SMART objectives**:

- **S**pecific – Objectives need to be precise and succinct rather than being vague.

- **M**easurable – Objectives should be quantifiable, e.g. to increase market share, raise sales revenue or reduce staff absenteeism by a certain amount.

- **A**chievable – Objectives must be practically feasible (attainable). One variation of this criterion is that objectives should be **A**greed, i.e. be accepted and understood by key stakeholders.

- **R**ealistic – Firms should ensure that their objectives are reasonable given their limited resources, e.g. it is irrational for a new business to strive to become the market leader within its first few months of operating in an established industry.

- **T**ime constrained – There should be a specified time frame within which the objectives should be achieved.

Strategies can then be devised to achieve these targets. For example, Drucker believed that effective communication and the development of people could prevent a 'them and us' culture at work (a psychological divide between management and subordinates). He also argued that employees need to be given opportunities to develop personally, which would ultimately benefit the business. Hence, managers and workers are dependent on each other to fulfil their functions. Very importantly, Drucker argued that business strategy only works if the people involved clearly know what the objectives are.

Drucker believed that every manager should be involved in **strategic planning**, especially as the business environment is always undergoing change. He felt that businesses ought to recognise the importance of change and embrace change. For example, in periods of difficult trading times, such as during a business start-up or during an economic downturn, the main organizational objective is survival. Struggling firms are not likely to worry too much about public opinion caused by job losses. Conversely, during favourable trading periods, businesses have to decide whether to expand for future growth or to reap the benefits of higher profits for its owners. Ultimately, there is no single organizational objective that is suitable for all businesses to follow. However, he recommended that businesses should avoid meaningless change, especially since change can be very expensive. Furthermore, change that is not communicated clearly to employees can cause major demotivation among the workforce. Nevertheless, having clearly defined and realistic objectives with sufficient resources to implement appropriate business strategies can make success more likely.

The concepts of globalization and culture have also impacted corporate social responsibility, which has become a major focus of business strategy for many organizations. With increased educational awareness and media exposure of ethical issues around the globe, it is increasingly important for organizations to adopt a socially responsible attitude to the way they conduct business. Firms such as The Body Shop have been able to use this strategy to their advantage by marketing their ethical code of practice as a unique selling point. A reputation for CSR that exceeds societal norms and expectations can provide a business with competitive advantages: an enhanced corporate image, motivational effects on the workforce, attracting high-calibre staff to join the organization and attracting investment in the business. Nevertheless, the financial costs of complying with ethical and socially responsible behaviour can be too much for many businesses. For example, a profit-seeking business is likely to shut down any unprofitable divisions of its business even if this results in job losses and negative effects on the local community.

IB Learner Profile – Be an Inquirer and Be Principled

Seconds from Disaster: The Deepwater Horizon is an excellent documentary looks at the events of the Deepwater Horizon rig in the Gulf of Mexico. BP's attempt to cut back on safety checks ultimately resulted in the world's largest accidental marine oil spill, costing BP billions of dollars. Watch the video here: https://goo.gl/6R1kTB

IB Learner Profile – Be an Inquirer

Take a look at this excellent website to learn more about Cadbury Schweppes's ethical business practices: https://goo.gl/UKyivQ

Theory of knowledge

To what extent do emotions and reason influence decision making in business organizations?

CUEGIS ESSAY

With reference to an organization of your choice, examine how **change** and **ethics** affect business decision making.   *[20 marks]*

CUEGIS ESSAY

With reference to an organization of your choice, examine how **culture** and **innovation** affect business decision making.   *[20 marks]*

CUEGIS ESSAY

With reference to an organization of your choice, discuss how **globalization** and **innovation** create both opportunities and threats.   *[20 marks]*

CUEGIS ESSAY

With reference to an organization of your choice, discuss how **culture** influences both organizational objectives and business **strategy**.   *[20 marks]*

REVIEW QUESTIONS

1. How do mission and vision statements differ from one another?

2. Why are aims and objectives important to business organizations?

3. Differentiate between strategic objectives and tactical objectives.

4. Why is there a need for organizations to change objectives?

5. What is meant by ethical objectives and corporate social responsibility (CSR)?

6. What are the advantages and disadvantages of ethical behaviour and CSR?

7. How does the evolving role and nature of CSR impact on business aims and objectives?

8. What does it mean to set SMART objectives?

9. Why do objectives have changing significance in different situations?

10. Outline two recent changes in society's expectations of business behaviour.

KEY TERMS

Aims are the long-term goals of a business, often expressed in the firm's mission statement. They are a general statement of a firm's purpose or intentions and tend to be qualitative in nature.

The **Ansoff matrix** (1957) is an analytical tool to devise various product and market growth strategies, depending on whether businesses want to market new or existing products in either new or existing markets.

Corporate social responsibility (CSR) is the conscientious consideration of ethical and environmental practices related to business activity. A business that adopts CSR acts morally towards its various stakeholder groups and the wellbeing of society as a whole.

Diversification is a growth strategy in the Ansoff matrix, which involves an organization launching new products in new markets, e.g. Honda producing lawnmowers and airplanes.

An **ethical code of practice** is the documented beliefs and philosophies of an organization, so that people know what is considered acceptable or not acceptable within the organization.

Ethical objectives are organizational goals based on moral guidelines, determined by the business and/or society, which direct and determine decision-making.

Ethics are the moral principles that guide decision-making and strategy. Morals are concerned with what is considered to be right or wrong, from society's point of view.

Market development is a growth strategy in the Ansoff matrix, which focuses on using customer loyalty to persuade them (and prospective customers) to purchase a new product from the business.

Market penetration is a growth strategy in the Ansoff matrix that focuses on developing existing markets with existing products, in order to increase the organization's sales revenue and market share.

A **mission statement** refers to the declaration of an organization's overall purpose. It forms the foundation for setting the objectives of a business.

Objectives are the relatively short term targets of an organization. They are often expressed as SMART objectives.

Business organization and esnvironment

CORE

Product development is a growth strategy in the Ansoff matrix that involves introducing new products to existing customers, by developing or replacing current products.

SMART objectives are targets that are specific, measurable, achievable, realistic and time constrained.

Strategic objectives are the longer-term goals of a business, such as profit maximization, growth, market standing and an improved corporate image

Strategies are plans of action that businesses use to achieve their targets, i.e. the long-term plans of the whole organization.

SWOT analysis is an analytical tool used to assess the internal strengths and weaknesses and the external opportunities and threats of a business decision, issue or problem.

Tactical objectives are short-term goals that affect a section of the organization. They are specific goals that guide the daily functioning of certain departments or operations, e.g. survival and sales revenue maximization.

Tactics are the short-term plans of action that firms use to achieve their objectives.

A **them and us culture** exists in the workplace if there is a psychological divide between senior management and subordinates.

A **vision statement** is an organization's long-term aspirations, i.e. where it ultimately wants to be.

Vision enables firms to know their long term aspirations

1.4 Stakeholders

"Just because we aren't all the same doesn't mean we have nothing in common." - Kirk Kerekes, US entrepreneur

SL/HL content	Assessment objective
Interests of internal stakeholders	AO2
Interests of external stakeholders	AO2
Possible areas of mutual benefit and conflict between stakeholders' interests	AO3

© IBO, 2017

Business organization and environment

CORE

Internal stakeholders

The interests of internal stakeholders. AO2

© IBO, 2017

A **stakeholder** is any individual, group or organization with a direct interest in, and is affected by, the activities and performance of a business. **Internal stakeholders** are members of the organization, i.e. the employees, managers, directors and shareholders of the organization.

Employees

The staff of a business will have a stake (an interest) in the organization they work for. Employees are likely to strive to improve their pay (and other financial benefits), working conditions (such as hours of work and the working environment), job security and opportunities for career progression.

Theorists such as Charles Handy argue that employees are an organization's best asset. It is the staff who produce goods and services for sale; they are the ones who communicate with the customers. Consequently, more employers have encouraged their workers to be involved in decision-making. A motivated workforce is more dynamic and loyal. Hence, it is important for managers to meet, as far as possible, the needs of their employees. As American comedian Fred Allen (1894–1956) said, "*Treat employees like partners, and they act as partners.*"

British entrepreneur Sir Richard Branson would agree with Charles Handy and Fred Allen. Branson famously declared that he puts his employees first, customers second and shareholders third. He claims that by doing this, customers and shareholders both benefit. After all, demotivated workers are unlikely to produce good quality products or deliver good customer service. Worse, disgruntled staff might take industrial action

(see Unit 2.6). For example, around 40,000 BMW workers went on a prolonged labour strike at its South Africa car plant in late 2013 causing export sales to fall by 75%. In 2016, a total of 36,500 workers from Verizon, an American telecommunications company, went on strike for 13 days.

Managers and directors

Managers are the people who oversee the daily operations of a business. Directors are senior executives who have been elected by the company's shareholders to direct business operations on behalf of their owners. Senior managers and directors might aim to maximize their own benefits, such as annual bonuses and other perks (see Unit 2.4). Hence, they are likely to aim for profit maximization. This would also please the shareholders, helping to safeguard the jobs of top executives. Moreover, senior staff will look at the long-term financial health of their organization, e.g. they might aim to retain profits for further investment in the business.

Shareholders (stockholders)

Limited liability companies (see Unit 1.2) are owned by shareholders. This stakeholder group invests money in a company by purchasing its shares. Stockholders are a powerful stakeholder group as they have voting rights and a 'say' in how the company is run. As the owners of the company, they are also entitled to a share of its profits. Shareholders have two main objectives:

- To maximise *dividends* (a proportion of the company's profits distributed to shareholders.

- To achieve a *capital gain* in the value of the shares, i.e. a rise in the share price.

Question 1.4.1   Nokia and Microsoft

Nokia was once the pride of Europe having been the market leader in the mobile phones industry from 1998 to 2008, enjoying up to 49.4% market share. In 2005, the Finnish company sold its one billionth mobile phone. By 2007, its market capitalisation was a staggering $150bn, making it the 5th most valuable brand in the world. However, the huge popularity of Apple and Samsung smartphones eventually forced Nokia to be sold to Microsoft for 'just' 5.4bn euros ($7.3bn) in November 2013. A staggering 99.5% of Nokia's 3,900 shareholders voted in favour of the deal after seeing its share price drop by 93% and its **market share** continually decline to 3%. The company's 32,000 employees were transferred to Microsoft in early 2014.

(a) Define the term **market share**.   *[2 marks]*

(b) Explain the difference between Nokia's **shareholders** and **stakeholders**.   *[4 marks]*

(c) Examine how different stakeholder groups were likely to be affected by Microsoft's takeover of Nokia.   *[6 marks]*

External stakeholders

The interests of external stakeholders. AO2

© IBO, 2017

External stakeholders do not form part of the business but have a direct interest or involvement in the organization, e.g. customers, suppliers, pressure groups, competitors and the government.

Customers

Customer care is very important in all aspects of business operations. Marshall Field (1834–1906), founder of Marshall Field & Company (a chain of USA department stores) said, "Right or wrong, the customer is always right." Sam Walton (1918–1992), co-founder of the world's largest retailer Walmart, also believed in this idea. He argued that customers can simply choose to spend their money elsewhere thereby threatening the survival of a business. In ever competitive markets, businesses have to increasingly listen to the opinions of their customers. Bill Gates, co-founder of Microsoft, built his fortunes by meeting the needs of customers all around the world. He said that dissatisfied customers are the best source of learning for any business.

Hence, it is vital that businesses pay attention to the needs of their customers, such as greater choice of better quality products at competitive prices. Businesses use market research (see Unit 4.4) to find out what customers want. For example, many businesses such as fast-food restaurants and hotels use customer 'suggestion schemes' and 'satisfaction surveys'. Complaints and suggestions can then be considered by the management team. Ultimately, these actions signify the organization's desire to keep customers happy and loyal.

Suppliers

Suppliers provide a business with stocks of raw materials, component parts and finished goods needed for production. They can also provide commercial services, such as maintenance and technical support. Suppliers strive for regular contracts with clients at competitive prices. They also request that customers pay any outstanding bills on time.

Businesses try to establish a good working relationship with suppliers in order to receive quality stocks on time and at a reasonable price, e.g. airlines rely on their catering suppliers as flights might be cancelled if there is a dispute between the airline and the caterers. A good relationship can also mean that suppliers offer preferential credit terms, which allow a business to buy today but pay at a later date, thus improving the firm's cash flow position (see Unit 3.7).

Pressure groups

Pressure groups consist of individuals with a common interest who seek to place demands on organizations to act in a particular way or to influence a change in their behaviour. Examples include organizations set up to campaign against smoking, deforestation and the harmful treatment of animals or the protection of the environment.

Pressure groups have increasingly influenced the decisions and actions of businesses directly or by influencing government policy, such as by lobbying for a change in legislation (see Box 1.4.a). Some pressure groups, such as Friends of the Earth and Greenpeace, do this by operating on an international level and getting support from the general public who are aware and concerned about damage to the environment.

A final example is the local community, putting demands on businesses to create jobs thus providing extra income and spending in the local community. It might also want businesses to be accountable for the impact of their activities on the local environment. Many popular holiday destinations, for instance, have been negatively damaged by the influx of tourists, e.g. litter, traffic congestion and ecological damage to beaches and rural areas. Finally, the local community might also put pressure on businesses to sponsor local fund-raising events. These considerations are paramount to the local community's acceptance of businesses operating in their location.

Box 1.4.a   Possible actions taken by pressure groups

- **Boycotting** is the refusal to buy products from a certain business as a sign of protest, by creating adverse publicity for the business.
- **Lobbying** means using the power of pressure groups to influence key issues with employers, legal representatives and the government, e.g. demanding government to legislate against socially undesirable business activities.
- **Public relations (PR)** means getting positive publicity about a specific opinion or cause, e.g. charities often use famous celebrity ambassadors to support their mission. PR is vital as it raises public awareness and support.
- **Direct action** means a pressure group takes action to achieve its cause, e.g. staging mass protests or taking legal action against firms that may have acted illegally.

Competitors

Competitors are the rival businesses of an organization. For example, the main rivals of Japan Airlines are Singapore Airlines, Qantas, Cathay Pacific and Air China. As a stakeholder group, competitors are interested in the activities of a business for several reasons, including:

- Businesses might benefit from some competition as rivalry can create an incentive to be innovative and/or to produce new products.

- To remain competitive, businesses need to be aware of and respond to the practices of their rivals.

- To benchmark performance, i.e. to compare key indicators against its main rivals such as sales turnover, profit and market share figures.

Case study

Pressure group campaigns such as anti-smoking or anti-littering have led to public and government support in many countries. For example, cigarette advertising is banned in Australia whilst littering carries a heavy financial and imprisonment penalty in Singapore. Animal protection groups, such as the World Wildlife Fund, use social marketing techniques (see Unit 4.1) to gain positive press coverage.

IB Learner Profile – Be an inquirer

Investigate the great rivalries between the likes of Coca-Cola and Pepsi, Ford and General Motors, Boeing and Airbus, McDonald's and Burger King, or Nike and Adidas. A good starting point is CNN's report on the largest rivalries in business history: http://goo.gl/vyYR74

Business organization and environment

CORE

Government

The government is an important external stakeolder as it can have a significant influence on business activity, including assurances that:

- Unfair business practices are avoided

- The correct amount of corporate tax is paid from net profits

- Health and safety standards at work are met

- Compliance with employment legislation occurs

- Consumer protection laws are upheld.

Governments might also have a financial stake in a business. For example, the largest shareholder of Hong Kong Disneyland is the HK government. Its 52% stake in the theme park is an attempt to boost leisure and tourism in Hong Kong. Hence, it will have a direct interest in the performance of the business.

Ultimately, the government aims to ensure that businesses act in the public's interest. It can stimulate business activity by lowering interest rates and/or taxes to create employment and investment opportunities. The government might also offer incentives to multinational corporations to locate in their country, such as subsidised rent and tax concessions. It might introduce initiatives that benefit organizations, such as investment in road building and communications networks. However, government intervention can also constrain businesses. For example, Microsoft was broken up into two smaller companies due to numerous law suits against the software giant for malpractice and unfair competition.

> ### IB Learner Profile – Be reflective and be a thinker
>
> Read the article 'Shareholders v Stakeholders – A new idolatry' from *The Economist* (http://goo.gl/XVQFjh). What answers does the article provide to the debate about which stakeholder group is the most important in the tweny-first century?

Figure 1.4.a Hong Kong relies heavily on leisure and tourism

Question 1.4.2

(a) Define the term **external stakeholder**. *[2 marks]*

(b) Examine how the performance of a school or college might impact on any **two** of its stakeholder groups.

[6 marks]

Stakeholder conflict

Possible areas of conflict between stakeholders' interests. AO3

© IBO, 2017

Stakeholder conflict refer to the inability of an organization to meet all of its stakeholder objectives simultaneously, due to differences in the varying needs of all its stakeholder groups. Stakeholder conflict exists in situations where people are in disagreement due to differences in their opinions, thus creating friction between stakeholder groups of the organization. Margaret Thatcher (1925 - 2013), former British Prime Minister, said that standing in the middle of a road would get you hit by traffic coming from both sides, i.e. some of her decisions pleased certain members of the public but she could not please all the people all of the time. This notion also applies to businesses.

Conflict arises because a business cannot simultaneously meet the needs of all its stakeholders. For example, if shareholders want more profit then this may come about by cutting staff benefits. However, this would obviously upset employees. Suppliers would like their customers to pay the full price in one transaction, in order to improve their own cash flow, but businesses would expect to receive discounted prices for regular purchases and for buying in large quantities.

A common cause of stakeholder conflict is the remuneration (pay and benefits) of the company directors. Shareholders and employees might argue that top management are 'overpaid' and that there should be a fairer distribution of profits to shareholders (in the form of dividends) and to staff (improved remuneration). However, senior executives would argue that their compensation needs to be adequate to pay for the higher risks involved in decision-making. They argue that this could ultimately increase profits for the business, leading to higher dividends and wages in the future.

Another source of potential conflict is that some stakeholders have more than one role or set of interests in an organization. For example, managers are employees too, whilst some employees might also be shareholders. A customer is also likely to be a member of the local community. Based on the differing objectives of these groups, some degree of conflict is likely to occur.

In deciding how to deal with conflicting stakeholder needs, leaders need to look at three key issues:

- The type of organization in question – A partnership might strive for profit whereas a charity is likely to have different priorities. So, the partners might see customers as the key stakeholder whereas the local community could be the most important group for the charity. A limited company will be accountable to its shareholders (owners), so will have to give them priority.

- The aims and objectives of the business – If a firm aims for expansion as part of its business strategy, then the proportion of profits allocated to its owners will be less than otherwise in the short term. Instead, the priorities of leaders is given a higher priority during the change process.

- The source and degree of power (influence) of each stakeholder group – Customers will have more power if the business is selling a product in a mass market where there are plenty of substitutes. Access to the media can also give power to pressure groups. Likewise, a united workforce will strengthen the influence of employees via their trade union.

Business organization and environment

CORE

Theory of knowledge

Discuss whether it is possible to 'know' which stakeholder group is the most important to an organization. What knowledge issues would be made in such a case?

Exam tip !

Be prepared to answer examination questions about:
- the differences between internal and external stakeholders
- the differences between stakeholders and shareholders
- the various aims of different stakeholder groups and how these might conflict with each other.

Question 1.4.3   The Royal Bank of Scotland Group

British banking and insurance company The Royal Bank of Scotland Group (*RBS Group*) has operations in Europe, North America and Asia. Before the global financial crisis of 2008, *RBS Group* was one of the largest banks in the world. However, its inability to deal with the turmoil in the financial industry led to the UK government buying over 80% of the company's shares. The share price of *RBS Group* dropped from £3.54 to just £0.11. To survive, *RBS Group* had to sell its 4.26% **stake** in Bank of China, but did not make any profit on the deal. *RBS Group* holds the record for the largest loss in British corporate history; a staggering £24.1bn ($39.1bn) in 2008.

(a) Outline the meaning of *RBS Group* having a "stake" in Bank of China.   *[2 marks]*

(b) Calculate the percentage change in *RBS Group's* share price.   *[2 marks]*

(c) Outline **two** reasons why the shareholders of *RBS Group* might be concerned about its performance.   *[4 marks]*

(d) To what extent should businesses like *RBS Group* listen to the views of its various stakeholder groups?   *[10 marks]*

Question 1.4.4   Škoda Auto

Founded in 1895, Škoda Auto is one of the oldest automobile manufacturers in the world. In early 2007, the Czech company, which became part of Volkswagen Group in 2000, entered China as part of its growth strategy. However, in the same year, its workforce in Europe went on strike over concerns regarding pay and benefits. It was reported that **industrial action** cost Škoda, the country's largest exporter, 60 million crowns ($2.9 million) per day in lost output. Nevertheless, China became Škoda's main market; by 2013, the company had produced its 1 millionth car in China.

(a) Identify **two** external stakeholder groups of Škoda Auto.   *[2 marks]*

(b) Define the term **industrial action**.   *[3 marks]*

(c) Explain one source of conflict between Škoda Auto's various stakeholders.   *[4 marks]*

(d) Examine how the conflict outlined in your answer above could have been minimized.   *[6 marks]*

Mutual benefits of stakeholders' interests

Possible areas of mutual benefit between stakeholders' interests.

AO3

© IBO, 2017

Stakeholder conflict is a potentially ever-present phenomenon. However, modern management thinking suggests that there are mutual benefits in simultaneously meeting the competing needs of different stakeholders. For example, addressing the needs of both employees and managers can lead to a highly motivated and productive workforce with low rates of absenteeism and staff turnover. This can lead to improved customer relations, corporate image, market share and profits.

As a result, shareholders will also be pleased. Greater output might also lead to more employment in the local community. Hence, it is argued that meeting the needs of all stakeholder groups *can* be achieved, although this might only occur in the medium to long term.

Theory of knowledge

Is it unethical if a business chooses to ignore the demands (or needs) of one particular stakeholder group?

Question 1.4.5   Royal Dutch Shell

Royal Dutch Shell (or *Shell* for short) is Europe's largest energy and oil company. It was formed by the merger of Holland's Royal Dutch and Britain's Shell in 1907. The BBC reported in early 2007 that the Anglo-Dutch company earns £1.5m ($2.5 m) per hour! This staggering figure obviously draws the attention of *Shell's* **internal stakeholders**. However, being a global energy and oil company also means that *Shell's* activities are carefully scrutinised by environmental and human rights groups, such as Greenpeace. In 2017, *Shell's* sales revenue exceeded $305 billion (about a third of the Netherland's GDP).

(a) Define the term **internal stakeholders**. [2 marks]

(b) To what extent should a global company such as *Shell* allow environmental and human rights groups to exert influence on their decision-making? [10 marks]

Stakeholders and the CUEGIS concepts

Conflict exists in every organization, to some extent. At times, employees will disagree with management decisions; customers will be disgruntled; suppliers will fail to deliver the right goods on time; shareholders will be unhappy with the performance of the business, and so forth. Given the potential mutual benefits of achieving the interests of various stakeholders, conflict resolution is an important aspect of any business strategy.

However, it is unlikely that a business can fulfil the aims of all its stakeholders at the same time; yet it is undesirable to maximise the needs of just one stakeholder group. If a particular group is not catered for, then it is possible that they will cause disruptions and problems for the business. Most strategies aim for a 'best fit' compromise so that the needs of all stakeholder groups are reasonably addressed. The outcome of any negotiation between various stakeholder groups will depend largely on the culture of the organization and the relative bargaining power of the different stakeholders. For example, large multinational producers such as Honda or Ford have better bargaining power with their suppliers than mechanics operating as sole traders trying to negotiate prices for motor vehicle parts.

Stakeholder mapping is a model that assesses the relative *interest* of stakeholders and their relative power (or influence) on businesses, as shown in Figure 1.4.b.

		Level of interest	
		Low	*High*
Level of power	*Low*	**A** (minimum effort)	**B** (keep informed)
	High	**C** (keep satisfied)	**D** (maximum effort)

Figure 1.4.b Stakeholder mapping

Stakeholder mapping lets managers assess how to deal with changing and conflicting stakeholder objectives. Whilst it is extremely difficult to please all stakeholders at the same time, managers can prioritise their actions by using this model. Stakeholders in quadrant A are unlikely to receive much attention from the decision-makers. Conversely, those in quadrant D will receive the most attention as they are the key stakeholders of an organization. Stakeholders in quadrant B need to be kept informed whilst those in quadrant C must be kept satisfied, perhaps by consulting them on strategic decisions.

In reality, managers will deal with stakeholder conflict in different ways depending on their leadership style and the organizational culture. For example, paternalistic leaders (see Unit 2.3) would argue that although customers are vital to any business, it is the needs of employees that have to be considered first. They believe that by hiring the right people and devoting time and money to train and develop employees, the result is that workers will automatically deliver a first-rate service to their customers.

Furthermore, external stakeholders such as pressure groups have become increasingly effective in influencing business activity through changes and innovations in digital social media. Due to public awareness of the detrimental effects of globalization (such as the exploitation of child labour or the impact on global warming), businesses are finding it ever more difficult to simply ignore ethical business behaviour and the views of their external stakeholders.

Theory of knowledge

Are the values and beliefs of some stakeholders more superior than those of others?

CUEGIS ESSAY

With reference to an organization of your choice, examine how **culture** and **ethics** impact both internal and external stakeholders. *[20 marks]*

REVIEW QUESTIONS

1. Explain the difference between internal and external stakeholders.

2. What is the difference between stakeholders and shareholders?

3. Explain why employees are often considered to be the key stakeholders in an organization.

4. Distinguish between a director and a manager of a company.

5. Why are stockholders a potentially powerful stakeholder group?

6. Why are customers, suppliers and competitors considered to be external stakeholders?

7. How might pressure groups affect the success of a business?

8. What is the role of the government as a stakeholder group in business activities?

9. Outline the sources of stakeholder conflict in a business.

10. How might businesses resolve stakeholder conflict in the workplace?

KEY TERMS

Competitors are the rival businesses of an organization. To remain competitive, businesses need to be aware of and respond to the practices of their rivals.

Conflict refers to situations where stakeholders have disagreements on certain matters due to differences in their opinions. This can lead to arguments and tension between the various stakeholder groups.

Customers are the clients of a business. They seek to have value for money, such as competitive prices and good customer service.

Directors are senior executives who have been elected by the company's shareholders to direct business operations on behalf of their owners.

Employees are the staff of an organization. They have a stake (an interest) in the organization they work for, e.g. improved pay, working conditions, job security and opportunities for career progression.

External stakeholders of a business are individuals and organizations not part of the organization but have a direct interest in its activities and performance, e.g. customers, suppliers, pressure groups and the government.

Financiers are the financial institutions (such as banks) and individual investors (such as business angels) who provide sources of finance for an organization. They are interested in the organization's ability to generate profits and to repay debts.

Government refers to the ruling authority within a state or country. As an external stakeholder group, the government is interested in businesses complying with the law, such as paying the right amount of taxes.

Internal stakeholders of a business are members of the organization, e.g. the employees, managers, directors and shareholders of the organization.

Local community refers to the general public and local businesses that have a direct interest in the activities of the organization. They are interested in the organization's ability to create jobs and to conduct its business in a socially responsible way.

Managers are the people who oversee the daily operations of a business. They aim to maximise their own benefits, such as annual bonuses and other perks.

Pressure groups consist of individuals with a common concern (such as environmental protection) who seek to place demands on organizations to act in a particular way or to influence a change in their behaviour.

Stakeholder conflict refer to the inability of an organization to meet all of its stakeholder objectives simultaneously, due to differences in the varying needs of all its stakeholder groups.

Stakeholder conflict exists due to incompatible goals

Stakeholder mapping is a model that assesses the relative *interest* of stakeholders and their relative *influence* (or power) on an organization.

Shareholders (or stockholders) are the owners of a limited liability company. Shares in a company can be held by individuals and other organizations.

Stakeholders are individuals or organizations with a direct interest (known as a stake) in the activities and performance of a business, e.g. shareholders, employees, customers and suppliers.

Suppliers provide a business with stocks of raw materials, component parts and finished goods needed for production. They can also provide commercial services, such as maintenance and technical support.

1.5 External environment

"The reasonable man adapts himself to the world; the unreasonable one persists in trying to adapt the world to himself." -
George Bernard Shaw (1856–1950), Irish author

SL/HL content	Assessment objective
STEEPLE analysis of a given organization	AO2, AO4
Consequences of a change in any of the STEEPLE factors for a business's objectives and strategy	AO3

© IBO, 2017

STEEPLE analysis

STEEPLE analysis of a given organization. AO2, AO4

© IBO, 2017

STEEPLE is an acronym for the **S**ocial, **T**echnological, **E**conomic, **E**nvironmental, **P**olitical, **L**egal and **E**thical opportunities and threats of the external business environment. These factors, unlike internal ones, affect all businesses yet are beyond the control of any individual organization. STEEPLE analysis is central to business strategy, such as assessing the feasibility of an overseas investment project.

External factors that present chances for businesses are called **opportunities**, such as lower tax rates and lower interest rates. External factors that can harm a business are called **threats**, such as a recession, oil crisis or major roadworks.

The importance of each opportunity and threat identified in a STEEPLE analysis can be weighted in a scientific way. This is useful when trying to examine the advantages and disadvantages of a decision. If the overall opportunities of a decision outweigh the threats, then the business is likely to pursue that option. However, in reality, external factors are subject to rapid and unforeseeable change. An exogenous shock, such as a war or an oil crisis, can reduce the chances of success despite what a STEEPLE analysis initially revealed.

The key advantage of STEEPLE analysis is that it is quite simple to use. The analysis helps managers to be thorough and logical in their analysis of the external opportunities and threats faced by the business. It is also a useful brainstorming and discussion tool. STEEPLE analysis promotes proactive and forward thinking rather than static views based on gut feelings. Hence, it is more likely that managers will be better informed and prepared to deal with external shocks.

A simplified example of a STEEPLE analysis is shown in the exam tip on the following page, which examines some of the opportunities and threats of multinational companies operating in India.

Figure 1.5.a   Road works are a major external constraint on businesses

Exam tip !

It is not always necessary to conduct a full STEEPLE analysis. In the corporate world, managers may prefer to use a **PEST analysis**, where political factors include (where appropriate) the legal opportunities and threats, and the social factors include ethical and environmental opportunities and threats.

Exam tip !
Worked example: STEEPLE analysis of multinational companies operating in India

Social
- Potential market of over 1.325 billion people (the second most populous country in the world)
- A large and well-educated English-speaking workforce of around 125 million people
- Large yet increasing discrepancies in the distribution of income and wealth
- Language barriers in rural cities, with potential clash of national cultures in a multilingual and multi-ethnic country.

Technological
- Growing number of technologically aware population (huge opportunities for firms providing products such as mobile phones, personal computers and Internet services)
- Major industries include communications technology, biotechnology, software, automobiles, petrochemicals and pharmaceuticals
- Technologies are easily copied due to a lack of appropriate legislation.

Economic
- Huge growth potential in financial markets
- Significant economic growth and rising disposable incomes (spending power) in India
- Improved infrastructure and market opportunities in Mumbai and New Delhi
- Relatively low costs of production (average wage rates are still very low)
- Most people are employed in the agricultural sector, with India being one of the world's top producers of cereals (wheat, rice and sugar), meat, fruits, vegetables, tea, coffee, cotton, coal and wool
- Infrastructure and economic stability are less attractive than in other countries such as China
- The vast majority of the Indian population is still very poor.

Environmental
- Major challenges for India include tackling air pollution, water pollution, littering, waste disposal and environmental degradation
- Indian government taking a more proactive approach to enforcing environmental protection.

Political
- Political reform in India will encourage better trade relations with other nations
- Legislation is less stringent than in other nations, thus placing fewer constraints on business activity
- Regarded as less politically stable and relatively corrupt compared with other countries in the region
- Poor enforcement of patents and copyrights might discourage technology transfer to India.

Legal
- Strict compliance laws for foreign bank accounts and heavy penalties for tax evasion
- Employment legislation is often overlooked, e.g. poaching of staff from competitors is common
- There are no specific data protection laws enforced in India.

Ethical
- Corruption is widespread, fuelling poverty and harming India's international competitiveness
- Slow business negotiations as the locals focus on establishing a trusting relationship as a prerequisite to doing business in India
- Indian culture is averse to critical disagreements, such as saying 'no', as this is seen as being rather rude; disagreements should be expressed in an ethical way, using diplomatic language
- Extremely difficult for foreign companies to penetrate the Indian economy without partnering with a local Indian company.

Question 1.5.1 Internal and external constraints

Examine the internal and external constraints for any **one** of the following business decisions:

(a) Kraft Foods announces takeover of Cadbury.

(b) Singapore Airlines plans to move call centre into India.

(c) Disney set to open new theme park in Shanghai.

(d) Virgin Atlantic unveils plans to start daily flights to Nairobi, Kenya.

[6 marks]

Social opportunites and threats

STEEPLE analysis of a given organization. AO2, AO4

Consequences of a change in any of the STEEPLE factors for a business's objectives and strategy. AO3

© IBO, 2017

Social, cultural and demographic factors can directly affect the activities of a business. The values and attitudes of society towards a wide range of different issues (such as business ethics, social welfare, women, religion or animal rights) can present both opportunities and threats for businesses. Examples include the following:

- The growing support for environmental protection has altered business behaviour immensely, with many organizations now reporting the non-financial aspects of their operations, such as recycling and waste management.

- With a more liberal and modern social attitude towards women in most societies, businesses have benefited from having a more flexible labour force.

- Migration and the increased awareness and acceptance of *multiculturalism* has created more choice for consumers, e.g. the most consumed take-out food in the UK is Indian curry, whilst the largest non-Asian importer of Malaysian Laksa (spicy noodle soup) is Finland.

- Societal pressures for businesses to act more ethically and socially responsibly can often result in higher costs.

- Demographic changes in society (see Unit 2.1), such as an ageing population in economically developed countries, have affected recruitment practices, marketing strategies and the products supplied by businesses. Women in modern societies are opting to have children at a later age as they give their careers priority, thereby providing further opportunities for businesses.

- Language can create opportunities and threats too. The largest multinational companies are aware that the most commonly spoken languages around the world are Mandarin, English, Spanish and Hindi. However, it is not always possible to translate marketing messages and other communications across different languages and cultures (see Unit 4.7).

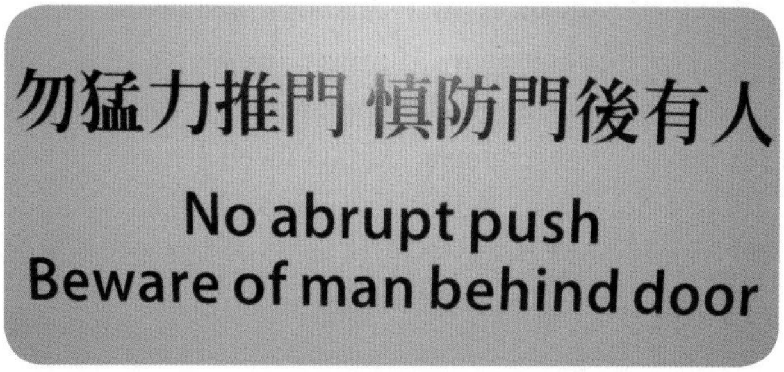

勿猛力推門 慎防門後有人

No abrupt push
Beware of man behind door

Figure 1.5.b *Language barriers can cause cultural misunderstandings*

Case study

In December 2013, Marks & Spencer announced that its Muslim employees would not have to sell pork or alcohol to customers. By contrast, supermarket chains Tesco and Sainsbury's said it made no business sense to hire checkout staff who refused to touch or serve certain items due to religious reasons.

Theory of knowledge

How do the words we use in different societies to describe 'equal opportunities' affect our understanding of the concept? Are there other meanings and does it matter which interpretation we use?

Question 1.5.2   Opportunities and threats

Comment on how the following demographic changes present both opportunities and threats to businesses.

(a) A growing number of self-employed people.   *[4 marks]*

(b) An increasing number of single-parent families.   *[4 marks]*

(c) Adults choosing to have fewer children and at a later stage in their lives.   *[4 marks]*

(d) An increasing number of people graduate with university degrees.   *[4 marks]*

Technological opportunities and threats

STEEPLE analysis of a given organization. AO2, AO4

Consequences of a change in any of the STEEPLE factors for a business's objectives and strategy. AO3

© IBO, 2017

The technological environment presents constant threats and opportunities. Advances in technology and work processes have improved productivity. However, the high cost of staying up to date with technological progress can cause problems for businesses. For example, Airbus faced lengthy delays in the production of the A380 (the world's largest commercial aircraft) and subsequently had to compensate its customers such as Emirates Airlines and Singapore Airlines.

Technology affects all aspects of business functions. For instance, the Internet has directly affected human resource management (in the recruitment process), marketing (such as e-commerce), finance (annual reports are published online) and operations management (such as access to benchmarking data).

Apart from the Internet, other opportunities that technology can bring to businesses include:

- New working practices – Many more people are working from home by using information communication technology (see Unit 2.1). Global businesses are also increasingly using video conferencing to cut the costs of face-to-face meetings and international recruitment. Marketing activities have also been affected, such as online advertising.

- Increased productivity and efficiency gains – Robots and machines are much faster and more accurate than humans, especially in the mass production of goods over a long period. Unlike humans, machinery can be made to work very long hours without the need for breaks, financial

rewards, motivation or maternity leave! Firms are also more likely to achieve zero defects (no wastage) from the use of technology. Automated stock control systems can automatically reorder stocks. Despite the large initial costs of automation and technology, capital-intensive firms can benefit from cost savings in the long run.

- Quicker product development time – The use of CAD/CAM technology (computer aided design and computer aided manufacturing) has allowed firms to produce prototypes quickly and cost-effectively, thereby accelerating the design, manufacturing and launch of new products.

- Job creation – Advances in technology bring about a need for maintenance and technical support staff. Examples include programmers, hardware and software engineers, graphic designers and ICT teachers/lecturers.

- New products and new markets – Technology is a source of innovation and brings about new products in the marketplace, e.g. wireless broadband services, smartphones, high-definition 3D smart televisions and electric cars. Apple's highly successful range of innovative products elevated the company to become one of the most valuable businesses on the planet.

The technological environment also presents certain threats to businesses, such as:

- Technology is not always reliable or secure – Computer failure or hacked files can present serious problems for businesses. For example, in December 2013, over 40 million credit and debit card records were hacked from US retailer Target. In 2018, Facebook was in trouble with the law due to a massive data scandal, with allegations of misuse of personal data to influence the 2016 US presidential elections and the Brexit vote (the UK leaving the European Union).

- Shorter product life cycles (see Unit 4.5) – Equipment and software may become obsolete increasingly quicker, and therefore need upgrading. This can make it increasingly difficult for smaller firms to compete.

- It can be costly – As products such as smartphones have shorter life cycles, businesses need to devote more resources to new product development.

- Job losses – Automation has led to unemployment in the primary and secondary sectors, e.g. commercial farming, oil extraction and car manufacturing. In the tertiary sector, many supermarket checkout assistants have been replaced with self-service checkout machines. Therefore, businesses need to carefully manage the process of staff redundancies.

When adopting certain technologies, managers need to consider several factors:

- Costs – such as the cost of purchase, installation, maintenance, depreciation, replacement and insurance of new technologies.

- Benefits – such as the expected gains in efficiency (as measured by productivity, flexibility and communications) and profits.

- Human relations – such as the impact of resistance to change, and the impacts on morale, flexible working patterns and workforce planning (see Unit 2.1).

- Recruitment and training – such as the costs of training workers to adopt the new technologies, the number of people who need training and where to find the time to train people.

Figure 1.5.c   Electric cars are becoming increasingly popular

Case study

In June 2010, Tesco opened the UK's first supermarket without any checkout staff. Instead, one person is hired at the store in Northampton to supervise the five checkouts, mainly to assist customers who have not used a self-service checkout before. Tesco, the UK's largest retailer with over 28% market share in the groceries industry, employs over 476,000 but critics argue that such technologies would cause mass job losses.

Table 1.5.a Opportunities and threats of Internet technologies

Opportunities	Threats
Speed of access to information Businesses and customers can gain access to up-to-date information from any part of the world through dedicated websites. There is also a huge range of news media that can provide invaluable information to users in a cost-effective way.	**Price transparency** Firms are exposed to the forces of competition as customers can easily compare the prices of different businesses without leaving their home or office. In addition, as there is no physical presence, it can be difficult to guarantee a product's quality.
Reducing language and cultural barriers Information on the Internet can be easily translated into different languages by using dedicated software. This can also help to reduce the costs of trading overseas.	**Online crime** Hackers have cost e-commerce businesses a huge amount of money. Internet banking and credit card fraud are quite common. This threat has therefore limited the number of online customers.
Reduced costs Firms with an online presence can benefit immensely from e-commerce. Trading can take place at any time from any part of the world without the need for a physical outlet. Staffing costs can therefore be reduced.	**Higher production costs** Other than the costs of online crime, businesses also face maintenance and training costs to ensure that employees are competent and confident in their use of the latest Internet technologies.
Overcome geographical limitations The Internet makes location less of an issue for many businesses. The use of mobile devices has fuelled e-commerce and virtually eliminated any limitations of geographical proximity to physical retailers.	**Reduced productivity** Surveys from around the world, from India to Indiana, have consistently shown that labour productivity is harmed by employees who access personal email and social networking sites during working hours.

Question 1.5.3   Nintendo and Apple

The Nintendo *Wii* and Apple iPod were huge hits with customers. Nintendo's games console appealed to new **market segments** such as women and the elderly. Demand was particularly high in Asia, Europe and the USA, helping Nintendo to outsell its two nearest rivals, the Xbox 360 and PlayStation 3. Its most popular game, *Wii Sports*, sold over 82 million copies worldwide. First sold in November 2006, the *Wii* was replaced by the *Wii U* in November 2012 (the Xbox One and PlayStation 4 were not released until November 2013). According to Nintendo, the company sold 425,000 unit of its *Wii U* in the first month of sale in the USA alone. In April 2007, Apple announced the sale of its 100 millionth iPod, making it the most successful music player in history. Over 300 million iPods were bought within the first ten years of its launch.

(a) Define the term **market segments**.   *[2 marks]*

(b) Explain how the technological environment can present opportunities for hi-tech firms such as Nintendo and Apple.   *[6 marks]*

Economic opportunities and threats

STEEPLE analysis of a given organization. AO2, AO4

Consequences of a change in any of the STEEPLE factors for a business's objectives and strategy. AO3

© IBO, 2017

The economic environment refers to the state of the economy in which businesses operate. This is determined by the government's ability to achieve four key economic objectives: to control inflation, to reduce unemployment, to achieve economic growth and to have a healthy international trade balance. Government policies used to achieve these fundamental goals will therefore present opportunities and threats for businesses.

1.   Controlled inflation

Inflation is the continual rise in the general level of prices in an economy. Most economists regard low and stable inflation as a prerequisite to achieving the other three government economic objectives, so it is an absolute priority for economic prosperity.

Inflation can complicate business planning and decision-making. For example, raw material costs, catalogue and menu prices, and wage claims are all affected by inflation. Essentially, inflation that is not controlled becomes a threat to businesses due to the higher costs and the uncertainties that are caused. Inflation also affects the international competitiveness of a country. A nation that has a relatively higher inflation rate tends

Question 1.5.4   Zimbabwe's hyperinflation problems

Zimbabwe suffered immensely from the impacts of hyperinflation for almost a decade, with annual rates reaching 231,000,000% in July 2008. This meant that prices of goods and services in the country were more than doubling each week! Back in June 2006, the country's Reserve Bank had issued a new bank denomination – the 100,000 Zimbabwean dollar note (less than $1 at the time). However, by January 2009 the government had launched the 100 trillion Zimbabwean dollar banknote (ZWD100,000,000,000,000)! The Zimbabwean dollar was eventually abandoned in favour of the US dollar as the nation's official currency. Economists warned that the problem would continue to be a major issue unless the government dealt with the root causes of **inflation**. An estimated 10.5 million Zimbabweans (around 80% of the population) live below the poverty line.

(a) Define the term **inflation**.   *[2 marks]*

(b) State **two** factors that could have caused inflation in Zimbabwe.   *[2 marks]*

(c) Examine the impact of uncontrollable inflation for businesses in Zimbabwe.   *[6 marks]*

to be less price-competitive when trading overseas. This would generally lead to a fall in export earnings, lower national output and higher unemployment.

Inflation can be caused by excessive demand in the economy (too much spending) or by higher costs of production (leading to a rise in prices so that firms can maintain their profit margins). Any factor that causes a rise in consumption, investment, government spending or international trade earnings will increase the economy's aggregate demand. For example, households and firms will spend more money and at a faster rate if income levels are very high, thereby fuelling inflation. Examples of higher costs include increased wages caused by trade union action, soaring raw material prices caused by an oil crisis or higher rents demanded by landlords.

2.   Reduced unemployment

The **unemployment rate** measures the proportion of a country's workforce not in official employment. Governments aim to deal with the problems of unemployment because there are social costs of high unemployment (which present threats to businesses). For example, the unemployed suffer from stress, depression and low self-esteem. The local community might suffer from poverty and increased crime levels. There is an increased burden on taxpayers to support government spending on welfare benefits for the unemployed. Overall, the country's international competitiveness is therefore likely to deteriorate.

In general, governments use a combination of policies to tackle unemployment, depending on the types and causes of the unemployment (see Box 1.5.a), thus providing opportunities for businesses. For example, the government can reduce taxes and/or increase its spending to boost the level of consumption in the economy. It can also reduce interest rates to encourage consumers and firms to borrow and spend more. Alternatively, it can use protectionist measures to safeguard domestic businesses (and jobs) from international competition. Lowering corporate tax and/or interest rates should stimulate business activity and investments in the long run. Government spending on education and training should help to make future generations of workers more skilled and flexible.

Box 1.5.a   Types of unemployment

- **Frictional unemployment** occurs when people change jobs as there is usually a time lag between leaving a job and finding or starting another.
- **Seasonal unemployment** is caused by periodic and reoccurring changes in demand for a product, e.g. beach resorts tend to suffer from a lack of tourists during the winter months.
- **Technological unemployment** results from the introduction of labour-saving (capital-intensive) technologies, which can cause mass-scale unemployment.
- **Regional unemployment** refers to the different unemployment rates in different areas of a country. Remote rural areas tend to have higher levels of unemployment than busy urban districts.
- **Structural unemployment** occurs when the demand for products produced in a particular industry continually falls, resulting in structural and long term changes in demand.
- **Cyclical unemployment** (or **demand deficient unemployment**) is caused by a lack of demand in the economy. It is the most severe type of unemployment, as it tends to affect all industries.

Case study

In 2013, the number of people unemployed in Spain exceeded 6 million for the first time in the country's history. Spain's unemployment rate hit a record 27.2% as the country struggled to get out of the recession. The number of people considered long-term unemployed (those out of employment for more than a year) increased to 3.5 million. The youth unemployment rate (for those aged under 25) was a staggering 57%. By 2018, Spain's official unemployment rate had fallen below 17%, with youth unemployment at over 35%.

Theory of knowledge

To what extent should governments be morally obliged to provide free education and health care?

IB Learner Profile – Be an inquirer

Investigate the causes and economic consequences of China's rising wages: http://goo.gl/lva9bG

3.   Economic growth

Economic growth is the increase in a country's economic activity over time. It is measured by the change in the value of the economy's total output (known as the **gross domestic product** or GDP) per year. Higher rates of economic growth suggest that the economy is more prosperous and therefore the average person is earning more income, creating more opportunities for businesses. The pattern of fluctuations in economic growth is known as the **business cycle** (see Figure 1.5.d).

- During a **boom**, the level of economic activity rises with consumer expenditure, investment and export earnings all increasing. At the peak, economic activity is at its highest level, so unemployment is low whilst consumer and business confidence levels are high resulting in higher levels of profit for businesses.

- A **recession** occurs when there is a fall in GDP for two consecutive quarters (6 months). Features of a recession include declining aggregate demand, lower investment, falling export sales and rising unemployment. Businesses most likely to suffer are those that have a small range of products and those that sell products that are sensitive to changes in incomes (e.g. houses, cars, jewellery and overseas holidays). Box 1.5.b outlines ways that businesses can deal with the threats of a recession.

- A **trough** (or **slump**) refers to the bottom of a recession and the last stage of decline in the business cycle, with high unemployment alongside very low levels of consumer spending, investment and export earnings. Businesses suffer from poor cash flow and many will have already closed down due to poor liquidity (insufficient money to run the business). Consumers have little confidence in the economy and workers suffer from a lack of job security.

- **Recovery** occurs when the level of GDP starts to rise again, after the economy has experienced a slump. Since national output and income begin to increase again, the level of consumption, investment, exports and employment will all gradually rise, creating opportunities for businesses.

Poorer countries and regions of the world have found it difficult to grow. Barriers to economic growth exist, such as a lack of infrastructure (transport and communications networks) and these could be a restraining force for many businesses that wish to expand overseas. Businesses operating in countries without basic electricity, road networks, schools, hospitals and housing find it relatively difficult to prosper.

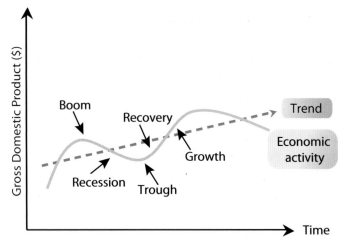

Figure 1.5.d The business cycle

Box 1.5.b   Coping with a recession

- **Cost reduction** to improve cash flow, e.g. efforts to cut lighting and energy bills, finding alternative suppliers who can offer better prices, relocating to cheaper premises or making some staff redundant.
- **Price reductions** to sustain or increase sales. People become more price sensitive during a recession, so lower prices will be very welcome by potential customers.
- **Non-pricing strategies** (such as repackaging, special offers or special after-sales care) to sustain or revitalise the volume of sales.
- **Branding** to maintain sales as customers become or remain loyal to a brand irrespective of changes in price or their incomes.
- **Outsourcing** production overseas where costs are lower to help the business to gain a competitive price advantage, thereby reducing the impact of a recession in the domestic economy.

Figure 1.5.e Poor communities lack infrastructure needed for growth

4. A healthy international trade balance

In broad terms, the internal trade balance records the value of a country's export earnings and its import expenditure. Governments strive to avoid a deficit on their international trade balance (i.e. try to avoid import expenditure exceeding export earnings). Just as an individual cannot spend more than s/he earns in the long run, the same applies to countries.

To correct an imbalance on its international trade balance, governments often attempt to alter their exchange rate, which can provide opportunities or threats for businesses. The **exchange rate** measures the value of the domestic currency in terms of foreign currencies. A higher exchange rate (known as an appreciation of the currency) means that export prices will be relatively higher, thereby reducing the exporter's price competitiveness. Although a lower exchange rate (known as a depreciation of the currency) should give domestic firms a relative price advantage, it also means that they have to pay higher prices for imported raw materials and components.

Continual and large fluctuations in exchange rates can create threats for businesses. Business planning and forecasting become very complex and perhaps impractical. For example, businesses may not be able to accurately forecast export sales or costs of imported materials due to exchange rate volatility. International trade deals could be postponed until the business can benefit from more favourable movements in the exchange rate (although there is no guarantee that this will ever happen).

Alternatively, governments can set up international trade barriers to correct any disparity in its international trade balance or to protect their domestic industries. **Protectionist measures** refer to any government policy used to safeguard domestic businesses from foreign competitors (see Box 1.5.c). Such measures pose a threat, or barrier to trade, for foreign businesses trying to establish themselves in overseas markets.

In addition to the four government objectives for the economy, consumer and business confidence levels affect the level of business activity. The actions and activities of competitors can constrain the performance of a particular business as well.

Box 1.5.c Examples of protectionist measures

- **Tariffs** (**customs duties**) are taxes on imported products, thereby raising their price to give domestic firms a price advantage, e.g. Japan imposes up to 778% import taxes on rice (the highest rate in the world) to protect its agricultural industry.
- **Quotas** are quantitative limits on the volume or value of imports, e.g. Hong Kong, India, China and the UK place quotas on the number of Hollywood movies released in their countries (to protect their respective film industries).
- **Subsidies** are payments made by a government to domestic businesses as a form of financial aid to reduce their costs of production, thereby giving them a competitive advantage.
- **Embargoes** are physical bans on international trade with a certain country, usually due to strategic reasons, severe health and safety concerns, or political conflicts. For example, Coca-Cola was able to open its bottling plant in Rangoon in June 2013 after the Burmese government lifted its embargo after more than 60 years(!)
- **Technological and safety standards** are strict administration and compliance costs in meeting industrial and health and safety regulations imposed on imported products. Compliance therefore raises production costs (and prices) of foreign producers.

Business organization and environment

CORE

Theory of knowledge

Is it possible to 'know' what is the most important government objective?

Theory of knowledge

Is economic growth always desirable? What does 'desirable' actually mean? To whom?

Question 1.5.5   JKL Jeans

JKL Jeans sell jeans throughout the UK. They buy an average of 15,000 pairs of jeans per month at a cost of $25 each from an American manufacturer. *JKL Jeans* then sell these to their customers at a price of £35 each.

(a) Define the term **exchange rate**.   *[2 marks]*

(b) Use the various exchange rates below to complete the table for *JKL Jeans*, rounding to the nearest whole number.

[4 marks]

Exchange rate	Purchase cost ($)	Purchase cost (£)	Sales revenue (£)	Profit or Loss (£)
£1 = $1.30				
£1 = $1.35				
£1 = $1.40				
£1 = $1.45				

(c) Comment on the relationship between changes in the exchange rate and the level of profits for *JKL Jeans*.

[4 marks]

(d) Explain two other costs that *JKL Jeans* might incur from using a foreign supplier.   *[4 marks]*

(e) Examine how a high exchange rate can be both an opportunity and a threat to a business such as *JKL Jeans*.

[6 marks]

Environmental opportunities and threats

STEEPLE analysis of a given organization. AO2, AO4

Consequences of a change in any of the STEEPLE factors for a business's objectives and strategy. AO3

© IBO, 2017

Individuals, organizations and governments are increasingly concerned about the negative impacts of business activity on the natural environment. Without government intervention, private sector businesses are unlikely to consider the *external costs* of business activity – the costs incurred by society rather than by the buyer or seller. Examples of external costs include passive smoking, air and noise pollution, packaging waste and global warming. Climate change has been blamed for the increase in natural disasters such as tsunamis and hurricanes.

Changes in social attitudes towards the environment have meant that businesses are increasingly reviewing their practices. Firms that do not respect the environment face ruining their reputation and long-term profitability. If compliance costs are too high, then firms may choose not to become more environmentally friendly. The extent to which businesses consider environmental issues also depends on their aims and objectives, the attitudes of workers and management, the likely impact on their profits and the available resources (financial, human and capital).

The weather and seasonal changes can also present opportunities or threats. For instance, torrential rain or flooding will affect a large number of businesses, e.g. theme parks, car wash firms and agricultural farmers. The Indian Ocean tsunami (Southeast Asia, 2004), Hurricane Katrina (USA, 2005), severe snow across Europe (December 2010), torrential floods (Australia, 2011) and Typhoon Haiyan (November 2013) caused major havoc to businesses. Extreme weather conditions in Russia reduced its GDP by more than 1% in 2010. Japan's 9.0-magnitude earthquake in 2011 (the worst in the country's history) caused damage of over $235 billion. Of course, some businesses might be able to exploit changes in the season, such as tour operators focusing on ski holidays in the winter and beach resorts in the summer.

Finally, health scares and epidemics also present threats to businesses. The outbreak of SARS (2003) and bird flu (2006 and 2017) caused turmoil in China, with many businesses collapsing. Mad cow disease (late 1990s), foot and mouth disease (2001) and swine flu (2009) had similar effects in Europe.

Figure 1.5.f Tourism is dependent on the weather

Theory of knowledge

Can anything good for businesses ever come out of major natural disasters?

Political opportunities and threats

STEEPLE analysis of a given organization. AO2, AO4
Consequences of a change in any of the STEEPLE factors for a business's objectives and strategy. AO3
© IBO, 2017

The political stability of a country and government policies (such as taxation and interest rate policies) can provide both opportunities and threats for businesses. A laissez-faire government adopts a free market approach to managing the economy as it rarely intervenes in business affairs. The advantage is that leaving businesses to their own devices should stimulate healthy competition and efficiency. It is also more likely to attract foreign direct investment as it is easier to conduct business in such countries. In reality, most countries adopt an interventionist approach to managing the economy by using legislation and policies to oversee business behaviour and to influence the level of business activity. Two commonly used government policies are fiscal policy and monetary policy.

Fiscal policy is the use of taxation and government expenditure policies to influence business activity. The government spends the tax revenue that it raises, in addition to other sources of government revenue, on a number of areas including social security, health care, education, transport and infrastructure.

Box 1.5.d Common examples of taxes

- **Income tax** – a levy on personal incomes from wages, salaries, rent, interest and dividends. It is the key source of tax revenue for most governments.
- **Corporate tax** – a levy on profits. Small businesses tend to be charged a lower tax rate on their profits than large multinational companies.
- **Sales taxes** – taxes on an individual's expenditure, such as Value Added Tax (charged in most European countries) and the Goods & Services Tax (used in the USA and other parts of the world).
- **Capital gains tax** – a tax on the surplus (known as 'capital gains') made from investments such as shares and property.
- **Inheritance tax** – a tax on the value of assets (such as cash or property) passed onto a third party following the death of the owner of the assets.
- **Excise duties** – levies on demerit goods such as alcohol, tobacco, petrol and gambling.
- **Customs duties** – taxes on foreign imports, which help to raise government revenue and give domestic businesses a relative price advantage.
- **Stamp duty** – a tax paid when commercial or residential property is bought. It tends to be progressive, so the higher the property value the greater the tax rate tends to be.

Figure 1.5.g Taiwan's high-speed rail line cost $18 billion

Deflationary fiscal policy is used when the economy experiences high rates of economic growth and inflation, so needs to be slowed down via a combination of higher taxes and reduced government expenditure policies. By contrast, **expansionary fiscal policy** is used to boost business activity, perhaps to get the economy out of a recession. This is done by a combination of tax cuts and increased public sector spending, thereby creating business opportunities.

Theory of knowledge

How do different stakeholders determine what a 'fair' tax is? How should we determine what is a fair tax rate for businesses to pay?

Monetary policy is the use of interest rate policy to affect the money supply and exchange rates in order to influence business activity. The interest rate is the price of money, both in terms of the cost of borrowing money and the return for saving money in a bank account. If the economy is believed to be growing too fast, the government or the Central Bank is likely to raise interest rates to combat the effects of inflation, and vice versa. For example, in 2018, the Argentinian government raised interest rates to 40% in order to combat inflation rates in excess of 25%.

Figure 1.5.h Monetary policy is about controlling the money supply

Raising interest rates makes borrowing less attractive because households and businesses face higher interest repayments on their loans. In addition, those with existing credit card bills, loans and mortgages face escalating interest repayments. Higher interest rates automatically reduce people's disposable income after all interest-bearing loans have been paid. Hence, those with existing loans may need to reduce their overall spending. An increase in interest rates is likely to reduce consumption and investment expenditure, therefore being a threat to businesses, even though this may help to control inflation in the economy.

An increase in interest rates in a country also tends to stimulate demand for its currency since foreign investors are attracted by better returns on their savings. If Germany and Australia have relatively higher interest rates than Japan or Taiwan,

then demand for Euros and Australian dollars would tend to rise thereby increasing the price (or exchange rate) of these currencies. This causes the price of exports to be relatively higher and therefore is likely to reduce the demand for exports. Hence, higher exchange rates tend to be a threat for domestic businesses in the long run.

Common mistake

Students often comment that higher interest rates create incentives for people to *save* more money. In reality, most governments only tend to change interest rates by 0.25% at a time; hardly an incentive to spend less in order to save more. Some people might save more (probably those without mortgages, credits cards bills and loans), but this is highly unlikely for households and businesses with outstanding loans. Thus, higher interest rates have a much larger impact on reducing the *spending* ability of households and firms.

The government can also use **deregulation** to provide opportunities for businesses to prosper. Deregulation is the removal of government rules and regulations (bureaucracy) which constrain business activity within a particular industry. It should therefore enhance efficiency and encourage more competition within the industry.

Political **corruption** can be a major and ongoing threat for businesses. Transparency International, a global non-governmental organization, claims that there is a strong correlation between corruption, poverty and international competitiveness, i.e. higher levels of corruption in a country jeopardise the nation's ability to alleviate poverty and to be competitive on an international scale. Box 1.5.e shows the most honest and least honest countries according to Transparency International, with a score of 0-9 being 'highly corrupt' and a score of 90-100 being 'very clean'.

Theory of knowledge

To what extent is business knowledge limited by uncertainty about the external environment?

Box 1.5.e   Top seven most honest and least honest nations

Rank	Country	Score
1	New Zealand	89
2	Demark	88
3	Finland	85
3	Norway	85
3	Switzerland	85
6	Singapore	84
6	Sweden	84
:	:	:
171	North Korea	17
175	Sudan	16
175	Yemen	16
177	Afghanistan	15
178	Syria	14
179	South Sudan	12
180	Somalia	9

Source: adapted from www.transparency.org

Theory of knowledge

How is it possible to know whether what the government says is actually true?

Legal opportunities and threats

STEEPLE analysis of a given organization. AO2, AO4
Consequences of a change in any of the STEEPLE factors for a business's objectives and strategy. AO3
© IBO, 2017

The government imposes rules, regulations and laws to ensure that the general public is protected from adverse business activity. Government intervention can also protect the interests of businesses. Common legislation affecting businesses include:

- **Consumer protection legislation**   Laws exist that make it illegal for businesses to provide false or misleading descriptions of their products and services (see Question 1.5.6). Products must meet certain quality standards and be fit for their purpose. Businesses are held liable for any damage or injury caused by their defective products.

- **Employee protection legislation**   These laws protect the interests and safety of workers (see Box 1.5.f). For instance, anti-discrimination legislation helps to ensure that businesses act fairly towards their employees, irrespective of their age, gender, religion or ethnicity.

- **Competition legislation**   Laws ensure that anti-competitive practices are prohibited to protect customers and smaller businesses from firms with monopoly power. The government takes action against businesses deemed to be acting against the public interest, such as large firms engaging in price fixing or charging unjustifiably high prices. Competition laws can also present opportunities. For example, copyright, trademark and patent laws give businesses legal protection against competitors replicating their works or inventions. This can stimulate innovation (see Unit 5.6), thereby improving the firm's competitiveness.

- **Social and environmental protection legislation**   Laws exist to prevent or reduce the consumption of *demerit goods* (products that cause additional costs to society), e.g. tobacco, petrol, alcohol, gambling and illegal drugs. The social costs (to the general public) of consuming demerit goods outweigh the private costs of consumption (incurred by the consumer). Without government legislation, the consumption of these products would be higher and therefore the costs to society would be greater (e.g. passive smoking, pollution, drink driving, and crime).

Figure 1.5.i Alcohol is a demerit good

Box 1.5.f   Legal employment rights

Although countries vary in their use of employment legislation, the laws typically found in most economically countries include:

- **Anti-discrimination laws** make it illegal to discriminate (show prejudice) against individuals because of their gender, race (ethnicity), religion, disability, marital status or age.
- **Equal pay legislation** makes it unlawful for an employer to reward employees differently if they are doing work or jobs deemed to be of equal value.
- **Health and Safety at Work Acts** (HASAWA) cover the provision of safe and adequate working conditions. Businesses need to offer a secure and hygienic working environment for their staff.
- **Statutory benefits** are the legal benefits that all businesses are obliged to offer to their workers, such as maternity leave, sick pay, holiday pay and retirement pension scheme.
- **National minimum wage legislation** requires all businesses to pay a legal minimum rate of pay to their workers, thus creating incentives to work for the poorest paid workers in the country.

Case study

Businesses can get into all sorts of trouble if they do not comply with employment legislation. In November 2000, Coca-Cola was made to pay out $192.5 m (worth around 300 million cans of Coke) in lawsuit allegations that they treated black workers unfairly.

Case study

The US state of Colorado legalised the sale of marijuana (cannabis) in 2014 at regulated retailers. The psychoactive drug became legally available for personal and recreational use for those aged 21 and above. Entrepreneurs in Colorado cashed in by attracting tourists to the area. Critics argued that legalisation sends the wrong message to youth around the world.

Case study

In 2013, the Turkish government introduced a series of strict trading laws of the sale of alcoholic products: alcohol cannot be sold within 100 metres of a place of worship or a school, all forms of alcohol advertising are banned, and alcohol cannot be bought or sold between 10 pm and 6 am.

Question 1.5.6   Findus horsemeat scandal

In 2013, the UK's Food Standards Agency (FSA) confirmed that meat found in some frozen beef lasagne products from *Findus* were made from 100% horsemeat. This led to a complete **product recall** of all meat products under the *Findus* **brand** in 13 countries, including the UK, France and Sweden. The FSA reported that there was no evidence to suggest that the horsemeat caused a food safety risk, but questions were raised about the unethical practice of the European food producer and its failure to comply with product description laws. The company made an official apology to customers and offered full refunds for products purchases.

(a) (i) Define the term **product recall**. *[2 marks]*

(a) (ii) Define the term **brand**. *[2 marks]*

(b) Explain how *Findus* may have acted unlawfully and unethically. *[6 marks]*

IB Learner Profile – Be knowledgeable and a thinker

Gender equality is the fifth Sustainable Development Goal (SDG) of the United Nations. Investigate the arguments in favour of gender equality - the UN website (www.un.org/sustainabledevelopment/) is a good starting point. Can businesses genuinely promote gender equality in the workplace? Justify your reasoning.

Theory of knowledge

Is 'business ethics' an oxymoron? How can we truly know if an organization's corporate social responsibilities are genuinely altruistic rather than for personal gain?

Question 1.5.7 Walmart

Global retailer *Walmart* was charged with breaking local labour laws in late 2006. *Walmart* had been found guilty of exploiting employees in Pennsylvania, USA by forcing them to work during their rest breaks without pay. The courts fined *Walmart* $78 million. The following year, 1.6 million female workers also filed for **discrimination** charges, claiming that *Walmart* denied them opportunities for promotion due to their gender. They also claimed that *Walmart* paid male counterparts higher wages. In November 2013, employees staged a protest to demand higher pay, calling for a minimum annual salary of $25,000 for full-time workers. *Walmart* defended its practices stating that its average worker earns $12 per hour – significantly higher than the federal **national minimum wage** of $7.25 per hour.

(a) (i) Define the term **discrimination**. [2 marks]

(a) (ii) Define the term **national minimum wage**. [2 marks]

(b) Justify why organizations such as *Walmart* need to be aware of the legal environment. [10 marks]

Ethical opportunities and threats

STEEPLE analysis of a given organization. AO2, AO4
Consequences of a change in any of the STEEPLE factors for a business's objectives and strategy. AO3
© IBO, 2017

Business ethics are the moral principles that are, or should be, considered in business decision-making, i.e. what is judged to be right or wrong. Ethical firms act in a socially responsible way towards their stakeholders (especially their customers, employees and the local community), e.g. protecting the natural environment by using resources efficiently and minimising waste. Ethical firms pay their workers on time, do not employ workers below the legal minimum age or allow their employees to operate in poor working conditions. They do not use misleading marketing or deal with corrupt suppliers, sponsors or governments. Although there are compliance costs in acting ethically, firms that are socially responsible can benefit in several ways:

- They attract and retain good quality workers. Google, for example, has a very loyal and dedicated workforce, largely because of the astonishing working environment, which includes free buffet meals, gym access, laundry and a host of other on-site benefits.

- They attract new customers and retain existing ones. To remain competitive, businesses need to consider the impact of their operations on society and the environment because customers are increasingly concerned about environmental protection and ethical business behaviour.

- Social responsibility generates good publicity and public relations. Organizations such as The Body Shop, The Co-operative and Friends of The Earth have used their ethical stance to propel their business and mission (cause).

Businesses are increasingly prepared to have external *social audits* conducted. These are reports on the ethical and social stance of a business, examined and reported by an external agency. The social audit reports both external matters (such as a firm's involvement in community projects and the level of pollution caused by the firm) and internal issues (such as the efficiency of its waste management processes and its ability to provide staff with a safe working environment).

Choosing to be ethical and socially responsible can bring benefits, but there are also compliance costs involved with such decisions. A business might not always be able to pursue the cheapest or the most profitable option due to the costs of being ethical and socially responsible. For example, the cheapest supplier might not be chosen if it is perceived (by customers and other stakeholders) to be an unethical business.

Case study

In 2013, the 'horsemeat scandal' spread throughout Europe and affected businesses in many other parts of the world. Food products advertised as containing beef were adulterated with horsemeat, by up to 100% in some cases. Horse DNA was found in frozen beef burgers in supermarkets in Ireland and Britain. Retailers such as Tesco and Burger King cut all links with the suppliers found guilty by the European authorities.

Theory of knowledge

How does cultural bias affect people's interpretation of what is and what is not considered to be ethical business behaviour?

Exam tip !

The external environment is a complicated topic, so it is advisable to revisit this unit towards the end of your course and when preparing for the Paper 1 (pre-released) Case Study.

The external environment and the CUEGIS concepts

STEEPLE analysis provides managers with an overview of the factors in the external environment that affect business activity and the issues that should be addressed in any business strategy. It is a useful and straightforward framework that aids management decision-making, such as:

- the potential costs and benefits of a joint venture, merger or acquisition (see Unit 1.6)

- marketing planning, e.g. the opportunities and threats of international marketing (see Unit 4.7)

- business propositions, e.g. whether to expand overseas or to outsource production (see Unit 5.4)

- investment opportunities, e.g. deciding on the location of business (see Unit 5.4).

Changes in the external environment, which are inevitable, present both threats and opportunities for businesses. Changes in social, cultural, technological and environmental factors will also affect business strategy. Different businesses are affected by different external factors and to varying degrees. This will largely depend on factors such as:

- The size of the business – Smaller and newer firms tend to be less able to cope with external shocks to the business environment.

- The ability of management – Experienced and skilled managers are able to predict and successfully react to changes in the external environment and potential crises (see Unit 5.7).

- The degree of brand loyalty – Businesses with a loyal customer base are less exposed to the threats of competition, so are less affected by external changes such as fluctuations in the exchange rate.

- The diversity of the firm's operations – Firms that have a diversified product portfolio and have overseas operations are more able to handle changes in the external environment. By contrast, firms that specialise in one or two products in a specific market are more vulnerable to external threats.

- The level of a firm's gearing - Gearing refers to the extent to which a business relies on external borrowing (see Unit 3.6). Businesses that are highly geared are more defenseless if there are adverse changes in the external business environment, e.g. if interest rates increase.

Change in the external environment also affect a firm's competitive strategy (its ability to compete against domestic and international rivals), such as exchange rates or government rules and regulations. Management guru Michael Porter believes that business strategy needs to focus on a chosen source of competitive advantage. This could be through low prices (such as Ryanair or IKEA) or via outstanding quality (such as BMW or Gucci). Such decisions allow businesses to devise appropriate strategies to maintain or improve their competitiveness in an ever-changing and dynamic and globalized business world.

IB Learner Profile – Be an inquirer

Investigate China's demographic changes and the effects on the country's modernising society: http://goo.gl/DNWocC.

Investigate the importance of establishing 'guangxi' as a cultural expectation for conducting business in China: http://goo.gl/IDYBqf.

CUEGIS ESSAY

With reference to an organization of your choice, examine how **change** in the external environment impacts on its **strategy**.   *[20 marks]*

CUEGIS ESSAY

With reference to an organization of your choice, discuss how **ethics** influence its business **strategy**.
[20 marks]

REVIEW QUESTIONS

1. What does the acronym STEEPLE analysis stand for?

2. Distinguish between opportunities and threats.

3. Outline the purpose of a STEEPLE analysis.

4. How does the technological environment present both opportunities and threats for businesses?

5. Why are inflation and unemployment threats for most businesses?

6. How do fluctuations in the exchange rate affect the sales revenues and profits of a business?

7. What are the various stages of the business cycle?

8. How does the government influence business activity?

9. How does the legal environment provide both opportunities and threats to businesses?

10. State three ways in which ethical considerations affect business activity.

KEY TERMS

Business cycle refers to the fluctuation in the level of business activity over time. Countries tend to move through the cycle of booms, recessions, slumps, recovery and growth.

Business ethics are the moral principles that are, or should be, considered in business decision-making, i.e. what is judged to be right or wrong.

Deregulation is the removal of government rules and regulations that constrain an industry to enhance efficiency and encourage more competition within the industry.

Economic growth measures changes in the Gross Domestic Product of a country over time. It occurs if there is an increase in GDP for two consecutive quarters.

Environmental factors are the ecological influences that have a direct impact on the operations of an organization, e.g. adverse weather, climate change and green technologies.

Business organization and environment

CORE

Ethics are the moral values and judgements (of what is right) that society believes businesses ought to consider in their decision-making.

The **exchange rate** is the value of a country's currency in terms of other currencies.

Fluctuations in the exchange rate affect business operations and profitability

The **external environment** refers to a framework of the (STEEPLE) factors that are beyond the control of any individual organization, but which affect all businesses and their operations.

Fiscal policy is the use of *taxation* and *government expenditure* policies to influence business activity.

Inflation occurs when the general price level in an economy continuously rises. It is measured by changes in the cost of living for the average household in a country.

Interest rate is a measure of the price of money in terms of the amount charged for borrowed funds or how much is offered on money that is saved.

Monetary policy is the use of interest rate policy to affect the money supply and exchange rates in order to influence business activity.

Political factors in a STEEPLE analysis refer to influences from the role that governments play in business operations, e.g. tax laws and rules or restrictions on trade.

Protectionist measures are any measure taken by a government to safeguard its industries from overseas competitors. They are a threat to businesses trying to operate in foreign markets.

Social factors in a STEEPLE analysis are the influences on business related to people in society, their lifestyles and their beliefs (or values).

STEEPLE analysis is an analytical framework used to examine the opportunities and threats of the external environment (social, technological, economic, environmental, political, legal, and ethical environments) on business activity.

Unemployment refers to the number of people in the workforce who are willing and able to work but cannot find employment.

1.6 Growth and evolution

"It is not the strongest of the species that survive, nor the most intelligent, but the one most responsive to change." -
Charles Darwin, English naturalist

SL/HL content	Assessment objective
Economies and diseconomies of scale	AO2
The merits of small versus large organizations	AO3
The difference between internal and external growth	AO2
The following external growth methods: • mergers and acquisitions (M&As) and takeovers • joint ventures • strategic alliances • franchising	AO3
The role and impact of globalization on the growth and evolution of businesses	AO3
Reasons for the growth of multinational companies (MNCs)	AO3
The impact of MNCs on the host countries	AO3

© IBO, 2017

Business organization and environment

CORE

Economies and diseconomies of scale

Economies and diseconomies of scale. AO2

© IBO, 2017

One major reason why businesses aim to grow is to benefit from **economies of scale** – the lower average costs of production as a firm operates on a larger scale due to an improvement in productive efficiency. Economies of scale can help businesses to gain a competitive cost advantage because lower average costs can mean a combination of lower prices being charged to customers and a higher profit margin earned on each unit sold.

The **average cost** (AC) is the cost per unit of output. It is calculated by dividing total costs (TC) by the quantity of output (Q), i.e. AC = TC ÷ Q. For example, if total costs of producing 10,000 t-shirts is $78,000 then the cost of each shirt is $7.80.

Average costs consist of two components: **average fixed costs** (AFC) and **average variable costs** (AVC). AFC is calculated by dividing the total fixed costs by the level of output, i.e. AFC = TFC ÷ Q. Similarly, AVC is calculated by dividing the total variable costs by the level of output, i.e. AVC = TVC ÷ Q.

The average fixed costs of a firm will decline continuously with larger levels of output. This is because the TFC remain constant but are spread over an increasing amount of output, i.e. the same (fixed) costs are being divided by a larger and larger number (level of output).

Case study

The Airbus 380, the world's largest passenger plane, has 49% more seating capacity than its rival Boeing 787 Dreamliner, yet burns 17% less fuel per seat. Hence, the average cost of fuel for Airbus is lower. This is particularly important for airline carriers operating in a highly competitive industry where fuel prices account for a large proportion of their costs (the A380 has a fuel capacity of 81,890 gallons or 310,000 litres), and where the price of aircraft is hugely expensive – the Boeing 787 Dreamliner costs more than $257 m and the Airbus A380 costs $418 m per plane!

79

Economies of scale that occur inside the firm and are within its control are known as **internal economies of scale**. Those that occur within the industry and are largely beyond an individual firm's control are known as external economies of scale.

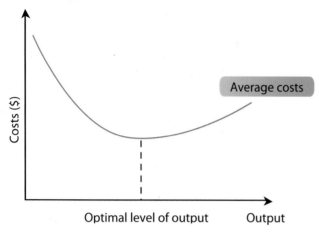

Figure 1.6.a Economies and diseconomies of scale

Internal economies of scale

By operating on a larger scale, a business can reduce its average costs of production due to any combination of the factors below. The relative importance of each depends on the actual firm under consideration.

- **Technical economies** Large firms can use sophisticated machinery to mass produce their products. For example, due to the huge scale of production, the Phillips factory in Shenzhen, China produces complete audio systems within a few seconds! The high fixed costs of their equipment and machinery are spread over the huge scale of output, thereby reducing their average costs of production. Small businesses do not find it feasible or cost-efficient to buy and use such technology.

- **Financial economies** Large firms can borrow massive sums of money at lower rates of interest compared to smaller rivals because the larger firms are seen as less risky to financial lenders. In addition, a large and established business looking to borrow money will probably choose a lender that offers the most attractive interest rate, i.e. there is rivalry amongst the financiers to lend to large businesses. By contrast, smaller firms often struggle to raise external finance and are charged higher interest rates on their borrowing.

- **Managerial economies** A sole trader (see Unit 1.2) often has to fulfil the functions of marketer, accountant and production manager. As people cannot be equally good

at everything, specialisation leads to higher productivity. Large firms divide managerial roles by employing specialist managers. Through growth, a business can avoid a duplication of effort in planning, communication, marketing, distribution and production processes. The higher productivity means that average costs can still fall.

- **Specialisation economies** This is similar to managerial economies of scale but results from division of labour of the workforce, rather than the management. Motor vehicle manufacturers that use mass production benefit from having specialist labour such as designers, production staff, engineers and marketers. These specialists are responsible for a single part of the production process and their skills and expertise mean that there is greater productivity.

- **Marketing economies** Large firms can benefit from lower average costs by selling in bulk, thus benefiting from reduced time and transactions costs. A small retail outlet might sell 1,000 cans of Coca-Cola in a month to hundreds of different customers. This will cost a lot more than Coca-Cola who can sell 1,000 cans in one transaction to a single customer (such as a supermarket). Global firms such as McDonald's and Nike can spread the high costs of advertising by using the same marketing campaign across the world (language translation is a minor cost as part of a global marketing budget).

- **Purchasing economies** Large firms can lower their average costs by buying resources in bulk. Note, however, that even relatively small firms can gain from purchasing economies because they gain discounts for bulk purchases. Of course, the larger the order the greater the bulk discount might be, so there is an advantage to being big in business.

- **Risk-bearing economies** These savings can be enjoyed by conglomerates (firms with a diversified portfolio of products in different markets). Conglomerates can spread their fixed costs, such as advertising or research and development, across a wide range of operations. Unfavourable trading conditions for certain products or industries can be offset by more favourable conditions in other sectors of the business. For conglomerates such as Cheung Kong Holdings, a loss in one area of their business does not jeopardise the business overall.

Case study

Cheung Kong Holdings, Hong Kong's largest company, has an incredibly diverse range of operations, including: supermarkets, mobile telecommunications, electronics, food and drink, Internet and broadband television services, media, hotels and property development. It is also the world's largest port operator and health and beauty retailer. The conglomerate was founded by Sir Li Ka-Shing, a Chinese migrant who arrived in Hong Kong penniless but went on to become Asia's richest man.

Exam tip !

Many students define economies of scale as "the benefits of bulk buying". However, even small businesses can buy in bulk; the term refers to the cost-reducing benefits enjoyed by firms engaged in large scale operations. Financial, technological and managerial economies of scale are probably far more important in reducing the average costs of production for most businesses than their ability to buy in bulk.

External economies of scale

External economies of scale are cost-saving benefits of large scale operations arising from outside the business due to its favourable location or general growth in the industry. Examples of external economies include:

- **Technological progress** increases the productivity within the industry. For example, the Internet has created huge cost savings for businesses engaged in e-commerce (see Unit 4.8).

- **Improved transportation networks** help to ensure prompt deliveries. Furthermore, employees who are late to work due to poor transportation links cost the business money. Customers want convenience, i.e. easy access to suppliers. Ultimately, congestion increases business costs and reduces sales revenues.

- An abundance of **skilled labour** might exist in the local area, perhaps through government aided training programmes or reputable education and training facilities in a certain location. This provides local businesses with a suitable pool of educated and trained labour, thereby

helping to cut recruitment costs without compromising productivity levels.

- **Regional specialisation** means that a particular location or country has a highly regarded and trustworthy reputation for producing a certain good or service. For example, Murano, in Venice, Italy, is famous throughout the world for its glass products such as vases, jewellery and chandeliers. This allows the industry to benefit from having access to specialist labour, subcontractors and suppliers, thus helping to reduce average costs of production for the industry. Its reputation also allows firms in Murano to charge higher prices.

Figure 1.6.b Murano is famous for its glass chandeliers

Internal diseconomies of scale

Contrary to popular belief, businesses can become too large. There comes a 'tipping point' when economies of scale can no longer be exploited. **Diseconomies of scale** are the result of higher unit costs as a firm continues to increase in size, i.e. the business becomes outsized and inefficient so average costs begin to rise. Internal diseconomies usually occur due to managerial problems. Examples include:

- As a firm becomes larger, managers may *lack control and coordination* as the span of control (see Unit 2.2) is likely to increase and cause communication problems. Ultimately, these difficulties slow down decision-making. Coordination and control problems also occur for businesses with operations in different locations throughout the world. Workers in larger organizations might feel a sense of alienation, which can harm staff morale (see Unit 2.4). These issues add to the firm's costs without any corresponding increase in productivity, thereby raising its unit costs.

- There is likely to be *poorer working relationships* in an oversized business. With a larger workforce, senior managers are more likely to become detached from those lower down in the hierarchy, thereby making them feel distanced or out of touch. This can damage communication flows and the morale of staff, thereby reducing their productivity thus leading to higher unit costs.

- Outsized organizations are likely to suffer from the disadvantages of specialisation and division of labour. Workers become bored with performing repetitive tasks. With a larger workforce, there may also be scope for *slack* (inefficiency and procrastination). This leads to lower productive efficiency and hence an increase in the average costs of production.

- The amount of *bureaucracy* (administration, paperwork and company policies) is also likely to increase as a business grows. This makes decision-making more time consuming and adds to the costs of the business, but is unlikely to contribute to any extra output of goods and services to the customer. Bureaucracy can also make communication more difficult, thereby worsening working relationships, again contributing to higher unit costs.

- *Complacency* with being a large and dominant player or even the market leader in the industry can also cause many problems. Complacency is most likely to reduce productivity thereby raising unit costs of production.

The potential for large firms to experience diseconomies of scale means that some businesses prefer to grow via **franchising** (covered later in this Unit). Multinational companies such as McDonald's and 7-Eleven have used this strategy to expand their businesses and to raise brand awareness, without having to face higher unit costs of being large.

External diseconomies of scale

External diseconomies of scale refer to an increase in the average costs of production as a firm grows due to factors beyond its control, i.e. problems that affect the whole industry, often because there are just too many firms. Average costs of production increase for all businesses in the industry. Examples include:

- Too many businesses locating in a certain area causes land to become more scarce thereby *increasing market rents.* This adds to the fixed costs of all businesses in the area without any corresponding increase in output. Hence, unit costs will rise. The high demand for businesses to locate in busy city districts such as Manhattan (New York), Causeway Bay (Hong Kong), Tokyo (Japan), and The City (London) has resulted in a sustained and continuous rise in the rental value of land in these prime locations.

- Since workers have greater choice from a large number of employers in the local area, businesses might have to offer *higher wages and financial rewards* to retain workers or attract new staff. This will increase costs without necessarily increasing output, thereby raising average costs of production.

- *Traffic congestion* results from too many businesses being located in an area. Deliveries are likely to be delayed due to the overcrowding. This increases transportation costs for businesses, thereby contributing to the increase in unit costs of production.

Case study

Amazon was founded in 1994 by Jeff Bezos, operating the business from his garage in Washington, USA. Originally an online bookstore, the business earned $20,000 in sales per week within its first two months of trading. However, it wasn't until 2001 when the company declared its first profit. Amazon has continued to grow across North America, Latin America, Europe, Africa and Asia. It employs over 180,000 workers in the USA and earns over $178bn in annual sales revenue. Bezos is now the world's richest man.

Figure 1.6.c Traffic congestion is a cause of external diseconomies of scale

Small versus large organizations

The merits of small versus large organizations. AO3
© IBO, 2017

All businesses have an appropriate scale of operation. For instance, the market for smartphones is enormous whereas that for IB textbooks is relatively small. The size of a business can be measured in several ways:

- Market share – a firm's sales revenue as a percentage of the industry's total revenue.

- Total revenue – the value of a firm's annual sales turnover per time period.

- Size of workforce – the total number of employees hired by the business.

- Profit – the value of a firm's profits per time period.

- Capital employed – the value of the firm's capital investment for the business to function.

An increase in the value of any of the above measures would suggest that the firm is growing. Essentially, the size of a business is measured in relative terms, i.e. compared to the size of rivals.

Table 1.6.a lists some of the benefits to an organization of being large.

Despite the benefits of being a large business, small firms can still thrive for several reasons. Table 1.6.b lists some of the benefits to an organization of being small.

Table 1.6.a Benefits to an organization of being large

Factor	Benefit
Brand recognition	Familiarity with the brand allows large businesses to sell to a wider market. Many firms are large and established enough to have global brand recognition.
Brand reputation	Larger firms tend to be more trusted due to their brand image and brand reputation.
Value-added services	Larger firms have the resources to provide a wider range of services, e.g. longer opening hours and interest-free credit instalments.
Lower price	Larger firms are able to offer customers greater price discounts through their ability to enjoy economies of scale.
Greater choice	Larger firms can provide more choice, e.g. Amazon sells a huge range of books, toys, music and DVDs compared to a small local book shop, toy store or music retailer.
Customer loyalty	The above benefits mean that more customers are likely to remain loyal to the business, its products and its brands due to the perceived trust and value for money.

Business organization and environment

CORE

Table 1.6.b Benefits to an organization of being small

Factor	Benefit
Cost control	Large scale operations can mean that a firm encounters diseconomies of scale due to problems of control, coordination and communication. Owners of small firms might not want to expand since they could face higher unit costs as their organizations grow. Growth can also require extra borrowing costs and/or a dilution of ownership and control.
Financial risk	Since the costs of running a large global business are huge (such as the costs of research and development, marketing or recruitment and training), the financial risks are also high. By contrast, owners of small businesses can better manage and control their finances.
Government aid	Financial support in the form of grants and subsidies can be offered to small businesses to help them start up and to develop. Funds for training may also be available for small businesses that provide employment opportunities in the local community.
Local monopoly power	Small businesses may enjoy being the only firm in a particular location, e.g. a local restaurant, a franchised petroleum retailer and a small convenience store located in a remote town. Large businesses may be reluctant to locate in remote areas (see Unit 5.4) so this provides an opportunity for smaller firms to establish themselves in the area.
Personalised services	Smaller firms are more likely to have the time to devote to individual customers. For example, staff at a small local convenience store can get to know its customers better as staff are not pressurised by high sales targets. By contrast, large supermarkets rely on a high number of customers being served with some using self-checkout services.
Flexibility	Small businesses tend to be more flexible and adaptive to change. IFor example, if a sole trader runs a beauty salon that is rather unsuccessful, then the business might be changed to something completely different, such as a children's toy shop. Large businesses have large financial commitments and conflicting stakeholder objectives (see Unit 1.4) which combine to reduce their ability to change.
Small market size	Some businesses, such as a local hair salon or private tuition firm, are unlikely to attract the attention of large firms due to the very limited size of the market. Large corporations may not find it financially worthwhile to compete with these small local firms, thereby allowing them to thrive.

Figure 1.6.d Small businesses can thrive despite the existence and benefits of larger firms

The optimal (most appropriate) size for a business depends on its internal structure, its costs, and its aims and objectives. For example, Mars and IKEA are privately owned companies (see Unit 1.2) since the owners want the businesses to remain in the control of the founding families rather than external owners (shareholders and directors). Firms minimise their costs by operating at the output level where average costs are at their lowest (see Figure 1.6.a). If a firm operates beyond its optimal size (i.e. it becomes too large) then diseconomies of scale will be experienced, thereby raising unit costs and reducing profits.

In reality, a firm might not operate at its optimal level due to a lack of resources. It cannot expand if it does not have appropriate and sufficient sources of finance. Furthermore, it cannot increase output if it lacks the productive capacity (see Unit 5.5) to do so. The firm will also choose not to expand output if there is insufficient demand, even if producing more means lower average costs.

Question 1.6.1   Small versus large

Businesses come in all different sizes. For example:

*   A vast number of sole traders only supply a limited number of products.
*   Airbus and Boeing manufacture commercial aircraft for airline companies only.
*   Ferrari and Rolex supply luxury goods to a relatively small consumer market.
*   Ford, General Motors and Toyota mass produce their cars.
*   Samsung, Apple and HTC collectively produce billions of mobile phones.
*   Burger King, KFC and McDonald's have outlets throughout the world.
*   Microsoft supplies computer software for over 90% of the world's personal computers.

Some businesses prefer to stay small. Rolex and Ferrari, for example, deliberately limit growth in their operations. Others, such as McDonald's and Toyota, continually strive for expansion.

(a) Explain why economies of scale might benefit customers.   *[2 marks]*

(b) Explain why economies of scale might be inappropriate, undesirable or inaccessible for certain businesses.   *[4 marks]*

(c) Explain why so many small firms continue to survive and thrive, despite their limited ability to access economies of scale.   *[4 marks]*

(d) To what extent do large businesses operate in the best interests of the general public?   *[10 marks]*

Figure 1.6.e   Small firms tend to sell a limited range of goods

Nevertheless, growth is a continual aim of most established businesses. There are several reasons why firms seek to grow:

*   To reap the benefits of larger scale production, i.e. *economies of scale*.

*   To gain a larger *market share* and *market power* (see Unit 4.1). This also allows the firm to charge higher prices (see Unit 4.5) yet gain more profit at the same time.

*   Growth is a means of *survival* as competitors are also likely to strive for growth. Businesses need to 'run faster to stay still', i.e. grow to compete with their growing rivals.

*   To *spread risk*s by diversifying into new markets rather than focusing only on one specific market. If there are detrimental changes in a particular market, then having operations in other markets might help to safeguard the firm's survival.

Case study

Blockbuster was a multinational company founded in 1985 and provided home entertainment rental services, such as DVD movies and video games. At its peak in 2004, the American company employed over 60,000 people in 9,000 stores across the world. Its failure to adopt internet technologies and to diversify, plus the competition from rivals such as Netflix and Amazon, led to Blockbuster's bankruptcy in 2010. Whilst acquisitions enabled the business to continue its operations, albeit on a much smaller scale, the company closed its remaining 300 stores in November 2013.

Question 1.6.2   Hoang Ngan

Hoang Ngan is a small business specialising in clothing products for men. Established in 2016, *Hoang Ngan* has expanded its operations in two other locations in South Vietnam. However, the owner has struggled to secure finance for its planned **growth** in neighbouring countries Laos and Cambodia.

(a) Define the term **growth**. [2 marks]

(b) Identify **two** reasons why banks might be reluctant to fund the expansion plans of *Hoang Ngan*. [2 marks]

(c) Explain **two** problems that *Hoang Ngan* might encounter operating in new overseas markets such as Laos and Cambodia. [6 marks]

Ultimately, the reasons for seeking growth can be summarised as the desire for businesses (especially those in the private sector) to gain more profit in the long run. However, growth is neither easy nor cheap to achieve. It requires access to more financial and non-financial resources, including human resources. Also, some firms can actually overtrade (expand too quickly by taking on more orders than they have the capacity to handle) or expand in the wrong direction (perhaps by entering markets where they lack local expertise). Such firms are therefore exposed to even greater risks of failure.

Internal (organic) growth

The difference between internal and external growth. AO2
© IBO, 2017

There are two categories of business growth: *internal growth* and *external growth* (considered in more depth in the next section). **Internal growth** occurs when a business grows organically, using its own capabilities and resources to increase the scale of its operations and sales revenue. It is typically financed through a combination of retained profits, borrowing and issuing of new shares. A business can grow internally in several ways such as:

- Changing **price** – More customers tend to buy a product at lower prices. However, if there are very few substitutes for the product, the business will earn more revenue by raising prices. For products in highly competitive markets, a price reduction should generate proportionately more sales revenue.

- Effective **promotion** – People are more likely to buy a product if they are informed, reminded and/or persuaded about its benefits. The Coca-Cola Company spends $1.9 billion each year on promoting its products, which is one reason why it is the world's most recognised brand with sales of 1.9 billion servings per day.

- Producing improved or better **products** – Through methods such as market research, innovation and new product development, businesses can produce products that are more appealing to the market, thereby raising their sales. Most new products on the market fail, so it is quite common for firms to improve on the design or features of an existing product. Nevertheless, innovation can be a lucrative source of internal growth.

- Sell through a greater distribution network (**placement**) – If a product is widely available, customers are more likely to buy it. One of the world's most expensive production cars is the Lamborghini Veneno, with a selling price of $4.5m. Apart from the price, the Lamborghini Veneno is very limited in supply, so this limits the potential number of customers. Coca-Cola, on the other hand, is widely available throughout the world in different places, e.g. supermarkets, restaurants, cinemas, airlines and vending machines.

- Offer preferential **credit** – Customers are more likely to make a purchase if they are offered the ability to 'buy now and pay later'. Allowing customers to pay in regular instalments perhaps over 12 or 24 months for the purchase of expensive products, such as motor vehicles or large-screen televisions, can attract more customers to the market. However, firms must be careful not to offer too much credit as this can affect their cash flow position (see Unit 3.7).

- Increased **capital expenditure** (investment) – This can be in the form of internal expansion of the business to new locations or the introduction of new production processes and technologies to improve productivity. However, investment risks might not pay off so careful planning, such as investment appraisal (see Unit 3.8), is required.

- Improved **training and development** – People (employees) are often said to be a firm's most important asset. Training and development (T&D) is vital as customers are unlikely to buy from people with little or no product knowledge. T&D not only helps to make staff more confident and competent in their jobs, it can also help to motivate the workforce as they feel more valued by the employer. This can improve the level of customer service, thereby contributing to greater customer loyalty and higher sales for internal growth.

- Providing overall **value for money** – Businesses that can provide perceived value for money are most likely to experience internal growth. Customers will tend to look at more than just price when making purchasing decisions. Other factors include: quality, after-sales care, brand image, maintenance costs and environmental considerations.

Table 1.6.c lists some advantages and disadvantages of internal growth.

Case study

Apple uses an internal growth strategy by focusing on new product development and launching new products. These products include the iPod Touch, iPad, iPhone, iMac Pro, MacBook Air, MacBook Pro, Apple TV, Apple Watch, HomePod and the App Store.

Case study

Maybach was an ultra-luxury car manufacturer before it ceased production in 2013. Founded by Wilhelm Maybach in 1909, the German carmaker struggled from a lack of sales. In 1997, the company planned for the revival of the Maybach brand to compete with Rolls Royce and Bentley. Parent company Daimler AG had predicted annual worldwide sales of 2,000 Maybach cars – only 3,000 cars had been sold since 2002.

Table 1.6.c Advantages and disadvantages of internal growth

Advantages	Disadvantages
Better **control and coordination** It is often easier to grow internally than to rely on external sources. Organic growth also means the firm maintains control, whereas external growth can lead to a loss of control and ownership of the business.	**Diseconomies of scale** Higher unit costs of production can arise from internal growth. Hierarchical structures (see Unit 2.2) tend to be a feature of internal growth, causing communication problems and slower decision-making as a business grows.
Relatively **inexpensive** The main source of organic growth is retained profits. There might also be a need to raise interest-bearing capital, but there is less risk with internal growth as the amount of capital involved is relatively lower. The higher cost of external growth means that for many firms internal growth is the only suitable method of growth.	A need to **restructure** Although a sole trader can control and coordinate the business quite easily, if it grows into a multinational company then the organizational structure has to be changed. Restructuring requires time, effort and money, e.g. it requires training and updating of skills. Specialist managers have to be hired as the firm and its workforce grows.
Maintains **corporate culture** A major problem for mergers and acquisitions occurs when two firms with potentially very different cultures form a new company. By contrast, internal growth means there are no problems related with culture clashes (see Unit 2.5) and conflicting management styles.	**Dilution of control and ownership** If a firm grows by changing its legal status, for example from a partnership to a public limited company, then the original owners (the partners) have to share decision-making with the new owners (the shareholders). With more owners, decision-making is prolonged and there is more likely to be conflict of interests between the different shareholders.
Less risky Due to the above reasons, internal growth is the easiest and least risky method of growth and evolution for most businesses. Furthermore, internal growth builds on the strengths of the firm, e.g. its brand and customer loyalty.	**Slower growth** Internal growth is slower than external growth. Despite the risks, shareholders may prefer more rapid methods of growth to boost their return on investment.

Question 1.6.3   Poundland

British discount retailer *Poundland* has built a reputation for organic growth. Founded in 1990, Poundland opened its 500th store in 2014 and enjoyed sales growth of 15%. *Poundland*, which sells all its items at £1 ($1.45) or less, serves 7 million customers each week and has reported annual increases in profits by as much as 29%. Its strategy is to focus on organic growth in Ireland, the Netherlands and the UK in order to gain greater **market share** – in 2017, it had already opened its 900th store.

(a) Define **market share**.   *[2 marks]*

(b) Describe **two** methods of organic growth that *Poundland* might have used.   *[4 marks]*

(c) To what extent is organic growth desirable for a business such as *Poundland*?   *[10 marks]*

Theory of knowledge

How do the concepts of change and innovation influence our knowledge of business management?

Exam tip !

Essentially, internal growth is about a business expanding and evolving by using its own capabilities and its own resources in three 'new' ways:

1. Selling to new customers in existing markets
2. Finding new markets (local and/or overseas)
3. Launching new products to existing and/or new markets.

Question 1.6.4   A.S. Watson Group

With a history dating back to 1828, *A.S. Watson Group* has evolved into an international retail and manufacturing business with operations in over 14,100 stores across 24 markets worldwide. It is the world's leading health, beauty and lifestyle retailer, with over 28 million customers per week. *A.S. Watson Group* employs over 120,000 staff and its **product portfolio** includes some of Asia's best known brands and retail chains: Watson's Your Personal Store (health and beauty), PARKnSHOP (supermarkets), FORTRESS (electrical appliances), Watson's Wine Cellar and Nuance-Watson airport duty free shops. It is also a major producer and distributor of water products and beverages, including brands such as Sunkist and Mr. Juicy. In Europe, its health and beauty brands include Superdrug, Rossmann, Trekpleister, Drogas, and Spektr. Its luxury perfumery cosmetics brands include ICI PARIS XL, Marionnaud and The Perfume Shop. Growing the business remains a long-term aim at *A.S. Watson Group*.

Source: A.S. Watson Group (www.aswatson.com)

(a) Define the term **product portfolio**.   *[2 marks]*

(b) Suggest the type of business organization that *A.S. Watson Group* might be classified as operating.   *[2 marks]*

(c) Explain how *A.S. Watson Group* benefits from synergy by its growth and evolution strategies.   *[4 marks]*

(d) Despite its enormous size and global presence, examine why *A.S. Watson Group* still aims to grow larger as part of its long-term strategy.   *[6 marks]*

External (inorganic) growth

The difference between internal and external growth. AO2

© IBO, 2017

External growth (or **inorganic growth**) occurs through dealings with outside organizations. Such growth usually comes in the form of alliances or mergers with other firms or through the acquisition (takeover) of other businesses. Mergers and acquisitions (M&As) are collectively known as the **amalgamation** or **integration** of firms. There are several general benefits of external growth:

- External growth is a faster way to grow and evolve, e.g. it is quicker for a supermarket to merge with or acquire another supermarket than to buy or rent land to open new outlets.

- It is a quick way to reduce competition. By taking over a rival, for example, a firm is able to eliminate a competitor. However, such strategies can be prohibited by the government because the lack of competition might not be in the best interest of the general public.

- It can bring about greater market share and market power (see Unit 4.1).

- Working with other businesses means sharing of ideas. Inorganic growth can therefore generate new skills, experiences and customers.

- External growth can help a firm to evolve, thereby spreading risks across several distinct markets. Hence, such firms can benefit from risk-bearing economies of scale.

The main disadvantage of external growth is the huge costs, which tends to be higher than that needed for internal growth. Takeover bids can be especially expensive. Disney's takeover of Pixar (see Question 1.6.6) cost $7.4bn – about the same value as Coca-Cola's annual profits!

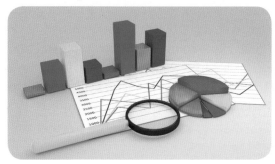

Figure 1.6.f External growth helps to build a firm's market share

External growth methods

The following external growth methods: mergers and acquisitions (M&As) and takeovers, joint ventures, strategic alliances and franchising. AO3

© IBO, 2017

Mergers and acquisitions

The phrase 'mergers and takeovers' or 'mergers and acquisitions' (M&As) refers to the amalgamation (integration) of two or more businesses to form a single company. The new firm will usually benefit from economies of scale and have a larger share of the market(s) that it operates in.

A **merger** takes place when two firms agree to form a new company, such as the merger between the UK's British Petroleum and USA's oil company Amoco in 1998 to form 'BP Amoco' – which has since been renamed and shortened to 'BP'. Other examples of large mergers include: Daimler Benz and Chrysler (1998), Glaxo Wellcome and SmithKline Beecham (2000), Hewlett–Packard and Compaq (2001), and American Airlines and US Airways (2013).

A **takeover** (or acquisition) occurs when a company buys a controlling interest in another firm, i.e. it buys enough shares in the target business to hold a majority stake. To entice shareholders of the target company to sell their shares, the offer price is likely to be well above the stock market value of the shares. Takeovers have been used as a method of business growth for a long time. For example, Heineken, the Dutch beer company established in 1864 by Gerard Adriaan Heineken, came to dominate the Dutch brewing industry by acquiring many of its competitors. Google acquired YouTube for $1.65 billion in 2006 – not bad for a business that was only 10 months old at that time! In 2017, 21st Century Fox was bought by the Walt Disney Company for $52.4 billion. With over 195 years of history, Cadbury was bought out by Kraft Foods in 2010 for a whopping £11.5 billion ($18bn); reasonable perhaps considering people spend over $9.5 million on chocolates per hour! Box 1.6.a outlines reasons why a certain business might become a takeover target.

Common mistake

Students will often claim that a business needs to buy at least 50% of the shares in another company in order to acquire it. Buying 50% plus 1 share will guarantee the acquisition but this might prove too expensive and is not a necessary condition. Buying a majority stake (which can be less than 50%) will ensure control of the acquired business.

Business organization and environment

CORE

Box 1.6.a   Reasons why businesses become takeover targets

- They have growth potential but lack sufficient funds for internal growth.
- They are seen as a small rival that has growth potential.
- They have a widely recognised corporate name or brand but are facing a financial crisis.
- They are vulnerable (an easy target for a takeover) due to a drop in profits and subsequent fall in their share price.

There are four types of integration that can occur in a merger or acquisition:

- **Horizontal integration** is the most common type of M&A, which occurs when there is an amalgamation of firms operating in the same industry. For example, Nike bought Umbro (both in the sports apparel industry) in 2007 for $580 million. Carlsberg, the Danish beer-maker, acquired China's largest beer producer Chongqing Brewery in December 2013. Horizontal M&As do not represent growth in the industry but a larger market share, and hence greater market power (dominance), for the amalgamated business.

- **Vertical integration** takes place between businesses that are at different stages of production. Forward vertical integration is the amalgamation of businesses that head towards the end stage of production (towards the consumer), e.g. a coffee manufacturer acquires a chain of cafés. Backward vertical integration means a merger or acquisition of businesses towards an earlier stage of production, e.g. a coffee manufacturer merges with its supplier of coffee beans. This growth strategy helps the manufacturer to secure lower costs of raw materials.

- **Lateral integration** refers to M&As between firms that have similar operations but do not directly compete with each other. For example, Tata Motors (considered a mass market brand) acquired Jaguar and Land Rover (both considered as luxury brands) in 2008, PepsiCo acquired Quakers Oats Company in 2001, and Microsoft bought LinkedIn in 2016.

- **Conglomerate M&As** (mergers and acquisitions) are the amalgamation of businesses that are in completely distinct or diversified markets (Table 1.6.d). For example, Berkshire Hathaway owns businesses in a vast range of industries, including: insurance, property, clothing, meat products, flight services, home furnishing, news media, confectionery, beverages and carpet making!

Synergy is a major reason why organizations seek to grown inorganically. Synergy occurs when the whole is greater than the sum of the individual parts when two or more business operations are combined. Synergy creates greater output and improved efficiency.

The degree of success of M&As depends on several factors. First, the level of planning involved is crucial. A clear rationale of the benefits of the merger or takeover must be communicated to key stakeholder groups to win their support. Success also depends on the aptitudes of senior leaders of the two firms involved. Conflict can easily lead to the demise of M&As. Managers need to exert their negotiation skills and be able to handle the added pressures and responsibilities that they will face. Finally, regulatory problems can also present a barrier to success. The government can step in to prevent M&As taking place in order to prevent the business from having too much market power, if this is deemed to be against the best interest of the general public.

Table 1.6.d on the following page lists some advantages and disadvantages of mergers and acquisitions.

Case study

Nokia was founded in 1865 – about 125 years before the commercialization of the mobile phone. The Finnish company started by manufacturing paper in its pulp mills in various locations, including the town of Nokia. The company diversified into rubber manufacturing before switching to electronics. At its peak, Nokia had 62.5% market share before Apple launched its iPhone 3G in 2008. Fierce competition from Apple and Samsung forced Nokia to be sold to Microsoft for 5.4bn euros ($7.2bn) in 2014, following a drop in its market share to just 3%, but still employs over 100,000 workers.

Table 1.6.d Benefits and drawbacks of mergers and acquisitions

Benefits	Drawbacks
Greater market share The integrated firm is likely to benefit from having greater market power and a larger customer base.	**Redundancies** Job losses are likely to occur due to cost savings in M&As, e.g. the new business will not need two finance directors.
Economies of scale Larger scale operations help to lower unit costs, thus improving the firm's competitiveness and/or profit margins.	**Conflict** There are potential disagreements and arguments between the firms involved in M&As, so conflict is inevitable.
Synergy The integrating firms have access to each other's resources, such as distribution channels, new technologies, human resources and management know-how. Hence, they are able to better use their combined resources to boost productivity and profits.	**Culture clash** People and processes will need to adapt to the desired corporate culture of the newly formed organization. This may entail changes to the firm's core values and mission statement. Staff might also need time to adapt to new methods of working.
Survival M&As are a fast method of growth to protect the survival of a business. As a defensive strategy, it allows the new firm to be in a stronger position to compete with its rivals.	**Loss of control** The original owners or management team will lose some degree of control as the new board of directors will need to be restructured.
Diversification Some M&As allow firms to diversify their product mix. This allows them to benefit from a larger customer base and reduced risks.	**Diseconomies of scale** The larger firm might suffer from increased bureaucracy and longer channels of communication, leading to less effective decision-making.
	Regulatory problems Governments may be concerned with, and hence prevent, M&As if they create a monopoly with too much power.

Question 1.6.5   The London Taxi Company

In 2013, the producers of the iconic black taxi, London Taxi International (*LTI*), was sold to China's largest carmaker *Geely* for just £11.4 million ($18.6 million). *LTI* went into administration in October 2012 after 5 years without making any profits, with most of its workers losing their jobs. The **acquisition** safeguarded production in the UK to secure the British association with the London black taxi as a global brand, although *Geely's* factory in Shanghai focuses on building taxis for the left-hand drive market. In a rare move following a takeover, *Geely* rehired the workers who were made redundant following *LTI's* successive losses between 2007 to 2012. *LTI* was re-branded to The London Taxi Company at the end of 2010.

(a) Define the term **acquisition**. *[2 marks]*

(b) Examine the winners and losers from *Geely's* takeover of *LTI*. *[6 marks]*

(c) Discuss the driving forces behind *Geely's* strategic move to acquire *LTI*. *[10 marks]*

Business organization and environment

CORE

Case study

On Valentine's Day 2013, US Airways and American Airlines agreed to merge in a deal worth $11 billion to create the world's largest airline, with 6,700 daily flights and annual revenues of over $42 billion. The airlines claimed the deal should offer passengers more travel options but probably at higher prices. Government regulators had initially blocked the merger as it was not deemed to be in the best interest of the general public, but the merger was completed in December 2013 with the airlines being renamed American Airlines Group Inc.

IB Learner Profile – Be an inquirer

Investigate recent mergers and acquisitions in your country, or a country of your choice. Who were the winners and losers?

Question 1.6.6   Disney's takeover of Pixar

In 2006, *The Walt Disney Company* agreed to a $7.4 billion deal to take ownership of *Pixar Animation Studios,* the firm responsible for movies such as *Toy Story, Finding Nemo, Cars, Monsters Inc.* and *Planes. Disney* said that high demand for Pixar's movie merchandise (such as Buzz Lightyear toys and DVD movie sales) had earned Disney over $3.2 billion. The real value to *Disney,* however, is the synergy that would be created from the **integration** of the two firms. In 2010, *Toy Story 3* became the highest-grossing animated movie of all time, earning over $1 billion at the box office. As part of its growth strategy, *Disney* acquired *Lucasfilm* in 2012, and scheduled production of a third trilogy of *Star Wars*, with Episode VII released in December 2015, and Episode IX in December 2019.

(a)   In the context of the case study, define the term **integration**.   *[2 marks]*

(b)   Examine **two** potential problems for businesses during an acquisition.   *[6 marks]*

(c)   Discuss the decision of *The Walt Disney Company* to acquire other firms such as Pixar.   *[10 marks]*

Joint ventures

A **joint venture** (JV) occurs when two or more businesses split the costs, risks, control and rewards of a business project. In doing so, the parties agree to set up a new legal entity. For example, Coca-Cola has a JV with San Miguel by shared ownership of Coca-Cola's bottling plant in the Philippines. BMW has a JV with China's Brilliance Automobiles in sharing paint facilities. An example is Sony Ericsson (see Question 1.6.7). Typically, a JV between two firms will involve a 50:50 split of costs, responsibilities and profits (or losses).

Joint ventures allow organizations to enjoy some of the benefits of mergers and acquisitions (such as higher market share) but without having to lose their corporate identity. Other advantages of joint ventures include:

- **Synergy**   The pooling of experiences, skills and resources of the collaborating firms should create synergy. The 50:50 joint venture between Lloyds Bank and Sainsbury's (a bank and a supermarket chain) between 1997 and 2014 meant that both parties could specialise in their area of expertise yet gain access to new technologies and customers to achieve larger profits for both organizations.

- **Spreading of costs and risks**   Financial costs, risks and losses are shared in a JV thereby helping to reduce the financial burden on any single organization. JVs also allow firms to diversify their products, also helping to spread risks.

- **Entry to foreign markets** Joint ventures are used by companies to enter foreign countries by forming an agreement with local firms. National laws make JVs the only option for businesses wishing to enter some foreign markets, e.g. many foreign firms have entered China and India by forming JVs with local Chinese and Indian businesses.

- **Relatively cheap** Joint ventures are relatively cheap compared with the costs of a hostile takeover (which are often unknown). It is also easier to pull out of a JV if necessary.

- **Competitive advantages** Competition can be reduced by forming a JV. Companies cooperating in a JV are unlikely to directly compete with each other, yet their pooled resources make them a stronger force against their rivals. Their collective size could also mean that further economies of scale can be enjoyed.

- **Exploitation of local knowledge** Firms that expand via international JVs can take advantage of each other's local knowledge and reputation. This might not be the case with mergers or acquisitions that are exposed to potential problems of overseas expansion (such as differences in business etiquette, cultural values, language and traditions).

- **High success rate** Joint ventures tend to be friendly and receptive. The parties pool their funds and resources, sharing responsibility for their mutual benefit. This positive attitude is more likely to lead to the success of a JV. By contrast, takeovers often fail due to their unfriendly and hostile nature.

Joint ventures and strategic alliances have similar drawbacks. Partners in a JV have to rely heavily on the resources and goodwill of their counterparts. There is also likely to be a dilution of the brands, yet firms spend huge amounts of money trying to develop their own brands (see Unit 4.5). Finally, whenever firms work together on a project, there is always the possibility of organizational culture clashes that can lead to operational problems for the joint venture.

Case study

Banking reforms and cost-cutting since the global financial crisis of 2008 meant that Barclays had to adapt its growth strategy. In 2014, the bank joined forces with Asda, the British supermarket chain owned by Walmart, to provide banking services. The move was in line with trends in the UK and USA where the number of traditional bank branches has been reduced by around 40% since 1989.

Question 1.6.7   Sony Ericsson

Established in 2001, Sony Ericsson was a **joint venture** between Japan's Sony and Sweden's Ericsson. The **synergy** created by combining Sony's consumer electronics expertise with Ericsson's technological knowledge in the communications industry meant the company was successful in reducing the market share of more established mobile manufacturers. Within the first five years of operation, the company had sold almost 75 million phones, making it the world's fourth largest mobile phone manufacturer (Sony had less than 1% market share prior to the joint venture). However, intense competition from market leaders Samsung and Apple led to falling profits and declining synergies at Sony Ericsson. In 2012, Sony acquired Ericsson's 50% share of the joint venture for $1.47 billion and was rebranded as Sony Mobile Communications. At its peak, Sony Ericsson sold over 103.4 million units in annual sales (2007), but this declined to a low of 14.6 million phones in 2016.

(a) (i) Define the term **joint venture**. [2 marks]

(a) (ii) Define the term **synergy**. [2 marks]

(b) Explain **two** reasons why a merger between Ericsson and Sony might not have been appropriate compared with the joint venture. [4 marks]

(c) Examine the costs and benefits of the joint venture to Sony and Ericsson. [6 marks]

Strategic alliances

A **strategic alliance** (SA) is similar to a joint venture in that two or more businesses cooperate in a business venture for mutual benefit. The firms in the SA share the costs of product development, operations and marketing. However, unlike JVs, forming a strategic alliance means that the affiliated businesses remain independent organizations. Typically, there are four key stages to the formation of a strategic alliance:

- *Feasibility study* – Investigate and establish the rationale, objectives and feasibility of the SA.

- *Partnership assessment* – Analyse the potential of different partners, such as what they have to offer to the alliance in terms of both human and financial resources and expertise.

- *Contract negotiation* – Negotiations take place to determine each member's contributions and rewards, thus forming a mutually acceptable contract.

- *Implementation* – Operations are initiated with commitment to the contract from all parties.

The main purpose of strategic alliances is to gain synergies from the different strengths of the members of the alliance by pooling their resources (to benefit from each other's expertise and financial support). Two airlines both with half-empty aircraft could directly compete or they could collaborate by using a single full aeroplane to cut staff and fuel costs and split the profits for mutual benefit. Strategic alliances also gain from economies of scale by operating on a larger scale. Customers are also likely to benefit from the added value services under a strategic alliance, such as the convenience of access to wider channels of distribution (see Unit 4.5).

Figure 1.6.g Strategic alliances are common in the airline industry

Exam tip !

You should be able to evaluate the use of different methods of external growth. A strategy that is suitable for one organization is not necessarily appropriate for others. It is important to put your answers in the context of the business and to consider short and long term factors in your evaluation.

Franchising

McDonald's, Subway and The Body Shop use **franchising** as a method of external growth. A franchise is a form of business ownership whereby a person or business buys a license to trade using another firm's name, logos, brands and trademarks. In return for this benefit, the purchaser of a franchise (called the **franchisee**) pays a license fee to the parent company of the business (known as the **franchisor**). The franchisee also pays a **royalty payment** (like commission) based on the sales revenue of the franchisee. The world's largest franchises are Subway, 7-Eleven, McDonald's, KFC and Burger King.

Tables 1.6.e and f on the following page list some of the franchising benefits and drawbacks to the franchisee and franchisor.

Case study

Star Alliance was set up in 1997 by five founding airlines: Lufthansa, Scandinavian Airlines, Thai Airways International, United Airlines and Air Canada who share the costs and benefits of airline operations. It was the first strategic airline alliance and has grown to 28 members, making it the largest alliance in the industry.

Case study

Burger King has used franchising as its key business strategy for growing nationally and internationally. The world's second largest fast food chain has more than 15,000 outlets, with around 90% of them being franchises. Its high success rate relies on the know-how, brand recognition and trust of a parent organization coupled with the incentives and enthusiasm of the franchisees to make it a success. Burger King's parent company is Yum! Brands, which also owns KFC and Taco Bell.

Table 1.6.e Benefits for the franchisor and franchisee

Benefits for the franchisor	Benefits for the franchisee
The company can experience rapid growth without having to risk huge amounts of money as the franchisee pays for the outlet itself. Hence, it can be cheaper than internal growth.	There is relatively low risk since the franchisor has a tried and tested formula so the chances of business success are high.
It allows the company to have a national or international presence without the higher costs of organic growth or M&As (as the franchisee helps to finance the expansion).	There are relatively lower start-up costs because the business idea has already been developed by the franchisor (such as market research and product development).
The franchisor benefits from growth without having to worry about running costs such as staff salaries, purchase of stocks, recruitment and training.	It is in the best interest of the franchisor to ensure that the franchise succeeds, so it will provide added-services to franchisees, e.g. training and advice on financial management.
Franchisors receive royalty payments from the franchisee, usually set as a percentage of the sales revenues. They can also charge a 'membership' (joining) fee to their franchisees.	The franchisee is likely to benefit from large scale advertising used by the franchisor, i.e. franchisees receive 'free' advertising and promotion, also helping to reduce their costs.
Franchisees have more incentives to do better than salaried managers, thereby increasing the chances of success for the franchisor.	Franchisees can have greater awareness of local market conditions and needs, further boosting their chances of success.

Table 1.6.f Drawbacks for the franchisor and franchisee

Drawbacks for the franchisor	Drawbacks for the franchisee
There is a huge risk in allowing others to use the franchisor's name. Unsuccessful franchisees can damage the reputation of the whole franchise business.	Franchisees cannot simply use their own initiative to try out new ideas as they are regulated by the franchisor. This constrains the entrepreneurial talents of the franchisee.
It can be difficult to control the daily operations of franchisees and to get them to meet the quality standards set by the franchisor.	Buying a franchise can be very expensive, yet there is no guarantee that this investment will ever be recouped.
Although franchising is faster than internal growth, it is not as quick as M&As.	Franchisees have to pay a significant percentage of their revenues to the franchisor.

Question 1.6.8 Pizza Hut

Founded in 1958, *Pizza Hut* is the world's largest chain of pizza restaurants. Within a year of opening, the company launched its first **franchise**. Today, its operations span the globe with over 16,000 restaurants in over 95 countries. The company plans to continue opening more stores in existing and new locations. *Pizza Hut's* homepage even has a section titled 'Become a Franchisee' with all the necessary information for potential franchisees.

(a) Define the term **franchise**. *[2 marks]*

(b) Explain **two** reasons for *Pizza Hut's* decision to use franchising as its main method of growth. *[4 marks]*

(c) Examine the potential problems of *Pizza Hut's* growth strategy. *[6 marks]*

The role and impact of globalization

The role and impact of globalization on the growth and evolution of businesses. AO3

© IBO, 2017

Globalization can be defined as the growing integration and interdependence of the world's economies. It has caused national economies to integrate towards a single global economy, where consumers have ever-increasingly similar habits and tastes. With globalization, economic and political decisions taken in one region of the world will affect those in other parts of the world too.

Multinationals such as Apple, BMW, Coca-Cola and IKEA design and market their products to a world audience. Consumers around the world easily recognise and have similar tastes for their products. In the case of McDonald's, even the production processes are largely the same throughout the world; burgers and fries are cooked in exactly the same way irrespective of where the McDonald's restaurant is located in the world. The Coca-Cola brand is the most recognised in the world. Thus, such firms are able to exploit global marketing and production economies of scale (see Unit 1.6) as they grow and evolve.

Case study

IKEA, the world's largest retailer of home furniture, was founded in 1943. It wasn't until 1963 that IKEA opened its first overseas stores in neighbouring Norway and later in 1969 in Denmark. The Swedish company has since grown to over 415 stores in 49 countries, and employing 195,000 people around the world.

Source: http://www.statisticbrain.com/ikea-statistics/

The role and impact of globalization on business growth and evolution

Globalization presents opportunities for growth and evolution of businesses as well as threats to their operations. Examples include the following:

- Globalization considerably increases the level of **competition**, such as Vodafone (UK) competing with mobile operators Telefónica (Spain), Reliance Communications (India), T-Mobile (Germany), Verizon Wireless (USA) '3', MegaFon (Russia), China Mobile (China) and Hutchison Telecom (Hong Kong). The Internet has also reduced costs for many industries, thereby reducing barriers to entry and attracting competition. For example, in many countries Expedia.com has successfully competed with more established travel agencies.

Box 1.6.b   Top 10 most globalized countries

KOF is a Swiss organization that conducts world rankings of the most globalized countries, as measured by economic, social and political indicators of globalization. The KOF Index of Globalization covers over 200 countries around the world.

Rank	2017	2016	2015	2014	2010
1	Netherlands	Netherlands	Ireland	Ireland	Belgium
2	Ireland	Ireland	Netherlands	Belgium	Austria
3	Belgium	Belgium	Belgium	Netherlands	Netherlands
4	Austria	Austria	Austria	Austria	Switzerland
5	Switzerland	Switzerland	Singapore	Singapore	Sweden
6	Denmark	Singapore	Sweden	Denmark	Denmark
7	Sweden	Denmark	Denmark	Sweden	Canada
8	United Kingdom	Sweden	Portugal	Portugal	Portugal
9	France	Hungary	Switzerland	Hungary	Finland
10	Hungary	Canada	Finland	Finland	Hungary

Source: KOF Index of Globalization http://www.globalization-index.org/

- Meeting **customer expectations** becomes increasingly more demanding. Businesses must now meet the ever-greater customer demands for quality, customer service, price and after-sales care in order to have any competitive advantage. Pressure groups and the media have provided another perspective on the potential threats of globalization.

Case study

In his book *Fast Food Nation: The Dark Side of the All-American Meal,* Eric Schlosser discusses how globalization of the fast-food industry has led to increased obesity in China and Japan. The documentary-movie *Supersize Me* and the film adaptation of Schlosser's book have highlighted some of the drawbacks from the globalization of US fast-food throughout the world.

- Multinationals and e-commerce businesses in particular benefit from the **increased customer base** that globalization brings. With China and India both embracing changes in the global business environment, there are vast opportunities for businesses that trade with the world's two most populous countries (around 35% of the world's population).

- Businesses that are able to build a global presence can benefit from **economies of scale,** such as the advantages of global marketing economies and risk-bearing economies (see Unit 1.6). These present clear opportunities for business growth. Jeff Bezos, the world's richest man, has a reported wealth of over $110 billion, mainly accumulated through the sheer diversity of the products sold on Amazon, the company he founded in 1994.

- Globalization presents multinationals with greater **choice of location**. Like many other global businesses, Apple chose to outsource production in China due to the relatively low costs of labour and rent. Apple's products are "Created in California and assembled in China." The increased choice of location can therefore help to reduce a firm's costs of production.

- **External growth opportunities** - Mergers, acquisitions, strategic alliances and joint ventures allow businesses to grow at a faster pace than if they were to expand organically. Globalization enables businesses to have more choice in their expansion plans. For example, BMW's joint venture with Brilliance China Automotive, established in 2003, gives the German carmaker direct access to the lucrative Chinese market, where more BMWs are sold than in any other country.

- **Increased sources of finance** Globalization presents many more opportunities for seeking external sources of finance to fund business growth and evolution. For example, Li Ka-Shing bought a 0.8% stake in Facebook for $120 million and another $50 million in Spotify, the music streaming service provider. Tycoon Warren Buffett bought a 10% stake in BYD, a Chinese manufacturer of cars and rechargeable batteries for $230 million.

The globalization of markets has meant the world is a smaller place (in terms of time, distance and conditions for international trade). Improved information and communications technology (ICT) and high-speed travel mean that businesses can trade even more efficiently. They have had a huge impact on converging lifestyles and tastes throughout the world economy – American fast-food, Brazilian coffee, German sports cars and Japanese electronic gadgets to name but a few. Businesses that have an international approach are therefore able to reap the benefits of globalization. A business that is able to expand overseas before its rivals may also gain a first-mover advantage (the competitive gains from being the first firm to enter a particular market) as it establishes itself and builds up a loyal customer base.

Exam tip !

Despite the uniformity brought about by globalization, countries still have their national identities through language, culture and other unique characteristics. Businesses are likely to need to adapt their products and services to meet the varying needs of their international clients (also see Unit 4.7).

Business organization and environment

CORE

Question 1.6.9 McDonald's

In 2006, *McDonald's* (the world's largest fast food chain) reported global **sales revenue** in excess of $20bn for the first time in its history. This was boosted by strong sales revenue in the USA, Japan, Russia and Europe. Another contributing factor was *McDonald's* revamp of its global business by adding salads and other healthy options to its traditional menu of burgers and French fries. The company communicated this change by publicising nutritional facts of its products. Sales exceeded $25 billion in 2017.

Critics have argued that *McDonald's* food and drinks remain unhealthy and high in calories. Their marketing strategies aimed at children, such as their trademark *Happy Meal*, have been attacked due to the soaring obesity levels amongst children.

(a) Define the term **sales revenue**.   *[2 marks]*

(b) Outline **two** possible problems created by the critics of *McDonald's* for the business.   *[4 marks]*

(c) Explain **two** reasons for *McDonald's* growth in global sales.   *[4 marks]*

(d) Discuss the extent to which the fast-food industry is a globalized industry.   *[10 marks]*

Question 1.6.10 Bollywood

Bollywood is the Hindi-language film industry– the largest in India, with an estimated 500 million viewers worldwide. Since 2000, Bollywood has grown in popularity around the world as **globalization** and the media make access to information much easier and faster. Bollywood movies are typically three to four hours long, with dozens of flamboyant songs and dances and always feature a happy ending. India is a country of 16 official languages although 24 languages are spoken by over a million people each. Indian cinema is the world's largest film industry as measured by ticket sales and film production.

(a) Define the term **globalization**.   *[2 marks]*

(b) Discuss the view that knowledge and awareness of local cultures are important aspects of successful global businesses.   *[10 marks]*

Case study

Katrina Kaif is a one of Bollywood's highest-paid actresses. She was born in Hong Kong in 1983, but soon moved to China, and then to Japan. By the time she was 8, she had moved to France and then onto Switzerland, Poland, Germany, Belgium, Hawaii and England. Her career eventually took her to Mumbai. As a UK passport holder and huge movie star, Kaif was honoured with a wax figure at Madame Tussauds in London in 2015.

Theory of knowledge

Do China and India present the most important competitive threat or opportunity for global brands and multinational companies?

The growth of multinational companies

Reasons for the growth of multinational companies (MNCs). AO3
© IBO, 2017

A **multinational company** (MNC) is an organization that operates in two or more countries. The terms MNC and transnational corporation are often used interchangeably, although some commentators say that a MNC has its Head Office based in the home country whereas a **transnational corporation** has regional head offices rather than a single international base. Examples of large MNCs include: Apple, Coca-Cola, Exxon, HSBC, Microsoft, Nike, Samsung, Toyota and Walmart, which all excel within their industries in terms of sales, profits, assets and market value.

The rise of MNCs and the ever growing importance of international trade have intensified globalization. Businesses may strive to become MNC for several reasons, including the following:

- An **increased customer base** allows businesses to increase their sales turnover by expanding internationally. For example, many businesses (such as HSBC, KFC, Starbucks, Lamborghini and Walmart) have expanded into China to benefit from the huge customer base. International brand recognition can also be enhanced by using global marketing strategies.

- Many MNCs expand overseas to benefit from **cheaper production costs**, especially inexpensive labour. For example, the relatively high cost of labour in Germany, partly due to the imposition of minimum wage legislation, has meant that businesses such as Adidas, BMW and Volkswagen have production facilities overseas with cheaper labour.

- As production levels increase, MNCs are able to benefit from **economies of scale**. MNCs might also want to locate overseas to benefit from the host country's infrastructure, such as its road, telecommunication and port networks. The host country may offer better quantity and quality of land in terms of the amount of space and/or the cost of land. There could also be financial incentives from the host country's government that help to reduce production costs whilst allowing the MNC to expand.

- By producing within a particular country, MNCs can usually avoid any **protectionist policies** that the country might impose (see Box 1.6.c). This is why many Japanese motor vehicle manufacturers, including Toyota, Honda and Nissan, have set up factories in the European Union and North America.

- MNCs are able to **spread risks**. Unfavourable market conditions in one country or region might not damage the overall business if it can spread risks internationally. Natural disasters (such as tsunamis), terrorist acts (such as the 9/11 attacks) and diseases (such as swine flu and mad cow disease) have affected different areas of the world. Over-specialization in any one of these regions could have led to a serious dent in profits for these businesses.

Box 1.6.c Protectionist policies (trade barriers)

- **Tariffs** are a tax on imports, thus adding to the price of foreign products. This makes imports less price competitive. MNCs can overcome this by establishing production facilities in the tariff-imposing nation.

- **Quotas** are quantitative limits imposed on the sale of imports. This results in a lower supply (or availability) of imported products, thereby forcing up import prices.

- **Restrictive trade practices** are acts that unfairly, although not illegally, discriminate against foreign firms since they do not apply to domestic firms. Examples include rigorous administrative procedures and strict safety standards, again raising the costs and limiting the availability of imports.

Business organization and environment

CORE

Question 1.6.11 Carlsberg

Founded in 1847, *Carlsberg* is one of the largest breweries in the world with around 45,000 employees and annual sales in the region of $11bn. The Danish beer company has a long-established market presence in Western Europe, giving it a competitive advantage albeit in a mature market. **Brand awareness** and **brand loyalty** have been secured by its sponsorship of prominent sporting events and teams. More recently, *Carlsberg* has relied on new markets, such as Eastern Europe and Asia, for sales and profits growth. In 2013, *Carlsberg* announced a joint venture to establish a beer production facility in Bago Region, Myanmar.

Source: www.carlsberg.com

(a) Outline the evidence that suggests *Carlsberg* is a multinational business. *[2 marks]*

(b) Distinguish between **brand awareness** and **brand loyalty**. *[4 marks]*

(c) Outline **two** factors that may have led to the globalization of the beer market. *[4 marks]*

(d) Discuss the possible opportunities and threats to *Carlsberg* operating in overseas markets. *[10 marks]*

The impact of MNCs on the host countries

The impact of MNCs on the host countries. AO3

© IBO, 2017

A **host country** is any nation that allows a multinational company to set up in its country. In addition to the reasons for the growth of MNCs, they have varying impacts on host countries, some of which are beneficial whilst others are detrimental.

Theory of knowledge

If globalization causes the loss of cultural identities, does this diminish our breadth of knowledge?

Table 1.6.g Advantages and disadvantages of MNCs to the host countries

Advantages	Disadvantages
MNCs **create jobs** in the host country. For example, Volkswagen's manufacturing plant in Kaluga, Russia created more than 3,500 jobs with an initial investment of $400m. Although some MNCs have been criticised for paying 'low' wages to staff in poorer countries, MNCs tend to offer higher pay than local firms in these countries.	MNCs are capable of causing **unemployment** in the host country as they can pose a threat to domestic businesses. Competition can be good if it causes local firms to improve their efficiency, but it can also be a setback if it means that domestic firms are unable to compete and end up making people redundant or even having to close down.
MNCs help to boost the host country's **gross domestic product** (the value of a country's annual output) by creating consumption expenditure (since more people are in paid employment) and by boosting export earnings for the host country, thereby improving its standards of living. For example, Hungary's largest exporter is German car manufacturer Audi, which has its Audi TT sports car produced in western Hungary.	Whilst MNCs can create wealth in a host country, the **profits are repatriated** to the home country. There is also a degree of insecurity as MNCs are increasingly footloose (see Unit 5.4), i.e. they are not tied to a specific location so can change at very short notice for cost advantages. For example, in 2012 French retailer Carrefour pulled out of Turkey, Poland, Romania, Malaysia, Taiwan, Indonesia and Singapore.

continued >>

Table 1.6.h Advantages and disadvantages of MNCs to the host countries (continued)

Advantages	Disadvantages
MNCs have **introduced new skills and technology** in production processes to host countries, e.g. Japanese firms have introduced the models of kaizen, kanban and andon (see Unit 5.3) to Western economies. With new ideas in management thinking and technology transfer, the efficiency of production in the host country is raised.	Anti-globalization groups are concerned about the **social responsibility** of MNCs in their attempt to grow and exploit Earth's scarce resources. Host nations are often unable to control the actions of large MNCs, due to their sheer market power, e.g. Walmart's sales revenues exceed the GDP of Indonesia, the world's fourth-most populous country.
MNCs intensify **competition** in the host country. This should lead to greater efficiency to the benefit of domestic customers. Also, it can be argued that without the threat from MNCs, domestic firms do not necessarily have the incentive to be innovative or to respond to market forces.	Due to fierce **competitive pressures**, domestic firms might be forced into reducing prices to remain competitive. Technology transfers present a further threat as domestic firms might not have the finance to compete, so they become prone to **takeover bids** or collapse outright.

Case study

Hollywood is a large threat to other movie industries around the world. Governments often intervene to protect domestic industries and jobs from foreign competition. For example, China and India limit the number of Hollywood movies that are released each month in their respective countries. China has an annual quota of 34 foreign movies whilst India is the largest producer of movies in the world.

Theory of knowledge

Should large and profitable multinational companies have an obligation to support the poor in society?

Question 1.6.12   MNCs in the UAE

Multinational companies are attracted to the United Arab Emirates (UAE) because of the low taxes, political stability and high gross domestic product per capita. Microsoft, Marriott Group, DHL and Ericsson all have operations in the UAE. The influx of engineering, law and accountancy firms brings managers from many countries and creates a demand for goods and services such as international schools. Dubai (one of the seven Emirates that make up the UAE) has gained a reputation as being a destination for shopping, attracting many tourists from around the world. Dubai is the largest and most populous city in the UAE, with over 2.8 million people. Dubai is one of the world's fastest growing economies.

(a) Define the term **multinational companies**. [2 marks]

(b) Explain how globalization might affect the location of multinational companies. [4 marks]

(c) Examine the benefits to MNCs operating in a foreign countries such as the UAE. [6 marks]

Business organization and environment

CORE

Growth and evolution and the CUEGIS concepts

Growth is a strategic aim for many businesses. In an ever-globalized business world, the driving force behind growth and evolution is not simply profit, but sustainable competitiveness – as the Chinese proverb goes *"Be not afraid of going slowly; be afraid only of standing still."*

The concepts of change, culture and globalization are central to any business strategy that involves growth in overseas markets. International trade and operations can cause major problems including adjusting to foreign languages, customs and cultures. There could also be a need to modify business practices to suit local laws and regulations.

This Unit has looked at the various business strategies that organizations often use to achieve growth. These strategies can be remembered by the mnemonic FUBED:

- **First-mover advantage**   This is the strategy of being the first in a market. This allows the business to establish market share, a good reputation and a loyal customer base before other firms have a chance to launch their products.

- **Unique selling point** (USP)   Offering products that have a USP makes a product stand out from other products that are available on the market.

- **Branding**   A well-established and recognised brand provides huge opportunities for business growth in local and international markets.

- **Economies of scale**   These enable a business to benefit from lower unit costs of production by operating on a larger scale. Lower average costs help to give the firm a price advantage.

- **Diversification**   This strategy involves the business selling new products in new markets to spread its risks (see Ansoff's Matrix, Unit 1.3). It enables the firm to gain revenue from an untapped market (as it is new to the industry), despite being a potentially high risk strategy.

M&As are common in today's fast-paced, highly competitive and continually changing business environment. Organizations are increasingly having to 'run faster to stay still', i.e. they have to grow and evolve in order to maintain their market share and competitiveness. As a strategy, M&As enable businesses to retain or enhance their competitiveness. The increasing number of people and organizations actively involved in stock markets, fuelled by the globalization of markets, has made M&As more attractive. Deregulation has also enabled M&As to take place more efficiently.

However, growth strategies do not always work, e.g. not all M&As are successful due to resistance to change and cultural clashes. In these cases, a **demerger** might take place. This happens when a company sells off a part of its business, thereby separating into two or more businesses. It usually happens due to conflicts, inefficiencies and incompatibilities following an earlier merger of two or more companies. In 2007, for example, IBM sold a large proportion of its investment in Lenovo, China's largest computer manufacturer (which acquired IBM's personal computing division in 2005). Global car manufacturer DaimlerChrysler (which merged in 1998) also demerged in 2007. Cadbury Schweppes (which merged back in 1969) split up in 2008. In 2018, Whitbread (the UK's largest hospitality company) sold off Costa Coffee. Firms might strategically choose to demerge in order to:

- Offload unprofitable sections of the business

- Avoid rising unit costs and inefficiency by being too large (diseconomies of scale)

- Raise cash to sustain operations in other parts of the business

- Have a clearer focus by concentrating their efforts on a smaller range of business operations.

For some businesses, growth and downsizing occur on a cyclical basis. Reductions in the size of a business create their own problems that need careful change management. For example, there is likely to be a reduction in staffing so redundancies have to be planned and managed (see Unit 2.1). The costs of redundancies could be quite considerable and cause short-term liquidity problems for the business (see Unit 3.7).

An alternative strategy to a complete merger or takeover of a target business is to buy one of its brands. This strategy is known as **brand acquisition**. For example, BMW bought the Rolls Royce brand in 2003 to enhance its product portfolio. This is a relatively low risk growth strategy. However, it can be expensive. For example, in 2013, Berkshire Hathaway bought the Heinz brand for $28 billion. Similarly, firms may decide to sell one of their brands if they are facing a liquidity problem, rather than be taken over by a third party company.

Exam tip!

To broaden your understanding of the complexities that multinational companies face when operating in overseas markets, read Unit 1.5 (the external environment). Make links between the content in Units 1.5 and 1.6, such as the political, legal and social environments, and how these affect a firm's growth strategy.

CUEGIS ESSAY

With reference to an organization of your choice, examine how **globalization** has influenced its growth **strategy**.   *[20 marks]*

CUEGIS ESSAY

With reference to an organization of your choice, examine how **innovation** has influenced its growth **strategy**.   *[20 marks]*

REVIEW QUESTIONS

1. Using examples, distinguish between economies and diseconomies of scale.

2. What is meant by the optimal size of a business?

3. What are the merits and limitations of small businesses?

4. Distinguish between internal and external growth.

5. Distinguish between joint ventures and strategic alliances.

6. What are the benefits of mergers and acquisitions as forms of external growth?

7. What are the advantages and disadvantages of franchising as a method of growth?

8. What is globalization and how does it impact on business growth and evolution?

9. What is a multinational company?

10. What positive and negative impacts do multinational companies have on host countries?

KEY TERMS

Acquisition (or **takeover**) is a method of external growth that involves one company buying a controlling interest (majority stake) in another company.

Backward vertical integration occurs when a business amalgamates with a firm operating in an earlier stage of production, e.g. a car manufacturer acquires a supplier of tyres or other components.

Conglomerates are businesses that provide a diversified range of products and operate in an array of different industries.

A **demerger** occurs when a company sells off a part of its business, thereby separating into two or more businesses. It usually happens due to conflicts, inefficiencies and incompatibilities following an earlier merger of two or more companies

Diseconomies of scale are the cost disadvantages of growth. Unit costs are likely to eventually rise as a firm grows due to a lack of control, coordination and communication.

Diversification is a high risk growth strategy that involves a business selling new products in new markets, i.e. spreading risks over a diverse variety of products and markets.

Economies of scale refer to lower average costs of production as a firm operates on a larger scale due to gains in productive efficiency, e.g. easier and cheaper access to finance.

External economies of scale occur when an organization's average cost of production falls as the industry grows. Hence, all firms in the industry benefit.

External growth (or **inorganic growth**) occurs when a business grows by collaborating with, buying up or merging with another firm.

Financial economies of scale are cost savings made by large firms as banks and other lenders charge lower interest to larger businesses (for overdrafts, loans and mortgages) because they represent lower risk.

First-mover advantage refers to the competitive gains from being the first business to enter a particular market, or market segment. The business benefits from being able to establish itself in the market and building up a loyal customer base.

Forward vertical integration is a growth strategy that occurs with the amalgamation of a firm operating at a later stage in the production process, e.g. a book publisher merges with a book retailer.

Franchise refers to an agreement between a franchisor selling its rights to other businesses (franchisees) to allow them to sell products under its name in return for a fee and regular royalty payments.

Globalization is the growing integration and interdependence of the world's economies, causing consumers around the globe to have increasingly similar habits and tastes.

Horizontal integration is an external growth strategy that occurs when a business amalgamates with a firm operating in the same stage of production.

Internal economies of scale is a category of economies of scale that occurs within a particular organization (rather than the industry as a whole) as it grows in size.

Internal growth (also known as **organic growth**) occurs when a business grows using its own capabilities and resources to increase the scale of its operations and sales revenue.

A **joint venture** is a growth strategy that combines the contributions and responsibilities of two different organizations in a shared project by forming a separate legal enterprise.

Lateral integration refers to M&As between firms that have similar operations but do not directly compete with each other, e.g. PepsiCo acquiring Quaker Oats Company.

Marketing economies of scale occur when larger businesses can afford to hire specialist departmental managers, thereby improving the organization's efficiency and productivity.

A **merger** is a form of external growth whereby two (or more) firms agree to form a new organization, thereby losing their original identities.

A **multinational company** (MNC) is an organization that operates in two or more countries, with its head office usually based in the home country.

The **optimal level of output** is the most efficient scale of operation for a business. This occurs at the level of output where average costs of production are minimised.

Purchasing economies of scale occur when larger organizations can gain huge cost savings per unit by purchasing vast quantities of stocks (raw materials, components, semi-finished goods and finished goods).

Risk bearing economies of scale occur when large firms can bear greater risks than smaller ones due to having a greater product portfolio. Hence, inefficiencies harm smaller businesses to a larger extent.

Specialization economies of scale occur when larger firms can afford to hire and train specialist workers, thus helping to boost their level of output, productivity and efficiency. This helps to cut average costs of production.

Strategic alliances are formed when two or more organizations join together to benefit from external growth, without having to set up a new separate legal entity.

Synergy is a benefit of growth, which occurs when the whole is greater than the sum of the individual parts when two or more business operations are combined. Synergy creates greater output and improved efficiency.

A **takeover** (or **acquisition**) occurs when a company buys a controlling interest in another firm, i.e. it buys enough shares in the target business to hold a majority stake.

Technical economies of scale are cost savings by greater use of large-scale mechanical processes and specialist machinery, e.g. mass production techniques to cut unit production cost.

Vertical integration takes place between businesses that are at different stages of production.

1.7 Organizational planning tools

"Those who say it cannot be done, should not interrupt those doing it." - Chinese proverb

HL content only	Assessment objective
The following planning tools in a given situation: • fishbone diagram • decision tree • force field analysis • Gantt chart	AO2, AO4
The value to an organization of these planning tools	AO3

© IBO, 2017

Fishbone diagram

Fishbone diagram as a planning tool in a given situation. AO2, AO4
The value of the fishbone diagram as a planning tool to an organization. AO3

© IBO, 2017

All businesses, irrespective of their legal status or size, have to plan how they are to achieve their organizational objectives. **Organizational planning tools** are the various methods that businesses use to aid their decision-making, e.g. fishbone diagrams, decision trees, force field analysis, and Gantt charts. These tools enable businesses to deal with their problems, issues or concerns in a systematic way.

The **fishbone diagram** is a graphical representation of the most likely causes and effects of an important decision. It was devised in the 1960s by Japanese quality guru Professor Kaoru Ishikawa (1915–1989). Ishikawa is also credited for coining the term 'quality circles' (see Unit 5.3).

As a qualitative organizational planning tool, the fishbone diagram is used to identify the root causes of a problem or issue. The fishbone diagram is also known as the **cause and effect diagram**. The problem or issue being investigated is shown on the right hand side of the diagram (see Figure 1.7.a).

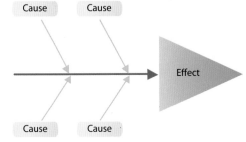

Figure 1.7.a Example 1 of a Fishbone diagram

The 4Ms (management, manpower, machines and materials) is one method that can be used to identify different categories of causes of a problem or issue, such as demotivated or unproductive employees.

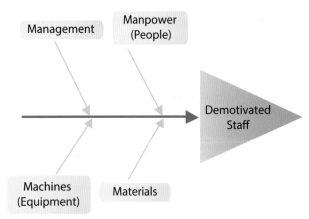

Figure 1.7.b Example 2 of a Fishbone

The following causes can be found from using the fishbone diagram:

• Management, e.g. unsuitable management style and miscommunication with the workforce

• Manpower, e.g. unskilled workers, a lack of training and insufficient personnel

• Machinery, e.g. technological failures, faulty equipment and the use of outdated machinery

• Materials, e.g. sub-standard (poor quality) materials and delayed deliveries.

Note that there is flexibility in the use of the nodes or 'bones' (not just the 4Ms). For example, *paraphernalia*, *policies*, *procedures*, and *people* (the 4Ps) are the bones often used for administrative and service-related problems (see Figure 1.7.c). Essentially, the categories used must meet the needs of the organization.

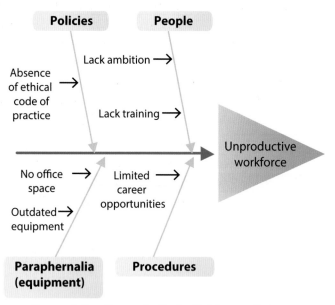

Figure 1.7.c Example 3 of a Fishbone diagram

When the fishbone diagram is completed, discussion takes place to decide on the most likely root causes of the problem. The ultimate purpose the fishbone diagram is to find the key source(s) of the problem so that they can be targeted for improvement. In Figures 1.7.b and 1.7.c, managers can identify the various aspects of the problem which must undoubtedly be addressed, such as providing adequate training and updating office equipment.

To successfully construct a fishbone diagram, the following steps must be observed:

1. The problem or issue must be clearly stated and agreed upon before further discussions begin.

2. Contributors must be concise and to the point. Causes rather than symptoms must be stated.

3. For each 'bone', brainstorm the possible causes and place these onto the node.

4. Consider combining nodes that are rather empty or scrapping them altogether.

5. Consider separating overcrowded nodes.

6. Consider which root causes warrant further investigation by circling these on the diagram.

7. Discuss how each circled item affects the problem or issue being investigated.

Once the root causes have been established, the fishbone is complete and decision makers move onto devising appropriate strategies to deal with the sources of the problem.

A key strength of the Ishikawa model is that it is easy to use and understand. It allows decision makers to brainstorm ideas in a systematic, holistic and logical way. It facilitates a visual diagnosis of a problem or issue. Today, computer programmes based on Ishikawa's ideas, such as SmartDraw, can be used to aid decision-making.

However, the fishbone diagram model tends to be rather simplistic for some real-world problems. In practice, the fishbone diagram is often used in conjunction with other decision-making frameworks to establish and quantify the root cause(s) of a problem.

Common mistake

Many students claim that certain decisions should not be pursued due to the risks involved, yet there is an element of risk associated with almost every business decision. It is the role of skilled managers to ensure that decision-making carries as much quantifiable, rather than unquantifiable, risk as possible.

Decision trees

Decision trees as a planning tool in a given situation. AO2, AO4
The value of decision trees as a planning tool to an organization. AO3
© IBO, 2017

A **decision tree** is a quantitative decision-making tool. It is a diagrammatic representation of the different options that are available to a business in the decision-making process, showing their probable outcomes. The tool allows managers to calculate the expected value of each decision in order to plan the best option to follow.

For example, consider the following options available to Chris McCorkell who is deciding whether or not to sell his apartment in New York. If he sells it this year, he could get $600,000. However, waiting until next year when the housing market is expected to improve increases his chances of selling the apartment at a higher price. Suppose the following factors need to be considered:

- Chris McCorkell could sell the property at the current market price of $600,000. This option would incur costs of $10,000 for estate agency and solicitors' fees, i.e. this option yields a return of $590,000.

- He could postpone the sale until next year with a 65% chance of receiving a higher price for the apartment. The estimated value of Chris McCorkell's property is $650,000 if he sells it next year. Costs would rise to $12,000, i.e. the net return would be valued at $638,000.

- However, reports suggest there is a 25% chance of house prices remaining stable and a 10% chance of the prices declining within the year. If property prices drop, Chris McCorkell's apartment is estimated to be worth $530,000 after associated costs.

Chris McCorkell can now use this information to calculate the expected value of each decision. This is done by multiplying the values of each outcome by its probability and then adding up the results. A decision tree is the diagrammatic version of this process (see Figure 1.7.d). The rules used to construct and interpret decision trees are:

- The diagram is constructed from left to right.

- **Decision nodes** are shown as squares. These are used when there is a decision to be made, e.g. whether to launch a new product, to invest in new machinery or to move into overseas markets. In the above example, Chris McCorkell has two options, one of which has a definite outcome (selling today). The decision maker has at least some control over decision nodes.

- **Chance nodes** are shown as circles. These are used to show the different possible outcomes of a decision. Typical outcomes include criteria such as 'failure or success' and 'improvements or deteriorations'. If Chris McCorkell, opts to sell his apartment next year (i.e. chance node B), there are three possible outcomes, none of which will definitely happen. Businesses and decision makers do not have direct control over chance nodes.

- For each chance node, there will be two or more routes (outcomes). These show the **probability** of the different outcomes for each chance node. The probabilities for each chance node must add up to 1.

- The actual values of each outcome are stated at the end of each **branch**. The costs of each option must be deducted when calculating the net figure for each outcome.

- Each unwanted branch of the decision tree is cut-off (rejected), indicated by two parallel lines. This will leave just one best option to follow.

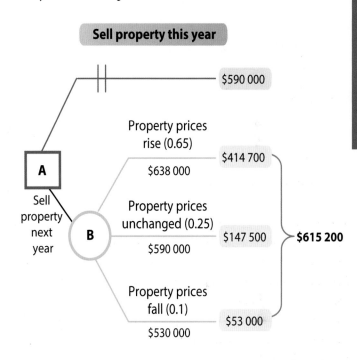

Figure 1.7.d Decision tree for Chris McCorkell

The expected values in Figure 1.7.d (those appearing at the end of each branch) are calculated as follows:

- The decision to sell the property today would generate a known value of $590,000, i.e. $600,000 minus the transactions costs of $10,000.

- For chance node B, the decision to postpone the sale has a 65% chance of earning $638,000 (after associated costs) so the expected value is $414,700 (i.e. $638,000 × 0.65).

- There is a 25% chance that property prices will remain unchanged in the next year. Hence the expected net outcome here is $147,500 (i.e. $590,000 × 0.25).

- Finally, there is a 10% chance that property prices will fall within the year. Therefore, the expected value in this case is $53,000 (i.e. $530,000 × 0.1).

- Therefore, the total expected value of chance node B is $615,200.

The above analysis suggests that Chris McCorkell should delay the sale of his property because the total expected value will be higher ($615,200 compared to $590,000, i.e. a net gain of $25,200). The expected value refers to the average outcome if the decision was made many times over and is calculated by multiplying the net value of a decision by its probability.

Figure 1.7.e Decision trees can help with investment decisions

Table 1.7.a Advantages and disadvantages of decision trees

Advantages	Disadvantages
They allow managers to set out problems in a clear and logical manner.	The probabilities given in a decision tree are only estimates and subject to forecasting errors.
All potential options can be seen at the same time, thereby speeding up decision-making.	They are based on quantitative data only, so qualitative issues (such as the effects on staff morale or the compatibility of a decision with the firm's aims) are ignored.
They consider the risks involved in decision-making, such as possible negative outcomes.	The technique does not necessarily reduce the amount of risk involved in decision-making.
They enable more scientific and objective decisions to be made as all likely costs of decisions are considered.	Delays in the planning process can void the data by the time a decision is actually made, yet time lags are often inevitable in the real business world.
As a visual stimulus, they provide a tangible insight to a problem, rather than having to rely on people's views or emotions of the problem.	The task of assigning probabilities is rather subjective so results can be deliberately biased to justify the preference of the management.

Question 1.7.1 Drisner Traders Ltd.

Drisner Traders Ltd. is considering a move into overseas markets. The Australian company is deciding between two locations: Kazakhstan or South Korea. Market research results are shown in the table below. All financial figures are expressed in $ for ease of comparison.

Kazakhstan	Probability	Costs/Revenues ($)
Cost		250 000
High return	0.6	400 000
Low return	0.4	250 000

South Korea	Probability	Costs/Revenues ($)
Cost		175 000
High return	0.75	300 000
Low return	0.25	180 000

(a) Construct a decision tree to show which of the two locations is best, based on financial grounds. *[5 marks]*

(b) Discuss the value of decision trees as an organizational planning tool for *Drisner Traders Ltd.* *[10 marks]*

Question 1.7.2   Ah-Tieng Beverages

Ah-Tieng Beverages produces traditional Chinese herbal drinks. The company's products are well known throughout the largest cities in China. With **secondary market research** data suggesting that sport and exercise are becoming increasingly popular, *Ah-Tieng Beverages* is considering entering the market for energy drinks.

The success of the proposal is largely dependent on the level of economic growth in the Asia Pacific region over the next five years. With operations currently only in China, *Ah-Tieng Beverages* is considering several options to expand overseas, although it can only afford to implement one of these initially. The estimated costs and benefits of the options are shown below:

Option	Economic growth	Chance	Return	Cost
Hong Kong	Improve	50%	$16 m	$10.6 m
	Unchanged	30%	$10 m	
	Worsen	20%	$4 m	
Taiwan	Improve	60%	$18 m	$9.8 m
	Unchanged	30%	$8 m	
	Worsen	10%	$2 m	
Japan	Improve	40%	$18 m	$11.3 m
	Unchanged	30%	$7 m	
	Worsen	30%	$(2 m)	

(a) Define the term **secondary market research**. *[2 marks]*

(b) Construct a fully labelled decision tree and calculate the predicted outcome for each option faced by *Ah-Tieng Beverages*. *[5 marks]*

Force field analysis

Force field analysis as a planning tool in a given situation. AO2 and AO4

The value of force field analysis as a planning tool to an organization. AO3

© IBO, 2017

Force field analysis (FFA) was developed by social psychologist Professor Kurt Lewin in 1951. Lewin argued that successful businesses tend to be constantly adapting and changing, rather than being fixed in outdated practices and unable to look forward. **Driving forces** push for change whilst **restraining forces** act against change. The relative strength of these forces determines whether the change should take place. There are several stages involved in a force field analysis (FFA):

1.   List the driving forces for change and the restraining forces against change.

2.   Allocate a weight to each of these forces, from 1 (weak) to 5 (strong).

3.   Draw a FFA diagram (see Figure 1.7.f), including the weights of each of the driving and restraining forces.

4.   Total the scores for the driving forces and restraining forces.

For example, a business deciding whether to relocate its production facilities in an overseas country might produce a FFA that looks similar to the one in Figure 1.7.f:

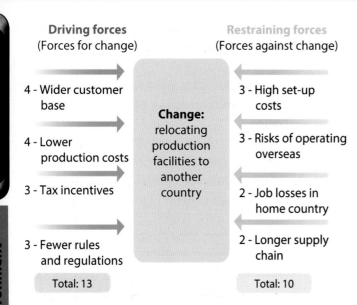

Driving forces
(Forces for change)

Restraining forces
(Forces against change)

4 - Wider customer base

4 - Lower production costs

3 - Tax incentives

3 - Fewer rules and regulations

Change: relocating production facilities to another country

3 - High set-up costs

3 - Risks of operating overseas

2 - Job losses in home country

2 - Longer supply chain

Total: 13

Total: 10

Figure 1.7.f Example of a force field analysis

Figure 1.7.f shows the driving forces for change outweigh the restraining forces against the change. Even if managers have already decided to go for this option, FFA can help to work out how to improve the project's chances of success. This is done by investigating how driving forces can be strengthened and how restraining forces can be minimised.

Whilst, the problems of change management are not solved by FFA it allows managers to examine the driving and restraining forces more clearly.

Lewin argued that progress is not the result of one-off changes but by many small changes and improvements. Nevertheless, there are two main weaknesses of this organizational planning tool:

- Weights attached to the driving and restraining forces might be done subjectively rather than based on facts or evidence.

- Not all relevant forces might be considered, perhaps deliberately to overemphasise the need for change.

Nevertheless, Lewin's force field analysis is a useful decision-making technique for looking at the forces acting for and against change. If change is desired, managers can analyse and influence the forces to make the change happen. FFA is essentially a specialised technique of weighing up advantages and disadvantages to help decide whether a proposed change is worth implementing.

Common mistake

Higher Level students should consider the use of decision-making tools, such as force field analysis, as part of the internal assessment (IA). However, ensure that the weights applied to the restraining forces and driving forces are from the decision-makers (e.g. CEO or senior managers at the organization). Too often, students assign the numbers (weights) so this adds very little, if any, value to the organization.

Gantt charts

Gantt charts as a planning tool in a given situation. AO2 and AO4

The value of Gantt charts as a planning tool to an organization. AO3

© IBO, 2017

A Gantt chart is a visual representation of all the tasks in a particular project plotted against the timescale. It is a management tool used to plan and schedule business projects, allowing project managers to monitor progress. It was created around 1910 by Henry L. Gantt (1861–1919), an American mechanical engineer. It was designed to help supervisors see whether factory workers were on target in meeting deadlines for manufactured output.

Figure 1.7.g Gantt charts are used to ensure projects finish on time

Project management allows managers to complete a project successfully in the quickest time available by overseeing a large number of activities and ensuring that each task is completed on schedule. If a deadline is missed, there is likely to be delays for the rest of the project. Late completion of a project or the late delivery of output to a client can be very costly to the business. Gantt charts show this information visually, giving project managers an instant overview of the project, the activities involved, their duration and when each individual activity needs to be finished. The rules used to construct and interpret Gantt charts are:

- It is presented as a bar chart showing all the scheduled tasks over a given time scale.

- The time scale is shown on the horizontal axis.

- Each activity is shown by a separate horizontal rectangular bar, with the length depicting the duration of the activity. Each bar shows the start date, duration and end date of an activity.

- Each horizontal bar show the start and finish dates.

- Both critical and non-critical activities (those with some slack time) are shown.

- Predecessor–successor relationships are shown, i.e. activities that must be preceded by others and activities that must follow others.

Today, project managers tend to use computer software, such as Microsoft Project, Visio and Excel, to generate Gantt charts.

The ultimate purpose of producing a Gantt chart is to identify the minimum (shortest) amount of time needed to complete a project. This requires the various tasks of a project to be planned in a logical order so that the different processes are completed with minimal delay and maximum efficiency. The process involves:

- Identifying all the activities required for the completion of the project.

- Breaking down the project into separate and clearly identifiable tasks.

- Determining how long each of these tasks will take.

- Identifying all **dependencies**, i.e. activities that cannot start until the completion of other tasks.

- Determining which tasks can take place concurrently (to minimise production time).

- Placing all tasks in the right sequence on the Gantt chart.

Consider Figure 1.7.h below, which is a simplified example that involves planning an end-of-year office party. Assume that the date for the party has already been set.

Without using a Gantt chart, the individual tasks amount to 24 days. However, the Gantt chart in Figure 1.7.i on the following page shows the project can be reduced to just 19 days.

- Task A takes 7 days to complete. So, the earliest activity B can start is after the 7th day.

- Task B takes 2 days to complete. So, activities C and D cannot start until after the 9th day.

- Task C starts after day 9 with a duration of 5 days, so it is completed on the 14th day at the earliest.

- Task D can take place at the same time as Task C. It takes 7 days to complete activity D.

- Although task C can be finished by the 14th day, task E cannot start until activity D is also completed. Hence, completion of task C can be slightly delayed (by 2 days) without there being a delay to the overall project.

- Task E can only start when tasks C and D are completed. Since task D starts on the 9th day and lasts 7 days, it will be completed on the 16th day after which task E can be started. Task E takes a further 3 days, so the shortest time the project can be completed is 19 days.

Project: End-of-year office party			
Task	Description	Preceded by	Duration (days)
A	Send out invites and wait for replies	-	7
B	Research and book suitable venue based on number of replies	A	2
C	Book entertainment (music and awards ceremony)	B	5
D	Order wines and cake for delivery	B	7
E	Set up hall and stage for the party	C, D	3

Figure 1.7.h Tasks for end-of-year office party

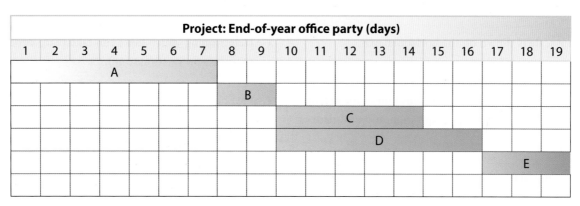

Figure 1.7.i Gantt chart (office party)

Consider the illustrative example below that uses a Gantt chart for a student's internal assessment in the HL Business Management course:

Project: BM SL Internal Assessment (weeks)															
1	2	3	4	5	6	7	8	9	10	11	12	13	14	15	16
A	Choice of firm and issue														
	B		Propose IA title for approval												
			C			Research Proposal & Action plan									
			D			Secondary research									
			E				Primary research								
						F		Analysis of findings							
									G	Conclusions and recommendations					
			H						Bibliography and Appendices						
										I	Submit first draft				
				Teacher marks first draft							J				
				Changes to first draft							K				
											Submit final draft				L

Figure 1.7.j Gantt chart (HL IA)

Notice the Gantt chart shows that the students can be working on the Research Proposal and Action Plan (Task C) alongside their primary and secondary research (Tasks D and E). The students can proofread their IA and make changes to their first draft (Task K) during weeks 12 and 13 whilst the teacher is marking the (hard copy) drafts. Final changes would take place from Week 14 when the marked drafts are handed back to the students.

Exam tip!

Gantt charts present problems for many students, but you can get around these by practising the construction of the charts. You might have created a Gantt chart to present your Action Plan in the Research Proposal of the HL Internal Assessment. Use this knowledge to reinforce your understanding of this organizational planning tool.

Similarly, the following illustrative example shows a Gantt for the SL IA:

								Project: BM SL Internal Assessment (weeks)							
1	2	3	4	5	6	7	8	9	10	11	12	13	14	15	16
A	IA title approval														
		B			Conduct secondary research										
		C		Primary research (if relevant)											
						D				Written commentary					
		E								Bibliography and Appendices					
										F	Submit first draft				
					Teacher marks first draft						G				
					Proofreading and corrections						H				
											Final draft submission			I	

Figure 1.7.k Gantt chart (SL IA)

Question 1.7.3 Constructing a Gantt chart

Construct a Gantt chart from the information below for Project X and identify the shortest time in which the project can be finished. [5 marks]

Task	Order (preceded by)	Estimated time (weeks)
A	–	3
B	–	3
C	–	3
D	A	2
E	B	4
F	C	1
G	D, E and F	6

Exam tip!

You may be required to construct a Gantt chart from given information in the exams. This tool can be very challenging for a lot of students, so the only way to improve is by practising your technique. Even if your Gantt chart is slightly wrong, marks are awarded for correctly interpreting and explaining the diagram.

IB Learner Profile – Be principled and be reflective

Discuss the extent to which it is possible for business decision-making to be simultaneously fair, honest and socially acceptable.

Theory of knowledge

Should intuition (gut feelings, hunch and/or instinct rather than quantitative or scientific techniques) play a more significant role in business decision-making?

Question 1.7.4 Kekerovic Contractors

Kekerovic Contractors specialises in the planning and construction of houses in Nîmes, southern France. The operations director, Bronco Kekerovic, has recently taken on a project to build a four-bedroom home with an outdoor pool. The project's tasks, duration and sequence are outlined below.

- A – Lay foundation to the house: 1 week.
- B – Construction of house: 6 weeks. B is preceded by A.
- C – Excavation and foundation for swimming pool: 2 weeks. C is preceded by A.
- D – Tiling and sealing of pool: 2 weeks. D is preceded by C.
- E – Internal décor and fixtures for the house: 3 weeks. E is preceded by B.
- F – Final testing and handing over keys to the new owner: 1 week. F is preceded by activities D and E.

(a) Construct a Gantt chart for *Kekerovic Contractors* using the above information and identify the quickest time in which the project can be completed. *[4 marks]*

(b) Explain why the use of Gantt charts can be important for businesses such as *Kekerovic Contractors*. *[6 marks]*

Organizational planning tools and the CUEGIS concepts

Decision-making is at the heart of Business Management, so organizational planning is central to this function. Managers are involved in making decisions each day (see Box 1.7.a). They have to make choices between competing alternatives.

Box 1.7.a The three levels of business decision-making

- **Operational decisions** are routine and day-to-day decisions, e.g. supervisors deciding when factory floor workers should go for their break or sales managers dealing with customer enquiries or complaints.
- **Tactical decisions** are regular and short-term decisions normally handled by middle management, e.g. decisions about pricing strategies or recruitment and selection of staff.
- **Strategic decisions** are high-level and long-term decisions that set the overall direction for a business. Such decisions are dealt with by senior managers as they carry more risk, e.g. which products to develop, which new markets to enter, and the review of salaries and benefits to staff.

The business environment is said to be dynamic in nature, i.e. it is exposed to continual change and nothing remains unchanged for very long, especially in an increasingly globalized and digital business world. It is the responsibility of the management team to forecast and plan change and to take appropriate action.

However, businesses are likely to face constraints on their strategic planning and decision-making, including:

- *The availability of finance* All decisions require funding. Whilst some options may seem favourable, they might not be financially feasible.

- *Organizational culture* The traditions and norms of an organization can create barriers to planning and decision-making. A culture that is resistant to change can prevent certain options from being pursued. By contrast, adaptive cultures are more receptive to change.

- *The dynamics of the workforce* A highly skilled workforce is able to adopt a wider range of options. Decision-making is less onerous if managers can rely on staff to implement decisions.

- *External constraints* (see Unit 1.5) Businesses may be constrained in their strategic decision-making by ethical considerations, government rules and regulations, and the state of the economy. The intensity of rivalry and pace of innovation in the industry can also create some problems for organizational planning and decision-making.

Nevertheless, the use of organizational planning tools (such as decision trees and the fishbone diagram), can help managers to make rational strategic decisions. After all, the quality of decision-making will affect the long-term prospects of an organization. Hence, the use of appropriate planning tools can help businesses to make better and more informed strategic decisions. As the Chinese proverb says, *"The rich man plans for tomorrow, the poor man for today"*.

CUEGIS ESSAY

With reference to an organization of your choice, discuss the ways in which **culture** and **ethics** can influence organizational planning and decision-making.

[20 marks]

REVIEW QUESTIONS

1. What are organizational planning tool?

2. What is meant by a 'cause and effect' (or fishbone) diagram?

3. What is a decision tree and why do businesses use this tool?

4. Distinguish between chance nodes and decision nodes when constructing decision trees.

5. Distinguish between driving forces and restraining forces in a force field analysis.

6. How are the weights in a force field analysis are assigned?

7. What are Gantt charts?

8. What is meant by a 'dependency' in a Gantt chart?

9. Why do project managers use Gantt charts?

10. What are the differences between operational, tactical and strategic decisions?

KEY TERMS

Chance nodes in a decision tree are used to show the different probable outcomes of a decision. They are shown as circles.

Decision nodes in a decision tree are used when there is a decision to be made. The nodes are shown as squares. The decision maker has at least some control over decision nodes.

Decision trees are a quantitative organizational planning tool that calculates the probable values of different options, helping managers to minimise the risks in decision-making.

Dependencies in a Gantt chart represent the activities that cannot start until the completion of other tasks.

Driving forces in a force field analysis show the benefits of change (such as reduced costs or improved productivity).

Force field analysis is an organizational planning tool that deals with the forces for and against change.

Fishbone diagram (or **cause and effect model**) is an organizational planning tool based on identifying and dealing with the root causes of a problem or issue facing a business.

Gantt charts are a visual representation of all the tasks in a particular project plotted against the timescale. As a planning and scheduling tool, it allows project managers to monitor progress.

Organizational planning tools are the various methods that businesses use to aid their decision-making, e.g. decision trees, fishbone diagrams, Gantt charts and force field analysis.

Restraining forces in a force field analysis show the causes of resistance to change.

2.1 Functions and evolution of human resource management

"A thousand workers, a thousand plans." - Chinese proverb

SL/HL content	Assessment objective
Human resource planning (workforce planning)	AO1
Labour turnover	AO2
Internal and external factors that influence human resource planning (such as demographic change, change in labour mobility, new communication technologies)	AO3
Common steps in the process of recruitment	AO2
The following types of training: • on the job (including induction and mentoring • off the job • cognitive • behavioural	AO2
The following types of appraisal: • formative • summative • 360-degree feedback • self-appraisal	AO2
Common steps in the processes of dismissal and redundancy	AO1
How work patterns, practices and preferences change and how they affect the employer and employees (such as teleworking, flexitime, migration for work)	AO2
Outsourcing, offshoring and re-shoring as human resource strategies	AO3
How innovation, ethical considerations and cultural differences may influence human resource practices and strategies in an organization	AO3

© IBO, 2017

Human resource planning

Human resource planning (workforce planning). AO1

© IBO, 2017

Human resource management (HRM) is the management function of using and developing people within a business to meet its organizational objectives. This entails interrelated roles, such as:

• Workforce planning (also known as human resource planning)

• The recruitment, selection and induction of new employees

• Training and development of staff

• Performance management and staff appraisals

• Reviewing pay and remuneration packages

• Disciplinary and grievance procedures

• Looking after the welfare (wellbeing) of employees.

People are important to an organization as they *add value* to its output. This can be achieved by increasing productivity (output per worker), improving quality, coming up with new ideas and providing better customer service to enhance the overall purchasing experience of customers. Consider, for example, the differences in your experience as an IB student with and without a classroom teacher.

Many entrepreneurs argue that people are a firm's most valuable resource. Employing the right people helps businesses to achieve their aims and objectives. To do this, a firm needs to use **human resource planning** (or **workforce planning**) – the management process of anticipating and meeting an organization's current and future staffing needs. Workforce planning can be short term or long term, although it is an ongoing process for most businesses:

- Short-term workforce planning deals with the existing and upcoming demands of an organization, e.g. employing workers to cover for staff who are about to resign, retire or go on maternity leave.

- Long-term workforce planning looks at the human resource needs of the business in the foreseeable future, e.g. the Walt Disney Company recruited and trained employees up to two years before Hong Kong Disneyland was opened.

Workforce planning can be achieved by looking at:

- Historical data and trends – such as the change in the size of the workforce over the past few years or the popularity of part-time and flexible working hours. However, past data is not indicative of what actually happens in the future.

- Sales and income levels – higher levels of income and spending in the economy will lead to more jobs being created.

- Labour turnover rates– measure the number of employees who leave a firm as a percentage of its workforce, per year. The higher the staff turnover rate, the more workers a firm will need to recruit.

- The flexibility and workload of staff – a highly flexible and skilled workforce may be able to cope if there is a sudden shortage of staff. In a firm where people are over-specialised and where workload is mounting, it might be necessary to employ more staff.

- Demographic changes – government data regarding changes in the demographics of the workforce, such as the changes in the number of female workers in the economy or the number of graduates, can help managers to forecast their human resource needs.

Workforce planning consumes a lot of time and money. For example, a recent report in the *South China Morning Post* revealed that poor recruitment practices in Hong Kong cost businesses HK$39 billion (US$5 billion) per year. The same report showed that managers in Hong Kong spent a fifth of their time correcting the mistakes made by their staff. Despite attempts to achieve effective workforce planning, external influences affect the accuracy of the forecasts. This is because businesses are constantly exposed to the forces of change, such as an economic recession which reduces the demand for human resources.

Exam tip !

The term *labour force* (or *workforce*) can mean one of two things, so it is important to put the term in the correct context. 'Workforce' can refer to the nation's labour force, i.e. all those available for work (the employed, the self-employed and the unemployed). It can also refer to the people employed in a particular organization, i.e. the firm's workforce.

Labour turnover

Labour turnover. AO2

© IBO, 2017

Labour turnover measures the percentage of the workforce that leaves the organization in a given time period, usually one year. For example, if twelve teachers in an IB World School left during the academic year when 96 teachers were employed, the labour turnover rate would be 12.5%. Thus, it is calculated using the formula (for each time period):

$$\text{Labour turnover} = \frac{\text{Number of staff leaving}}{\text{Total number of staff}} \times 100$$

Some organizations tend to have higher rates of staff turnover than others. Firms that hire lots of part-time and temporary staff, such as McDonald's and Burger King, are likely to accept higher rates of labour turnover, mainly due to the nature of the job (such as the relatively low wages paid to unskilled workers). The main reasons why people leave their jobs can be summed up by internationally best-selling author MJ Yate who used the acronym CLAMPS as the six acceptable reasons: **C**hallenge, **L**ocation, **A**dvancement, **M**oney, **P**ride (or **P**restige) and (**J**ob) **S**ecurity.

A low labour turnover rate suggests that managers have recruited the right people for the job and that the existing employees are content and motivated at work. By contrast, a high labour turnover rate suggests that staff are incompetent or lack job satisfaction. It might also be caused by better job opportunities and remuneration packages offered by other employers. A high labour turnover rate will clearly add to the costs of recruiting and training new staff in addition to the lost productivity when experienced staff leave. For example, *ACAS* reported in 2017 that the average cost of replacing just one worker in the UK exceeds £30,000 ($43,500). CBS News reported in 2013 that the cost of replacing someone earning less than $50,000 per year amounts to around 20% of the person's annual salary.

The opposite of labour turnover is staff retention. The benefits of high staff retention are the opposite of the drawbacks of high staff turnover. For example, consider if your IB Business Management teacher left the school at the end of your first year in the IB Diploma Programme. For students, there is a lack of continuity and a period of time to adjust to the new teacher in your second (final) year of the IBDP. For the school, there are the costs of recruitment to replace the teacher. The successful recruit may need time to adjust to the school culture and have a period of training to learn about the policies and processes at the school.

Firms with high staff retention tend to be those that motivate their workers and develop a positive organizational culture. They regularly offer staff training for both personal and professional development. There is sound leadership, and workers are made to feel valued. All this helps to boost morale as staff see their employers valuing their contributions and development. Employers also benefit from the resulting employee loyalty.

CORE

Question 2.1.1   Trump Organization's Golf Links

Several years before he became the President of the USA, Donald Trump announced a £1billion ($1.45bn) golf development at Balmedie, near Aberdeen, Scotland. The local community was understandably excited about the prospects of the 6,000 jobs that would be created. Trump's plans included two championship golf courses, a five-star hotel and hundreds of holiday homes. Trump, who popularised the phrase *"you're fired!"* on reality television programme *The Apprentice*, said that **labour turnover** was not a problem at the *Trump Organization*.

(a) Define the term **labour turnover**.   *[2 marks]*

(b) Explain **two** reasons why a business such as the *Trump Organization* might need to hire new workers.   *[4 marks]*

(c) Explain the importance of understanding labour turnover for the *Trump Organization*.   *[4 marks]*

Human resource management

Internal and external factors that influence human resource planning

Internal and external factors that influence human resource planning (such as demographic change, change in labour mobility, new communication technologies). AO3

© IBO, 2017

Internal factors (such as labour mobility) and external factors (such as new communications technologies) both influence human resource planning.

Demographic change

The supply of human resources in a country is affected by demographic changes in the workforce. Demography is the statistical study of population characteristics and trends. Businesses need to understand these changes so that they can respond appropriately. Demographic changes can be caused by changes in various factors:

- The **net birth rate** – the difference between the number of births and deaths per period of time. Countries with a high net birth rate will, in the long term, have a larger supply of human resources.

- The **net migration rate** – measures the difference between the number of people entering a country (immigrants) and the number of people leaving (emigrants). If the net migration figure is positive, the supply of human resources will increase.

- The **retirement age** – the legal age when people can stop work and claim money from their pensions. If the retirement age is raised, it automatically increases the number of people in the labour force, i.e. those of legal working age. Many Western economies, faced with an increasing number of elderly people, have considered increasing the retirement age. For example, in 2011 France controversially raised its retirement age from 60 to 62. France, Ireland, Japan, Taiwan and the UK have plans to gradually increase their retirement age to 68.

- **Women** entering or returning to the workforce – this boosts the supply of human resources. In modern societies, there has been an increase in the number of women working part-time. This gives businesses and staff greater flexibility in determining working hours.

A distinct demographic change in economically developed societies is increased longevity, i.e. people, on average, are living longer. Coupled with a declining birth rate in these countries, an **ageing population** (when the average age of the population increases) has the following effects:

- *Increased dependent population* The dependent population consists of people who are below the legal working age, those out of work and the retired population. They are 'supported' by the working population of taxpayers. With an ageing population, less people will be working in proportion to those who have retired, which adds further pressure on taxpayers to contribute towards government expenditure.

- *Reduced labour mobility* Young people tend to be more geographically and occupationally mobile. They have fewer reservations about moving to different places and jobs, including those overseas. Labour immobility reduces the flexibility and international competitiveness of a country's workforce.

- *Changes in consumption patterns* Different age groups have different spending patterns. Children, for example, may spend much of their money (or that of their parents!) on toys and schooling. Retired people are likely to spend a larger proportion of their money on holidays and healthcare related goods and services. Hence, an ageing population can create opportunities for firms to cater for more mature age groups.

- *Change in employment patterns* With more people going to university, the average age of people entering the workforce has also risen. Coupled with an ageing population, this means that firms are more likely to retain staff beyond their retirement age due to labour supply shortages. Some firms might even consider relocating overseas if domestic labour supply is insufficient or not suitable.

Changes in labour mobility

The **mobility of labour** is the extent to which labour can move to different locations (known as *geographical mobility*) and their flexibility in changing to different jobs (known as *occupational mobility*). The more mobile workers are (both geographically and occupationally) the higher the supply of labour tends to be. Labour can be geographically mobile, especially within a country, but there are limitations:

- Friends and family ties tend to be the key constraint for most people's geographical mobility.

- Relocation costs (moving expenses) such as remortgaging property and consideration of different house prices.

- Fear of the unknown means that people might prefer 'home comforts' (familiarity), e.g. uprooting the family and finding a new school for the children can be daunting for many people.

- The cost of living in a particular area such as the higher cost of housing and other expenses in cities can deter people from relocating in these areas, thus reducing the potential supply of labour.

- Language and cultural differences tend to limit international mobility.

The limitations on occupational mobility include:

- Occupational mobility tends to be greater with acquired attributes of a worker (such as education, qualifications, skills, experience and training).

- Younger people tend to be more occupationally mobile as they often change careers. Mature workers may think they are too 'old' to retrain or may have more financial commitments so are less willing to take risks by changing careers.

- Some workers are immobile because they are highly specialised in their area of expertise. These people find it difficult to seek employment opportunities in other industries.

- If employers discriminate against people's age, gender, religion or race then this will also hinder the occupational mobility of workers.

New communication technologies

Advances in communications technologies, such as email, e-commerce and video conferencing, can bring both opportunities and threats to human resource planning. For example, there are more opportunities for people to work from home, due to advances in mobile and Internet technologies. By contrast, businesses that are capital-intensive might not require as many workers. Information and Communications Technologies (ICT) in human resource planning can be used to support current practices (activities) in workforce planning and/or to change (improve) workforce planning processes.

Examples include:

- Recruitment – Almost all firms use ICT in their recruitment practices, e.g. the use of company websites or commercial providers such as LinkedIn to advertise jobs; the use of online application forms to speed up communication and to reduce costs; and the increased use of video-conferencing for job interviews.

- Meetings – Businesses with branches or facilities in different locations, including overseas, can reduce the costs of meetings by using video-conferencing technologies. For smaller businesses, providers such as Skype also help to cut their costs of communications.

- Appraisals – Collaborative tools such as Google Docs can be used by the line manager and appraisees to set targets and review progress. Such technologies are more efficient than emailing appraisal documents to and from the different parties.

- Flexitime and teleworking – Mobile technologies have enabled many more people to work away from the office or at home. This can help to cut costs for both the business and the employees. Effective use of flexitime and teleworking also helps boost labour productivity.

- Online training courses - These courses tend to be cheaper than off the job training courses with a specialist trainer, e.g. IB teachers can enrol for online courses for a fraction of the cost of a face-to-face IB workshop held overseas in a 5-star hotel venue. Participants can also work online from the comfort of their office or at home.

CORE

IB Learner Profile – Be a thinker

Discuss with a friend whether you think that ICT can simultaneously achieve all of the following: reduce administrative costs, increase labour productivity, enhance communication, improve decision-making and enhance customer service.

Human resource management

Question 2.1.2   327 million Americans

In October 2006, the population of the USA reached a new milestone figure of 300 million, making it the third-most populated nation on Earth. The last milestone of 200 million people was recorded in November 1967. The population had exceeded 327 million by 2018, with the population increasing by 1 person per 18 seconds. Some people question America's ability to sustain its population growth, given that it is the largest consumer of the planet's scarce resources, despite its **ageing population**. Concerns mount as forecasts show that the population will reach 400 million by 2050.

(a) Define the meaning of **ageing population**.   *[2 marks]*

(b) Explain **two** threats created by the demographic changes in the USA.   *[4 marks]*

(c) Explain **two** business opportunities provided by the demographic changes in the USA.   *[4 marks]*

Recruitment and selection

Common steps in the process of recruitment. AO2
© IBO, 2017

The recruitment and selection of employees is vital to the running of a business. Labour is an essential factor of production needed for the provision of any good or service. Hiring the right people helps to ensure that businesses can function effectively. As the recruitment and selection process is likely to be time consuming and rather expensive, managers must ensure the steps in the process of recruitment are effective.

The recruitment and selection process (see Box 2.1.a) starts when a job becomes available within the organization, perhaps due to expansion of the business or to replace staff who have decided to leave the organization. People might leave a job for all sorts of reasons, such as to start a new job, to go into higher education, to spend more time with their children or being fired for misconduct.

Before a business recruits new workers, managers usually carry out a **job analysis**. This involves scrutinising the different components of a job, such as the routine tasks and responsibilities of the post holder, to determine what the job entails. The job analysis helps to create two important documents needed for the recruitment and selection of staff – the *job description* and the *person specification*.

Managers might also want to verify:

* the skills and training required to do the job

* the qualifications and personal qualities needed to carry out the job

* the rewards needed to recruit and retain the post holder.

Once the initial job analysis has been done, the human resources manager will produce a **job advertisement** to get as many suitable people as possible to apply for the vacant job. There are usually two documents that are produced before writing a job advertisement: the job description and the person specification. Both these documents are important in objectively assessing the suitability of applicants. They can also be used to gauge training needs and for conducting job appraisals.

A **job description** is a document that outlines the details of a particular job. It refers specifically to what the job entails rather than the type of person required for the job. It includes the job title and the roles, duties and responsibilities of the post holder. Good job descriptions also have an element of flexibility in order to exploit the skills of employees; a rigid job description can limit the potential of workers especially as businesses constantly experience organizational change. A typical statement in a job description that allows such flexibility is 'and any other reasonable job assigned by the employer'.

A **person specification** is a document that profiles the ideal candidate, such as the qualifications, skills, and experiences sought by the employer. It also lists the personal attributes that the successful applicant should have, such as the ability to lead a team and to think critically. For some jobs, such as fashion models, news readers or professional sports people, the person specification may even state physical attributes of the ideal candidate.

Once the job description and person specification have been finalised, the job can be advertised. This usually includes important information, e.g. hours of work, the rate of pay and fringe benefits (see Unit 2.4). It is also important to have contact details for the business and to set a deadline date for receiving applications. It is usual to advertise a job both internally (within the organization) and externally. A good job advertisement will ultimately attract only suitable applicants who have the potential to do the job. Therefore, human resource managers consider the 5 'TRAPS'© in designing effective job advertisements:

- **Truthful** – The advertisement should not make exaggerated or misleading claims about the job, the pay or the organization. Exaggeration and dishonesty might attract more applicants, but is unethical and can create many problems for the business in the long term.

- **Relevant** – Job advertisements need to be succinct in order to attract people's attention and interest.

- **Accurate** – To minimise the number of unsuitable applicants for a job, the person specification and job description must be precise.

- **Positive** – An encouraging and upbeat job advertisement helps to attract people to apply for the job.

- **Short** – Given that advertising space is expensive, only appropriate and necessary information should go in a job advertisement.

Box 2.1.a   Summary of the recruitment process

1. Conduct a job analysis to determine the firm's need to hire new employees

2. Produce a job description and person specification

3. Advertise the vacant post

4. Check applications and shortlist suitable candidates

5. Interview the shortlisted candidates

6. Perform aptitude testing (if applicable)

7. Check references for shortlisted candidates

8. Job offer made to the best candidate

9. Issue and sign the contract of employment

10. Carry out induction of new recruit.

Question 2.1.3   Fonthill Primary School job advertisement

Fonthill Primary School, Belgium is seeking to hire an Educational Assistant (€22 per hour) to work up to 17 hours a week in the Learning Support Department. The successful candidate will be required to facilitate specially designed educational resources and activities working in collaboration with a classroom teacher and the Head of Department. Applicants should demonstrate patience, initiative and preferably have previous experience working with young children with specific learning difficulties. This position involves working with a single child on a one-to-one basis. Send your completed application form and CV to the principal, Ms. Danielle Franzén Daoudy. Closing date: Friday, 18 May.

(a) Explain why it is important for *Fonthill Primary School* to produce a well-defined job description. [4 marks]

(b) Examine whether the above would make an effective job advertisement. [6 marks]

CORE

Human resource management

The application process

Applicants for a job usually apply using a combination of three methods:

- **Application form** – a standardised form produced by the business for selecting appropriate applicants for a job. Employers can tailor questions on the form to meet their specific needs. Such forms make candidates answer the same questions in a consistent format, allowing employers to compare like-with-like.

- **Curriculum vitae** – a document outlining an applicant's education, employment history, skills and professional qualifications. The curriculum vitae (CV), also known as a résumé, allows employers to see what the candidate has achieved and to judge whether the experiences meet the requirements of the job.

- **Cover letter** – an introductory letter written by the applicant, stating which position is being applied for and why the applicant should be considered for the job. The cover letter (or **letter of application**) allows the HR manager to browse through potential applications, without having to first read all the CVs or application forms (many of which will be unsuitable).

Traditionally, businesses would mail application forms to prospective applicants. However, it is more common today for candidates to email their CV or to apply using an online application form, which speeds up the recruitment process and helps to cut costs (printing and mailing) for the business.

The selection process

Once the completed application forms and CVs have been received by the business, the HR manager checks these to identify suitable candidates for the job (a process known as **shortlisting**). The shortlisting process involves comparing the application form and the CV of a candidate against the job description and person specification. This helps to identify the most suitable applicants to invite for a job interview. The three main methods used to select the best candidate for a job are: interviews, testing and references.

Interviews

Interviews are the most common method of selection. An interview is a two-way dialogue between the interviewer (representing the employer) and the interviewee (the candidate applying for a job) to help managers make more informed decisions when selecting the best candidate for a job. However, to get the most out of the interview process, all other prerequisites (such as job analysis) must have been carried out effectively. Interviews provide the chance for an employer to meet with the applicant face to face, whether in person or via video-conferencing. The interview will allow the employer to get a better idea about what the applicants are like, whether they are suitable for the job(s) being offered and whether they will fit into the organization. Interviews also allow applicants to get more information about the job and the business to assess whether they would be happy to work at the organization.

Figure 2.1.a Interviews are an essential part of the recruitment process

Interviews need to be well planned and conducted professionally. For example, interviewers must organize an appropriate venue where there will be no disruptions; appropriate questions need to be prepared to avoid negative discrimination; the job description and person specification must be readily available for the interviewing panel; and the interviewers should have studied the candidate's CV and references to get to know something about the applicant before the interview commences. Successful interviews also require managers to have good interview skills. Interviews can take various forms:

- *Video-conferencing interviews* use ICT technology to save on the costs of people having to physically meet. Video-conferencing interviews are increasingly being used to recruit people from overseas to fill middle and senior management posts.

- *Telephone interviews* take place over the telephone. These interviews can be useful for those involved in telesales.

- *Face-to-face interviews* are usually carried out at the business, allowing the manager to meet and talk with the applicants. These interviews can range from having just one interviewer to several people interviewing the candidate at the same time (known as a *panel interview*).

- *Group interviews* involve a number of candidates being interviewed simultaneously. The panel of interviewers can judge how individual candidates behave in such a situation, e.g. which candidates are timid, assertive or extroverted, and perhaps identify those that are natural leaders.

Research has shown that the most effective interviews tend to follow a structured approach, with the same core questions being asked of each candidate. These interviews have some flexibility, such as asking further questions based on what the respondent says in the interview. However, if the same fundamental questions are asked to all candidates, interview bias can be reduced.

The purpose of the interview process is to find and appoint the best candidate for the vacant job. Applicants can improve their chances of success at interview by reflecting on common sense protocol (see Box 2.1.b). Interviews are conducted by asking a series of questions (see Box 2.1.c) that link to the job description and the person specification. There are two categories of interview questions:

- **Behavioural-based questions** are used to assess a candidate's behavioural pattern and initiative. Such questions typically start off as "*Explain an example of when you . . .*" or "*Tell me about...*"

- **Situational-based questions** are used to assess an applicant's judgmental ability. The interview starts with a hypothetical scenario and asks the interviewee for a response, e.g. "If one of your team members was constantly late to work, what would you do?" The purpose is to evaluate the critical thinking ability of the applicant in each given scenario.

One drawback of interviews is that they are very time-consuming. Many interviews last between 30 minutes and an hour, with some jobs requiring candidates to have further interviews with other key personnel. Another limitation is that a person's actual ability is not tested; interviews can be unreliable in selecting the best applicant because candidates can lie or hide the truth. Even if a candidate performs well during an interview, the lack of desired qualities, experience or skills needed for the job may not have been picked up in the interview. Hence, other forms of selection are also used, such as testing and references.

Box 2.1.b   Interviewee etiquette

Do …

- Prepare - research the organization and the industry; plan on how to get to the venue (on time!); re-read your CV and letter of application; prepare answers to questions that are likely to be asked at the interview.

- Dress appropriately - first impressions count and can have a major impact on the interviewers.

- Practice interview skills - helps you to answer questions more concisely and confidently.

Don't …

- Be late - this will give a very bad first impression and no one likes waiting!

- Be critical - condemning others (such as previous bosses and colleagues) will not impress the interviewing panel.

- Falsify answers - dishonesty to interview questions may eventually surface, with devastating consequences.

Box 2.1.c   Ten common interview questions

1. Why do you want this job?

2. What do you know about this organization?

3. Why do you think that you will fit into this organization?

4. What are your key strengths?

5. What are your main weaknesses and what have you done about them?

6. Which leader/person do you admire most? Why?

7. Describe your key responsibilities in your last job.

8. Who was the most difficult person you had to work with and how did you manage this?

9. What are your key interests and how might these help you in this job?

10. Why did you leave your last job?

CORE

Human resource management

Testing

Although testing is time consuming, it increases the chances of hiring the best candidate for a job. This reduces costs incurred in the long run if the wrong applicant is hired. The main types of testing used in recruitment are:

- **Psychometric tests** assess a candidate's personality to gauge the attitude of potential recruits and their level of motivation. It is important to recruit people who will fit into the culture of the organization, so many large firms use psychometric tests especially for more senior positions.

- **Aptitude tests** examine the ability and skills of potential employees. For example, applicants for a secretarial job might be tested on the speed and accuracy of their typing, in-tray exercises to test their ability to cope under pressure and their problem solving skills.

- **Intelligence tests** calculate the mental ability of an applicant, such as their skills of numeracy, literacy, reasoning and general knowledge.

- **Trade tests** are used to examine a candidate's skills in a specific profession. These are useful when standards or skills cannot be judged from an interview or from a candidate's application form. For example, voice tests are used when recruiting television newsreaders and radio presenters.

References

References are written statements about an applicant from an independent source, such as a previous employer. *Referees*, the people who write references, may be asked to confirm the strengths and suitability of an applicant. They serve as a final safety check to ensure the information given by candidates in their application form, CV and interview are accurate and truthful. Employers can then determine the suitability of the applicant for the advertised job(s).

The contract of employment

Once a suitable candidate has been appointed (offered the job), the new recruit is entitled by law (in most countries) to receive either a signed contract of employment or a written statement of the terms and conditions of their employment (see Box 2.1.d).

Induction

The final stage of the recruitment process is to provide induction for new recruits to help them settle into their new roles. This also applies to internally recruited staff, perhaps due to a promotion or due to restructuring within the organization. The duration and breadth of induction will be less for internal recruits as they are already familiar with the policies, practices and culture of the organization.

Recruitment can be categorised as internal or external. **Internal recruitment** involves hiring people who already work for the business to fill a vacant post. This might happen when a business restructures its organization of human resources (see Unit 2.2) or when internal candidates are successful in applying for promotional posts within the firm. Internal posts are usually advertised on staff notice boards, in newsletters or via staff emails.

Box 2.1.d Contents of an employment contract

1. Job title

2. Specific duties of the job

3. Date the job starts (and ends, if the agreement is a finite contract)

4. Hours and days of work

5. Rate(s) and method of pay

6. Holiday and sick pay entitlements

7. Pension scheme arrangements

8. Outline of disciplinary procedures

9. Period of notice that must be given when employment is terminated (from either party)

10. Names and signatures of both parties, and dated on the contract.

Table 2.1.a Advantages and disadvantages of internal recruitment

Advantages	Disadvantages
Cost effective It is usually cheaper and quicker to recruit from within an organization as suitable candidates may be readily available.	**Fewer applicants** This limits the number of potential applicants but external candidates could be of better quality but are overlooked.
Less down-time Internal people are already familiar with the culture of the business and how it operates. They are able to adapt and settle into the new post quickly. Hence internal recruits can take up their new role with minimal down-time (time used to get familiar with the operations of a business rather than time actually spent on getting work done).	**'Dead wood'** Without external recruits, it might be difficult to get new ideas into the business. Firms lose out from having outdated working practises (known as dead wood) as staff have been there for too long. Quite often, managers discover that their staff lack the necessary skills and qualities to take up an internal promotion, so have to use external recruitment.
Less risk Employing a new worker from outside the organization could be risky in that their actual abilities and skills may not have been truly tested in the recruitment process. By contrast, recruiting internally might ensure that the job is filled with a highly suitable candidate.	**Time-consuming** Redeploying, relocating or promoting an internal candidate usually leads to another unfilled vacancy in the organization. Therefore the process could potentially be more time consuming than if external recruitment had been used from the outset.
Motivational Internal recruitment, especially for promotional posts, can act as a form of motivation. Providing internal people with opportunities for promotion suggests that managers value their employees. Hence, internal promotion can create employee loyalty and commitment to the firm.	**Internal politics** There could be resentment and conflict amongst fellow workers who were unsuccessful for the internal post. This can create an uncomfortable working environment for the people involved. Also, if no internal candidates are suitable then the business will still have to use external recruitment.

External recruitment is the process of hiring people from outside the business. The various methods of doing this include:

- *Newspaper advertising* – a common method as it has a wide audience. However, targeting the right people can be difficult and the advertising costs are high.

- *Specialist trade publications* – used to better target the right audience, e.g. management jobs in the UK supermarket industry are advertised in 'The Grocer' (www.thegrocer.co.uk) and teaching jobs are published in the 'Times Educational Supplement' (www.tes.com).

- *Internet advertising* – more businesses are using the internet to advertise their jobs. They may use specialist recruitment websites (such as LinkedIn, SimplyHired, Job.com and Glassdoor) or their own company website to advertise vacancies. Internet advertising can have a global reach yet only incurs relatively low costs.

- *Commercial employment agencies* – these agents advertise and interview suitable applicants for a job and make recommendations for selection to the hiring firm. Using agencies costs money (as they charge a fee for their services) but saves a huge amount of time for the employer who might also prefer to rely on the recruitment expertise of the employment agency.

- *Job centres* – non-profit organizations funded by the government to help people find employment. Businesses can advertise their vacancies at job centres free of charge. However, job centres tend to be used for advertising relatively low paid jobs so might not be suitable for some businesses.

- *Headhunting* – the poaching of a person from his or her current employer. The person is sought for their experience, expertise and knowledge. To entice them to leave their current job, the hiring company will try to offer a contract, including a pay deal, that is simply too good to resist.

- *University visits* – businesses go to specific universities to advertise their jobs. These jobs tend to be for junior management posts. Visiting universities means that there is a large pool of potentially suitable and talented people to choose from.

- *Employee referrals* – personal recommendations made by a current employee who knows people with the necessary skills and qualities to fill a vacancy. As is so often the case in the business world, sometimes it really is who you know rather than what you know that matters.

CORE

Human resource management

Table 2.1.b Advantages and disadvantages of external recruitment

Advantages	Disadvantages
'New blood' People hired from outside the organization can bring in new ideas and ways of thinking. They can contribute to the sharing of best practise and give the business insight to how a rival firm might have done things.	**Greater degree of uncertainty** When hiring external recruits, managers take a risk as they do not really know the candidates or their ability to do the job effectively. Even if they are able, they might not fit into the corporate culture.
Wider range of experiences Similarly, external recruits might be more qualified or more suitable than any of the internal candidates, perhaps because they have gained the experiences and skills required by the business from their previous employer.	**Time-consuming** External recruitment takes longer than internal recruitment. Advertising, shortlisting, interviewing and checking references all take up valuable management time. Adhering to anti-discrimination laws in recruitment further lengthens the process.
Larger pool of applicants Businesses will have a wider range and larger number of people applying for the job. This increases their chance of finding the ideal candidate for the job.	**Expensive** External recruitment can be very expensive, e.g. costs of job adverts in newspapers. There is also the time used up by managers involved in the recruitment process.

Training

The following types of training: on the job (including induction and mentoring), off the job, cognitive and behavioural. AO2

© IBO, 2017

Training is the process of providing opportunities for workers to acquire employment-related skills and knowledge. The amount and nature of training required will vary from one job to another. Some jobs require constant training or updating of skills and qualifications (such as those in the law or medical professions). Other jobs only require basic training to be carried out (such as unskilled machine operators in a factory). Training is regarded as an important investment in what is perhaps the organization's most valuable asset.

Figure 2.1.b Aspects of training

The general **objectives of training** and development include:

- To enhance the efficiency and effectiveness of staff.

- To improve the quality of work (including customer service) by the employees.

- To facilitate career and personal development of employees.

- To develop a multiskilled and productive workforce.

- To help staff adapt to change (such as technological, organizational, social and legal changes).

The general **benefits of training** include:

- A better skilled and more flexible workforce leads to organizational targets being met.

- Improved competence leads to (having to do things again due to errors the first time round). Hence, greater efficiency and better productivity help to reduce costs.

- Higher morale as workers progress within the organization. This may help to reduce absenteeism and to reduce staff turnover, as staff feel valued by employers who have invested in them. Workers also have improved chances of promotion as they become more skilled.

- By having a good reputation for training and developing staff, businesses might find it easier to attract good quality workers.

- As staff become more confident and competent in their roles, the quality of output and level of customer service are likely to increase.

- Training helps employees adjust better to change. By updating their skills and being multiskilled, workers are better able to cope with organizational change.

The largest drawback of providing training opportunities is the financial costs, i.e. the course fees for training and loss of output whilst workers are being trained. For example, the costs of sending an IB teacher to a workshop held overseas include: air fares, taxi transfer, travel insurance, hotel accommodation, meal allowances, course fees paid to the IBO, and payment for a cover (substitute) teacher whilst person attends the training. Another limitation is that effective training takes time to plan and this often consumes a large amount of a manager's valuable time. Furthermore, there is no guarantee that employees will stay at the business after being upskilled (gaining new skills, knowledge and qualifications through training).

Ultimately, the benefits of training mean that the workforce becomes more flexible, motivated and productive. If the benefits of training are greater than the costs, it is deemed to be financially justified.

Note that whilst training tends to be specific to the tasks and responsibilities of a certain job, development focuses on enhancing the personal skills of a person. Developing these personal skills helps the employee to be more effective and flexible in their jobs. Examples of personal skills development include: assertiveness, counselling, time management, stress management, first-aid and foreign language courses. Employees wishing to attend such courses must be able to justify how their

personal development helps to improve their performance in the workplace.

There are four broad types of training: on the job (including induction and mentoring), off the job, cognitive and behavioural (see Figure 2.1.c).

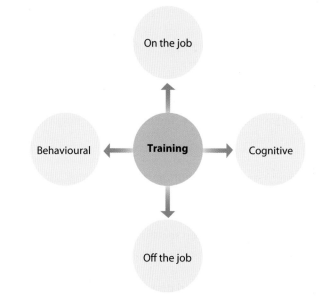

Figure 2.1.c Types of training

Question 2.1.4   Northern Ireland's hotel industry

In a recent report on the **recruitment** situation in Northern Ireland's hotel industry, it was found that workers suffered from low wages (earning little much more than the national minimum wage), very limited career and promotion prospects and a lack of training and professional development. Professor Tom Baum and Frances Devine's report also showed that most hoteliers felt that staff training and development are a burden rather than a benefit, and so should be kept at a minimum. Nevertheless, the *Irish Times* reported that more jobs were created in the hotel industry, with Dublin enjoying high hotel occupancy rates.

(a) Define the term **recruitment**.   *[2 marks]*

(a) Explain why "limited career and promotion prospects" might create problems for hoteliers.   *[4 marks]*

(c) Discuss the view that training and development are a burden rather than a benefit in Northern Ireland's hotel industry.   *[10 marks]*

On-the-job training

On-the-job training refers to training carried out whilst at the workplace. For example, the training can be delivered by a head of department, supervisor or other specialist. The trainees learn from the skilled colleague delivering the training at the place of work. Essentially, this type of training involves 'learning by doing'. As Confucius said, *"I hear and I forget. I see and I remember. I do and I understand".*

Induction training is a type of on-the-job training aimed at introducing new employees to the organization. The purpose of induction training is to help new recruits to settle in quicker. It can help to avoid costly mistakes being made by new employees who are not aware of the procedures or code of behaviour required to carry out their duties. It can also help new recruits to integrate into the corporate culture of the organization (see Unit 2.5).

Induction training might require a new recruit to:

- Meet key personnel, such as the employee's line manager and members of the department.

- Tour the premises including the recruit's main areas of work.

- Learn about the new job role and other relevant duties and specific procedures.

- Look at company policies and practices, e.g. rest breaks, health and safety policy, and fire or emergency evacuation procedures.

Mentoring is another type of on-the-job training involving a partnership between two people – the mentor and the mentee. The mentor is a more experienced member of staff who helps the mentee gain and develop specific skills and knowledge. The Oxford School of Coaching and Mentoring defines mentoring training as "to support and encourage people to manage their own learning in order that they may maximise their potential, develop their skills, improve their performance and become the person they want to be".

As part of their on-the-job training, junior managers might shadow (observe and learn from) more senior managers. For example, an aspiring senior teacher might shadow the school principal who acts as the mentor in training the mentee to prepare for principalship. Essentially, the mentor acts as a 'guide on the side', providing advice and pointing the mentee in the right direction in terms of career opportunities and development. Mentors ask questions and challenge mentees to reflect on their career progression and to take proactive responsibility for their own career development. A useful acronym to remember the role of a mentor is MENTOR: someone who motivates, encourages, nurtures, trains, observes and records (the progress of) the mentee.

Table 2.1.c Advantages and disadvantages of on-the-job training

Advantages	Disadvantages
Can be relatively cheap as the firm uses in-house specialists to facilitate the training.	Trainees may pick up bad working practices (short cuts and lazy habits) from the trainer.
Relevant as the training is targeted at issues directly related to the firm's needs.	Internal trainers may lack the most up-to-date training experience and skills.
Fewer disruptions to daily operations as the trainee is still 'at work' rather than being trained overseas, for example.	Trainers will not be able to conduct their own work whilst facilitating the training; thus on the job training can prove to be expensive.
Can help to establish relationships at work as team working is involved.	On the job training is often rather piecemeal and incomplete due to a lack of resources.
The location is convenient for workers and trainers, rather than them having to go off-site.	Productivity is initially low as workers undergo the process of learning new skills.

Table 2.1.d Advantages and disadvantages of induction training

Advantages	Disadvantages
Establishes clear expectations and good working habits from the start.	Planning, delivering and overseeing an induction programme can be very time consuming.
Helps new recruits to understand the *corporate culture* of the organization.	Key staff need to be 'freed' from their other duties as they are involved in providing induction.
By settling in more quickly, new recruits can contribute to the organization more promptly.	Information overload is counter-productive for new staff who have to absorb new information.
Morale is boosted as new staff feel welcome and are more confident and competent in their jobs.	The length of induction programmes can be very long, especially in large and disparate firms.

Table 2.1.e Advantages and disadvantages of mentoring training

Advantages	Disadvantages
Synergy is created as the mentor shares personal experiences, skills and knowledge with others, thus expanding staff development.	Planning, delivering and overseeing a mentoring programme can be very time consuming for senior managers.
Mentoring can be informal, thus benefiting the organization indirectly, as well as formally (where goals are recorded and progress monitored).	Mismatched pairing of mentor and mentee can cause major problems, such as stress, anxiety and conflict; thus can be counterproductive.
There is a qualitative difference between a mentor-mentee relationship and a manager-subordinate relationship; the former is more authentic and has longer lasting benefits.	Effective mentoring requires long-term commitment from both mentor and mentee. This can negatively impact on their workload; making time to meet is not always easy in busy firms.
Effective mentoring creates a safe environment for mentees to reflect and discuss issues openly and honestly, without fear of negative consequences on their jobs.	Using internal employees as mentors might require training (mentors should have opportunities to be trained too), thus added to the costs of the business.

Off-the-job training

Off-the-job training refers to training carried out off-site, e.g. at a tertiary college or hotel conference room. First-aid training, for example, might require specialist trainers and equipment that are not available in the business. Although internal trainers can be used to lead the training, external specialists are usually used for their particular expertise. For example, IB Workshop Leaders train and upskill teachers working in IB World Schools. Off-the-job training may involve day-release for training or attendance at evening classes. It is common that key personnel (e.g. middle managers) are chosen to attend these training courses and are then expected to *cascade* (pass on) the skills and knowledge that they have acquired to the rest of their team members.

It is common for those who attend off-the-job training to give the employer and service provider some form of official feedback. For example, a questionnaire can be used to assess the suitability of the course content and the extent to which participants feel the training will help to improve their work.

This can also help employers to determine whether the training could be extended to others in the organization.

Case study

The IBO offers a range of off the job training courses for teachers in IB World Schools. These are offered as online courses or face to face workshops, based on three different categories:

- **Category 1** – training that focuses on IB philosophy and implementation, for schools and teachers new to the IB.
- **Category 2** – training that focuses on the delivery of an IB Programme for experienced teachers of the PYP, MYP, CP or DP.
- **Category 3** – training targeted at educators to build on and enhance their professional development portfolios in delivering an IB programme, such as workshops that focus on the Extended Essay, or a new syllabus for the subject.

Table 2.1.f Advantages and disadvantages of off-the-job training

Advantages	Disadvantages
Experts, who might not exist or be available internally, are used to provide the training.	There is a potential loss of output whilst workers attend the off-site training course.
A wider range of training can be provided, e.g. first aid, ICT, customer relations management, health and safety, risk management, or even foreign languages (for certain professions).	Hiring specialist trainers and the venue can be very expensive. There may also be a need to reimburse staff for transportation and accommodation costs (for residential courses).
There are no distractions or disruptions from colleagues and customers as the training is conducted off-site.	It is debateable whether all the skills and knowledge learnt are relevant and therefore transferable to the business.
Networking can take place, whereby employees get to meet other people who form the basis of business contacts.	Finding the time for staff to cascade the information and knowledge from the off-site training course can be difficult.

CORE

Human resource management

Cognitive training

Cognition is the ability of the brain to learn and to think. **Cognitive training** is about training and developing mental skills to improve work performance. It is based on the notion that the ability to learn is fundamental to success in the workplace. Hence, cognitive training includes learning activities designed to help improve memory, attention, listening skills, logic and reasoning, visual and auditory processing, self-control, time management and problem solving. All these cognitive skills are important in the learning process. Such training is designed to help workers improve their mental processes, acquire new knowledge, aid decision-making and solve work-related problems.

Cognitive training in used in many professions, such as accounting, finance and insurance that use cognitive courses and tests to develop their workers' mathematical skills. For example, accountants use cognitive training to improve the speed and accuracy of bookkeeping tasks. Research by psychologists has shown that highly skilled individuals benefit the most from cognitive training.

However, there are several limitations. For example, many cognitive training courses do not cater for the needs of trainees who have different needs or goals. Developing relevant and applicable cognitive training can also be expensive; whilst commercial programmes are available, they might not meet the specific needs of the organization. It is also somewhat difficult to measure the impact of the training and how long the effects last.

Nevertheless, supporters of cognitive training argue that improvements from such training are key determinants of job performance and career advancement. After all, it is agreed that the development of the brain is the key to our learning capacity and therefore our ability to perform at work.

Theory of knowledge

State the ten traits of the IB Learner Profile. To what extent does the IB Learner Profile promote cognitive learning?

Behavioural training

Behavioural training deals with identifying functional issues that could improve performance in the workplace by developing behavioural change in the workforce. Training is meaningless unless a desirable change in behaviour takes place. Behavioural training enables participants to move towards this desired change. For example, if the firm's goal is improved customer satisfaction, then behavioural training focuses on enhancing customer relations and customer service. The aim of behavioural training, like all types of training, is to advance both personal and professional effectiveness. Examples of behavioural training include:

- Team building – developing team cohesiveness to improve productivity

- Ethical business practice – raising awareness of business ethics and codes of practice

- Emotional intelligence – identifying, assessing, and controlling the emotions of individuals

- Motivation training – motivating individuals, teams and the workforce

- Conflict resolution – managing conflict in the workplace

- Stress management – identifying and handling stress, including staff wellbeing

- Anger management – understanding and controlling anger

- Leadership skills – understanding and leading others in the organization

- Business etiquette – organizational, regional, national and international cultural norms.

Human behaviour is, however, a product of innate human nature (e.g. some people are naturally shy whilst others are spontaneous, stubborn or sociable) and of individual experiences and environments (such as their family upbringing or the type of school they attended). Critics of behavioural training argue that the benefits, if any, are short-lived as people naturally default to their innate behaviour. As the Chinese proverb goes, *"It is easier to move a mountain that to change a person's personality"*.

Nevertheless, supporters of behavioural training believe that such training provides people with the necessary skills, knowledge and tools to solve work-related problems. Empirical studies have shown that social and psychological factors play important roles in labour productivity. Whilst learning often stops when job training courses end, this is not necessarily the case with behavioural training. As Mahatma Gandhi (1869–1948) said, "*Leadership at one time meant muscles, but today it means getting along with people.*"

Theory of knowledge

If employees are so diverse in their thinking, personalities and behaviour, what exactly is 'human nature'?

Figure 2.1.d Opportunities for team-building can improve morale and motivation

CORE

Appraisal

The following types of appraisal: formative, summative, 360-degree feedback and self-appraisal. AO2

© IBO, 2017

An **appraisal** is the formal assessment of an employee's performance in fulfilling his/her job based on the tasks and responsibilities set out in their job description. It is common for appraisals to be conducted on an annual or quarterly basis by a more senior member of staff, although interim meetings often take place between the appraiser and appraisee. The main reasons for appraisals are to:

- assess and record an employee's performance in line with his/her job description and targets

- assist staff in reflecting on their performance at work

- provide an opportunity to praise staff for their good work

- identify any barriers hindering the performance of an employee

- identify appropriate training and development needs of the appraisee

- set new targets and goals for continuous improvement

- aid professional development, helping employees to plan their careers

- aid management in assessing the suitability of individuals for a pay rise or promotion.

Human resource management

Section 2 Human resource management

Appraisals are part of **performance management** – the continuous process involving the planning, reviewing and mentoring of employees in order to enhance their performance at work. Managers will use a range of data, information, meetings and interviews to assess each employee (see Box 2.1.e).

The appraisal system usually enables employees to respond to professional discussions. Communication is two-way, allowing worker to inform the employer about their training needs and professional aspirations. Line managers provide constructive feedback to the appraise in order to provide support to continuous professional reflections and development.

Box 2.1.e   Typical questions asked in appraisal meetings

- What has gone well for you this year? What has not gone so well for you?
- What are your key strengths and weaknesses (areas for development)?
- What can be done to help improve your overall performance in the workplace?
- What are your training and development needs to help your professional development?
- Where do you see yourself in five years' time?

Table 2.1.g Advantages and disadvantages of appraisals

Advantages	Disadvantages
They are used to set targets, leading to changes for personal and professional development.	Appraisals are time consuming and can be a costly exercise.
Appraisals allow managers to objectively praise staff on their strengths and for their contributions in the workplace.	Confidential feedback must be given, and follow-up action requires funding and monitoring; otherwise the process is meaningless.
Managers can use appraisals to provide constructive feedback to employees, so allows staff to focus on areas for improvement.	By their very nature, appraisals can be rather subjective as perceptions and relationships at work can interfere with the process.
Appraisals can be a useful method of getting valuable feedback from the staff.	Staff may get offended by comments from the appraiser, especially about areas of weakness.
Managers often aggregate the findings of appraisals to identify common strengths and areas in need of improvement. Thus training and development needs can be better planned.	Many appraisers lack the skills, experience and confidence to carry out appraisals effectively. This diminishes the credibility of the process and the findings.
Appraisals can be used as part of job evaluation to work out levels of pay. This can be done by looking at the different tasks, responsibilities, skills, qualifications and challenges that a job entails. The appraisal process can then allow a business to objectively reward more demanding jobs with higher rates of pay.	Employees can experience unnecessary anxiety and stress if appraisals are linked to pay. It can also be a daunting experience for both the employee and the appraiser, especially with upwards appraisals (where a worker appraises his or her line manager).

Types of appraisal

Formative

Formative appraisal is a planned (formative) and ongoing process in which appraisal evidence is used by employees to inform them about what to do to improve their work practices. It enables managers and appraisees to engage in performance management conversations, encouraging employees to think about their own contributions to the workplace. Formative assessment is commonly used in schools, e.g. teachers mark an end-of-topic test, grade it, and add written comments to inform students about how to improve.

Formative appraisal is often used for appraising staff hired for a probation (trial) period, e.g. formative assessment of a junior doctor, beginning teacher or graduate bank manager at the beginning, middle and end of their training placement. The process helps the appraisee to modify work practices to improve overall attainment. Like most types of appraisals, the goals of formative appraisal include to:

- monitor the performance of employees' learning

- help employees to identify their strengths and weaknesses (areas that need developing)

- help managers to recognise areas where staff are struggling so that any problems can be addressed promptly.

CORE

Human resource management

It doesn't really matter what methods are used in formative appraisal, so long as the information is helpful for the employee to make adjustments to improve their productivity, e.g. observations of the worker, aptitude testing or a full diagnostic appraisal.

Summative

A summative appraisal is a written description of an employee's performance at work, summarising personal performance and achievements during the year. The summative appraisal usually has recommendations for improvement (targets for a subsequent appraisal). It is used to hold staff accountable for their work, often testing the knowledge and competence of employees. For example, summative appraisals of teachers usually involve lesson observations carried out by line managers. They are similar to a summative report that students might get in schools, often following a major test or end-of-year examination, showing them what they have learned during the semester or the academic year. The goal of summative appraisal is to evaluate the performance or contribution of workers by comparing this with a predetermined standard or benchmark, i.e. to make a professional judgement of a worker's competency and to identify areas in need of improvement.

360-degree feedback

360-degree appraisal involves collecting evidence about the appraisee's job performance from peers, subordinates, line managers or other parties (such as suppliers or customers) who have direct contact with the employee. Opinions and comments are usually obtained by the use of questionnaires or interviews. The questions are mainly focused on the core competencies of the appraisee. 360-degree appraisals are a popular method of appraising managers, with the aim of providing useful and practical feedback to improve managerial effectiveness. However, such appraisals often rely heavily on opinions rather than factual evidence. Hence, this is not suitable for all businesses and it is important for managers to consider group norms and subcultures before embarking with 360-degree appraisals. In some cultures, 360-degree appraisals are inappropriate as subordinates do not appraise their seniors.

Self-appraisal

Self-appraisal involves employees appraising themselves based on predetermined criteria. Appraisees are expected to be honest about their strengths and weaknesses. They also need to set realistic targets for improvement. Some self-appraisal systems require workers to rate themselves. This is easier for some workers to do (the extroverts, for example) than it is for others who find it personally or culturally awkward to rate themselves. Quite often, the self-appraisal is compared to the assessment carried out by the line manager and then used as a basis for subsequent discussions.

Whichever type of appraisal is used, a performance appraisal usually includes the following steps:

- *Staff records and reports* are used to evaluate the performance of an employee over the past year.

- A formal and structured *appraisal meeting* is conducted to allow the appraisee to reflect on personal performance. Feedback is important and an action plan might be formulated by both parties.

- Appraiser completes a *written report* of the appraisal. There is often a rating system used to judge the performance of the appraisee, perhaps ranging from 'Outstanding' to 'Unsatisfactory'.

- Both appraiser and appraisee *sign* the final written report.

- At times, there might also be a *countersignature* from a more senior manager, such as the supervisor of the appraiser to ensure that the appraiser has carried out the assessment accurately and objectively.

If an appraisee has an overall rating that is below 'Moderate', then the following actions can be taken:

- Issue an advisory letter to the employee (similar to issuing a warning letter).

- Counselling the appraisee and giving advice on shortcomings in the appraisee's job performance, i.e. discussion of strategies for improvement.

- Dialogue concerning the consequences if there is no improvement in job performance.

- Closely monitor the performance of the appraisee, perhaps by calling for quarterly reports or more frequent updates.

- If no improvements are made within the agreed time period, action is taken to dismiss the employee.

CORE

Human resource management

135

Dismissal and redundancies

Common steps in the processes of dismissal and redundancy. AO1

© IBO, 2017

Whilst the human resources department has the crucial role of attracting and recruiting workers, it also has to ensure that the termination of employment contracts is carried out efficiently. Employment can be terminated in one of four situations: dismissal, redundancy, retirement (when workers, due to their age, withdraw from the workforce) and resignations (when the employee chooses to leave their job).

Dismissal means the termination of a worker's employment due to incompetence (unsatisfactory performance) or a breach of contract. In everyday language, this is when a person is 'sacked' or 'fired'. Managers have to present a good case for dismissing an employee and act in a fair manner in handling the case. Dismissal is usually seen as being fair in the following situations:

- **Incompetence** – a lack of ability, usefulness or effectiveness required to carry out the job, i.e. underperformance in the job.

- **Misconduct** – unacceptable behaviour such as being constantly late for work, harassing other employees, rudeness to customers or frequently missing deadlines. Employees will usually get a series of warnings for their misconduct before being dismissed.

- **Gross misconduct** – major misdemeanours (wrong doings) such as theft, fraud, endangering others or being drunk at work. Gross misconduct can lead to instant dismissal without any warning.

- **Legal requirements** – if an employee does not have the necessary skills or requirements for their job, then the employer can legally dismiss the worker. For example, a worker may have been dishonest about their qualifications, abilities and experiences.

In most countries, dismissing a worker is usually a three-step process:

- Initial verbal warning about misconduct or unacceptable conduct at work – This can be put in writing as a record of the warning. It is common for this verbal warning to be valid for one year, after which the warning is void if there is no reoccurrence of the misconduct.

- Official written warning for repeated misconduct – A formal meeting takes place for the employer to issue the warning to the employee, who may be allowed to bring a colleague to the hearing (for morale support). An action plan and timeframe for improvement are discussed and put in writing.

- Any further repeated cases of misconduct results in the worker being dismissed. This may or may not involve severance pay (a final payment for employment services), depending on the specific circumstances and the legal system. Both parties sign the letter of termination. It is common for the employer to have a witness so the aggrieved employee does not make false accusations later.

Box 2.1.f   You're fired!
Grounds for immediate dismissal

- The employee is unfit for the position during the probation (trial) period.
- There is a significant breach of the rules and regulations set by the employer, e.g. violation of health and safety at work.
- Neglect of duty.
- Corruption that leads to substantial damage to the employer's financial interests.

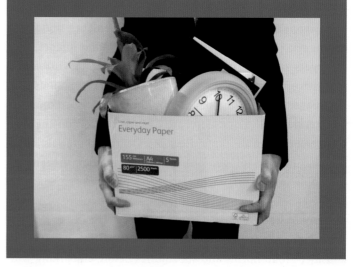

Evidence must be gathered and presented at all stages of the dismissal process. Examples include: records of appraisal meetings, email records, customer feedback, witness statements, or even closed-circuit television (CCTV) recordings. Employers also need to show evidence of providing support and opportunities for the employee to make improvements. It is also important for managers to communicate the dismissal with the rest of the team who may be concerned about their own job security and to prevent rumours spreading.

Figure 2.1.e Security cameras are used to safeguard the interests of the business

However, not all cases of dismissal are justified. **Unfair dismissal** occurs when an employee is dismissed without a valid or legal reason. For example, the employee may have been wrongly accused of gross misconduct such as theft. In most countries, the employee would have the legal right to take the case to a court hearing. If the employee can prove his or her innocence, the court can demand reinstatement of the employee (they get their job back) and/or financial compensation for the loss of earnings and the mental stress caused.

The two main causes of unfair dismissal are **discrimination** and **constructive dismissal**. For instance, an employer might discriminate against a worker's age, race, gender, ethnicity, sexual orientation or religion (that does not affect their job) so dismisses the person for such reasons. In countries with equal opportunities legislation, women cannot be dismissed because they are pregnant. To do so would be seen as unfair dismissal. Constructive dismissal occurs when a worker is forced into resignation because the employer has made it very difficult for the worker to continue in the job. For example, the employer might have changed the terms and conditions of employment without any consultation with the employee, such as a change in responsibilities or hours of work. In all cases of unfair dismissal, the employee has the legal right to seek compensation from the business.

Redundancies (also known as **retrenchments** or **lay-offs**) occur when a business can no longer afford to employ the worker or when the job ceases to exist. For example, many retail workers are hired temporarily during the busy trading period prior to Christmas but are thereafter laid-off (made redundant). When a business has to retrench workers, there are two main options:

- **Voluntary redundancies** take place when the employer asks for volunteers to leave. They are offered a *redundancy package* (severance pay), such as three months' pay. The amount of redundancy pay depends on the workers' salary and benefits and the length of time that they have worked for the organization. Voluntary redundancy is the least likely option to cause conflict and hardship to the workforce.

- **Compulsory redundancies** (or **involuntary redundancies**) occur when the employer has to choose which workers to make redundant. There are two main ways they can do this: the *LIFO* method (last-in-first-out), which makes the newest recruits in the team redundant, or by the *retention by merit* method whereby the least productive workers are made redundant first. The LIFO method is perceived by employees to be fairer, although productive workers might be lost this way. Retention by merit can be perceived to be highly subjective (a worker might be laid off because the manager doesn't like him rather than because of his ability to do his job), but it can be beneficial if unproductive and inefficient workers are removed from the business.

- In some countries and some jobs, it is possible for the employer to issue finite (fixed term) contracts. At the end of the contract, the employer can assess whether it is worth rehiring the worker, based on past performance and on the financial position of the business. Alternatively, some businesses choose to reduce pay instead of making some staff redundant. For larger businesses, another option is to **redeploy** staff. This means transferring employees from a department or branch that no longer requires their services to other areas of the business where vacancies exist. In reality, redeployment is not usually an option for most businesses. Furthermore, redeployment can cause anxiety and demotivate workers who are transferred to an unknown environment.

CORE

Theory of knowledge

Which of the ways of knowing is most dominant when dismissing workers?

Theory of knowledge

In some countries, such as the USA, it is illegal to fire a whistleblower (an employee who openly criticises the illegal activities of the employer, e.g. sexual harassment in the workplace or violation of health and safety laws). Is it ethical to protect whistleblowers? Should society encourage whistleblowers to reveal the 'truth'?

Human resource management

Question 2.1.5   Myspace

Social networking service provider *Myspace* was founded in 2003. It was once the world's most popular social media website. However, it was overtaken by Facebook in 2008, although *Myspace* did generate $800 million in revenue that year from its workforce of 1,600 employees. Since then, the number of users has steadily declined. In 2011, *Myspace* announced redundancies for half its workforce in the USA as part of the social entertainment firm's cost-cutting exercise. By 2018, *MySpace* employed less than 500 people. In an attempt to remain popular, *Myspace* diversified to allow unsigned musicians to post and sell music on their website.

(a) In the context of the case study, distinguish between **redundancy** and **dismissal**.   *[4 marks]*

(b) Examine how redundancies might enable *Myspace* to better achieve its workforce planning targets.   *[6 marks]*

Changing employment patterns and practices

How work patterns, practices and preferences change and how they affect the employer and employees (such as teleworking, flexitime, and migration for work). AO2

© IBO, 2017

In modern societies, there have been a number of observable changes in employment patterns and work practices, such as the increase in the number of people working flexitime.

Employment sector

There are four employment sectors in an economy – primary, secondary, tertiary and quaternary (see Unit 1.1). Generally, as a country develops and prospers, the proportion of workers employed in the primary sector falls, with a shift to secondary industries and finally the tertiary and quaternary sector. In developed economies, the tertiary sector accounts for the largest proportion of employment, with many highly skilled people employed in the quaternary sector. For example, less than 2% of people in the USA, UK and France work in agriculture, whereas over 75% of the working population are employed in the services sector.

Figure 2.1.f Paddy fields (rice fields) are part of the primary sector

Ageing population

The net birth rate in many developed economies has been falling. This means that the size of the future workforce will also fall. Yet people are living longer, so the average age of workers will tend to rise (known as an ageing population). Hence, the shortage in labour supply will affect workforce planning, recruitment and training. Firms will be more willing to appoint and retain older employees. They will also be more flexible in keeping staff beyond retirement age. Women and part-time staff, who help to provide more workforce flexibility, will also be sought after. Training opportunities will be provided for existing staff to enhance their performance and to offer them the prospect of internal promotion, i.e. training is used as a means of retaining staff.

Theory of knowledge

Why is it that despite having a lower average life expectancy and the existence of equal opportunities laws, no country allows men to retire earlier than women?

Flexible work structures

Charles Handy's theory of the shamrock organization (see Unit 2.2) suggests that businesses will gradually use fewer core staff to improve their flexibility. For example, firms are increasingly outsourcing projects and using consultants. Reducing the number of the core staff and employing more part-time workers also helps businesses to reduce their labour costs. Greater flexibility might mean that a larger number of people work from home.

Flexible working patterns have many implications for employers and employees, including:

- *Organizational restructuring*   There is less likely to be a traditional organizational structure (see Unit 2.2) as firms employ various combinations of core, part-time and peripheral staff.

- *Flexitime*   Consultants, contractors and part-time employees are more likely to be allowed to work the hours that suit their individual needs. Businesses offer flexible working hours to cater for people who have to balance work with other priorities such as childcare or higher education.

- *Changing recruitment practices*   Firms shift to hiring more flexible workers (in terms of location, working hours and skills). Hence, they are likely to employ more part-time and temporary staff.

- *Retention of core staff*   Key employees of an organization will need to be retained for their outstanding skills and expertise, perhaps by offering first-rate financial rewards. In 2011, Google gave its staff a $1,000 bonus plus a 10% basic salary increase to prevent staff being poached by Facebook and other rivals.

- *Training*   Firms will be less likely to invest in training, except for their core staff. However, there will be pressure for staff to constantly update their skills. Firms can pay for this (for their core staff at least) or people may have to update employment skills at their own expense (such as enrolling for online training courses).

Likewise, workers will have to be more flexible and adaptable. There is no such thing as a 'job for life' and people have to be prepared to move between occupations and perhaps industries to maintain employment. However, a multiskilled and flexible worker will be highly attractive to potential employers. Examples of flexible working practices include: teleworking, homeworking, portfolio working, part-time employment and flexitime.

Teleworking

Teleworking, a term coined by management consultant Jack Nilles in 1973, refers to working away from the office by using electronic forms of communication, e.g. telephones, the Internet and email. It is popular in the USA, Canada, Sweden, Finland and the UK. The trend has been partly due to increasing problems commuting in central business districts but mainly due to the technological advances in ICT.

Examples of businesses that use teleworking include insurance firms, banks, market research firms and airlines. These businesses have 'call centres' where a dedicated team of workers deal with customer enquiries and complaints on the telephone. This frees up management time at individual branches as they do not have to deal with so many enquiries from customers. Teleworkers can be mobile, such as sales people who spend most of their time commuting and visiting clients.

Homeworking is a category of teleworking whereby people work from their own home. According to the International Telework Association and Council (ITAC), the number of Americans working from home (during business hours) at least one day per month rose from approximately 20% in 2004 to around 33% (over 40 million people) by 2010. With advances in technology which allow employees to operate in almost any location (such as wireless broadband, Wi-Fi and mobile technologies), the number of teleworkers will continue to rise.

Figure 2.1.g An increasing number of people are choosing to work from home

CORE

Human resource management

Table 2.1.h Advantages and disadvantages of teleworking and homeworking

	Advantages	Disadvantages
Employees	• Job opportunities, especially for those living in remote areas. • Suitable for those who have to care for family members, e.g. parents of young children or elderly parents. • Flexible working hours. • Benefits of not having to commute, e.g. travel costs, time and stress. • Autonomy in decision-making and choice of how teleworkers organise their work. • Income tax allowances for using personal property for conducting business activity. • Reduction in costs of ICT systems means more people can afford to work from home.	• There is a huge dependence on the use and reliability of ICT software and hardware. • Teleworkers, partly due to the nature of their work, often exceed working time directives. • Teleworkers might suffer from social isolation (including boredom). • There is often less job security and less trade union representation for teleworkers. • Employees are likely to face distractions working at home, especially those with young children. • Teleworkers and homeworkers tend to suffer from a lack of training opportunities and career development.
Employers	• Reduced office overheads as less prime office locations and space are needed. • Flexible and extended working hours can be offered to customers. • Flexible working practises enable the firm to cater for peak and off-peak trade. • Continuity of service from those with young children or other dependents. • Research shows teleworkers have a lower absenteeism rate than office workers. • Flexibility to deal with working time directives (laws), which govern the maximum hours of work per time period.	• Set up costs, such as the cost of ICT equipment, can be very high. • Teleworking requires tight control in recruitment as not everyone has the right profile, e.g. initiative, experience, and self-motivation. • Management, monitoring and control are more difficult as staff are off-site. • Technological breakdowns can cause major disruptions to the business. • Teleworking is not always possible, e.g. lack of space at home or lack of security and confidentiality of data being held at home.

Portfolio working

A **portfolio worker**, a description coined by Charles Handy (1990), is a person employed in a number of different jobs, carried out simultaneously, usually on a part-time or temporary basis. For example, the portfolio worker might be completing a project for one business, whilst conducting market research for another and providing consultancy services for yet another organization. The portfolio worker charges a fee for each unit of work carried out.

Portfolio working increases the flexibility and mobility of an organization's human resources. An advantage for the portfolio worker is that the variety of experiences can contribute to a more fulfilling career. The key drawback is the lack of job security. Ad hoc employment opportunities mean that the portfolio worker might not have any contracts at a particular point in time whilst being very busy at other times with several projects being undertaken concurrently. For instance, plumbers, electricians and landscape gardeners tend to have many projects going on

at the same time in the summer, but are less busy during the winter months.

William Bridges wrote about similar trends in his book, *Job Shift* (1994). He used the term *dejobbing* to explain the increasing number of people becoming independent workers rather than the conventional meaning of being an employee. Couriers, for example, are often classed as 'self-employed' and are responsible for their own costs, although they carry out work for various organizations.

Part-time employment

In many countries, an increasing number of people work part-time. This is partly due to the greater number of females and students opting to work part-time and the benefits of labour flexibility. A key advantage to a business hiring more part-time staff is that they are cheaper to employ. Part-timers are generally entitled to lower remuneration (pay and benefits) compared with their full-time counterparts and are easier to replace if need be. There is also a large pool of people that can work part-time, such as working mothers or full-time college and university students. This helps to keep wages relatively low and gives the employer plenty of choice. Hence, part-timers are said to be 'easy to hire and fire'. Perhaps more importantly though, is that part-time employment gives a business more flexibility, i.e. it is easier to adjust working hours to accommodate fluctuations in demand. Hours can be reduced during off-peak periods and raised again during busier trading times.

However, part-time employees tend to feel less valued and therefore are less loyal to a business. This can negatively affect the level of motivation, productivity and labour retention. Second, a huge amount of time and resources are consumed in hiring, inducting and training new part-time staff. Since labour turnover tends to be higher among part-timers, this on-going process can be expensive and it uses up a lot of valuable management time. It may therefore be more cost effective for some firms to hire full-time workers from the outset.

Flexitime

The traditional working hours for many industries in Western economies was from 9 am until 5 pm. This rigid system no longer applies to the vast majority of businesses. One alternative is to have **shift work** with different groups of people working at different time allocations, such as a team of workers on a 9 am to 5 pm shift and another team on a 12 pm to 8 pm shift. Another alternative is to use **flexitime**, a system which requires employees to work for a core period (say from 9 am to 1 pm) but the rest of the time is 'flexitime'. This means that staff determine when they will work, subject to them getting their

work completed by set deadlines. For example, a worker who is required to work a 36-hour week might be able to work 9-hour shifts from Monday to Thursday and have Friday off.

Both shift work and flexitime can help to extend normal working hours of a business (thereby generating more sales or getting more work done). They also help to reduce the need for paying staff to work overtime. Offering flexitime can improve a firm's image as it is seen to be providing equal opportunities to staff who are unable to work standard hours due to their other important commitments. Flexitime can also be beneficial to employees as it gives them a greater degree of freedom to balance their work and personal life.

Flexitime is increasingly popular in the UK and USA, where more than 25% of women are employed on a flexitime basis. Legislation in the UK, introduced in 2003, made flexitime more accessible to parents of young and/or disabled children. The law was extended in 2007 to give carers of adults the right to request flexitime from their employers.

Flexible work patterns, practices and preferences, such as portfolio working and teleworking, have meant that the average number of hours worked has increased. This has happened despite the employment laws in some countries, such as within the European Union where there is a maximum working week of 48 hours. This trend can provide opportunities for businesses to earn more money for each extra hour that they stay 'open' for trading.

Question 2.1.6 McDonald's

McDonald's is the most globalized fast food restaurant in the world, with over 37,000 outlets in 120 countries. Part of its successful growth strategy has been the ability to adopt **flexible work patterns**. Most of the workers at *McDonald's*, consisting mainly of students and women, are in **part-time employment.** In Australia, the company uses the catchphrase *"Your money, Your hours, Your way"* as part of its recruitment plan. *McDonald's* actively encourages students to apply for jobs at their stores by using slogans such as '*Learn While You Earn'* and '*Work with mates, buy what you want'*. Their careers webpage (www.mcdonalds.co.au/careers) even has sections titled 'Send Site to Friend' and 'Info for your parents'. In countries which encourage flexible work patterns, *McDonald's* has been able to open some of its stores on a 24-hour basis.

(a) (i) Define the term **flexible work patterns**. [2 marks]

(a) (ii) Define the term **part-time employment**. [2 marks]

(b) Examine the costs and benefits of flexible work structures to *McDonald's* and its employees. [6 marks]

(c) Discuss the likely consequences of flexible work patterns on the workforce planning, recruitment and training of *McDonald's*. [10 marks]

Migration of workers

In a globalized world, ever more people are migrating for work purposes. The United Nations defines a migrant worker as "a person who is engaged in a remunerated activity in a State of which he or she is not a national", i.e. anyone working outside their home country. For example, millions of Filipino and Indonesian women work overseas as domestic helpers in countries such as Hong Kong, Singapore, Taiwan, Malaysia and Dubai. Migrant workers contribute to the economic growth of the host country through their production, consumption and the payment of taxes. Many migrant workers also remit a significant proportion of their pay back to their home country, thus benefiting the country of origin. There are numerous reasons for the migration of workers, such as:

- Pay and remuneration – Many multinationals attract migrant expatriate workers, especially those in senior posts, by offering them better pay and remuneration (e.g. relocation allowance, subsidised housing, medical cover and education allowance for those with children). Migrant workers might also choose certain countries for their low tax rates (see Table 2.1.i).

- Employment opportunities – Unemployment and poverty may prompt many workers in low income countries to seek work elsewhere. At the same time, high income countries experiencing economic growth have an increased need for labour, especially unskilled labour.

- Seasonal factors – Farm workers, for example, might migrate during off-peak seasons to find employment in other countries.

- Domestic instability – Political instability, the lack of security and limited business opportunities in the domestic economy are key drivers for migrant workers.

- Higher standard of living – Migrant workers seek a better lifestyle so immigration provides such a possibility. Working overseas may provide better career prospects for migrant workers and more educational opportunities for their children.

Outsourcing, offshoring and re-shoring

Outsourcing, offshoring and re-shoring as human resource strategies. AO3
© IBO, 2017

Globalization has intensified competition in many industries. To compete internationally, firms need to have a competitive advantage. Cost advantages, for example, mean that the firm can reduce prices to gain market share. Alternatively, prices can be left unchanged but the cost advantage from operating on a larger scale (see Unit 1.6) creates greater profit margins.

One strategic way that businesses have strived to gain a cost advantage is by **outsourcing** – the practice of transferring internal business activities (functions) to an external firm as a method of reducing costs. For instance, Sony, Microsoft and Nintendo outsource the production of their games consoles to Taiwan's Foxconn. Subcontractors (the outsourced firms) are able to carry out the outsourced work for less than their clients are able to, without compromising quality (see Box 2.1.g).

Source: http://www.worldwide-tax.

Table 2.1.i Tax rates (max. % rate for selected countries)

Country	Corporate tax	Income tax	Sales tax
Australia	30.0	45	10
Canada	15.0	36	25
China	25.0	45	17
Hong Kong	16.5	17	0
India	40.0	30	15
Mexico	30.0	30	16
Qatar	10.0	0	0
Romania	16.0	16	24
Spain	25.0	45	21
Turkey	20.0	35	18
United Arab Emirates	0.0	0	0
United Kingdom	19.0	45	20
Vietnam	20.0	35	10

CORE

Human resource management

Outsourcing tends to be used for three interrelated reasons:

- When activities are not core to the functions of the business – For example, many firms outsource marketing and security functions. A school may outsource catering services to allow the school to concentrate efforts on its core activities, i.e. teaching and learning.

- When the business lacks specific skills or expertise – For example, subcontractors are often hired to maintain the ICT functions of a business, such as networking and systems upgrades. The services of market research organizations, lawyers and accountants are further examples.

- To cut costs of production – Outsourcing is used if it leads to productivity gains and cost advantages. Many multinational companies, both manufacturers and service providers, have outsourced operations abroad in order to benefit from significantly lower labour costs.

Figure 2.1.h School catering services are often outsourced

> ## Box 2.1.g   Typical business activities/ functions that are outsourced
>
> - Catering
> - Cleaning
> - Customer service call centres
> - Maintenance of information communications technology (ICT) systems
> - Manufacturing of parts and components
> - Property management and maintenance
> - Public relations
> - Recruitment and selection (recruitment agencies)
> - Security systems
> - Training and development (continuous professional development).

Table 2.1.j Advantages and disadvantages of outsourcing

Advantages	Disadvantages
Specialists are hired to carry out the work to high quality standards. This is particularly important if the business does not have the necessary skills and expertise available internally to carry out the outsourced functions.	In their aim to cut costs, subcontractors have been known to 'cut corners' by hiring under-aged, illegal and unqualified workers. This has led to substandard quality and conflict between the contractor and subcontractor.
Different subcontractors will bid (or tender) for the outsourced work. The one with the most attractive overall package will be awarded the contract. This means that the subcontracted work is provided at competitive rates, enabling the business to control its own costs without jeopardising quality assurance.	Quality management can become more difficult. Subcontractors are relied upon for the quality of the outsourced work. Things can go wrong, such as conflicting views about the quality of the output. Allowing external parties to have such a large influence on the reputation of a business can be potentially disastrous.
It helps to reduce labour costs as outsourced workers are not employees of the organization, e.g. they are not remunerated with holiday pay, bonuses, sick leave or pension contributions.	Subcontractors need to be monitored to ensure that deadlines are met and quality standards are observed. This will increase the costs of administering all outsourced activities.
Outsourcing allows the business to concentrate on its core activities, i.e. what it is best at doing. This can therefore help to improve the overall efficiency of the organization.	Outsourcing can initially cause redundancies in the organization. This needs to be managed carefully as it will affect the level of staff morale and motivation within the firm.
Outsourcing improves workforce flexibility. For example, there is no need to recruit employees during busier trading periods as subcontractors can be used to increase output. Conversely, during less busy periods, there is no need to reduce (internal) staffing as the outsourced firm is responsible for staffing.	Outsourcing and offshoring have often been associated with unethical practises, such as the exploitation of labour in less economically developed countries. This may involve poor working conditions, long working hours, low pay, the use of child labour and an absence of health and safety policies.

CORE

Human resource management

143

Question 2.1.7 British school outsources teaching to India

In late 2010, *Ashmount Primary School* in Islington, north London became the first school in the UK to **outsource** its teaching to India. Staff located more than 4,000 miles away are being used to teach children struggling in mathematics. The service, provided by *BrightSpark Education*, costs £12 ($7.5) an hour for each student, which is significantly cheaper than employing private tutors at a cost of £40 ($64) an hour. The service involves students using www.brightsparkeducation. com to complete their work on the computer. They can also talk online to a teacher in India via a headset.

Ashmount Primary School was approached by *BrightSpark Education* to pilot the system. The school claimed that the service had made a considerable improvement to student learning in mathematics, but critics argued the move would undermine teaching standards. They suggested that quality assurance could be an issue, depending on the quality of the tutor's English and cultural awareness. *BrightSpark Education* said that all its tutors are maths graduates with relevant teaching experience.

(a) Define the term **outsource**.   [2 marks]

(b) Evaluate the decision of *Ashmount Primary School* to outsource some of its teaching to tutors in India.   [10 marks]

Offshoring

Offshoring is an extension of outsourcing that involves relocating business activities and processes abroad. It is possible to offshore work but not to outsource it, e.g. moving employees and certain manufacturing activities overseas to take advantage of lower costs and taxes. American and British firms dominate the practice of **offshore outsourcing**. This has made countries such as India and the Philippines highly attractive locations due to their large pool of educated English-speaking workers who earn significantly less than their western counterparts. For example, popular outsourced activities in the Philippines include call centres, financial management, computer software development, and legal transcriptions. New Balance, Puma and Reebok outsource the production of their footwear to China's Yue Yuen Industrial Holdings, the world's largest manufacturer of sports shoes.

Offshore outsourcing of production activities and human resources can help a business to get around protectionist measures used by foreign governments (see Unit 1.5). For example, Nike and Adidas outsource the manufacturing of their sports apparel to firms in China and Indonesia. This helps them to get around the problem of import taxes and other trade restrictions being imposed on the sale of their products in these countries. It also allows the firm to access the latest technologies and developments in manufacturing activities that it does not have an expertise in.

However, critics of offshoring (including offshore outsourcing) have complained about quality management issues. For example, can someone in India really address 'local' banking issues from clients in London, Paris or New York? A survey reported in the *Scotsman* revealed that almost 15% of businesses surveyed had or were switching production back to the UK because output was falling below the expected quality standards.

The benefits of offshoring are also subject to changes in the external environment (see Unit 1.5). For example, the cost savings from offshoring may be wiped out simply because of adverse fluctuations in the exchange rate. Similarly, if the host country experiences high rates of inflation and continual rises in minimum wages, then the business may need to reconsider the use of offshoring.

Re-shoring

Re-shoring is the reverse of offshore outsourcing, i.e. the transfer of business operations back to their country of origin.

Figure 2.1.i Offshore outsourcing is popular among sports shoes manufacturers

For example, US toy firm Wham-O re-shored production of its highly popular Frisbee (flying disc toy) from China to California in 2010. Re-shoring has become more popular as the cost-effectiveness of offshoring has declined for many European and American companies. For example, the *Wall Street Journal* reported that wages in China's manufacturing sector increased by 71% in the first five years following the global financial crisis in 2008. Toyota pulled out of Australia in 2017, citing rising costs of production largely caused by the strength of the Australian dollar. In 2012, The Boston Consulting Group (BCG) found that over a third of American manufacturing companies with annual sales above $1 billion had or were planning to move their production facilities away from China and back to America. The Wall Street Journal reported that wages in China's manufacturing sector increased 71% in the first five years following the global financial crisis in 2008. In 2014, The Financial Times reported similar findings for British firms. Reasons for re-shoring as a human resource strategy include:

- Product recalls and mass-media coverage of outsourced business practices that are unethical have caused concerns for multinational companies. Improving and monitoring the quality and consistency of output is perhaps easier if production is re-shored.

- China losing its status as the 'workshop (factory) of the world'. Labour costs in China have risen sharply as the country continues to experience phenomenal economic growth. Rising wage demands in China mean that it is cheaper to produce in other Asian countries such as Vietnam and Bangladesh. The rising value of China's currency, the renminbi, has also taken its toll.

- Transportation costs continually rising means that is has become more cost-effective for businesses to be located nearer to their customers.

- The increased demand for customization of products has meant the need for businesses to be more responsive to customer demands and market changes, e.g. Starbucks coffee compared to regular coffee from a convenience store, or Subway sandwiches instead of batch produced ready-made sandwiches from a supermarket.

- Domestic governments have also supported and encouraged re-shoring, in order to bring back jobs and balance government budgets. This was particularly important following the aftermath of the global financial crisis of 2008.

Figure 2.1.j Despite a trend in re-shoring, China remains an attractive choice for offshoring

CORE

Human resource management

Human resource planning and the CUEGIS concepts

How innovation, ethical considerations and cultural differences may influence human resource practices and strategies in an organization. AO3

© IBO, 2017

Highly effective managers consider the cultural impacts of human resource planning. For example, although upwards appraisals (that involve subordinates appraising someone more senior in the organization) are used in some countries, they are unpopular in other countries due to their subjective nature. In some cultures, appraising senior staff is regarded as disrespectful and intimidating (for both appraiser and appraisee). Many subordinates are often unwilling to criticise their line managers for fear of being reprimanded at a later date. In some organizations, the culture means that appraisees might also lack the experience to conduct 360 degree feedback or upwards appraisals.

Globalization and innovation require human resource managers to think about how information communication technologies (ICT) contribute to workforce planning. For example, in addition to their own websites, an increasing number of businesses are using commercial websites such as LinkedIn and Facebook as part of their recruitment practice. In a globalized and increasingly complex business world, organizations have used ICT to solve many of their problems and to improve productivity. Managers in multinational companies face growing difficulties in coping with workforces that may be geographically spread across many different countries, with huge culturally differences and working in contrasting political and legal systems. Given such trends, ICT is increasingly used as a tool to improve the capabilities, efficiency and functions of the organization and its workforce.

IB Learner Profile – Be an inquirer and be knowledgable

Investigate how innovations such as Twitter, Facebook and LinkedIn are changing the way that businesses recruit workers. A good starting point is this article from The Hindu Business Line: http://goo.gl/1Fv1R2. You can also read about an innovative way to recruit casual, part-time and temporary workers, launched by the 23-year old CEO of *OneShift* in Australia and New Zealand: http://goo.gl/pcfgop.

IB Learner Profile – Be a thinker

How might the use of new communications technologies encourage collaboration, communication and empowerment in the workplace?

Strategically, managers are increasingly seeking and developing a flexible workforce who are able to adapt to changes in the external business environment. For example, businesses that employ a large proportion of part-time workers, such as fast-food restaurants and supermarkets, are able to take advantage of workforce flexibility according to the needs of the firm. This is also a key reason for the growth in the number of teleworkers and homeworkers in the service sector.

Human resource planning is an essential part of any business strategy. If managers do not make the most of their human resources, the organization will face a number of problems (the 5 Rs):

- *Recruitment* – Higher costs of recruitment, induction and training.

- *Resources* – Increasing amount of resources and time spent on dealing with personnel problems, rather than on achieving organizational objectives.

- *Reservations* – Lower morale and higher levels of uncertainty suffered by existing staff who experience continual change in staffing.

- *Returns* – Lower levels of labour productivity, competitiveness and profits.

Case study

LinkedIn is the world's largest social networking website for people in professional occupations. It launched in 2003 and had over 20 million users within its first three years and almost 260 million users within ten years. By 2018, it had over 530 million registered users in over 200 countries (or over 96,800 members joining each day during its first 15 years of operation!) Employers can list jobs on the website and recruit top workers in a cost-effective way, whilst employees can look for jobs, make connections with other professionals and find business opportunities.

- *Reputation* – Poorer corporate image as the business cannot retain its staff.

Managers are increasingly keen to know why staff leave their firm through the use of exit interviews. These are interviews with staff who have resigned from the organization to establish the true reasons about why staff choose to leave the business. For example, employers might think that the remuneration package offered is competitive, although this might not be the view of the majority of the workers. Data and information from exit interviews can then be used by managers to improve staff retention and strategic human resource planning.

Whilst there are costs associated with improving staff retention, most strategists believe that the long-term benefits are far greater. Theorists and entrepreneurs such as Charles Handy, and Richard Branson argue that human resources should be viewed as an investment and that training and development are an essential part of successful human resource planning.

Successful business strategy also requires managers to acknowledge the need for ongoing training (known as continuous professional development or CPD). Symptoms of poor training or a lack of training include: higher staff absenteeism, low morale, higher staff turnover, poorer quality output, greater waste and more mistakes being made. Hence, provision and adequate funding of CPD is vital for the long-term success of the firm. However, not all CPD programmes are effective.

IB Learner Profile – Be an inquirer and be knowledgable

Visit the ACAS website (www.acas.org.uk) and investigate the costs, causes and consequences of absenteeism to the economy. According to ACAS, which groups of workers are most likely to be absent from work and why?

A successful training strategy should:

- Show commitment to the training and development needs of all staff, perhaps through the discussions in appraisal meetings

- Assess the operational requirements of the organization against the skills of the staff

- Link training and development needs to departmental and organizational objectives

- Help to promote a culture of continuous learning and professional development relevant to the context of the business

- Be cost-effective yet provide equal opportunities for training and development for all staff.

Training programmes also help organizations to achieve a flexible workforce. *Workforce flexibility* refers to the ability of workers to multi-task (carry out a range of different tasks or jobs simultaneously) and to adapt to changes in the business. For example, many retailers have benefited enormously from hiring part-time workers as it means they can open for longer periods. Flexibility allows a business to be more efficient and can help to cut costs (part-time workers, for instance, cost less to employ).

CUEGIS ESSAY

With reference to an organization of your choice, examine how **ethics** and **culture** impact on human resource planning.   [20 marks]

REVIEW QUESTIONS

1. What is meant by human resource management?

2. What is workforce planning?

3. What is labour turnover and how is it calculated?

4. What are demographic changes and how do these influence workforce planning?

5. What is an ageing population and what are the consequences of this for workforce planning?

6. How do new communications technologies influence human resource planning?

7. Why do businesses need to recruit people?

8. Identify the general steps in the recruitment and selection process.

CORE

Human resource management

9. What is a job analysis and why is it important?

10. Differentiate between internal recruitment and external recruitment.

11. What are the objectives and benefits of training?

12. Distinguish between cognitive and behavioural training.

13. Distinguish between formative and summative appraisal.

14. What is the difference between dismissal and redundancy?

15. Why do business use outsourcing and offshoring, whilst others choose re-shoring?

KEY TERMS

360-degree appraisal is a type of appraisal system that provides feedback from a range of employees who work with or have interactions with the person being appraised, e.g. line manager(s), co-workers, subordinates and (sometimes) customers.

An **ageing population** is a demographic change that tends to occur in high-income countries, with the average age of the population getting higher.

Appraisal refers to the formal process of evaluating the contributions and performance of an employee, usually conducted through observations and interviews with the appraisee's line manager.

Behavioural training deals with identifying functional issues that could improve performance in the workplace by developing behavioural changes in the workforce. It is based on the notion that training is meaningless unless a desirable change in behaviour takes place.

Cognitive training is about training and developing mental skills to improve work performance. It is based on the notion that the ability to learn is fundamental to success in the workplace.

Contract of employment refers to the legal agreement between an employer and an employee, detailing the terms and conditions of employment.

Demography is the statistical study of population characteristics, using data such as birth rates, death rates, ageing populations and net migration rates.

Dismissal is the termination of a worker's employment due to employee incompetence (unsatisfactory performance) or a breach of contract.

External recruitment involves hiring staff from outside the organization to fill vacant posts.

Flexible work patterns means the trend in using less core staff and more peripheral workers and subcontractors to improve the flexibility and productivity of the workforce.

Formative appraisals is a type of appraisal system that takes place on a continual basis, rather than at the end of the trading year, in order to allow workers to improve their performance and effectiveness.

Gross misconduct refers to major misdemeanours, such as theft, fraud, endangering others or being drunk at work. Such acts can lead to instant dismissal.

Human resource management (HRM) refers to the role of managers in planning and developing the organization's people. This is done through interrelated functions such as the recruitment, selection, dismissal and training and development of employees.

Human resource planning (or **workforce planning**) is the management process of forecasting an organization's current and future staffing needs.

Induction is training aimed at introducing new staff to the business to get them familiar with the policies, practices and culture of the organization.

Internal recruitment is the practice of hiring people who already work for the firm to fill a position, rather than employing someone new to the organization.

A **job analysis** is part of the recruitment process that involves scrutinising the different components of a job (such as the routine tasks and responsibilities of the post holder) to determine what it entails.

A **job description** is a document that outlines the nature of a particular job, i.e. the roles, tasks and responsibilities. It is used for the recruitment and performance appraisal of employees.

Job evaluation is an assessment of a particular job in relation to other jobs in the organization, so that the remuneration and other rewards and benefits can be determined in an objective, transparent and fair manner.

Labour turnover measures the number of workers who leave a firm as a percentage of the workforce, per year. It is often used to gauge the level of motivation in an organization.

Mentoring is a type of on-the-job training involving a partnership between a mentor and a mentee to help the mentee gain and develop specific skills and knowledge.

Migrant workers are people who move to other countries in search of better job prospects and opportunities.

The **mobility of labour** is the extent to which workers are flexible enough to move to different locations (geographical mobility) and/or their flexibility in changing to different jobs (occupational mobility).

Offshoring is an extension of outsourcing that involves relocating business activities and processes abroad. It is possible to offshore work but not to outsource it, although the practice is dominated by offshore outsourcing.

Off-the-job training refers to training carried out off-site, such as at a tertiary college or training centre. It often requires specialist trainers and equipment that are not available within the business.

On-the- job training refers to training carried out whilst at the workplace, with the training delivered by an in-house specialist, such as a head of department or more experienced colleague.

Outsourcing refers to the practice of using external providers for certain non-core business activities. These firms are able to carry out the outsourced work for less than the business would be able to.

Performance management is the continuous process involving the planning, reviewing and mentoring of employees in order to enhance their performance at work.

A **person specification** is a document that gives the profile of the ideal candidate for a job, such as their skills, qualifications and experience.

Portfolio working means to simultaneously carry out a number of different jobs, often for various employers, usually on a part-time or temporary basis. Examples include freelance editors and management consultants.

Promotion refers to the career advancement of workers, in terms of their hierarchical ranking and professional roles and responsibilities.

Recruitment refers to the process of hiring suitable workers. This entails a thorough job analysis to ensure that the best candidate is hired.

Redeployment means transferring a staff member from a department or branch that no longer requires his/her services to other areas of the business where a vacancy exists.

Redundancies (**retrenchments** or **lay-offs**) occur when the employer can no longer afford to hire the worker or when the job ceases to exist following the completion of a project.

Re-shoring is the reversal of offshore outsourcing, i.e. the transfer of business operations back to its country of origin.

Retention is the opposite of labour turnover, as it measures the ability of a firm to keep its employees at the organization, per time period.

Self-appraisal is a type of appraisal system that involves an individual worker reflecting on and rating his or her own performance against the pre-agreed or benchmark performance standards.

Shortlisting is the process of sifting through applications to identify suitable candidates for a job. It is the stage that precedes the interview in the recruitment process.

Teleworking is a method of workforce planning whereby employees work in a location away from the workplace, such as those working from home or at a call centre.

Training is the process of providing opportunities for workers to acquire employment-related skills and knowledge.

Workforce refers to the number of employees at any one point in time for a particular organization. It is often used to measure the size of businesses.

CORE

Human resource management

2.2 Organizational structure

"The best executive is the one who has sense enough to pick good men to do what he wants done, and self-restraint enough to keep from meddling with them while they do it." - Theodore Roosevelt (1858–1919), 26th President of the USA

SL/HL content	Assessment objective
The following terminology to facilitate understanding of different types of organizational structures: • delegation • span of control • levels of hierarchy • chain of command • bureaucracy • centralization • decentralization • de-layering	AO1
The following types of organizational chart: • flat/horizontal • tall/vertical • hierarchical • by product • by function • by region	AO2, AO4
Changes in organizational structures (such as project-based organization, Handy's 'Shamrock Organization')	AO2
How cultural differences and innovation in communication technologies may impact on communication in an organization	AO3

© IBO, 2017

Organizational structure

Businesses organize their human resources in various ways. In a small business, such as a sole proprietorship, there may be an informal organizational structure; the owner has a range of functions including marketing, operations and finance. Roles can be changed depending on the demands of the job at a particular point in time. The owner also carries out more mundane tasks such as being a sales person and a stock controller. However, in most businesses there is a need for a more formal and organized structure. This helps a business to function more efficiently, due to:

- **Accountability** – shows who is held responsible (or answerable) for each particular job, e.g. the marketing staff are held accountable to the marketing director for their performance.

- **Responsibility** – shows who is in charge of whom and in what role or capacity, e.g. the operations director being in charge of all production workers.

Figure 2.2.a shows a typical structure for a secondary (high) school. The Headteacher (Principal) is at the top of the organizational structure and is ultimately responsible for all the staff in the school. Managers are responsible for their own teams, such as the Head of Modern Foreign Languages who is in charge of the language teachers. S/he is accountable to the Deputy Headteacher (Vice Principal) in charge of the school curriculum. Likewise, the Coordinator of PSE (personal and social education) is accountable to the Heads of Year and responsible for working with the form tutors.

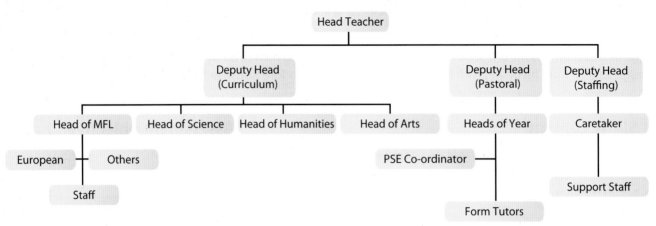

Figure 2.2.a Example of an organization chart for a secondary school

As a business gets larger and more complex, it has to become more structured for tasks and roles to be fulfilled in a manageable and coherent way (see Box 2.2.a). Although businesses differ in their formal structures, the typical configuration consists of different levels of directors, managers and workers (see Figure 2.2.b).

Figure 2.2.b Human resources in an organization

Box 2.2.a   Job roles within an organization

- Chief Executive Officer (CEO) or Managing Director (MD) – The CEO represents the head of the Board of Directors (BOD) and is ultimately responsible for the success of the business and implementing corporate strategy. The CEO is accountable to the company's BOD and shareholders.
- Board of Directors (BOD) – Directors are responsible for the overall running of the business. In a large firm, there is likely to be directors responsible for each key functional area: marketing, human resources, finance and operations management. Collectively, they advise and support the CEO.
- Middle management – Managers are typically responsible for a team of people and/or certain tasks. They are decision makers with responsibility for the day-to-day operations. They assist and are accountable to the BOD. They take on roles and responsibilities as delegated to them by the directors.
- Supervisors and team leaders – Supervisors and team leaders carry out some, but not all, of the duties of middle management. They are involved in making operational decisions (daily or routine decisions) for the organization. They work directly with the workers, for whom they are responsible.
- Other employees (Operatives) – In a large organization, these people form the majority of the workforce. In a school, operatives include: the majority of teachers (those not in a management position), office staff (e.g. secretary and administration staff), technicians, caterers for the canteen, caretaker, cleaners and janitors, and security staff.

Theory of knowledge

Why are there more male Chief Executive Officers than female CEOs?

Delegation and span of control

The following terminology to facilitate understanding of different types of organizational structures: Delegation and Span of control.
AO1
© IBO, 2017

Delegation

As a business grows, managers need to relinquish some of their roles and responsibilities because they are not able to effectively control all aspects of the organization. This passing on of control and authority to others is called **delegation**. It involves the line manager entrusting and empowering staff to complete a task or project but holding them accountable for their actions. The responsibility still remains with the line manager although the actual work is done by the authorised person.

The art of effective delegation is one of the most important skills of managers. Given time and other constraints, managers cannot and should not deal with every single matter themselves. Effective delegation (see Box 2.2.b) has major benefits for both managers and employees:

- The manager saves time by not having to tackle every single task, so can focus more on the strategic issues facing the organization.

- Delegation can motivate and develop employees who feel that they are trusted and that their talents have been recognised.

By contrast, poor delegation causes confusion and a feeling of inadequacy. This leads to demotivated staff, resulting in a failure to achieve the tasks set.

Common mistake

Students often claim that delegation motivates people because of the associated financial rewards. However, delegation does not always involve monetary compensation, but is instead a form of empowerment and so can act as a non-financial motivator (see Unit 2.4).

Box 2.2.b   SMARTER delegation

- **S**pecific – Tasks must be clearly defined so that subordinates can carry them out.
- **M**easurable – Results must be quantifiable to measure the extent to which the delegated task has been achieved.
- **A**greed – Both managers and subordinates must agree to the delegated task to avoid any potential conflict. They should also agree on the amount of power and freedom that goes with the assigned work.
- **R**ealistic – Delegated tasks must be reasonably achievable, otherwise workers will not be dedicated to completing them.
- **T**ime-bound – A timeframe must be set so that tasks are completed in a timely manner.
- **E**thical – Tasks must be delegated fairly to prevent dissatisfaction and resentment. Delegating only dull and unchallenging tasks simply demoralises and demotivates staff.
- **R**ecorded – Tasks should be documented to provide guidance and to aid recognition of them being accomplished. This also allows staff to be credited for their achievements.

Span of control

The span of control refers to the number of people who are directly accountable to a manager. Hence, the higher up a person is in a hierarchy, the wider his/her span of control tends to be. The CEO of a company is directly responsible to the Board of Directors and is also indirectly in charge of all workers in the organization. Hence, the CEO's direct span of control is narrow, but the indirect span of control in very wide.

An advantage of a wide span of control (see Figure 2.2.c) is that fewer layers are needed in the hierarchy. This helps with cost control as there are less managerial positions in the firm. The flatter structure also means that communications between the different levels of the hierarchy should be more effective (in terms of speed and accuracy).

By contrast, a narrow span of control means that there are fewer subordinates who are accountable to a manager (see Figure 2.2.d). It is therefore easier to communicate with and control the team. Smaller teams might also be more productive since there is likely to be better team spirit and cohesiveness. Larger teams tend to suffer from communication problems which

CORE

Human resource management

may cause tension and conflict. However, due to more levels of management in the structure, this system tends to be more costly.

So what is the ideal span of control for a business? Management consultants have been debating this question for decades. It stems from the works of Henri Fayol (1841–1922). It was V.A. Graicunas (1898–1947), a Lithuanian management consultant, who first used empirical evidence to address the question of the optimal span of control. Graicunas suggested that the maximum number of subordinates should be four (in most cases) or five to one manager. He argued that the span of control should be limited because *"One of the surest sources of delay and confusion is to allow any superior to be directly responsible for the control of too many subordinates."* However, there is no consensus on the optimal span of control.

As the business environment continues to evolve, many businesses have opted for wider spans of control. In essence, the decision is judgmental. The degree of control granted to a manager depends on several factors, which can be remembered by the acronym MOST:

- **M**anager – The more skilled and experienced the manager is more likely to have a wider span of control. By contrast, junior managers have a narrower span of control.

- **O**rganizational culture – Narrower spans of control may be required in cultures that require managers to closely monitor and control their subordinates. By contrast, managers in democratic cultures tend to delegate and empower their subordinates, thereby allowing for a wider span of control. Such cultures prefer the term 'span of support'.

- **S**ubordinates – Highly skilled staff are more likely to work in smaller, dynamic teams with their line manager having a relatively wider span of control. Google uses an innovative approach, with a 60:1 span of control.

- **T**ask – Complex, urgent and important tasks tend to require a narrower span of control as communication will be more important, i.e. it is often more effective to have smaller teams where both accountability and responsibility can be clearly identified. By contrast, products that can be mass-produced means that less supervision is needed. Hence, the span of control can be widened as workers have relatively simple tasks that can be done with minimal supervision.

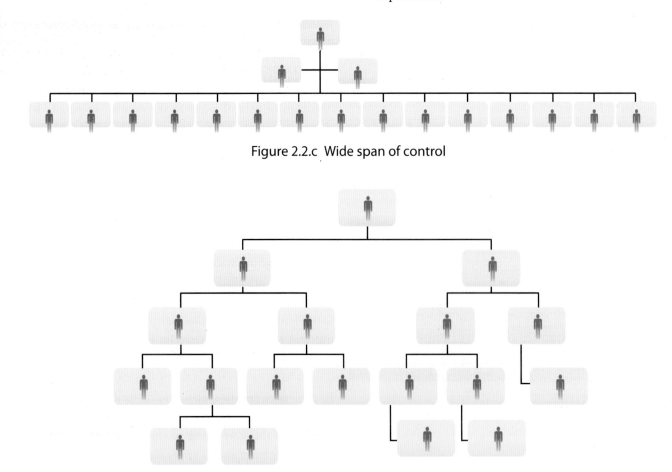

Figure 2.2.c Wide span of control

Figure 2.2.d Narrow span of control

CORE

Human resource management

However, hierarchical structures also have their limitations. Departmentalisation can mean workers are isolated to their official teams (see below for benefits of informal structures). Hierarchical structures also tend to be rather inflexible. This might prove problematic when there are changes in the external business environment that require flexible structural changes in the organization.

Levels of hierarchy

The following terminology to facilitate understanding of different types of organizational structures: Levels of hierarchy, Chain of command and Delayering. AO1
© IBO, 2017

The **hierarchy** in a business refers to the organizational structure based on a ranking system. Those at the top of the hierarchy include the CEO, Chairperson and the Board of Directors. At the other extreme, the most unskilled employees in the organization appear at the bottom of the hierarchy. Each hierarchical level refers to a different rank with its associated degree of authority and responsibility. Figure 2.2.e shows an organization with 5 levels in its hierarchical structure.

The person directly above an employee on the next hierarchical level is known as the **line manager**. For example, in Figure 2.2.e, those on level 5 (the bottom level) of the chart report directly to their line manager on level 4. A line manager is responsible for the day to day management of the people (known as *subordinates*) who are directly on the next level down the hierarchy.

There are two main advantages of using hierarchical structures. First, they show clear lines of communication within the organization. This can improve the coordination and productivity of workers. Second, hierarchical structures establish departments or teams to create a sense of belonging in the workplace so act as a form of motivation (see Unit 2.4).

Chain of command

The chain of command refers to the formal line of authority through which orders are passed down in an organization. This can be seen through a firm's organization chart. Businesses that have only a few levels of hierarchy have a short chain of command. By contrast, the chain of command is long in businesses that have many levels in the hierarchical structure.

For example, in Figure 2.2.a (on page 152), if the Headteacher wanted to get a message to all teachers of Spanish and French, the formal chain of command would be communication via the Deputy Head (of Curriculum) to the Head of Modern Foreign Languages and to the Head of European Languages.

Delayering

Many large businesses have opted to delayer their organizations. Delayering is the process of removing one or more levels in the hierarchy to flatten the organizational structure. This reduces the number of layers and widens the span of control in the hierarchy.

CORE

Human resource management

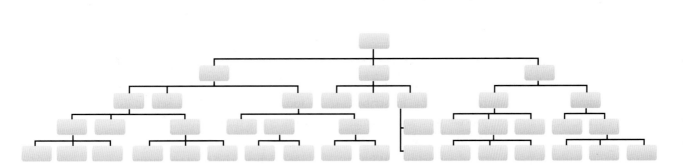

Figure 2.2.e Hierarchical structure

Table 2.2.a Advantages and disadvantages of delayering

Advantages	Disadvantages
Reduces costs by removing levels of management - Cost savings are made on the salaries and benefits previously received by middle management.	**Creates anxiety and a sense of insecurity** among workers who are worried about their jobs, e.g. some are made redundant and others are demoted. These issues harm morale and productivity.
Improves the speed of communication flows by flattening hierarchical structures, i.e. chains of command are reduced.	**Overloads staff** as their workload increases – This can have a counter-productive effect on the quality of work and staff motivation.
Encourages delegation and empowerment as wider spans of control should provide more opportunities for employees to take on wider responsibilities.	Managers deal with larger teams, so **decision-making can take longer**. It can also create problems for meeting deadlines.

Case study

Haier is the world's largest producer of domestic appliances, including air conditioners, washing machines, microwave ovens, cookers, fridges, freezers and televisions. In late 2013, the Chinese company's CEO Zhang Ruimin delayered the firm by removing the company's entire middle management layer from the organizational structure. The move was driven by Zhang's desire to encourage innovation and teamwork.

Common mistake

Many students confuse the terms **downsizing** and **delayering**. Whilst downsizing involves a reduction in the workforce, perhaps due to mass redundancies, delayering simply means removing at least one level in the hierarchical structure, without anyone necessarily losing their job.

Question 2.2.1   Restructuring at Southmead College

More than 50 teachers at *Southmead College* went on strike over staff restructuring plans set out by Trish Dagg, the principal. She argued that restructuring was necessary to cut costs and to generate funds to invest in equipment and staff **training**. The restructured organization would generate minimal redundancies and some middle managers would be demoted to classroom teachers to cut costs. Staff at *Southmead College* were angry as the restructuring meant that some teachers would get a pay cut of up to $11,200 a year.

(a) Define the term **training**.   *[2 marks]*

(b) Discuss the decision to restructure *Southmead College*.   *[10 marks]*

Bureaucracy

The following terminology to facilitate understanding of different types of organizational structures: Bureaucracy. AO1

© IBO, 2017

Bureaucracy is the execution of tasks that are governed by official administrative and formal rules of an organization. Bureaucratic organizations are characterised by prescribed rules and policies, standardised procedures, and formal hierarchical structures. Bureaucracy is often associated with excessive administration, paperwork and formalities. Within an organization, this might include:

- the frequent requirement to fill out unnecessary or tedious paperwork

- staff working in multiple departments and therefore having to report to several managers

- too many committees set up to investigate issues of concern to the organization

- long, official chains of command

- managers with duplicate or overlapping roles and responsibilities.

Figure 2.2.f Bureaucracy involves a lot of paperwork, policies and procedures

Karl Marx (1818–1883), a philosopher and political economist, argued that bureaucracy has a cost to organizations and society. However, as a socialist, he believed that the cost could be justified if bureaucracy is enforced properly. Max Weber (1864–1920), a German economist and socialist, built on the work of Marx, believing that bureaucracy was the ideal organizational structure. He argued that bureaucracy can be synonymous with efficiency because it is simply division of labour being applied to the administrative tasks within an organization. This is why many private sector firms have dedicated administrative departments. He suggested that a bureaucratic organization is governed by several principles, including:

- Continuity – The establishment follows official rules and regulations rather than taking high risks that could jeopardise its survival and continuity.

- Rules and regulations – Business activity is conducted in accordance with the official policies of the organization, such as clear lines of authority, responsibility and accountability.

- Hierarchical structures – Authority and responsibilities are part of a formal hierarchical structure with line managers carrying out their tasks in an impersonal way.

- Accountability – Business activity is conducted with written evidence of compliance with the firm's policies. Formality therefore makes every worker accountable for their own performance.

However, the main drawback of bureaucracy can be summarised by Parkinson's Law (1955): "*Work expands so as to fill the time available for its completion.*" In many organizations, bureaucracy hinders and/or prevents creativity and risk-taking, and often slows down decision-making. Bureaucratic organizations tend to be highly inflexible since formal decision-making becomes slow and perhaps overly cautious.

Centralization and decentralization

The following terminology to facilitate understanding of different types of organizational structures: Centralization and Decentralization. AO1
© IBO, 2017

Decision-making power can be either kept in the hands of a few people or it can be shared out among the workforce. The extent to which authority is concentrated or diluted within an organization depends on the traits and skills of managers and workers, the degree of trust and the corporate culture.

In a **centralized structure**, decision-making is made by a very small number of people. These decision makers, usually the senior management team, simply hold onto decision-making authority and responsibility. Decisions are made through the person(s) in the centre (see Figure 2.2.g) without consultation with other members of the organization. This model was favoured by scientific management practitioners (see Unit 2.4) such as Henri Fayol, Frederick Taylor and Henry Ford.

Some advantages and disadvantages of decentralized structures are given in Table 2.2.b.

The alternative organizational structure is to use **decentralized structures**, whereby decision-making authority and responsibility is shared with others (see Figure 2.2.h). For example, departments or regional offices might be empowered to make decisions on behalf of the overall organization. However, key strategic decisions are still concentrated in the hands of the CEO and the board of directors.

Theory of knowledge

To what extent do organization charts limit our knowledge about an organization?

Table 2.2.b Advantages and disadvantages of centralization

Advantages	Disadvantages
Rapid decision-making There is no need to consult staff on decisions and therefore quick decision-making can take place.	**Added pressure/stress for senior staff** Decision-makers do not delegate authority so could face huge pressures from the extra workload.
Better control Centralization allows managers to have a better overview and tighter control of what is happening in their organizations. This is particularly important in large firms where communications can break down due to a lack of overall control and authority.	**Inflexibility** The organization becomes rather bureaucratic and inflexible as workers have very limited autonomy. They lack opportunities to be creative and simply follow the orders of the decision-makers. Hence, the skills and talents of employees are not exploited.
Better sense of direction Decisions are made by senior managers, i.e. the people who are most qualified to lead the organization. As there are fewer decision-makers, consistency in approach is also more likely to be achieved.	**Possible delays in decision-making** Since a centralized group makes all the decisions, it is likely that many decisions will eventually be delayed. This is simply due to the sheer number of decisions that the group needs to make.
Efficiency Centralized control means that tasks are less likely to be repeated by different people or departments in the organization.	**Demotivating** Employees lack opportunities to make a genuine contribution so motivation and productivity suffer as workers feel less valued.

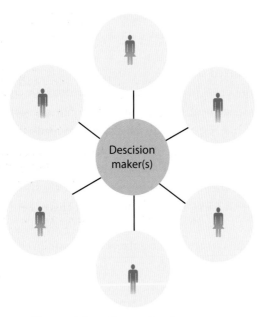

Figure 2.2.g Centralized structure

So the question is whether businesses ought to become more centralized or decentralized. The decision depends on several factors:

- The size of the organization – The larger the firm becomes, the greater the need for decentralization. For example, multinational conglomerates (see Unit 1.6) cannot be efficiently operated by highly centralized structures.

- The scale of importance of the decision – Decisions that have high-cost implications and/or consequences will be centralized.

- The level of risk – High-risk decisions will again remain in the hands of the key decision makers, i.e. remain centralized.

- The corporate culture – Organizations such as computer software companies that rely on the creative and innovative skills of employees tend to be decentralized.

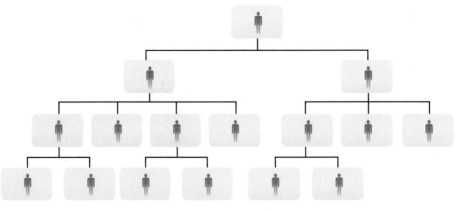

Figure 2.2.h The decentralized structure

By contrast, factory operatives in low-skilled jobs producing mass-produced goods are organized through centralization.

- Management attitudes and competencies – Managers who have a positive outlook towards workers' attitudes and abilities are more likely to delegate authority and responsibility. By contrast, managers who are unwilling to let go of their control or status will centralize decision-making authority.

- The use of information communication technologies (ICT) – Firms that adopt up-to-date methods of ICT are able to decentralize to a greater extent. For example, firms that have a significant number of teleworkers (see Unit 2.1) empower their staff to work from home.

Some advantages and disadvantages of centralized structures are given in Table 2.2.c.

Table 2.2.c Advantages and disadvantages of decentralization

Advantages	Disadvantages
Input from the workforce Firms can benefit from the skills and expertise of their employees, especially their middle managers.	**Costly** Empowerment and delegation often require financial incentives, e.g. better pay and remuneration for middle managers.
Speedier decision-making Planning and execution are more efficient as there is delegation of authority and responsibility.	**Inefficiencies** In decentralized organizations, middle managers might carry out duplicate functions as there is no overview of what everyone else is doing.
Improved morale Empowered staff are more likely to feel valued and motivated as they have some input into decision-making. The autonomy also means that they can use their initiative and feel a sense of ownership for their work, so productivity also improves.	**Greater chances of mistakes** Decentralizing authority and responsibility only works if the empowered are sufficiently competent. With more decision makers, it becomes more difficult to track where mistakes were made or where things went wrong.
Improved accountability Staff are held directly accountable for their input which can lead to improvements in the quality of their work.	**Loss of control** By decentralizing decision-making, authority is diluted. Thus, senior managers have less direct control over the operations of the business.
Teamwork A feature of decentralization is collaborative work across teams and departments. The sharing of ideas can foster harmonious relationships and generate innovative ideas.	**Communication issues** By decentralizing decision-making power, there is a greater need for efficient communication. This might require additional time and resources, thereby adding to overall production costs.

CORE

Question 2.2.2   Ferrari

Ferrari, the Italian sports car manufacturer, was founded in 1947 by Enzo Ferrari. The company prides itself on the outstanding build quality of its prestigious cars. Workers are exceptionally skilled and have a high degree of decision-making power due to **decentralization**. According to *Ferrari,* 88.5% of its 2,695 workers in Maranello, Italy have attended training programmes to develop their managerial and professional skills.

(a) Define the term **decentralization**. *[2 marks]*

(b) Explain why skills training is important to firms such as *Ferrari*. *[4 marks]*

(c) Examine the factors that influence the degree of decentralization at *Ferrari*. *[6 marks]*

Human resource management

Organizational charts

The following types of organization charts: flat/horizontal, tall/vertical, hierarchical, by product, by function and by region.

© IBO, 2017

An **organization chart** is a diagrammatic representation of a firm's formal structure. Formal groups are set up to carry out specific functions, such as a team of finance specialists or a department of marketers (see Figure 2.2.i). Most formal groups are permanent although businesses can set up temporary groups to investigate a particular issue or problem. An organization chart shows five important features of a business:

- The different *functional departments* within a business – In Figure 2.2.i there are four functional departments shown: Marketing, Production, Finance and Human Resources. Each of these is headed by a Director. It shows how different areas of the business link to one another and verifies staff positions in the overall organization.

- The *chain of command* – This shows the various positions of authority in the organization. In particular, it shows which people have direct line authority over others, e.g. the Production Director has line authority over all employees in the Production Department, i.e. the Operations Manager, the Security Director, the Quality Controller, Production operatives and the Security staff.

- The *span of control* – This measures the number of staff directly accountable to a single line manager, e.g. the CEO has a direct span of control of four people (the Directors). Each Director has a direct span of control of one (their deputy manager) except the Production Director who has a span of control of two (the Security Director and the Operations Manager). It shows which people have authority and the extent of the responsibility they have for others.

- The official *channels of communication* – This is the route that messages are communicated within the organization, e.g. communications that concern only the Finance team would go through the CEO, Finance Director, Finance Manager and the Finance staff.

- The *levels of hierarchy* – Figure 2.2.i also shows there are five hierarchical levels. The CEO is at the top level whereas production operatives are on the bottom (fifth) level. It shows which line manager different workers report to, so that there is formal accountability.

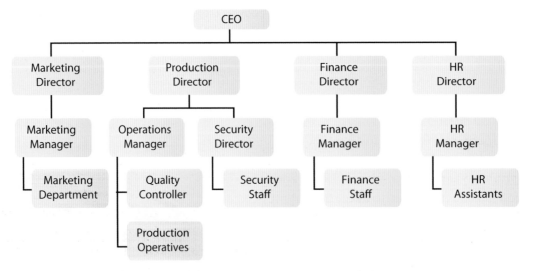

Figure 2.2.i Example of an organizational chart

Question 2.2.3 Organization charts

(a) Construct two organization charts based on the following information:

(i) A partnership with two owners, each with a 50% stake in the business, who have direct control over their five employees. *[2 marks]*

(ii) A private company with three people on the board of directors, three department managers, each with a team of three people. *[4 marks]*

(b) Contrast the two organization charts from above by referring to the span of control and the chain of command. *[4 marks]*

(c) Explain **two** consequences to a business that chooses to adopt a wider span of control. *[4 marks]*

Flat and tall organization charts

Tall organization charts (or **vertical organization charts**) have many levels in the organizational hierarchy. Therefore, managers tend to have a narrower span of control. By contrast, in **flat organization charts** (or **horizontal organization charts**) there are fewer levels (see Figure 2.2.j). Thus, each manager tends to have a wider span of control. Table 2.2.d gives advantages of these structures.

Case study

In 2014, the Bank of Italy flattened its organizational structure, with decision-making power decentralized to the central bank's eight directors. The restructuring was part of the bank's five-year plan to cut its staff by 10%.

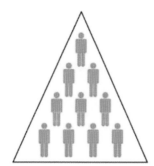
Tall hierarchical structures have narrow spans of control

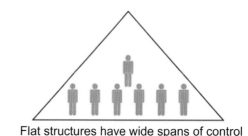
Flat structures have wide spans of control

Figure 2.2.j Tall and flat hierarchical structures

Table 2.2.d Advantages of tall and flat hierarchical structures

Advantages of tall (vertical) structures	Advantages of flat (horizontal) structures
There tends to be quicker and more effective communication within smaller teams. By contrast, a wide span of control means the manager has to communicate with many more people.	Delegation becomes a relatively important part of managing the organization. Hence, there are opportunities for subordinates to take on extra responsibilities and to develop their careers.
Smaller teams are generally easier to control and manage, with greater team cohesiveness.	Communication should be improved overall since there are fewer layers in the hierarchy.
Greater specialization and division of labour can help to increase efficiency and productivity. Hence, managers do not have to spend as much time monitoring their teams.	It is cheaper to operate because there are fewer managers to be hired due to fewer levels in the hierarchy. Many of these managerial functions are either eliminated or delegated.
There are greater opportunities for more people to be promoted as more levels exist in the organizational hierarchy. This can motivate some employees to work harder, thus improving staff retention and labour productivity.	Flat structures can help to eliminate a 'them and us' culture so workers do not feel alienated from senior management, i.e. there is less of a psychological distance between senior managers and those at the bottom of the hierarchy.

CORE

Human resource management

Question 2.2.4 Departments or faculties?

Many IB World Schools are organised by functional departments, who are held accountable to the Senior Leadership Team. For example, Group 3 subjects (such as Business Management, Economics, Geography, History, Philosophy and Psychology) can be organized as completely separate departments (see below). However, in other schools these subjects are grouped together as an Individuals and Societies (or Group 3) Faculty, whereby the individual subjects are coordinated by Head of Subjects who are accountable to the Head of Faculty.

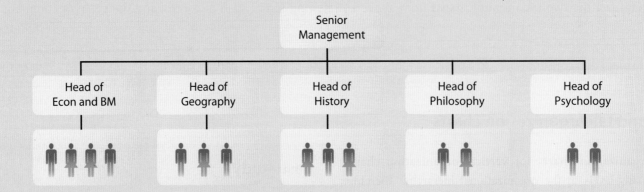

(a) Explain how the above organization chart would be affected if the separate departments were to be line managed by a Head of Faculty.   *[4 marks]*

(b) Discuss whether it is better for schools to be organized as departments or as faculties.   *[10 marks]*

Hierarchical organization charts

A hierarchical structures is a traditional approach to organizing human resources in a business where emphasis is placed on subordinates reporting to their line manager. The position of workers in the hierarchy indicates their rank, status and level of authority. Those at the top of the hierarchy (the CEO and Directors) are the most vital to the organization and are remunerated with a larger salary and benefits as they carry the most responsibility.

Tall hierarchical structures are bureaucratic as there are many levels in the rigid hierarchy, with work processes formally regulated by rules and procedures. Such structures promote specialization as each level has a relatively narrow focus. By contrast, a flat hierarchical structure has only a few levels between the operatives and the CEO.

Organizational structure by product, function and region

- **Organization by product** Most large businesses have a broad range of products. Hence, they might choose to structure their human resources according to the various types of product, e.g. US restaurant giants Yum! Brands Incorporated uses this organizational structure for its various strategic business units (SBU) such as Pizza Hut, Taco Bell and KFC.

- **Organization by function** Most businesses are organized by function, i.e. the different operational roles within a business such as Marketing, Production, Finance and Human Resources. Some businesses will also have functional departments in charge of Administration, ICT and Research and Development (R&D).

- **Organization by region** Multinational companies (see Unit 1.6) are often organized by geographical region. This allows the business to be more aware of and responsive to local cultural differences and consumer needs. Such organizational structures allow regional managers to have better overall control over staffing and training issues.

CORE

Human resource management

The organizational chart in Figure 2.2.k shows organization by product, function and region.

- *Function*: There are three vice presidents of the business, each in charge of one functional area (Marketing, Production and Finance).

- *Region*: Plant managers are located in Taiwan, Singapore and Vietnam. They are accountable to the vice president in charge of production. The same structure exists in these locations for the marketing and finance departments.

- *Product*: Within each region, there is organization based on either consumer products or industrial products.

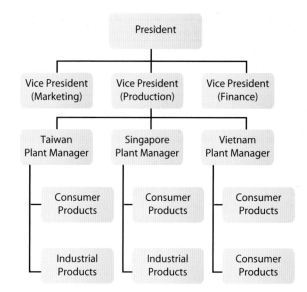

Figure 2.2.k Multi-forms of organizational structure

Question 2.2.5   Organizations and spans of control

(a) With reference to Figure 2.2.k, identify who the plant managers are accountable to and who they are responsible for.   *[2 marks]*

(b) Using Figure 2.2.k, describe what is meant by **span of control** and **levels of hierarchy**.   *[4 marks]*

(c) Explain how an organization chart might be used in a firm's induction programme.   *[4 marks]*

Project-based organization

Changes in organizational structures, such as project-based organization. AO2

© IBO, 2017

In a **project-based organization**, human resources are organized around particular projects. Many businesses use a project-based organization chart, such as those in construction, software engineering, entertainment, aerospace and oil exploration. Project-based structures allow such businesses increased flexibility to adjust quickly to market changes and to adopt rapid innovations. Each project is led by a project manager supported by a team of workers (see Figure 2.2.l). For example, a construction company might have several teams working on different projects such as the building of a bridge, motorway and hospital.

In many businesses, project-based organization is used for a temporary period to execute specific projects, with teams focusing on their assigned project rather than on their position in the firm itself. The workers are often from different functional departments but come together to focus

on completing a particular project. Project managers can have several project groups reporting to them on projects such as product development or expansion in an overseas market.

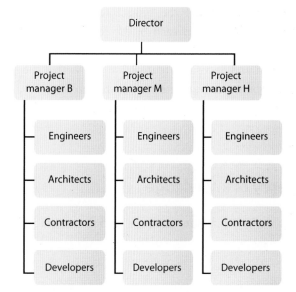

Figure 2.2.l Project-based organization chart

CORE

Human resource management

163

Table 2.2.e Advantages and disadvantages of project-based organization

Advantages of project-based organization	Disadvantages of project-based organization
Flexibility As projects are time-limited by definition, project-based organizational structures continuously change as projects are completed and new ones initiated.	**Discontinuity** As workers always move between projects, with different teams and project managers, there could be fewer opportunities to develop personally and professionally.
Productivity Projects are focused on solutions rather than functionality. Project managers focus on implementation, striving to meet deadlines and operating within the assigned budget.	**Isolation** Each project team is self-sufficient yet only operates temporarily. There are very limited opportunities to work with other teams or people in the rest of the organization.
Efficiency As the project manager has direct control and authority over the project, tasks get done quicker. Efficiency is further improved if the project manager can assemble the team, made up of people most suited to the project.	**Inefficiencies** Each project needs its own finances and team of experts, resulting in a duplication of resources and effort. As people continuously move from one project to another, there can be added pressures/stress for staff.
Motivational Project-based organization can be a source of motivation because individuals are able to work on different projects, so this adds interest and variety to their work. It also broadens their professional experiences.	**Conflicting interests and priorities** Project teams are formed on a temporary basis, so there is less obligation to make sure that team members get along, especially if the members come from departments with different cultural norms.

A common form of project-based organization is the **matrix structure**. This is the flexible organization of employees from different departments within an organization temporarily working together on a particular project. Functional departments still exist, although the project team has the opportunity to work with colleagues from other departments. Each member in the matrix organization is held accountable to two managers - their official department (line) manager and the project manager. Teams work better if the team members are highly skilled and experienced, so the project manager does not need to micro-manage individuals. Hence, it is the capability of team members in matrix structures that is important, rather than their formal rank in the official organizational structure.

Suppose, for example, that a project team was set up to investigate the best way to launch the opening of a new store. The members of the project team might consist of one representative from each of the following departments: Board of Directors, Marketing, Finance, Human Resources, Production and Security. Figure 2.2.m shows that the project team members communicate in a non-hierarchical way instead of the traditional, formal chains of command.

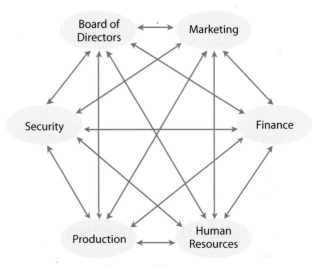

Figure 2.2.m Matrix structure

Handy's Shamrock organization

Changes in organizational structures, such as Handy's Shamrock Organization. AO2

© IBO, 2017

Charles Handy (born 1932), co-founder of the London Business School in 1967, believes that people are the most important resource in any organization. His ideas differed markedly from those of F. W. Taylor (see Unit 2.4) who believed in tall hierarchical structures with close supervision of workers. By contrast, Handy recommends that businesses ought to place greater emphasis on meeting the needs of workers through methods such as *job enrichment* (giving workers more interesting and challenging tasks) and *flexible working practices*. For example, students in part-time employment and mothers with young children would have more choice over the hours that they work. Handy believes this helps to improve the wellbeing and morale of workers.

Theory of knowledge

How do organization structure and communications influence our knowledge of businesses?

CORE

Human resource management

Handy also emphasised the dynamic nature of change within organizations and the external business environment, thus requiring changes in organizational structures. He did not believe in 'jobs for life' but that short-term contracts were more appropriate. He argued that non-essential work (i.e. jobs that can be done by other organizations) should be contracted out to specialists who can do the work more productively and cost efficiently. The trend in the number of businesses that subcontract business activities supports Handy's beliefs. For example, schools might subcontract their non-core services such as security, catering and buildings maintenance.

Figure 2.2.n A shamrock

Due to these structural changes, Handy coined the concept of the **Shamrock organization**. The model gets its name from the shamrock plant (a three-leafed clover). Handy suggested that there are three groups of workers within a Shamrock organization:

- **Core staff**   This group consists of full-time professional workers (such as managers and technicians) who handle the daily operations of the business. They are crucial to the organization's operations, survival and growth. With developments in teleworking and e-commerce (see Unit 4.8) the core staff are becoming an increasingly smaller group. This has led to downsizing and restructuring of the workforce in many businesses.

- **Peripheral workers**   Also known as the **contingent workforce**, this group consists of part-time, temporary and portfolio workers who are employed as and when they are needed. They tend to be paid by piece rate for short periods of employment, thus helping to reduce labour costs for the firm The peripheral group forms the flexible workforce for an organization and constitutes a greater proportion of the workforce for large businesses, e.g. supermarkets such as Walmart, Tesco and Carrefour employ far more part-time staff than full-time workers.

- **Outsourced workers**   This group consists of individuals or businesses that are not employed by the organization but are paid to complete particular and specialized tasks, such as advertising campaigns or skills training. Freelance workers, subcontractors, agencies and the self-employed are examples of outsourced workers; they are hired by an organization for their expertise. For instance, most large firms use marketing agencies to design appropriate promotional campaigns.

The three parts of the Shamrock organization have their own advantages and limitations for a business. The core workers, vital to the organization, must be well paid and remunerated. They are likely to enjoy some degree of job security, be well motivated and highly productive. The peripheral workers will suffer from a lack of job security thereby negatively affecting their morale. However, they present flexibility for an organization and are easier to 'hire and fire'. The outsourced workers are experts in their field but are therefore likely to be relatively expensive.

Although Handy introduced the idea of the Shamrock organization back in the early 1990s, time has shown that businesses are indeed restructuring to become more flexible in their structures, reducing the core staff and using more peripheral and outsourced workers. The trend in modern businesses that use increasingly more part-time workers and teleworkers supports Handy's foresight.

Impact of culture and ICT on communication in organizations

How cultural differences and innovation in communication technologies may impact on communication in an organization.
AO3

© IBO, 2017

Communication is the transfer of information from one party to another. Managers spend a significant part of their time communicating with both internal and external stakeholders. The purposes or objectives of communication include to instruct, clarify, interpret, notify, warn, receive feedback, review and, above all, to inform. Effective communication is vital to the success of any business so that staff are aware of their roles and the expectations of them, and so that managers can gather and act upon feedback from employees, customers and other stakeholders. In other words, effective communication enables people to have a better understanding and control of what they do.

CORE

Human resource management

However, cultural differences have an impact on communication in an organization. For example, language proficiency is a highly valued communication skill in today's ever-more competitive labour market. For instance, English is the official business language in much of Southeast Asia but fluency in native languages such as Mandarin, Hindi and Spanish are also vital in many occupations in that part of the world. Similarly, accents can hinder communication as different pronunciations and tone of voice can cause messages to be misinterpreted or misunderstood.

Cultural ignorance can cause offense to others. For example, KFC's global slogan "We do chicken right" is literally translated into Chinese as 'It's good for us to be prostitutes' – not exactly the best slogan for a family-orientated restaurant! KFC did not take cultural factors into consideration when communicating its marketing message. They clearly did not understand that different cultures have different understandings towards the same thing. By contrast, HSBC's slogan "The world's local bank" suggests they are aware of cultural differences in the countries where they operate.

Figure 2.2.p In Paris, tourist operators employ staff who are fluent in both French and English

Figure 2.2.o The Kingdom of Bhutan did not introduce TV broadcasts until 1999

Innovation in communication technologies also has an impact on communication in organizations. Internet technologies have reduced the cost of domestic and international communications. However, strategic planners need to consider the communication problems that can still occur on an international level where language and culture (see Unit 4.7) can present barriers to effective strategic implementation. Examples of ICT-based communication systems are considered below.

One common way to deal with communication problems on an international scale is to recruit bi-lingual or multi-lingual employees. This trend has been fuelled by globalization and the huge growth in world tourism, which have led to language skills being highly demanded in many tertiary sector industries. For example, staff at Hong Kong Disneyland must be tri-lingual in English, Cantonese and Mandarin. This helps to reduce the impact that language and cultural differences can have as a barrier to effective communication.

IB Learner Profile – Be knowledgeable and be an inquirer

What do the following words all have in common: avatar, bangle, cheetah, cot, guru, juggernaut, jungle, loot, pundit, pyjamas, shampoo, shawl, veranda and yoga? They are all 'English' words from India! Find out what other words from other countries and cultures have made it into the Oxford English Dictionary.

Question 2.2.6 The importance of body language

The key factor to good **communication** is to pay attention to what others have to say. Good communicators are not those who simply speak at others. In business, effective communication is all about establishing a rapport with customers, colleagues and management. Not listening to customers can be a costly mistake; dissatisfied customers mean a loss of sales and less loyalty to the organization. Most experts feel that effective management involves listening to what employees have to say and having consideration for their needs.

In addition to listening skills, good communicators also show positive body language, such as a warm smile and making eye contact when speaking to someone. Research has shown communication is 7% dependent on spoken words, 38% on the tone of the voice whilst the remaining 55% is on non-verbal signals, such as body language.

(a) Define the term **communication**. *[2 marks]*

(b) Outline **two** benefits of good communication to a business of your choice. *[4 marks]*

Electronic mail (email)

Electronic mail is the process of using computer wide area networks (WAN) as a mailing system. Data is electronically transmitted from one computer device to another. It is a very fast method of communication because all the data (text, graphs, charts and images) are already in electronic form. Data can also be transmitted to many different recipients at the same time. The widespread use of mobile devices such as smartphones and tablet computers has cemented the use of email for communication in businesses.

However, the set-up costs can be high, such as the purchase of computer equipment and the maintenance of the system. There is also the ongoing cost of using an Internet service provider.

Data transmission via email is not always secure as it can be hacked into. This is one reason why many people still shy away from using e-commerce and credit cards for online shopping (see Unit 4.8). Also, computer systems and networks can fail (or 'crash'), causing communication failure.

Theory of knowledge

"If a manager cannot communicate something, this is not knowledge." Discuss the extent to which you agree with this statement.

CORE

Question 2.2.7 Email usage at work

Research has shown that most **electronic mail** is accessed at work. However, many of the emails sent are informal (personal) messages, such as arranging social gatherings, rather than official work-related issues. Email usage in the workplace varies from country to country. For countries where email communication is widely used, the result has been an increase in the number of people who are using the Internet to communicate with their colleagues. Some argue that using email in the workplace can improve overall efficiency whilst others believe that it is open to abuse and is an excuse to avoid talking to people.

(a) Outline what is meant by **electronic mail**. *[2 marks]*

(b) Describe how email might encourage informal communication in the workplace. *[2 marks]*

(c) Examine whether email improves the efficiency of communication in the workplace. *[6 marks]*

Human resource management

Mobile devices

The traditional telephone is still immensely popular as a means of communication in organizations, but smartphones and tablet devices such as the iPad are becoming ever more popular for business use. The top four mobile phone producers surpassed one billion units in a year for the first time in 2007; the average Finnish person owns more than two mobile phones; whilst the average Japanese person has a replacement mobile phone every nine months. Mobile devices are used by managers and employees who are 'on the go', such as real estate agents, sales representatives, insurance brokers, teleworkers (see Unit 2.1) and those travelling abroad for business. Technological progress, such as Wi-Fi and digital camera technology, has also further popularised the use of mobile devices as a form of information communication technology.

Figure 2.2.q A tablet PC

Video-conferencing

Video-conferencing uses a combination of telephone, computer and video technology. It allows meetings to take place when staff are in different locations, thereby cutting out travel time and costs. Video-conferencing allows people to talk to each other and see each other as they are being filmed (rather similar to an online conversation using a webcam). More and more multinational companies are using this method for interviewing overseas recruits.

Once the initial start-up costs have been paid for, video-conferencing has the advantage of being much quicker and cheaper than bringing people together in one location. An added advantage over ordinary face-to-face meetings is that video recordings can be made for future reference. However, a major disadvantage is that video-conferencing systems are expensive. Meetings can also be more difficult to conduct due to time zone differences and the over-reliance on technology. Due to possible time lags between sending and receiving messages, large meetings involving many people from numerous locations may have a slightly different 'feel'.

Theory of knowledge

Management guru Peter Drucker said that the most important thing in communication is to hear what isn't being said. To what extent do you agree with this?

Question 2.2.8   Edexcel examination paper blunder

Edexcel is one of the main examination boards in the UK. In 2013, students were forced to sit an incomplete GCSE Maths exam because *Edexcel* failed to include the first seven questions, despite some questions being repeated. The blunder was blamed on a printing error. In the same week, *Edexcel* issued the wrong A Level Maths examination to some schools, giving them an allegedly harder examination paper. The mistakes enraged teachers and parents as *Edexcel's* slip-ups placed extra stress on students. *Edexcel* responded by stating that it had launched an investigation into how the errors occurred and would ensure students would not be penalised during the marking process.

(a) In the context of the case study, explain **two** causes of communication failure.   *[4 marks]*

(b) Examine the importance of effective communication to *Edexcel*.   *[6 marks]*

CORE

Human resource management

Organizational structure and the CUEGIS concepts

Human resources are undoubtedly essential to any business strategy. Effective control and organization of people requires careful strategic human resource planning (see Unit 2.1). An organization chart is an important aspect of strategic planning as it allows people to see:

- The overall structure of human resources in the organization

- Each manger's scope of responsibility

- Those who must report to a certain line manager

- The formal chain of command.

An inefficient organizational structure can cause staff demotivation, a duplication of effort, communication problems, difficulties in coordination and poor decision-making.

As an organization evolves and grows, it is inevitable that change creates new job roles. The increased need for human resources means that managers may have to restructure the organization as part of their overall strategic implementation. For example, it is likely that larger firms require longer chains of command and taller hierarchical structures. Tall structures, which were popularised in the 1930s, have given way to flatter structures in many large organizations today. Delayering not only cuts costs and unnecessary management roles (financial rewards for managers are typically based on their hierarchical rank), but also leads to more effective communication. Delegation of decision-making authority is also pushed down and spread out amongst those lower in the hierarchy. As a result, productivity should improve. For example, Japanese companies found that the strategic implementation of matrix structures and quality circles (see Unit 5.3) creates synergy, thereby improving their overall efficiency and competitiveness. However, overseas expansion also means that managers have to be aware of potential cultural differences and approaches to organizational structures.

Although there has been extensive research into the optimal organizational structure, the conclusion is that there simply isn't a model that suits all organizations. Each model has its own strengths and weaknesses and every business is unique in its character and culture. The 'best' strategy depends on several key factors, including:

- The size of the business – Larger firms require more formal structures.

- Employee competencies – Organizations with highly skilled workers can adopt relatively flat, informal or project-based structures, whereas those with unskilled workers require a more formal and rigorous structure.

- Management attitudes – Managers who are able to trust their staff and are willing to relinquish decision-making power are more likely to implement flatter and flexible work structures.

- The culture of the organization – Innovative firms that are accustomed to change, for example, might opt for more flexible, project-based structures.

In today's fast-paced business environment, where change is unavoidable, flexibility is a key feature of an organization's business strategy. Since many decisions and actions need to be spontaneous, the decision-making process can no longer be heavily centralized. For example, if firms choose as part of their strategy to adopt Handy's Shamrock organization, then the internal structure of the business needs to be reviewed. Change has also led to delayering being caused by **downsizing** (when the size of the core workforce in the Shamrock organization is reduced). This can further reduce a firm's costs because there are fewer staff who are remunerated on full benefits (such as statutory sick pay, holiday pay and contributory pensions). This strategy can lead to more flexible working practices (see Unit 2.1) as firms hire more peripheral and temporary workers. These people are not entitled to the same remuneration as core full-time staff.

Theory of knowledge

Can mass redundancies and downsizing ever be considered as an ethical business practice?

Exam tip!

The examination may require you to apply the CUEGIS concepts in the context of business communication. An example is to ask you to examine how innovation in technology has impacted on communications in a business organization that you have studied.

CORE

Human resource management

Innovation has also meant that electronic methods of communications have a growing importance in the global business world. ICT has allowed for faster yet cheaper communication over long distances. However, this can mean the need to purchase and maintain expensive equipment. Whilst email can be cost effective, the use of mobile phones for international calls is still rather expensive although innovative apps such as Viber, WhatApp, Skype and FaceTime are increasingly popular with small businesses. Nevertheless, business strategy needs to consider contingency plans as organizations that rely heavily on ICT find that operations come to a halt when electronic equipment fails.

CUEGIS ESSAY

With reference to an organization of your choice, examine how **culture** and **change** influence the organizational structure of the business.   *[20 marks]*

REVIEW QUESTIONS

1. What is meant by organizational structure and what is its purpose?

2. What is the difference between accountability and responsibility?

3. What is delegation and how does it relate to the span of control?

4. Distinguish between a wide and a narrow span of control.

5. Explain the difference between flat and tall hierarchical structures.

6. What is the chain of command?

7. Distinguish between centralized and decentralized structures.

8. What is bureaucracy?

9. What is an organization chart?

10. Differentiate between organization by product, function and region.

11. What is project-based organization?

12. Explain how Charles Handy's Shamrock organization changes traditional organizational structures.

13. In the context of human resources, what is meant by communication?

14. Outline how cultural differences have an impact on communication in an organization.

15. How have innovations in technology impacted on communication in businesses?

KEY TERMS

Accountability describes the extent to which a person is held responsible for the success or failure of a task. It allows senior managers to have better control over the running of their organizations.

Bureaucracy is the official administrative and formal rules of an organization that govern business activity. It involves prescribed rules and policies, standardised procedures, and formal hierarchical structures.

Centralized structures occur when the majority of decision making is done by a very small number of people (usually the senior management team) who hold decision making authority and responsibility.

Chain of command refers to the formal line of authority, shown in an organization chart, through which formal orders are passed down.

Communication is the transfer of information from one party to another. The purposes or objectives of communication include to instruct, clarify, interpret, notify, warn, receive feedback, review and, above all, to inform.

Culture refers to the norms, attitudes, values, goals, and practices that characterises an organization. As a concept, the definition can be expanded to a country or a region of the world.

Decentralization occurs when decision making authority and responsibility is shared out with others in the organization.

Delayering is the process of removing levels in the hierarchy to flatten the organizational structure, thereby widening the span of control in the hierarchy.

Delegation is the empowerment of a person lower down in the organizational structure by passing on control and authority to complete a certain task or role.

A **flat organizational structure** means that there are only a few layers in the formal hierarchy and hence managers have a relatively wide span of control.

The **hierarchy** in a business refers to the organizational structure based on a ranking system. Each hierarchical level refers to a different rank with its associated degree of authority and responsibility.

Innovation refers to the process of creating a product (good or service) that is new, better and of commercial value. A **matrix structure** refers to the flexible organization of representatives from different departments temporarily working together on a particular project.

Levels of hierarchy refer to the number of layers of formal authority in an organization. The number of levels is shown in an organizational chart.

Line manager refers to the person directly above an employee in the organizational structure.

Managers are the people responsible for the day-to-day running of the business or a department within the organization.

A **matrix structure** refers to the flexible organization of representatives from different departments temporarily working together on a particular project.

Organization by function refers to structuring a workforce according to business functions, i.e. specialised roles or tasks.

Organization by product refers to structuring a workforce according to the goods or services produced or sold. Each department focuses on a different product within the organization's overall product portfolio.

Organization by region refers to structuring a workforce according to different geographical areas, based on where the firm's operations are.

Organization chart is a diagrammatic representation of a firm's formal structure.

Outsourced workers (or the **contractual fringe**), in Charles Handy's Shamrock organization, are the individuals or organizations hired on a contract basis to carry out a specific but non-core roles in an organization.

Peripheral workers, according to Charles Handy, are the contingent workers consisting of part-time and temporary staff hired by the organization.

A **project-based organization** organizes human resources around particular projects, each led by a project manager. Such structures allow businesses increased flexibility to adjust quickly to market changes and to adopt rapid innovations.

Responsibility refers to who is in charge of whom and in what role or capacity, such as a finance director being responsible for the staff and the operations in the finance department.

The **Shamrock organization** refers to Charles Handy's model that organizations are increasingly made up of core staff who are supported by peripheral workers, consultants and outsourced staff and contractors.

Span of control refers to the number of subordinates overseen by a manager, i.e. the number of people who are directly accountable to the manager.

A **tall organization structure** means that there are many layers in the hierarchy and hence managers have a narrow span of control.

CORE

Human resource management

171

2.3 Leadership and management

"Some are born great, some achieve greatness, and some have greatness thrust upon 'em." - William Shakespeare (1564–1616), British author and playwright

SL/HL content	Assessment objective
The key functions of management	AO2
Management versus leadership	AO2
The following leadership styles: • autocratic • paternalistic • democratic • laissez-faire • situational	AO3
How ethical considerations and cultural differences may influence leadership and management styles in an organization	AO3

© IBO, 2017

Key functions of management

The key functions of management. AO2

© IBO, 2017

The term functions of management refers to the roles and responsibilities of managers. French economist Henri Fayol (1841–1925) investigated the scientific management of labour organization and production. He identified the five functions of management as: to plan, command, control, coordinate and organize business activities.

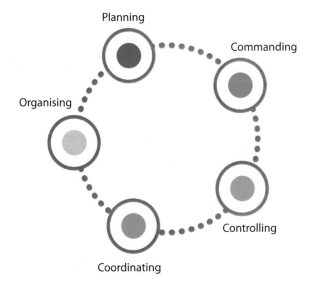

Figure 2.3.a Key functions of management

• Planning Managers are responsible for setting the course of action to achieve organizational objectives. They are involved in setting both tactical plans (short-term plans) and strategic plans (long-term plans).

• Commanding Managers give instructions and orders to their teams and subordinates in order to achieve business objectives. They should enforce discipline in the workplace to prevent slack and to prevent non-compliance.

• Controlling Managers are responsible for the performance and health and safety of their teams. Corrective measures should be taken if targets are not being met.

• Coordinating Managers have the responsibility for ensuring that all departments strive to achieve the goals of the organization.

• Organizing Managers organize resources in order to achieve corporate objectives. This might include delegating or allocating tasks to workers to ensure that deadlines are met.

Human resource management

An alternative perspective on the functions of management was proposed by Charles Handy (born 1932), who outlined three key roles of management:

- *Managers as general practitioners* Handy compared personal health problems with the wellbeing of a firm, such as the level of staff turnover, productivity and customer satisfaction. If there are health problems in the business, then managers must deal with these. For example, if low productivity is a concern, then managers might hire more people, retrain staff and/or dismiss unproductive workers. Alternatively, low productivity could be a result of poor morale so financial incentives might be used to resolve this.

- *Managers as confronters of dilemmas* Handy suggested that managers are relatively well paid because they have to deal with a constant flow of dilemmas (problems). For example, managers are required to let go of some authority when delegating work to their teams, but they must also retain responsibility for the assigned tasks. Other dilemmas include the management of stakeholders (see Unit 1.4) and organizational conflict (see Unit 2.6).

- *Managers as balancers of cultural mixes* Handy argued that it is the manager's role to balance the cultural mix in an organization to get the best out of each individual. Whilst Fayol would have suggested a hierarchical and formal structure to shape and embrace the culture of an organization, Handy argued that organizations should become flatter to improve communications and enhance decision-making.

Handy suggested that effective management of the above roles requires the helicopter factor, i.e. managers and leaders need to rise above situations to see the 'big picture'. Ineffective management, he argued, takes place when there is micro-managing in an organization, i.e. managers get caught up or too involved in every small aspect of the business. Instead, they need to delegate by being generalists rather than specialists.

A third perspective on the functions of management is that of Peter F Drucker (1909–2005). Drucker believed that people are the key to the success of a business. He argued that managers should not get too involved in the daily activities of employees as they have more knowledge in certain areas than their line manager or other colleagues. Hence, Drucker encouraged decentralisation in the workplace (see Unit 2.2). According to Drucker, managers have five basic functions:

- Setting organizational objectives Managers are involved in setting and communicating organizational objectives (see Unit 1.3).

- Organizing tasks and people Managers establish systems (such as an appropriate organizational structure) to ensure the different functional areas of the business are integrated to achieve its objectives.

- Communicating with and motivating people For the workforce to be efficient and productive, managers must build teams that are motivated to achieve the organization's objectives.

- Measuring performance Drucker suggested that job performance should be measured by the extent to which each employee meets performance objectives.

- Developing people Managers are responsible for bringing out the best in people. This might be done through giving workers opportunities to take on extra responsibilities.

Case study

Charles Handy is renowned for being one of Britain's greatest management gurus, having been credited in 2001 as the second most influential management thinker (after Peter Drucker). A graduate from Oxford University, Handy argued that trying to define a manager is less meaningful than examining what a manager actually does. Handy is widely recognised as Europe's best known and most influential social and management philosopher.

Case study

Peter Ferdinand Drucker is widely credited as the father of modern management. During the course of his career as a management consultant and university professor, Drucker wrote 39 books in 65 years. One of his major contributions to business management was the concepts of *SMART objectives* (see Unit 1.3) and *management by objectives* – the idea that what gets measured gets done.

Question 2.3.1 Vinayak Textiles

Vinayak Textiles is a clothing manufacturer that employs 30 people in Hyderabad, India. Wages at the firm exceed the minimum wage in the city and staff have come to expect annual pay rises. The current management team, who adopt a **laissez-faire** approach, has expressed a desire to export the firm's products overseas to gain higher sales and market share. However, mismanagement over the years has led to falling profits and lower competitiveness. Part of the problem is that many of the workers have become complacent, as there is very little supervision.

The new incoming Managing Director, Ritu Vinayak, has hinted at restructuring the organization. She intends to introduce a system whereby staff are remunerated based on their attainment of certain targets. Pay increments would no longer be a right ,but a reward for improved performance.

(a) (i) Define the term **laissez-faire**. *[2 marks]*

(a) (ii) Define the term **sales revenue**. *[2 marks]*

(b) Apply the theories of authors such as Fayol, Handy or Drucker to explain the functions of management at *Vinayak Textiles*. *[6 marks]*

The difference between management and leadership

Management versus leadership. AO2

© IBO, 2017

A leader is someone who influences and inspires others to get things done. A leader fosters motivation, respect, trust and loyalty from the workforce. Leadership is the process of influencing and inspiring others to achieve organizational goals. Leaders tend to focus on achieving broader goals or visions with no definitive time frame in mind.

Mary Parker Follett (1868–1933) famously defined management as *"the art of getting things done through people"*. It is essentially about problem-solving and decision-making, so involves a process of planning, organising and coordinating human and capital resources to achieve organizational objectives. Managers tend to focus on achieving specific goals within a definite time frame.

The terms *management* and *leadership* are often used interchangeably because they serve similar purposes. At times, this is acceptable. However, there are some significant differences and it is important to consider these when referring specifically to either management or leadership:

- *Time and devotion* Management is often described as a '9 am to 5 pm' job whereas leadership is about being responsible 24-hours each day. Professor Warren Bennis argues that managers have a short-term view whereas leaders have a much longer term perspective. In essence, managers deal with tactical decisions whereas leaders handle strategic decisions.

- *Roles and responsibilities* Leaders are accountable for a much broader range of roles and responsibilities. They deal with what and why questions, such as the strategic direction of the organization. Hence, leaders are innovative thinkers; Steve Jobs constantly reminded his staff at Apple that they were *"changing the world"*. By contrast, managers deal with routine how and when questions. They know how best how to administer the day-to-day operations of a business. However, leaders know what the best thing to actually do is.

- *Influence on others* Instructions and orders from managers are listened to because they come from an official position of authority. Leaders, however, inspire and motivate their followers through action. They focus on people rather than concentrating on tasks. Hence, leaders are more socially engaged than managers. Bennis claims the key to competitiveness rests with the ability of leaders to generate intellectual capital (the skills and competencies of the workforce). This means that people can no longer be seen as resources that are simply managed as this would be 'as difficult as herding cats' – a phrase that means it is impossible to manage the unmanageable. Instead, leaders inspire and entrust creative and talented people to help develop the organization.

- *Risk-taking* Managers follow predetermined rules and policies set by the organization. They tackle a particular task by keeping order and control, complying with company policies. Hence, their focus tends to be on accomplishing tasks. Leaders are more radical in their thinking. They take risks by challenging the status quo (the organizational norms) to move the organization forward.

- *Vision* Some theorists argue that it is the vision that leaders have which ultimately separates them from managers. French emperor Napoleon Bonaparte (1769–1821) said, *"A leader is a dealer in hope."* Leaders create a culture of hope, getting people to where they have not been before, whereas managers abide by the procedures and culture of an organization. Managers can do well in stable business environments, but leaders are the ones who shine during times of change.

Despite their differences (see Table 2.3.a), both management and leadership are essential for a business to be successful. It is possible for a manager to also be a leader (and vice versa),

but this is not necessarily desirable. They provide different traits and strengths to enable an organization to meet its objectives.

In essence, the differences between leadership and management can be explained by the differences in their characteristics, roles and outcomes. Large businesses in particular rely on the complementary roles of management and leadership to ensure the efficient running of their organizations.

Exam tip !

Despite the distinction made between leaders and managers, they are not mutually exclusive given that the skills required to be an effective leader or manager are essentially the same. After all, managers have to lead their teams in order to achieve the strategic goals of the organization.

Theory of knowledge

Do leaders and managers apply the (eight) Ways of Knowing differently?

Table 2.3.a Differences between the skills and roles of leaders and managers

Leaders	Managers
Do the right thing (sets goals)	Do things right (achieve goals)
Knowing what's right	Doing what's right
Asks why?	Asks how?
Motivating and inspiring others	Directing and controlling others
Empowering 'followers'	Delegating tasks to subordinates
People orientated	Task orientated
Create and foster a culture of change	Conform to organizational norms
Innovators	Implementers
Action	Position
Takes risks	Averts risks
Strategic decision-making	Tactical planning and monitoring
Respected by others	Listened to by others
Decisiveness	Analysis
Natural instincts	Learned skills

IB Learner Profile – Be principled

Identify someone in the media (such as a politician or business leader) who has demonstrated a lack of moral principles. Discuss the actions of that person and what could have been done better.

Question 2.3.2 School leadership and management

A school is typically led by a Principal (the Head teacher) and a senior **leadership** team. Middle managers are recruited to fill job roles such as Heads of Department and Heads of Year. There might also be a Business Manager, who is in charge of administering the non-teaching aspects of a school, such as buildings maintenance and the **management** of non-teaching staff.

(a) (i) Define the term **leadership**. [2 marks]

(a) (ii) Define the term **management**. [2 marks]

(b) Comment on how the roles of a manager and a leader differ in organizations, such as schools. [4 marks]

(c) Discuss how different management and leadership styles can influence the level of staff motivation in organizations such as schools. [10 marks]

Leadership styles

The following leadership styles: autocratic, paternalistic, democratic, laissez-faire and situational. AO3

© IBO, 2017

Leadership style refers to the ways in which decision makers behave or reveal their behaviour. There are five common styles of leadership:

Autocratic

An autocratic leader is one who makes all the decisions and prefers not to delegate any responsibility. Instead, the autocratic leader (or the authoritarian) simply tells subordinates what to do. This style is suitable in situations that require quick decision-making or when critical decisions have to be made, e.g. during a crisis or when dealing with a hostile takeover. The style is also appropriate when the workers are unskilled so depend on the directions and instructions of leaders.

One drawback is that communication is top-down, so any opinions or suggestions of the workers are ignored. This can cause resentment amongst employees as they have little opportunity to make a real contribution. Hence, authoritarians can alienate and demotivate the workforce that can cause high levels of absenteeism and labour turnover.

Theory of knowledge

Is it possible for employees to thrive under autocratic leadership? Do autocrats necessarily suppress creativity?

Paternalistic

Paternalistic leaders treat their employees as if they were family members by guiding them through a consultation process and acting in the best interest of their subordinates. They have exceptional organizational skills and build trust with their teams. There are two different types of behaviour depending on the perceptions or beliefs of the leader:

- A negative paternalistic style occurs when the leader perceives the workers as less than capable, so leads by guidance and control.

CORE

Human resource management

- A positive paternalistic style occurs when the leader perceives the workers as highly capable, so nurtures and develops the workers.

Whichever approach is taken, the paternalistic leader acts in a fatherly (pater is Latin for 'father') manner to guide and protect the workers. The workers are expected to be loyal and obedient. This style of leadership has worked well in countries such as Japan and India where the cultural setting has enabled people to work hard out of gratitude to their leaders. However, in other cultures and situations, this approach does not work well as workers do not necessarily want their perceived interests to be dictated by someone else – do parents always really know what is best for their children?(!) It is also inappropriate in organizations that have flatter, informal structures where creative thinking is required.

Figure 2.3.b Hyderabad, India, where a paternalistic style tends to work

Democratic

A democratic leader is one who involves employees in the decision-making process. They consult staff and consider their views before making any final decision. Democrats can bring about better morale and job satisfaction as employees are able to express their views and have some input into decision-making. The sharing of ideas can also lead to improved decisions. This leadership style might work more effectively if the leader cannot always be present to ensure that employees remain on task.

However, the main limitation of this approach is that it can delay decision-making because more people are involved in the process. Furthermore, such a style is not suitable when dealing with a very large workforce (since communication would be severely affected) or when there is a high dependence on clear leadership, such as dealing with trade union strike action or a public relations crisis.

Laissez-faire

Laissez-faire leaders are those who have minimal direct input in the work of employees. Instead, they allow subordinates to make their own decisions and to complete tasks in their own way. The leader sets the objectives but it is up to employees to decide how best to achieve these using the resources available to them. This can cause high levels of motivation as staff may feel trusted and highly valued by their employer. Workers might feel that they have control over their work and can contribute to the success of the organization. This style is suitable in businesses or situations where creativity is important, such as in computer software firms or advertising agencies.

A key limitation is that coordination and decision-making can be time-consuming since there is a lack of direct supervision or support. Hence, execution of business strategy can be prolonged, so this style can be unsuitable for businesses or situations that require quick decision-making. It also relies heavily on teamwork and the goodwill of employees to achieve the organization's goals. Laissez-faire leadership might also encourage *slack*, i.e. people ay be less proactive if they know they are not being directly monitored by senior management.

Exam tip !

Students often write in the exams that laissez-faire management is 'good' whilst autocratic management is 'bad' without any substance or justification. Avoid writing such subjective comments. There are circumstances when autocratic leadership is preferred to a laissez-faire approach, such as during a crisis or when dealing with imminent deadlines.

Theory of knowledge

In business management, is trust irrational?

Situational leadership

Situational leadership is a leadership style that, unlike the others above, is not based on any single dominant approach. In essence, it is about using the right leadership style for the right situation. For example, a crisis requires a more autocratic style whereas a laissez-faire approach can be adopted by leaders who have highly skilled and empowered staff.

Situational leadership also suggests that managers and leaders must be able to change and adapt their style to different situations. CLOTS® is a useful acronym for remembering the factors that can affect situational leadership styles:

- **Culture** What type of culture exists within the organization and what are the group norms?

- **Leader** How much trust do leaders have in their employees, how experienced are they as leaders and what is their preferred (or natural) leadership style?

- **Organizational structure** Are hierarchical structures tall or flat? How large is the span of control?

- **Task** To what extent are the tasks difficult, urgent and important? Are the tasks routine and low skilled or highly complex?

- **Subordinates** What are the level of skills, motivation and unity of the employees? How many employees are there?

Warren Bennis, who has devoted all of his professional life to the qualitative study of leadership, showed that leaders find their own style that suits them best. Although they may have a natural or preferred style, it is unlikely that effective managers and leaders will use a single style as different situations require them to adapt. This will depend on several factors such as:

- The traits, personality and experiences of the manager or leader

- The level of skills, experience, motivation and confidence of the employees

- The time frame, i.e. how quickly decisions need to be made

- The task, e.g. whether the task is routine or a crisis

- The degree of importance of the decision, e.g. tactical or strategic decision-making.

Theory of knowledge

To what extent should equity (fairness) inform business decision-making?

CORE

Question 2.3.3 Leadership and management styles

Explain which form of leadership and management style might be most appropriate for the following organizations.

(a) A small local restaurant with 13 employees. *[4 marks]*

(b) The armed forces (military). *[4 marks]*

(c) A typical IB World School that offers the IB Diploma Programme. *[4 marks]*

Human resource management

Question 2.3.4 Situational leadership

Using situational leadership theory, explain how the following situations should be handled by an effective manager or leader.

(a) Yoann is seeking permission to take 2 weeks off work to look after his father who is critically ill. [4 marks]

(b) Kiran is highly demotivated so is not putting in much effort, causing huge concerns for her team. [4 marks]

(c) Monisha has complained that her line manager is using bullying tactics and is not observing the equal opportunities policy of the organization. [4 marks]

Leadership, management and the CUEGIS concepts

How ethical considerations and cultural differences may influence leadership and management styles in an organization. AO3

© IBO, 2017

The preferred style of a leader depends on several factors including cultural styles of leadership. For example, a consensus model of leadership is found in countries like Japan and the Netherlands where group decision making is the norm. By contrast, the charismatic model of leadership is observed in other countries such as the UK, USA or Australia where there is a tradition and expectation that leaders make decisions with decisiveness and transparency.

Ethical considerations are based on the leader's personal values and moral judgement, which in turn determine the extent to which leaders accept responsibility for ensuring the ethical conduct of their organization. Due to the increasing external pressures for businesses to act in a socially responsible manner (see Unit 1.3), there has been greater scrutiny of business activities. Thus, more leaders have been focusing on ethical considerations in their decision-making and in the ways they influence others.

Theory of knowledge

Are paternalistic leaders more ethical than those who adopt an autocratic, democratic or laissez-faire style?

The leadership styles adopted by a business have a direct effect on the levels of morale, commitment and competence in the workplace. In turn, this affects the productivity and profitability of the organization. Hence, it is vital that any business strategy considers effective leadership, especially when implementing changes to the organization.

The trend for modern organizations is a shift away from autocratic leadership (as advocated by the likes of Henri Fayol and FW Taylor) towards a more democratic style of leadership; although this does not imply that organizations cannot thrive under a more authoritarian leadership system. Effective managers and leaders have been observed to trust their staff by delegating responsibility and empowering their subordinates rather than to micro-manage their work. Modern management practices see employees having a role in the decision-making process. Mahatma Gandhi (1869–1948) said, *"I suppose leadership at one time meant muscles; but today it means getting along with people"*. This is not seen as a weakness of leaders but an amplification of their ability to lead others in an everchanging business world where the skills of creativity and service to others are increasingly more important (see Figure 2.3.c).

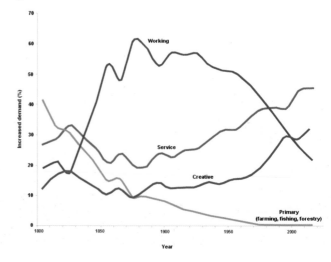

Source: Adapted from www.huffingtonpost.com/richard-florida/creativity-is-the-new-eco_b_1608363.html

Figure 2.3.c The increased demand for creativity

Delegation and empowerment also free up time for leaders and managers to fulfil other strategic responsibilities. Note, however, that not everyone is suitable or wants to take on extra responsibility. Also, managers still retain overall accountability for the delegated work so still need to monitor the progress of their subordinates. The Chinese proverb *"Talk does not cook rice"* suggests that managers and leaders, irrespective of the organizational culture, must set an example by their actions, rather than through talk or positions alone. Albert Einstein said, *"Setting an example is not the main means of influencing another; it is the only means."* Take the children's fable in Box 2.3.a as an illustration of why this is important.

Box 2.3.a   Children's tales and leadership

A mother crab disliked and disapproved of her offspring for walking sideways. Confused, the little crab asked the mother crab for a demonstration on how to perfect his walk. Eventually, the mother crab had to apologise for criticising the little crab as she herself was unable to walk straight.

The occurrence of globalization brings additional complexities to management and leadership. Using a preferred style might not be appropriate in a foreign country where language, cultures and lifestyles are different. Social psychologist Geert Hofstede investigated the links between international cultures and organizational cultures, concluding that people in different cultures expect different things from leaders. He found that knowledge and understanding of such differences can largely affect how managers and leaders behave in a cross-cultural situation.

Figure 2.3.d Culture, traditions and norms have a direct impact on leadership styles

IB Learner Profile – Be a thinker and be reflective

Leaders and entrepreneurs need to have qualities such as confidence, passion, global competency, uniqueness, empathy, creativity, risk-taking ability and alertness to opportunities. Why are most of these entrepreneurial qualities not part of the IB Learner Profile?

IB Learner Profile – Be an inquirer

Leadership styles can vary across national and regional cultures. Read the insightful BBC article (http://goo.gl/Px1HJP) about the CEO of Haier, China's consumer electronics giant. To what extent do you think the sledgehammer and catfish management approaches to leadership would work in your own country.

Case study

Steve Jobs (co-founder of Apple) and Ray Kroc (founder of McDonald's) were known to be autocratic leaders. Hollywood has made movies about these men, showing their drive for success, and the way in which they handled people who dared to question their approach or vision. You can watch the trailer of Jobs (2013), starring Ashton Kutcher as Steve Jobs, here: https://goo.gl/LXgxMA. The trailer for The Founder (2016), starring Michael Keaton as Ray Kroc, can be viewed here: https://goo.gl/LfFFRe.

Theory of knowledge

To what extent do leaders and managers always know what is 'best'?

CORE

Human resource management

CUEGIS ESSAY

With reference to an organization of your choice, examine how **ethics** affect the leadership **strategy**.

[20 marks]

CUEGIS ESSAY

With reference to an organization of your choice, discuss how **globalization** and **cultural** differences may influence leadership styles.

[20 marks]

CUEGIS ESSAY

Discuss how **globalization** and **cultural** differences may influence leadership styles in an organization.

[20 marks]

REVIEW QUESTIONS

1. What are the differences between 'management' and 'leadership'?

2. What are the main functions of management?

3. Distinguish between autocratic, democratic, paternalistic, laissez-faire and situational styles of leadership.

4. What are the five factors that affect situational leadership styles? (Hint: think of the mnemonic CLOTS).

5. How do cultural differences and ethical considerations affect leadership style?

KEY TERMS

Autocratic leadership refers to leaders who adopt an authoritarian approach by making all the decisions rather than delegating any authority to their subordinates. Instead, the autocrat simply tells others what to do.

Democratic leadership refers to leaders who take into account the views of others when making decisions. This participative leadership style means that decision-making is decentralised.

Functions of management refers to the roles of managers, e.g. the planning, organising, commanding, coordinating and controlling of business operations.

Laissez-faire leadership is based on having minimal direct input in the work of employees. Instead, they allow subordinates to make their own decisions and to complete tasks in their own way.

Leadership is the skill of getting things done through other people by inspiring, influencing and invigorating them.

Leadership style refers to the way in which leaders tend to function, such as in an autocratic, paternalistic, democratic, laissez-faire or situational manner.

Management is the practice of achieving an organization's objectives by effectively using and controlling the available human and non-human resources of the business.

A **manager** is someone with decision-making authority within an organization, and has responsibility for problem solving in order to achieve specific organizational goals.

Paternalistic leaders treat their employees as if they were family members, guiding them through a consultation process and acting in the perceived best interest of their subordinates. The leader makes decisions on behalf of the team, building trust and loyalty in the process.

Situational leadership refers to the belief that there is no single leadership style that suits all situations. The 'best' style depends on situational factors, such as the attitudes, behaviour and competencies of managers and workers.

CORE

Human resource management

2.4 Motivation

"If you think you can do a thing or think you can't, you're right." - Henry Ford (1863–1947), US carmaker

SL/HL content	Assessment objective
The following motivation theories: Taylor, Maslow, Herzberg (motivation–hygiene theory), Adams (equity theory) and Pink	AO3
The following types of financial rewards: salary, wages (time and piece rates), commission, profit-related pay, performance-related pay (PRP), employee share ownership schemes, fringe payments (perks)	AO2
The following types of non-financial rewards: job enrichment, job rotation, job enlargement, empowerment, purpose/the opportunity to make a difference, and teamwork	AO2
How financial and non-financial rewards may affect job satisfaction, motivation and productivity in different cultures	AO2

© IBO, 2017

Motivation

Motivation refers to the desire, effort and passion to achieve something. It is the willingness to complete a task or job with enthusiasm. The UK Institute of Management defines motivation as "getting someone to do something you want or, on an individual basis, wanting to do something for yourself for a particular reason."

Many businesses argue that people are their most valuable (and expensive) asset. Therefore, such businesses seek to get the most out of their human resources. Motivation theory looks at how managers seek to motivate their workforce to maximise job satisfaction, staff morale and labour productivity. Businesses need to understand what motivates people in order to achieve their organizational objectives. Box 2.4.a outlines some of the benefits of a motivated workforce. By contrast, a demotivated workforce will hinder the performance of a business. Signs of poor motivation are summarised in Box 2.4.b.

Box 2.4.a   Generic benefits of increased worker motivation

- Higher morale and job satisfaction (which leads to improved productivity and quality)
- Better industrial relations (reduces the chances of conflict in the workplace)
- Lower absenteeism (staff have incentives to turn up for work)
- Lower staff turnover (reduces the costs of hiring replacement staff)
- Improves corporate image (helps to attract customers and potential employees)
- Higher profitability (generated from combining the above benefits).

Theory of knowledge

What knowledge issues arise when attempting to measure the level of motivation in an organization?

Box 2.4.b Warning signs of poor motivation in the workplace

- High absenteeism rate (percentage of workforce that miss work without valid reasons)
- High labour turnover rate (number of staff who leave as a percentage of the total workforce, per year)
- High wastage level (a high percentage of defective output or substandard work)
- Increasing number of customer complaints (due to the poorer quality of output)
- Low quality output (workers are more likely to make mistakes and care less about quality)
- Poor punctuality (poor timekeeping)
- More disciplinary problems (corrective measures are required to deal with less productive staff.

Motivation theories

The following motivation theories: Taylor, Maslow, Herzberg (motivation–hygiene theory), Adams (equity theory) and Pink. AO3

© IBO, 2017

Taylor (1911)

Frederick Winslow Taylor (1856–1915), an American engineer and inventor, advocated the use of piece-rate payment systems, suggesting *"What the workmen want from employers beyond anything else is higher wages."* Taylor's **principles of scientific management** assumed that employees are primarily motivated by money and that productivity could be improved by setting output and efficiency targets related to pay.

Taylor believed it was a manager's duty to decide how each and every individual task should be completed, i.e. it was the manager's role to plan, direct and control. He suggested that *"In the majority of cases, man deliberately plans to do as little as possible"* and that factory workers were ill-equipped to plan their own work but only sought to maximise their economic rewards from work. Hence, Taylor promoted the use of *division of labour* (breaking down different aspects of a job or task and assigning different people to each particular part of the work) thus specialising in the production process to improve efficiency and output.

Taylor also advocated the use of **differentiated piecework** whereby workers are paid a standard level of output and receive a higher rate if they exceed that level. Essentially, it is an incentive scheme that rewards more productive workers. Taylor suggested that workers ought to be scientifically selected for jobs, based on their abilities rather than managers subjectively making decisions based on their perceptions of potential employees.

Taylor's theory of scientific management was highly influential in the 1920s. It was most famously adopted by Henry Ford who used conveyor belt technology to mass produce his Ford Model T cars. Today, McDonald's still uses a system of scientific management. Its catering procedures, such as cooking temperatures and cooking times, are the same all over the world. McDonald's even has its own university to ensure that senior managers are trained to perform their tasks in exactly the same way, wherever they work in the world. It is the managers who routinely inspect production processes in their restaurants to ensure that things run smoothly. Waged-staff are paid using a differentiated piecework system and have no input into how things are done.

Taylor's theory has been criticised for ignoring the *non-physical* contributions of workers. It can be difficult to measure physical output in some professions, e.g. teachers, doctors and social care workers. Hence, scientific management is rather ineffective when referring to jobs that focus on mental rather than physical output. Subsequent studies have also shown that people are not only and simply motivated by money. Taylor's theory ignored non-financial factors that motivate people. Due to higher levels of educational attainment in modern societies, workers do not simply want to be told what to do but prefer to have a say in how things are done. Taylor failed to acknowledge that workers can be innovative and independent thinkers. A final criticism is that scientific management can entail repetitive and monotonous tasks, thereby leading to job dissatisfaction. Although it rewards hard work, employees do not necessarily feel that the financial compensation is sufficient relative to the drawbacks of such a system.

Nevertheless, Taylor's research on how to increase productivity and efficiency levels has stood the test of time. Introduced in the early twentieth century, Taylor's work proved to be highly influential and relevant to businesses at the time. Taylor assumed that people are rational (sensible) so would work harder if they were better paid. US firms introduced mass production and employed low-skilled migrants who were probably most interested in the pay. Today, many businesses throughout the world still use Taylor's approach. The culture, values and beliefs of relatively low paid workers in India, Vietnam and Indonesia make it ideal to use scientific management.

Figure 2.4.a Vietnam's culture is ideal for scientific management

Maslow (1943)

American psychologist Abraham Maslow (1908–1970) focused on the psychological (emotional and mental) needs of workers as he believed that people are motivated by more than just money. He suggested that people would need to be satisfied with their lower level needs before they could progress to higher level needs, e.g. a person suffering from hunger (physiological needs) would not worry about trying to gain recognition (esteem needs). Maslow's hierarchy of needs revealed five levels of needs:

1. **Physiological needs** (or **basic needs**) are the needs that must be met for people to survive, e.g. water, food, air, warmth and sleep. In business terms, the amount of money workers earn determines the extent to which they are able to meet these basic needs.

2. **Security needs** (or **safety needs**) are the demands necessary to make people feel safe and stable, e.g. Christians believe the source of security is found in God. Security needs include predictability (daily structure and routine) and order (protection from harm). For example, businesses can provide job security, sick pay, maternity leave and pensions (retirement income).

3. **Social needs** (or **love and belonging needs**) refer to the human desire to be accepted as part of a friendship group or a family. It is human nature to want to be loved and accepted by others. These needs can be satisfied by communications, social gatherings, weddings, having children and other opportunities to be with people. Business applications of social needs include opportunities to work in teams, and compliance with antidiscrimination laws (which help to promote a sense of worth and belonging at work).

4. **Esteem needs** (or **ego needs**) refer to the desires for recognition and self-respect. *Internal esteem needs* indicate that people need to feel good about themselves (perhaps from a sense of achievement) whereas *external esteem needs* signify the desire for recognition by others (such as having status at work). As Henry Ford (1863–1947) said, *"There is no happiness except in the realisation that we have accomplished something."* Job titles, such as 'Regional Director', can help to boost internal and external ego needs. Schemes such as 'employee of the month' may or may not come with a financial reward, but for many people the recognition is more important than any financial gain. Sincere praise and positive reinforcements can also meet these needs. Internal promotion, rather than recruiting someone from outside the organization, can improve staff morale as this shows that employers have faith in the existing workforce. Training and development opportunities suggest that the organization values its people.

5. **Self-actualisation** is the highest level in Maslow's hierarchy of needs. It refers to the forces that drive people to become the best that they can be. Businesses can encourage this by providing opportunities for personal development and promotion. Maslow argued that people who achieve self-actualisation are democratic in their outlook because to reach self fulfilment, a person must have the freedom over what they do to exploit their talents and in a way that only they know best. Maslow explained this by saying, *"A musician must make music, an artist must paint, a poet must write, if he is to be ultimately happy."*

CORE

Human resource management

Figure 2.4.b Maslow's hierarchy of needs

Case study

Charle Co., a Japanese lingerie maker with a workforce of over 320 people, pays for an all-expenses annual visit to one of Disneyland's theme parks (including flights, entrance and hotel costs). This is in recognition of the contributions of the company's workers during the year.

In reality, it might not be feasible for a business to motivate all workers up the hierarchy of needs. For example, it might be more realistic to satisfy only physiological and security needs of the sales workforce of a large factory or supermarket. It might be more appropriate to concentrate on meeting the higher level needs of core staff such as senior managers. Critics of Maslow's theory also claim the following limitations:

- Levels of needs are somewhat difficult to measure. Maslow was a psychologist and not a scientist, mathematician or entrepreneur. How accurate can businesses really measure and quantify the level of security, ego, esteem and love or belonging in the workplace?

- Maslow assumed that everyone is motivated in the prescribed and chronological order of his model. However, do freelance artists and writers or volunteer workers fit this model? Homeworkers, authors, artists, and self-employed drivers do not get the social interaction of working in an office, but this does not mean they cannot be highly motivated. Some people are willing to sacrifice pay and benefits for better working conditions and job security. Indeed, subsequent studies by the Minneapolis Gas Company from 1945 to 1965 found that people placed security needs as their number one motivator. These extensive studies revealed that advancement, the type of work and being proud of working for the company were the next three key motivators (the latter two do not feature in Maslow's model).

- There is no explanation of what motivates people once they have achieved self actualisation. What drives those who have perhaps already reached self actualisation, such as the likes of Carlos Slim or Bill Gates? What motivates them to continue in their lines of business if they have already achieved so much in their prolific careers? What encourages wealthy people who are past retirement age, (such as Warren Buffet and Larry Ellison) to continue working?

Question 2.4.1   The world's richest billionaires

	Billionaire	Net Worth (US$bn)	Company
1.	Jeff Bezos	$112.0	Founder of Amazon.com
2.	Bill Gates	$90.0	Founder of Microsoft
3.	Warren Buffett	$84.0	CEO of Berkshire Hathaway (conglomerate)
4.	Bernard Arnault	$72.0	CEO of LVMH (Louis Vuitton Moët Hennessy)
5.	Mark Zuckerberg	$71.0	Co-founder and CEO of Facebook
6.	Amancio Ortega	$70.0	Co-founder of Inditex (fashion group)
7.	Carlos Slim Helú	$67.1	America Movil (telecommunications)
8.	Charles Koch	$60.0	Co-owner CEO of Koch Industries (diversified)
9.	David Koch	$58.5	Co-owner of Koch Industries (diversified)
10.	Larry Ellison	$58.5	Co-founder and CEO of Oracle (software)

Source: adapted from *Forbes* magazine World's Richest People Survey (www.forbes.com)

(a) Define the term **motivation**.   *[2 marks]*

(b) Applying the theories of Taylor and Maslow, examine whether people are motivated simply by money.
                                                                                                                                         [6 marks]

(c) Discuss the factors that drive the world's richest people to continue working despite their age or their wealth.
                                                                                                                                         [10 marks]

Expert Tip!

One way to remember Maslow's hierarchy of needs is the 5S model: survival (basic or physiological) needs, security (safety) needs, social needs, self-esteem, and self-actualisation.

Maslow's hierarchy of needs:
The 5S model

Self-actualisation
Self-esteem
Social needs
Security needs
Survival needs

Herzberg (1959)

Professor Frederick Herzberg (1923–2000) investigated the factors that caused satisfaction and dissatisfaction at work. Herzberg focused on the sociological and psychological aspects of work. His research was conducted by a series of interviews with accountants and engineers that resulted in two categories of factors affecting the level of motivation in the workplace: hygiene factors (mainly physical aspects) and motivators (mainly psychological aspects). (Refer to Box 2.4.c.)

Hygiene factors (or **maintenance factors**) are aspects of work that do not motivate but must be met to prevent dissatisfaction, i.e. they must not fall below the level considered to be acceptable by the workforce. Essentially, they are the factors that meet people's basic needs.

NO SMOKING 不吸煙
NO RUNNING 不能運行
NO EATING 不能食品
NO GOSSIP 不能八卦

JUKE RESISTANCE MATERIALS LTD. 繞樹有限公司

Figure 2.4.c Rules, regulations and policies are hygiene factors

Herzberg cited organizational rules, regulations, policies, supervision, working conditions and pay as examples of hygiene factors. So, for example, a business that pays less than average wage, offers no job security and has poor working conditions will negatively affect its employees. Herzberg argued that a pay rise does not in itself motivate as workers can come to expect further pay rises in the future. He suggested that hygiene factors become an expectation and are taken for granted, such as employer contributions to a worker's pension fund. Hence, maintenance factors do not motivate an employee to work any harder.

Motivators are factors that can lead to the psychological growth of workers and hence increase satisfaction and performance at work. Herzberg showed that achievement, recognition, responsibility and advancement of the worker lead to increased worker satisfaction. He argued that the use of motivators would help to improve the nature and content of a job.

Herzberg believed that firms ought to motivate employees by using a democratic leadership style (see Unit 2.3). He argued that businesses should train staff to perform tasks that they were not capable of doing when they were recruited. He suggested that managers could achieve this and worker motivation through three key areas:

- **Job enlargement** involves giving workers more variety in what they do, thus making the work more interesting. This does not necessarily mean that the work is any more challenging.

- **Job enrichment** involves giving workers more complex and challenging tasks to exploit their potential. This should therefore contribute to workers feeling a sense of achievement.

- **Job empowerment** entails delegating decision-making power to workers over their areas of job, helping to boost their overall morale.

Herzberg also looked at the crucial difference between what he called 'movement' and what he understood to be 'motivation'. **Movement** occurs when people do something because they *need* to, perhaps because it is part of their job so they feel obliged to do so, i.e. movement is an extrinsic incentive. By contrast, **motivation** happens when people do something because they *want* to, i.e. it is based on intrinsic reasons. Unlike many theorists who believed that people are motivated by financial rewards, Herzberg felt that workers are motivated by being responsible for their work, i.e. the work itself can be rewarding.

Herzberg's theory allowed managers to think in a different way from previous motivational theorists. The existence of hygiene factors meant it might be better for managers to ensure that workers are not demotivated, rather than hypothesising what might motivate them. Herzberg's arguments also presented problems for managers as he claimed that individuals are unique and therefore what motivates one worker does not necessarily motivate others. Furthermore, people's moods and priorities affect their level of motivation, so what motivates someone today does not necessarily motivate the same person tomorrow.

Critics of Herzberg's two factor theory argue that it does not apply to many occupations, especially those in low-skilled and low-paid jobs, where job enrichment and empowerment are not features of the work. He used professional workers and skilled engineers in his research sample, so the findings might not be representative of other workers. Moreover, some employees may not want enriched jobs as this involves extra responsibility and stress.

Box 2.4.c Herzberg's motivators and hygiene factors

Hygiene factors (job context - causes of dissatisfaction)
- Job security
- Organizational policies, rules and regulations
- Pay – salaries and wages
- Physical security
- Physical working conditions
- Relationship with peers, subordinates and supervisors
- Status
- Supervision and coordination.

Motivators (job content - causes of satisfaction)
- Achievement
- Advancement
- Interesting tasks
- Opportunities for promotion
- Personal growth
- Recognition
- Responsibility
- Work itself.

Question 2.4.2 Richer Sounds

Julian Richer (born 1959) is the Managing Director and founder of Richer Sounds, a hi-fi and home cinema retailer specialising in audio equipment such as LCD televisions, DVD players and amplifiers. In 1978, aged just nineteen, Richer opened his first store in London Bridge. The company has 53 retail outlets throughout the UK. In 1994, his flagship store in London Bridge set a new Guinness World Record for the highest sales per square metre of any retail outlet in the world – a staggering £195,426 ($322,450) per square metre – a record held for over two decades. Richer Sounds has also won many awards, including *Which?* magazine's Best Retailer Award and the *Sunday Times* award for Britain's best employer. The company is also one of the UK's most generous donors, allocating 15% of its annual profits to charitable organizations.

Richer believes it is vital that his staff have fun and enjoy their work. He is renowned for empowering staff to make a difference to the company. Each week, he looks at employee suggestions and awards up to £20,000 ($33,000) for an idea. Each month, the top three sales people get to use his personal Bentley or Rolls-Royce for a weekend. He only promotes people internally. Richer argues that businesses with demotivated staff face lower productivity due to higher absenteeism, labour turnover, theft and customer complaints.

Sources: www.richersounds.co.uk, www.richerstudentszone.co.uk and *The Richer Way*, by Julian Richer

(a) Describe the meaning of **empowering**. *[2 marks]*

(b) Explain how motivation can lead to improved labour productivity. *[4 marks]*

(c) Examine how the views of leaders, such as Julian Richer, can affect the successful implementation of motivation in the workplace. *[6 marks]*

CORE

Human resource management

Theory of knowledge

How can we possibly know the true meaning of a motivation theory if the theorist (such as Taylor, Maslow or Herzberg) is no longer alive?

Adams's Equity theory (1963)

Behavioural psychologist John Stacey Adams suggested that workers will naturally compare their efforts or rewards to those of others in the workplace (subordinates, peers and superiors). Each worker should receive remuneration (salary plus fringe benefits) that reflects their efforts. The degree of equity in an organization is based on the ratio of inputs (contributions made by the employee) to outcomes (financial and non-financial rewards). Typical inputs include expertise, experience, enthusiasm and effort. Outcomes typically include remuneration, recognition (praise), rank and responsibilities.

Adams argued that workers will only be motivated if their input to outcome ratio is seen to be equitable (fair) in relation to others in the workplace (see Table 2.4.a). He suggested that the degree of equity in the workplace has a direct impact on the level of motivation on three levels:

- *Equity norm* Workers expect an equitable remuneration for their contributions in their jobs. Adams proposed that businesses strive to ensure staff perceive equity in the workplace.

- *Social comparison* Workers determine what is fair based on comparisons of their inputs and outcomes with those of their peers (co-workers). Inequities exist if those who put in relatively more effort (or have to contribute more as part of their job) are paid comparatively less.

- *Cognitive distortion* Workers who feel under-compensated (inputs are greater than outcomes), become demotivated so might withdraw any goodwill. They can seek a balance by altering their inputs (such as putting in less effort) and/or outcomes (negotiate a pay rise).

Exam tip !

To contextualise equity theory, consider how you might feel if your teacher gives you a lower predicted grade for Business Management despite you putting in a huge amount of effort, yet your friend who has put in very little effort is given a higher predicted grade from the same teacher.

If inequities are not dealt with, absenteeism will increase (see Box 2.4.d) and workers can become disruptive to the organization. In severe cases of inequities, workers might even resign from their jobs. Therefore, an equitable balance in the ratio of inputs to outcomes means workers should have greater satisfaction in their jobs, helping to ensure positive, productive and professional relationships at work.

Table 2.4.a Examples of perceived equity and inequity

Perceived equity	Perceived inequity
Senior managers getting higher compensation packages because the value of their experience and skills (inputs) is greater.	A worker gets greater recognition and remuneration for his/her contributions, although other colleagues have done the same amount and quality of work.
More productive sales people are paid more. The pay differential acts as an incentive to work harder.	A colleague getting more time than others to complete the same tasks.
Part-time workers, such as full-time university students or mothers of young children, earn lower monetary compensation.	Workers get a 5% pay rise due to record profits being earned, but a rival firm grants its workers an 8% pay rise.
The captain or most valued player of a professional sports team gets paid more than other members of the team due to the skills and leadership qualities.	Two similarly ranked managers have different sized offices, one with air conditioning and a nice view whilst the other does not.

Box 2.4.d Costs of high absenteeism

- Hiring temporary staff to cover for absent workers.
- Overtime costs and disruptions to staff who take on the workload of absent personnel.
- Lower productivity since the absent worker's expertise is missed.
- Understaffing which causes detrimental effects on output, staff morale and customer service.

Exam tip !

Equity (fairness) is not the same as equality (sameness). Achieving equity in the workplace means the organization is fair, attentive, and appreciative. Equality would mean all workers being paid exactly the same, which might not be fair for a range of reasons.

However, critics of equity theory point out that the concept of fairness is highly subjective. Two people with the same qualifications and skills, performing the same jobs for the same remuneration might have very different perceptions of what is 'fair'. Some people are more sensitive to issues of equity than others; the theory ignores demographic, psychological and cultural variables that can affect perceptions of fairness. Furthermore, whilst workers can accept that senior staff are compensated more, there is a limit to the scales of equity so it can be highly demotivating if executive directors are excessively remunerated. Therefore, these issues and perceptions need to be managed effectively.

Box 2.4.e Perceptions of equality in the workplace

- Is it fair that the average salary is higher for men that for women?
- Is it fair that women can typically retire earlier than men, even though men in general have a shorter life span?
- Is it fairer for the boss to leave work before his/her employees?
- Is it fair to impose differentiated minimum wage rates that are dependent on a person's age?
- Why don't some countries have anti-discrimination laws regarding a person's age, race, gender, sexual orientation, religion, national origin or physical disability?

CORE

Human resource management

Question 2.4.3 Tanusankar Business School

Tanusankar Business School (TBS) is a **non-government organization** that provides professional courses in Business Management. Tanusankar Chakrabor, the founding president of *TBS*, is seeking to employ a new vice president and a marketing lecturer on a two-year renewable contract by mutual agreement and subject to performance. As a prestigious business school, *TBS* requires all successful applicants to have a minimum of four years full time relevant experience. The following information was collated for the advertised posts:

	Vice president	Marketing lecturer
Salary	$78,000	$45,000
Housing allowance	$10,000	$18,000
Gratuity *	22%	22%
Pension ^	$1,250	$1,250

* Gratuity is paid as an end of contract bonus, based on the percentage of a worker's salary.
^ Employer's contribution towards employee's pension fund.

(a) Define the term **non-government organization**. *[2 marks]*

(b) Using the data above, and with reference to equity theory, evaluate the extent to which the remuneration package at *TBS* might motivate its employees. *[10 marks]*

Pink (2009)

American author Daniel H. Pink challenges twentieth century thinking about the effectiveness of traditional rewards to motivate people in the twenty-first century. Motivation theorists of the last century, such as FW Taylor, suggested that monetary rewards such as bonuses and commission could be used to motivate workers. However, Pink argues that such traditional rewards simply 'dulls' and 'blocks' the essential skill of creativity, required from today's workforce.

In his book *Drive: The Surprising Truth About What Motivates Us*, Pink argues extrinsic factors no longer work because humans are not the same as horses so you can't get people to move *"by dangling a crunchier carrot or wielding a sharper stick."* His theory is based on three innate factors that drive (or motivate) people at work, school and in their personal lives:

- **Autonomy** – Self-sufficient to direct our own lives

- **Mastery** – Self-improvement to learn and create new things

- **Purpose** – Self-esteem and drive to do better by ourselves.

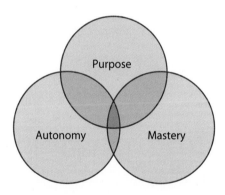

Figure 2.4.d Pink's intrinsic driving motivators

Autonomy Organizations can provide employees with autonomy in various aspects of their work:

- Task refers to what workers do, e.g. Google allows employees the space, time and resources to work on projects and problems in a creative way. New initiatives and innovations are often generated when workers have time to be creative, yet most organizations are far 'too busy' to allow this to happen.

- Time refers to when workers do their tasks. Businesses of the 21st Century are far more flexible organizations, allowing employees to have greater flexibility over when they complete tasks rather than working to fixed schedules, e.g. freelance personnel working from home.

- Technique refers to how workers do their tasks. Pink argues that traditional command and control techniques are no longer effective in modern society; instead only initial guidance is needed. Workers should be empowered and entrusted to tackle the task in the way they see fit rather than being told how to do things.

- Team refers to whom employees work with to complete a task. Organizations can promote some degree of autonomy by allowing workers to assemble their own teams or to have some choice over who they work with on certain projects.

Mastery This innate driver of motivation allows people to become better at something that matters to them as individuals. For example, not all teachers aspire to become senior leaders or principals as their passion remains in teaching their subject rather than leading an educational establishment. Mastery is important to motivation simply because people generally want to improve their work as it makes them feel better. This is critical to motivation because the risks of providing tasks below an employee's capabilities are boredom and demotivation, whilst anxiety and demotivation are the result of providing tasks that are beyond their capabilities (from being unable to do the job effectively). Pink advocates the use of 'Goldilocks tasks' (those that aren't too demanding or too simple) so that employees can extend and develop their skills and expertise. To create a work environment where mastery is possible, Pink suggests four essential elements: autonomy, crystal clear goals, immediate feedback and Goldilocks tasks. Type I behaviour, Pink argues, ensures efforts are made by people to improve at something that really matters to them, whether they are athletes, academics, authors or astronomers.

Purpose This is the third leg in the tripod of Type I behaviour. Purpose gives context to autonomy and mastery. Many students are demotivated in class because they don't understand the purpose – 'Why do I need to learn this?' and 'Will I ever use this in my future career?' are the sorts of questions that suggest there is a mismatch between the teacher's and students' perception of purpose. For Pink, purpose maximisation is as important as profit maximisation to inspire and guide people. In modern societies where corporate social responsibilities (CSR) are the norm, the use of profits must have a real purpose. Pink argues that enabling employees to have autonomy over how their organization gives back to the community can improve their motivation far more than using the profits for individual

CORE

Human resource management

rewards and bonuses. As the English proverb goes, *"It is better to give than to receive."* To ensure this psychological need is met, managers must clearly communicate the purpose to make sure employees know and understand the firm's purpose goals. Pink argues that employees who understand how their individual roles contribute to the purpose (vision) of their organization are far more likely to be satisfied in their work. Unlike managers, workers are not motivated by profit maximisation as it has no real impact on their wellbeing; instead the pressure to achieve profit maximisation is likely to have the opposite effect and contribute to their ill-being.

Figure 2.4.e Employee wellbeing room, where staff can relax and recharge

Pink distinguishes between Type X (extrinsic) and Type I (intrinsic) people. Type X people are motivated by extrinsic desires such as money and other rewards. Pink provides plenty of empirical evidence to show that Type I (intrinsically motivated people) usually outperform Type X people (their reward-seeking counterparts). For example, he quotes a Cornell University study on workers' autonomy at 320 small businesses concluding that firms that offered autonomy grew at four times the rate of the control-oriented businesses.

Although Pink's theory does not focus on financial rewards, he acknowledges that without adequate 'baseline rewards' (such as salaries and perks), people cannot satisfy their basic human needs. Pink argued that baseline rewards need to be both internally fair (workers want to know they are being paid fairly in comparison to their colleagues) and externally fair (being paid fairly in comparison to those working in the same industry). However, Pink's theory argues that financial remuneration and rewards are not and should not be the primary way of motivating people.

Whilst Pink argues that the rewards and punishments approach is not relevant for today's workforce, critics are not convinced that the theory applies across professions, national borders and cultures. For example, do top professional footballers switch between clubs (employers) primarily because of intrinsic values such as being able to play for a more prestigious club or to play in the first team each week (as Pink would argue) or mainly because of the financial rewards offered by the larger football club?

Case study

In August 2017, Neymar da Silva Santos Júnior (aged 25) became the world's most expensive football player having switched from Spanish club Barcelona to French club Paris Saint-Germain, who paid a world record €222 million ($268.7 million) for his services.

The Brazilian football player's weekly wages were reported to be around £600,000, i.e. $118,600 per day or over $83 every minute, even when asleep! A day's work for Neymar equated to about eight times the annual salary of the average person in Brazil!

Only Neymar himself truly knows the driving forces behind his move from Barcelona to PSG.

IB Learner Profile – Be a thinker

To what extent do you think that Pink's theory of motivation applies in the context of your country?

Watch Pink's entertaining TED Talk about his Drive theory before you answer this question: https://goo.gl/z6MZsv

Theory of knowledge

What do we really 'know' about motivation? Why is there no dominant motivation theory?

Table 2.4.b Summary of motivational theorists and their main findings

Theorist	Theory	Main findings
F.W. Taylor	Scientific management	Pay, above all, is the main source of motivation
A Maslow	Hierarchy of needs	Levels of human needs, from physiological to self-actualisation
F Herzberg	Two factor theory	Hygiene factors (which do not motivate alone) and Motivators
J.S. Adams	Equity theory	Workers are motivated if there is fairness in remuneration packages
D.H. Pink	Drive theory	Autonomy, mastery and purpose are the drivers of motivation in modern societies of the 21st century

Financial rewards

The following types of financial rewards: salary, wages (time and piece rates), commission, profit-related pay, performance-related pay (PRP), employee share ownership schemes, and fringe payments (perks). AO2

© IBO, 2017

Financial rewards are methods that businesses can use to motivate workers by using some form of monetary payment. The main methods of financial reward systems are considered below.

Salary

Salaries are financial rewards set at a fixed annual rate but paid on a monthly basis, e.g. a person earning $36,000 per year is paid $3,000 per month. Salaries can improve a firm's cash flow as workers are paid a fixed amount just once a month, usually directly into the worker's bank account. This is also safer and more convenient since there is no need to pay workers in cash. Salaried workers often have to work more than their contracted hours but are unlikely to be paid for this extra work as any overtime is usually considered to be part of the job (just ask your teachers!) By contrast, those earning wages might be paid in cash on a daily basis.

Salaries are used where output or productivity is not easy to measure and where linking pay with speed can lead to lower quality standards, e.g. as in the case of teachers and doctors. However, salaries suffer from two key disadvantages:

- Since it is not easy to distinguish the efforts or output of different workers, it can be difficult to reward those who are more productive.

- There is little, if any, incentive to work harder since people are paid the same amount for their time. This can encourage slack or procrastination in the workplace.

One way to deal with these problems is to introduce a system of *performance management* and *performance appraisal* (see Unit 2.1).

Wages (time and piece rates)

Wages are the reward for labour services, usually expressed as an hourly rate (time) or as a measurable quantity of output (piece rate). Wages based on time can be paid per hour, per day or per week. Unskilled workers tend to be paid by hourly rates. The wage rate is likely to depend on the worker's experience and responsibilities.

In many countries, a **national minimum wage** is set by the government, so all employers must pay their workers no less than the stated rate. Wage earners are often paid an **overtime rate** for the hours they work in excess of their contracted hours. It is common for overtime to be paid at time and a half (50% extra pay per hour) or double pay (100% extra pay per hour) to compensate the employee for sacrificing more leisure time.

The advantage of using wages is that it is a straightforward method that is easily understood by the employees. The key disadvantage, however, is that workers are not rewarded for their efforts but their time. This might encourage slack and poor productivity.

CORE

Human resource management

Figure 2.4.f The more hours worked, the more wages a worker receives

Piece rate is a payment system that can get around the problem of wages by rewarding more productive workers. Piece rate, advocated by FW Taylor, pays workers for each item that they produce or sell per time period, e.g. if a machinist in a clothing factory gets paid $1.20 per garment and manages to produce 200 items of clothing in a week, then the gross earnings would be $240. This ensures that workers are paid for the amount of work they actually do, e.g. the more rides taxi drivers complete, the higher their incomes become.

The key advantage is that employees have an incentive to work hard to maximise their incomes. However, there might

be a trade-off between the quantity and quality of output so there tends to be a need for supervision and quality control. Staff might also be demoralised due to the uncertain level of income, often caused by factors beyond their own control (such as mechanical failure), which would reduce their productivity and hence their pay.

Common mistake

Students often use the terms 'salary' and 'wage' interchangeably. However, salaries are a fixed cost whereas wages are a variable cost. Instead, it might be better for you to use the terms 'remuneration' and 'earnings'.

IB Learner Profile – Be an inquirer

Go to the KPMG website (www.kpmg.com) or a similar website to investigate which countries charge the highest rates of income tax and which countries charge a *zero* rate of income tax.

Question 2.4.4 Calculating financial rewards

(a) Outline the meaning of a time-rate financial reward system. *[2 marks]*

(b) Pravin earns $5 per hour as a part-time worker at a fast-food restaurant. His contracted hours are 12.5 hours per week. Calculate his weekly gross pay.

[2 marks]

(c) Marj earns $2,400 per month. Income tax rate is 15% and his personal tax allowance is $15,000 per year. Use these figures to calculate Marj's:
(i) annual gross income *[2 marks]*
(ii) annual taxable income *[2 marks]*
(iii) annual take-home pay. *[2 marks]*

(d) Buki is a salaried teacher at a school, earning $3,400 per calendar month. Calculate how much she earns per week.
[2 marks]

(e) As a salesperson, Phil earns a basic salary of $1,250 per month. Last month, he sold goods to the value of $12,000 for which he earns 5% commission. Calculate Phil's gross pay for the month. *[3 marks]*

The earnings of most employees are subject to personal income tax and other deductions. The total amount earned during a period of time is called the gross earnings. The government allows people to earn a certain amount of money (known as the tax allowance) before they pay income tax. The amount received after all deductions are paid is known as net earnings, i.e. the take-home pay.

Commission

Commission pays workers based on a proportion (percentage) of sales or output contributed by a worker. This contrasts with *piece rate* which is a fixed amount per unit made or sold. For example, real estate agents might get paid 1% (the commission) of the value of each property personally sold. So, an agent that sells a $500,000 property would earn $5,000 in commission. This payment system is commonly found in jobs where financial rewards act as an incentive to sell more, e.g. insurance brokers receive a percentage of the premiums paid on policies that they have arranged.

It is common for those on piece rate or commission to receive a basic salary. To some extent, this helps to meet their physiological needs so even if the person does not manage to sell anything, then they will still be paid a basic amount. However, for each item sold, salespeople will earn commission thereby boosting their overall earnings.

Output-based reward systems such as commission can overcome the problems of time-based systems such as wages. However, they suffer from their own limitations:

- Speedy production or aggressive selling techniques do not necessarily correlate with high quality output or good customer care.

- There is added pressure on workers to sell more or to perform at a faster pace.

- Tasks can be quite repetitive and monotonous, thereby causing boredom.

- As commission depends on fluctuating sales or output levels, it is difficult to meet security needs because workers do not know how much they will be paid.

- There could be a need to hire more quality controllers, especially in manufacturing jobs.

Profit-related pay

As a form of financial motivation, profit-related pay involves linking pay to the level of profits in the firm, i.e. the greater the profits, the higher the pay. Profit-related pay is usually paid as an annual bonus.

In 2018, Southwest Airlines paid its workers an extra 11.3% (the equivalent of 5 weeks' extra pay) as part of its $543 million profit-sharing scheme with its employee. Some some airline companies pay a thirteenth month bonus, paid along with the employee's December salary. The amount paid will usually be linked to the employee's salary and length of service, so those on higher salaries and who have been with the firm the longest are rewarded the most. This is seen to be a fairer way to share any profits with the workers.

Profit-related pay is used to strengthen employee loyalty and to foster team spirit (since profits can only be achieved by combined team efforts rather than by an individual's input). Hence, profit sharing should boost labour efficiency and limit the possibility of labour conflict. Another advantage is that it can help to break down a 'them and us' culture (see Unit 2.5) since managers and employees work together to achieve higher levels of profit.

However, the proportion of profits paid to employees is often seen as too small to provide an incentive to work any harder. Walmart, the world's largest retailer, announced in 2007 that it was to bring back annual bonuses paying an average of $651 to its 1.3 million hourly-paid workers (but the Walmart payout equated to under $1.80 per day for each worker!) Also, individual efforts are not explicitly recognised by this payment system, so there is no reason for any individual to improve their performance. In reality, profit sharing is often used to reward senior managers rather than for the whole workforce, especially as individuals lower down in the hierarchy have no direct influence in changing the firm's overall level of profits.

Performance-related pay (PRP)

Performance-related pay (PRP) is more flexible than profit-related pay as a reward system. PRP rewards employees (as individuals, teams or as a whole workforce) who meet certain goals. These goals may be related to sales targets, competence in a job or successful completion of a contract. PRP can be paid in various ways:

- Pay rise – an increase in a person's pay due to meeting or exceeding his/her performance targets.

- Performance bonus – paid to workers who have reached output or quality targets, e.g. sales staff might receive a cash bonus for reaching their sales targets.

- Gratuity – paid to staff who complete their employment contracts, e.g. international schools typically pay teachers hired from overseas a gratuity (an end-of-contract bonus based on a predetermined percentage of the employee's annual salary).

A key advantage of PRP is that it creates incentives for people to work and perform better, especially if targets are clearly set. PRP is also seen as a fair system since hard work is rewarded (see Adams's equity theory above). Furthermore, PRP helps to develop a performance culture where people strive to achieve their targets in return for the benefits of PRP, such as opportunities for promotion or a financial bonus.

However, PRP does suffer from several disadvantages:

- Targets might be unrealistic or unachievable so this can cause resentment and hinder job performance.

- The pressure imposed on workers to meet their targets can cause stress (especially if their pay is linked to achieving set targets).

- PRP is not appropriate for some professions where quality is more important than quantity, e.g. public sector doctors and teachers because it is difficult to quantify their level of 'performance'.

- It might not encourage teamwork since individual targets are set in performance appraisal meetings (even though team targets can be set). This can lead to workers feeling rather alienated and demoralised, especially if they feel their colleagues are being better rewarded.

- Non-financial motivators are ignored.

Employee share ownership schemes

This payment system rewards workers, managers and directors by giving them shares in the company or by selling the shares at a discounted price. It is often used as an alternative to awarding a cash bonus or profit sharing. The motive for using share ownership schemes is that employees (who become shareholders of the company) will have a more direct interest in the wellbeing of the organization. Subsequently, employers benefit from lower rates of absenteeism and staff turnover.

In reality, share ownership schemes tend to be used for rewarding those in the senior leadership team. The majority of employees do not qualify for share ownership, and even if they did the amount distributed is hardly sufficient to sustain their level of motivation. Hence, this reward system might prove to be impractical for many businesses.

Fringe payments (perks)

Fringe payments (or perks) are the financial benefits to employees in addition to their wage or salary. Examples include health insurance, housing allowance, contributions to the worker's retirement fund, staff discounts, subsidised meals, gym membership, paid holidays and paid sick leave. Perks vary from one firm to another and might depend on the employee's position or rank in the organization.

Figure 2.4.g Gym membership is a financial perk

A key advantage of using fringe payments is that they encourage employee loyalty. Perks can help to meet an employee's safety needs (see Maslow's hierarchy of needs theory) and make workers feel more valued as the employer provides these extra benefits to enhance their overall remuneration.

The main disadvantage of using fringe payments is the potentially high costs. For example, it is likely that all employees qualify to receive basic fringe benefits, such as annual paid leave (holiday pay), free uniforms and private medical cover. In addition, senior managers might qualify for further benefits, such as business-class air travel and company cars. These expenses can be an enormous burden on a firm's cash flow position (see Unit 3.7).

Figure 2.4.h Healthcare benefits are a fringe benefit

Case study

Google offers its full-time US-based employees a $5,000 subsidy on the purchase of a Toyota Prius, Honda Civic Hybrid or Honda Insight. Google's corporate image of innovation is coupled with its aim to preserve the environment by subsidising workers who buy environmentally friendly cars. Other perks include free food (breakfast, lunch and dinner), a fully equipped gym, free laundry, electric scooters for on-site use, and $12,000 per year for reimbursement of private tuition fees. If a Google employee dies, the spouse gets half of the salary for the next 10 years and the children get $1,000 per month until they turn 19!

Case study

According to *Forbes*, Tim Cook (who took over from Steve Jobs as CEO of Apple Inc.) is the world's highest remunerated person, having a reported total annual compensation of $377,996,537 (that's more than $1 million per day)!

Question 2.4.5   Camden International Consultants

Camden International Consultants (*CIC*) was set up in 1983 and is a highly successful private management consultancy firm. In addition to their salaries, consultants at *CIC* enjoy **perks** such as housing allowance, profit related pay and a company car.

Mairead Taylor, the new chief executive officer (CEO) who joined a year ago, has decided that there needs to be some radical changes to ensure that *CIC* remains competitive. Annual pay increments would now be based on **performance-related pay**, based on a performance appraisal system carried out by line managers. Mairead Taylor also stated that consultants would get a 5% pay cut, to bring salaries in line with the industry norm. This would also allow the firm to cut its fees by up to 3% within the next year in order to attract new clients.

(a) (i) Define the term **perks**.   *[2 marks]*

(a) (ii) Define the term **performance-related pay**.   *[2 marks]*

(b) Using relevant motivation theory, examine the possible consequences of implementing Mairead Taylor's plans at *CIC*.   *[6 marks]*

(c) Evaluate the CEO's proposal to remunerate management consultants by using performance-related pay.
                                                                                                                                           [10 marks]

Non-financial rewards

The following types of non-financial rewards: job enrichment, job rotation, job enlargement, empowerment, purpose/the opportunity to make a difference, and teamwork. AO2

© IBO, 2017

Non-financial rewards are non-monetary factors that motivate people by offering psychological and intangible benefits, i.e. factors not directly linked to money. The theories of Maslow, Herzberg and Pink advocate non-financial methods of motivation. Examples are explained below.

Job enrichment

Herzberg emphasised that making a job more interesting or challenging was a key motivator. **Job enrichment** (or **vertical loading**), gives workers more *challenging* jobs with more *responsibilities*. Hence, people have greater autonomy and authority in their work and have better opportunities to accomplish their jobs. It can also result in the psychological growth of workers, so they become more committed to their work. Furthermore, the ability to do a range of tasks means that workers have a better sense of achievement.

A limitation of job enrichment is the added expenses of time and money needed to train and develop workers to fulfil these extra responsibilities of their job. Another drawback is job enlargement increases the workload of employees which can result in anxiety, stress and lower productivity. Managers must also ensure that jobs are not too challenging or too complex for an employee who does not have the right skills set because it will not only lead to disastrous outcomes, but can also destroy the confidence and morale of the worker.

Job rotation

Job rotation is a type of job enlargement that involves workers performing different tasks at the same level of complexity in a systematic way. This means that employees perform a number of different tasks in order. For example, supermarket employees might work at the checkouts as cashiers one day, then rotate to work in other areas such as the delicatessen, bakery or stacking shelves on other days.

The intention of job rotation is to provide more variety to avoid the problems of overspecialisation (such as boredom caused by performing the same tasks over and over). Job rotation also makes it easier for people to cover for absent colleagues as they become more familiar with a breadth of tasks. However, multiskilling requires greater training costs and can be regarded by some employees as simply adding to their workload without real career development opportunities.

Figure 2.4.i Job rotation is commonly found in large supermarkets

Job enlargement

Job enlargement (also known as **horizontal loading**) refers to broadening the *number of tasks* that an employee performs, although the job itself remains essentially unchanged. For example, an administrative worker might spend most of the day looking after the reception area dealing with customer enquiries but also spend some time on data input, photocopying documents, filing and other clerical tasks.

One purpose of job enlargement is to reduce the monotony (repetitiveness) of tasks that can cause boredom and demotivation. Job enlargement can make a job more interesting as it involves workers having a wider range of tasks. However, some employees might view this as a way to get them to do more work for the same amount of pay, thus leading to demoralised workers. In addition, any benefits of job enlargement are likely to diminish after a period of time if the roles become mundane (unexciting). Finally, the continual enlargement of a job over time can lead to unmanageable workloads for staff, thus causing demotivation in the workplace.

Exam tip !

Be sure you know the difference between 'job enrichment' and 'job enlargement'. Job enrichment (vertical expansion of roles) is largely dependent on job enlargement (horizontally expansion of roles) whereas job enlargement can take place without job enrichment. It is job enrichment which is most helpful for employees to advance in their professional careers.

CORE

Human resource management

Empowerment

Empowerment is about developing the potential of workers or teams to achieve the best they can. It involves granting workers the *authority* to be in charge of their own jobs and to execute their own ideas to solve business problems. Hence, workers have some autonomy in decision-making and can decide for themselves the best way to deal with a task or issue. Empowerment can boost motivation as workers can take initiative and have a say in how things are done. Thus, they have a greater sense of pride in their work, e.g. in the teaching profession, the principal usually allows teachers to deliver lessons in a way that they see most appropriate.

Empowerment requires giving workers the necessary authority, skills, resources and opportunities to achieve personal and organizational goals. As Chinese philosopher Confucius (551 BCE–479 BCE) said, "*I hear and I forget. I see and I remember. I do and I understand*". Empowerment can be achieved through methods such as:

- *Delegation*   This occurs when managers pass on authority to their subordinates, allowing them to take charge of a task and to get recognition for their accomplishments. Delegation works best when subordinates have the competence (ability) and desire (willingness) to take on extra responsibility. Managers must also ensure that staff are given sufficient time and resources to accomplish the delegated tasks. Successful delegation can therefore boost morale and help people to gain invaluable experiences to progress in their careers.

- *Worker participation*   This occurs when workers have opportunities to participate in decision-making so they feel empowered, e.g. through employee suggestion schemes or the use of quality circles (see Unit 5.3) when dealing with a particular task or problem. Worker participation allows people to become more involved and interested in their work.

- *Continuous professional development* (CPD)   Employers who provide opportunities for their staff to undertake ongoing training tend to find that the costs of providing CPD are far less than the benefits reaped from having a more loyal, empowered and productive workforce. Workers feel more valued if the firm provides them with training and development opportunities. This can help workers to progress in their career and help to fulfil their potential.

However, empowerment must be used appropriately. Delegating tasks to empower staff can only be successful if the workers have adequate skills and have received the necessary training to independently tackle given tasks. Managers are still held responsible for the tasks they delegate, so inappropriate use of empowerment can lead to expensive mistakes being made.

Exam tip!

Delegation can empower a worker by giving the worker authority to take charge of a particular task or project. However, the responsibility of success or failure ultimately stays with the chief executive officer, i.e. authority can be delegated but responsibility cannot.

Purpose (the opportunity to make a difference)

Whilst some employees are driven by self-interest, others are motivated by using their work to help others thereby making a difference to the world we live in. Such employees are altruistic (selfless) and see the purpose of work being to make a positive change in other people's lives. Doctors, nurses, social care workers and teachers are examples. History has shown that during times of crises, people cooperate to help each other.

Very importantly, purpose is about the role or job itself rather than acts of altruism such as donating money to an external charity (which only generates perceived impacts on beneficiaries). The motivation to make a difference occurs when people have the opportunity to build ongoing relationships with the beneficiaries. This is apparent with charity and social care workers who are fully committed to their work in making a difference to others.

McKinsey & Company, the American global management consultancy firm, has shown through numerous studies that people with satisfactory salaries need more than financial rewards to sustain motivation. Their studies show some non-financial rewards are more effective than extra pay. The opportunity to help others or to make a difference to society can be motivational and give workers a real sense of purpose. Financial rewards, such as bonuses or share options, generate short-term gains in motivation, but can have negative unintended consequences such as the perception that these rewards become the norm. Philanthropy and alumni donations are common examples of how all employees can make a difference to others.

Case study

The world's top philanthropists have given billions to help others. Since 1999, Bill Gates has topped the list, having donated over $28b! The next four largest philanthropists are Warren Buffet ($21.5bn), George Soros ($8.5bn), Azim Premji ($8bn), Charles Francis Feeney ($6.3bn) and Sulaiman bin Abdul Aziz Al Rajhi ($5.7bn).

Source: http://www.therichest.com

Teamwork

Teamwork occurs when employees work with fellow colleagues. Examples include:

- *Departmental teams* – organising people into functional teams (see Unit 2.2) such as finance, marketing and operations management.

- *Cellular manufacturing* – teamwork to complete part of a production process (see Unit 5.2).

- *Quality circles* – team members meet regularly to discuss solutions to problems regarding quality within the production process (see Unit 5.3).

Teamwork can reduce boredom (of working alone) and help to meet the social needs of employees. Teamwork can help workers to build a sense of belonging, thereby reducing absenteeism and labour turnover whilst boosting productivity. It can also lead to greater flexibility and multiskilling as workers learn from other team members. Hence, workers can cover for one another during times of absences without delaying the production process or reducing the quality of the service being delivered.

Figure 2.4.j Teamwork helps to solve problems more effectively

CORE

Human resource management

IB Learner Profile – Be principled

Discuss the qualities needed to be a good team player. Given the benefits of group dynamics, what sort of people would make an ideal team?

Exam tip !

As a critical thinker, remember that these financial and non-financial rewards do not apply to everyone or to every business. Some will work in some situations and not in other scenarios. The important exam skill is to apply the various financial and non-financial rewards sensibly and in a way that is aligned with the specific business in question.

Box 2.4.f Characteristics of successful motivators

The Institute of Management in the UK has observed three key characteristics of successful motivators:
- They are positive thinkers (the glass is half full, rather than half empty). Having a positive attitude can go a long way in helping to achieve the strategic aims and objectives of an organization.
- They have and show gratitude and appreciation to their staff. This fosters harmony and trust in the workplace, thereby helping to bring out the best in employees.
- They believe in the self-worth of all workers. It is human nature to yearn for acceptance and love (see Maslow's theory). When each employee's self-worth is boosted through motivation, the business is more likely to flourish.

Theory of knowledge

Is it possible to quantify motivation in the workplace in order to acquire knowledge of what motivates employees?

Question 2.4.6 Pfizer

Pfizer, the multinational pharmaceutical giant, employs around 96,500 people around the world. The firm uses the motto CANI (Continuous and Never Ending Improvement) as a guiding principle to motivating the workforce. *Pfizer* uses both financial and non-financial methods to encourage employee loyalty. Having a relatively small workforce in Hong Kong, it is quite easy for the company to devise Individual Development Plans for each worker's training and development needs. The firm claims that 80% of management positions are filled using **internal recruitment**. The culture is one of encouragement and risk-taking rather than name and shame (blame).

(a) Define the term **internal recruitment**.   *[2 marks]*

(b) Explain **two** likely benefits for *Pfizer* in using internal recruitment.   *[4 marks]*

(c) Explain why a culture of risk-taking is important to pharmaceutical companies such as *Pfizer*.   *[4 marks]*

(d) To what extent do managers over-estimate the importance of using financial rewards to motivate their employees?
                                                                                              [10 marks]

Case study

Recent studies from global management consultancy firm McKinsey & Co. found that respondents view three non-financial rewards (praise from line managers, leadership attention to the work being done, and a chance to lead projects) to be more effective in motivating and engaging workers than the three highest-rated financial rewards (cash bonuses, increased base pay, and share options).

Common mistake

Many students seem to think that non-financial benefits do not cost a business any money. In fact, some of these can be quite expensive, e.g. the provision of training opportunities for the workforce. Praise and recognition might not be as costly but will still take up management time if such practices are to be genuine and valued by workers.

Motivation and the CUEGIS concepts

How financial and non-financial rewards may affect job satisfaction, motivation and productivity in different cultures. AO2
© IBO, 2017

One of the earliest recorded English proverbs is *"You can take a horse to water but you cannot force it to drink the water."* This is because the horse will only drink if it is thirsty. Likewise, people will only perform their jobs well if they are motivated to do so. Motivation is undoubtedly a strategic issue, especially as people are such an important aspect of any business strategy. Productivity is dependent on an employee's level of ability and motivation. Failure to motivate workers can lead to a range of problems, such as higher absenteeism, increased labour turnover, poor customer service and lower quality output. By contrast, a culture that fosters motivation leads to better labour retention and its associated benefits (see Box 2.4.g). Retention is the opposite of labour turnover, i.e. it measures the proportion of the workforce that choose to remain working at the organization, rather than leaving it.

CORE

Human resource management

201

Box 2.4.g Benefits of higher staff retention

- Lower costs of recruitment, selection, induction and training of new staff.
- Better corporate image, thereby making it easier to recruit new staff when necessary.
- Skills and knowledge are kept within the firm.
- Strong corporate culture.
- Improved competitiveness, due to the above benefits.
- Ultimately, helps to improve the firm's profitability.

However, there is no general strategy that bests motivates employees. This is largely because each and every worker is different in what motivates them. People are likely to be motivated by a combination of both intrinsic and extrinsic factors. **Intrinsic motivation** occurs when people engage in an activity out of their own desire, e.g. the enjoyment of pursuing a hobby or an interest because the person finds it to be challenging, stimulating or fun. Thus, intrinsically motivated students would want to master a subject rather than rote learn the subject simply to get good examination grades. Intrinsic motivation can also occur due to altruistic reasons, i.e. there is a sense of commitment to others. In many Asian cultures, intrinsic motivation occurs due to family reasons, e.g. students seek to work hard partly due to family pressures and partly to avoid letting down their parents. By contrast, **extrinsic motivation** occurs when people participate in an activity because of the benefits and rewards associated with doing so. These incentives might be tangible (e.g. wages, salaries and bonuses) or intangible (e.g. recognition and praise). Extrinsic motivation can also arise from organizational cultures that use pressure and threats, i.e. workers engage in an activity to avoid punishments.

Change also has a major impact on motivation, productivity and job satisfaction. In reality, motivating the workforce is an extremely complex task because there are so many different factors, each of which is subject to change, that affect the level of motivation of each individual. What motivates one person does not automatically motivate another, e.g. the threat of redundancy can be both a motivator and a demotivator. For some people and cultures, the fear of losing their job might drive them to ensure that they keep their jobs. For others, the insecurity does not motivate (refer to Maslow's safety needs).

Cultural norms also mean that some people are better suited to a system of scientific management, such as unskilled workers

in a manufacturing plant or a fast-food chain. Managers must therefore weigh up the costs of using various methods of motivation (e.g. profit-related pay) with the expected benefits (e.g. higher productivity). Some managers do not see any value in using non-financial motivators for workers who do not want responsibility or lack skills and ambition.

Finally, consider how the CUEGIS concepts apply across the content discussed in this unit on the different theories of motivation and the various methods of financial and non-financial motivation. For example, consider the following questions in relation to an organization of your choice:

- **C**hange: how has motivation changed over time?

- **Cu**lture: how does organizational culture influence motivation?

- **E**thics: what is the role of ethics in motivating employees?

- **G**lobalization: how has globalization influenced motivation?

- **I**nnovation: what role does innovation have in improving employee motivation?

- **S**trategy: to what extent do all stakeholders gain from a more motivated workforce?

Exam tip !

Motivation is not an isolated issue, nor is it a stand-alone topic within the syllabus. Instead, it is an integral part of the complex nature of strategically managing people within an organization.

Theory of knowledge

Is motivation driven by ethics or by the lack of ethics?

CUEGIS ESSAY

With reference to an organization of your choice, discuss the impact of **culture** and **ethics** on the level of staff motivation.   *[20 marks]*

REVIEW QUESTIONS

1. What is meant by motivation?

2. What are the benefits to a business in having a highly motivated workforce?

3. What are the signs of a demotivated workforce?

4. Distinguish between the theories of Taylor and Pink.

5. Compare and contrast the theories of Maslow and Herzberg.

6. State five methods of financial and non-financial ways to motivate individuals.

7. Distinguish between job enlargement, job enrichment and job rotation.

8. Explain how different methods of non-financial rewards work in different circumstances.

9. Explain the benefits of high staff retention.

10. Distinguish between intrinsic and extrinsic methods of motivation.

11. Distinguish between wages and salaries.

12. Distinguish between profit-related and performance-related pay.

13. Why are fringe benefits a form of financial reward?

14. Why is job empowerment a form of non-financial motivation?

15. Why can teamworking be motivational?

KEY TERMS

Commission is a type of financial payment system that rewards workers a certain percentage of the sales of each good or service that they are responsible for completing.

Delegation refers to managers passing on authority to subordinates to carry out a task or project. This can motivate workers who wish to be entrusted and recognised for their abilities.

Employee share ownership scheme is a type of financial payment system that involves giving workers shares (stocks) in the company they work for, either free of charge or at a discounted price.

Empowerment is a non-financial motivator that involves developing the potential of workers or teams to achieve the best they can by granting them the *authority* to make various decisions and to execute their own ideas to solve business problems.

Equity theory is J.S. Adams' theory of motivation, which suggests that people make comparisons of perceived fairness in the workplace (based on the ratio of their input (effort) to output (rewards).

Esteem needs in Maslow's hierarchy of needs refers to the desire of people to feel respected, having value and having self-respect.

Fringe payments (or **perks**) are the financial rewards paid in addition to a worker's wages or salaries, e.g. free uniforms, subsidised meals, housing benefit, pension fund contributions and company cars.

Herzberg's two factor theory looked at the factors that motivate employees, namely *hygiene factors* (that must be met to prevent dissatisfaction) and *motivators*.

Hierarchy of needs refers to A. Maslow's theory of motivation, that people are motivated by different levels of needs: physiological, safety, social (love and beginning), esteem and self-actualization.

Hygiene factors are parts of a job that Herzberg referred to that do not increase job satisfaction but help to remove dissatisfaction, such as reasonable wages and working conditions.

CORE

Human resource management

Job enlargement refers to increasing the *number of tasks* that an employee performs, thereby reducing or eliminating the monotony of repetitive tasks.

Job enrichment involves giving workers more *responsibilities* and more *challenging jobs*.

Job rotation is a form of job enlargement whereby workers are given different tasks, but of the same level of complexity, to help reduce the problems caused by performing repetitive tasks.

Job security is the assurance given to employees that they will keep their current job for the foreseeable future, as stated in an employment contract.

Maslow's hierarchy of needs outlines five levels of needs, from satisfying physiological needs to self-actualisation. Lower order needs must be met before people progress up the hierarchy.

Motivation refers to the inner desire or passion to do something. The driving forces could be intrinsic (e.g. to have a sense of achievement) and/or extrinsic (e.g. due to financial rewards).

Motivators are the factors that Herzberg considered to increase job satisfaction and motivation levels, e.g. praise and recognition.

The **national minimum wage** is the lowest hourly pay, as stipulated by the government, that employers can remunerate their workers.

Performance-related pay (PRP) is a payment system that rewards people who meet set targets over a period of time. The targets can be on an individual, team or organizational basis.

Piece rate is a payment system that rewards people based on the amount that they produce or sell. Thus, their pay is directly linked to their level of productivity.

Pink's drive theory suggests that people in modern societies are motivated by three key factors: autonomy, mastery and purpose.

Productivity measures the level of output per worker. It is an indicator of motivation as employees tend to be more productive with increased levels of motivation.

Profit-related pay is a type of financial reward system which remunerates workers a certain percentage of the annual profits that the firm earns.

Physiological needs (or basic needs) in Maslow's hierarchy of needs are the requirements for human survival, e.g. food, water, shelter and warmth.

Remuneration means the overall package of pay and benefits offered to an employee, such as salaries, commission, profit-related pay, performance-related pay, share ownership schemes, and fringe benefits.

Safety needs (or security needs) in Maslow's hierarchy of needs are the requirements that make people feel safe, e.g. job security.

Salary is a type of financial payment that rewards workers a fixed annual amount of money, but paid in monthly instalments.

Scientific management, developed by F.W. Taylor, suggests that specialisation and division of labour help to increase the level of productivity. This is especially the case if pay is linked to a piece-rate reward system.

Self-actualisation in Maslow's hierarchy of needs refers to the highest level of needs, which occurs when people become the very best that they can be and fulfil their potential.

Social needs (or love and belonging needs) in Maslow's hierarchy of needs refers to the requirements about being accepted by others.

Teamwork is a form of non-financial motivation, which involves the combined efforts of a group of workers to achieve of an organizational goal.

Time rate is a payment system that rewards staff for the time (rather than output) that they put into work. It is expressed per period of time, e.g. $10 per hour or $5,000 per month.

Wages are a type of financial reward payment system based on time or output. Wages are paid as time rate (hours) or piece rate (output).

2.5 Organizational (corporate) culture

"A people without the knowledge of their past history, origin and culture is like a tree without roots." -
Marcus M Garvey (1887–1940), Jamaican entrepreneur and political leader

HL content	Assessment objective
Organizational culture	AO1
Elements of organizational culture	AO2
Types of organizational culture	AO2
The reasons for, and consequences of, cultural clashes within organizations when they grow, merge and when leadership styles change	AO3
How individuals influence organizational culture and how organizational culture influences individuals	AO3

© IBO, 2017

Organizational culture

Organizational culture. AO1

© IBO, 2017

Culture can be defined as what is considered 'normal' to an organization, such as the way that workers behave within the business. Corporate culture is largely based on the beliefs, values and attitudes of the management and employees. It includes a range of things such as the approach towards punctuality, dress code or whether smoking is acceptable in the workplace. In essence, corporate culture represents the character or personality of an organization.

IB Learner Profile – Be reflective, and be a communicator

Cultures in songs Decide on a list of 5–10 popular songs that represent you as an individual and your culture. Explain to a classmate why you chose these songs. For example, *Under Pressure* by Queen because as an IB student, you constantly feel 'under pressure' or *Try* by P!nk as you feel you should always try your best, and no matter how hard life gets, you have to keep trying.

Elements of organizational culture

Elements of organizational culture. AO2

© IBO, 2017

The acronym NORMS© can be used to remember the interrelated determinants of organizational culture:

- **Nature of the business** Culture is shaped by the purpose and direction of the organization, derived from its mission, aims and objectives (see Unit 1.3). For example, there is likely to be a very different culture in a non-profit organization (such as a charity) than one found in an organization that thrives on aggressive selling (such as a real estate firm).

- **Organizational structure** Firms with tall structures tend to have lots of small teams that work well independently. By contrast, flatter structures may benefit from collaborative teamwork. Organizations made up of highly skilled and innovative staff have a different culture from those with demotivated staff who have no input in decision-making.

- **Rewards** If employees are appropriately remunerated for their efforts, the organization is more likely to develop a strong and united culture. Hence, a motivated workforce results in a culture of productive workers who strive to achieve organizational objectives.

205

- **Management styles** The culture in decentralized organizations (see Unit 2.2) tends to benefit from workers able to deal with most problems themselves, rather than taking all their problems to the management. Conversely, in firms where managers maintain centralized decision-making power, a different culture exists with the use of threats and sanctions. In extreme versions of this culture, much of management time is spent on checking employee emails, monitoring their telephone calls or even using surveillance cameras to observe the staff.

- **Sanctions** An organization with few sanctions can encourage staff to be slack, e.g. to be late for work, or even miss work, and to provide poor customer service. However, if an organization is too rigid in its policies and is extremely harsh in reprimanding workers, staff may feel resentful of the management.

To some extent, each classroom has its own culture. The culture is largely influenced by the members of the group (the students) and the attitude of the group leader (the teacher). Individual students might work better in some classes than in others because of the group dynamics and different expectations set by teachers.

The importance of understanding organizational culture

Cultural intelligence, or **cultural quotient** (CQ), is the ability of an individual to blend into occupational, corporate and national cultures. The term was coined by Professor Christopher Earley and Professor Elaine Mosakowski in the *Harvard Business Review* (2004). Cultural quotient is important as it measures the ability of people to understand and adjust to unfamiliar situations such as a hostile takeover (see Unit 1.6) or a crisis (see Unit 5.7).

The strength of an organization's culture depends on the degree of unity among the staff. If staff are unified in their beliefs and values, the culture will be stronger, i.e. a strong culture exists when the staff understand, believe and support the vision and mission of the organization. By contrast, a culture gap exists if organizational values are not aligned. Subsequently, managers may need to exercise control by formal and perhaps bureaucratic procedures. Advantages to a business that has a strong corporate culture include:

- Creating a sense of belonging and security for staff because they feel part of the organization. This helps to improve teamwork and to raise motivation in the organization.

- Promoting cohesiveness so people do things as they feel that it is the right thing to do.

Figure 2.5.a Children learning outside the classroom in Sri Lanka

- Reducing mistakes and misunderstandings as staff are familiar with the processes at work.

- Minimising problems associated with a culture gap so that conflict (see Unit 2.6) and misunderstandings between different groups are curtailed.

Types of organizational culture

Types of organizational culture. AO2

© IBO, 2017

Organizations are vastly different in the ways that they operate. This means there is no single dominant theory of the different models of organizational culture. Various theorists have put forward models of the types of organizational culture:

> **Exam tip !**
>
> The theorists covered in this section are not mentioned by name in the BM Guide, so you will not be explicitly examined on their work. However, some do appear in previous mark schemes, and their theories will help you to gain a better understanding of organizational culture.

Edgar H. Schein

Professor Edgar Henry Schein is credited for coining the term *corporate culture*. He argues that there are three levels of corporate culture:

- **Artefacts** are superficial and behavioural aspects of an organization that can be easily seen but not necessarily easy to understand. Examples include the organization's history, facilities, buildings, dress code and how people are seen to interact with each other.

- **Espoused values** are the desired or expected corporate culture. These are the values that the organization feels are important and staff are (ideally) committed to. Metaphors and symbols are used to express the culture among staff, e.g. the firm's mission statement, brands and slogans.

- **Shared basic assumptions** represent the deepest level of culture – the culture that is unseen and not easily identified as it is so well integrated in the organization. This reveals the actual values demonstrated through behaviour, rather than espoused values and philosophies. It includes subcultures inside the business and a culture

invisible to those new to the organization. Schein argued that it is at this level that culture drives an organization.

Charles Handy

In his book *The Gods of Management* (1978) Professor Charles Handy argued that different cultures are needed for different business activities. He stated that the culture used to run an efficient chocolate plant is different from that used to run a primary school or a construction site.

Handy described four types of organizational culture:

- **Zeus - Power cultures** exist when there is a dominant individual (such as the founder of the organization, or a figurehead like Zeus), or group holding decision-making power. For example, Steve Jobs, co-founder of Apple, led the company in a power-culture way. The organizational structure is likely to be flat with a relatively wide span of control (see Unit 2.2). Formal job titles or positions may not be highly regarded because decision-making power only exists with very few. Thus, decision-making is very swift, especially as there is little bureaucracy. Signs of power cultures come in various forms, e.g. parking spaces and private toilets (washrooms) reserved only for senior executives.

- **Apollo - Role cultures** exist in highly structured organizations with formal rules and procedures. Job roles are clearly stated in formal job descriptions and there is clear accountability. Power is devolved depending on the formal position that the individual holds in the organization. Role cultures are often found in schools and colleges.

Figure 2.5.b   Handy used a temple to symbolise a role culture, for it is old, strong and well established

207

- **Athena - Task cultures** exist in organizations where the focus is on getting results from the work done. Unlike power cultures, there is no single source of power. Hence, individuals and teams are empowered and have some discretion over their responsibilities. Teamwork is therefore vital in a task culture. Unlike in role cultures, formal job titles are seen as less important than the contribution that individuals make to completing tasks. Such cultures promote problem-solving through flexible and dynamic teams, often made up of representatives from different departments based on their expertise.

- **Dionysian - Person cultures** exist in organizations when staff in similar positions with similar expertise form groups to share their knowledge and skills. This type of culture is found in larger organizations with different branches, such as in commercial retailing, or in certain professions such as accountants, surgeons and lawyers. Hence, a person culture consists of independent professionals within an organization. Person cultures only exist for the benefit of the individuals involved, although the organization can indirectly benefit from the creativity and the sharing of good practise amongst the members.

Deal and Kennedy

Terrence Deal and Allan Kennedy (1982) described corporate culture as the way things get done within an organization. Their research was based on a two-dimensional framework:

- **Feedback and reward** looks at the speed of feedback and the level of rewards within an organization. If feedback is rapid (immediate), any unproductive conduct and inconsistent culture is quickly removed, e.g. those who slack at work will be dismissed. In a competitive team sports match, feedback and reward will be rapid. For a business exploring new technologies, feedback and reward is likely to be slow. Deal and Kennedy argue that rapid feedback and reward are likely to lead to a consistent corporate culture.

- **Risk** refers to the degree of uncertainty (the level of risk-taking) in an organization. Risk is something that either drives workers or it demotivates them. High-risk organizations, such as stock brokerage firms, are more likely to employ people with a high-risk profile. These can be very stressful businesses to work in, such as the emergency services, so those that do not fit the culture will not last very long in the job.

		Feedback and reward	
		Rapid	*Slow*
Risk	*High*	Tough-guy macho	Bet-the-company
	Low	Work-hard, play-hard	Process

Figure 2.5.c Deal and Kennedy's organizational culture model

Deal and Kennedy suggested four types of organizational culture:

- **Tough-guy macho culture** occurs in organizations where feedback is rapid and risks are high. It often applies to fast-paced organizations such as financial markets, stock exchanges, the police force, surgeries and professional sports clubs. It can be highly stressful to work in such a culture due to the high risks.

- **Work-hard, play-hard culture** exists where there is rapid feedback with low or few risks. Such a culture is typical in large organizations and in fast-paced customer-orientated businesses such as restaurants and hotels. Stress is more likely to come from the scope and pace of work rather than risk or uncertainty.

- **Bet-the-company culture** occurs in firms that take high risks but without rapid feedback or immediate rewards. Examples include the oil exploration and pharmaceutical industries, where it can take many years before getting any results. It can also be stressful working in such organizations because there is a high degree of risk and uncertainty – results take so long to materialise, if at all.

- **Process culture** exists in organizations where there is slow, little or no feedback with low risks. Bureaucracy exists and people become caught up with *how* things are done (paying attention to detail) rather than focusing on *what* should be done, i.e. achieving the aims and objectives of the organization. Government departments and insurance companies are examples.

Kotter and Heskett

In their book *Corporate Culture and Performance*, John Kotter and James Heskett (1992) suggested their are two types of corporate culture:

- **Adaptive cultures** are receptive to change and exist in organizations that adapt themselves to change. Staff and management are encouraged to be entrepreneurial and to take risks by not having a culture of blame. Adaptive cultures are often found in innovative organizations such as Google.

- **Inert cultures** are resistant to change and inward looking. They exist in organizations that hold negative values of any change to their culture. Such organizations promote inertia (disinterest and opposition) rather than being proactive to changes in the business environment.

Goffee and Jones

Rob Goffee and Gareth Jones devised the double-S model of organizational culture, which looks at two dimensions of culture: sociability and solidarity. They argue that the ideal culture has both high sociability and high solidarity.

- **Sociability** refers to the extent to which people have concerns for their colleagues. A culture with *high sociability* tends to focus on 'people' whereas a *low sociability* culture places greater focus on completing tasks.

- **Solidarity** refers to the degree of unity in an organization, such as whether people share the same values and have common interests. Hence, *high solidarity* aids harmony and efficiency in the workplace, whereas *low solidarity* implies self-interest takes priority. This is detrimental as it can promote high levels of internal conflict, uncooperative behaviour and/or inefficiencies.

HIGHER LEVEL

Question 2.5.1   Warwick Park School

Warwick Park School (WPS) failed its latest school inspection. The government inspectors had commented that teachers and students at the school failed to engage in active teaching and learning. Examination results were very poor with only 15% of the students achieving the expected national standards. Although the school was a happy community, staff and students at WPS had grown accustomed to failure when it came to examinations. Paramesh Murali, the new principal was hired to improve the quality of teaching and learning at WPS. He was known for his outstanding vision and entrepreneurial ability to turn around the fortunes of failing schools. At his first staff meeting, Paramesh Murali announced his radical plan for change, which included:
- Restructuring the senior management team
- Introducing a system of monthly staff performance appraisals
- Linking teachers' pay with performance management targets set by the principal
- Lesson observations to be carried out on a random and unannounced basis
- Changes to the school timetable to allow for more meetings, planning and extra-curricular activities.

Not surprisingly, the teachers at WPS were worried about dismissals, the manner in which change was being imposed, and the way that staff were to be managed.

(a) With reference to WPS, outline the meaning of organizational culture.   [2 marks]

(b) Explain why Paramesh Murali felt the need to change the organizational culture at WPS.   [4 marks]

(c) Suggest how staff concerns could be dealt with to foster the desired change in organizational culture.   [6 marks]

Human resource management

Geert Hofstede

Unlike the other theorists mentioned above, Geert Hofstede, a Dutch expert in corporate culture, studied the links between international cultures and organizational cultures. He found five dimensions (types) of culture:

- **Power distance** This measures the extent to which subordinates (or citizens) expect and accept unequal distribution of power within the organization (or country). A low power-distance rating, as found in Scandinavian countries, reflects the society's view that people should have equal rights. Hofstede found that high power-distance cultures tend to have centralized decision-making, whereas low power-distance cultures tend to be decentralized, with delegation and empowerment.

- **Individualism versus collectivism** This measures the extent to which people feel they should care for themselves (individualism) or be cared for by the family network and society (collectivism). It considers the extent to which people feel it is their responsibility to look after others or whether they feel that this is the responsibility of government.

- **Masculinity versus femininity** This dimension focuses on the extent to which a culture conforms to traditional gender values. *Masculinity* refers to values usually dominated by males, e.g. aggressiveness, competitiveness, ambition, selfishness and materialism. *Femininity* refers to values traditionally associated with females, e.g. placing focus on relationships and overall quality of life.

- **Uncertainty avoidance** This measures the extent to which people in an organization or country prefer structured routines (predictability) over flexible structures. Hofstede found that high uncertainty avoidance cultures have strong customs and habits. Hence, they tend to favour formal structures, rules and regulations. Those who hold a high degree of uncertainty avoidance tend to remain loyal to their employers.

- **Long-term versus short-term orientation** This final dimension of culture looks at the extent to which a particular culture values making sacrifices today for the benefits to be reaped in the future. Countries and companies with a culture of long-term orientation invest for the future, have perseverance and are patient with the results.

Figure 2.5.d Collectivism is part of Chinese culture

Hofstede's research gives some insight into how organizational cultures may differ from one country to another. National culture has a direct impact on organizational culture. For example, Universal Studios Singapore opened its theme park in 2010 on 18 March at precisely 8.28 am with eighteen Chinese lions blazing through the entrance. The number 8 is auspicious in Chinese culture. It is important for organizations with operations in overseas markets to consider the cultural differences that exist. What works well in one culture or country does not necessarily apply to others (also see Unit 4.7).

Figure 2.5.e Universal Studios, Singapore

In reality, although one type of culture might dominate in a particular organization, there may be other groups that conform to subcultures. These groups may have different opinions, beliefs and interests. This discrepancy among subgroups can also cause a culture gap – the difference between the desired culture of a business and the culture that actually exists.

Theory of knowledge

How might different cultures and beliefs affect knowledge claims in Business Management? How do these influence decision-making in in your home country?

Cultural clashes within organizations

The reasons for, and consequences of, cultural clashes within organizations when they grow, merge and when leadership styles change. AO3
© IBO, 2017

Cultural clashes exist when there is conflict or incompatibility between two or more cultures within an organization. This can exist when firms merge, when a business expands overseas (if workers are ignorant of international cultural differences) or when there is a change in leadership.

Reasons for organizational cultural clashes

- **Growth of firms**   The internal growth of firms is likely to lead to a more formal and hierarchical organizational structure (see Unit 2.2). This can result in organizations becoming more bureaucratic and power orientated in order to maintain control and coordination. In other organizations, an adaptive culture acts as the source of growth and evolution, rather than being the result of growth. Culture clashes often occur when businesses expand into overseas markets.

Case study

In 2005, McDonald's introduced the drive-thru service to China. However, this American culture was so abstract to Chinese drivers who actually bought food at the drive-thru, parked their cars and then ate their meals inside the McDonald's restaurants!

- **Mergers and acquisitions**   Organizational cultures can clash or change when there is external growth, e.g. a merger or takeover. In theory, mergers should help the organizations to gain from economies of scale (see Unit 1.6). However, mergers can fail due to culture clashes (see Question 2.5.2). Even if the merger goes ahead, the culture of the more dominant firm tends to prevail or a new hybrid culture develops. In reality, those who cannot adapt to the new culture are likely to leave the organization.

- **Change in leadership**   Leadership style (see Unit 2.4) is a factor affecting corporate culture: a change in leadership can easily result in a change in the organizational culture. Consider how your school principal shapes the culture of the school and what might happen if that person resigned. Leaders drive the strategic direction of the organization (see Unit 1.3), so a change in the leadership team can result in culture clashes (see Question 2.5.3).

Consequences of organizational cultural clashes

- **Misunderstandings and miscommunications** Cultural clashes and culture gaps often result in problems due to employees not understanding the reasons for change or if these have not been communicated effectively with the workers.

- **Unhappy staff** Cultural clashes and the potential conflict that results will tend to make people unhappy in the workplace.

- **Compromises must be reached** In order for the business to move forward, conflict needs to be resolved. Compromises may therefore need to be made in the negotiation process (see Unit 2.6).

- **Resistance to change** This happens because staff are likely to resent changes to the culture that they are used to, perhaps due to fear of the unknown or due to a lack of understanding of the benefits of change.

- **High costs of training staff and implementing change** For example, training costs may be necessary for businesses that adopt teleworking or diversify their operations.

- **National culture clashes/disputes** National cultures may be so strong that any attempts to change the way

things are done can cause conflict and resentment, e.g. cosmetic firms may find it difficult to expand into Muslim countries as the attitudes towards female liberation and freedom of expression are still very conservative.

Internally, cultural clashes can be the result of historical conflict (see Unit 2.6). **Conflict** refers to disagreements that result from differences in the attitudes, beliefs, values or needs of people. Cultural clashes can also arise from past rivalries and personality clashes. Ultimately, whatever the cause, businesses that ignore cultural differences do so at their own peril.

Box 2.5.a   Cultural clashes and place names
- Accident, Maryland (USA)
- Buttzville, New Jersey (USA)
- Great Snoring, Norfolk (England)
- Hardzardville, Connecticut (USA)
- Hospital, County Limerick (Ireland)
- Idiotville, Oregon (USA)
- Little Snoring, Norfolk (UK)
- Lost, Aberdeenshire (Scotland)
- No Place, County Durham (UK)
- Odd, West Virginia (USA)
- Ogre, Ogre District (Latvia)
- Pukë, (Albania)
- Rough and Ready, California (USA)
- Scratchy Bottom, Weymouth (UK)
- Wedding, Berlin (Germany)

Question 2.5.2   Organizational culture at Lenovo

Founded in 1984, *Lenovo* is the world's largest computer maker. In 2005, the Chinese computer giant bought US IBM's personal computer division for $1.25 billion. Workers at the *Lenovo* plant in China are used to stringent manufacturing systems, with only 18 seconds to add components before they are moved on in the assembly line. This ensures more than 400 laptops are produced each hour. Workers are expected to show respect to their seniors (higher ranked staff). Unlike in Western economies, *Lenovo's* staff are not generally encouraged to voice their opinions or to think independently. They would certainly shy from questioning the decisions made by senior management. Hence, mergers and joint ventures with Western firms have often proved difficult due to international cultural clashes.

(a) Define the term **mergers**. *[2 marks]*

(b) In the context of the case study, outline the meaning of cultural clashes. *[2 marks]*

(c) Examine the problems that *Lenovo* might have faced in the integration of two different corporate cultures. *[6 marks]*

Question 2.5.3   Wahaha and Danone's joint venture

China's largest drinks producer, Wahaha, formed a joint venture with France's largest food company, *Danone*, in 1996. When Wahaha's founder stepped down in 2007, several disputes broke out between the two companies, including the choice of a new chairman. Both companies wanted their own representative to take over as the new chairman. *Danone* then claimed that the Chinese had illegally copied some of its drinks. Under the joint venture agreement, Wahaha is not allowed to make products that directly compete with *Danone's* range of drinks products. *Danone* also faced pressures from Chinese officials when thousands of bottles of its Evian water were seized on accusations that they contained unsafe microorganisms.

(a) Define the term **joint venture**.   *[2 marks]*

(b) Explain the importance of understanding corporate and international cultures for the success of a cross-border joint venture.   *[4 marks]*

(c) Examine the consequences of culture clashes within organizations when leadership styles change.   *[6 marks]*

Theory of knowledge

Since our own experiences and cultural background play a vital part in how and what we understand, discuss whether it is possible to have objective knowledge across different cultures.

Theory of knowledge

Gantt (Unit 1.7), Levinson (Unit 4.5) and all the motivational theorists in the IB syllabus (Taylor, Maslow, Herzberg, Adams and Pink) were/are all American entrepreneurs and/or academics. Ansoff (Unit 1.3) was Russian-American and Lewin (Unit 1.7) was German-American. The people behind the Boston Matrix (Unit 4.5) were American. Ishikawa (Unit 1.7) was Japanese. How does cultural bias affect our knowledge and understanding of Business Management?

Case study

Euro Disney opened in Paris in April 1992. The management was faced with staff protests after having insisted on English being the language of communication at its meetings. They had also enforced a strict dress code, based on US practices. Analysts blamed the huge losses made by the theme park in 1994 on this major culture clash. Disney's management subsequently adopted French working practices whilst keeping the core product 'American'. In October 1994, the theme park was renamed 'Disneyland Paris'. . Today, about 8.5 million people visit Disneyland Paris, making it the most popular theme park in Europe.

IB Learner Profile – Be a thinker and be open-minded

How do national cultures affect corporate cultures? Is there a strong relationship between the two in your country?

Individuals and organizational culture

How individuals influence organizational culture and how organizational culture influences individuals. AO3

© IBO, 2017

Individuals, usually leaders, can have a huge influence on organizational culture. This ultimately results in the organizational culture influencing individuals within the organization. The qualities of effective leaders, such as their vision and interpersonal skills, influence staff members to develop the knowledge, skills, and values needed to shape the desired corporate culture. Equally, the unique element of any organizational culture is its diversity. The various mix of ethnicity, languages, gender and socioeconomic groups within a business means that individuals can shape the culture of the organization.

A strong and effective culture can be shaped by an individual, such as a principal in a school or the CEO of a finance company. Within the workplace, the organizational culture depends on rules and policies, social interactions, communications, collaboration, and informal friendship groups. The challenge for leaders is to influence people within the organization to follow or to shape a shared vision and corporate culture. Strategies to achieve this include being a MOVER:

- **M**entor – Leaders act as mentors (see Unit 2.1) by sharing knowledge and expertise, and supporting their people to mould a healthy organizational culture. This also helps to build trust within the organization.

- **O**utreach – Communicating the vision (and desired culture) to all members of the organization, so everyone moves in the same direction and stands for the same values.

- **V**ision – Without knowing where the business wants to be, it is impossible and pointless trying to guide and motivate staff.

- **E**ngaging – The desired corporate culture must engage and excite the workers; perhaps by the leader nurturing a sense of self-worth and commitment to the strategic goals of the organization. Empowering others (see Unit 2.4) also means a greater number of individuals can help to shape the organizational culture.

- **R**ole modelling – As Mahatma Gandhi said, *"You must be the change you wish to see in the world"*; that is, effective leaders lead by example. By being a role model to others in the organization, the leader can drive and develop the desired culture.

Case study

Following his death in October 2011, aged just 56, Steve Jobs was acknowledged by political and business leaders as an iconic entrepreneur who helped to transform the daily habits of millions of people across the globe. Steve Jobs is remembered for being the visionary who reinvented computing, music and mobile phones during what he called the 'post-PC era', changing the way we do things at home, school, work or leisure.

Figure 2.5.f   An effective leader, like Steve jobs, is a "MOVER"

Organizational culture can have a direct impact on individuals. For example, a *power culture* requires centralized decision-making whereby managers keep hold of authority and control. Hence, the organizational structure is likely to be tall with a narrow span of control (see Unit 2.2). By contrast, in *adaptive cultures* where workers are receptive and can adjust to change, flexible or decentralized structures are likely to be found to facilitate employees and managers to adopt a more entrepreneurial role. Similarly, flatter structures are likely to exist in *innovative cultures* which exist in firms that empower workers to make important decisions and to act on their own initiative. Flexible structures are also likely to be found in *task cultures* where the focus is on using the talents of team members, often from different departments, to achieve organizational objectives.

In power cultures where employee input is not really valued, it can prove difficult for individuals to fulfil their motivational needs. In such cultures, managers might also see staff training and development needs as irrelevant since employees do not have any decision-making rights. Similarly, if staff are earning low incomes, they might develop a culture of low or no risk taking as they feel that they are not being paid enough to justify making such important decisions.

The organization's culture also affects its approach to ethical business behaviour. For example, if recycling is part of a firm's culture, then staff are more likely to conserve the use of energy and other resources as this is the expected norm in the organization. However, a profit-seeking business might take a completely different stance on ethics.

IB Learner Profile – Be reflective and be a thinker

Discuss with a partner how your classroom teacher (as an individual) influences the culture of learning within your BM lessons. Also. consider how the students in your BM class (the collective individuals) affect the culture of the classroom. Finally, discuss how the cultural norms in your BM classes influence the individual members of the class. You could discuss:

- Accepted behaviours, the rules of the classroom, for example, the use of language, expectations of conduct and homework deadlines.
- Classroom norms – what does teaching and learning look like in your classroom?
- Values, for example, the degree of diversity, inclusion, equal opportunities, support and collaboration.

What do these discussions tell you about the link between individuals and organizational culture?

Case study

In December 2013, US car giant *General Motors* (GM) announced Mary Barra had been internally promoted to chief executive officer. Barra became the first female CEO of the company, having joined the company as an engineering student in 1980. The aftermath of the global financial crisis caused the US government spend $49.5bn bailing out GM, taking a 61% stake in the company. A week after Barra's promotion, the US government had sold all its shares in GM.

Theory of knowledge

Many business leaders value diversity in human affairs. Is globalization therefore bad for the global society?

Question 2.5.4   The Body Shop

The Body Shop was founded by Dame Anita Roddick in 1976. The company prides itself on being 'green' and socially responsible. Its ethical stance has propelled its operations to over 65 countries worldwide, serving almost 80 million customers each year. *The Body Shop* has five core values that are instilled in everything the company does:

- Against animal testing
- Support local community trade
- Activate self-esteem
- Defend human rights
- Protect the planet.

Logo and information reproduced with the kind permission of The Body Shop International plc.

(a) Describe the corporate culture at *The Body Shop*. *[2 marks]*

(b) Examine how ethical business behaviour can shape corporate culture and provide *The Body Shop* with a competitive advantage. *[6 marks]*

Human resource management

Organizational culture and the CUEGIS concepts

Organizational cultures change, develop and strengthen over time. Beliefs, norms, attitudes and values are more likely to be shared within the organization if they are given the time to do so. This makes any attempt to change the organizational culture a more difficult task. Nevertheless, as markets become more competitive and globalized, organizations are forced into being more adaptive to change and innovation. In addition, political, economic, social, technological and legal changes (see Unit 1.5) may require organizational cultures to adapt and embrace changes in the external business environment.

Organizational culture impacts on the attitude of workers towards change. If employees are not interested in pursuing change, this could harm the business's ability to achieve its goals. A weak, negative and undesirable culture can lead to increased absenteeism, lateness and conflict, thereby intensifying costs for the business. By contrast, a strong culture of acceptance to change and adoption of innovations will aid a business in responding to the changing needs of the market. Cultural harmony within an organization can only come about if all staff understand and share the same values. Without a shared vision, culture gaps and conflict (see Unit 2.6) can cause major problems for the organization.

Theory of knowledge

Have Internet technologies disrupted indigenous cultures?

Edgar Schein argued that cultural understanding is desirable for an organization's business strategy. He suggested that cultural understanding is a prerequisite to effective leadership. Management are often viewed as people who establish the corporate culture, i.e. it is the management that sets the rules, beliefs and norms within an organization in order to shape the corporate culture. There are several interrelated strategies to create a positive and harmonious culture:

- **Develop a sense of history** – Large and well-established organizations create a sense of belonging by developing historical accounts of their businesses. Past successes are glorified in publications and literature. Photographs and artefacts are prominently displayed within the organization. The history of most companies can now be found on the Internet. Multinationals such as Coca-Cola, MINI and Cadbury have their own museums, which help to connect the past to the present and to shape the future direction of the organization.

- **Create a sense of unity** – Managers can create a sense of harmony and unity by establishing SMART objectives (see Unit 1.3) for the business and the workforce. This can help to foster a culture of collaborative teamwork and mutual understanding.

- **Promote a sense of value** – A strong and positive culture is more likely to prevail if there are established systems to reward and recognise the efforts of workers, e.g. the organization might enforce a policy of internally promoting staff to help them in their careers (see Unit 2.1) and firms that encourage a quality culture (see Unit 5.3) invest in the training and development of their staff.

- **Encourage a sense of responsibility** – Staff need to feel dedicated and responsible for their work. This is more likely to happen if there is a sense of unity and purpose. This could be achieved by creating opportunities for staff to work in interdepartmental teams or participate in social events for people to get to know each other better.

The main problem for managers trying to foster an improved or desired corporate culture is that culture is established over long periods of time. Culture is largely formed by the subjective views of people and how they perceive the organization becomes ingrained in the workers' minds. Of course, it is not always easy to change the views of people and this task is more difficult for an organization with a large global workforce. There can be considerable resistance to change of corporate culture as workers argue that 'things have always been done that way here'. Employees who are rational, motivated and attentive help to foster the desired corporate culture.

In fostering a desired culture, management usually use mission statements (see Unit 1.3) to provide a common purpose and clear strategic direction for the staff. The mission statement usually provides some indication of the corporate culture. Without a clear mission statement or effective management, a culture may develop which prevents the organization from achieving its strategic goals. For example, an understanding and awareness of corporate culture is important for workforce planning (see Unit 2.1). As part of strategic planning, especially for organizations striving to reduce their staff turnover, it is important to hire the right staff who will 'fit' into or help to positively develop the culture.

Finally, it is important to recognise that it might not be possible to have just one culture within an organization, especially in large ones where subcultures may exist. Indeed, the dominant culture may not be suitable for certain groups or individuals within the business. This is further complicated when organizations operate on an international scale. A recent report from the UK and Hong Kong Chambers of Commerce found that 20% of jobs in developed societies are directly tied to international trade (a proportion that is continually increasing). Today, societies face greater influences from other cultures, especially with the cultural diversity of people in many countries. Competitiveness is therefore centred on being able to work effectively with those in other countries. An understanding and appreciation of different cultures is essential for business strategy. After all, there is no right or 'best' culture for all organizations, especially as they are constantly exposed to the forces of change. An awareness of the differences in sub cultures that exist within an organization can empower leaders to lead and enhance their strategy.

Theory of knowledge

Are there any areas of Business Management not impacted by culture? What does this enable us to know about the discipline of Business Management?

IB Learner Profile – Be reflective, knowledgable and open-minded

Traditions unify people within and across cultures. How might this statement apply to the discipline of Business Management?

IB Learner Profile – Be an Inquirer and Reflective

As a class, describe the organizational culture at your school by using Answer Garden (http://answergarden.ch/). You can type words up to 20 characters for each answer. Reflect on the extent to which the results align with your school's mission statement.

CUEGIS ESSAY

With reference to an organization of your choice, examine how **globalization** influences organizational **culture**.   [20 marks]

CUEGIS ESSAY

With reference to an organization of your choice, discuss how **change** influences its organizational **culture**.   [20 marks]

CUEGIS ESSAY

With reference to an organization of your choice, discuss how **culture** influences its organizational **strategy**.   [20 marks]

REVIEW QUESTIONS

1. What is meant by organizational culture?

2. What are the five elements (or determinants) of organizational culture? (hint: NORMS).

3. Why is it important to understand organizational culture?

4. Explain the meaning of cultural intelligence and why high CQ is important.

5. What are the various types of organizational cultures?

6. What are cultural clashes and why do they occur?

7. What is a 'culture gap'?

8. How might organizational culture be affected following a takeover or merger?

9. How do individuals influence organizational culture?

Human resource management

HIGHER LEVEL

10. How does organizational culture influence individuals within an organization?

11. In C. Handy's *The Gods of Management*, what is meant by a Zeus (or Power) culture?

12. In Deal & Kennedy's theory of organizational culture, what is meant by a "tough guy macho culture"?

13. Distinguish between adaptive and inert organization cultures.

14. In Geert Hofstede's theory of organization culture, what is meant by uncertainty avoidance?

15. What are culture clashes, and why do they occur?

KEY TERMS

Adaptive cultures exist in organizations that are responsive and receptive to change. Such organizations tend to be innovative and are able to foster change.

Corporate culture, or **organizational culture**, describes the traditions and norms within an organization. It is largely based on people's beliefs, values and attitudes in the workplace.

Cultural intelligence, or **cultural quotient** (CQ), measures the ability of an individual to blend into occupational, organizational and national cultures. CQ is an indicator of a worker's ability to cope with change.

Culture clash exists when there is conflict or incompatibility between two or more cultures within an organization, e.g. when two firms integrate via a hostile takeover.

Culture gap refers to the difference between the existing culture of an organization and its desired culture. Management strive to reduce this gap.

Inert cultures are the opposite of adaptive cultures as people are negative about and resistant to change.

Innovative cultures exist in organizations that empower workers to make important decisions and to act on their own initiative.

Person cultures exist in organizations when staff in similar positions, with similar expertise and training establish groups to share their knowledge.

Power cultures exist when there is one dominant individual or group that holds decision-making power. Hence, the organizational structure is likely to be flat with a relatively wide span of control.

Role cultures exist in highly structured firms with formal rules, policies and procedures. Job roles are clearly stated in job descriptions and power is devolved to middle managers.

Task cultures exist in organizations where the focus is on getting results. Individuals and teams are empowered and have some discretion over their responsibilities.

Values are the organization's beliefs and moral standards, which form an essential part of its organizational culture.

Values are the beliefs and moral standards of an organization

Human resource management

2.6 Employer and employee relations

"The voice of the people is louder than the boom of a canon." - Armenian proverb

HL content	Assessment objective
The role and responsibility of employee and employer representatives	AO2
The following industrial/employee relations methods used by: • employees: collective bargaining, slowdowns/go-slows, work-to-rule, overtime bans and strike action • employers: collective bargaining, threats of redundancies, changes of contract, closure and lock-outs	AO3
Sources of conflict in the workplace	AO2
The following approaches to conflict resolution: • conciliation and arbitration • employee participation and industrial democracy • no-strike agreement • single-union agreement	AO3
Reasons for resistance to change in the workplace (such as self-interest, low tolerance, misinformation and interpretation of circumstances)	AO2
Human resource strategies for reducing the impact of change and resistance to change (such as getting agreement/ownership, planning and timing the change and communicating the change)	AO3
How innovation, ethical considerations and cultural differences may influence employer–employee relations in an organization	AO3

© IBO, 2017

Employee and employer representatives

The role and responsibility of employee and employer representative. AO2

© IBO, 2017

Managers usually strive to ensure that there are good working relationships at work. This is often much easier to do in theory than in practice. Poor working relationships often lead to low morale and conflict (disagreements). Industrial unrest can subsequently arise, i.e. employer and employee relationships worsen. This means that workers are displeased with issues at work, such as pay and working conditions. Extreme actions taken by the disgruntled workforce include strike action or even rioting. Employee and employer representatives deal with sources of disputes on behalf of their members (employees and their employers) and conflict resolution.

Some individuals might not want to negotiate alone so they use 'agents' such as lawyers or trade union representatives to act on their behalf. **Collective bargaining** refers to the process by which pay and conditions of work are settled by negotiations between employers and employees, or by their respective representatives. **Negotiation** is a bargaining process whereby two or more parties attempt to achieve a mutually acceptable result. The negotiations tend to focus on the terms and conditions of employment, such as wage rates, hours of work and working conditions. The ultimate goal of negotiation is a 'win–win' outcome for all parties concerned. For example, employees via their trade union representatives may promise higher levels of productivity in return for better financial rewards. The outcome should benefit both employees and employer.

Employees are usually represented by a **trade union** (or **labour union**). This is an organization whose members unite to protect their rights and welfare. An individual is unlikely to have much bargaining power compared with a union of workers due to the strength in numbers. From an employer's perspective, it is also cheaper and quicker to bargain with just one trade union representative than many individual workers. Box 2.6.a describes the main types of labour unions.

Box 2.6.a Types of labour unions

- **Craft unions** These were the original labour unions with members sharing a particular skill or craft, such as engineers or printers.
- **Industrial unions** These unions accept members from the same industry, irrespective of their skills, qualifications, ranking or the nature of their work.
- **General unions** Such unions accept members from any industry, regardless of their skills or qualifications, so they tend to have a very large membership.
- **White-collar unions** These unions admit clerical, administrative and professional staff, i.e. members are non-manual workers. They exist in professions such as teaching and banking.

Members of a trade union must pay an annual fee to contribute towards the costs of running the union. Union subscription fees also cover the costs of legal advice and representation for members in a grievance or other industrial dispute. The primary role of labour unions is to protect the interests of their members, i.e. the employees who belong to the union. This is done mainly through collective bargaining on behalf of their members for improved pay and working conditions and/or through persuading governments to pass legislation in favour of workers (such as minimum wage legislation). Examples of the main issues that labour unions are occupied with include:

- Negotiating with employers for increased pay and benefits.

- Improving the conditions of work for their members, e.g. working hour and rest breaks.

- Supporting members with necessary legal advice, as and when needed.

- Providing financial support and legal advice to members who might have been unfairly dismissed or made redundant.

- Upholding the rights of their members to have professional training and development.

- Pressuring employers to ensure that equipment and machinery at work are safe to use, to protect members' health and safety at work.

Figure 2.6.a Labour unions fight for health and safety laws in the workplace

Employer representatives are individuals or organizations that represent the management team in the collective bargaining process. Some employers use a specialist management consultancy firm, whilst others prefer to use a small team of highly skilled individuals on the senior management team. In large organizations, the employer representatives are often from the company's head office. These representatives act as authorised representatives and contact people for the employer. Employers can also use **employers' associations**. These are organizations that represent the general views and interests of all businesses within a certain industry by negotiating with unions and influencing government action.

The outcome of the negotiation and collective bargaining process depends on the relative bargaining strengths of the employer and employee representatives. These in turn depend on several factors, including:

- The level of experience and skills of the negotiators.

- The number of members and the degree of unity within the trade union – Unions tend to be more powerful if members are united and if a majority of the workforce belong to the union.

- The state of the economy – For example, employees are in a weaker position to negotiate pay deals if there is high unemployment.

- Demand for labour is derived from the demand for the products that labour is used to supply – Thus, the demand for labour is unsustainable if prospects for a good or service are unfavourable, thus weakening the bargaining power of employee representatives.

- The degree of substitution between labour and capital – If unions continually push for pay rises without any benefit to the firm, the business will be more likely to use *capital intensive* production methods and/or make staff redundant due to the higher costs of production.

- Public and media opinion – Support for the business or labour union may determine which party has stronger negotiating powers.

- Government involvement – Government rules and regulations often determine the parameters within which negotiations take place.

Nevertheless, trade unions have steadily declined in popularity across all modern societies. Fewer people tend to be joining unions, for a variety of reasons. For example, automation and mechanisation in some organizations have led to redundancies in the manufacturing sector (traditionally the largest segment of union workers). A range of government rules and legislation has also led to weakening trade union powers, thereby making them less attractive to members. Finally, more part-timers in the workforce have led to a decline in union membership (as they tend not to be unionised). As a consequence, many organizations have developed **staff associations**. These have similar roles to a trade union except that they operate only within the organization. Hence, the issues dealt with by a staff association are more relevant to the workers, although their bargaining strength is weaker than that of a labour union.

Industrial/employee relations methods used by employees

The following industrial/employee relations methods used by employees: collective bargaining, slowdowns/go-slows, work-to-rule, overtime bans and strike action. AO3
© IBO, 2017

Workers can have a mix of objectives that they hope to achieve:

- Increased pay or the prevention of pay cuts

- Improved remuneration, such as fringe benefits and paid holidays

- Better working terms and conditions, such as hours of work and rest breaks

- Training and development opportunities

- Better-quality staff facilities, such as an improved canteen or office.

Trade unions use the following methods to help achieve their objectives: collective bargaining (negotiations), go-slows (slowdowns), work-to-rule, overtime bans and strike action.

Collective bargaining

Individual employees are unlikely to be in a good position to negotiate with management. However, this weakness is removed when the workforce is united, via trade union representation. Subsequently, senior managers are more pressured to listen to the views of the workers. A united workforce benefits from an increase in its collective bargaining power during the collective bargaining process.

Go-slows (slowdowns)

Under this form of industrial action, employees work at the minimum pace allowable in their employment contract. This reduces productivity yet employers find it difficult to discipline staff who work at a slow but contractually acceptable pace. Overtime work is avoided and urgency ceases as employees seek to minimise the speed of their work. Go-slows can be highly effective when firms face imminent deadlines or during periods of high seasonal demand because their operations become extremely disrupted.

Figure 2.6.b Go-slow is about working at the slowest pace possible

Work-to-rule

This occurs when employees do the absolute minimum required according to the rules set by the employer. Workers adhere precisely to all rules and regulations to delay production and to reduce productivity. Any goodwill from staff is withdrawn; workers do no more than they absolutely need to. For example, office staff may refuse to answer telephone calls during lunch breaks or choose to leave work as soon as their shift finishes. Such industrial action is considered less disruptive than strike action as workers are simply just obeying rules and regulations. Hence, employers find it more difficult to discipline staff who work to rule.

Overtime bans

This refers to a directive from the labour union for members to disengage in any overtime activity (operating beyond contracted hours of work). Overtime is not usually part of a worker's employment contract. By prohibiting overtime work, labour unions cause disruptions to business activity in the hope that management will listen to their views. Like go-slows, overtime bans can be highly effective during peak seasons and when businesses have impending deadlines.

Strike action

This refers to the collective refusal of employees to work. Strike action is usually the result of major industrial unrest such as widespread pay disputes or serious grievances. A strike is only considered to be official if it has the backing of the majority of members of a trade union. The union usually carries out a vote on strike action beforehand and then gives notification of such intent to the management. Workers carry out strike action as a sign of protest or disapproval of management decisions and actions. It is hoped the strike action forces an agreement to be reached with the management.

Strike action used to be a powerful tool used by unions to get their demands met. However, changes in social attitudes and legislation in many countries have meant that there are laws to protect employers from the potential power and threat of trade unions. Strike action can obviously be very disruptive to a business and governments try to ensure that businesses can operate fairly and competitively, without the added pressures imposed by trade unions. For example, in many countries it is illegal for a union to call for strike action from its members without giving prior notice to the employer. This allows the management to formulate contingency plans (see Unit 5.7) as the business will obviously be disrupted by the proposed industrial action.

A variation of strike action is a **walk-out**. A walk-out is a form of industrial action that happens when employees independently or collectively leave (or walk out of) their place of work as a sign of protest or disapproval of management decisions and actions.

Figure 2.6.c Public protests are a method of expressing employee rights in the workplace

Whichever method of industrial action is used, the output and efficiency of the business suffers at least temporarily. This reduces the competitiveness and profits of the organization, with the intention of making the employer listen to the demands of the workforce.

Question 2.6.1 Industrial action

In 2011, more than 250,000 people participated in a general march and rally in central London over **public sector** spending cuts and government failure to deliver promised labour and pension reforms. Trade unionists protested against the severe cuts which they argued would harm people's jobs and lives. Many people were particularly displeased with cuts in education and the police force.

In 2011, the unemployment rate of 18 to 24 year olds had risen to 20.3%, the highest rate since records began. The British government responded by saying that the **industrial action** was only temporary and had limited consequences on the economy, especially with the run-up to the London Olympic Games in 2012. With debt close to 60% of the nation's GDP, the government argued that public spending cuts were in the best interest of the country in the long term.

(a) (i) Define the term **public sector**. *[2 marks]*

(a) (ii) Define the term **industrial action**. *[2 marks]*

(b) Examine how mass-scale industrial action can affect the business opportunities of a country. *[6 marks]*

Box 2.6.b Reasons for a pay rise

Trade unions demand higher wages on behalf of their members due to a combination of reasons:

- An increase in the *cost of living* (due to inflation) which effectively reduces people's real income level.
- Workers in similar occupations in the industry have received a pay increase.
- Higher profits, contributed by the input of workers, provide a justification for higher pay.
- The productivity of labour has increased so workers 'should' be rewarded accordingly.
- A significant increase in *staff turnover* means that a pay rise may be needed to recruit and retain workers.

IB Learner Profile – Be an inquirer and be knowledgeable

Investigate a major industrial dispute for a company of your choice. What did the management team learn from this process?

Theory of knowledge

How much maternity leave (paid and unpaid) should a woman get?

Industrial/employee relations methods used by employers

The following industrial/employee relations methods used by employees: collective bargaining, threats of redundancies, changes of contract, closure and lock-outs. AO3

© IBO, 2017

Employer objectives include: lower production costs to remain competitive, improved productivity levels and lower rates of absenteeism and higher staff retention. The objectives of workers, if they are to be met, will raise the costs for an organization. Hence, employer objectives are likely to conflict with those of employees. Employers are usually represented in the negotiation process by a management team or by employers' associations (organizations that represent the general views and interests of all member businesses within a certain industry). Their function is to influence government action, rather like

Human resource management

a pressure group, and to negotiate with trade unions and the media. Employer associations can also offer advisory business-related services.

The senior management team and employers' associations are likely to consist of highly skilled negotiators who use a combination of tactics, such as: collective bargaining (negotiations), threats of redundancies, changes to employment contracts, closures and lock-outs.

- **Collective bargaining (negotiations)** This differs from other forms of conflict resolution in that it does not require the involvement of third parties to establish a win–win situation. Skilled negotiators representing the employers often use deadlines as a tactic. Setting short deadlines often gives the opposition little time to prepare or fight for its case.

- **Threats of redundancies** Some negotiators use intimidation to pressure or threaten employees. For example, during times of conflict, senior managers might use the threat of redundancies to pressure workers into complying with their demands. However, this does not mean that employers can simply mistreat or fire employees as they are protected by employment laws.

- **Changes of contract** It may be possible to legally change people's contracts of employment, if administered fairly. For example, if staff are on finite contracts then it is possible to change the terms and conditions of pay when renewing the contract. This gives the business a degree of flexibility in its pay structure. However, this can be seen as coercion as those who do not accept the new terms and conditions of the contract are simply denied the opportunity to extend their employment.

- **Lock-outs** A lock-out occurs when the employer temporarily stops employees from working during an industrial dispute. This is different from a strike where it is the employees who refuse to work. The business may hire security guards and/or change the locks of the premises to prevent employees from entering the premises. The lock-out will, in theory, eventually put pressure on some people to want to return to work in order to get paid. A divided trade union soon becomes a dysfunctional union.

Figure 2.6.d A lock-out prevents workers from accessing the workplace

Case study

In 2001, Cathay Pacific Airways fired 49 of their 1500 pilots due to industrial unrest. The purpose was to send a warning to all other union members to refrain from taking further industrial action.

Question 2.6.2 Indonesia's national strike action

In late 2013, **labour unions** in Indonesia called for nationwide **strike action** over poor pay for workers in the world's fourth most populous country. Employee representatives argued that the cost of living had risen sharply due to a combination of inflation (mainly caused by rising fuel prices and higher rents) and wages being capped by the government. Factory workers complained about being among the lowest-paid in Asia, earning less than their counterparts in China and India do. Government representatives responded by stating that the minimum wage had soared by 44% in a year to 2.2 million rupiah ($200) per month for workers in Jakarta.

(a) (i) Define the term **labour unions**.   *[2 marks]*

(a) (ii) Define the term **strike action**.   *[2 marks]*

(b) Examine **two** alternative methods that labour unions could use to protect the interests of their members.
                                                                                         [6 marks]

- **Closure** One way that managers can deal with strike action is to close the business. This is a rather extreme method, which is used when other approaches have been exhausted and when unions reject the employer's final offer. At best, closure means that workers will not receive any wages. In the worst case scenario, closure can mean that workers are made redundant. This ultimatum might be enough to persuade employees to renegotiate or to settle for a compromise.

> ### Theory of knowledge
>
> The EU's Working Time Directive states that all workers must not be required to work more than 48 hours in a week, with a minimum rest period of at least 11 hours a day.
> How can we know if this is beneficial to businesses?

Conflict

Sources of conflict in the workplace. AO2

© IBO, 2017

Conflict refers to a situation of friction or mutually exclusive goals between two or more parties, such as employees and employers. It is caused by disagreements or incompatibilities between these groups and results in a lack of cooperation. Conflict can arise at different levels, ranging from interpersonal conflict between individuals to international conflict between regional directors of a company.

Sources of conflict in the workplace include:

- *Needs and wants* – Conflicts arise when people's needs and desires are ignored, e.g. workers want job security and attractive pay and remuneration. Conflict often arises due to differences in opinions over rates of pay and working conditions. For instance, introducing flexible working practices (see Unit 2.1) may suit some people, such as part-time staff, but not others who might face restructuring or redundancies.

- *Perceptions* – Different people interpret things differently. What annoys one person does not necessarily annoy others. Misunderstandings and misperceptions can easily lead to conflict, e.g. some people are receptive to change whilst others are opposed to change perhaps due to their ignorance. Hence, there is a crucial role for effective communication to unite perceptions if conflict is to be minimised.

- *Values* – Conflict can arise when people hold incompatible beliefs, values or principles. If people are unwilling to compromise, this can make the management of conflict a very challenging task.

- *Power* – Conflict can arise when people in a position of power try to make others do something against their will or benefit. The unfair or exploitative use of authority causes friction in the workplace, e.g. managers might place pressure on employees to meet unrealistic sales targets.

- *Feelings and emotions* – Conflict often occurs because people ignore the feelings of others in the organization. It is quite natural for a person to feel let down or upset when others disagree with their ideas or opinions. It is not easy to simply separate professional life from personal life so feelings and emotions can become a major influence over how people deal with conflict. For example, grievances in the workplace or gossiping often lead to permanent conflict as people find it hard to forget and forgive those who they feel have been unfair or unreasonable.

Conflict in the workplace becomes a problem if it is not managed properly, because it can:

- Hinder productivity (there is less focus on completing the task at hand)

- Reduce the level of staff morale due to added stress and anxieties

- Cause inappropriate conduct, such as unethical behaviour

- Fuel the internal politics (incompatible differences) within an organization

- Hamper opportunities for collaborative teams.

Note that conflict is not necessarily a negative thing. Some analysts believe that conflict is often needed in organizations. For instance, conflict can help to raise and address real problems that are bothering people. It can also help people to recognise and benefit from their personal differences. Having a better understanding of each other's differences and needs can actually foster better working relationships in the future. Conflict itself is not the true problem; it is the way in which conflict arises and how it is managed that can become problems.

Human resource management

Question 2.6.3   Deutsche Telekom

Deutsche Telekom is one of Europe's largest telecommunications company, with over 235,000 workers and sales in excess of €58 billion ($79.3 billion). Although the German company experienced short-term **walk-outs** in the past, it had not experienced full **strike action** until 2007 when more than 11,000 employees went on strike over proposed pay cuts and increased working hours.

Deutsche Telekom, parent company of mobile phone giant T-Mobile, argued that the proposals were necessary as almost a million customers had left its fixed-line business, having switched to cheaper rivals. In 2012, Deutsche Telekom and T-Mobile workers across the USA and Germany went on strike again over further pay disputes.

(a) Distinguish between a **walk-out** and **strike action**. [4 marks]

(b) Comment on the sources of conflict at Deutsche Telekom. [4 marks]

Theory of knowledge

How might emotions affect our perceptions on inequalities in the workplace?

Theory of knowledge

Which way of knowing (perception, emotion or reasoning) is the main source of conflict?

Theory of knowledge

In business management, is compromise irrational?

Figure 2.6.e Conflict resolution is an important managerial skill

Conflict resolution

Conflict resolution refers to the course of action taken to resolve conflict and differences in opinions. It is considered to be successful if each party's interests are addressed, resulting in a satisfactory outcome for all sides. Given that employers and employees may have conflicting interests, it can be difficult for both sides to reach a settlement. There are several ways to approach conflict resolution, including: conciliation and arbitration, employee participation and industrial democracy, no-strike agreements and single-union agreements.

Conciliation and arbitration

Conciliation is a process whereby the parties involved in a dispute agree to use the services of an independent mediator. This person meets with the parties separately (a practice known as caucusing) in an attempt to resolve their disputes and differences. The conciliator's role is to encourage the parties to negotiate and compromise to reach a solution that is mutually acceptable (see Figure 2.6.f). The parties are unlikely to actually meet so it is important for conciliators to be highly skilled negotiators and effective communicators. Conciliators will almost always get the parties to commit their compromise in writing, which makes the resolution legally binding.

Arbitration is similar to conciliation in that an external entity is used as part of conflict resolution. However, the process involves an independent arbitrator deciding on an appropriate outcome. The arbitrator acts rather like a judge by listening to and examining the arguments put forward by both parties before making a final decision or recommendation. The arbitrator's final decision becomes legally binding.

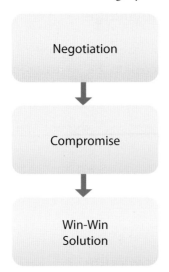

Figure 2.6.f The three step conciliation process

An extreme case of arbitration is **pendulum arbitration** which requires the arbitrator to decide completely in favour of one party or the other, i.e. there is no compromise made. The idea behind this approach is that both parties in the dispute are forced to make more realistic and/or conservative demands. For example, suppose that there is conflict over the rate of pay rises, with the labour union pushing for 6% but employers arguing for only 3%. The arbitrator will need to assess both sides of the argument. If the arbitrator calculates that 4% is the correct level for pay increments, this is closer to the 3% advocated by the employer and therefore the decision will be to raise pay by 3%.

Employee participation and industrial democracy

Employee participation is an example of **industrial democracy**. This means that employees are given responsibilities and authority to complete tasks and are involved in the decision-making process. An example of employee participation is team working (see Unit 2.4). Motivation theorists such as Maslow and Herzberg (also see Unit 2.4) point out that employee participation and industrial democracy help to increase productivity because workers are more involved so are happier. Furthermore, employers benefit from a more cooperative workforce that is less likely to engage in industrial action. Employees benefit from higher levels of morale and an increase in job satisfaction. As a result, absenteeism and labour turnover rates are also likely to fall. These benefits lead to a 'win–win' situation for both the employer and employees.

No-strike agreements

Many trade unions have been negatively affected by their image for being disruptive to the business community. Union membership throughout the world has also been declining. In response to these trends, many unions have tried to improve their image by having a *no-strike agreement*, i.e. members agree not to take strike action as a form of industrial action. For example, the American Federation of Teachers with around 1 million members across the USA has a no strike policy. This has helped the union to sustain its membership and reassured employers and other stakeholder groups that the teachers will not strike at the expense of their students.

Figure 2.6.g The Association of Teachers and Lecturers is a union for educators in the UK

Single-union agreements

A single-union agreement occurs when an organization agrees to participate in the negotiation process with a sole labour union that represents the workers. The benefit of a single-union agreement is that it causes fewer disruptions to the employer as there is no need to spend as much management time and resources dealing with a multitude of problems from various inter-union disputes.

In reality, the approach taken to deal with conflict largely depends on people's concern for their own outcomes and that of others. This means that there are five possible outcomes:

- High concern for personal outcome leads people to **compete** for a win–only outcome.

- High concern for others only means **surrendering**, which leads to a win situation for the other party.

- Low or no concern for either party's outcomes simply means there is **avoidance** of the issue.

- High concern for the outcome of both parties leads to **collaboration** (cooperation) to find a mutually beneficial solution.

- Moderate concern for the outcome of both parties leads of some sort of **compromise**.

Most experts believe that high concern for the outcome of both parties (and hence efforts to find a mutually beneficial resolution) leads to the most satisfactory result. Note that each strategy will be appropriate in different circumstances, at different times. Collaboration, for example, does not work for all cases of conflict.

		Concern for self		
		Low	Moderate	High
Concern for others	High	Surrender		Collaborate
	Moderate		Compromise	
	Low	Avoidance		Compete

Figure 2.6.h Outcomes of conflict

Theory of knowledge

What are the knowledge issues involved in determining what is considered to be a reasonable salary to remunerate workers?

Theory of knowledge

Is there ever a case for senior managers to surrender to, or to avoid conflict? Are these signs of poor leadership?

Question 2.6.4 Human Rights Watch and Walmart

Human Rights Watch is an international **non-governmental organization** based in New York. In 2007, it carried out its first ever survey on how American companies treat their workers (having previously conducted studies in other countries). Human Rights Watch found that *Walmart*, the largest employer in the USA, had violated federal laws by its aggressive efforts to shut out trade unions. The report found that none of the 1.3 million *Walmart* staff was associated with a labour union. Independent reports also suggested that *Walmart* employees were disgruntled over the lack of **corporate social responsibility**, especially the poor pay and working conditions. In late 2012, following protests by thousands of *Walmart* workers, Human Rights Watch claimed, "Walmart has repeatedly used tactics that run afoul of US law and directly infringe on workers' right to freedom of association."

Walmart responded by defending its labour policies. The retailer argued that it provided open channels of communication to allow employees to express their ideas, comments and concerns. *Walmart* also claimed that its labour practices meant that none of the workers needed to join labour unions, further testifying that the accusations made in the Human Rights Watch report were outdated and misleading.

(a) (i) Define the term **non-governmental organization**. *[2 marks]*

(a) (ii) Define the term **corporate social responsibility**. *[2 marks]*

(b) Explain how a perceived lack of corporate social responsibility at *Walmart* can cause conflict. *[4 marks]*

(c) Evaluate alternative approaches to conflict resolution at *Walmart*. *[10 marks]*

Human resource management

Resistance to change

Reasons for resistance to change in the workplace (such as self-interest, low tolerance, misinformation and interpretation of circumstances). AO2

Human resource strategies for reducing the impact of change and resistance to change (such as getting agreement/ownership, planning and timing the change and communicating the change). AO3

© IBO, 2017

One of the major barriers to effective change management is the resistance to change from the workforce. According to Professor John Paul Kotter (1979) of Harvard Business School, there are four main reasons why people are resistant to change in the workplace:

- Self-interest often takes priority over organizational objectives. People may be more interested in (concerned with) the implications of change for themselves rather than the benefits that change might bring for the organization. Hence, they may feel that change simply involves extra effort.

- Low tolerance of change happens because people prefer familiarity to disruptions and uncertainties. A lack of security is sensed when people are out of their norms or comfort zone. There could also be an element of fear from being made redundant, perhaps with the introduction of new production techniques. Staff might also fear failure in adapting to change, such as not being able to work within an automated environment.

- Misinformation causes misunderstandings because the purpose of change has not been communicated properly. Staff often feel that change is not necessary, especially if things are going well – as the saying goes, 'If it isn't broken, don't fix it'. Uncertainties can also arise due to the anxieties of the unknown caused by misinformation.

- Different assessments of the situation occur when there are different interpretations of circumstances, i.e. management and staff disagree on the purpose and merits of change. Managers may feel that restructuring of the workforce is necessary, for example, but workers might disagree as they are the experts in their roles and do not see the need for such change.

There is also the possibility of ambivalence (the internal conflict surrounding change where some people do not necessarily voice their concerns) which could underestimate the actual degree of resistance to change. When people are in a group situation, for example, they may conform to the majority view but would prefer to act differently themselves. Others might feel that if they resist change then they are overlooked in future for any promotional opportunities within the organization.

Professor Kotter proposed the six change approaches model to deal with resistance to change (see Figure 2.6.i):

1. **Education and communication** This approach aims to inform and educate staff (and other stakeholders) about the change beforehand. Early communication and clarification can help stakeholders to see the rationale for change and establish a degree of trust. Perhaps more importantly, this reduces any unsubstantiated claims and rumours about the proposed change.

2. **Participation and involvement** This approach links with several motivation theorists such as Maslow and Herzberg (see Unit 2.4) who argue that employee involvement in decision-making can motivate and improve morale amongst the workforce. Kotter argued that by involving employees in the change process, perhaps by a series of consultations, formal agreements and giving staff a sense of ownership of the change, they are more likely to accept change instead of resisting it.

3. **Facilitation and support** This approach is paternalistic in style as managers become supportive of staff during difficult times, thereby averting potential resistance to change. Managerial support can be in numerous forms, such as planning and timing the change effectively. For example, staff may need retraining to accommodate the new changes. If change involves redundancies, then support systems need to be implemented to help workers find alternative employment. Counselling employees to deal with their fears and apprehensions is another example.

4. **Negotiation and agreement** This is the 'carrot' approach whereby managers use incentives to remove or limit resistance to change. This can be done by 'inviting' workers to accept amendments in their employment contracts to accommodate the new changes, for example. Alternatively, staff who resist change might be offered early retirement or redundancy incentives to leave the organization. At other times, managers may be willing to compromise to provide an incentive for staff to settle for the change.

HIGHER LEVEL

Human resource management

5. **Manipulation and co-option**   This approach involves bringing a representative of those resisting change into the change process. The purpose, in theory, is to give them representation but in fact the underlying reason is to convert the representative's thinking so that the advantages of change can be communicated to those resisting change (whatever their reason). These representatives, such as trade union leaders, are quite often given a symbolic role but the reality is that their view will not affect the desire of management to push for the change. This approach is, of course, seen as rather unethical and can backfire if those resisting change discover what the management is really trying to do.

6. **Explicit and implicit coercion**   This is the 'stick' approach to dealing with resistance to change and is typically used as a last resort. Managers can use coercion (bullying tactics) to force staff into accepting change, by threatening disciplinary action, dismissals, job losses, redeployment (transferring employees to other jobs), or not promoting employees. Due to employment legislation that exists to protect employees, coercion is likely to be carried out implicitly by managers.

Figure 2.6.i Kotter's six change approaches

Theory of knowledge

How do individuals, organizations and societies cope with change in the modern business world? How does culture influence how they cope?

Industrial/employee relations and the CUEGIS concepts

How innovation, ethical considerations and cultural differences may influence employer–employee relations in an organization.
AO3
© IBO, 2017

Innovation in the workplace involves the implementation of new processes and technologies in an organization. This includes technologies that support or improve the performance of employees and the quality of their work. Consider, for example, how learning technologies in education has changed the way that teachers and students work. Such innovations can therefore improve employee motivation and commitment. However, labour-saving technologies and innovations can harm employer–employee relations. This can result in poorer quality work, demotivation and lower productivity.

Ethical considerations include the implementation of corporate social responsibilities (see Unit 1.3), such as the ethical treatment of workers. For example, employers who provide workers with adequate rest breaks, equal opportunities and training prospects are likely to get the best out of their employees, who get to enjoy a good work–life balance (see Box 2.6.c). By contrast, employees who are mistreated, discriminated against or overstretched struggle to have a positive working relationship with their employers.

Box 2.6.c   Work practices that support employees' work–life balance

- Policies and practices to reduce workload
- Flexible working practices, e.g. part-time, flexitime and homeworking (see Unit 2.1)
- Job-sharing (a form of part-time work with two people sharing the work of a single full-time job)
- Flexibility in the allocation of paid vacation time
- Allowing leave of absence from the workplace for a variety of reasons, e.g. maternity, paternity and adoption leave or for sickness.

Cultural differences (see Unit 2.5) can also influence employer–employee relations. People tend to be more cooperative, creative and productive when they are happy. This is clearly dependent on the organizational culture. For example, industrial relations depend very much on the dominant leadership and management styles within an organization, e.g. managers that have low concern for people and only focus on completing tasks tend to foster poor employer–employee relations. In some cultures, managers believe that creating fear is the best way to keep employees working and not to slack off. By contrast, other cultures foster a culture of trust and empowerment. They develop a culture that values the importance of consultation in the decision-making process. They value the contributions that workers can make to devise more informed strategic judgments. Julian Richer the founder of Richer Sounds (see Question 2.4.2) believes it is vital that his staff have fun, are able to contribute ideas, enjoy their work and feel valued. This will have a positive impact on employer–employee relations, which ultimately leads to improved performance in the workplace.

It is also important for managers to be aware of international cultural differences when trying to deal with conflict at work. For example, US and European companies are used to dealing with confrontational issues, whereas the Japanese and Indians find outright confrontation a barrier to negotiations. Another example is that of gestures such as shaking hands; in some cultures the shake of hands means 'farewell' or 'nice to meet you' but in other situations it also means 'we have a deal'. In some Asian countries, physical contact between men and women is discouraged, but this should not be seen as being an unfriendly mannerism (also see Box 4.7.c).

Theory of knowledge

Is it possible to measure happiness in the workplace in a truly objective way? Can we therefore measure the correlation between happiness and productivity, or do we simply know by intuition?

Employers have often used **public relations** (PR) as a strategy to deal with industrial disputes. PR is the function of a business that deals with comments, complaints and criticisms from the general public, including the firm's customers. PR specialists (whether internally or externally hired) deal with the media and are responsible for issuing press releases and other information that portray the business in a positive manner. PR is different from advertising in that it aims to achieve favourable publicity without the cost and it does not primarily aim to boost sales. Instead, PR is more about building goodwill and restoring industrial relations.

Finally, it is an imperative part of strategic thinking to consider the needs of workers and to treat staff in an appropriate manner if they are truly regarded as the organization's most valuable asset. After all, it is the employees who persuade and serve customers to part with their money. Therefore, open and trusting employee–employer relations enhance the strategic direction and prosperity of an organization.

Theory of knowledge

Conflict creates change. To what extent do you agree with this statement in the context of Business Management?

CUEGIS ESSAY

With reference to an organization you have studied, examine how **change** and **culture** have influenced employer-employee relations. *[20 marks]*

REVIEW QUESTIONS

1. Distinguish between negotiations and collective bargaining.

2. What are labour unions (trade unions)?

3. What are employer's associations?

4. The outcome of any negotiation or collective bargaining process depends on several factors. State five of these factors.

5. What is a trade (labour) union?

6. What is the main purpose of a labour union?

7. Distinguish between 'go-slow' and 'work-to-rule'.

8. Differentiate between 'lock-outs' and 'closures'.

9. What is meant by conflict?

10. Why does conflict become a problem if not managed properly?

11. Distinguish between conciliation and arbitration.

12. Why might employee participation and industrial democracy lead to a win-win outcome?

13. How might no-strike agreements help to improve the image of a labour union?

14. What are the reasons for resistance to change in the workplace?

15. Outline the human resource strategies for reducing the impact of change and resistance to change.

KEY TERMS

Arbitration is a process that involves an independent person or body (the arbitrator) deciding on an appropriate outcome to a dispute. The arbitrator's final decision is legally binding.

Collective bargaining is the negotiation process whereby trade union representatives and employer representatives discuss issues with the intention of reaching a mutually acceptable agreement.

Conciliation is a process whereby the two parties involved in a dispute agree to use the services of an independent mediator to help in the negotiations.

Conflict refers to disagreements that result from differences in the attitudes, beliefs, values or needs of people. It can also arise from past rivalries and personality clashes.

Conflict resolution refers to the course of action taken to manage and resolve conflict or differences in opinions.

Employers' associations are a type of employer's representatives. The association is an organization that represents the general views and interests of all businesses within a certain industry by negotiating with unions and influencing government action.

Employer representatives are individuals or organizations that represent the management team in the collective bargaining process.

Go-slows, or **slowdowns**, are a form of industrial action that involve employees working at the minimum pace allowable under their employment contract.

Industrial action refers to the activities taken by disgruntled employees due to disputes over working conditions and practices, e.g. hours of work or pay disputes. It is a result of poor employer–employee relationships or conflict at work.

Industrial democracy means that employees are given responsibilities and authority to complete tasks, i.e. they have opportunities to be involved in the decision-making process.

Negotiation is a bargaining process whereby separate parties attempt to achieve a mutually acceptable outcome, i.e. a 'win–win' situation.

A **no-strike agreement** is a method of conflict resolution involving members of a labour union agreeing not to strike as a form of industrial action.

Overtime bans are a form of industrial action with workers complying with a labour union directive for members to disengage from working beyond their contracted employment hours.

Single-union agreement refers to an organization agreeing to participate in collective bargaining with a sole trade union that represents the workers.

Staff associations strive to uphold the welfare of their staff members (although their bargaining power is weaker than that of trade unions) by dealing with issues that are directly relevant to staff in their actual workplace.

Strike action is a form of industrial action that involves employees refusing to work. This is usually the result of major industrial unrest such as large-scale pay disputes or serious grievances.

A **trade union** (or **labour union**) is an organization of worker-members who unite to protect their rights and wellbeing in the workplace.

Work-to-rule occurs when employees do the absolute minimum required, as stated in their employment contracts, i.e. they adhere precisely to all rules and regulations in order to reduce productivity.

3.1 Sources of finance

"A business that makes nothing but money is a poor kind of business."   Henry Ford (1863–1947), founder of the Ford Motor Company

SL/HL content	Assessment objective
Role of finance for businesses: • capital expenditure • revenue expenditure	AO2
The following internal sources of finance: • personal funds (for sole traders) • retained profit • sale of assets	AO2
The following external sources of finance: • share capital • loan capital • overdrafts • trade credit • grants • subsidies • debt factoring • leasing • venture capital • business angels	AO2
Short, medium and long-term finance	AO1
The appropriateness, advantages and disadvantages of sources of finance for a given situation	AO3

© IBO, 2017

Finance and accounts

CORE

The role of finance for business

Role of finance for businesses: capital expenditure and revenue expenditure. AO2

The appropriateness, advantages and disadvantages of sources of finance for a given situation. AO3

© IBO, 2017

All businesses need money to finance their various activities. This could be for the initial setting up of the business, for its day-to-day running or for expansion purposes. Businesses can obtain their finance from a range of sources, such as loans from a bank or by selling shares.

The appropriateness of the various sources of finance depends on several factors, including the size and type of business organization, the time scale involved and the purpose of the finance. For example, a sole trader is likely to use personal finance for setting up the business, whereas a multinational might seek external sources of finance to expand in overseas markets.

Figure 3.1.a Sources of finance help to raise cash for business expenditure

The role (purpose) of finance can be categorised either as capital or revenue expenditure:

- **Capital expenditure** is the finance spent on **fixed assets**. These are items of monetary value that have a long-term function so can be used repeatedly, e.g. land, buildings, equipment, machinery and vehicles. Fixed assets determine the scale of a firm's operations. They are not intended for resale (in the short term) but for the purpose of generating money for the business. The sources of finance for capital expenditure tend to come from medium and long-term sources because of the high cost of financing fixed assets. These assets can also provide collateral (financial guarantee) for securing additional loan capital.

- **Revenue expenditure** refers to payments for the daily running of a business, e.g. wages, raw materials, rent and electricity. It also includes the payment of indirect costs (see Unit 3.2) such as insurance and advertising. Costs must be controlled so that the business can generate enough revenue to earn a profit.

Different businesses have different access to an array of finance (see Table 3.1.a). Typically, the main source of finance for sole traders is their personal savings. By contrast, larger and more established businesses can seek other sources of finance for expansion purposes, e.g. by issuing shares or by selling debentures.

Internal sources of finance

The following internal sources of finance: personal funds (for sole traders), retained profit and sale of assets. AO2

The appropriateness, advantages and disadvantages of sources of finance for a given situation. AO3

© IBO, 2017

Sources of finance can also be categorised as *internal* or *external*. **Internal sources of finance** come from *within* the business. These include:

Personal funds

This is the main source of finance for sole traders and for partnerships (see Unit 1.2). Jamie Oliver, the famous British celebrity chef, hired fifteen unknown recruits for his restaurant 'Fifteen', using £500,000 ($725,000) of his own money to finance the project.

Retained profits

This is the value of profits that the business keeps (after paying taxes to the government and dividends to its shareholders) to use within the business. Retained profits are often used for purchasing and/or upgrading fixed assets. Some retained profit might also be kept in a contingency fund (see Unit 5.7) in case of emergencies and unforeseeable expenditure in the future. The benefit of retained profit as a source of finance is that it does not incur any interest charges.

Sale of assets

Businesses can sell their dormant assets (unused assets), such as selling old machinery and computer equipment that have been replaced. If a business has chosen to relocate (see Unit 5.4), it might be able to raise finance through the sale of land and buildings. In more extreme cases, businesses can raise finance by selling some of their fixed assets to survive a liquidity problem.

Question 3.1.1   London Olympic Games

London made history by becoming the first city to host the modern Olympic Games three times (1908, 1948 and 2012). The commercial benefits were welcomed by the UK construction industry, with around half a million new jobs added to the industry in preparation for the global sporting event. Transport for London also funded numerous improvements in preparation for 2012, including expansion of railway networks and the introduction of Britain's first 'bullet' (high-speed rail) trains.

(a) With reference to the case study, distinguish between *revenue expenditure* and *capital expenditure.*   [4 marks]

(b) Examine the benefits to various stakeholder groups of the Olympic Games being held in London.   [6 marks]

External sources of finance

The following external sources of finance: share capital, loan capital, overdrafts, trade credit, grants, subsidies, debt factoring, leasing, venture capital and business angels. AO2

The appropriateness, advantages and disadvantages of sources of finance for a given situation. AO3

© IBO, 2017

External sources of finance come from outside the business. These include:

Share capital

This is the main source of finance for most limited liability companies, as shown in a firm's balance sheet (see Unit 3.4). Share capital is the money raised from selling shares in the company. The key advantage is that it can provide a huge amount of finance. For example, Brazilian oil company Petrobras raised a world record $70 billion from a public share issue in September 2010.

Private limited companies cannot sell their shares to the general public whereas public limited companies can issue their shares on a stock exchange. The main functions of a stock exchange (or stock market) are to enable companies to raise capital and to provide a market for second-hand shares and government stocks. The London, Tokyo and New York Stock Exchanges are among the biggest in the world.

Many businesses decide to 'go public' by floating their shares on a stock exchange for the first time. This is known as an **initial public offering** (IPO). Popular IPOs are heavily oversubscribed, which pushes up the share price. Existing companies can raise further finance by selling more sales in a **share issue** (or a **share placement**). However, by issuing shares, ownership and control of the business becomes diluted. The process also involves many legalities and administrative procedures, with their associated costs.

Exam tip !

When shareholders sell their shares, the company does not receive any of this money as these shares are traded on the secondary market of the stock exchange; no new shares have been issued by the company.

Figure 3.1.b The New York Stock Exchange

CORE

Box 3.1.a   The world's five largest IPOs

Company	Country	Year	Funds raised (USD)
Alibaba.com	China	2014	$25.00bn
Agriculture Bank of China (ABC)	China	2010	$22.10bn
Industrial and Commercial Bank of China (ICBC)	China	2006	$21.97bn
American International Assurance (AIA)	USA	2010	$20.51bn
Visa Inc.	USA	2008	$19.65bn

Sources: adapted from Reuters.com and *Forbes*

Question 3.1.2   Agricultural Bank of China (ABC)

In August 2010, Agricultural Bank of China (*ABC*) completed its **initial public offering** (IPO) in Shanghai and Hong Kong, raising $22.1 billion. Despite the weak market sentiment in Asian stock markets and fears that Chinese bank shares were overvalued, investors poured money into China's third largest lender, with more than 325 million customers across 24,000 branches. *ABC*'s flotation proved to be the world's largest ever, beating the previous record of $21.97 billion set by the IPO of China's largest bank, Industrial and Commercial Bank of China (ICBC) in October 2006.

(a) Define the term **initial public offering**.   *[2 marks]*

(b) Comment on why *ABC* might have decided to float its shares on the stock market.   *[4 marks]*

(c) Explain why investors might have been so keen to buy shares in *ABC*, despite the weak market sentiment in Asian stock markets at the time.   *[4 marks]*

Loan capital

These are medium- to long-term sources of finance obtained from commercial lenders such as banks. Interest charges are imposed and can be fixed or variable, depending on the agreement between borrower and lender. The amount borrowed is paid back in instalments over a predetermined period, such as 5, 10 or 25 years.

An example is a **mortgage** that is a secured loan for the purchase of property such as land or buildings. If the borrower *defaults* on the loan (fails to repay) then the lender can repossess (take back) the property. Another example is a **business development loan**, catered to meet the specific development needs of the borrower. Businesses can use these highly flexible loans to start or expand their business, to purchase equipment and other assets, or even to boost working capital (see Unit 3.7).

A third example is **debentures**. These are essentially long-term loans issued by a business. Debenture holders (individuals, governments or other businesses) receive interest payments even if the business makes a loss and before shareholders are paid any dividend. The interest payment can be fixed or variable depending on the type of debenture. They are used by a vast range of organizations, from Arsenal Football Club for its Emirates Stadium in London to private schools in Hong Kong (see Question 3.1.3). Unlike shareholders, debenture holders do not usually have ownership or voting rights. Therefore, debentures provide a long-term source of finance, without the business losing any control. However, issuing debentures increases a firm's gearing (see Unit 3.6). This means the firm has more borrowing as a percentage of its capital employed, so this raises interest payments to the lender and increases the firm's exposure to risk if interest rates increase.

Figure 3.1.c
Debentures were used to help build The Emirates Stadium, London

Question 3.1.3   Kellet School

In 2013, *Kellett School* in Hong Kong introduced record-breaking **debentures** up to the value of HK$10 million (US$1.29 million), being refundable when students eventually leave the school. Parents with more than one child at the school would get a small discount. Its school fees ranged from HK$123,500 to HK$168,800 (US$15,930 to US$21,775). The timing coincided with the school's move to a new HK$200 million (US$25.8 million) campus with its much improved facilities such as a large auditorium, swimming pool, Astroturf multisport areas, an extensive library and state-of-the-art classrooms.

Critics argued the enormous cost of education would diminish Hong Kong's international competitiveness by putting off highly skilled expats and their families coming to Hong Kong. Rival school *Harrow International* offers non-interest bearing debentures of up to HK$3 million (US$387,000). Capital expenditure and the costs of land construction mean that debentures are common in international schools in Hong Kong.

Source: adapted from www.thestandard.com.hk

(a)   Define the term **debentures**.   *[2 marks]*

(b)   Outline why *Kellett School* decided to sell debentures.   *[2 marks]*

(c)   Despite the high price, suggest why most parents might agree to purchase *Kellett School's* debentures.   *[4 marks]*

(d)   Explain **two** potential drawbacks to a school that chooses to raise finance through the sale of debentures.   *[4 marks]*

(e)   Examine **two** alternative sources of finance that *Kellett School* could have used to finance its capital expenditure.   *[6 marks]*

Overdrafts

This allows a business to temporarily overdraw on its bank account, i.e. to take out more money than it has in its account. Overdrafts are commonly used when businesses have minor cash flow problems (see Unit 3.7). Although overdrafts can demand a relatively high rate of interest, they are usually more cost-effective than bank loans. This is because, unlike bank loans, overdrafts are used as short-term sources of finance and interest is charged on a daily basis if, and only if, a business overdraws on its account. They are suitable when there is a need for a large cash outflow, such as retailers stocking up for peak trading periods. They are also suitable for businesses that have sold items on credit and are awaiting payments from their customers. However, a major disadvantage is that overdrafts are repayable on demand from the lender. Nevertheless, overdrafts provide flexibility for businesses that might occasionally face cash flow problems.

Trade credit

This source of finance allows a business to 'buy now and pay later'. Although a sale is made at the time of purchase, the seller or credit provider does not receive any cash from the buyer until a later date. Organizations that offer trade credit (known as **creditors**) usually allow between 30–60 days for their customers (known as **debtors**) to pay. **Credit cards** are similar to trade credit except that the creditor is not a supplier but a financial institution such as banks that offer electronic funds transfers through providers such as American Express and Visa. Essentially, this acts as a cash advance to the credit card holder. Credit cards are a vital source of external finance for sole traders and partnerships.

Grants

This refers to government financial gifts (non-repayable funds) to support business activities. Grants are usually offered to eligible businesses as one-off payments and do not need to be repaid. This might be for small business start-ups or to help stimulate economic activity in regions or industries that may be facing particular problems such as high unemployment. However, government grants may be hard to obtain.

Subsidies

These are similar to grants in that the purpose is to reduce costs of production, although the focus of subsidies is to provide extended benefits to society. For example, farmers are often provided with subsidies so that food prices can be stabilised.

Subsidies are often approved for essential products and services, such as health and education services. Subsidies do not cut into profit margins. Although firms charge lower prices, profit is made up by the financial support of the government subsidy.

Debt factoring

Debtors are people or organizations that owe money to the business. For example, a business might have sold supplies to a customer on 30 days credit, so the business will not receive any payment until the following month. However, if the business gives too much credit to its clients, it faces a higher chance of **bad debt** – debtors who are unable to repay the money owed, perhaps due to their own financial problems. Banks often experience an increase in bad debts when there is a sudden and unexpected downturn in the economy.

Debt factoring is a financial service that allows a business to raise funds based on the value owed by its debtors, i.e. customers who have bought on credit. Most debt factoring service providers offer between 80–85% of the outstanding payments from debtors within 24 hours once the application has been approved. This can be beneficial compared to receiving money in 30 or 60 days' time – typical credit periods. Hence, debt factoring can act as an immediate source of finance for businesses that have cash flow problems. The service provider takes over the legal responsibility of chasing up debtors. The main disadvantage of debt factoring is the high fees charged by the service providers. There are additional charges for management, administration and maintenance of accounts. The larger the value of debtors, the higher the charges tend to be due to the increased risks involved. Also, not all businesses are eligible to use the service, especially smaller firms.

Leasing

This is a form of hiring whereby a contract is agreed between a leasing company (the lessor) and the customer (the lessee). The lessee pays rental income to hire assets from the lessor, who is the legal owner of the assets. It can be cheaper to lease assets such as machinery, equipment, vehicles and buildings, especially in the short to medium term. Hence, leasing is suitable for business customers who do not have the initial capital to buy such assets. This consequently releases cash for other purposes within the business. Another benefit to the lessee is that repairs and maintenance are the responsibility of the lessor. Also, as spending on leased assets is classed as a business expense, the tax bill of the lessee is reduced. The main disadvantage to the customer is that in the long term, leasing is more expensive than hire purchase or the outright purchase of the assets. **Sale-and-leaseback** involves a business selling a particular fixed asset (to raise finance) and immediately leasing the property back. In essence, the business transfers ownership although the asset does not physically leave the business.

Figure 3.1.d Police cars are often financed by leasing

Question 3.1.4 Bradylee Diamonds

Bradylee Diamonds has a forecast cash flow deficit of $140,000 in two months' time. It also has debtors totalling $180,000. The firm decides to use a **debt factoring** service that advances 80% of the debtor balance.

(a) Define the term **debt factoring**. *[2 marks]*

(b) Calculate and outline whether this decision would resolve the cash flow problem for *Bradylee Diamonds*. *[4 marks]*

Instead of leasing, **hire purchase** (HP) allows a business to pay its creditors in instalments, perhaps over 12 or 24 months. The asset is legally the property of the creditor until all payments have been made. Quite often, a deposit (or down payment) is required to secure a HP deal from the lender. Also, if the buyer defaults on the agreement (falls behind on repayments) then the lender can repossess the asset. HP is a form of buying on credit, so interest is charged by the lender on the amount borrowed. It is different from leasing because the buyer eventually owns the asset on payment of the last instalment.

Venture capital

This is a form of high-risk capital, usually in the form of loans or shares, invested by venture capital firms, usually at the start of a business idea. Venture capitalists seek to invest in small to medium-sized businesses that have high growth potential. There is a considerable chance of business failure but also significant returns if the business succeeds. Hence, those who aim to secure venture capital must present a coherent and convincing business plan (see Unit 1.1) with supporting data to show venture capitalists that the risks are worth taking. Venture capitalists can also provide invaluable advice about the strategic direction of the business.

Venture capitalists and business angels (see below) look at a number of criteria before committing their capital in an investment project, including:

- **Return on investment** Investors demand a return on their capital. Venture capitalists know that a huge majority of business start-ups fail outright, so each business in their investment portfolio has to have good potential to be highly profitable.

- **The business plan** This should outline the long-term aim and purpose of the business venture. The purpose creates *direction* and an *identity* for the business, which is central to securing finance from investors. Investors must feel confident that the business fully understands the market in which it operates. They want to see that the idea allows the business to compete in a high-growth market with few competitors. Innovative and original ideas can convince investors to part with their capital.

- **People** It is extremely difficult for any individual to have all the skills, experiences and contacts required to run a business successfully. Essentially, no matter how good an idea might be in the business plan, success will only materialise if the business has a good team of people. Ineffective people management is a major cause of business failure (see Unit 1.2) so this is an aspect that venture capitalists will examine carefully.

- **Track record** Investors will assess the past track record of a business and its management before investing any capital. This might include an investigation into the firm's ability to pay back previous lenders and the success record of the entrepreneurs.

Question 3.1.5   Wizz Air

In late 2013, Hungary low-cost airline carrier *Wizz Air* signed a **sale-and-leaseback** agreement with Chinese CDB Leasing Co. to finance six Airbus A320 aircraft. The deal raised $549 m to finance the airline's expansion plans with new routes to Barcelona, Bologna, Dortmund and Rome from 2014. Established in 2003, the airline flies to over 144 destinations in 42 countries. As is common with low-cost budget airlines, *Wizz Air* operates a buy on board system where food and beverages are paid for on board rather than included in the ticket price.

(a) Define the term **sale-and-leaseback**. *[2 marks]*

(b) Explain **two** advantages to businesses such as Chinese CDB Leasing Co. leasing assets to established organizations such as *Wizz Air*. *[4 marks]*

Business angels

These are extremely wealthy individuals who choose to invest their own money in businesses that offer high growth potential, i.e. high-risk, high-return business ventures. By contrast, venture capital is typically a pool of professionally managed funds. Business angels provide funding for firms that are unable to secure loans from banks and/or too small to attract the attention of venture capitalists.

Business angels are likely to take a proactive role in the setting up or running of the business venture. This means that the owner loses some control to the business angel. Another disadvantage is that the organization might eventually have to buy out the stake owned by the business angel. However, with their wealth of experience and financial backing, angel investors can be a major advantage to the survival and success of a new business.

Case study

According to the UK Business Angels Association (UKBAA), approximately 18,000 business angels invest about £1.5 billion ($2.1bn) in the UK each year. The typical business angel invests about £40,000 ($65,500) and is driven by being able to help others to succeed in business, and invests in a business for up to eight years. Interestingly, only about 5% of Britain's angel investors are female.

Source: https://www.ukbaa.org.uk/

Theory of knowledge

Does the lack of access to sources of finance for businesses hinder their innovation?

Question 3.1.6   MG Rover

In May 2000, four British businessmen, nicknamed the *Phoenix Four,* bought MG Rover from previous owners BMW for just £10 ($14). They each put in £60,000 ($84,000) of their own money but were also given £1bn ($1.4bn) in cash and assets from BMW, despite the owners losing £1m ($1.4m) each day from MG Rover! The British public saw the *Phoenix Four* as heroes, having saved the former British company from extinction.

However, five years later, the business announced 5,000 job losses. The Phoenix Four were condemned for their gross mismanagement of MG Rover and for their extravagant financial rewards. MG Rover had struggled to survive in a highly competitive and rapidly changing industry. Whilst BMW retained the highly successful MINI brand, Range Rover was sold off (now owned by India's Tata Motors). MG Rover is now owned by Chinese firm Nanjing Automobile, having been bought out in 2005 for £53 m ($74.2 m).

(a) Define the term **acquisition**. [2 marks]

(b) Describe why the members of the *Phoenix Four* might be classed as business angels. [2 marks]

(c) Explain the dangers outlined in the case study concerning the use of business angels. [4 marks]

(d) Analyse how the profitability of a business, such as MG Rover, affects its ability to raise external sources of finance. [6 marks]

Table 3.1.a Summary of business ownership and sources of finance

	Sole traders	Partnerships	Private limited company	Public limited company	Non-profit organization
Business angels	✓	✓	✓		
Debt factoring	✓	✓	✓	✓	
Donations/gifts					✓
Grants & subsidies	✓	✓	✓	✓	✓
Leasing & HP	✓	✓	✓	✓	✓
Loans	✓	✓	✓	✓	✓
Overdraft	✓	✓	✓	✓	✓
Personal funds	✓	✓			
Retained profit (surplus)	✓	✓	✓	✓	✓
Shares			✓	✓	
Trade credit	✓	✓	✓	✓	✓
Venture capital	✓	✓	✓		

Short-, medium- and long-term finance

Short, medium and long-term finance. AO1

© IBO, 2017

Effective managers pay careful attention to the cash-flow situation of their business (see Unit 3.7) by ensuring the cash coming into the business covers the cash going out. However, problems occasionally arise so managers consider different forms of finance to deal with short-, medium- and long-term needs for finance. Business analysts do not have a common definition for the short, medium and long term. However, the following definitions are in line with accounting terminology:

- **Short term** refers to the current fiscal (tax) year. In terms of external sources of finance, this means anything that has to be repaid to creditors within the next twelve months. Examples include trade credit and overdrafts.

- **Medium term** refers to the time period of more than twelve months but less than 5 years. Medium term sources of finance include leasing, commercial loans, and hire purchase agreements in excess of a year.

- **Long term** refers to any period of five years or longer. The longer the time period in question, the harder it becomes to plan effectively. Examples of long-term sources of finance include long-term loans such as mortgages and debentures.

Nevertheless, it is important to remember that these definitions tend to vary between businesses and industries. What is important is how these definitions link to the overall aims and

objectives of a business. For example, firms that are heavily involved in research and development such as space technology or pharmaceuticals might view the medium term as ten years, whereas fast-paced industries such as ICT and fashion might see five years as relatively long term. Table 3.1.b categorises, in a simple way, the different sources of finance under the headings of the short, medium and long term.

Table 3.1.b Summary of sources of finance by timeframe

	Short term	Medium term	Long term
Internal sources			
Personal funds	✓		
Retained profits	✓	✓	✓
Sale of fixed assets (divestment)	✓		
Sale of dormant (unused) assets	✓		
External sources			
Business angels	✓	✓	✓
Debentures			✓
Debt factoring	✓		
Government grants & subsidies	✓	✓	✓
Leasing	✓	✓	✓
Loan capital		✓	✓
Overdrafts	✓		
Share capital			✓
Trade credit	✓		
Venture capital	✓	✓	✓

Sources of finance and the CUEGIS concepts

Different sources of finance are used in different business situations. However, they all serve the same purpose – to fund business activity. This is important because serious cash-flow problems (when a business is unable to pay its short-term debts) can cause liquidation or bankruptcy. This is especially the case if creditors chase debtors for the money owed but they do not have the finance to immediately repay their debts. Hence, any effective business strategy must consider the various sources of finance to ensure there are sufficient funds to run the organization in the short, medium and long term.

Whilst family and friends are not explicitly featured in the Business Management syllabus as a source of finance, it is a popular source in many cultures, especially for sole traders and partnerships. For example, it is common in China and India for owners of small businesses to raise a significant amount of finance from friends and family. Borrowing money from family and friends is often reasonably straight forward and inexpensive compared with borrowing from a bank, which might require collateral (security) before a loan can be authorised. However, this source of finance is usually very limited, and borrowing from family and friends often provokes disputes, irrespective of culture.

Business failure is largely attributed to the lack of strategic financial planning and control. Effective financial management is essential for the successful daily running of a business and for its long term prosperity, especially in a business environment with continual changes taking place. Managers consider a number of interlinked factors when examining the strategic choice between alternative sources of finance. These factors can be remembered by the acronym SPACED:

- **S**ize and status of firm A well-known and large multinational corporation will find it much easier to raise finance from a wider range of sources than a sole trader. Despite a stock market crash during 2006, the Industrial and Commercial Bank of China (ICBC) was able to raise the most substantial amount of finance for any initial public offering in history at that time. This was largely due to consumers and businesses having confidence in the share issue of China's largest bank. Large organizations are also able to obtain cheap finance due to financial economies of scale (see Unit 1.6), especially as they are able to offer higher levels of collateral than smaller firms.

- **P**urpose of finance - The choice of finance depends on whether it is intended for the daily running of the business (short-term purposes) or for the replacement of fixed assets over a longer time period. For example, overdrafts are more suitable for improving working capital whereas leasing might be more appropriate for financing expensive equipment.

- **A**mount required - large amounts of finance might be raised through an initial public offering or through secured long-term loans from banks. If only a small amount is needed then retained profit or an overdraft might be sufficient. Lenders also assess the firm's existing gearing (long-term external borrowing as a percentage of its capital employed). Firms with a high gearing ratio are relatively high risk because they have existing debt commitments, so are more vulnerable at times when interest rates increase (which would raise their repayments).

- **C**ost of finance - Managers need to consider the purchase cost of assets and the associated costs, such as administrative fees and maintenance charges. Higher costs tend to require longer term sources of finance, e.g. mortgages for the purchase of land and buildings.

- **E**xternal factors Factors beyond the control of a business can have a huge impact on the strategic choice of finance. Businesses will be affected by the state of the economy and consumer confidence levels (see Unit 1.5). Interest rate and stock market volatility also affect the level of consumer and producer confidence levels, thereby affecting the level of business investments. Low interest rates tend to stimulate investment as borrowing costs are lower.

- **D**uration - if the finance is needed for a long period of time for fund *capital expenditure*, such as for the purchase of new buildings, then long-term loans such as mortgages or debentures are suitable. If finance is needed to help fund *working capital* (see Unit 3.7), then short term sources such as trade credit and overdrafts are more appropriate.

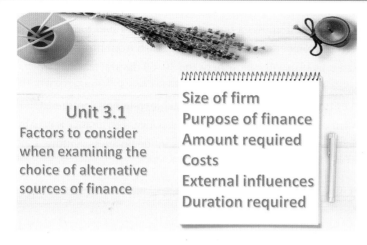

Unit 3.1
Factors to consider when examining the choice of alternative sources of finance

Size of firm
Purpose of finance
Amount required
Costs
External influences
Duration required

Like so many aspects of business, managers are aware that the strategic choice and control of finance will have repercussions on the firm's financial performance. The financial accounts (profit and loss account and the balance sheet – see Unit 3.4) reveal, in quantitative terms, the degree of success of the firm's business strategy.

CUEGIS Essay

With reference to an organization of your choice, examine how sources of finance influence **change** and **strategy**.   *[20 marks]*

REVIEW QUESTIONS

1. Distinguish between capital expenditure and revenue expenditure.

2. Distinguish between internal and external sources of finance.

3. State 3 sources of internal finance.

4. State 5 sources of external finance.

5. What is the difference between a creditor and a debtor?

6. What are the differences between share capital and loan capital?

7. What is the difference between trade credit and leasing?

8. Distinguish between venture capital and business angels.

9. What is the difference between short, medium and long-term finance?

10. What factors do managers need to decide on before choosing their source(s) of finance?

KEY TERMS

Business angels are wealthy entrepreneurs who risk their own money by investing in small to medium-sized businesses that have high growth potential.

Capital expenditure is investment spending on fixed assets such as the purchase of land and buildings.

Debt factoring is a financial service whereby a factor (such as a bank) collects debts on behalf of other businesses, in return for a fee.

External sources of finance means getting funds from outside the organization, e.g. through debt (overdrafts, loans and debentures), share capital, or the government.

Grants are government financial gifts to support business activities. They are not expected to be repaid by the recipient.

Initial public offering (IPO) refers to a business converting its legal status to a public limited company by floating (selling) its shares on a stock exchange for the first time.

Internal sources of finance means getting funds from within the organization, e.g. through personal funds, retained profits and the sale of assets.

Leasing is a form of hiring whereby a contract is agreed between a leasing company (the lessor) and the customer (the lessee). The lessee pays rental income to hire assets from the lessor, who is the legal owner of the assets.

Loan capital (also known as **debt capital**) refers to medium to long-term sources of interest-bearing finance obtained from commercial lenders. Examples include mortgages, business development loans and debentures.

Long-term finance refers to sources of finance of more than five years, used for the purchase of fixed assets or to finance the expansion of a business.

Finance and accounts

CORE

Medium-term finance refers to sources of finance of one to five years in duration, used mainly to pay for fixed assets, i.e. capital expenditure.

Overdrafts allow a business to spend in excess of the amount in its bank account, up to a predetermined limit. They are the most flexible form of borrowing in the short term.

Personal funds are a source of internal finance, referring to the use of an entrepreneur's own savings. Personal funds are usually used to finance business start-ups.

Retained profit is the value of surplus that the business keeps to use within the business after paying corporate taxes on its profits to the government and dividends to its shareholders.

Revenue expenditure refers to spending on the day-to-day running of a business, such as rent, wages and utility bills.

Sale-and-leaseback is a source of external finance involving a business selling a fixed asset (such as its computer systems or a building) but immediately leasing the asset back. In essence, the lessee transfers ownership to the lessor but the asset does not physically leave the business.

Share capital is the money raised from selling shares in a limited liability company, from its initial public offering (IPO) and any subsequent share issues.

Share issue (also known as a **share placement**) exists when an existing public limited company raises further finance by selling more of its shares.

Short-term finance refers to sources of finance needed for the day-to-day running of a business, i.e. revenue expenditure.

Sources of finance is the general term used to refer to where or how businesses obtain their funds, such as from personal funds, retained profits, loans and government grants.

A **stock exchange** is a highly regulated marketplace where individuals and businesses can buy and/or sell shares in public limited companies (joint stock companies).

Subsidies are funded by the government to lower a firm's production costs as output provides extended benefits to society, e.g. farmers are often provided with subsidies to stabilise food prices.

Trade credit allows a business to 'buy now and pay later'. The credit provider does not receive any cash from the buyer until a later date (usually allow between 30–60 days).

Venture capital is high-risk capital invested by venture capital firms, usually at the start of a business idea. The finance is usually in the form of loans and/or shares in the business venture.

Venture capital is used to finance business ideas withhigh potential returns

3.2 Costs and revenues

"Better go home and make a net, rather than dive for fish at random." - Chinese proverb

SL/HL content	Assessment objective
The following types of cost, using examples: • fixed • variable • semi-variable • direct • indirect/overhead	AO2
Total revenue and revenue streams, using examples	AO2

© IBO, 2017

Types of cost

The following types of cost, using examples: fixed, variable, semi-variable, direct and indirect/overhead. AO2

© IBO, 2017

In everyday language, a consumer might say that a shirt 'cost $25'. In business language, the correct terminology is 'the **price** is $25'. **Cost** refers to the expenditure in producing the shirt (see Table 3.2.a), not the amount paid by the customer to buy it.

Businesses need to pay for both set-up costs and running costs. **Set-up costs** are the items of expenditure needed to start a business, e.g. obtaining premises, purchase of machinery and equipment, and deposits to utilities companies (gas, water, electricity and telephone).

Running costs are the ongoing costs of operating the business, e.g. wages and salaries, insurance premiums, and the cost of purchasing stocks.

Exam tip !

Remember that cost refers to the cost of production (which is paid by the producer) whereas price refers to the amount the product is sold for (which is paid by the customer).

Table 3.2.a Examples of business costs for a clothes retailer

Set-up costs	Running costs
Premises, e.g. down payment on a mortgage or rent deposit	Regular mortgage, rent and/or lease payments
Buildings, e.g. physical alterations to the building, as required	Packaging materials, e.g. wrapping paper, gift tags and carrier bags
Fixtures and fittings, e.g. changing rooms for customers, signage, counters and shelving	Repairs and maintenance costs
Equipment, e.g. cash registers, computers, phones, office equipment and stationery	Depreciation costs on capital equipment and replacement costs
Connection and installation of utilities and power, e.g. telephone lines and electricity	Utility bills, e.g. for electricity and telephone lines
Legal and professional fees, e.g. for licenses	Marketing costs, e.g. in-store promotions
Initial stock of supplies (inventories)	Replenishing stocks from suppliers
Recruitment costs of hiring and inducting staff	Wages, salaries and other staffing costs such as clothing or uniform

Fixed costs

Fixed costs are the costs of production that a business has to pay regardless of how much it produces or sells. Examples include rent on leased premises, interest payments on bank loans, advertising expenditure, market research, management salaries, stationery, security and professional accountancy fees. These costs have to be paid even if there is no output. Figure 3.2.a shows a business with total fixed costs (TFC) of $5,000.

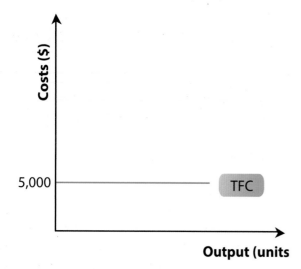

Figure 3.2.a Fixed costs of a business

Note that fixed costs can change, but this happens *independently* from the level of output. For example, a landowner might raise rents due to higher property prices in the economy, or company directors being paid higher salaries due to rising costs of living. In both cases, fixed costs increase but are not directly linked to the firm's output level.

Variable costs

Variable costs are the costs of production that change in proportion with the level of output or sales. As output increases, so too do the total variable costs (TVC) as seen in Figure 3.2.b. This means that if the level of output or sales doubles, then variable costs would also double. For example, raw material costs will increase if a textiles firm makes more curtains. Other examples include the commission earned by sales staff and the packaging costs directly associated with output. In theory, if there is no production then the value of variable costs should be zero.

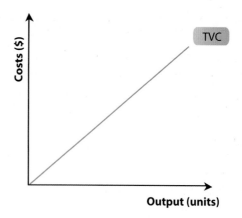

Figure 3.2.b Variable costs of a business

Adding the total variable costs to the fixed costs gives the value of **total costs** (TC), i.e. TC = TVC + TFC. It can be seen in Figure 3.2.c that the TC line starts at the same value as fixed costs because these have to be paid even if there is no output. Notice that the numerical difference between the TC and TVC lines at each level of output is equal to the value of total fixed costs.

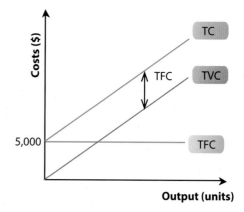

Figure 3.2.c Total costs of a business

Common mistake

Avoid writing 'circular answers' in your script, i.e. do not repeat the question in your answers. For example, when asked to distinguish between fixed and variable costs, many students simply state that "fixed costs are fixed and variable costs are variable". Review the key terms that you are unable to define in your own words.

Semi-variable costs

Semi-variable costs contain an element of both fixed and variable costs. They tend to change only when production or sales exceed a certain level of output. For example, mobile telephone and Internet service providers often allow a user to have a predetermined number of 'free minutes' or a limit on data usage. However, there is also a 'standing charge' which means no matter how much (or little) the person uses the phone or Internet, there is a fixed minimum monthly charge. If the user exceeds the quota, then the telephone and Internet bills become variable.

In reality, many costs could be classified as semi-variable costs. The payment for labour services is not necessarily as straightforward as either a wage (variable cost) or salary (fixed cost). For example, sales people tend to earn a fixed basic pay in addition to their commission (a variable element). Machinery and vehicles are usually classed as fixed costs, but the more they are used (due to higher levels of output) the higher their maintenance and depreciation costs tend to be.

Direct costs

A direct cost is specifically related to an individual project or the output of a particular product; without which the costs would not be incurred. This can include variable costs such as raw materials. However, unlike variable costs, direct costs are not necessarily related to the level of output, i.e. they can be fixed costs. For example, the direct costs of purchasing a commercial building include: consultancy costs, solicitor's fees, telephone bills, postage, photocopying costs, mortgage fees and bank charges. Essentially, direct costs can be traced back to the output of a product and/or to a specific cost centre (see Unit 3.9).

Note that what is a variable cost for one business is not necessarily so for another. For instance, catering costs for a flight on a mainstream airline carrier, such as Singapore Airlines, would be classed as variable costs. This is because the more passengers on the aeroplane, the more food and drinks will be required since these are included in the ticket price. However, for a 'no-frills' budget airline such as Ryanair, easyJet and AirAsia, the catering costs are considered to be direct costs. The cost of food and drinks is directly related to the flight, but passengers do not all demand meals and drinks since these are paid for on an individual basis.

Case study

IHS, a US electronics and media research company, reported that the Sony PlayStation 4 costs $372 to build plus $9 for direct labour, bringing the total cost of each unit to $381. This is just $18 below the retail price of $399 at its launch in November 2013.

Indirect costs (overheads)

Indirect costs, also known **overheads**, are those that cannot be clearly traced to the production or sale of any single product. For example, rent and lighting costs can be associated with all areas of a business rather than being directly linked to the output of a particular product. Other examples of overheads include: advertising, legal expenses, administrative staff salaries, insurance, security, stationery, shipping and postage costs, utility bills and accounting fees. Indirect costs can be fixed costs since they do not directly relate to the level of output. However, unlike fixed costs, indirect costs are not easily identified with a particular business activity.

Question 3.2.1 Airline costs

(a) Classify the following costs for a mainstream airline company in terms of fixed or variable costs:
- Advertising and promotions
- Airport charges
- Fuel
- Meals and drinks onboard
- Remuneration of administrative staff
- Remuneration of pilots and flight attendants.

[3 marks]

(b) With reference to the airline industry, distinguish between direct and indirect costs. [4 marks]

Exam tip !

The terms *indirect costs* and *direct costs* are used when referring to businesses that produce or sell a range of products and therefore operate 'cost centres' and 'profit centres' (see Unit 3.9). These costs can be either fixed or variable costs, depending on the nature of the business.

The terms *fixed costs* and *variable costs,* as used in break-even analysis (see Unit 3.3), are used when referring to the sale or production of just a single type of product.

Box 3.2.a   Costs formulae

Key: Q = Quantity (or level of output)
- Total Cost (TC) $TC = TFC + TVC$
- Total Variable Costs (TVC) $TVC = AVC \times Q$
- Total Fixed Costs (TFC) $TFC = AFC \times Q$

Where AVC is the average variable cost and AFC is the average fixed cost.

Note: The above cost formulae are *not* given to candidates in the examination.

Question 3.2.2   Calculating business costs

(a) Complete the table below for the costs of producing fine glass ornaments.   *[5 marks]*

(b) Using graph paper, plot the TFC, TVC and TC curves.   *[4 marks]*

(c) Explain the reason for the shape of each of the three cost curves in your diagram.   *[6 marks]*

Output (Units)	Total fixed costs ($)	Total variable costs ($)	Total costs ($)	Average costs ($)
0	20 000			-
100		5 000		
200		10 000		
300			34 500	
400			38 000	
500				90.0
600				97.0

Revenue

Total revenue and revenue streams, using examples. AO2

© IBO, 2017

Revenue refers to the money coming into a business, usually from the sale of goods and/or services (known as sales revenue). The formula for calculating revenue is:

Sales revenue = Price × Quantity sold

For example, if Church's charges $300 on average for each pair of its shoes and sells 300 pairs in a week, its total sales revenue will be $90,000 (i.e. $300 × 300) for that time period. A business earns profit if there is a positive difference between its revenues and costs.

Case study

Church's is an English producer of high-end luxury shoes. Founded in 1873 by Thomas Church and his three sons, its main operations are in Northampton, UK. It can produce up to 5,000 pairs of shoes per week, with around 70% of the output being exported. From humble beginnings, Church's now has retail outlets around the world including New York, Milan, Paris, Rome, Madrid, Hong Kong Singapore and Shanghai.

Theory of knowledge

Discuss the view that there is no role for imagination, memory, faith or intuition as Ways of Knowing about a firm's costs and revenues.

Box 3.2.b   Revenue formulae

- Total Revenue (TR) $TR = P \times Q$
- Average Revenue (AR) $AR = \dfrac{TR}{Q}$

  since: $P = \dfrac{TR}{Q}$

  then: $AR = P$

Note: The above revenue formulae are *not* given to candidates in the examination.

Revenue streams

Revenue does not only come from the sale of goods and services. Money can come into a firm from other means, known as **revenue streams**, depending on the type of firm and its activities. Other sources of non-sales revenue for a business include:

- **Advertising revenue** Companies such as Google, Twitter and Facebook rely heavily on advertising revenue as a revenue stream. For example, over 80% of the revenues from social media firm Twitter comes from text and display advertising. Google and Facebook offer cost per click (advertisers pay only when customers actually click on the advert) and cost per thousand impressions (advertisers pay based on the number of times their adverts are displayed).

- **Transactions fees** Ryanair, for example, charges customers who pay by American Express credit card €7 ($9.50) *and* 2% commission. Other budget airlines such as AirAsia and easyJet charge fees for checked baggage and pre-assigned seats. According to the *Wall Street Journal*, low-cost airlines earn around 20% of their revenue from these alternative revenue streams (see Box 3.2.c).

Finance and accounts

CORE

Question 3.2.3   Big Bao

Big Bao sells a range of lunchtime snacks in Bristol town centre, UK.
In 2019, the business sold 31,790 units of its lunchtime snacks. This represented a 10% increase in its **sales volume** from the previous year, when price per unit was $6.50

(a) Outline the meaning of **sales volume**.   [2 marks]

(b) Calculate the value of *Big Bao's* sales in 2018.   [2 marks]

Box 3.2.c Revenue streams in the budget-airline industry

- SpiceJet Ltd. charges for hot meals, snacks and beverages
- Jetstar and Scoot loan iPads for a fee
- AirAsia customers can pay for the privilege of being seated in a children-free quiet zone!
- Ryanair failed in its attempt to charge passengers for the use of toilets, but now offers advertising space on its planes, including on the wing tips.

- **Franchise costs and royalties**   McDonald's, Burger King and KFC all operate franchises (see Unit 1.6). Franchisees pay a fee to the franchisor to purchase the right to use its brand name, logos and trademarks. The franchisee also pays a royalty payment based on the sales revenue of the franchised business. Royalties are also received by the holder of patents and copyrights from others who are granted the use of their inventions and creations.

- **Sponsorship revenue**   Sponsorship is a form of below-the-line promotion (see Unit 4.5) whereby the sponsor financially supports an organization in return for prominent promotional display of the donor's brand trademark. For example, Arsenal Football Club received a €132 million ($178.4m) sponsorship deal in 2006, lasting 15-year with Emirates Airline. In 2012, this deal was extended with another $242m, and another $200m in 2018. In return, Arsenal's football shirt would carry the 'Fly Emirates' slogan until 2024 and name its ground the Emirates Stadium until 2028.

Table 3.2.b World's most expensive football shirt sponsorship deals (per year)

Football Club	Shirt Sponser	£ million
FC Barcelona	Nike	100.0
Manchester United	Adidas	75.0
Chelsea FC	Nike	60.0
Bayern Munich	Adidas	42.5
Real Madrid	Adidas	34.0
Arsenal FC	Puma	30.0
Tottenham Hotspurs	Nike	30.0
Liverpool FC	Warrior	25.0
Juventus	Adida	20.0
AC Milan	Adidas	19.0

Source: adapted from *sillyseason.com* (all figures are per year for the duration of the sponsorship contract)

Question 3.2.4   Goff's Organic Fresh Fruits (GOFF)

Ian Goff owns and manages a fresh fruits and vegetables store (GOFF – Goff's Organic Fresh Fruits) in a small town in California, USA. Each morning, he drives his delivery van to an out-of-town **wholesale market** to buy fresh, organic fruits and vegetables. During peak seasons, Ian Goff employs two people to help him at the store for which he pays $1,200 rent to his landlady each month. In addition, Ian Goff has to pay for the loan on his one-year old vehicle plus other running costs such as power and lighting.

(a) Define the term **wholesale market**.   *[2 marks]*

(b) Apart from the loan, outline two other indirect costs that GOFF might have to pay.   *[4 marks]*

(c) *GOFF* buys its tomatoes at $0.80 per kg. Calculate the monthly cost, revenue and profit on tomatoes if GOFF buys 50 kg of tomatoes, and sells them at $1.20 per kg.   *[3 marks]*

(d) GOFF bought 100 kg of apples this month and manages to sell 80 kg of apples at the usual price of $2 per kg. To get rid of the excess supply, GOFF reduces the price of the remaining stock to $1.5 per kg. Calculate the revenue from the sale of apples if GOFF manages to sell all of its apples.   *[2 marks]*

Question 3.2.5   Manchester United Football Club

In 2013, Manchester United Football Club *(MUFC)* become the world's first sports club to be valued at over $3 billion. Being one of the most widely supported sports teams in the world, the English football club attracts a huge amount of sponsorship money including its world record shirt sponsorship deal with US carmaker Chevrolet. It also benefited from sponsorship deals with the Commercial Bank of Qatar, Emirates NBD Bank and Pepsi. Back in 2006, *MUFC* chose to reject a sponsorship deal with Mansion, an online gambling company, worth up to £70m ($101m), opting instead to sign a four-year sponsorship deal with American International Group (AIG) in a deal worth $90.5m. Data from *Forbes* shows that match day revenues account to less than 30% of *MUFC's* total **revenue stream**, which also includes broadcasting rights, sponsorship deals and merchandise sales across the globe. In 2015, *MUFC* signed a new 10-year shirt sponsorship deal with Adidas, worth £75m per year ($108.75m).

(a) Define the term **revenue stream**.   *[2 marks]*

(b) Explain why businesses such as Adidas and Pepsi might want to sponsor a large football club such as MUFC.
                                                                                                              [4 marks]

(c) Examine the view that the senior management at *MUFC* were correct to choose *AIG* as their sponsor despite the larger offer from *Mansion* at the time.   *[6 marks]*

Finance and accounts

CORE

- **Subscription fees**   These charges are imposed on customers who use or access a good or service, based on a formal agreement. For example, fitness and leisure clubs charge yearly membership fees, many credit card companies charge annual fees, telephone companies charge a basic service fee on a monthly basis but extra for additional services (such as overseas calls and pay-per-call services), as do cable and satellite television providers. Manchester United Football Club has operated its subscription television channel since 1998.

- **Merchandise**   Service providers in the entertainment industry (such as cinemas, concerts, theatres and theme parks) rely on selling merchandise (such as popcorn, beverages, souvenirs and memorabilia) in addition to admissions charges. Facebook customers can use its gift card for spending at different retailers such as Burger King, Outback Steakhouse, Staples and Target.

- **Dividends**   Being a shareholder of other companies entitles a business to payments of any declared dividends. Dividends are a share of the net profit distributed to shareholders at the end of the tax year. For example, Europe's largest carmaker Volkswagen holds shares in Porsche, Suzuki, and Scania (the Swedish maker of heavy trucks and buses).

- **Donations**   These are financial gifts from individuals or other organizations to a business. Charities and non-profit organizations (see Unit 1.2) such as schools, hospitals and universities rely heavily on donations as a regular revenue stream. There are usually no direct benefits to the donor (except the feel-good factor in donating to a worthwhile cause), although some donations have terms and conditions attached, such as an appropriate acknowledgement of the donors' names in recognition of their gift. Donations are not a likely source of revenue for most private sector businesses.

- **Interest earnings**   Businesses can earn interest on their cash deposits at the bank. For highly cash-rich businesses this can be an important revenue stream. *Forbes* reported that Apple had a total cash balance of $137.1 billion in 2013, whilst Microsoft had $68.3 billion, Google had $48.1 billion, and pharmaceutical company Pfizer had $46.9 billion. Depositing $1 billion in a bank account that pays just 1% interest per year still yields $27,397 per day! At an interest rate of 3%, the daily revenue stream would be $82,192!

Figure 3.2.d Apple's cash balance enables it to have an additional revenue stream

- **Subventions** These are subsidies offered from the government to certain businesses to help reduce their costs of production. They are usually given to organizations that generate benefits to society, such as private schools and hospitals. For example, the Hong Kong government agreed to pay the English Schools Foundation a fixed annual subvention of HK$283 million ($36.5 million) as a revenue stream in addition to its school fees from 2003 to 2016. Subventions are also often given to help fund research and development.

IB Learner Profile

Which parts of the IBLP are most important in compiling cost and revenue information? Which components of the IBLP are least applicable? Why?

Costs, revenues and the CUEGIS concepts

Being aware of costs allows managers to be in control of their finances, especially during times of change. Cost control is crucial if a business is to maintain and/or improve its profitability. Large firms in particular benefit from being able to measure the financial performance of each division of their organization. Some businesses use the 'FORCE' approach (Focus On Reducing Costs Everywhere) as a strategy for staying competitive. This does not mean that cost-cutting

will automatically raise profitability, but it can help to keep costs under control. The extent to which businesses focus on cost control depends on their organizational culture and management preferences. Cost-cutting can be justified if it leads to improved efficiency and profitability. Ethical considerations occur if cost-cutting has negative impacts on staffing, such as poorer working conditions, pay cuts or job losses.

Whilst cost control is vitally important, raising revenue is just as important, if not more so. The UK Institute of Management suggests that successful businesses focus 80% of their business strategy on ways to raise revenues and only 20% on cost-cutting. Indeed, forward-looking businesses can afford to spend more money provided that the revenues and profits allow it to do so. For example, Kering (the French multinational owner of luxury brands such as Gucci and Yves Saint Laurent) bought out mass-market sports brand Puma in order to earn more revenue - not to save on its costs.

In monitoring and overseeing a firm's costs and revenues, managers use a variety of strategies in addition to the use of cost and profit centres (see Unit 3.9). For instance, budgets and variance analysis are critical (see Unit 3.9) in controlling business activity. Human resources also have a key role in helping the business to control costs and to raise revenues. Managers must have the means to measure and assess the performance of staff, and to reward them appropriately (see Unit 2.4). Again, these strategic issues highlight the interrelated nature of Business Management.

CUEGIS Essay

With reference to an organization of your choice, examine how **innovation** and **globalization** have influenced its costs and revenues.   *[20 marks]*

CUEGIS Essay

With reference to an organization of your choice, examine how **change** and **strategy** impact on its costs and revenues.   *[20 marks]*

REVIEW QUESTIONS

1. Explain the difference between price and cost.

2. How do set-up costs differ from running costs?

3. Distinguish between fixed and variable costs of production.

4. How are fixed cost and variable cost curves shown diagrammatically?

5. Distinguish between direct and indirect costs of production.

6. What are semi-variable costs?

7. How are total costs calculated?

8. What is revenue and how is it calculated?

9. What is meant by average revenue?

10. Explain, with the use of examples, the meaning of revenue streams

KEY TERMS

Average cost (AC) refers to the cost per unit of output. It is calculated by using the formula: $AC = TC \div Q$, where TC is total cost and Q is quantity (or output level).

Average revenue (AR) refers to the value of sales received from customers per unit of a good or service sold. It is calculated by using the formula: $AR = TR \div Q = P$, where TR is total revenue. It is essentially the same as the average price.

Cost refers to the sum of money incurred by a business in the production process, e.g. the costs of raw materials, wages and salaries, insurance, advertising and rent.

Direct costs are costs specifically attributed to the production or sale of a particular good or service. Direct costs can be traced back to the product and/or to a cost centre.

Dividends are a share of the net profit distributed to shareholders at the end of the tax year.

Fixed costs are the costs that do not vary with the level of output. They exist even if there is no output, e.g. the cost of rent, management salaries and interest repayments on bank loans.

Indirect costs (or **overheads**) are costs that do not directly link to the production or sale of a specific product, e.g. rent, wages of cleaning staff, and lighting.

Price refers to the amount of money a product is sold for, i.e. the sum paid by the customer.

Revenue is the money that a business collects from the sale of its goods and services. It is calculated by multiplying the unit price of each product by the quantity sold.

Revenue stream refers to the money coming into a business from its various business activities, e.g. sponsorship deals, merchandise, membership fees and royalties.

Running costs are the ongoing costs of operating the business, e.g. wages and salaries, insurance premiums, and the cost of purchasing stocks.

Semi-variable costs are those that have an element of both fixed costs and variable costs, e.g. power and electricity or salaried staff who also earn commission.

Set-up costs are the items of expenditure needed to start a business, e.g. obtaining premises, purchase of machinery and equipment, and deposits to utilities companies (gas, water, electricity and telephone).

Total costs are the sum of all variable costs and all fixed costs of production.

Total revenue is the sum of all revenue streams for a business. It is calculate by multiplying the price of a product with the quantity sold.

Variable costs are costs of production that change in proportion to the level of output, e.g. raw materials and piece-rate earnings of production workers.

Finance and accounts

CORE

3.3 Break-even analysis

"He who has no thirst has no business at the fountain" - Dutch proverb

SL/HL content	Assessment objective
Total contribution versus contribution per unit	AO2
A break-even chart and the following aspects of break-even analysis: • break-even quantity/point • profit or loss • margin of safety • target profit output • target profit • target price	AO2, AO4
The effects of changes in price or cost on the break-even quantity, profit and margin of safety, using graphical and quantitative methods	AO2, AO4
The benefits and limitations of break-even analysis	AO3

© IBO, 2017

Finance and accounts

CORE

Contribution

Total contribution versus contribution per unit. AO2

© IBO, 2017

Contribution refers to the sum of money that remains after all direct and variable costs have been taken away from the sales revenue, i.e. the amount available to contribute towards paying fixed costs of production. The formula for contribution per unit is therefore:

Contribution per unit = P – AVC

where P is the price and AVC represents the average variable costs. Similarly, the total contribution is simply the unit contribution multiplied by the quantity of sales (Q):

Total contribution = (P – AVC) × Q

So, for example, if a firm sells chairs at $100 each whilst the variable costs are $45 per chair, then the business makes a contribution of $55 per chair. Note that this is not the actual profit made because fixed costs have not yet been accounted for. However, each chair sold 'contributes' (adds) $55 towards the payment of the firm's total fixed costs (TFC). Once these have been covered, further sales will contribute towards the profit of the business. In other words:

Profit = Total contribution – TFC

Hence, profit can be increased in the following ways:

• Increasing sales of the product, which raises the total contribution (or gross profit).

• Reducing variable costs, perhaps through negotiating better deals with current suppliers or seeking new suppliers that offer more competitive prices.

• Reducing fixed costs and overheads, perhaps through better financial control or the use of cost and profit centres (see Unit 3.9).

Contribution analysis can help a business to identify products that are relatively profitable and ones that might need more attention. Consider the data in Table 3.3.a that shows how contribution analysis might be used.

Exam tip !

It is quicker to use the total contribution to calculate profit than it is to calculate the difference between total costs and total revenue,
i.e. gross profit = (P – AVC) x Q, or TR – TVC.

255

Table 3.3.a Contribution analysis for Café Cuppa

Product	Cappuccino	Latte	Mocha	English tea	Orange Juice	Spring Water
Average unit price ($)	5.50	5.75	6.55	3.20	2.55	1.80
Average variable cost ($)	2.25	2.75	3.15	0.95	1.05	0.80
Unit contribution ($)	3.25	3.00	3.40	2.25	1.50	1.00

Examination of the data in Table 3.3.a suggests that all products are profitable because the unit contribution is positive. Hence, the sale of each product contributes positively towards the fixed costs of Café Cuppa. The strongest product is the Mocha; despite its relatively high unit cost of production, it earns the firm $3.40 contribution per unit sold. The most vulnerable product is the Spring Water which only earns Café Cuppa $1 contribution per unit sold. It is important to also know the number of units sold before concluding which product is the most profitable. However, it is clear that twice the number of units of Orange Juice needs to be sold in order to earn the same contribution as one unit of Latte. In general, any product that makes a positive contribution is worth considering as it helps towards the payment of the firm's fixed costs (and hence profits).

Contribution analysis has several uses for businesses:

- **Pricing strategy**   Contribution analysis helps a business to set prices for each of its products to ensure there is contribution being made towards payment of fixed and indirect costs.

- **Product portfolio management**   The analysis can help managers to decide which products should be given investment priority. In general, products with a higher total contribution tend to be given precedence. Products that earn a low unit contribution rely on high sales volumes to avoid being withdrawn or replaced by other products.

- **Allocation of overheads to cost and profit centres** (see Unit 3.9)   The use of contribution analysis can ensure that cost allocation is done in a fair manner.

- **Make-or-buy decisions** (see Unit 5.5)   Contribution analysis can help a business decide whether it should produce (make) the products or purchase them (buy) from suppliers. The relative difference between the unit contribution of making or buying the product is likely to determine the decision.

- **Special order decisions**   These occur when a customer places an order at a price that differs from the normal price charged by the business. The price could be higher (although the customer will request added benefits for this, such as shorter delivery times) or lower (probably because the customer is buying a significant amount of the product). Whether the business takes on this special order will largely depend on the total contribution made from such a deal.

- **Break-even analysis**   A business breaks even when neither a profit nor a loss is made. This occurs at the level of output where *total costs equal total revenue*, i.e. TC = TR. Break-even is a key objective of new and unestablished firms. Hence, businesses need to pay careful attention to their cash-flow situation (see Unit 3.7) by monitoring and controlling the money coming into the business (revenues) and the money leaving the firm (costs).

Common mistake

Students who claim that a product should be discontinued or reduced in price (to sell more) because it has the smallest amount of contribution in a firm's product portfolio do not understand the concept clearly. Even the tiniest contribution can be used to pay towards a firm's fixed costs. By contrast, discontinuing the product would mean less total contribution and hence, less profit per unit sold.

Break-even analysis

A break-even chart and the following aspects of break-even analysis: break-even quantity/point, profit or loss, margin of safety, target profit output, target profit and target price. AO2, AO4
© IBO, 2017

Managers of all businesses are concerned with the difference between revenue and costs. A business can only survive in the long term if its revenues exceed its costs, i.e. if it is profitable. New firms in particular will want to determine the level of sales that must be made in order to earn a profit. **Break-even analysis** is a management tool that can be used for this purpose.

In financial terms, a business can be in one of the following situations at any point in time:

- **Loss** – when costs of production exceed the revenues of the business

- **Break-even** – when the revenues of the business equal the costs of production

- **Profit** – when revenues exceed costs of production.

Carrying out a break-even analysis (BEA) can inform managers of two things:

- Whether it is financially worthwhile to produce or launch a particular good or service

- The expected level of profits that the business will earn if all goes according to plan.

Consider the following numerical example. A jeans retailer has fixed costs of $3,500 per month. Variable costs are $10 per pair of jeans, and the selling price is $30. There are three ways that can be used to determine the **break-even point** (see Box 3.3.a for break-even formulae):

1. Using the **TR = TC** rule

    The break-even quantity (BEQ) can be calculated by comparing total sales revenues with total costs. Recall from Unit 3.2 that total revenue is calculated as Price × Quantity sold and that Total Costs consist of both fixed and variable costs. The BEQ can then be calculated as:
    TR = TC
    P × Q = TFC + TVC
    30Q = 3,500 + 10Q
    20Q = 3,500
    Q = 175 pairs of jeans.

2. Using the contribution per unit rule

    Break even = Fixed Costs ÷ Contribution per unit

    This is the quicker of the two quantitative methods of calculating break even.

    Using the above figures, we get:
    Unit contribution = Price *minus* average variable costs, i.e. $30 – $10 = $20
    Therefore, the BEQ = $3,500 ÷ $20 = 175 pairs of jeans.

3. Interpretation from a break-even chart.

In Figure 3.3.a below, the break-even level of output can be seen on the *x*-axis at the point where TC = TR, i.e. 175 pairs of jeans.

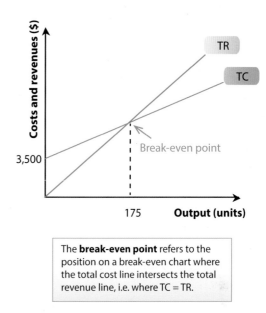

> The **break-even point** refers to the position on a break-even chart where the total cost line intersects the total revenue line, i.e. where TC = TR.

Figure 3.3.a Break-even chart

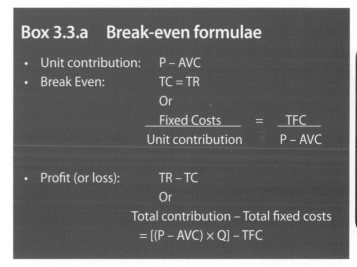

Box 3.3.a   Break-even formulae

- Unit contribution: P – AVC
- Break Even: TC = TR
    Or
    $$\frac{\text{Fixed Costs}}{\text{Unit contribution}} = \frac{\text{TFC}}{\text{P} - \text{AVC}}$$

- Profit (or loss):   TR – TC
    Or
    Total contribution – Total fixed costs
    = [(P – AVC) × Q] – TFC

All three methods give the same answer – the business needs to sell 175 pairs of jeans each month to reach break-even. The chart also shows that any sales beyond the break-even level of output generates a **profit**, whereas selling less than the BEQ means the firm makes a **loss** for that month (see Figure 3.3.b).

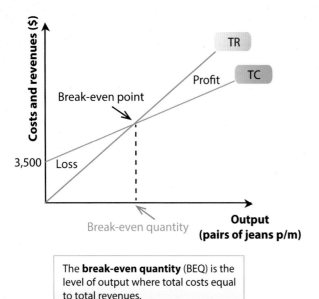

The **break-even quantity** (BEQ) is the level of output where total costs equal to total revenues.

Figure 3.3.b Break-even chart

Exam tip !

Break-even analysis is a popular examination topic. Therefore, it is important that you are able to accurately construct and interpret information shown in a break-even chart. Perhaps more importantly, you must be able to modify a break-even chart and examine its implications for a business.

Common mistake

Many students seem to think that calculating the break-even point will actually ensure the firm covers its costs and makes profit. Of course, calculating the BEQ does not mean the firm has actually sold anything(!) BEA is simply a management decision-making tool based on expected sales and cost.

The margin of safety

The margin of safety (MOS) measures the difference between a firm's sales volume and the quantity needed to break-even, i.e. it shows the extent to which demand (for a product) exceeds the BEQ. A positive MOS means that the firm makes a profit, whereas a negative safety margin means the firm makes a loss. The greater the positive MOS, the safer the firm will be in terms of earning profits, especially if there are adverse changes in the marketplace. It is calculated using the formula:

MOS = Level of demand *minus* Break-even quantity

Common mistake

Candidates often label the axes on a break-even graph inaccurately. In particular, the *y*-axis is often labelled as 'Costs' although BEA clearly also considers revenues. The unit of measurement ($) is also often missing. Hence, the correct label should be 'Costs and revenues ($)'.

Question 3.3.1 Graham Go-Karts!

Steve Graham is the owner of *Graham Go-Karts!* The firm has fixed costs of $20,000 per month. He charges $35 per ride, which allows customers to go round the track for 20 minutes. The cost of operating each ride, including the fuel costs, averages $10. In an average month, *Graham Go-Karts!* has 855 riders.

(a) Calculate the break-even quantity (number of riders) for *Graham Go-Karts!* *[2 marks]*

(b) Calculate the value of total revenue at the break-even quantity. *[2 marks]*

(c) Calculate the value of total costs at the break-even quantity. *[2 marks]*

(d) Calculate the level of profit for *Graham Go-Karts!* in a typical month. *[2 marks]*

For example, if the demand for the jeans retailer in the previous example is 280 pairs per month, then the safety margin is 105 units (i.e. 280 minus 175). This means that the business can sell 105 pairs of jeans less than its current level without making a loss (see Figure 3.3.c). Hence, the smaller the MOS, the more vulnerable a business becomes to changes in the market. Many businesses prefer to express the margin of safety as a percentage of the BEQ because this puts the MOS figure into context and allows better comparisons to be made. In this case, the MOS is 60% higher than the break-even level of output, i.e. $(105 \div 175) \times 100$. Hence, the MOS can reveal the degree of risk involved in a business decision.

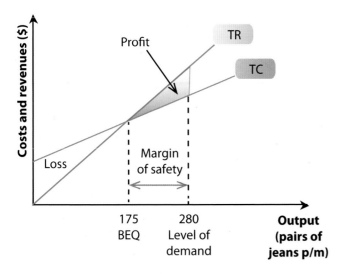

Figure 3.3.c The margin of safety

Common mistake

Far too often, candidates express the margin of safety as a monetary value. This clearly shows a lack of understanding and application of the concept. The MOS is calculated and shown on the x-axis of a break-even chart, i.e. the unit of measurement is the volume of output rather than the value of that output.

Constructing a break-even chart

To construct an accurate break-even chart, use the following rules:

1. Although not necessarily required to show break-even, it is conventional to draw and label the total fixed costs (TFC) line.

2. The total costs (TC) line is drawn and labelled. Recall that even when there is no output, fixed costs still have to be paid. Hence, the TC line starts at the same level as TFC.

3. The total revenue (TR) line is drawn and labelled. When there is no output, the sales revenue is zero, so the TR line starts at the origin.

4. The x-axis is labelled as 'Output' and measured in the appropriate units, per time period.

Finance and accounts

CORE

Question 3.3.2   Calculating the margin of safety

Tread-it is a manufacturer of hiking shoes. Play-it produces wooden toys for children. Cost and revenue data for both businesses are shown in the table below.

	Tread-it	Play-it
Break-even quantity	250	500
Output	500	(i)
Margin of safety (units)	(ii)	300
Margin of safety (%)	100	(iii)

(a) Calculate the missing figures for (i), (ii) and (iii) in the table above.   *[3 marks]*

(b) Comment on which firm has the better margin of safety.   *[4 marks]*

5. The *y*-axis is labelled as 'Costs and revenues', expressed in terms of a currency.

6. A title, put into the context of the business, should also be added.

Consider the following worked example. Suppose that Katia Torralba Jewellery Ltd. sells handmade necklaces at an average price of $260 with variable costs averaging $120 per unit. The fixed costs are $3,500. To plot the break-even chart, it is necessary to first calculate:

- The BEQ: Using the contribution per unit method, the BEQ is worked out as 3,500 ÷ (260 − 120) = **25 units.**

- The value of costs and revenue at the BEQ: Since the value of TC and TR are the same at the BEQ, it does not matter which component is worked out. For example, TC = $3,500 + ($120 × 25) = $6,500. Equally, if we calculate the TR, the figure would be $260 × 25 = **$6,500.**

Using this information, it is now possible to plot the break-even chart as shown in Figure 3.3.d. We know that the *x*-axis must go to beyond 25 units and that the *y*-axis must go beyond $6,500.

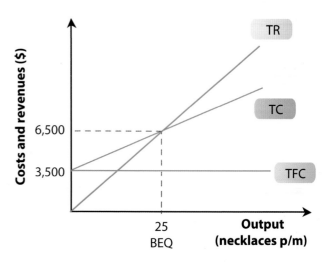

Figure 3.3.d Break-even chart for Katia Torralba Jewellery Ltd.

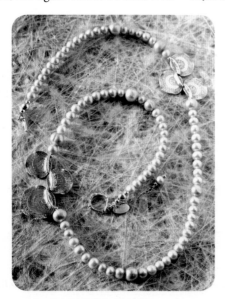

Figure 3.3.e Bespoke jewellery
© Photo courtesy of Katia Torralba Jewellery Ltd.

Question 3.3.3   TMR Day-Care Centre

Thuy and Mark Rees run a children's day-care centre in Hanoi, Vietnam. The main clients are working parents, who pay a fixed $20 per child for the whole day. Children learn through play and are engaged in activities, such as art, music, dance and physical education, at *TMR Day-Care Centre*. The business is open for an average of 22 days each month. The firm's expected costs and revenue for the next year are as follows:

Capacity	25 children per day
Demand	80% of capacity
Price	$20 per child per day
Materials	$4 per child
Rent	$600 per month
Salaries	$1,000 per month
Administration	$100 per month
Utility bills	$140 per month

(a) Calculate the sum of the fixed costs.   *[2 marks]*

(b) Calculate the break even quantity per month.   *[2 marks]*

(c) If *TMR Day-Care Centre* works at 80% of its capacity, calculate the margin of safety.   *[2 marks]*

(d) Construct a fully labelled break even chart for *TMR Day-Care Centre*.   *[5 marks]*

(e) Identify the break even point, the break even quantity and the margin of safety on your chart.   *[3 marks]*

(f) Examine the strengths and weaknesses of using break-even analysis for a business such as *TMR Day-Care Centre*.   *[6 marks]*

Finance and accounts

CORE

Exam tip !

To calculate the target profit output level of a firm, use the following formula:

Target profit output = (Fixed costs + Target profit) ÷ Contribution per unit

Theory of knowledge

Do theoretical models, such as break-even analysis, support or hinder our search for knowledge?

Continuing from the earlier example of Katia Torralba Jewellery Ltd., it is possible to use a break-even chart to work out the level of sales needed to earn a certain amount of (or target) profit. For example, for the firm to earn a target profit of $5,600 per month, it can be seen from Figure 3.3.f that the firm needs to sell 65 necklaces.

Target profit can also be worked out manually, without the use of a break-even chart by using the following steps:

Target profit = TR *minus* TC
5600 = 260Q − 3,500 − 120Q (as $260 is the target price)
9,100 = 140Q

Hence, Q = **65 units** (the target profit output)

The target revenue can then be worked out as
TR = $260 × 65 = $16,900

The total costs at 65 units of output = $3,500 + ($120 × 65)
= $11,300

Therefore the target profit is $16,900 – $11,300 = **$5,600**

Alternatively, the total contribution method can be used to work out profits at this level of output. Recall that **Profit = Total contribution – TFC.**

Total contribution = ($260 – $120) × 50 = $7,000
TFC = $3,500
Hence, profit = **$3,500**

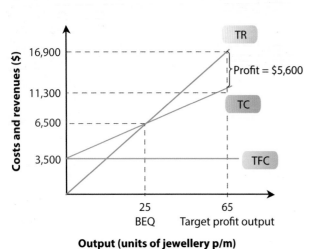

Figure 3.3.f Break-even chart for Katia Torralba Jewellery Ltd.

Figure 3.3.g Profit is what remains after all costs have been paid

Whilst profit can be seen from a break-even chart, it is typically calculated by working out the difference between total revenues and total costs. For example, suppose that Katia Jewellery Ltd. sells 50 necklaces per month. Profit can be worked out using the TR – TC rule:

TR = $260 × 50 = $13,000
TC = $3,500 + ($120 × 50) = $9,500
Profit = **$3,500**

Exam tip !

It is often quicker to calculate profit using total contribution than to use the alternative profit formula (total revenue minus total costs).

Question 3.3.4   Creighton Tours

Edward Creighton is a tour operator for holidaymakers in China. His business specialises in arranging English-speaking tours to remote areas of China. *Creighton Tours* has monthly **fixed costs** of $3,500. The cost of operating each tour averages $120. Edward's monthly sales target is 60 clients, and the firm has a target profit of $2,500.

(a) Define the term **fixed costs**.   *[2 marks]*

(b) Calculate the target price of the average tour for *Creighton Tours*.   *[2 marks]*

Question 3.3.5   RT's Hotdogs

Rhys Thomas runs a hot dog stall outside a busy shopping mall. His expected costs and revenues for the next few months are shown below:

Capacity	200 hotdogs per day
Sales volume	110 hotdogs per day
Unit price	$2.50
Ingredients and materials	$0.8 per hotdog
Rent	$200 per month
Salary	$500 per month
Other overhead costs	$320 per month

(a) Construct a break-even chart for *RT's Hotdogs*, showing the monthly break-even quantity.   *[5 marks]*

(b) Assume that the average daily sales volume increases to 70% of capacity and that rent rises by 50%. Determine the effect of these changes on your break-even chart and comment on your findings.   *[5 marks]*

Question 3.3.6   Mendoza Taxi Services

José Mendoza runs a taxi service in Manila, Philippines. The average fare paid by customers is 330 pesos. *Mendoza Taxi Services* has fixed costs of 6,400 pesos, and the average cost of each journey is 130 peso. The average number of taxi journeys each month is 66.

(a) Calculate the break-even quantity for *Mendoza Taxi Services*.   *[2 marks]*

(b) Calculate the margin of safety for *Mendoza Taxi Services*.   *[2 marks]*

(c) Calculate the current annual profit for *Mendoza Taxi Services*.   *[2 marks]*

(d) Calculate the target price of each journey if José Mendoza has a monthly target profit of 8,000 pesos.   *[2 marks]*

Finance and accounts

CORE

Changes in break-even

The effects of changes in price or cost on the break-even quantity, profit and margin of safety, using graphical and quantitative methods. AO2, AO4

© IBO, 2017

One criticism of break-even analysis is that the model is static, i.e. it represents only a snapshot position of the business. Manual calculations of changes in break-even due to changes in prices or costs can also be onerous. However, computer software packages can show managers the effects of these changes on the BEQ, profit and MOS. This makes BEA a little more flexible and useful.

Nevertheless, actual break-even, profits or losses are likely to be different from those predicted in a BEA because there are so many factors that can affect the profit (or loss) of a business. These factors include:

- *The difference between short-term and long-term profits* It might be necessary to reduce prices (subsequently increasing the break-even quantity) in order to attract customers. In the long term, prices can be increased once a loyal customer base has been established.

- *The level of demand is subject to change* Factors that affect demand, such as changes in income or fashion, will alter the BEQ and hence the value of profits.

- *Profit depends on the level of risk involved* Whilst low-risk projects generally lead to a quicker BEQ, the value of the profits is likely to be low. High-risk projects, such as the Airbus A380 (see Question 3.3.8), have the potential of huge amounts of profits but have a high BEQ.

- *Innovation and the introduction of new technologies* Dell computers, Dyson vacuum cleaners and Apple iPads have generated sales and profits far in excess of their original forecasts.

- *Luck!* Every business needs a little bit of luck to succeed. External factors, such as changes in exchange rates, unemployment, national income and interest rates (see Unit 1.5), can have a direct impact (positive or negative) on the profitability of businesses.

Benefits and limitations of break-even analysis

The benefits and limitations of break-even analysis. AO3

© IBO, 2017

Break-even analysis is a useful management decision-making tool for asking 'what if' questions. The model provides a quick graphical focus on the cost and revenue structures of different scenarios and projects. For example, it allows managers to

Question 3.3.7   Eleanor Art Studio Ltd.

Eleanor Flesher owns *Eleanor Art Studio* in Beijing, China. The firm has overhead costs of $3,000 per month. The variable cost and price are $5 and $20 respectively, per person per lesson. There are typically 500 customers each month, although the firm's maximum capacity is 600 clients.

(a) Calculate the break-even quantity for *Eleanor Art Studio*.   *[2 marks]*

(b) Calculate the margin of safety for the *Eleanor Art Studio*.   *[2 marks]*

(c) Construct a fully labelled break-even chart for *Eleanor Art Studio*.   *[5 marks]*

Suppose in the subsequent time period that rent increases, thus raising the firm's overheads to $4,000 per month. Also, Eleanor Flesher reduces her price to $17, which raises demand to 520 clients per month.

(d) Calculate the new break-even quantity, and comment on your findings.   *[4 marks]*

(e) Illustrate the new break-even level of output on your original chart.   *[1 mark]*

(f) Explain whether the change in price was a sensible decision by Eleanor Flesher.   *[4 marks]*

quickly visualise the impact of changes in price and/or costs on the profits of the business.

BEA analysis can also be used to make realistic predictions rather than relying on simple guesswork. For example, a restaurateur can use past data and experience to estimate the average cost of a meal, the average number of customers on different days and the average price paid for each meal. This data can therefore help a multi-product firm to work out its break-even level of sales, albeit somewhat inaccurately perhaps.

BEA is particularly beneficial to businesses that:

- Produce and/or sell a single, standardised product.

- Operate in a single market.

- Make products to order (see Box 3.3.b), i.e. all output is sold.

Common mistake

Students often think that a benefit of calculating the break-even point ensures that the business will cover its costs and hence make a profit. This is not the case, as BEA is a management tool to help decision-making; it does not guarantee a profit will be made and it is possible for the safety margin to be negative.

However, the assumptions of the break-even model are hardly ever met by most businesses:

- BEA assumes that all cost functions are linear. In reality, cost curves are unlikely to be linear because *economies of scale* (and hence lower average costs of production) can be gained by operating on a larger scale. Fixed costs might also change, perhaps due to an increase in rent.

- BEA assumes the sales revenue function is linear. In reality, customers would demand discounts for larger orders, thereby distorting the sales revenue line. Indeed, managers know that to sell more, a business might need to reduce its prices. Also, a linear sales revenue function ignores *price discrimination* (see Unit 4.5) used by many businesses (charging different prices to different groups of customers, such as adults and children).

- It assumes that the business will sell all of its output. However, in reality most businesses will have some unsold stock, which do not generate cash but cost the firm money (storage and insurance costs, for example). Furthermore, unsold stock might need to be sold at a discount (thereby reducing the profits) to make space for new incoming stocks.

Other limitations of break-even analysis include:

- As a *static* model, BEA might not be very useful in a dynamic business environment. For example, it ignores the possibility that production costs can and do change at short notice, such as fluctuating exchange rates which affect the costs and revenues of exporting firms. The use of dedicated computer software, such as spreadsheets, can help to update data more easily, but each set of break-even calculations will only be valid for one point in time.

- As with all financial and numerical predictions, the principle of *garbage in, garbage out* (GIGO) applies. Unrealistic and obsolete data input will generate unconvincing results. Hence, the accuracy of BEA largely depends on the validity of the original data (used to generate the calculations) and on management skills and experiences (to estimate costs and revenues).

- Other quantitative and qualitative factors that can alter the costs, revenues and output of the business are ignored. For example, BEA ignores the impacts of staff working under increased pressures to maximise output, such as demotivation and declining productivity. The reaction of competitors, the availability of spare capacity and access to finance are also ignored in BEA.

- BEA is really only suitable for single-product firms that sell all of their output. For firms with a broad product portfolio, overheads have to be split between the various products in a rather subjective way. Although there are software programmes that can help managers to calculate multiproduct break-even, these do not truly represent the break-even for each product.

Exam tip !

Break-even analysis is a particularly popular topic for SL students. Whilst it is important to practise how to construct break even charts, it is equally important to be able to examine the benefits and limitations of breakeven analysis.

Finance and accounts

CORE

Figure 3.3.h BEA is not so useful for vendors that sell a range of products

Theory of knowledge

What is the definition of a number? What role does mathematics have as an area of knowledge in the study of Business Management?

Theory of knowledge

Does it matter if the assumptions of break-even analysis are actually flawed? Is 'knowledge' diminished in any way?

Question 3.3.8 Airbus A380

Prior to its first commercial flight in 2007, the Airbus A380 – the world's largest passenger airliner – was estimated to break-even on 270 orders with an average price of $375.3 m depending on the equipment installed. However, the company later announced the **break-even quantity** had been revised to 420 aircraft following production delays and soaring costs that had plagued the European aircraft giant. At that time, *Airbus* had only sold 159 A380s, with the first plane delivered two years behind schedule.

By 2013, the average list price of the A380 was $390m with a total of only 317 orders by 2015. *Airbus* had expected to sell 1,200 A380 planes during its first 20 years

(a) Define the term **break-even quantity**.   [2 marks]

(b) Calculate the revised margin of safety for the Airbus A380.   [2 marks]

(c) Comment on how the change in the margin of safety is likely to affect *Airbus*.   [4 marks]

(d) Explain how the delays and soaring production costs might affect the profits of *Airbus*.   [6 marks]

(e) Examine the value of break-even analysis as a management tool for businesses such as *Airbus*.   [6 marks]

Break-even analysis and the CUEGIS concepts

The concept of contribution is crucial to the understanding of break-even analysis. Recall that *unit contribution* is the difference between a product's price and its variable costs of production, i.e. unit contribution = P – AVC. Any product that makes a positive contribution will help towards paying some of the fixed costs of the business. Therefore, contribution analysis suggests three broad strategies for improving profits:

- Increasing sales revenue, e.g. by using appropriate marketing strategies (see Unit 4.5) or growth strategies (see Unit 1.6) to attract more customers.

- Reducing variable costs, e.g. by seeking more cost-effective production methods, thereby helping to raise the contribution made from selling each unit of output.

- Reducing fixed costs, e.g. negotiating cheaper rents or limiting extravagant company expenses, thereby helping to reduce the break-even level of output.

Despite its limitations, BEA is a useful quantitative organizational planning tool for presenting cost and revenue data to aid strategic decisions, such as:

- *Product portfolio management* BEA helps to assess the expected BEQ prior to the launch of a new product, thereby helping firms to manage their product portfolio. Although the analysis works best for single-product firms, allocating overheads (see Unit 3.9) can help to alleviate this issue.

- *Risk assessment* Calculating the margin of safety helps managers to gauge the level of risk involved in a particular project. A predicted MOS of 250% might justify the go-ahead for a project, whereas a negative safety margin can prevent a loss being made had the firm intuitively invested in the project.

- *Make-or-buy decisions* As the name suggests, these decisions refer to a firm's choice of whether to produce a product itself or to buy it from a supplier (see Unit 5.5). BEA shows the relative benefits of either decision.

- *Special order decisions* These are atypical and/or one-off orders for which a business will charge a price that differs from the norm. For example, some customers might demand speedier delivery times or changes to the product specification, thereby raising production costs. BEA helps to assess whether the change in profits – by accepting the special order – is worthwhile. Hence, BEA can be quite a flexible tool in an ever-changing business environment.

As with all quantitative tools, it is important to consider the analysis in the context of the business, e.g. its organizational culture and business strategy. It is also essential to remember that break-even analysis should be used with caution, bearing in mind the assumptions of the model. In addition, BEA ought to be used alongside other tools such as SWOT analysis (see Unit 1.3) and investment appraisal (see Unit 3.8) to form more comprehensive and coherent strategic decision-making.

Box 3.3.b Special order decisions – a numerical example

Suppose a charity wishes to buy 10 computers at a price of $500 each instead of the usual $800. Unit variable costs of the computers are $200 and fixed costs are allocated at $3,000. Assuming the business has spare capacity, recommend whether it take on this special order.

Break-even analysis shows that the BEQ is 10 computers, i.e. $3,000 ÷ ($500 – $200).

There are three possible outcomes:

- Based on financial grounds, the firm only breaks even. For some managers, this will not be worthwhile, especially if production costs turn out to be higher than expected.
- Based on qualitative factors such as corporate social responsibility, the business might take on the order as it feels that the charity is supporting a worthwhile cause.
- Based on contribution analysis, the fixed costs exist with or without this special order. So by taking it on, there is a contribution of $300 per computer. Hence, some managers would accept the special order.

Theory of knowledge

Do you think there is ever a justification in business for taking on a special order solely because of ethical reasons, rather than for profit?

CUEGIS Essay

With reference to an organization of your choice, discuss the extent to which **change** and **strategy** limits the usefulness of break-even analysis as a business management tool.

[20 marks]

REVIEW QUESTIONS

1. Explain the meaning of break-even.

2. What is contribution per unit?

3. How is contribution per unit used to calculate break-even output?

4. What are the three generic ways that profits can be increased?

5. State the two formulae used to calculate break-even.

6. Outline the difference between the break-even point and the break-even quantity.

7. What is a safety margin?

8. How is the margin of safety calculated?

9. What are the assumptions made when carrying out a break-even analysis?

10. Outline the benefits and limitations of break-even analysis.

KEY TERMS

Break-even analysis is a management tool used to calculate the level of sales needed to cover all costs of production. Thereafter, further sales generate a positive safety margin, and hence profit for the business.

Break-even chart is the name given to the graph that shows a firm's costs, revenues and profits (or loss) at various levels of output.

Break-even point refers to the position on a break-even chart where the total cost line intersects the total revenue line, i.e. where TC = TR.

Break-even quantity refers to the level of output that generates neither profit nor loss. It is shown on the x-axis on a break-even chart.

Contribution per unit (or **unit contribution**) is the difference between the selling price of a product and its variable costs of production, i.e. P – AVC. The surplus goes towards paying fixed costs.

The **margin of safety** (MOS) is the difference between a firm's level of demand and its break-even quantity. A positive MOS means the firm can decrease output (sales volume) by that amount without making a loss. A negative MOS means the firm is making a loss.

Profit is the positive difference between a firm's revenue and its costs. On a break-even chart, profit is shown at all levels of output beyond the break-even quantity.

A **special order decision** occurs when a customer places an order at a price that differs from the normal price charged by the business.

Target price is the price set by a firm in order to reach break-even or a certain target profit.

Target profit is the amount of surplus a firm intends to achieve, based on price and cost data. It can been calculated by taking estimated total costs from expected sales revenues. It can also be identified from a break-even chart.

Total contribution is the unit contribution (P – AVC) multiplied by the quantity of sales (Q), i.e. total contribution = (P – AVC) × Q. It is, essentially, a firm's gross profit.

3.4 Final accounts

"Nothing speaks more eloquently than money." - French proverb

SL/HL content	Assessment objective
The purpose of accounts to different stakeholders	AO3
The principles and ethics of accounting practice	AO3
Final accounts: • profit and loss account • balance sheet	AO2, AO4
Different types of intangible assets	AO1

HL content	Assessment objective
Depreciation using the following methods: • straight line method • reducing/declining balance method	AO2, AO4
The strengths and weaknesses of each method	AO2

© IBO, 2017

The purpose of final accounts

The purpose of accounts to different stakeholders. AO3

© IBO, 2017

All businesses need to keep records of their financial statements. Whilst proper accounting allows managers have better financial control and planning, it can also be a legal requirement. Where there is a *divorce of ownership and control* (see Unit 1.2), much of the firm's finances will have probably come from shareholders. Financial reporting is a way to account for the money of the business, whether it belongs to the owners, investors or lenders. Hence, having to produce final accounts ensures that all payments and receipts of a business have to be officially accounted for. All companies (businesses owned by shareholders) must provide a set of final accounts to their various stakeholders. These accounts consist of two statements:

- The **profit and loss account** which the trading position of a business at the end of a specified accounting period.

- The **balance sheet** which the assets and liabilities of a business at a particular point in time.

It is a legal requirement in most countries for companies to have their final accounts audited by independent and chartered accountants who certify the financial statements to be accurate and truthful. Incorporated businesses are legally obliged to produce final accounts, which act to ensure transparency in their use of funds. However, as there is no universal method to present the final accounts, there is some degree of flexibility in reporting the 'actual' financial position of a company; much of this comes down to the auditor's professional judgement.

Internal stakeholders (see Unit 1.4) can use final accounts to manage the business and to aid strategic decision-making. The purpose of final accounts for external stakeholders is to aid evaluative judgments, such as the firm's ability to pay suppliers or financiers. The purpose of final accounts for different stakeholders is considered below:

- **Shareholders** The owners of a company are interested to see where their money was spent and the return on their investments. Based on its financial performance, shareholders can decide whether to hold, sell or buy (more of) the company's shares.

Finance and accounts

CORE

- **Employees**   Staff are interested in their organization's financial accounts to assess the likelihood of, or present a case for, pay increments. The final accounts can also enable employees to assess the degree of job security.

- **Managers**   Managers use financial accounts to judge the operational efficiency of their organizations. Financial analysis can also be useful for target setting and strategic planning.

- **Competitors**   Rivals are interested in the final accounts of a business to make comparisons of their financial performance (see Unit 3.5).

- **Government**   The tax authority examines the accounts of businesses, especially large multinationals, to ensure that they pay the correct amount of tax.

- **Financiers**   Financial lenders such as banks or business angels (see Unit 3.1) scrutinise the accounts of a firm before approving any funds.

- **Suppliers**   Suppliers examine a firm's final accounts to decide the extent to which trade credit should be given.

- **Potential investors**   Private and institutional investors use final accounts and ratio analysis to assess whether an investment would be financially worthwhile, i.e. by calculating its profitability ratio, measuring its gearing ratio, and determining the organization's liquidity position (see Units 3.5 and 3.6).

Figure 3.4.a Financiers use final accounts to judge on the creditworthiness of their clients.

The principles and ethics of accounting practice

The principles and ethics of accounting practice. AO3
© IBO, 2017

When compiling the final accounts, accountants and financial professionals must abide by the principles and ethics of accounting practice established by a regulatory body. This is important for maintaining a positive reputation of their businesses and to prevent fraudulent practices. The Association of Chartered Certified Accountants (ACCA) is a global regulatory body for professional accountants, assuring that its members are appropriately regulated. The ACCA's Code

Question 3.4.1   Nestlé

Nestlé is the world's largest food company, founded by Henri Nestlé in 1866. Many of the Swiss company's brands are internationally renowned, such as Kit Kat and Smarties (confectionery), Dreyer's (ice cream), Nescafé, Nespresso, Nestea, Nesquik, Vittel and Perrier (beverages), Gerber (baby food products) and Maggi (seasoning and sauces). A huge proportion of *Nestlé's* revenues come from the sale of confectionery, a market also dominated by rivals such as Mars (with brands such as Snickers and M&Ms) and Cadbury's (who own brands such as Time Out, Crème Eggs and Diary Milk). *Nestlé* is listed on the Swiss **stock exchange** in Zurich and employs over 335,000 people worldwide. Since 1974, *Nestlé* has owned a large share in L'Oreal, the world's largest cosmetics company.

(a) Outline the meaning of a **stock exchange**.   *[2 marks]*

(b) Identify two stakeholder groups of *Nestlé*.   *[2 marks]*

(c) Examine the importance of final accounts to both stakeholder groups mentioned in your answer to part **(b)**.

[6 marks]

of Ethics and Conduct sets out five guiding principles for accounting practice:

- *Integrity* Accounting practice should be "straightforward and honest in all professional and business relationships." Integrity also implies fair and truthful behaviour.

- *Objectivity* Accounting practice should be free from bias and any conflict of interest. Professional judgement should not be compromised by undue influence from other people.

- *Professional competence and due care* Accountants are obliged to maintain their professional knowledge and skills to ensure they provide a competent professional service. They must also act diligently when providing professional accounting services.

- *Confidentiality* Accountants must respect the confidentiality of information they acquire in their professional duties and must not disclose any of this information (unless they have permission or a legal obligation to do so). Very importantly, accountants must not use the confidential information for their personal gain.

- *Professional behaviour* Accounting practices must comply with relevant laws and regulations. Accountants must avoid any action that could discredit their profession. They should, in their professional capacity, behave with courtesy and consideration towards others.

Figure 3.4.b ACCA's principles and ethics of accounting practice

Principles and ethics of accounting practice
- Ethics
- Integrity
- Objectivity
- Confidentiality
- Professional conduct

Case study

Enron was a huge America energy company, with annual sales in excess of $100 billion, and a workforce of over 20,000 people. However, its dishonest accounting practices led the company to go bankrupt in December 2001, with some of the top executives being jailed for accounting fraud. The scandal caused Enron's share price to drop from over $90 to less than $1 prior to its bankruptcy.

S

Common mistake

The principles and ethics of accounting practices are not a relatively new phenomenon as some students claim. Despite the rise in the number of cases of fraudulent practices exposed in the news media, Luca Pacioli, regarded as the 'Father' of accounting, first wrote about accounting ethics in 1494!

The profit and loss account

Final accounts: profit and loss account. AO2, AO4
© IBO, 2017

The **profit and loss account** (or the **income statement**) is a financial statement of a firm's trading activities over a period of time, usually one year. Most businesses that operate in the private sector aim to make a profit. Even for non-profit organizations and those in the public sector, it is important to make a surplus in order to survive. The main purpose of the profit and loss (P&L) account is to show the profit or loss of a business during a particular trading period.

Profit, in its simplest form, is the positive difference between a firm's revenues and its costs. **Revenue** is the inflow of money from ordinary trading activities, e.g. cash sales, credit sales, charges/fees and royalties (see Unit 3.2). **Costs** are the outflow of money from a business due to its operations, e.g. wages, salaries, rent and the purchase of stock. Profit creates an incentive for most businesses to do well. After all, if a business does not earn profit, it could struggle to survive.

There are three sections to an income statement: the trading account, the profit and loss account, and the appropriation account.

Finance and accounts

CORE

Finance and accounts

CORE

Trading account

The trading account is the first section of the P&L account and shows the difference between a firm's sales revenue (the value of products sold to customers) and its costs of producing or purchasing those products to sell. Hence, the trading account shows the **gross profit** of a firm:

Gross profit = Sales revenue – Cost of goods sold

The **cost of goods sold** (COGS) is the accountant's term for the direct costs of the goods that are actually sold, e.g. raw material costs. COGS (or **cost of sales** when referring to services) is worked out by the formula:

COGS = Opening stock + Purchases – Closing stock

For example, if a business opens trading this morning with $5,000 of stock (the cost value) and receives a delivery of stock for which it pays $25,000 then the business has costs of stock valued at $30,000. At the end of the trading day, it has $3,800 of stock remaining. Using the formula, the calculation of COGS then becomes:

COGS = $5,000 + $25,000 – $3,800 = $26,200

Thus, the COGS is $26,200. Assume that the stocks sell for three times their cost - this would generate sales revenue of $78,600 (i.e. $26,200 × 3). Thus, the value of the firm's gross profit is: $52,400 – $26,200 = **$52,400**

Using this example, the trading account is shown in the following format

Trading account for Company Y for the year ended 1 April 20xx

	$	$
Sales		78 600
Cost of Goods Sold:		
Opening Stock	5 000	
Purchases	25 000	
Closing Stock	3 800	
		26 200
Gross Profit		52 400

Question 3.4.2 Trading account for Clockworks Ltd.

The information below represents data for *Clockworks Ltd.*

- 3,000 clocks sold at $35 each
- **Closing stock** valued at $20,000
- Purchases totalled $50,000
- Stock at 1 April 2018 was valued at $15,000

(a) Define the term **closing stock**. *[2 marks]*

(b) Construct a trading account for *Clockworks Ltd.* for the year ended 31 March 2019. *[4 marks]*

A business can improve its gross profit by reducing costs and/or raising revenue, such as:

- Using cheaper suppliers – This reduces the COGS, although finding cheaper suppliers without hindering quality can be problematic.

- Increase selling price – This raises the value of each item sold, but is likely to cause a fall in the volume of sales.

- Enhanced marketing strategies – Methods such as promotions and repackaging can be used to make the product more appealing. However, this will raise the firm's expenses.

Profit and Loss (P&L) account

The profit and loss account, or the **profit statement**, shows the **net profit** (or loss) of a business at the end of a trading period. Net profit is the surplus, if any, from sales revenues after all expenses are accounted for. Hence net profit is the actual profit made from a firm's normal trading activities.The gross profit is used to deduct all expenses to calculate net profit:

Net profit = Gross profit – Expenses

Expenses are the indirect or fixed costs of production, e.g. administration charges, management salaries, insurance premiums (for buildings, vehicles and stock) rent of land and property, and stationery costs.

Suppose that a florist sold $230,000 of stock with a market value of $460,000 during the fiscal (tax) year ended on 31st December

2018. Rents payable amounted to $90,000 whilst utility bills (gas, water, electricity and telephone) totalled $60,000. Other overheads amounted to $15,000. The profit statement would then be as shown below.

There are several ways that a business might try to reduce its expenses in order to increase its net profit. For example:

- Rent charges could be negotiated or the firm could move to cheaper premises; although relocation might not prove feasible due to *industrial inertia* (see Unit 5.4).

- Fuel consumption such as heating and lighting could be targeted, e.g. businesses could turn down the heating temperature during the winter, use less air conditioning in the summer and turn off lights when not required. Such actions help to reduce electricity bills and can give firms a better image with environmentalists.

- Administration costs could be examined by reviewing the work of clerical staff to reduce costs. This might be achieved by combining jobs or employing fewer people to carry out such tasks.

Exam tip !

What's the correct format?
Different firms in different countries use slightly different methods to present their P&L accounts. For your IB exams, use the format shown in Table 3.4.1. Remember to place an appropriate title at the top.

P&L account for Florists-R-Us, for the year ended 31 December 2018

	$	$
Sales revenue		460 000
Cost of Goods Sold		230 000
Gross Profit		230 000
Less Expenses:		
Rents	90 000	
Utility bills	60 000	
Other overheads	15 000	
		165 000
Net profit		65 000

Profit & Loss account for (*Company name*), for the year ended (*date*)

	$m
Sales revenue	700
Cost of Goods Sold	350
Gross Profit	350
Less Expenses:	200
Net profit before interest and tax	150
Less Interest	10
Net profit before tax	140
Less Tax	25
Net profit after interest and tax	115
Dividends	35
Retained profit	80

© IBO, 2017

Table 3.4.a Format of the Profit & Loss account

Question 3.4.3   Masks-R-Us Ltd.

An extract of this year's financial data for *Masks-R-Us Ltd.* for the period ended 31 August is shown below:

- Sales turnover: 14,000 masks @ $10 each
- Opening stock: $10,000
- Purchases: $35,000
- Closing stock: $12,000
- Overhead expenses: $17,000
- Interest: $5,000
- Tax: 15% of net profit after interest

(a) Construct a full Profit & Loss account for *Masks-R-Us Ltd.*   *[5 marks]*

(b) Discuss whether the financial performance of *Masks-R-Us Ltd.* can be judged solely on this quantitative information.   *[10 marks]*

Interest charges and taxes, despite being expenses, are shown as separate items in the P&L accounts. This is because both interest and tax rates change over time and are beyond the control of the business. Profit might be lower this year only because tax or interest rates were raised. This practice allows a firm to compare like-with-like and to enable historical comparisons of financial performance. Interest is a cost as it represents the charge or fee that a business pays to its lenders for loans. Corporate tax is the levy payable on a company's profits. Suppose that Florists-R-Us has $8,000 of interest to repay to the bank and that corporate tax is charged at 10%. By including interest and tax, the P&L account is shown as:

Profit & Loss account for Florists-R-Us, for the year ended 31 December 2018

	$
Sales revenue	460,000
Cost of Goods Sold	230,000
Gross Profit	230,000
Less Expenses:	165,000
Net profit before interest and tax	65,000
Less Interest	10,000
Net profit before tax	55,000
Less Tax (10%)	5,500
Net profit after interest and tax	49,500

Appropriation account

The final section of the P&L account is called the appropriation account. There are two parts to this account, which show how the net profit after interest and tax is distributed:

- **Dividends** This shows the amount of net profit after interest and tax that is distributed to the owners (shareholders) of the company. The share of net profit (after interest and tax) allocated to shareholders is based on the decision of the Board of Directors and is approved at the company's Annual General Meeting. It is usual for dividends to be paid biannually. An interim dividend is paid approximately half way through the year and then the final dividend is declared and paid at the end of the firm's fiscal year. The figures are transferred to the balance sheet and shown under current liabilities.

- **Retained profit** This shows how much of the net profit after interest and tax is kept by the business for its own use, such as reinvesting it in the company or to expand the business. This figure is transferred to the "Financed by" section of the firm's balance sheet.

In reality, the three parts of the P&L account are combined into one final account. Assume that Florists-R-Us allocates 30% of its net profit after interest and tax to shareholders and retains the rest. Combining the three parts of the account will produce a P&L account like this:

Profit & Loss account for Florists-R-Us, for the year ended 31 December 2018

	$	
Sales revenue	460 000	Trading account
Cost of Goods Sold	230 000	
Gross Profit	230 000	
Less Expenses:	165 000	
Net profit before interest and tax	65 000	
		Profit & Loss account
Less Interest	10 000	
Net profit before tax	55 000	
Less Tax (10%)	5 500	
Net profit after interest and tax	49 500	
Dividends (30%)	14 850	Appropriation account
Retained profit (70%)	34 650	

Question 3.4.4 TOYS

The data below refers to the profit and loss account for TOYS, for the years ended 31st March.

	Year 1 ($'000)	Year 2 ($'000)
Sales	**450**	(i)
Cost of Goods Sold	(ii)	200
Gross Profit	270	300
Expenses	90	100
Net profit before interest and tax	**180**	(iii)
Interest payable	0	10
Taxation	(iv)	48
Net profit after interest and tax	135	142
Dividends	15	10
Retained profit	(v)	132

(a) Complete the missing figures in the above profit and loss account for TOYS. *[5 marks]*

(b) Discuss whether the owners of TOYS would be pleased with the performance of the company. *[10 marks]*

The P&L account is important as it shows the profit (if any) that is generated after all costs are accounted for. The gross profit might seem appealing, but if the expenses are higher than the gross profit, the business makes an overall loss. Clearly, a business cannot survive for long without making any actual profit.

There are, however, several limitations of the P&L account:

- The P&L account shows the historical performance of a business. There is no guarantee that future performance is linked to past performance or success.

- As there is no internationally standardised format for producing a P&L account, it might be difficult to compare the profit or loss of different firms in different countries, be they in the same or dissimilar industries.

- Window dressing can occur, i.e. the legal manipulation of final accounts to make them look financially more attractive. This disguises the underlying financial position of the company. For example, a firm might include the sale of some fixed assets or non-operating income in its P&L account to boost the value of profits, thereby impressing its shareholders.

Figure 3.4.c Window dressing is about making a firm's products or accounts look more attractive

The balance sheet

Finance accounts: balance sheet. AO2, AO4
© IBO, 2017

A balance sheet is one of the annual financial statements that all companies are legally required to produce for auditing purposes. It contains information on the value of an organization's assets, liabilities and the capital invested by the owners. As it shows the financial position of a business on one day only (usually the last day of the accounting year), it is often described as a 'snapshot' of a firm's financial situation.

It is called a balance sheet because the document shows a firm's sources of finance (shown as the equity) and where that money has been used (shown as the net assets), i.e. it reveals where a firm's money has come from (e.g. share capital and retained profit) and what it has been spent on (assets). For example, if a firm's building has a market value of $550,000 but has an outstanding mortgage of $350,000, the difference of $200,000 is the firm's equity, representing the portion of the property that the business actually owns. Thus, the balance sheet helps to ensure that all monies within the organization are properly accounted for.

A balance sheet must contain three essential parts: assets, liabilities and equity.

Assets

Assets are items of monetary value that are owned by a business, e.g. cash, stocks and buildings. To purchase assets, firms need different sources of finance (see Unit 3.1). Assets can be classified as fixed assets or current assets.

A **fixed** asset is any asset used for business operations (rather than for selling) and is likely to last for more than 12 months from the balance sheet date, such as premises, machinery and equipment. A **current asset** refers to cash or any other liquid asset that is likely to be turned into cash within twelve months of the balance sheet date. The three main types of current assets are cash, debtors and stocks.

> **Exam tip !**
>
> An asset belongs to a business but this does not mean that it has been paid for. A building (asset) could be worth millions of dollars, but is funded mainly by debt with the remaining amount being the equity.

Finance and accounts

CORE

Liabilities

A liability is a legal obligation of a business to repay its lenders or suppliers at a later date, i.e. the amount of money owed by the business. There are two main classifications of liabilities: long-term liabilities and current liabilities.

Long-term liabilities are debts that are due to be repaid after twelve months, i.e. they are sources of long-term borrowing. Examples include debentures, mortgages and bank loans (see Unit 3.1). **Current liabilities** are debts that must be settled within one year of the balance sheet date, e.g. taxes owed to the government, and bank overdrafts.

The value of a firm's **net assets** is therefore the value of all assets minus its liabilities. This must be equal to (balance with) its **equity** on the balance sheet. Net assets are calculated using the formula:

Net assets = Fixed assets + Working capital − Long-term liabilities

Or

Net assets = Total assets − Total liabilities

Equity (capital and reserves)

This section of the balance sheet shows the value of the business belonging to the owners. It can appear in a balance sheet as **shareholders' equity** (for limited liability companies) or as **owners' equity** (for businesses other than limited liability companies). There are two main sections to this part of the balance sheet:

- **Share capital** refers to the amount of money raised through the sale of shares. It shows the value raised when the shares were first sold, rather than their current market value.

- **Retained profit** is the amount of net profit after interest, tax and dividends have been paid. It is then reinvested in the business for its own use. This money, of course, belongs to its owners so appears under owners' equity or shareholders' equity. The figure for retained profits comes from the firm's P&L account.

From a balance sheet, we can see that:

Total assets − Total liabilities = Net assets = Owners' Equity

This means that the owners own the value of the assets of the business after deductions have been made for all its debts.

The example opposite shows a balance sheet for a hypothetical chain of restaurants for a particular year, illustrating the format and concepts used to construct a balance sheet. The key terms are explained on the right-hand side of the table.

Exam tip !

Retained profit appears in both the balance sheet and profit and loss account. The figure in the P&L account shows the net profit (after interest and tax) that is kept within the business for its own use, rather than being distributed to the owners or shareholders. Retained profit also appears in the "Financed by" section of the firm's balance sheet, as an internal source of finance.

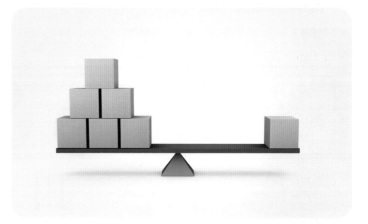

Figure 3.4.d A firm's equity must balance with its net assets

Balance sheet for Bellamkonda Restaurants Ltd. as at 30th Sept 20XX

	$'000	$'000	
Fixed assets			Fixed assets are items owned by the business that are not intended for resale within the next 12 months but are used to generate output and sales, e.g. the physical restaurants (premises), equipment, tables, chairs, drinks machines, fridges, cash registers, and air conditioning.
Premises	1 700		
Machinery and equipment	500		
		2 200	
Accumulated depreciation	200		This refers to the provisions made for the fall in the value of fixed assets over time, e.g. due to wear and tear of the machinery and equipment used in the restaurants.
Net fixed assets		2 000	The value of the restaurant's fixed assets after provisions are made for depreciation.
Current assets			Current assets are items owned by the business that are in the form of cash or what it intends to change into cash within one year of the balance sheet date, e.g. stock (food and drinks) and debtors (customers who have paid by cheque or credit card).
Cash	250		
Debtors	30		
Stocks	200		
	480		
Current liabilities			Current liabilities are debts that the business must pay to its creditors within 12 months of the balance sheet date, e.g. money owed to trade creditors (suppliers of food and drinks), to the bank for overdrafts (short-term borrowing), corporate tax owed to the government.
Short-term loans	15		
Trade creditors	250		
Taxation	55		
	320		
Net current assets (working capital)		160	Net current assets, also known as *working capital*, is calculated as the difference between a firm's current assets and its current liabilities.
Total assets less current liabilities		2 160	This is the sum of fixed and current assets minus the value of current liabilities.
Long-term liabilities			Long-term liabilities (or loan capital) are the debts owed by a firm, repayable after 12 months from the balance sheet date. Examples include mortgages and debentures (see Unit 3.1) to buy the premises and the outstanding bank loans (which may have been used to purchase the machinery and equipment).
Mortgage	500		
Debentures	500		
Bank loans	100		
		1 100	
Net assets		**1 060**	This figure is the sum of total assets less total liabilities. It must match (or balanced with) the figure for the firm's equity.
Financed by:			This section shows the capital and reserves of the business, i.e. the money that belongs to its owners. Here, 1 million shares were issued at $1 each, raising $1m for the restaurant (note that this is not the current market price of the shares). Accumulated retained profit (or reserves) refers to the surplus appropriated to the company from previous years.
Ordinary share capital (1 m shares at $1 per share)	1 000		
Accumulated retained profit	60		
Equity		**1 060**	Equity (or *shareholders' funds* refers to the sum of money that belongs to the owners of the restaurant, i.e. the owners' equity. It is equal to share capital plus reserves (accumulated retained profits).

Finance and accounts

CORE

Exam tip !

What's the correct format?

Different firms and different countries use slightly different methods to present their balance sheets. In the IB exams, use the format presented in Table 3.4.b. Remember to place an appropriate title at the top of the balance sheet.

Exam tip !

The main difference between the balance sheet of incorporated and unincorporated businesses is that *share capital* does not appear as part of their equity, because the latter do not have shareholders. The vast majority of examination questions will ask you to interpret the balance sheet of a limited liability company.

Balance sheet for (*Company Name*) **as at** (*Date*)

	$m	$m
Fixed assets	500	
Less accumulated depreciation	20	
Net fixed assets		480
Current assets		
Cash	10	
Debtors	12	
Stocks	35	
Total current assets	57	
Current liabilities		
Overdraft	5	
Creditors	15	
Short-term loans	22	
Total current liabilities	42	
Net current assets (working capital)		15
Total assets less current liabilities		495
Less **Long-term liabilities** (debt)	300	
Net assets		**195**
Financed by:		
Share capital	110	
Accumulated retained profit	85	
Equity		**195**

© IBO, 2017

Table 3.4.b Format of the balance sheet

It is common practice, and a legal requirement in many countries, to report the balance sheet figures for two consecutive years. This allows different stakeholder groups to make comparisons regarding the performance of the business.

The balance sheets of sole traders and partnerships differ slightly to those produced by limited companies. For example:

- Sources of finance will differ. Limited companies can raise finance through the sale of *debentures* (recorded under long-term liabilities), whereas this would not appear on the balance sheet of unincorporated businesses.

- *Shareholders' funds* is replaced with *owner's equity* including the personal funds of sole traders and partners (unincorporated firms do not have shareholders).

- Since there are no shareholders in a partnership or sole proprietorship, dividends will not appear under their current liabilities. Instead, the sole trader or partners might take out funds from the business for their personal use (known as *drawings* to accountants).

Limitations of Balance Sheets

- As balance sheets are static documents, the financial position of a business might be very different in subsequent periods. For example, the value of capital and reserves can change the next day due to the business using the funds for expansion purposes.

- The figures are, at best, only 'accurate' estimates of the value of assets and liabilities. The *market value* of an asset is not necessarily the same as its *book value* (the value shown on the balance sheet). The true market value of a fixed asset is only known once the item has been sold. Also, the values shown do not show a detailed breakdown of a firm's assets, so the information is somewhat incomplete.

- Since there is no specific format required for producing a balance sheet, different businesses (or their accountants) will produce accounts in varying formats and include different assets and liabilities. This can make it difficult to compare the financial position of different firms, even those that operate in the same industry.

- Not all assets are included in a balance sheet, especially intangible assets and the value of human capital. For example, professional sports clubs do not include the market value of their players in their balance sheet. To do so would be difficult as each organization would need to determine which players to include in their valuation. Similarly, the club's manager or coach has a market value but this is not shown on the balance sheet. If the saying that 'workers are a firm's most valuable assets' is true, this means that the financial position of a business is not accurately represented in a balance sheet.

Theory of knowledge

Is it possible to know if the finances of a company are truly represented in the final accounts of a business?

Question 3.4.5 Marc Brothers Motor Repairs

The financial data for *Marc Brothers Motor Repairs* are shown below. The company's reporting day for the **balance sheet** is 31st March.

Property = $630,000, Machinery and vehicles = $230,000, Depreciation = $144,000, Stock = 30,000, Cash = $12,000, Debtors = $16,000, Overdraft = $13,000, Loan capital = $380,000, Share capital = $300,000, and Accumulated retained profit = $81,000.

(a) Define the term **balance sheet**. *[2 marks]*

(b) Use the data above to construct a balance sheet for *Marc Brothers Motor Repairs*. *[5 marks]*

Question 3.4.6   Bajaj Electronics

Bajaj Electronics is an importer and exporter of consumer electronic products, and computer accessories. Selected financial data from the company on 31 December are shown below.

	2019 ($'000)	2018 ($'000)
Bank overdraft	20	10
Cash	25	20
Creditors	50	50
Debentures	50	50
Debtors	70	50
Fixed assets	250	250
Long-term liabilities	50	80
Retained profit	75	75
Share capital	200	150
Stock	100	95

(a) Identify one example of fixed assets and one example of stocks for *Bajaj Electronics*. *[2 marks]*

(b) Construct a balance sheet for *Bajaj Electronics* for both years. *[5 marks]*

(c) State the value of working capital *Bajaj Electronics* for both years. *[2 marks]*

Question 3.4.7   Senjaya Fabrics Ltd.

Hendra Senjaya runs *Senjaya Fabrics Ltd.*, a garments manufacturer in Indonesia. Hendra has provided excerpts from the finance department which shows the following (all figures are in millions of Indonesian rupiah as at 31 March this year):

Cash = IDR32 m

Creditors = IDR45 m

Debtors = IDR35 m

Mortgage = IDR127 m

Overdraft = IDR30 m

Property = IDR350 m

Accumulated retained profits = IDR100 m

Share capital = IDR175 m

Stocks = IDR60 m.

(a) Define the term **share capital**. *[2 marks]*

(b) Using the above data, construct the balance sheet for *Senjaya Fabrics Ltd*. *[5 marks]*

Intangible assets

Different types of intangible assets. AO1

© IBO, 2017

Intangible assets are non-physical fixed assets that have the ability to earn revenue for a business, e.g. brand names, goodwill, trademarks, copyrights and patents. They are legally protected by **intellectual property rights** (see Unit 5.6). Intangible assets can account for a large proportion of a firm's asset value, although it is usually difficult to place an objective and accurate price on such assets. The main intangible fixed assets that can appear in a balance sheet include:

- **Brand** recognition and brand value help to drive global sales for companies such as Apple and Coca-Cola, year after year. Hence, branding is an indefinite asset as brand recognition and brand loyalty stay with the company for as long as it operates. According to *Forbes*, the Apple brand is worth $104 billion. The Microsoft, Coca-Cola and IBM brands are all worth more than $50 billion.

- **Patents** provide legal protection for inventors, preventing others from copying their creation for a fixed number of years. For example, compact disks were patented by electronics firm Philips. Patents act as an incentive to stimulate innovation. If rivals could simply copy the invention, there would be no need for them to spend large amounts of money on research and development. Patents allow the inventor to have exclusive rights to commercial production for a specified time period. Other firms must apply and pay a fee to the patent holder if they wish to use or copy the ideas, processes or products created by the inventor.

- **Copyright** (©) provides legal protection for the original artistic work of the creator, such as an author, photographer, painter or musician. Media sources such as newspapers, sound recordings, computer software and movies are examples of such works. Anyone wishing to reproduce or modify the artist's work must first seek permission from the copyright holder, usually for a fee. The copyright holder of this textbook is IBID Press.

- **Goodwill** is the value of an organization's image and reputation. It can also include the value of the firm's customer base and its business connections. A business that treats its workers well is likely to see a lot of goodwill from its staff, i.e. employees are loyal to the firm and consequently add greater value. Goodwill is then the sum of customer and staff loyalty and can provide a major competitive edge for any business. As US entrepreneur Marshall Field (1834–1906) said, 'Goodwill is the one and only asset that competition cannot undersell or destroy'.

- **Registered trademarks** (®) are distinctive signs that uniquely identify a brand, a product or a business. Trademarks can be expressed by names, symbols, phrases or an image, such as the Nike 'swoosh' mark. Like copyrights and patents, trademarks provide legal protection against those who might try to copy their creations and inventions. Registered trademarks can be sold so ownership can be transferred for appropriate fees, and is reflected in the firm's balance sheet. For example, in 1998 Volkswagen bought the Bentley brand (luxury automobiles) for £430 million ($625m).

Theory of knowledge

In 2014, *Forbes* estimated Google's brand value to be around $47bn, whereas *Interbrand* estimated Google's brand value to be in excess of $93bn. Given this huge difference, is there any substance in the knowledge claims of brand values?

Intangible assets are not always shown in a balance sheet because their value is very difficult to measure. For example, what are the Google or Coca-Cola brands really worth? How do we value the goodwill of staff in a school or hospital? No two firms are likely to answer these questions in exactly the same way. The subjective nature of valuing intangible assets renders it unnecessary or even impossible to include on a balance sheet. For example, goodwill is only truly realised when a takeover or merger has taken place with the buyer paying a premium for the purchase of the business. This premium represents the goodwill – the difference between the value of the business and the purchase price. Adding intangible assets on a balance sheet can be seen as a form of window dressing to artificially inflate the value of a business, e.g. Vodafone managed to turn an €11 billion ($15 billion) loss into a €10 billion ($13.7 billion)

profit in 2006 by legal use of creative accounting to include goodwill. There is no doubt that intangible assets add value to a business beyond its book value; the uncertainty lies in how to place an accurate value on such assets.

Figure 3.4.e Times Square, New York, where many global brands are instantly recognisable

IB Learner Profile – Be an inquirer

Branding consultancy firm *Interbrand* publishes an annual ranking of the 'Best Global Brands' by market value. Visit their website (www.interbrand.com) to identify the current top 10 global brands and to investigate the criteria used by *Interbrand* to determine the value of these brands.

Theory of knowledge

To what extent do the financial data of a business reflect the "truth" about the organization?

Question 3.4.8   Harry Potter (JK Rowling)

JK Rowling was unemployed at the time when she wrote her first Harry Potter fantasy novel, back in 1994. She has certainly come a long way since then. In 1998, Warner Bros purchased the rights for film adaptations of the Harry Potter novels. By 2007, Warner Bros and Universal Studios announced the construction of 'Harry Potter World' at the Universal Islands of Adventure theme park in Orlando, Florida. Prior to the release of Rowling's seventh and final instalment of the series, global sales of her books had already exceeded 400 million copies and been translated into more than 65 languages. According to *TIME,* the Harry Potter brand is worth over $25 billion. The huge commercial success and high market value of the *Harry Potter* franchise means that Rowling, her publishers and Warner Bros are keen to protect their **intellectual property rights**.

(a) Describe what is meant by **intellectual property rights**.   *[2 marks]*

(b) In the context of the case study, explain **two** benefits of protecting copyrights.   *[4 marks]*

(c) Comment on how the $15 billion valuation of the Harry Potter brand might be affected by the subjective nature of placing values on intellectual property rights.   *[4 marks]*

Depreciation [Higher Level]

Depreciation using the following methods: straight line method and reducing/declining balance method. AO2, AO4

The strengths and weaknesses of each method. AO2

© IBO, 2017

Property and land tend to rise in value over time. The increase in the value of fixed assets is known as **appreciation**. However, most fixed assets tend to depreciate over time. **Depreciation** is the fall in the value of fixed assets over time, due to:

- **Wear and tear** Fixed assets such as computers and motor vehicles are used repeatedly over time, so they tend to wear out and raise maintenance costs. Hence, the value of these fixed assets declines over time.

- **Obsolescence** As newer and better products become available, the demand and hence the value of existing fixed assets will fall. Obsolete assets are out-of-date assets such as old versions of vehicles, computers or software.

Depreciation spreads the **historic cost** (purchase cost) of fixed assets over their useful lifespan. The change in the value of fixed assets is shown by reassessing their value on a balance sheet. Depreciation needs to be recorded in order to:

- Calculate the value of a business more accurately. Depreciating fixed assets will reduce the value of net assets to better reflect the true value or financial position of a business. Similarly, revaluing assets that have appreciated will increase the net asset value.

- Realistically assess the value of fixed assets over time. The historic cost of fixed assets such as machinery and vehicles is unlikely to be equal to its current market value.

- Plan for the replacement of assets in the future. Provisions are made for purchasing new fixed assets. Depreciation is recorded on the P&L account as an expense because it reflects the fall in the value of fixed assets that will eventually need to be replaced.

Figure 3.4.f Depreciation is the fall in the value of an asset over time

There are two main methods of calculating depreciation: the *straight line method* and the *reducing balance method*. In practice, it does not really matter which method is used but in order to allow for meaningful and historical comparisons, it is vital to be consistent in the choice of method used.

Question 3.4.9 Safarie Air Tours

Safarie Air Tours is owned by Achmad Safarie. The company recently paid $5.2 million for a second-hand airplane. The asset has an estimated useful life of 5 years, with an expected **residual value** of $1.6m

(a) Define the term **residual value**. *[2 marks]*

(b) Calculate the value of the annual depreciation for *Safarie Air Tours*. *[2 marks]*

Straight line method

This is the simplest and most commonly used of the two methods. It is popular amongst European companies. The annual depreciation is calculated using three key variables: the *life expectancy of the asset* (how long it is intended to be used before it needs to be replaced), the scrap or *residual value* of the asset (how much it is worth at the end of its useful life) and the *purchase cost* of the asset. The following formula is used:

$$\text{Annual depreciation} = \frac{\text{Purchase cost}}{\text{Lifespan}}$$

For example, if an electronic security system is bought for $25,000 and is expected to last five years (i.e. when it will be replaced), the annual depreciation is a fixed amount of $5,000 (i.e. $25,000 ÷ 5 years). The value of the asset at the end of each year is shown in Table 3.4.c and represented diagrammatically in Figure 3.4.g.

Table 3.4.c   Straight line depreciation at $5,000 per annum

Year end	Depreciation ($)	Book value ($)
0	–	25 000
1	5 000	20 000
2	5 000	15 000
3	5 000	10 000
4	5 000	5 000
5	5 000	0

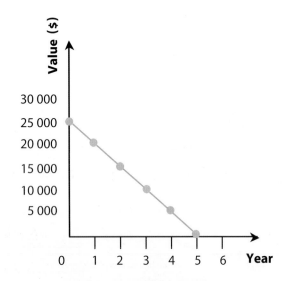

Figure 3.4.g Straight line depreciation

The **residual value** is an estimate of the scrap or disposal value of the asset at the end of its useful life. Many firms simply use a zero residual value since estimates may prove to be inaccurate. However, it is unusual for a fixed asset to lose all of its value because it can fetch a minimal price when sold. In such a case, the formula becomes:

$$\text{Annual depreciation} = \frac{\text{Purchase cost } \textit{less } \text{Residual value}}{\text{Lifespan}}$$

So, if the electronic security system is expected to fetch a second-hand value of $5,000 in 5 years' time, then the annual amount of depreciation is worked out as ($25,000 – $5,000) ÷ 5 years = $4,000 per annum, i.e. a difference of $1,000 each year compared with the depreciation charge if there is no residual value.

The key advantage of the straight line method is that it is simple to calculate and to understand. However, the main weakness is that depreciating fixed assets by an equal amount each year is not realistic, e.g. motor vehicles lose a much larger percentage of their value at the beginning of their useful life cycle. The straight line depreciation method does not account for the loss of efficiency or the higher repair costs of fixed assets over time.

Reducing balance method

The reducing balance method (or the **declining balance method**) depreciates the value of an asset by a predetermined percentage for the duration of its useful life. This reduces the value of an asset by a larger amount in the earlier years of its useful life. The book value of the asset is calculated by deducting the accumulated (cumulative) depreciation from the historic cost (purchase cost) of the asset, i.e.

$$\text{Net book value} = \text{Historical cost } \textit{less } \text{Accumulated depreciation}$$

The reducing balance method is more realistic in representing the falling market value of fixed assets over time. This method is preferred by most US companies. However, it is not as straightforward to calculate and deciding on the annual rate of depreciation is somewhat subjective. Also, it is unnecessary if the purpose is to simply spread the cost of an asset over its useful lifespan.

Continuing with the above example, assume the business chose to use the reducing balance method to depreciate the electronic security system at an annual rate of 25%. This depreciation charge is shown in Table 3.4.d (figures rounded to the nearest dollar). The graphical representation of this is shown in Figure 3.4.h.

This method leaves a residual value of $5,933 for the electronic security system after five years.

Amortisation is similar to depreciation but is used to reduce the value of non-physical fixed assets (intangible assets) on a balance sheet. For example, as copyrights and patents near their expiry date the value of such intellectual property rights tends to fall.

Table 3.4.d   Reducing balance depreciation at 25% per annum

Year end	Depreciation ($)	Book value ($)
0	-	25 000
1	6 250	18 750
2	4 687	14 063
3	3 516	10 547
4	2 637	7 910
5	1 977	5 933

Theory of knowledge

Scottish writer Thomas Carlyle, (1795-1881) said that *"You may prove anything by figures"*. To what extent does this claim apply to knowledge in Business Management?

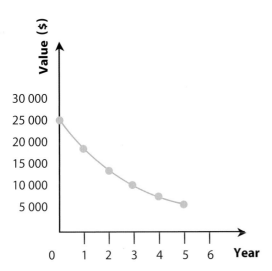

Figure 3.4.h Reducing balance depreciation

Exam tip !

HL students are expected to know both methods of calculating depreciation: the straight-line method and the reducing-balance method. Make sure you practise both methods thoroughly.

Question 3.4.10   Neville Stibbs Stationers (NSS)

Neville Stibbs Stationers (NSS) purchased five printing machines for $200,000 with an expected useful life of 5 years. The management at NSS uses a **depreciation** rate of 30%.

(a) Define the term **depreciation**.   *[2 marks]*

(b) Calculate the residual value of the laser printing machines after 5 years.   *[3 marks]*

Question 3.4.11 Chard-Reid Enterprise Inc.

Chard-Reid Enterprise Inc. recently bought a new company car for $35,000. The firm expects to replace it in five years' time. The current market resale value of the car in five years' time is approximately $5,800. The company uses an annual 30% depreciation rate.

(a) Use the reducing balance method of depreciation to calculate the book value of *Chard-Reid Enterprise Inc.'s* new company car after the first *two* years.   *[2 marks]*

(b) Calculate the estimated value of the car after two years, if *Chard-Reid Enterprise Inc.* had used the straight line method of depreciation.   *[2 marks]*

(c) Explain which method of depreciation would reduce the net book value of the car the most by the end of the third year.   *[4 marks]*

(d) Examine the strengths and weaknesses of both methods of depreciation for *Chard-Reid Enterprise Inc.*   *[6 marks]*

Limitations of final accounts

- Using a single year's accounts in isolation is of little value since there is no way of judging financial performance over time. Instead, a series of final accounts would be more useful to show any trends.

- Human resources are totally ignored. The skills, loyalty and motivation of staff are overlooked in financial analyses. The inability to retain or motivate staff can have major repercussions on the future financial position of the firm.

- Final accounts do not reveal anything about the firm's non-financial matters, such as its organizational culture. Qualitative factors can be equally important in decision-making. For example, ethical objectives and the location of industry are affected by both financial and non-financial factors.

- There needs to be access to the accounts of other businesses in order to benchmark the financial performance with rivals in the industry (see Unit 5.3).

- Whilst final accounts must be lawfully produced, this does not mean that they reveal the whole truth. Companies will limit, within reason, the financial information that they disclose since their accounts will be in the public domain and hence accessible by their rivals.

- The final accounts are historical accounts of the financial position of a firm. Past performance is not necessarily indicative of current or future performance.

Exam tip !

As always with quantitative techniques, it is vital to look beyond the financial data. You should consider qualitative issues, such as organizational objectives, the state of the economy and corporate culture. Final accounts are just one part of the quantitative analyses required to give an accurate appraisal of the firm's financial position. Budgeting is an important consideration for the daily operation of a business, whilst investment appraisal assesses the financial gains on growth and expansion plans. So, the importance of any single financial statement in strategic planning and analysis should be handled with prudence.

Final accounts and the CUEGIS concepts

Final accounts can provide invaluable data for strategic planning and analysis. The financial documents are important for two key reasons: *disclosure* and *accountability* of financial matters of a business. Used properly and ethically, they can reveal the profitability of a business. If profit has been declared due to a one-off sale of fixed assets such as land or property, then there is likely to be low profitability.

As part of a firm's business strategy, managers examine the working capital and liquidity of the organization (see Unit 3.7). The balance sheet reveals the ability of the firm to meet its daily running costs. Indeed, both the balance sheet and P&L accounts are often used by businesses seeking to secure external funding for growth and expansion (see Unit 1.6).

One strategy could be to develop the firm's intellectual property rights (IPR). The use of IPRs such as patents and copyrights can act as an effective form of barrier to entry. Global businesses such as Coca-Cola, Toyota and The Walt Disney Company have used IPRs to erect artificial entry barriers to protect their market share. Aristotle Onassis, a Greek business mogul, said that the secret to corporate success is to have or know something that no one else does. This means that innovation and new product development (see Unit 5.6) are important strategies for long-term survival. The legal protection of new products, designs and processes can therefore increase the firm's value on its balance sheet. In today's ever-more competitive environment, many organizations no longer see IPRs as a defensive strategy, but as an offensive business strategy for corporate success.

However, one problem is that different countries have different laws and cultural norms regarding the construction of the final accounts. Nevertheless, the consensus in modern societies is that all business decisions, including the reporting of financial accounts, have ethical or moral implications for various stakeholder groups.

> ## CUEGIS Essay
>
> With reference to an organization of your choice, discuss how **change** and **strategy** have influenced its final accounts (the balance sheet and the profit and loss account). *[20 marks]*

REVIEW QUESTIONS

1. What are the two sets of final accounts that all companies are obliged to report to their shareholders?

2. Outline how four different stakeholder groups might make use of financial accounts.

3. What are the main principles of accounting practice?

4. Why is there a need for accounting practice to be ethical?

5. What is the purpose of a profit and loss account?

6. What is a balance sheet and why is it said to be a static financial document?

7. What are intangible assets?

8. Why do firms depreciate the value of their fixed assets?

9. Distinguish between the reducing balance and the straight line methods of depreciation.

10. What are the limitations of the final accounts?

KEY TERMS

The **appropriation account** refers to the final section of a P&L account and shows how the net profit after interest and tax is distributed, i.e. dividends to shareholders and/or retained profit kept by the business.

A **balance sheet** contains financial information on an organization's assets, liabilities and the capital invested by the owners on one specific day, thus showing a 'snapshot' the firm's financial situation.

Book value is the value of an asset as shown on a balance sheet. The market value of assets can be higher than its book value because of intangible assets such as the brand value or the goodwill of the business.

Cost of goods sold (COGS), also known as **cost of sales** (COS), is shown in the trading account and represents the direct costs of producing or purchasing stock that has been sold.

Creditors are suppliers who allow a business to purchase goods and/or services on trade credit.

Current assets are the short-term assets that belong to a firm, which are expected to remain in the business for up to 12 months, e.g. cash, debtors and stock (inventory).

Debtors are a category of current assets, referring to customers who have bought goods or services on credit, i.e. they owe money to the business, which is due (payable) at a later date.

Depreciation is the fall in the value of fixed assets over time, from wear and tear (due to the asset being used) or obsolescence (outdated or out of fashion).

Final accounts are the published annual financial statements that all limited liability companies are legally obliged to report, i.e. the balance sheet and the P&L accounts.

Fixed assets are items owned by a business, not intended for sale within the next twelve months, but used repeatedly to generate revenue for the organization, e.g. land, premises and machinery.

Goodwill is an intangible asset which exists when the value of a firm exceeds its book value (the value of the firm's net assets).

Gross profit is the difference between the sales revenue of a business and its direct costs incurred in making or purchasing the products that have been sold to its customers.

The **historic cost** refers to the purchase cost of a particular fixed asset.

Intangible assets are fixed assets that do not exist in a physical form, e.g. goodwill, copyrights, brand names and registered trademarks.

Long-term liabilities are the debts owed by a business, which are expected to take longer than a year from the balance sheet date to repay.

Net assets show the value of a business by calculating the value of all its assets minus its liabilities. This figure must match the equity of the business in its balance sheet.

Net profit is the surplus (if any) that a business makes after all expenses have been paid for out of gross profit.

The **profit and loss account** (or **income statement**) is a financial record of a firm's trading activity over the past 12 months, consisting of three parts: the trading account, the P&L account and the appropriation account.

Reducing balance method is a method of depreciation that reduces the value of a fixed asset by the same *percentage* each year throughout its useful life. This is the more realistic method to use.

The **residual value** of an asset is an estimate of the scrap or disposal value of the asset at the end of its useful life.

Retained profit is the amount of net profit after interest, tax and dividends have been paid. It is then reinvested in the business for its own use.

Share capital refers to the amount of money raised through the sale of shares. It shows the value raised when the shares were first sold, rather than their current market value.

Shareholders' funds show the equity of the owners, i.e. the share capital invested by the owners and the retained profit and reserves that have been accumulated.

Straight line method is a method of depreciation that reduces the value of a fixed asset by the same *value* each year throughout its useful life. This is the relatively easier method to calculate.

The **trading account** is the first section of the P&L account, showing the difference between a firm's sales revenue and its direct costs of trading, i.e. it shows the gross profit of a business.

Window dressing refers to the legal act of creative accounting by manipulating financial data to make the results look more flattering.

3.5 Profitability and liquidity ratio analysis

"Many of the things you can count, don't count. Many of the things you can't count, really count." - Albert Einstein (1879–1955), mathematics genius

SL/HL content	Assessment objective
The following profitability and efficiency ratios: • gross profit margin • net profit margin • ROCE	AO2, AO4
Possible strategies to improve these ratios	AO3
The following liquidity ratios: • current • acid test/quick	AO2, AO4
Possible strategies to improve these ratios	AO3

© IBO, 2017

Ratio analysis

In its simplest sense, a ratio is one number expressed in terms of another. For example, in an organization with 30 women and 20 men, the male to female ratio is 2:3, i.e. for every two male employees, there are 3 female workers. **Ratio analysis** is a quantitative management tool for analysing and judging the financial performance of a business. This is done by calculating financial ratios from a firm's final accounts (see Unit 3.4). To assess whether financial performance has improved, current figures are normally compared with historical figures. Alternatively, the same ratios can be compared with those of rivals to judge whether the business has improved against its competitors.

Exam tip !
Don't just simply learn the formulae for the ratios without understanding what they actually mean. Instead, focus on why or how the ratios could be used in the context of the given business. Address issues such as:
• How is the business performing (based on financial data)?
• How has the business performed over time (trends)?
• What else needs to be considered that is not presented in the data? For example, think about business objectives and any external constraints on the organization's performance.

The purpose of ratio analysis

The purpose of ratio analysis is to:

• Examine a firm's financial position, e.g. its short- and long-term liquidity position

• Assess a firm's financial performance, e.g. its ability to control expenses

• Compare actual figures with projected or budgeted figures (known as variance analysis)

• Aid decision-making, e.g. whether investors should risk their money by investing in the business.

Ratios are compared in two ways:

• Historical comparisons involve comparing the same ratio in two different time periods for the same business. Such comparisons show trends, thereby helping managers to assess the financial performance of a business over time.

• Inter-firm comparisons involve comparing the ratios of businesses in the same industry. For example, two businesses might have the same amount of profit although their sales revenue may be quite different. Ratio analysis can therefore show the relative financial performance of a business.

In reality, businesses use both historical and inter-firm comparisons when analysing their financial ratios. However, it is important to remember that ratio analysis is only of value if managers compare like with like. For example, McDonald's should only compare its financial ratios with rivals of similar size in the same industry. There is little value in McDonald's comparing its financial ratios against a sole trader who runs a single fast-food restaurant or comparing its figures to manufacturers of furniture.

Exam tip !

When learning the different financial ratios, make sure that you understand the various *units of measurement* used. Some ratios are expressed as a number in terms of another (e.g. 2:1), whilst others are shown as a percentage, or even as 'number of days'. The important thing is to understand the meaning of the ratio and to be able to write about the ratio into the context of the organization.

Profitability and efficiency ratios

The following profitability and efficiency ratios: gross profit margin (GPM), net profit margin (NPM) and return on capital employed (ROCE). AO2, A04

Possible strategies to improve these ratios. AO3

© IBO, 2017

Profitability ratios examine profit in relation to other figures, such as the ratio of profit to sales revenue. These ratios tend to be relevant to profit-seeking businesses rather than for not-for-profit organizations. Managers, employees and potential investors are interested in profitability ratios as they show how well a firm has performed in financial terms.

Efficiency ratios show how well a firm's resources have been used, such as the amount of profit generated from the available capital used by the business. For example, the two firms in Table 3.5.a generate the same amount of absolute profit but Firm A is more efficient. This is because it generates $100 million profit from using capital worth $200 million (a return of 50%) whereas Firm B earns the same amount profit from using $250 million worth of capital resources (a smaller return of 40%).

Table 3.5.a   Efficiency and the use of capital resources

	Firm A	Firm B
Profit	$100 m	$100 m
Capital employed	$200 m	$250 m
Efficiency ratio	50%	40%

Profit is a key objective for most businesses and acts as a measure of a firm's success. **Profit** is defined as the surplus earnings of an organization once all costs have been deducted from sales revenue. Profitability ratios measure profit in relation to other variables such as sales turnover. The main profitability ratios are the gross profit margin (GPM) and net profit margin (NPM).

The absolute amount of profit, as declared in a profit and loss account, tells us little about the financial performance of a business. For example, is a business financially successful if it earns $10 million profit? The answer might be 'yes' for a small partnership selling computer accessories, but the answer would be a definite 'no' for a much larger business such as Lenovo or IBM. We can draw this conclusion when comparing the ratio of profit to the huge sales turnover of, or the amount invested by, Lenovo and IBM. Hence, to assess the profitability of a business, it is necessary to compare and relate profit to other financial aspects of the business. A key limitation of using profitability ratios is that they only apply to profit-orientated businesses.

Exam tip !

When dealing with finance, it is important to look at the bigger picture and to put the figures into context. For example, in February 2007, sportswear manufacturer Puma announced a 26% drop in profits to €38.2 million ($43m). Does this represent poor performance? Not necessarily. This very limited information can, on its own, be misleading. In fact, Puma was undergoing expansion and was using its retained profits to finance its growth (hence the fall in its declared profits). Puma's sales had actually increased by more than 33%. Ten years later, Puma declared net profit of €135.2 million.

Gross profit margin (GPM)

The gross profit margin shows the value of gross profit as a percentage of sales revenue. The figures for working out the GPM are found in the profit and loss account, using the formula:

$$GPM = \frac{Gross\ profit}{Sales\ revenue} \times 100$$

The GPM ratio is expressed as a percentage. For example, if a business has a gross profit of $120 million from sales of $200 million, then the GPM is 60%. This means that for every $100 of sales, $60 is gross profit (with costs of goods sold accounting for the other $40). The higher the GPM, the better it is for a business as gross profit goes towards paying its expenses. The GPM ratio can be improved in two main ways:

- **Raising revenue** by
  - Reducing the selling price of products for which there are many substitute products - this enables the firm to gain a competitive advantage by having lower prices.
  - Raising the selling price of products for which there are few if any substitutes - if customers are not very responsive to changes in price (due to strong brand loyalty or a lack of close substitute products), then the business can gain higher sales revenue by charging a higher price.
  - Using marketing strategies to raise sales revenue - for example, special promotions (see Unit 4.5) and product extension strategies can help to boost sales.
  - Seeking alternative revenue streams (see Unit 3.2) - this can enable the business to improve its sales revenue, particularly when it is affected by fluctuations in seasonal demand.

Figure 3.5.a Holiday and beach resorts are prone to seasonal fluctuations in demand

- **Reducing direct costs** by
  - Cutting direct material costs - for example, businesses might choose to use cheaper suppliers and/or cheaper materials. Some airlines have saved millions of dollars each year by cutting back on the amount of chocolates or snacks that they offer on-board. However, cost cutting can have a negative impact on the perceived quality of the good or service.
  - Cutting direct labour costs -businesses might choose to reduce staffing costs by cutting the number of staff, or by getting staff to do more (for the same pay). Either way, the productivity of staff may increase, thereby reducing unit labour costs. However, this method can cause resentment and demotivation.

In reality, a business is likely to strive to raise its GPM ratio by a combination of methods to reduce costs and to raise revenues.

Net profit margin (NPM)

The net profit margin shows the percentage of sales turnover that is turned into net profit. A NPM ratio of 35% means that for every $100 of sales, $35 is net profit. This is the amount of profit that is left after all production costs are accounted for (both direct and indirect costs). NPM is calculated using the formula:

$$NPM = \frac{Net\ profit}{Sales\ revenue} \times 100$$

The NPM ratio is a better measure of a firm's profitability than GPM as it accounts for both cost of sales (direct costs) and expenses (indirect costs). The difference between a firm's GPM and its NPM represents the expenses, and therefore the larger the difference between these two ratios, the more difficult overhead control tends to be. As with the GPM, the general rule is that the higher the NPM, the better it is for the organization.

It is common for high volume products, such as confectionary and fast food, to have a relatively low profit margin. However, the high sales volume compensates for this. Conversely, for low volume products, such as aircraft and luxury wines, the profit margin tends to be relatively high to compensate for the lower volume of sales.

The NPM can be improved by financial and non-financial strategies such as those mentioned above for the GPM. However, costs can be examined further to reduce business expenses. For example, it may be possible to:

Finance and accounts

CORE

- negotiate preferential payment terms with trade creditors and suppliers. By delaying payment, a business may be able to improve its working capital. Alternatively, it might be possible to negotiate discounts for paying creditors on time.

- negotiate cheaper rent. Trustworthy and creditable businesses may be able to negotiate lower rents or delay payment of rent to improve their cash flow position.

- reduce indirect costs. Careful examination of an organization's expenses might reveal areas where costs can be cut without detrimental effects to the business. For example, many businesses no longer pay senior managers to fly first class, choosing business class or economy class travel instead. Other overheads that might be reduced include advertising, stationery and insurance premiums.

Figure 3.5.b Business class air travel is an expensive cost for firms

Note: It is common practice to use 'Net Profit *before* interest and tax' to calculate the NPM because it allows historical comparisons to be made. Net profits are subject to change, caused by fluctuating interest rates and tax rates (both factors are beyond the control of a business).

To calculate financial ratios, such as the GPM and the NPM, it is usually necessary to use a **balance sheet** and a **profit and loss account** (see Unit 3.4). For illustrative purposes, the numerical questions that follow in Units 3.5 and 3.6 will refer to the numbers given in Tables 3.5.a and 3.5.b for *JKL Ltd.*, a fictitious company.

Balance sheet for JKL Ltd as at 31 December

	Year 2	Year 1
Fixed assets	600	500
Current assets		
Cash	200	50
Debtors	150	200
Stock	350	250
Total current assets	700	500
Current liabilities	300	200
Net current assets (working capital)	400	300
Total assets less current liabilities	1 000	800
Long-term liabilities (debt)	250	250
Net assets	**750**	**550**
Financed by:		
Ordinary share capital	500	500
Retained profits	250	50
Equity	**750**	**550**

Table 3.5.b Balance sheet for JKL Ltd. as at 31 December (figures in $'000s)

Profit & Loss account for JKL Ltd. for the year ended 31 December

	Year 2	Year 1
Sales revenue	1 000	850
Cost of goods sold	500	450
Net profit before interest and tax	400	360
Tax	100	90
Dividends	50	220
Retained profits	250	50

Table 3.5.c Excerpts from JKL Ltd.'s Profit and Loss Account for years ended 31 December (figures in $'000s)

Question 3.5.1   Calculating profitability

(a) Determine the value of *JKL Ltd.*'s gross profit and its expenses in both years.   *[2 marks]*

(b) (i) Calculate the GPM and the NPM ratios for *JKL Ltd.* in both years (show all your workings).   *[4 marks]*

(b) (ii) Explain your findings from the previous question.   *[4 marks]*

(c) Comment on further information that could be used to determine the profitability of *JKL Ltd.*   *[4 marks]*

Exam tip !
Worked example

Explain how a price reduction for a product could reduce the gross profit margin (GPM), but actually boost the net profit margin (NPM). Use a numerical example to help explain your answer.

Answer

	Before ($)	After ($)
Turnover	1 000	1 200
Cost of goods sold	600	740
Gross profit	400	460
GPM	40.0%	38.3%
Indirect costs	300	300
Net profit	100	160
NPM	10.0%	13.3%

The fall in price will automatically reduce the profit margin, other things being equal. However, the price reduction has attracted more customers and since indirect costs are constant, the NPM has increased.

Efficiency ratios

Efficiency ratios look at how well a firm's financial resources are being used. The only efficiency ratio that both SL and HL students to learn is the most important one, the **return on capital employed (ROCE)**. The ROCE ratio measures the financial performance of a firm compared with the amount of capital invested. ROCE is also an indicator of the profitability of a firm, i.e. it is considered to be both a profitability and an efficiency ratio. It is calculated using the formula:

$$\frac{\text{Net profit before interest and tax}}{\text{Capital employed}} \times 100$$

The figure for capital employed can be seen on a firm's balance sheet. Capital employed is the sum of shareholders' funds plus retained profits plus long-term liabilities, i.e. it is the sum of total internal sources of finance plus all external sources of finance.

Capital employed = loan capital + share capital + accumulated retained profit

Recall that loan capital is shown as long-term liabilities on the balance sheet. The ROCE figure shows profit as a percentage of the capital used to generate it. The higher the ROCE figure, the better it is for the business. Some sources refer to a 20% ROCE as being a target benchmark, although this needs to be put into the context of the business and the industry in which it operates. A 20% ROCE figure shows that for every $1,000 invested in the business, $200 profit is generated. As a general rule, the ROCE should at least exceed the interest rate offered at banks; otherwise it would be better to simply deposit the capital in an interest-bearing bank account. In addition, bank deposits would probably carry less risk compared with other investment projects. Hence, ROCE must be high enough to create an incentive for investors to part with their money.

295

Figure 3.5.c   An ROCE of 20% means $200 is earned per $1,000 invested

ROCE is calculated by using *net profit before tax and interest* as this allows for better historical comparisons (since interest and tax rates are subject to change over time and are beyond the control of the business). Many people regard the ROCE as the single most important financial ratio as it measures how well a firm is able to generate profit from its sources of funds. Hence, the ROCE is often referred to as the **key ratio**.

The ROCE ratio can be improved mainly by strategies to boost net profits (see above). Mathematically, the ROCE ratio will also increase if capital employed falls whilst net profits remain constant; although in reality this is probably not desirable.

Liquidity ratios

The following profitability and efficiency ratios: current ratio and acid test (quick) ratio. AO2, A04

Possible strategies to improve these ratios. AO3

© IBO, 2017

Liquidity ratios look at the ability of a firm to pay its short-term liabilities, such as by comparing working capital to short-term debts. Creditors and financial lenders are interested in liquidity ratios to help assess the likelihood of getting back the money they are owed. Shareholders and potential investors may also be interested as these ratios can reveal a firm's ability to repay its debts.

Certain assets of a business can be turned into cash quickly, without losing their value. These assets are known as **liquid assets** and can be in the form of *cash* itself, stocks (finished goods, ready for sale) and *debtors* (see Unit 3.4). Liquidity ratios calculate how easily an organization can pay its short-term financial obligations from its current assets. The two main liquidity ratios are the current ratio and the acid test ratio.

Current ratio

The current ratio deals with a firm's liquid assets and short-term liabilities, i.e. its working capital. It reveals whether a firm is able to use its liquid assets to cover its short-term debts. The current ratio is calculated by using the formula:

$$\frac{\text{Current assets}}{\text{Current liabilities}}$$

Question 3.5.2   Calculating ROCE

(a) Calculate the ROCE ratio for *JKL Ltd*. for both years.   *[2 marks]*

(b) Explain what the figures suggest about the efficiency and profitability of *JKL Ltd*.   *[6 marks]*

Question 3.5.3   Dan & Glover

Dan & Glover has a **gross profit** of $150m, expenses of $30m and capital employed of $400m.

(a) Define the term **gross profit**.   *[2 marks]*

(b) Calculate Dan & Glover's return on capital employed (ROCE).   *[2 marks]*

For example, if a business has current assets (cash, debtors and stocks) of $300,000 and current liabilities (such as overdrafts and trade creditors) of $120,000, then the current ratio would be 2.5:1. This means the firm has $2.50 of current (liquid) assets for every $1 of current liabilities.

It is generally accepted that a current ratio of 1.5 to 2.0 is desirable. This allows for a safety margin because in reality it might not be possible to sell assets quickly without losing some value. It also means that there is likely to be sufficient working capital. Clearly, if the current ratio is below 1:1 then the short-term debts of the business are greater than its liquid assets, which could jeopardise its survival if creditors demand payment. Equally though, a firm can have too high a current ratio. A high current ratio suggests that there is too much cash (which could be better spent to generate more trade), too many debtors (which increases the likelihood of bad debts) or too much stock (which increases storage and insurance costs). As always, it is important to put ratios into context. Supermarkets hold a huge amount of stock so may have a current ratio of over 2:1 but this is acceptable as their stocks are highly liquid.

The current ratio can be improved by a combination of raising the value of current assets and reducing the value of current liabilities. For example, overdrafts can be reduced by opting for long-term loans that offer more attractive rates of interest. This will also free up working capital in the short term. However, this option may, of course, affect the long-term liquidity of the firm.

Acid test ratio (Quick ratio)

The acid test ratio (or the quick ratio) is similar to the current ratio except it ignores stock when measuring the short-term liquidity of a business. The formula for working this out is:

$$\frac{\text{Current assets} - \text{Stock}}{\text{Current liabilities}}$$

This approach can be more meaningful than the current ratio because stocks are not always easily converted into cash, i.e. not all stocks are highly liquid. For example, *work-in-progress* (semi-finished) goods do not have much *value added*, so would not fetch a very good price. Highly expensive stock, such as Boeing aircraft, also cannot be turned into cash quickly.

As a general guideline, the quick ratio should be at least 1:1 otherwise the firm might experience working capital difficulties or even a liquidity crisis (a situation where a firm is unable to pay its short-term debts). As with the current ratio, too high an acid test figure can suggest that the firm is holding onto too much cash rather than using it more effectively. As always, however, this ratio must be put into the context of the business and the industry in which it operates.

Potential investors and short-term lenders are likely to be interested in a firm's acid test ratio. Since the ratio measures the ability of a firm to cover short-term debts with its cash and debtors, this will help reduce the expossure of risk to investors and lenders.

Question 3.5.4 Bjorn Bowls

Bjorn Perera Inc. operates a bowling centre. The company has reported the following financial data:

- Cash = $50,000

- **Debtors** = $35,000

- Inventories = $45,000

- Overdrafts = $15,000

- Tax = $25,000

- Trade creditors = $50,000

(a) Define the term **debtors**.   *[2 marks]*

(b) Calculate the current ratio for *Bjorn Bowls*.   *[2 marks]*

Mathematically, the quick ratio can be improved by either raising the level of current assets (cash or debtors) or lowering the amount of current liabilities. It can be dangerous for a firm to increase debtors since this increases the likelihood of bad debts occurring. There is also a potentially large opportunity cost in holding too much cash. Hence, it is more practical for a business to concentrate on reducing its short-term liabilities, such as overdrafts and trade creditors. For example, it might be possible to negotiate delayed payment to trade creditors.

Uses and limitations of ratio analysis

Ratio analysis provides useful data for the various stakeholders of a business who have a direct interest in its financial performance. Essentially, stakeholders use financial ratios to aid decision-making by assessing the relative financial strengths and weaknesses of a business. For example:

- Employees and trade unions can use financial ratios to assess the likelihood of pay rises and the level of job security (possibly revealed by profitability and liquidity ratios).

- Managers and directors can assess the likelihood of getting management bonuses for reaching profitability, liquidity and efficiency targets. They can also use ratios to identify areas that need improving.

- Trade creditors look at short-term liquidity ratios to ensure that their customers (i.e. other businesses) have sufficient working capital to repay them.

- Shareholders use ratios to assess the return of their investment compared with other investments, such as holding shares in other companies or in a bank account.

- Financiers use ratios to consider if the business has sufficient funds and profitability to repay any loans that may be approved.

- The local community can use a range of financial ratios to gauge job opportunities for local residents. They might also use ratios to secure sponsorship for local community projects.

However, financial ratio analysis does have its limitations:

- Ratios are a historical account of a organiztion's performance. They do not indicate the current or future financial situation of a business (although they do give an indication of the financial health of the firm).

- Changes in the external business environment (see Unit 1.5) can cause a change in the financial ratios without there being any underlying change in the performance of a business. For example, higher interest rates will reduce profitability, although sales revenues may have actually increased.

- There is no universal way to report company accounts so this means that businesses may use different accounting policies. This makes inter-firm comparisons more difficult. For example, some firms use the *straight-line method* for depreciating assets whilst others use the *reducing balance method* (see Unit 3.4).

- Qualitative factors that affect the performance of an organiztion are totally ignored. For example, the level of staff motivation and customer perceptions of quality are not considered in ratio analysis.

Question 3.5.5   Calculating ratios

(a) Refer to the accounts for *JKL Ltd.* shown in Tables 3.5.a and 3.5.b to calculate the current ratio and acid test ratio for both years.   *[4 marks]*

(b) Comment on the liquidity position of *JKL Ltd.*   *[4 marks]*

(c) Explain what other information might be needed to judge the liquidity position of *JKL Ltd.*   *[4 marks]*

- Organizational objectives differ between businesses, so comparing results from a ratio analysis could be meaningless. For example, there should be some reservation in comparing the financial performance of a state-owned airline with that of a private sector airline.

As with any financial analysis (such as cash flow forecasts and investment appraisals), ratio analysis is only partial, i.e. it does not provide a complete picture of a firm's performance. Other quantitative and qualitative factors can help make a better assessment of an organization's financial performance, such as:

- *Historical comparisons* – The same ratio should be compared year on year to identify any trends and, perhaps more importantly, the reasons for such trends. This can help stakeholders to determine any improvement or deterioration in the firm's financial performance.

- *Inter-firm comparisons* – Ratios should be benchmarked (compared) with those of close rivals to assess the relative performance of the business. A firm's ratio analysis may reveal pleasing results, but this might be less attractive if it had been outperformed by its competitors.

- *The nature of the business and its aims and objectives* – A profit-seeking multinational company may understandably have very different ratios from those of not-for-profit organizations. Similarly, businesses with a prominent social and ethical stance might strive to have somewhat lower profitability ratios.

- *The state of the economy* – A firm's financial performance may at first seem to have deteriorated but when put into the context of the business cycle (booms, peaks, recessions and slumps) may paint a different picture.

- *Social factors* – A firm's activities might be highly profitable but ratio analysis does not consider the natural environment or society. Examples of side effects of business activity include: air pollution, excess packaging and job losses; none of which are examined in ratio analysis.

Figure 3.5.d Pollution in Mumbai, India

Whilst ratio analysis aids management decision-making, there are limitations to what it can do and reveal. It is therefore important to consider other quantitative and qualitative factors when measuring the performance of a business.

Exam tip !

Often in ratio analysis questions it is more important to consider what data are not given rather than just to examine the financial data provided. Good management decision-making considers a range of information, both quantitative and qualitative.

Finance and accounts

CORE

Table 3.5.d Ratio analysis summary

Type	Ratio	Formula
Profitability	Gross Profit Margin	$\dfrac{\text{Gross profit}}{\text{Sales revenue}} \times 100$
	Net Profit Margin	$\dfrac{\text{Net profit}}{\text{Sales revenue}} \times 100$
Liquidity	Current ratio	$\dfrac{\text{Current assets}}{\text{Current liabilities}}$
	Acid test	$\dfrac{\text{Current assets} - \text{Stock}}{\text{Current liabilities}}$
Efficiency	Return on Capital Employed	$\dfrac{\text{Net profit before interest and tax}}{\text{Capital employed}} \times 100$

Question 3.5.6   D. McCleod & Co. vs K. Tang & Son

Study the data below regarding the performance of two companies, *D. McCleod & Co.* and *K. Tang & Son*, and then answer the questions that follow.

	Firm	Year 1	Year 2	Year 3
Gross Profit Margin (%)	McCleod	50	45	40
	Tang	50	40	45
Net Profit Margin (%)	McCleod	20	20	20
	Tang	19	18	20
Return on Capital Employed (%)	McCleod	15	13	14
	Tang	12	10	15
Quick ratio	McCleod	2.5	2.2	1.5
	Tang	1.5	1.9	1.1
Gearing (%)	McCleod	45	47	50
	Tang	45	43	40

Note: SL students are not expected to use the gearing ratio in this question. HL students might want to refer to Unit 3.6 before tackling this question.

(a) Define the term **quick ratio**.   *[2 marks]*

(b) Distinguish between **gross profit** and **net profit**.   *[4 marks]*

(c) Comment on why it is important for potential investors to consider non-financial factors when making investment decisions.   *[4 marks]*

(d) Discuss the relative attractiveness of *D. McCleod & Co.* and *K. Tang & Son* to potential investors.   *[10 marks]*

Theory of knowledge

Is the use of quantitative data and information more important than qualitative knowledge claims to managers?

Profitability and liquidity ratios and the CUEGIS concepts

Changes in the external business environment (see Unit 1.5) will cause changes to the financial ratios of a business. For example, higher interest rates and/or corporate taxes will tend to reduce profitability ratios, even if sales revenues have actually increased in this time period. Hence, financial ratios can change without there being any underlying change in the performance of a business. The global financial crisis of 2008 caused major havoc to businesses worldwide with many businesses going bankrupt and caused unemployment in countries such as Spain and Greece to reach historical highs. Such changes will have harmed the financial performance, and hence ratios, of many businesses. By contrast, favourable changes in the economy or advances in technology can help businesses to improve their profitability and liquidity ratios.

It is important to note that there is no internationally accepted standard in reporting the final accounts (the balance sheet and P&L account). This can make international comparisons of financial ratios very difficult, and somewhat meaningless, due to the different accounting conventions used. For example, in some countries and cultures, it is perfectly acceptable for sole traders who work from home to claim personal income tax deductions on the costs of electricity, rent (or mortgage), telephone, petrol and the Internet.

As with all aspects of finance and accounts, there is an ethical dimension to ratio analysis. Businesses have been known to manipulate their final accounts and presentation of their financial ratios, thus misinforming their stakeholders. In 2013, a study by researchers at the University of Toronto and the University of Chicago found that the probability of businesses involved in accounting fraud in any given tax year is 14.5%, costing investors an average of 22% of the funds in the fraud-committing firms. The British Prime Minister George Canning (1827) put this nicely by saying, *"I can prove anything by statistics except the truth"*.

IB Learner Profile – Be an inquirer and be principled

Investigate the financial fraud committed by any one of the following institutions: Bear Stearns, Enron, Dewey & LeBoeuf, Lehman Brothers and WorldCom. A good starting point is this infographic: http://goo.gl/zCCjk0. What lessons can business leaders learn from the mistakes of others?

Nevertheless, used correctly, ratio analysis is a useful management tool for strategic analysis. It is used to assess the financial health of a business, which in turn depends on a combination of profitability, liquidity (both short-term and long-term) and financial efficiency. Many managers today place great emphasis on short-term liquidity ratios, since a lack of working capital is the single largest cause of business failure (see Unit 3.7). However, all categories of financial ratios are important as they are interrelated. For example, adequate gearing and sufficient liquidity should help a firm to increase its profitability. Profitable businesses that lack sufficient liquidity are unlikely to survive. Hence, firms with good overall financial performance succeed and survive in the long run.

Whilst financial ratios can be used to judge the success of business strategy, they pose a slight problem for judging the success of non-profit organizations (NPOs) such as charitable organizations and non-government organizations (see Unit 1.2). As NPOs are not run to make a profit, non-financial factors need to be considered, such as using examination results to judge attainment in state-funded schools. If the school has achieved better results over time, this could suggest that its performance has improved.

Another measure could be to look at how well (efficient) the school operates within its allocated budget. It might also be difficult to compare like-with-like since schools can be different in so many ways - there are religious schools, different levels of funding, different catchment areas and demographics, selective and non-selective schools, single-sex schools, and so on. Hence, schools are likely to have different organizational objectives. As 'success' is judged by the extent to which organizational objectives are met, the criteria for judging success in NPOs will vary from those used for profit-seeking businesses. Hence, in judging business strategy, there is a need to consider a range of qualitative factors and not just financial ones.

CUEGIS Essay

With reference to an organization of your choice, discuss the role of profitability and liquidity in formulating business **strategy** and **change**. *[20 marks]*

REVIEW QUESTIONS

1. What is meant by ratio analysis?

2. What are the main purposes of carrying out financial ratio analysis?

3. When conducting ratio analysis, why is it important to compare like-with-like?

4. What are profitability ratios? What are efficiency ratios?

5. What do the GPM and NPM ratios tell us about a firm's profitability?

6. How might a business raise its GPM and NPM ratios?

7. What are liquidity ratios?

8. Why do many businesses prefer to use the acid test ratio rather than the current ratio?

9. What are the limitations of ratio analysis?

10. How might changes in the external business environment affect the financial performance of a business?

KEY TERMS

The **acid test ratio** is a liquidity ratio that measures a firm's ability to meet its short-term debts. It ignores stock because not all inventories can be easily turned into cash in a short time frame.

Capital employed is the value of all long-term sources of finance for a business, e.g. bank loans, share capital and accumulated retained profit.

The **current ratio** is a short-term liquidity ratio that calculates the ability of a business to meet its debts within the next twelve months.

Efficiency ratios indicate how well a firm's resources have been used, such as the amount of profit generated from the available capital used in the business.

Gross profit margin (GPM) is a profitability ratio that shows the percentage of sales revenue that turns into gross profit.

Liquid assets are the possessions of a business that can be turned into cash quickly without losing their value, i.e. cash, stock and debtors.

Liquidity crisis refers to a situation where a firm is unable to pay its short-term debts, i.e. current liabilities exceed current assets.

Liquidity ratios look at the ability of a firm to pay its short-term liabilities, such as by comparing working capital to short-term debts.

Net profit margin (NPM) shows the percentage of sales revenue that turns into net profit, i.e. the proportion of sales revenue left over after all direct and indirect costs have been paid.

Profitability ratios examine profit in relation to other figures, e.g. the GPM and NPM ratios. These ratios tend to be relevant to profit-seeking businesses rather than for not-for-profit organizations.

Ratio analysis is a quantitative management tool that compares different financial figures to examine and judge the financial performance of a business. It requires the application of figures found in the final accounts (the balance sheet and the profit and loss account).

Return on capital employed (ROCE) is an efficiency ratio (although it also reveals the firm's profitability) measuring the profit of a business in relation to its size (as measured by capital employed). ROCE is often referred to as the **key ratio.**

Financial ratios help firms to determine their return on investment

3.6 Efficiency ratio analysis

"A good decision is based on knowledge and not on numbers." - Plato (427–347 BCE), Greek philosopher

HL content	Assessment objective
The following further efficiency ratios: • inventory/stock turnover • debtor days • creditor days • gearing ratio	AO2, AO4
Possible strategies to improve these ratios	AO3

© IBO, 2017

Efficiency ratios

The following further efficiency ratios: inventory/stock turnover, debtor days, creditor days and gearing ratio. AO2, AO4

Possible strategies to improve these ratios. AO3

© IBO, 2017

Efficiency ratios show how well an organization's resources have been used, such as the amount of time taken by the business to sell its stock (inventory) or the average number of days taken to collect money from its debtors. Supermarkets, for example, sell their stocks faster than luxury jewellers. There are four main additional efficiency ratios for HL students to learn: stock turnover, debtor days, creditor days and the gearing ratio.

Stock turnover

The stock turnover ratio (or **inventory turnover** ratio) measures the number of times an organization sells its stocks within a time period, usually one year. The ratio therefore indicates the speed at which a business sells and replenishes all its stock. There are two alternative ways to calculate stock turnover:

$$\text{Stock turnover (number of times)} = \frac{\text{Cost of goods sold}}{\text{Average stock}}$$

Or

$$\text{Stock turnover (number of days)} = \frac{\text{Average stock}}{\text{Cost of goods sold}} \times 365$$

When looking at stock turnover, *cost of goods sold* is used (rather than sales turnover) as stocks are valued at *cost* value

of the inventory (to the business) rather than *selling price*. For example, if a business has COGS equal to $100,000 and an average stock level valued at $20,000 then the stock turnover ratio is 5 times a year (or every 73 days on average). This means that the business sells all of its inventory, which is then replenished, five times a year. Using this calculation, the higher the ratio the better it is for the business because more stock is sold and therefore the more efficient it is in generating profit. A high stock turnover also means that perishable stock such as fresh milk or freshly baked cakes, do not expire or stocks do not become out-dated.

Figure 3.6.a Firms selling perishable products need to have a high stock turnover rate

There are several ways that a organization's stock level can be reduced to improve its stock turnover ratio:

• Holding lower stock levels requires inventories to be replenished more regularly (which can have both advantages and disadvantages – see Unit 5.5).

- Divestment (disposal) of stocks which are slow to sell, i.e. getting rid of obsolete stock and unpopular products in the firm's portfolio.

- Reduce the range of products being stocked by only keeping the best-selling products.

When comparing this ratio, it is important (as always) to compare like-with-like. Different businesses have different benchmark figures for stock turnover. For example, a restaurant should expect a significantly higher stock turnover ratio than a seller of luxury motor vehicles. A stock turnover rate of 5 is perhaps acceptable to suppliers of consumer durables, but unacceptable to a florist or fresh fish monger. Hence, a low stock turnover ratio is not necessarily a bad sign; all ratios must be put into context.

Debtor days

The debtor days ratio measures the number of days it takes a business, on average, to collect money from its debtors. Hence, it is sometime referred to as the debt collection period. Debtors are the customers who have purchased items on trade credit and therefore owe money to the business. It is calculated using the formula:

$$\text{Debtor days} = \frac{\text{Debtors}}{\text{Sales revenue}} \times 365$$

For example, if an organization's debt (shown on its balance sheet) totals $1 million whilst its sales turnover is $5 million, then the ratio is 73 days, i.e. it takes the business an average of 73 days to collect debts from its customers who have bought items on credit. Logically, the less time it takes for customers to pay their debts, the better it is for the business. There are two reasons for this: first, the business improves its cash flow if customers pay on time and second, due to the opportunity cost of holding onto money, the business could invest this money in other revenue-generating projects. However, a ratio that is too high or too low can also be problematic:

- Although businesses may allow customers to buy on credit, it is important that the credit period granted is not too long otherwise the businesses could face liquidity problems (see Unit 3.7).

- Equally, too low a ratio suggests customers may seek other suppliers if the credit period given to them is uncompetitive because clients prefer better credit terms.

It is quite common to allow customers 30–60 days trade credit. The organization's ability to collect debts within a suitable timeframe is known as credit control. A business is generally seen as having good **credit control** if it can collect debts within 30–60 days. Businesses can improve their debt collection period in several ways:

- Impose surcharges on late payers. For example, banks and utility companies add a fine to those who pay their bills late. In some countries, such as Hong Kong, the government will impose a surcharge on income tax bills for late payers.

- Give debtors incentives to pay earlier, such as giving a discount to those who pay their bills before the due date. Many businesses encourage their credit customers to use *direct debit* or *autopay*. These are financial services that involve transferring money owed to creditors by using funds directly from the client's bank account on designated days. This saves customers having to remember when to pay their bills and hence avoid penalties for paying late.

- Refuse any further business with a client until payment is made. This may include stopping supplies to a customer or suspending an order until payment is received.

- Threaten legal action. The threat of taking a customer to court is rather extreme but is often used for clients who repeatedly pay late.

Some businesses, such as suppliers of expensive luxury goods, rely more on credit sales than others. Hence, for these businesses it is more acceptable to have a higher debt collection period. Fast food restaurants or hair salons, on the other hand, have customers paying for their goods at the time of purchase so their debt collection period would be much lower.

Figure 3.6.b Suppliers of luxury goods, such as yachts, rely on credit sales

Creditor days

The creditor days ratio measures the number of days it takes, on average, for a business to pay its trade creditors. The formula for this ratio is:

$$\text{Creditor days} = \frac{\text{Creditors}}{\text{Cost of goods sold}} \times 365$$

For example, if a business has $225,000 owed to its suppliers (as seen from its balance sheet) with $2 million worth of cost of goods sold (COGS), then the creditor days ratio is 41 days. This means the business takes 41 days on average to pay its suppliers. It is common to provide customers with 30–60 days credit, so a creditor days ratio in this range would seem acceptable.

A high creditor days ratio means that repayments are prolonged. This can help to free up cash in the business for other use (in the short term). However, a high ratio might also mean that the business is taking too long to pay its creditors so suppliers may impose financial penalties for late payment. In this case, a high creditor days ratio will harm the firm's cash flow position.

The efficiency position of a business can be enhanced by improving any of its efficiency ratios, i.e. increasing stock turnover, reducing debtor days, and increasing creditor days. Strategies to achieve this include:

- Developing closer relationships with customers, suppliers and creditors, thereby helping to reduce the debt collection time and extend the credit period.

- Introduce a system of just-in-time production (see Unit 5.5) to eliminate the need to hold large amounts of stock and to improve stock control.

- Improve credit control, i.e. managing risks regarding the amount of credit given to debtors. For example, giving customers an incentive to pay earlier or on time helps to reduce the chances of bad debts (loans that do not get repaid).

Gearing ratio

The gearing ratio is used to assess an organization's *long-term liquidity* position. This is done by examining the firm's capital employed that is financed by long-term debt, such as mortgages and debentures (see Unit 3.1). Gearing enables managers to gauge the level of efficiency in the use of an organization's capital structure.

The gearing ratio formula is:

$$\text{Gearing ratio} = \frac{\text{Loan capital}}{\text{Capital employed}} \times 100$$

For example, a business with long-term liabilities totalling $5 million whilst its capital employed is $15 million has a gearing ratio of 33.3%. This means that one-third of the organization's sources of finance comes from external interest-bearing sources, whilst the other two-thirds represent internal sources of finance. Recall from Unit 3.5 that Capital employed = loan capital (or long-term liabilities) + share capital + retained profit. The higher the gearing ratio, the larger the firm's dependence on long-term sources of borrowing. This means that the business incurs higher costs due to debt financing, such as interest repayments to banks or debenture holders. This can therefore limit the net profit for the firm.

Finance and accounts

CORE

Question 3.6.1

(a) Use Tables 3.5.a and 3.5.b to calculate the following ratios for *JKL Ltd.*, for both years:

(i) stock turnover [2 marks]

(ii) debtor days and [2 marks]

(iii) creditor days. [2 marks]

(b) Examine the ways in which *JKL Ltd.* could improve its efficiency position. [6 marks]

(c) Using your answers from part (a) above, explain the efficiency position of *JKL Ltd.* [6 marks]

Creditors and investors are interested in the level of gearing of a business. A firm is said to be *highly geared* if it has a gearing ratio of 50% or above. Such businesses are more vulnerable to increases in interest rates. This situation is similar to an individual who has a large mortgage with a bank. A rise in interest rates will mean such individuals will have higher monthly interest repayments on their outstanding mortgages. Similarly, a highly geared business will be more exposed to interest rate increases or if there is a downturn in the economy as loan repayments remain high, while cash inflow from sales will tend to fall in a recession. Other financiers are less likely to lend money to firms that are already highly geared due to their large loan commitments. Such businesses are more prone to experience financial difficulties and may be taken over by larger rivals.

Shareholders and potential investors are also interested in the gearing ratio as it helps to assess the level of risk. Since financiers have to be repaid first (with interest), this may reduce the amount paid to shareholders and the amount retained for reinvestments. However, if the profitability of the business is high, then potential returns can be very attractive even in highly geared firms.

Although gearing can make profits more volatile, businesses tend to require external finance to fund their expansion. The phrase 'you need money to make money' suggests that external financing can help businesses to grow. Many years before becoming US President, Donald Trump made his wealth largely through high gearing as internal sources of finance are rarely sufficient to fund the rapid growth of a business. The problem facing finance managers is how much debt the business can handle before the benefits of growth outweigh the costs of high gearing and financial risks. The level of gearing that is acceptable to a business will depend of several factors such as:

- The size and status of the business – Generally, there is a positive correlation between a firm's size and status and its ability to repay long-term debts. Most stakeholders would

not worry too much if McDonald's had a gearing ratio of 50% as it is likely to be able to repay the debt.

- The level of interest rates – If interest rates are low, then businesses are less vulnerable (at least in the short term) even with high gearing. For example, during Japan's recession in the 1990s, interest rates were close to zero per cent. This would minimise the interest repayments on long-term external finance.

- Potential profitability – If businesses have good **profit quality** (long-term prospects of earningg profit) then high gearing is less likely to be an issue. This applies to many businesses in high-tech industries that invest heavily in research and development. They may need external finance to fund the expenditure on R&D but the potential for high returns can minimise their exposure to gearing.

Theory of knowledge

At what time does a business decide to expand?

Efficiency ratios and the CUEGIS

Exam tip !

Examination questions typically ask students to use financial ratios to comment on an organization's:
a)   profitability
b)   liquidity position
c)   efficiency position
d)   gearing
These are the main categories of ratios! Make sure that you know their meaning and the different types of ratios within each category.

Question 3.6.2

(a)   Calculate the gearing ratio for *JKL Ltd.* for both years.   *[2 marks]*

(b)   Explain what the gearing ratios tell you about *JKL Ltd.*'s long-term liquidity position.   *[4 marks]*

(c)   Examine whether high gearing can actually be beneficial to organizations like *JKL Ltd.*   *[6 marks]*

Question 3.6.3   Ocean Deco Limited

Ocean Deco Limited is a company that specializes in the renovation of commercial properties, such as painting, decorating, repairs and maintenance of retail outlets. The company was started in 1999 by Chris DelPreore and his son, who had graduated from London Business School in the same year.

As a relatively small business, Ocean Deco Limited has faced problems in securing **external finance** although it did manage to take out an $80,000 mortgage this year to fund its expansion plans. Ocean Deco Limited has been approached by a larger company, *Shanghai Commercial Ltd.*, with an offer of a takeover. Chris DelPreore is reluctant to sell the family business that he helped to establish. However, his son is attracted by the lucrative deal and has advised his father that *Ocean Deco Limited* can no longer compete with its larger rivals that use the latest industrial tools and equipment to enhance their productivity.

Extract from the profit and loss account and balance sheet of *Ocean Deco Limited:*

	$'000
Revenue	532
Cost of sales	248
Expenses	132
Fixed assets	145
Current assets	85
Less current liabilities	62
Owners' Capital	88
Long-term liabilities	80

(a) Define the term **external finance**.   [2 marks]

(b) Calculate the following ratios for *Ocean Deco Limited:*

   (i)   Gross profit margin (GPM)   [2 marks]

   (ii) Return on capital employed (ROCE)   [2 marks]

   (iii) Gearing.   [2 marks]

(c) Using the above ratios, explain why *Shanghai Commercial Ltd.* is interested in taking over *Ocean Deco Limited*.   [4 marks]

(d) Considering both numerical and non-numerical factors, recommend to the owners of *Ocean Deco Limited* whether they should accept or reject the takeover bid.   [10 marks]

Table 3.6.a   Efficiency ratio analysis summary

Type	Ratio	Formula
Efficiency ratios	Stock turnover	Stock turnover (number of days) $= \dfrac{\text{Cost of goods sold}}{\text{Average stock}}$ Or Stock turnover (number of days) $= \dfrac{\text{Average stock}}{\text{Cost of goods sold}} \times 365$
	Debtor day	Debtor days $= \dfrac{\text{Debtors}}{\text{Sales revenue}} \times 365$
	Creditor days	Creditor days $= \dfrac{\text{Creditors}}{\text{Cost of goods sold}} \times 365$
	Gearing	Gearing ratio $= \dfrac{\text{Loan capital}}{\text{Capital employed}} \times 100$

Question 3.6.4   ACS Playframes Limited

ACS Playframes Limited (ACSPL) specialises in manufacturing and distributing children's playframes. The privately owned company, set up by Pamela Ng, employs five full-time staff and several part-time staff.

ACSPL has enjoyed several years of expansion in the provision of their products to hotels, schools and local government. However, several larger foreign rivals have recently established a presence in the market. The booming economy has also meant that interest rates are on an upwards trend.

Pamela has been informed by Alka Hingle, her accountant, that the company's costs of external financing have risen dramatically. Alka presented the following financial information for *ACSPL* (as of 31 March of this year) which raised some working capital and liquidity issues:

Cost of sales	$900 000
Current assets of sales	$600 000
Current liabilities	$550 000
Expenses	$600 000
Fixed assets	$7 500 000
Long-term liabilities	$3 200 000
Retained profit	$850 000
Sales revenue	$3 500 000
Shareholders' funds	$3 500 000

(continued) …

... *(continued)*

(a) Define the term **long term liabilities**. *[2 marks]*

(b) Construct a profit and loss account for *ACSPL* using the figures above. *[5 marks]*

(c) (i) Calculate the value of the current ratio. *[2 marks]*

    (ii) Calculate the value of the gearing ratio. *[2 marks]*

    (iii) Using your answer from part (i) and the information in the case study, explain why *ACSPL* is said to have 'some working capital and liquidity issues'. *[4 marks]*

(d) Examine **two** financial strategies that Pamela could use to deal with her company's working capital and liquidity issues. *[6 marks]*

Theory of knowledge

Is the use of quantitative data and information more important to managers than qualitative knowledge claims?

Theory of knowledge

Numbers can be manipulated in such a way that they can reveal any 'truth' that a manager wishes. To what extent do you agree with this statement?

CORE

---

concepts

The CUEGIS concepts were applied to profitability, liquidity and efficiency ratios in Unit 3.5. Additionally, innovations can help businesses improve their efficiency and profitability. Apple, for example, became the world's largest company from January 2012 to April 2013 after hugely successful product launches such as the iPad and iPhone. By contrast, the inefficiencies and lack of profit quality of Sony has led to its market decline in the consumer electronics industry.

Globalization also present many business opportunities, thus having a generally positive impact on financial ratios. However, with a wider customer base across the globe, managing debtors can become increasingly difficult. Multinational companies trying to exploit the benefits of globalization will also need finance to fund their growth. This can have a detrimental effect on their gearing, at least in the short run.

Finally, it is important to be reminded that when analysing the financial performance of a business, the calculations should always be put into the context of the market in which the firm operates, and its organizational culture. A gearing ratio of over 50% is perhaps acceptable to a large multinational company that is expanding into overseas markets with huge growth potential. This may be less acceptable to a business that sells products in niche markets, such as hand-made ukuleles. Similarly, producers of solar panel units may grant a longer credit period to property developers, whereas this is unlikely for supermarkets and retailers of fast-moving consumer goods.

Figure 3.6.c Hand-made ukuleles are niche market products

A 'high' ROCE figure is not necessarily indicative of good business strategy either as the ratio should be compared with historical performance, inter-firm performance, interest rates offered by banks and the expected returns from alternative projects. The context also includes consideration of the economic, social and political environments (see Unit 1.5) in which the business operates. Poorer liquidity is expected during a recession, for example. There is also a time lag between strategic implementation and the realisation of profits; this lag will vary from one industry to another. Nevertheless, ratio analysis can provide some invaluable information for the implementation of business strategy.

REVIEW QUESTIONS

CUEGIS Essay

With reference to an organization of your choice, examine the role of **innovation** and **globalization** on its operational efficiency.   *[20 marks]*

1. What are efficiency ratios?

2. What is meant by stock turnover?

3. What are the two ways to calculate the stock turnover ratio?

4. What is meant by the debt collection period?

5. How can the efficiency position of an organization be enhanced?

6. What is credit control and why is it important?

7. Explain whether a high or low figure is preferable for i) debtor days and ii) creditor days.

8. What is the gearing ratio?

9. How is capital employed calculated?

10. Why are highly geared businesses generally considered to be risky?

KEY TERMS

Credit control refers to the ability of a business to collect its debts within a suitable timeframe.

Creditor days ratio is an efficiency ratio that measures the average number of days it takes for a business to pay its creditors.

Debtor days ratio is an efficiency ratio that measures the average number of days it takes for a business to collect the money owed from debtors.

Efficiency ratios show how well an organization's resources have been used, such as the amount of time taken by the firm to sell its stock (inventory) or the average number of days taken to collect money from its debtors.

The **gearing ratio** measures the percentage of an organization's capital employed that comes from external sources (long-term liabilities), such as debentures and mortgages. Businesses that have at least 50% gearing are said to be highly geared.

Profit quality refers to the ability of a business to earn profit in the foreseeable future. A business with good profit quality is able to earn profit in the long run.

Stock turnover ratio (or inventory turnover ratio) measures the number of times a business sells its stocks within a year. It can also be expressed as the average number of days it takes for a business to sell all of its normal inventory.

Stock turnover is important for firms that sell fresh products

3.7 Cash flow

"Don't empty the water jar until the rain falls." - English proverb

SL/HL content	Assessment objective
The difference between profit and cash flow	AO2
The working capital cycle	AO2
Cash flow forecasts	AO2, AO4
The relationship between investment, profit and cash flow	AO2
The following strategies for dealing with cash flow problems: • reducing cash outflow • improving cash inflows • looking for additional finance	AO3

© IBO, 2017

The difference between cash and profit

The difference between profit and cash flow. AO2

© IBO, 2017

Cash is often described as the lifeblood of a business because every organization needs cash to keep functioning. Cash is needed to pay for daily costs such as wages and electricity charges. Failure to pay suppliers and utility bills may eventually result in a business being declared bankrupt. Cash is a current asset. It is the money that a business actually receives from the sale of goods and services. It can be either held 'in hand' (actual cash in the business) or 'at bank' (cash held in a bank account).

Profit in its simplest form is the positive difference between a firm's total sales revenue and its total costs of production. When a sale is made, this contributes towards paying the firm's costs. When enough products are sold to pay for all costs, the firm reaches its break-even point (see Unit 3.3). Any sales beyond a firm's break-even point generates profit for the business.

Profit = Revenues – Costs

When making a purchase, customers might have several payment options, e.g. cash, cheque or credit. Paying by credit means that customers can buy now but pay later. For example, a credit period of 30 days means that customers do not need to pay for their purchase until a month later. This might attract customers but can also cause cash flow problems for the business since it will need to operate without immediate payment from its credit customers.

When a firm sells its products on credit, it automatically earns a profit on the sale (assuming price exceeds unit costs of production). However, as customers pay on credit, the firm does not receive the cash at the time of purchase. Hence, profit is made before the cash is received, i.e. profit is not the same as cash. For example, if a firm sold $50,000 of goods in a month, with 60% of its customers paying by cash, then only $30,000 cash is received. The other 40% (or $20,000) is not received until the end of the credit period. Hence, the sales revenue ($50,000) is not the same as the cash inflow ($30,000) during the month. Profit is made if all production costs are paid for.

It is therefore possible for a firm to be profitable but cash deficient. The classic reason is because there is poor credit control, which damages the firm's cash flow position. Another case is when a profitable business tries to expand too quickly, so runs out of cash. Seasonal variations in demand can also mean that there are certain times in the year when the firm might experience short-term liquidity problems. Ultimately, a business cannot operate without sufficient cash to pay its suppliers, employees and financiers, i.e. a lack of cash will eventually lead to a firm going bankrupt.

Conversely, it is also possible to be cash rich but unprofitable. The initial hype for a new product may bring in plenty of cash

311

for a business but unless the firm is able to control its costs, including its fixed and indirect costs (see Unit 3.2), the business will not be profitable. Hence, all businesses, however profitable, must manage their cash flow position in order to survive.

Exam tip !

There is also a difference between **sales revenues** and **cash inflows**. The former comes from a single source, i.e. customers. Cash inflows can come from non-revenue sources, e.g. selling dormant (unused) assets to generate cash, using bank loans, or receiving donations and government grants.

Case study   Marks & Spencer

In 2018, UK retailer Marks & Spencer (M&S) announced it would close 100 stores by 2022 due to declining profits and cash flow problems. The chief executive officer, Steve Rowe, said customer preference for online shopping and the growing presence of no-frills retailers (such as Primark, Aldi and Lidl) were to blame.

Rowe also announced that the first phase of store closures would cost M&S, which was established in 1884, over £321 million ($465 million).

Question 3.7.1   McDonald's

In keeping with the times, fast-food giant *McDonald's* has revamped its traditional menus since 2003. It has added healthier options such as salads, pastas, soups, smoothies and bottled water. The company's strive to gain more revenue led to its global "I'm lovin' it" slogan, extended opening hours and new facilities to allow customers to pay with their credit cards. In 2012, *McDonald's* reported its annual sale revenues had increased to $27.5 billion, although **net profits** were only $5.5 billion, its first decline in nine years. In 2014, *McDonald's* opened its first restaurant in Vietnam as part of its continued expansion plans.

(a) Define the term **net profits**.   *[2 marks]*

(b) Explain how it is possible for *McDonald's* to report an increase in sales revenues but a fall in its net profits.   *[4 marks]*

(c) Explain how the use of credit cards might help to increase sales yet prolong the working capital cycle for *McDonald's*.   *[4 marks]*

The working capital cycle

The working capital cycle. AO2
© IBO, 2017

Working capital refers to the cash or liquid assets available for the daily running of a business. It shows the funds that are available for a business to pay for its immediate costs and expenditure, e.g. raw materials, wages and paying suppliers. A lack of working capital means that the firm has insufficient cash to fund its routine operations.

The term **liquidity** refers to how easily an asset can be turned into cash. Highly liquid assets are those that can be converted into cash quickly and easily without losing their monetary value, e.g. cash deposits at a bank. Raw materials, on the other hand, would be relatively illiquid assets as they cannot be changed into cash as easily or quickly.

Evidence from around the world consistently shows that insufficient working capital is the single largest cause of business failure, rather than a lack of profitability. Inadequate working capital leads to **insolvency** (a situation where working capital is insufficient to meet current liabilities). This can lead to the collapse of the business as creditors will take legal action to recover their money. This causes **liquidation** of the firm, i.e. it will need to sell off its assets to repay as much of the money owed to its creditors.

Working capital (or **net current assets**) is calculated using the formula:

Working Capital = Current assets – Current liabilities

Current assets are the liquid resources belonging to a business that are expected to be converted to cash within the next twelve months. There are three main types of current assets:

- **Cash**   This is the money that is held in the business or at the bank.

- **Debtors**   This refers to people or other organizations that owe money to the business as they have purchased goods on credit. The value of debtors is a current asset because the money is owed to (or belongs to) the business.

- **Stock**   This is unsold supplies of raw materials, semi-finished goods (work-in-progress) and finished goods. Finished stocks are relatively liquid in comparison to raw materials.

Figure 3.7.a Work-in-progress is a type of current asset

Current liabilities refers to the money that a business owes that needs to be repaid within the next twelve months. Some of the more common examples include:

- **Overdrafts**   This short-term source of finance (see Unit 3.1) needs to be repaid quickly as interest rates tend to be very high.

- **Creditors**   Suppliers need to be repaid for items that have been purchased on trade credit.

- **Tax**   Businesses pay a variety of taxes to the government, such as corporate tax and stamp duty (see Unit 1.5).

For most businesses, there is a delay between paying for costs of production (such as the purchase of stock and payment of wages) and receiving the cash from selling their products. This is because the production process takes time – consider the time lag from receiving an order for a Ferrari and actually receiving the cash once the car is finally handed over to the customer. The interval between cash payments for costs of production and cash receipts from customers is known as the **working capital cycle** (see Figure 3.7.b). The delay means that businesses must manage their working capital very carefully to continue functioning.

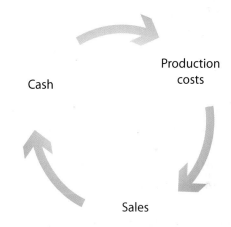

Figure 3.7.b The working capital cycle

Whilst it is important for businesses to have sufficient working capital, there are drawbacks to holding too much cash and liquid assets. This is because the assets, such as stocks and cash, could have been used more productively and profitably elsewhere, such as growth and expansion.

A common measure of liquidity is the current ratio (see Unit 3.5) which compares the values of current assets with current liabilities. For example, if current assets are valued at $3 million and current liabilities at $2 million, the current ratio is 1.5:1. This means that for each $1 of current liabilities, the firm has $1.50 in liquid assets. If the ratio is below 1:1, then the firm has a liquidity problem as its working capital cannot cover its current liabilities.

Finance and accounts

CORE

Cash flow forecasts

Cash flow forecasts. AO2, AO4

© IBO, 2017

A **cash flow forecast** is a financial document that shows the expected movement of cash into and out of a business, per time period. It is based on three key concepts:

- **Cash inflows** refers to cash that comes into a business, usually from sales revenue when customers pay for the products that they have purchased. Cash inflow can also come from payments made by debtors, loans from a bank, interest received from savings deposits, the sale of fixed assets or the rental income charged on property owned by the business. Predicting cash inflows requires accurate sales forecasting (see Unit 4.3).

- **Cash outflows** refers to cash that leaves a business, e.g. when invoices or bills have to be paid. A cash flow forecast therefore requires a detailed budget with itemised expenses such as: rent, wages, purchase of stocks, taxes, payments to creditors, advertising, loan and interest repayments and dividends.

- **Net cash flow** refers to the difference between cash inflows and cash outflows, per time period. Ideally, net cash flow should be positive, although it is possible for a firm suffering from negative net cash flow to survive temporarily. Even if a firm is profitable, it can only survive in the long run if its receipts (cash inflows) are greater than its expenses (cash outflows).

Suppose that a business buys imported digital cameras from Japan at an average cost of $100 and sells these at an average price of $350. Each camera sold earns the business $250, irrespective of whether customers pay by cash. However, if some customers pay by trade credit then this will reduce the value of cash inflows for this particular trading period.

Reasons for cash flow forecasts

- Banks and other lenders require a cash flow forecast to help them assess the financial health of the business seeking external finance.

- They can help managers to anticipate and identify periods of potential liquidity problems, i.e. cash deficiency. Managers can then plan accordingly, perhaps by arranging bank overdrafts or adjusting the timing of cash inflows and cash outflows to avoid liquidity problems.

- They aid business planning. Good financial control is not only socially responsible but can help a business to better achieve its organizational aims and objectives. Forecasts can be compared with actual cash flows to improve future predictions and planning.

Constructing cash flow forecasts

Consider the following numerical example in Table 3.7.a, which shows a simplified six-month cash flow forecast for Fabrice Vanegas Trading Company. Assume that the firm receives $4,000 of rental income in November. It is common to show negative numbers in brackets.

Question 3.7.2 Le Royal Méridien Hotels

Le Royal Méridien is a luxury five-star hotel chain that operates in many parts of the world, including Bristol (UK), Hamburg (Germany), Ko Samui (Thailand), Mumbai (India), and Toronto (Canada). The parent company, Starwood Hotels & Resorts, has plans for continued expansion in the world's top cities. However, the construction of a typical *Le Royal Méridien* hotel takes between 2 to 3 years. This means the hotel group must maintain sufficient **working capital** at all times.

Le Royal Méridien in Dubai

(a) Define the term **working capital**. *[2 marks]*

(b) Explain why *Le Royal Méridien* needs better cash flow management when there is a long working capital cycle during the construction of its new hotels. *[4 marks]*

Question 3.7.3 Pranab & Co.

Pranab & Co. is a shoe retailer in Morocco. The data below are excerpts from *Pranab & Co.'s* cash flow statement for last month. All figures are in Morocco dirham (MAD).

> Opening balance: MAD33,000
>
> Total **cash inflows**: MAD135,000
>
> Total cash outflows: MAD103,000

(a) Define the term **cash inflows**. *[2 marks]*

(b) Calculate the net cash flow for *Pranab & Co.* *[2 marks]*

In addition to the three key components in a cash flow forecast, there are two other important parts:

- **Opening balance** is the amount of cash at the beginning of a trading period. Notice that the opening balance is the same value as the preceding month's closing balance, e.g. at the close of business on 31 July, the cash balance was $3,000 so it is logical that the opening balance on 1 August is the same value, i.e. $3,000.

- **Closing balance** is the amount of cash at the end of a trading period. It is calculated by the formula:

  Closing balance = Opening balance plus Net cash flow.

For example, although the net cash flow (the difference between cash inflows and cash outflows) is negative $2,000 in July, the closing balance is positive $3,000 due to the opening balance of $5,000 in July.

Notice that the company has a negative closing balance in September and October. A business cannot survive without sufficient cash, so the cash flow forecast can help the firm to devise plans to deal with cash shortages.

Fabrice Vanegas Trading Company might, for example, seek to take out a bank overdraft (see Unit 3.1) as a short-term measure to deal with this liquidity problem.

Table 3.7.a Simplified cash flow forecast for Fabrice Vanegas Trading Co.

	Jul	Aug	Sept	Oct	Nov	Dec
Opening balance ($)	5,000	3,000	300	(1,400)	(2,600)	600
Inflows ($)						
Cash sales revenue ($)	6,000	5,000	6,500	6,800	7,500	9,500
Other income ($)	0	0	0	0	4 000	0
Total cash inflows ($)	6,000	5,000	6,500	6,800	11,500	9,500
Outflows ($)						
Stock ($)	2,500	2,200	2,700	2,700	3,000	3,300
Labour costs ($)	3,500	3,500	3,500	3,500	3,500	3,500
Other costs ($)	2,000	2,000	2,000	1,800	1,800	2,200
Total cash outflows ($)	8,000	7,700	8,200	8,000	8,300	9,000
Net cash flow ($)	(2,000)	(2,700)	(1,700)	(1,200)	3,200	500
Closing balance ($)	3,000	300	(1,400)	(2,600)	600	1,100

CORE

Exam tip !
Worked example: Cash flow forecast

Study the cash flow forecast below to complete the missing values for (a)–(e).   *[5 marks]*

	Sept ($)	Oct ($)	Nov ($)	Dec ($)
Cash sales	2,000	2,000	**(d)**	4,000
Stock purchases	600	600	900	1,200
Rent	1,000	0	1,000	0
Other costs	600	600	800	1,000
Opening cash balance	1,000	**(c)**	1,600	1,900
Net cash flow	**(a)**	800	300	1,800
Closing cash balance	**(b)**	1,600	1,900	**(e)**

Answers:

(a) Cash inflow in September is $2,000. The total cash outflow is $2,200 (the sum of stock, rent and other costs). Net cash flow is the difference between cash inflows and cash outflows for the month, so the value of (a) = **($200)**, i.e. there is negative net cash flow of $200.

(b) The closing balance = opening balance plus net cash flow, i.e. the value of (b) = $1,000 + ($200) = **$800**.

(c) The opening balance in October is the same value as the closing balance in September, i.e. (c) = **$800**.

(d) The total cash outflow in November is $2,700 (i.e. $900 + $1,000 + $800). The net cash flow is given as $300. This means the cash sales exceeded the cash outflow figure by $300, so (d) = **$3,000**.

(e) The closing balance at the end of December is worked out in the same way as part (b), i.e. opening balance plus net cash flow for the month. Hence, the value of (e) = $1,900 + $1,800 = **$3,700**.

Question 3.7.4   Wincent Wines

Morten Wincent has recently opened a wine retailing business in a busy location. He expects most of his customers will purchase the wines using credit. He has created the following cash flow forecast for the next three months of trading. He feels this is optimistic but realistic, especially as the firm has yet to spend any money on marketing. Whilst *Wincent Wines* allows its customers up to 60 day pay for their items, its suppliers only give the business trade credit of 14 days.

	Month 1 ($)	Month 2 ($)	Month 3 ($)
Sales revenue	25,000	20,000	22,000
Overdraft		8,000	0
Cash inflow	28,000		22,000
Cost of goods sold	16,250		14,300
Staff wages	4,000	4,500	4,300
Expenses	5,000	5,000	5,000
Other costs		1,600	1,850
Cash outflow	26,750	24,100	
Net cash flow	1,250		(3,450)
Opening balance	(1,750)	(500)	3,400
Closing balance		3,400	(50)

(a) Complete the missing figures in the cash flow forecast for *Wincent Wines*.   [4 marks]

(b) Explain **two** possible causes of cash flow problems for *Wincent Wines*.   [4 marks]

(c) Explain **two** ways that Morten Wincent might be able to resolve his anticipated cash flow problems.   [4 marks]

Question 3.7.5   Menelao Stationers

Denise Menelao has recently received her licence to set up a stationery outlet, *Menelao Stationers* in Long Beach, California. Her main clients would be from the business sector as well as local schools. She plans to commence trading on 1 August and has initial capital of $6,500 that she puts into her business bank account. Denise Menelao has also gathered the following information:

- Sales for the first four months are forecast to be: $2,000 (Aug), $5,500 (Sept), $3,200 (Oct) and $3,000 (Nov).
- Stock purchases cost exactly half the value of sales each month.
- Rent is paid every two months, starting in September. Each payment is $2,000.
- Utility bills are predicted to average $500 per month.
- Other expenses are expected to be $1,800 for the first month and $1,100 per month thereafter.

(a) Construct a cash flow forecast for *Menelao Stationers*.   [5 marks]

(b) Comment on the liquidity position of *Menelao Stationers*.   [4 marks]

Causes of cash flow problems

All businesses must have healthy cash flow in order to generate sufficient working capital to pay their staff, suppliers, financiers and landlords. The main causes of cash flow problems include:

- **Overtrading** This situation occurs when a business attempts to expand too quickly (or aggressively), without the sufficient resources to do so. For example, it accepts more orders than it has the capacity to handle. The excess orders add to production costs without any corresponding revenue (which only comes after the product has been manufactured and sold to customers). The purchase of fixed assets as part of rapid expansion also consumes cash, thus reducing the working capital of the business.

- **Overborrowing** The larger the proportion of capital raised through external sources of finance, the higher the cash outflow on loan interest payments. During times of rising interest rates, cash outflow on loan interest increases, putting further pressure on a firm's working capital and liquidity position.

- **Overstocking** This means that a business holds too much stock as a result of an ineffective stock control system (see Unit 5.5). Stocks cost money to buy, produce and store. In addition, excess stocks represent a waste of scarce resources, i.e. the money could have been better spent elsewhere.

- **Poor credit control** Cash flow problems can arise when a firm offers customers an extended credit period, leading the business to trade for long periods without cash inflows. It can also arise if too many customers are offered credit, which increases the chances of bad debts being experienced, i.e. debtors who fail to pay.

- **Unforeseen changes** Unexpected and erratic changes in demand can cause serious cash flow problems. Machinery breakdown, which lengthens the working capital cycle, is one example. Conversely, seasonal fluctuations in demand cause temporary, albeit perhaps predictable, cash flow issues. This affects businesses that face highly seasonal demand, such as producers of Valentine's cards, Easter eggs, Halloween products and Christmas cakes.

Figure 3.7.c Seasonal demand causes fluctuations in cash flow

Question 3.7.6   Bereti's Boutique

Nicole Bereti is planning to open a perfume boutique in Vancouver, Canada which will commence business at the beginning of August this year. Consider the following information and then answer the questions that follow:

- Nicole has $15,000 from her personal bank account that she wishes to use for her business in August.
- She estimates that the first four months of sales revenue will be: $5,000, $5,800, $7,000 and $9,500.
- The cost of buying the perfumes is estimated to cost: $3,000, $3,480, $3,850 and $4,750 respectively.
- Anticipated expenditure on advertising is $1,500 for the first month and $1,000 every month thereafter.
- Nicole intends to hire four members of staff, who will each earn a **salary** of $1,200 per month.
- Other costs (such as rent and utility bills) amount to an average of $600 per month.

	Aug ($)	Sept ($)	Oct ($)	Nov ($)
Opening balance				
Owner's capital				
Cash inflows (sales)				
Total cash inflows				
Cash outflows:				
Cost of sales				
Advertising costs				
Staffing costs				
Other costs				
Total cash outflows				
Closing bank balance				

(a) Define the term **salary**. [2 marks]

(b) Complete the cash flow forecast for *Bereti's Boutique* by using the format above. [5 marks]

(c) Examine the cash flow position faced by *Bereti's Boutique*. [6 marks]

Investment, profit and cash flow

The relationship between investment, profit and cash flow. AO2
© IBO, 2017

As previously mentioned cash is not the same as profit. A business could be making a loss, but has plenty of cash, or it could be profitable but lack working capital. For example, a new franchisee might run a cash-rich business (as there are lots of customers) but is unprofitable because of the huge costs involved, e.g. purchase costs of the franchise (including buildings and equipment), training and recruitment costs, and supplies of stocks (inventory). Over time, the franchisee may become profitable, but financing growth (buying more franchised outlets) means the owner becomes cash deficient.

Examples of how investment, profit and cash flow are interlinked include:

- When a business sells an investment, it experiences an increase in its cash flow position. The opposite happens when a business buys an investment.

- When a firm obtains finance for investments, the cash inflow improves its liquidity position.

Note that in the above examples, the uses of cash for investments are not directly linked to a firm's trading activities. Hence, these cash inflows and outflows do not directly affect the firm's profitability.

Investment expenditure requires the use of cash, so net cash flow is likely to be negative in the short term. For example, China's Lenovo bought Motorola from Google for $3 billion in 2014. Lenovo is hoping to repeat its success of investing in the personal computer market when it bought the PC division of IBM in 2005. In 2013, Lenovo overtook HP to become the largest maker of PCs. It is important to remember that investment does not guarantee profit; Google lost more than $9 billion in the deal with Lenovo as it had bought Motorola for $12.5 billion in 2011.

The importance of how investment is financed also affects the cash flow position of a business. Diversified companies with a broad product portfolio (see Unit 4.5) can rely on alternative revenue streams (see Unit 3.2) for working capital. For example, Microsoft bought Skype for $8.5 billion in 2011 in a deal worth 32 times more than Skype's operating profits at the time. However, the software giant could rely on the cash flow from its broad product portfolio of over 100 other companies it had already acquired.

Cash flow is vital for investment opportunities because poor cash flow results in missed opportunities for investment. The pharmaceutical industry is an example. It can quite easily take around 17 years to commercialise a drug. Effective cash flow management and product portfolio management are therefore necessary prerequisites before the business can turn an investment into profit for the owners.

Case study

Amazon was founded in 1994 in Seattle, USA. Initially, the e-commerce company had forecast that it would take up to 5 years to return a profit to its investors. It was not until 2001 that Amazon finally earned a profit of $5 million on sales revenue of over $1 billion. Today, its annual sales revenue is in excess of $89 billion with good cash flow and profit.

Theory of knowledge

Scottish writer Thomas Carlyle, (1795–1881) said, *"You may prove anything by figures"*. To what extent does this claim apply to knowledge in Business Management?

Strategies to deal with cash flow problems

The following strategies for dealing with cash flow problems: reducing cash outflow, improving cash inflows, and looking for additional finance. AO3

© IBO, 2017

Improving the cash flow position of a business requires effective working capital management, i.e. the business must successfully manage its current assets (cash, debtors and stocks) and its current liabilities. Quite often, the solution to a problem is to deal directly with the causes. There are three generic ways to deal with cash flow problems:

- Reducing cash outflows

- Improving cash inflows

- Seeking alternative sources of finance.

Reducing cash outflows

These methods of improving the cash flow position of a firm deal with reducing costs and/or delaying the payment of costs.

- **Seek preferential credit terms** A business can negotiate extended credit terms, i.e. to lengthen the time taken to pay its suppliers and creditors. Alternatively, it can seek alternative creditors who can offer preferential credit terms. One limitation with this approach is the administrative costs and the time needed to investigate and negotiate better deals, which might not result in significant differences to the cash flow position of the firm.

- **Seek alternative suppliers** Different suppliers may be able to offer more competitive prices, which would help to reduce cash outflows. However, cheaper raw materials and stocks could equate to lower quality, so the business might need to change its marketing strategies as a result of this.

- **Better stock control** Reducing stock levels by using a just-in-time system (see Unit 5.3) can help to reduce liquidity being tied up in stocks. This method works well for manufacturers of mass market products such as motor vehicles and consumer electronics. However, it might not work as well for businesses that offer a service and do not hold much stock, such as airline carriers and hair salons.

- **Reduce expenses** Scrutinising expenses can help to identify overhead costs that can be reduced, without compromising quality. For example, airlines have saved huge amounts of money by reducing the number of drinks and snacks that are available on economy class travel. Some costs might not be necessary at all, including extravagant (non-essential) expenses for senior executives such as luxury company cars.

- **Leasing** Leasing, rather than buying, reduces the burden on cash flow. Buying land, machinery, vehicles and capital equipment will clearly be more expensive than renting or leasing (see Unit 3.1), at least in the short to medium term.

Figure 3.7.d Cash flow can be improved by cutting extravagant expenses such as luxury cars for business executives

Improving cash inflows

- **Tighter credit control** Firms can limit trade credit to their customers or reduce the credit period. Both methods mean that the business receives cash sooner which helps to improve its cash flow. However, customers might switch to rivals due to the worsened trade credit terms. Instead, debtors can be encouraged to pay earlier or on time by offering incentives, such as price discounts. Accepting interim payments can also help.

- **Cash payments only** Requiring customers to pay by cash only removes the delay in receiving cash from credit sales. However, the drawback is that customers might prefer to buy from competitors who offer trade credit. After all, if business customers paid by cash, this could negatively affect their own cash flow position.

- **Change pricing policy** Cutting prices can help to convert stocks into cash. In addition, it can help to offload excess stocks. This tactic works best for products that have lots of substitutes or are at the end of their product life cycle (see Unit 4.5).

- **Improved product portfolio** By providing a wide and varied product portfolio (see Unit 4.5), a business is more likely to generate increased sales revenue. Poor sales in one product market can be offset by better sales in other markets. Limitations are that broadening the product portfolio raises costs and risks, yet does not guarantee higher net cash flows.

Case study

Agnès B, the French fashion design label, has diversified its product portfolio to gain a wider revenue stream and improved cash inflow. Its product portfolio includes: clothing, fashion accessories, shoes, handbags, chocolates, patisserie and fresh flowers.

Seeking alternative sources of finance

- **Overdrafts** Banks provide this service which allows a business to temporarily take out more money than exists in its bank account. This gives the firm immediate access to cash during times of negative cash flow. However, the firm needs to pay interest on the amount that has been overdrawn. Firms facing a liquidity crisis might also find it difficult to obtain an overdraft.

- **Selling fixed assets** The sale of dormant assets (obsolete or unused assets) can generate much-needed cash, although it is only a one-off (as the asset cannot be resold by the business). However, selling fixed assets is not advisable, unless totally unavoidable, as these are needed for a business to operate and to expand.

- **Debt factoring** This financial service involves an external party taking over the collection of money owed by debtors. The debt factoring provider (see Unit 3.1) passes on the money owed to its client (minus the handling charges), thus giving the business immediate access to cash.

Finance and accounts

CORE

Finance and accounts

CORE

- **Government assistance** Some businesses qualify for grants, subsidies or low-interest loans. This helps to boost the cash flow position of a business. Governments are often reluctant to ignore struggling businesses as this could lead to job losses and higher social welfare costs.

Note: as cash flow forecasts and cash flow statements do not show the *profitability* of a business, the above solutions are based purely on cash flow problems (rather than profitability problems). Instead, the profitability of a firm can be seen in its profit and loss account (see Unit 3.4) and via ratio analysis (see Units 3.5 and 3.6).

Case study

In July 2014, Puma became Arsenal Football Club's new shirt sponsors, ending the London football club's 20-year association with Nike. The deal was worth over £30m a year ($45m) over 5 years. In 2019, Arsenal replaced Puma with Adidas as their new kit sponsor, in a deal worth £40m ($58m), with the cash helping to boost the English Premier League club's ability to compete in the most lucrative league of the world's most lucrative sport. Manchester United Football Club also have a shirt sponsorship deal Adidas, worth £75m.

Table 3.7.b Summary of dealing with cash flow problems

Lower cash outflows	Raise cash inflows	Additional finance
Preferential credit terms	Tighter credit control	Overdraft
Seek alternative suppliers	Cash payments only	Sale of fixed assets
Better stock control	Change pricing policy	Debt factoring
Reduce unnecessary expenses	Broaden product portfolio	Government assistance
Leasing or renting		

Exam tip !
Watch out for credit sales

When dealing with credit sales, be aware that the cash from such transactions are not received until the end of the credit period. For example, if $10,000 of goods were sold in July with 30 days credit, then the cash for this is not received until August. Hence, the $10,000 cash inflow is recorded in August (not July) in the cash flow statement.

Question 3.7.7   Ducie's Dance Studios Ltd

Marj Ducie runs a profitable dance company. However, she is concerned about the latest **cash flow forecast** for the business. Marj used the following data to prepare her cash flow forecast:
- Sales revenue: $12,000 in March; $10,000 in April; $9,000 in May; $11,000 in June.
- Payment from customers for sales are 50% paid for in cash and 50% paid for on one month's credit.
- Direct costs: $5,500 in April; $4,950 in May, and $6,100 in June.
- Indirect costs are $50,00 per month.
- The opening cash balance in April is $1,000.

(a) Define the term **cash flow forecast**.

[2 marks]

(b) Outline a possible reason why profitable firms might experience cash flow problems.

[2 marks]

(c) Construct a cash flow forecast for *Ducie's Dance Studios Ltd.* for the period April to June.

[5 marks]

(d) Examine the options available to *Ducie's Dance Studios Ltd.* in dealing with its liquidity problems.

[6 marks]

Limitations of cash flow forecasting

Movie mogul Sam Goldwyn (1879–1974) once joked that making predictions is difficult, especially if it concerns the future. Cash flow forecasting attempts to predict the liquidity position of a business in the future, based on certain assumptions. Inaccuracies can occur due to a number of reasons, such as:

- **Marketing**   Inaccurate or poor market research can lead to incorrect sales forecasts (see Unit 4.3). A distasteful or undesirable marketing campaign could offend customers, thereby harming the firm's cash flow position.

- **Human resources**   A demoralised workforce becomes a less productive workforce that delivers poor customer service. Disputes that are not managed can lead to industrial action. The result of unmanaged conflict will be an unfavourable effect on the firm's cash flow position.

- **Operations management**   Machine failure can cause production delays to the detriment of a firm's cash flow.

- **Competitors**   The behaviour of rival firms can be difficult to anticipate yet is likely to directly affect a firm's cash flow position and its level of success. For example, Toyota's aggressive but appealing marketing in the USA has threatened the sales and cash flow position of American car giants General Motors and Ford.

- **Changing fashion and tastes**   A favourable change in demand means that actual cash flows will be more positive than originally forecast, vice versa. Some products may become unpredictably popular and this would boost their cash inflow.

- **Economic change**   Changes in economic factors can also present opportunities or threats (see Unit 1.5). For instance, lower interest rates tend to encourage borrowing which boosts consumer expenditure and investment expenditure. Over time, this should increase employment and stimulate economic growth, thus boosting sales

and cash inflows. By contrast, higher rates of inflation can harm consumer and producer confidence, possibly leading to an economic downturn.

- **External shocks**   Events such as wars, oil crises, stock market crashes, health scares or adverse weather will make initial cash flow forecasts less accurate.

Figure 3.7.e Adverse weather conditions can cause cash flow problems

There is no guarantee that predictions and assumptions made in a cash flow forecast will materialise. Hence, forecasts tend to be for the immediate and foreseeable future only because predictions of the distant future tend to be highly inaccurate and therefore meaningless. Cash flow forecasting is also a continuous, ongoing process with regular updates being made when necessary. This helps to ensure that the cash flow position is carefully monitored to identify potential problems before they occur.

Common mistake

Many students seem to think that a positive cash flow figure means the business is profitable. This is fundamentally incorrect as a profit and loss account is used to show whether a business is profitable. The usefulness of a cash flow forecast depends on how well prepared and accurate the estimates are.

Theory of knowledge

To what extent do cash flow statements reveal the 'truth' about a business?

Finance and accounts

CORE

Cash flow and the CUEGIS concepts

In reality, businesses are likely to use a combination of cash-boosting and cost-reducing methods to improve their cash flow. The *Pareto Principle* (or the *80–20 Rule*) suggests that forward-looking businesses ought to focus 80% of their time and resources to boosting cash inflows and only 20% on cost-cutting strategies. Firms are also likely to have a *contingency fund* which sets aside cash for unexpected changes and emergency use. The greater the level of uncertainty faced by a business, and the more exposed it is to change, the higher its contingency fund tends to be.

Financial difficulties, caused by poor management of working capital and cash flows, will bring about problems for employees, customers, suppliers and investors of the organization. Working capital is essential for many aspects of business strategy. For example:

- Human resources strategy – Working capital is needed to pay staff on time. Motivation theory (see Unit 2.4) suggests that pay is a key motivator for many people. Indeed, a lack of pay is seen as a demotivator and can lead to industrial disputes (see Unit 2.6). Therefore insufficient working capital can lead to a demoralised and unproductive workforce.

- Marketing strategy – Marketing mix activities (see Unit 4.5) such as new product development or extension strategies require sufficient cash. Only the largest firms can afford to advertise via the mass media such as television and national newspapers. Marketing activities can be funded from products, known as *cash cows*, which generate a large and regular stream of cash.

- Production strategy – Manufacturers with long working-capital cycles, such as producers of luxury yachts or construction companies, need huge amounts of cash to complete their projects. Cash is also required to pay suppliers so that the supply chain process is efficient (see Unit 5.5).

Figure 3.7.f   Construction firms tend to have a long working capital cycle

Cash flow forecasting can be an effective management tool to oversee and control a firm's working capital. However, the forecasts and calculations are static, i.e. they only represent the cash flow situation of a business at one point in time. Changes in the external environment will alter cash flows, perhaps in a detrimental way. Hence, the results of any cash flow forecast to aid business strategy must be handled with some caution. Indeed, forecasts should be updated regularly to ensure that decision-making is based on the most up to date and relevant information. The critical factor is to ensure that the organization has sufficient liquidity to meet its costs and current liabilities, such as the money owed to suppliers, financiers and tax authorities.

However, managers face a dilemma in balancing the conflict between the desire for sufficient working capital and the desire for profits. Larger profits can be made by granting credit to more customers, to encourage them to buy. Since credit incurs administrative charges, many retailers require customers to spend a minimum amount before they can benefit from offering credit to customers. However, credit will prolong the firm's working capital cycle. By contrast, demanding cash payments only will ultimately drive away many customers. The balance then depends on the organizational culture, customer expectations and the actions of competitors. For example, increased competition in a globalized and digitised world has led customers to expect credit. It is also expected for purchases of expensive consumer durables such as jewellery, motor vehicles and home furniture.

In summary, cash is regarded as being more important than profit in the short run. Profitable firms will not survive in the long run if they lack sufficient working capital. There is no doubt that profit is vital and that it leads to the long-term prosperity and survival of a business. However, cash flow problems can occur at any time due to changes in the external environment, thereby causing huge disruptions to even the most established and globalized businesses.

CUEGIS Essay

With reference to an organization of your choice, discuss how **innovation** and **globalization** have influenced its use of finance. *[20 marks]*

REVIEW QUESTIONS

1. What is the difference between cash and profits?

2. Why might a profitable business lack cash, whilst a business with cash might lack profit?

3. What is meant by working capital?

4. Distinguish between insolvency and liquidity.

5. What are three examples of current assets

6. Distinguish between current assets and current liabilities.

7. What is the working capital cycle.

8. Distinguish between cash inflows and cash outflows.

9. What is meant by net cash flow?

10. Why do businesses produce cash flow forecasts?

11. Explain the link between a firm's closing balance and its opening balance in a cash flow forecast.

12. What are the main causes of cash flow problems?

13. What is the relationship between investment, profit and cash flow?

14. What are the three generic ways that a firm can deal with cash flow problems?

15. What are the imitations of cash flow forecasting?

KEY TERMS

Assets are items with a monetary value that belong to a business. They can either be *fixed assets* (e.g. machinery, tools and buildings) or *current assets* (e.g. cash, stock and debtors).

Bad debts exist when debtors are unable to pay their outstanding invoices (bills). This reduces the cash inflows of the vendor (the business that has sold the products on trade credit).

Cash is a current asset and represents the actual money a business has. It can exist in the form of *cash in hand* (cash held in the business) or *cash at bank* (cash held in a bank account).

Cash flow refers to the transfer or movement of money into and out of an organization. Cash *inflows* mainly come from sales revenue whereas cash *outflows* are for items of expenditure.

A **cash flow forecast** is a financial document that shows the predicted future cash inflows and cash outflows for a business during a trading period.

A **cash flow statement** is the financial document that records the actual cash inflows and cash outflows of a business during a specified trading period, usually 12 months.

Closing balance refers the value of cash left in a business at the end of each month, as shown in its cash flow forecast or statement, using the formula: Closing balance = Opening balance plus Net cash flow.

Current assets are liquid resources owned by a business, i.e. cash, debtors and stocks.

Finance and accounts

CORE

Current liabilities represent the money that a business owes that needs to be repaid within the next twelve months, e.g. overdraft, creditors and taxes.

Credit control is the process of monitoring and managing debtors, such as ensuring only suitable customers are permitted trade credit and that customers do not exceed the agreed credit period.

Creditors are businesses that have sold goods or services on trade credit, so will collect this money from its debtors at a future date.

Debt factoring is a financial service provided to businesses that have struggled to collect money from their debtors who have experienced major liquidity problems.

Debtors are customers who have purchased goods or services on credit, so owe the business money which is collected at a later date.

Expenses represent the expenditure in the working capital cycle, i.e. costs of production such as salaries, rent, advertising and distribution.

Fixed assets are illiquid resources owned by a business and are not intended for resale within the next twelve months but are used to generate revenue, e.g. land, vehicles and trademarks.

Insolvency is a situation where a firm's working capital is insufficient to meet its current liabilities. It can lead to the collapse of the business as creditors will take legal action to recover their money.

Liabilities are debts owed by a business. Current liabilities are short-term debts that need to be repaid within twelve months of the balance sheet date, e.g. overdrafts. Long-term liabilities, such as mortgages and bank loans, are repayable over a longer period.

Liquidity is the ability of a business to convert assets into cash quickly without a fall in its value.

A **liquidity problem** occurs where a business does not have enough cash to pay its current liabilities (short-term debts).

Net cash flow refers to the cash that is left over after cash outflows have been accounted for from the cash inflows, per time period.

Opening balance refers the value of cash in a business at the beginning of each month, as shown in its cash flow forecast or statement. It is equal to the closing balance in the previous month.

Overdrafts are a financial service that allow pre-approved customers to temporarily take out more money than is available in their bank account.

Overheads are the costs not directly associated with the production process yet necessary for providing and maintaining business operations, e.g. lighting, rent, security and insurance.

Overtrading occurs when a business attempts to expand too quickly without the sufficient resources to do so, usually by accepting too many orders, thus harming its cash flow position.

Profit in its simplest form is the positive difference between a firm's total sales revenue and its total costs of production.

Sales revenue is the value of goods and/or services sold by a business to its customers. It is calculated by using the formula: Sales revenue = Price × Quantity sold.

Short-term loans are advances (loans) from a financial institution that need to be repaid within 12 months of the balance sheet date.

Stock (or **inventory**) is the physical goods that a business has in its possession for further production, (raw materials and unfinished goods) or for sale (finished goods).

Tax refers to the payments made by a business to the government if it earns profit (net profit after all costs and expenses have been paid).

Working capital (or **net current assets**) is the amount of finance available to a business for its daily operations. It is calculated by current assets minus current liabilities.

The **working capital cycle** refers to the time interval between cash outflows for costs of production and cash inflows from customers who receive their finished goods and services.

3.8 Investment appraisal

"Never let a poor man advise you on investments." - Spanish proverb

SL/HL content	Assessment objective
Investment opportunities using payback period and average rate of return (ARR)	AO3, AO4

HL content	Assessment objective
Investment opportunities using NPV	AO3, AO4

© IBO, 2017

Payback period

Investment opportunities using payback period. AO3, AO4

© IBO, 2017

Investment refers to the purchase of an asset with the potential to yield future financial benefits, e.g. upgrading computer equipment or the purchase of a building. With most investments, resources are risked in a venture that might or might not bring about future advantages. For example, Hollywood movie *The 13th Warrior* starring Antonio Banderas cost around $160 million to produce in 1999 but proved to be the biggest flop as world box office sales totalled only $61.7 million. By contrast, *Avatar* (which cost almost $500 million in 2009) was a huge success; it took just three weeks to reach break-even and overtook *Titanic* to set a new world box-office sales record of over $2.78 billion. In June 2015, Universal Studios' Jurassic World earned a record $511.8 million in global sales during its first weekend around the world - the movie was budgeted at $150 million, so, the return on investment was 341.2% in a single weekend!

Investment appraisal refers to the quantitative techniques used to calculate the financial costs and benefits of an investment decision, i.e. the different methods used to assess the risks involved in investment decision-making. The three main methods of investment appraisal are: payback period, average rate of return and net present value.

The **payback period** (PBP) refers to the amount of time needed for an investment project to earn enough profit to repay the initial cost of the investment. The formula for calculating the PBP is:

$$PBP = \frac{\text{Initial investment cost (\$)}}{\text{Contribution per month (\$)}}$$

For example, suppose a firm is considering the purchase of new photocopier equipment at a cost of $10,000. The anticipated financial gain is $6,000 of revenue per year after maintenance costs are paid for. Hence, the payback period would be:

$$\frac{\$10,000 \text{ for purchase}}{(\$6,000 \div 12 \text{ months})}$$
$$= 20 \text{ months}$$

Most investment projects would only be considered if they have a relatively short PBP. In the above example, 20 months (or 1 year and 8 months) might be acceptable; the business will not want to purchase the photocopying equipment if it becomes obsolete before the payback period.

In reality, it is unlikely that the contribution will be constant each year. In this case, the PBP is calculated using the cumulative cash flow method (see the worked example on the following page).

Question 3.8.1 Verton Coffee

Elvy Verton is considering spending $300,000 on new machinery for her coffee shop business. The annual contribution from this investment is forecast to be $45,000. Elvy is keen for *Verton Coffee* to have a short **payback period**.

(a) Define the term **payback period**.   [2 marks]

(b) Calculate the payback period for *Verton Coffee*.   [2 marks]

(c) Explain why Elvy Verton is keen to have a short payback period.   [4 marks]

Finance and accounts (side tab)

CORE (side tab)

Exam tip !
Worked example: Payback period

Suppose the construction of a new sports complex costs $1m and is expected to generate the following net cash flows during the first four years:

Year 1 $200,000
Year 2 $340,000
Year 3 $430,000
Year 4 $430,000

The project will obviously not break-even in the first year (the cash outflow was $1 m whereas the net cash inflow in Year 1 is only $200 000). By calculating the cumulative cash flow, we get the following figures:

	Net cash inflow	Cumulative cash inflow
Year 1	$200,000	$200,000
Year 2	$340,000	$540,000
Year 3	$430,000	$970,000
Year 4	$360,000	$1,330,000

(continued) ...

(continued) ...

We can now see that the payback period (for the initial $1m) happens in the fourth year (the cumulative cash flow at the end of the third year is only $970,000).

To work out the PBP:

(a) Calculate the shortfall at the end of Year 3, i.e. $1,000,000 minus $970,000 = $30,000

(b) Calculate the average monthly cash inflow in Year 4, i.e. $360,000 divided by twelve months = $30,000

(c) Divide (a) by (b) to find the number of months, i.e. $30,000 into $30,000 = 1 month

Therefore, the payback period for the sports complex is forecast to be 3 years and 1 month.

Question 3.8.2 Mark Allegro Leasing Co.

Mark Allegro is considering spending $50,000 to purchase new power tools for his leasing company. The expected net cash flow from renting the new power tools to customers over the next 5 years is shown in the table below. Mark is keen to know the payback period before deciding whether to proceed with this investment.

Year	Net cash flow
1	$12,000
2	$14,000
3	$15,000
4	$14,000
5	$12,000

(a) Calculate the payback period for *Mark Allegro Leasing Co.* [2 marks]

(b) Comment on whether Mark Allegro should go ahead with this investment. [4 marks]

Question 3.8.3 Chelsea Football Club

Chelsea Football Club has enjoyed plenty of title successes since Russian oil tycoon Roman Abramovich took over the sports club in June 2003. He poured in an estimated £440 million ($640m) into the club that year. *Chelsea Football Club* went on to win the 2004-2005 season for the first time in 50 years. Abramovich invested a further £240 million ($350m) for the purchase of new players in 2006.

However, huge financial losses have weighed down *Chelsea Football Club*, with reported annual losses of £140 million ($203m), £88 million ($128m) and £80 million ($117m) in his first three years as owner of the club. Just as *Chelsea Football Club* had predicted, the investment reached it payback period target in 2010. By 2014, it became the seventh most valuable football club in the world, earning a profit of £18.4 million ($27m). In 2018, Forbes reported that *Chelsea Football Club* was valued at over $1.85 billion.

(a) Identify **two** possible reasons behind Roman Abramovich's decision to buy *Chelsea Football Club*. [2 marks]

(b) Explain, using the above case study, why investment can be risky. [4 marks]

(c) Comment on the usefulness of the payback period as an investment tool for *Chelsea Football Club*. [4 marks]

Table 3.8.a   Advantages and disadvantages of using the payback period

Advantages	Disadvantages
The PBP is the simplest and quickest method of investment appraisal; hence, it is the most commonly used method.	Contribution per month is unlikely to be constant as demand is prone to seasonal fluctuations so the PBP might take longer.
It can be useful for firms with cash flow problems as they can identify how long it would take for the cash to be recouped.	PBP focuses on time as the key criterion for investment, rather than on profits– the main aim of most private sector businesses.
It allows a firm to see whether it will break-even on the purchase of an asset before it needs to be replaced. This can be important in today's fast-paced business environment.	It can encourage a *short-termism* approach to investment, i.e. managers only focus on the short-term benefits and ignore the potential gains in the longer term.
The payback period can be used to compare different investment projects with different costs by calculating the quickest PBP of each option.	PBP might not be highly suitable for some firms, e.g. property developers and airline manufacturers are unlikely to recoup their investments for many years.
It helps to assess projects that will yield a quick return for shareholders.	Calculations are prone to errors as it is difficult to accurately predict future cash flows.

Figure 3.8.a It can take several years to recoup the investment costs of a cruise liner

Case study

In 2008, multibillionaire Warren Buffett (CEO of Berkshire Hathaway) bought a 10% stake in BYD, an investment worth $230 million at the time. BYD, the Chinese manufacturer of automobiles, phone components and rechargeable batteries opened its first manufacturing facilities in the USA in 2014. Its first order in Los Angeles was worth $12.1 million for ten zero-emission, all-electric buses.

Exam tip !

Students often conclude that because something is 'high risk' or 'risky', a business should avoid it. This is not reflective of the real business world where entrepreneurs have to regularly make decisions that involve an element of risk. Many businesses have become highly successful by taking huge risks. The decision is not whether to take risks but whether the benefits of the risk are likely to outweigh the costs involved.

Exam tip !

Probably the biggest potential mistake made by those relying on the use of the payback period is the decision to reject a project simply because it is not expected to pay off quickly, even though it may be very profitable in the long run. Context is important, so consider this when writing your responses.

Theory of knowledge

What is the definition of time? How much relevance does time have in the study of Business Management?

Average rate of return (ARR)

Investment opportunities using average rate of return (ARR). AO3, AO4

© IBO, 2017

The average rate of return (ARR) calculates the *average profit* on an investment project as a percentage of the amount invested. The formula for calculating the ARR is:

$$\frac{\text{Total profit during project's lifespan (\$)} \div \text{number of years of project}}{\text{Initial amount invested (\$)}} \times 100$$

Expressed as a percentage, the ARR enables managers to compare the return on other investment projects. As a basic benchmark, the ARR can be compared with the interest rate to assess the rewards for the risk involved in an investment. For example, if the ARR of a project for a large established multinational such as McDonald's is 7% whilst the interest rate on savings is 3%, then the real rate of return is 4%. This might well be worth the risk for multinationals. However, if it were for a new firm entering a niche market selling horse saddles, then a 4% real return might not be enough to convince decision makers to implement the investment plan, especially as banks are offering a (guaranteed) 3% return.

The main advantage of the ARR method is that it enables easy comparisons (in percentage terms) of the estimated returns of different investment projects. For example, if two projects are predicted to yield the same ARR, then the relatively cheaper project might be more desirable given that it carries less financial risk.

However, a weakness of the ARR method is that it ignores the timing of cash inflows and hence is prone to forecasting errors when considering seasonal factors. In addition, the project's useful life span (which might be a pure guess) is needed before any meaningful calculations can be made. Finally, as with all time-based forecasts, errors are more likely the longer the time period under consideration; we might know what is likely to happen tomorrow but we are less sure about the events in five years from now.

Exam tip !
Worked example: Average rate of return

Suppose the purchase of a new computer system that costs $350,000 is forecast to generate the following net cash flows over the next five years (when it needs to be replaced):

Year 1	$100,000
Year 2	$130,000
Year 3	$180,000
Year 4	$150,000
Year 5	$100,000

There are several steps needed to calculate the ARR for this project:

- Total net cash inflow over the five years is $660,000
- Projected profit = $660,000 minus $350,000 (for the initial investment) = $310,000
- Average annual profit = $310,000 ÷ 5 years = $62,000 per year
- Hence the ARR = $62,000 ÷ $350,000 = 17.7%

Comparing this figure with interest rates helps to assess whether the project is worth the risk. If the return on savings is 3.54%, then this particular project seems attractive, as the return on investment is five times as large.

Finance and accounts

CORE

Question 3.8.4   DeRogatis Computing Inc.

DeRogatis Computing Inc. is considering investing $100,000 in new machinery. The company expects the annual profits from the **capital expenditure** will be $50,000 per year for 4 years before the machinery needs to be scrapped.

(a) Define the term **capital expenditure**.   *[2 marks]*

(b) Calculate the average rate of return (ARR) for *DeRogatis Computing Inc.*   *[2 marks]*

Question 3.8.5 Payback period and average rate of return

Study the information in the table below and then answer the questions that follow.

Year	Net cash flow	
	Project Atlanta ($)	Project Boston ($)
0	(140 000)	(140 000)
1	80 000	60 000
2	60 000	60 000
3	20 000	60 000

(a) State the cost of the investment projects under consideration.   *[1 mark]*

(b) Calculate the payback period for both projects, and comment on your findings.   *[4 marks]*

(c) (i) Calculate the average rate of return on both projects.   *[2 marks]*

(c) (ii) Assuming that the savings interest rate is 4.75%, comment on your findings.   *[2 marks]*

(d) Examine which investment project is more attractive.   *[6 marks]*

Net present value [Higher level]

Investment opportunities using net present value (NPV). AO3, AO4

© IBO, 2017

Suppose you had the option of receiving a university scholarship to the value of $30,000 in either one lump sum today or over a 4-year period. Which would you opt for? Most people would go for the first option rather than the deferred payment option. The reason is linked to the saying "time is money". Money received today can be invested or simply saved in a bank to earn compound interest, whereas money received in the future will have lost some of its value.

For example, if you have $100 and decide to place it into a bank account paying 5% interest, at the end of the year you will have $105. Therefore, $105 in a year's time is worth the same as $100 today. If this was saved for a further year, then the present value would be $110.25 (i.e. $105 plus another 5% interest).

Figure 3.8.b The present value of $105 received in a year's time if the rate of interest is 5% is $100

Discounting is the reverse of calculating compound interest. A discount factor is used to convert the future net cash flow to its present value today. Given that receiving money today is worth more than it is in the future, the discount factor can represent inflation and/or interest rates.

As an example, suppose an organization expects to receive $100,000 in three year's time whilst today's interest rate is 5%. What is the present value of the $100,000? From Table 3.8.b, we can see that the discount factor for 5% interest over 3 years is 0.8638. Hence, the present value of the $100,000 received in 3 years' time is $100,000 × 0.8638 = $86,380. This is the equivalent of receiving $86,380 today and leaving it in the bank to earn compound interest of 5% for 3 years, which would equate to $100,000 received at the end of year 3.

Case study

The producers of television show *America's Got Talent* put a disclaimer on the $1m prize money for the winner of the competition. The total prize winnings of $1,000,000 is actually payable in financial annuities over 40 years! That equates to just $25,000 a year for 40 years. If interest rates averaged 5% in this time, and after state and federal taxes have been paid, the present value of the prize money is only worth around $375,000 – which is about the cost of a 30-second advert on AGT!

Box 3.8.a Calculating discount factors

- Determine the interest rate, e.g. 5%
- Work out the cumulative interest rate, e.g. 5% for 3 years = $(1.05)^3$
- Place this value as the denominator, with 1 as the default numerator: $1 / (1.05)^3 = 0.8638$ (to 4 d.p.)

(Note: students will *not* be expected to calculate discount factors; discount tables will be given for examination questions).

Table 3.8.b Discount factors

	1%	2%	3%	4%	5%	6%	7%	8%	9%	10%
Year 1	0.9901	0.9804	0.9709	0.9615	0.9524	0.9434	0.9346	0.9259	0.9174	0.9091
Year 2	0.9803	0.9612	0.9426	0.9246	0.9070	0.8900	0.8734	0.8573	0.8417	0.8264
Year 3	0.9706	0.9423	0.9151	0.8890	0.8638	0.8396	0.8165	0.7938	0.7722	0.7513
Year 4	0.9610	0.9238	0.8885	0.8548	0.8227	0.7921	0.7629	0.7350	0.7084	0.6830
Year 5	0.9515	0.9057	0.8626	0.8219	0.7835	0.7473	0.7130	0.6806	0.6499	0.6209
Year 6	0.9420	0.8880	0.8375	0.7903	0.7462	0.7050	0.6663	0.6302	0.5963	0.5645
Year 7	0.9327	0.8706	0.8131	0.7599	0.7107	0.6651	0.6227	0.5835	0.5470	0.5132
Year 8	0.9235	0.8535	0.7694	0.7307	0.6768	0.6274	0.5820	0.5403	0.5019	0.4665
Year 9	0.9143	0.8368	0.7664	0.7026	0.6446	0.5919	0.5439	0.5002	0.4604	0.4241
Year 10	0.9053	0.8203	0.7441	0.6756	0.6139	0.5584	0.5083	0.4632	0.4224	0.3855

HIGHER LEVEL

Finance and accounts

The net present value (NPV) is the sum of all discounted cash flows minus the cost of the investment project. Money received in the future is worth less than if it were received today, i.e. the longer the time period under consideration, the lower the present value of that future amount of money. The NPV is calculated using the formula:

NPV = Sum of present values – Cost of investment

The original amount invested is often referred to as the principal. The NPV will be positive (greater than the principal) if the discounted (future) cash flows are enough to justify the initial investment. Similarly, if the NPV is negative, then the investment project is not worth pursuing.

Theory of knowledge

Is there ever a case for a profit-seeking business to pursue a project that has an expected negative net present value?

Exam tip !

All students are expected to be able to calculate the Payback Period and ARR from given data. HL students also need to learn to calculate and interpret the NPV. More importantly, as this is not an accounts or finance examination, you are expected to be able to analyse the results of their calculations and explain the implications for business decision-making. From time to time, students will be asked directly to use a method of investment appraisal. Students may be asked to calculate the payback period, ARR and NPV (to 2 decimal places). You might also be asked to evaluate specified investment options and to recommend which investment option to pursue.

Theory of knowledge

To what extent can quantitative investment appraisal support knowledge claims in Business Management?

Exam tip !
Worked example

Suppose that new mechanisation for a firm is estimated to cost $300,000 and should last for five years. It will cost an estimated $50,000 per annum to maintain but will increase the value of the firm's output by an estimated $150,000. Interest rates are currently 5%. Calculate the NPV on the proposed investment.

Working out (figures in $)
The net cash flow in each year is simply the total cash inflow minus the total cash outflow, i.e. $150,000 minus $50,000 = $100,000.

Period	Net cash flow	Discount factor	Present value
Year 1	100,000	0.9524	95,240
Year 2	100,000	0.9070	90,700
Year 3	100,000	0.8638	86,380
Year 4	100,000	0.8227	82,270
Year 5	100,000	0.7835	78,350
Total	500,000		432,940

Notice that although the net cash flow is expected to be the same throughout the life of the project, a sum of $100,000 received in 5 years' time is worth a lot less than the same amount received this year.

Answer:
Add the total present value figures and minus the initial investment cost.
i.e. NPV = $432,940 – $300,000 = $132,940.
Notice that without using NPV the estimated return would be much higher at $200,000 (i.e. $500,000 – $300,000). However, the NPV method shows that each of the $100,000 net cash flow received in the future is worth less than the value today, i.e. the real return is only $132,940.

In the above example, since the NPV has a positive value of $132,940 the investment project should go ahead. However, the business must take care not to over-rely on the NPV figure, as it would be reduced if interest rates were to go up during the next five years. Other limitations are that NPV calculations can be complex and that results are only comparable if the initial investment cost is the same between competing projects.

Question 3.8.6   Calculating net present value

(a)   Calculate the net present value (NPV) by completing the table below. Discount factors for 6% are given to 4 d.p. Both projects cost $300,000. Explain which of the two projects should be pursued.   *[5 marks]*

Year	Investment Colorado			Investment Detroit		
	Net cash flow ($)	Discount factor	Present value ($)	Net cash flow ($)	Discount factor	Present value ($)
0	(300,000)	1.00			1.00	(300,000)
1	50,000	0.9434		100,000	0.9434	
2	100,000	0.8900		200,000	0.8900	
3	200,000	0.8396		200,000	0.8396	
4	200,000	0.7921		50,000	0.7921	
NPV						

(b)   Suggest what other information should be considered before deciding which investment project to pursue.   *[5 marks]*

Question 3.8.7   Which project?

Study the data below and answer the questions that follow. Refer to Table 3.8.b for the relevant discount factors. Each project costs $300,000. Assume the average interest rate is 4%.

Year	Net cash flow	
	Project England ($)	Project France ($)
1	100,000	100,000
2	120,000	200,000
3	150,000	150,000
4	200,000	100,000
Total	570,000	550,000

(a)   Define the term **net cash flow**.   *[2 marks]*

(b)   Using relevant investment appraisal methods, recommend which of the above projects would be the most attractive to investors.   *[10 marks]*

Question 3.8.8   Karoo Garments Limited

Karoo Garments Limited is a manufacturer of fashion garments for well-known retailers in Europe. It has a labour force of 85 people with over half of the workers employed on a part-time contract. Staff retention has been an on-going problem for *Karoo Garments Limited*.

The continuous changes in the fashion industry in Europe have led *Karoo Garments Limited* to devote more of its resources to reducing the new product development time. The company is deciding whether to invest in new machinery to improve productivity at its factory. The cost of the investment is forecast to be €230,000 with an expected lifespan of four years. Current data suggests that the machinery will fetch a **scrap value** of €10,000.

The projected net cash flows from the investment are given below:

Year	€'000
0	(230)
1	140
2	180
3	150
4	100

Karoo Garments Limited uses an 8% discount factor for the cost of capital. The corresponding discount factors are as follows:

Year 1: 0.9259   Year 2: 0.8573   Year 3: 0.7938   Year 4: 0.7350

(a) Define the term **scrap value**.   *[2 marks]*

(b) **(i)**   Calculate the payback period for the proposed investment project.   *[2 marks]*

　　　 (ii) Calculate the average rate of return on the proposed investment project.   *[3 marks]*

　　　 (iii) Calculate the net present value of the proposed investment project.   *[4 marks]*

(c) Using relevant numerical and non-numerical factors, evaluate whether *Karoo Garments Limited* should invest in the new machinery to improve productivity.   *[10 marks]*

Common mistake

Make sure you use the correct units of measurement for the different methods of quantitative investment appraisal as marks are often lost for making careless mistakes. The PBP is measured by time (e.g. 2 years and 5 months), the ARR is expressed as a percentage (e.g. 12.6%), and the NPV is stated as a monetary value (e.g. $3.65 million).

In summary, when assessing the value of investment projects, it is important to consider how the value of money changes over time. Cash received in the future is not of the same value as if it were received today because the money could have been invested. Inflation also reduces the value of money in the future. So, it is important to calculate the present value of money in order to distinguish between the yields of investments over different time periods. American poet and philosopher Ralph Waldo Emerson (1803–1882) made this point clear in his quote: *"Money often costs too much."*

Investment appraisal and the CUEGIS concepts

Quantitative investment appraisal can be a useful strategic tool as decision-making becomes more objective. Risks are not eliminated but decisions are less prone to inaccuracies and subjectivity. Managers can use such techniques in order to justify their capital expenditure, as part of their business strategy.

Nevertheless, the accuracy of any quantitative investment appraisal is only as good as the quality and reliability of the data used. As the phrase "Garbage in, garbage out" implies, the use of inaccurate or biased data will reduce the validity of the estimated figures. In addition, changes in interest rates will affect the potential net gains of any quantitative investment appraisal. A final point is that investment appraisal may not capture all the relevant costs and benefits, further diminishing the value of such calculations and raising possible ethical questions about the firm's strategy.

For investments to flourish, businesses need to have a culture of risk taking, led by innovative entrepreneurs. In some countries such as Ethiopia and Bhutan, businesses are risk-averse (where the cultural norm is to avoid risks), whereas American and Singaporean companies are used to promoting entrepreneurial activity. Thus, they are more likely to generate innovative output and have more productive and profitable businesses despite the risks associated with investments.

The investment appraisal methods discussed in this chapter are all quantitative techniques. Business strategy does not, however, rely only on numerical data because the figures do not necessarily reveal the full picture. **Qualitative investment appraisal** methods that affect investment decisions can be remembered by the mnemonic PORSCHE©:

- **P**redictions (or gut feelings) – investment decisions are often based on the intuition of changes in the future, e.g. predictions and expectations of changes in interest rates.

- **O**bjectives – a profit-seeking firm, for example, will prefer to use quantitative methods but a firm with a strong ethical stance may not give numerical data such a high priority.

- **R**isk profile – firms with a low risk profile are less likely to opt for high-risk high-return investments, choosing instead to opt for lower risk projects with more certainty

and returns. This approach protects the business from change, especially if the risks do not pay off.

- **S**tate of the economy – if the level of business confidence is high, then higher risk projects might be undertaken. However, if interest rates are forecast to rise over the medium to long term, managers become less receptive to implementing change, so put off investment plans.

- **C**orporate image – organizations need to consider how an investment project might affect their public relations and corporate image. For example, will the attention and response of pressure groups such as Greenpeace be an ethical issue if the investment project goes ahead?

- **H**uman relations – for example, how will the change affect staff morale? Are the workers receptive to change, based on the organizational culture and workplace norms? Will automation cause mass redundancies?

- **E**xogenous shocks – external influences or events such as hurricanes, oil crises and other natural disasters of unquantifiable risk may have to be considered when making investment decisions.

Figure 3.8.c Destruction in Tacloban, Philippines caused by Typhoon Haiyan in 2013

In summary, investment decisions are not purely based on numerical calculations. Even if an investment appraisal suggests that a particular project is financially feasible, qualitative concepts such as ethics might be more important in making a final decision. For example, in 2006 the shareholders of Manchester United Football Club voted against a £70 million ($102m) sponsorship deal with Mansion, an online gambling company. Although the deal was lucrative, it went against the ethical principles of the Club. Hence, when it comes to strategic investment decisions, it is necessary to consider the wider context and the impact on the various stakeholders of the organization.

Finance and accounts

Theory of knowledge

Can quantitative investment appraisal ever be free of cultural bias?

CUEGIS Essay

With reference to an organization of your choice, examine how **ethics** and **globalization** have influenced the organization's investment decisions.

[20 marks]

CORE

REVIEW QUESTIONS

1. What is meant by investment?

2. What is investment appraisal?

3. What is the payback period and how is it calculated?

4. State the benefits and drawbacks of the payback period as a method of investment appraisal.

5. What is the average rate of return and how is it calculated?

6. What is meant by a discount factor? [HL only]

7. What is net present value (NPV) and how is it calculated? [HL only]

8. What are the advantages of the ARR and NPV over the payback period as methods of investment appraisal? [HL only]

9. Distinguish between quantitative and qualitative investment appraisal.

10. What does the mnemonic PORSCHE© stand for when referring to qualitative investment appraisal?

KEY TERMS

The **average rate of return** (ARR) calculates the average annual profit of an investment project, expressed as a percentage of the initial sum of money invested.

The **cumulative net cash flow** is the sum of an investment project's net cash flow for a particular year plus the net cash flows of all previous years.

A **discount rate** is the number used to reduce the value of a sum of money received in the future in order to determine its present (current) value.

Discounted cash flow uses a discount factor (the inverse of compound interest) to reduce the value of money received in future years because money loses its value over time.

Investment refers to the purchase of assets with the potential to yield future financial benefits, e.g. upgrading computer systems or the purchase of property (such as land and buildings).

Investment appraisal is a financial decision-making tool that helps managers to calculate whether certain investment projects should be undertaken based mainly on quantitative techniques.

Net present value (NPV) calculates the total discounted net cash flows minus the initial cost of an investment project. If the NPV is positive, then the project is viable on financial grounds.

The **payback period** (PBP) is an investment appraisal technique that calculates the length of time needed to recoup (earn back) the initial expenditure on an investment project.

The **principal** (or **capital outlay**) is the original amount spent on an investment project.

Qualitative investment appraisal refers to judging whether an investment project is worthwhile through non-numerical means, e.g. is the investment consistent with the corporate culture?

Quantitative investment appraisal refers to judging whether an investment project is worthwhile based on numerical (financial) interpretations, i.e. the PBP, ARR and NPV.

3.9 Budgets

"If you buy things you don't need, you'll soon be selling things you do." - Filipino proverb

HL content	Assessment objective
The importance of budgets for an organization	AO2
The difference between cost and profit centre	AO1
The roles of cost and profit centres	AO2
Variances	AO2, AO4
The role of budgets and variances in strategic planning	AO2

© IBO, 2017

The importance of budgets

The importance of budgets for organizations. AO2

© IBO, 2017

A budget is a financial plan of expected revenue and expenditure for an organization, or a department within an organization, for a given time period. Budgets can also be stated in terms of financial targets such as planned sales revenues, costs, cash flow or profits. Budgeting is an essential part of managing organizations. Budgets are needed when a business grows beyond a size that prevents the owner or controller from making all expenditure decisions.

Budgets should be set in line with the aims of the business. They allow resources to be allocated according to the expected level of business activity for a specified period of time, usually one year. This frees up time for the senior leadership team as they do not need to check and authorize all items of expenditure. However, if a budget holder is not operating within the allocated budget, then corrective measures can be taken to improve the situation.

Being a forward-looking financial plan, a budget is prepared in advance, usually on a monthly, quarterly or annual basis. The specific purpose of a budget depends on the type of budget used within an organization (see Box 3.9.a), although they all serve to help managers plan, monitor and control business activities.

Budgets are produced for four interrelated reasons: Planning and Guidance, Coordination, Control and Motivation.

Planning and guidance

Budgeting requires managers to plan for the future and to anticipate financial problems before they occur. This should help organizations be better prepared to overcome the problems should they arise. During the planning stage of budgeting, the following questions might be asked:

- How much should the firm spend on marketing activities in the forthcoming year?

- How many workers are needed and how much will they cost?

- How much money should be set aside as a *contingency fund* (for emergency use)?

These questions help to allocate budgets to different departments and divisions of the organization. They can also help to provide some guidance for managers and budget holders in their decision-making.

Coordination

A budget enables managers to control the organization's money, instead of the money controlling the business. Effective budgeting requires managers to match budget allocations with the aims of the organization. For example, the budget typically allocated to the Science and ICT departments in a school is understandably greater than that planned for the Psychology or History department.

A budget helps the entire workforce to focus on common goals. Without proper **budgetary control** (corrective measures taken to ensure that actual performance equals the budgeted performance), budget holders might make decisions that conflict with those made in other departments. For example, the marketing department might unknowingly budget sales revenue beyond the organization's productive capacity (see Unit 5.5). Likewise, the production department might budget to expand beyond the firm's financial means. Hence, coordinated and controlled budgeting leads to consistent and coordinated decision-making.

Box 3.9.a   Types of budgets

- **Flexible budgets** enable a business to adapt to changes in the business environment, e.g. rapid and sudden unexpected changes will result in actual outcomes being very different from budgeted outcomes.
- **Incremental budgets** add a certain percentage onto the previous year's budget, usually linked to the inflation rate, due to increased costs of production. Expenditure items are literally the same as before.
- **Marketing budgets** allow managers to plan their marketing activities, such as the amount planned for advertising, sponsorship, and sales promotion.
- **Production budgets** are plans for the level of output, including forecasts for the cost of stocks that need to be purchased. Overheads are included to help plan and manage capacity utilization (see Unit 5.5).
- **Sales budgets** are forecasts of the planned volume of sales and the value of sales revenue.
- **Staffing budgets** are financial plans of the monetary costs of staff for the organization over the next twelve months, e.g. the number of staff and the cost of labour, including training costs.
- **Zero budgeting** sets each budget holder's account to zero. The budget holder must seek prior approval for any planned expenditure. This helps to identify areas or departments that require large amounts of essential expenditure and those that require less. It also ensures budgets do not grow automatically.

In practice, whichever type of budget is used, budgets are consolidated into the overall budget, known as the **master budget**. The Chief Financial Officer (CFO) has general control and management of the master budget, including financial plans for capital expenditure on fixed assets that the business intends to purchase.

Control

Just as people cannot continually live beyond their means (i.e. spend more than they earn), budgeting helps to control business expenditure. Many businesses do not have proper cost control and therefore end up overspending. Without budgeting, managers are not held accountable for their actions and expenditure. This subsequently leads to all sorts of financial and cash flow problems (see Unit 3.7).

Figure 3.9.a Budgets help businesses to have better financial control

Budgets are used to keep better financial control. Budget holders are constrained by what they can do and are held accountable for their expenditure. Budgetary control and variance analysis (covered later in this Unit) help to identify areas where a department is perhaps overspending. Having tighter financial control can prevent a business going into debt, particularly in large organizations that delegate budgets to their middle and senior managers. As part of their performance appraisal (see Unit 2.1), budget holders will discuss their budgets with the appraiser. This provides an opportunity for the budget holder to express any areas of concern.

Motivational

According to motivational theorists such as Frederick Herzberg (see Unit 2.4), recognition, responsibility and employee participation can motivate workers. Delegating budgetary control to budget holders can therefore boost their level of morale as they feel valued and trusted. Involving staff in the budgeting process also helps to promote teamworking (a form of non-financial motivation). This leads to further benefits such as higher productivity and reduced absenteeism.

For businesses, budgetary control can help allocate and clarify responsibilities. For example, senior managers are placed in charge of larger budgets. It can also be linked to performance management, to recognise and reward those who achieve their performance targets.

Collectively, the four purposes of budgets provide benefits that lead to the improved operational efficiency of an organization. Having to work within a realistically set budget encourages managers to seek efficiency gains by drawing attention to wastage and inefficiencies, thereby possibly giving the business a competitive advantage over its rivals.

Theory of knowledge

Does the budgeting process allow for imagination? Is it necessary, or even possible, to have the same budgeting process in every country?

IB Learner Profile – Be a thinker

Do you think it is better to be principled or open-minded as a budget holder? Why?

Question 3.9.1   Budgeting for a holiday

Kay Edwards is a college student who has plans to visit Shanghai with her friends in the summer holidays. The cost of the vacation is expected to be around $500, all inclusive. Kay has a part-time job working in a local supermarket for which she is paid $150 per week. She spends an average of $110 per week, although this can vary. There are ten weeks until the summer holidays.

(a) Calculate and comment on whether Kay Edwards is likely to be able to afford her overseas holiday.   *[4 marks]*

(b) Outline how budgeting can help Kay in her financial plans.   *[4 marks]*

Shanghai skyline by night

Question 3.9.2   Tsingtao Brewery Company

The Tsingtao Brewery Company (*Tsingtao* for short) is China's second largest brewery. Founded in 1903, the company has been export-orientated since the 1980s with sales in more than 50 countries. *Tsingtao* is one of the top brands of consumer products exported from China. It has been the top selling Chinese beer in the USA since the early 1970s. To further enhance its brand development, *Tsingtao's* **budgeting** allocated funds to officially sponsor the 2008 Beijing Olympics, which was watched by 4.7 billion viewers worldwide. In 2013, *Tsingtao* confirmed a sponsorship deal with the British Superbike Championship, further widening its **brand awareness** and capitalising on the global sports audience.

(a) (i) Define the term **budgeting**.   *[2 marks]*

(a) (ii) Define the term **brand awareness**.   *[2 marks]*

(b) Examine the importance of budgeting to *Tsingtao Brewery Company*.   *[6 marks]*

Setting budgets

Bearing in mind the purpose and importance of budgets, there are several considerations when setting budgets:

- The available finance – The greater the financial strength of a business, the greater the budgeted expenditure can be allocated to each budget holder.

- Historical data – Budgets are often based on past trends, such as last year's budgeted figures. If economic forecasts are positive, then budgets may be set at a certain percentage above last year's figures.

- Organizational objectives – If a business is planning external growth, for example, then budgets need to be raised accordingly as both marketing and production budgets need to be significantly higher.

- Benchmarking – Businesses often set their budgets based on the budgets of their nearest competitors. Therefore, if Cadbury budgets for a $2 million marketing campaign, rivals Nestlé and Mars are likely to follow.

- Negotiations – Some budgets are set through discussions between budget holders and the senior manager in charge of the master budget.

Figure 3.9.b Data, such as crime rates, are used to set budgets for the Police Force

Limitations of budgeting

Despite the potential benefits of budgets (such as improved planning, coordination and control), there are numerous potential limitations:

- As with all forms of quantitative forecasts, there may be unforeseen changes that can cause large differences between the budgeted figures and the actual outcomes. This can make some budgets unrealistic and targets unachievable.

- There is a natural tendency for managers to overestimate their budgets because it becomes easier to meet their targets by doing so. However, this can cause complacency and wasteful or excessive expenditure.

- Budgets are often not permitted to be carried forward to the following tax year. This means that any surplus (known as a favourable variance) does not appear in the subsequent budget. Such practice gives little incentive for budget holders to spend within their budgets.

- Budgets can be set by senior managers who have no direct involvement in the running of the department. This can cause resentment and discontent as senior managers might not fully understand the needs of the department. Ideally, senior managers and budget holders should discuss and set budgets together.

- Whilst budgeting is useful for businesses with stable sales and costs, it is less useful for businesses with seasonal fluctuations in demand and where costs are harder to predict. This is especially the case for businesses that source their materials from overseas (due to fluctuations in exchange rates).

- Rigid and poorly allocated budgets can harm quality, e.g. a lower production budget might lead to the use of substandard raw materials and components being used. Lower quality output will affect sales and could damage the reputation of the business. Cutting the staffing budget can lead to pay cuts and/or job losses, which creates poor industrial relations (see Unit 2.6).

- The process of planning, setting, controlling, monitoring and reviewing budgets can be extremely time-consuming.

- Since finances are limited, one department's gain is another's loss. Budget holders compete to increase their own budgets, at the expense of their colleagues. Hence, budgeting can cause conflict in the workplace and perceptions of inequity (unfairness).

- Budgeting ignores qualitative factors that affect the financial performance of an organization, e.g. corporate social responsibilities (see Unit 1.3); responsibilities towards the natural environment (see Unit 1.5); non-financial motivation of staff (see Unit 2.4); and brand development (see Unit 4.5).

- The budgeting process is rather inflexible in today's fast-paced and constantly changing business environment. Hence, budgeting can be an inappropriate management tool.

Cost and profit centres

The difference between cost and profit centres. AO1

The roles of cost and profit centres. AO2

© IBO, 2014

As a business grows, managing its finances becomes more difficult. Costs and revenues from different areas of the business become harder to account for. Hence, different sections of the business are divided up into either cost centres or profit centres with a manager being held responsible for the costs and/or revenues incurred for each department (or centre).

A **cost centre** is a department or unit of a business that incurs costs but is not involved in making any profit. These costs are clearly attributed to the activities of that department, e.g. salaries, wages, lighting, components and capital expenditure. Making these different sections of a business aware and accountable for their contribution towards the firm's costs can help managers to have better cost control. Hence, a manager will be assigned to monitor and manage the expenditure of each cost centre. This allows the business to see which centres are costing the firm the most money.

A **profit centre** is a department or unit of a business that incurs both costs and revenues. Profit centres tend to be used by large diversified businesses that have a broad product mix. Again, a manager is responsible for each profit centre, including having to produce an independent profit and loss account. Each profit centre is responsible for contributing to the overall profits of the business. For example, a bank might split its profit centres based on geographical locations, i.e. branch by branch (Starbucks and McDonald's operate profit centres in this way). Alternatively, it might be based on the source of revenue, such as private banking, commercial banking, foreign exchange, mortgages, loans, insurance and financial planning. Having profit centres allows an organization to identify the areas that generate the most (and least) revenues. Ultimately, improved financial accountability and efficiency lead to improved cost control and therefore higher profits for the business.

Exam tip!

It is possible for businesses to operate both profit centres and cost centres. For example, retailers such as Marks & Spencer, 7-Eleven and Zara operate profit centres for each of their outlets, but operate cost centres in their own head office, market research teams and advertising departments.

Question 3.9.3   Cathay Pacific Airways Limited

Cathay Pacific, Hong Kong's national flag carrier, is one of Asia's largest airline companies. It operates over 200 routes worldwide in over 60 countries. *Cathay Pacific's* operations are varied and include divisions that are responsible for in-flight entertainment, food catering, Members Lounge, The Marco Polo Club (frequent flyer programme) and Codeshare Agreements (a **strategic alliance** with Oneworld member airlines). It also wholly owns *Cathay Dragon* (formally Dragonair), an international airline based in Hong Kong. *Cathay Pacific* is one of just six airline companies that has received the prestigious 'Airline of the Year' from Skytrax, specialists in commercial air transport research and consultancy.

(a) Define the term **strategic alliance**.   [2 marks]

(b) Explain why businesses such as *Cathay Pacific* use cost and profit centres.   [4 marks]

(c) Comment on the likely difficulties involved in allocating *Cathay Pacific's* overheads.   [4 marks]

Table 3.9.a   Advantages and disadvantages of cost and profit centres

Advantages	Disadvantages
Managers are forced to be more accountable for their department's contribution towards the organization's costs, especially as the direct costs of production can easily be allocated to cost and profit centres.	Allocating indirect costs (such as rent, insurance and administrative costs) is a subjective task. Hence, it can be difficult to accurately calculate the overheads attributable to each cost or profit centre.
Managers can identify areas of weakness. It is not always clear if a certain part of a business is making a loss, especially if the organization as a whole is profitable. Using cost and profit centres allows a business to identify loss-making sections or products of the business.	The profits of a department can change simply because of the apportionment of fixed costs. Allocating a greater proportion of costs to a particular centre will reduce its profits, although this does not represent its underlying trading position.
Departments and smaller teams tend to work better than larger ones which may suffer from disorganization and a lack of communication. Accountability can promote better team spirit and productivity within the different areas of an organization.	The performance of a department can change because of external factors beyond its control, such as higher raw material prices. This therefore bears no reflection of the productivity and efficiency of the individual departments.
There is no need to fuss about whether a cost is fixed, variable, indirect or direct. All costs can be allocated or spread across the various cost and profit centres of a business.	Data collection is required to accurately account for all costs and revenues of each cost or profit centre. This is likely to be expensive and time consuming.
Benchmarking with the most efficient cost and profit centres within the organization can help to improve its overall efficiency.	Managing cost and profit centres can add to the pressure and stress on staff. This might lead to motivational and productivity issues.
Delegating power to those in charge of cost and profit centres can help to motivate these people. Delegation also helps to speed up decision-making in the organization.	Departments are less likely to consider social responsibilities and ethical objectives if they are run as profit centres. This is because compliance costs lower their profits.
The performance of cost and profit centres can be used to encourage and reward teams. Teams that achieve their targets and/or operate effectively within their budget may be rewarded accordingly.	In an attempt to cut costs and/or raise revenues, unnecessary internal competition might result. This can create tension and conflict between the various sections of an organization.

Variance analysis

Variances. AO2, AO4

The role of budgets and variances in strategic planning. AO2

© IBO, 2017

Recall that budgetary control is the use of corrective measures taken to ensure that actual outcomes equal the budgeted outcomes. A **variance** exists if there is a difference between the budgeted figure and the actual outcome. Budgetary control requires managers to investigate the cause(s) of any variance.

Variance = Actual outcome – Budgeted outcome

There are two types of variance:

- **Favourable variances** exist when the discrepancies are financially beneficial to the organization. For example, if actual marketing costs amount to $220,000 but the budgeted value was $250,000, then the business has a favourable variance of $30,000. Alternatively, if sales revenue was budgeted at $500,000 but the actual sales were $520,000, then there would be a favourable variance of $20,000.

- **Adverse variances** (or **unfavourable variances**) exist when the discrepancies are financially detrimental to the organization. They occur when actual costs are higher than expected (i.e. overspending) or when actual revenue is lower than budgeted (i.e. underselling).

Budget holders need to investigate the causes of any variance. For example, if an adverse variance is the result of overspending, then senior management will demand an explanation. There could be valid reasons for this, such as a supplier hiking prices after the budget had been set or because the business switched to using better-quality inputs in the production process (which cost more than budgeted).

Exam tip !
Favourable or positive?

There is no such thing as a positive (or negative) variance. Mathematically, a 'positive' variance exists when the actual outcome exceeds the planned or budgeted outcome. However, this might not be beneficial if we are referring to production and marketing budgets (as this would mean incurring higher costs than planned). Therefore, for clarity, we only talk about favourable (and adverse) variances.

Variance analysis helps managers to monitor and control budgets. Adverse variances provide warnings of falling revenues and/or rising costs. Managers can then implement corrective measures to offset these unfavourable variances. Variance analysis also helps in the review and revision of annual budgets. For example, if there is an adverse variance in the production budget due to rising raw material costs, then more funds can be allocated to the production department.

Consider the data in Table 3.9.b, which shows the budgeted and actual figures for Sharma Visual Arts Company. It is common in variance analysis to use the abbreviations (F) for favourable variances, and (A) for adverse variances.

Theory of knowledge

Is variance analysis an art or a science?

From the table, we can see the following:

- Sales are $5,000 higher than budgeted (planned), so this is financially beneficial to the organization, i.e. there is a favourable variance of $5,000.

- Staffing costs were budgeted at $25,000 but the business only spent $23,000 thus saving $2,000, i.e. a favourable variance.

- There is an adverse variance of $3,000 for raw materials as the company planned to spend $15,000 but actually spent $18,000.

- Since there is overspending of $2,000 on the marketing budget, this represents an adverse variance for the company.

- Finally, the planned expenditure on rent matches the actual spending on rent, so no variance exists in this instance.

Variances do not have to be expressed in monetary terms. Some businesses prefer to use percentage figures to show discrepancies between budgeted and actual values. For example, the sales variance for Sharma Visual Arts Company is 10% (F) higher than the budgeted figure ($55,000 compared with $50,000). Either way, once variances have been calculated managers need to investigate the causes and to implement corrective measures. It is common for managers to place greater emphasis on investigating the areas with adverse variances.

Table 3.9.b   Variance analysis for Sharma Visual Arts Company, period ending 31 March

	Actual value ($)	Budgeted value ($)	Variance ($)
Sales	55,000	50,000	5,000 (F)
Staffing	23,000	25,000	2,000 (F)
Raw materials	18,000	15,000	3,000 (A)
Marketing	14,000	12,000	2,000 (A)
Rent	20,000	20,000	0

Exam tip!
Worked example

Question: Complete the missing figures in the 'Variance' column and state whether the variance is adverse or favourable.

[5 marks]

Budget variances for The Wok Express

	Budgeted figure ($'000)	Actual figure ($'000)	Variance
Sales	500	495	
Cost of sales	200	210	
Gross profit	300	285	
Expenses	100	90	
Net profit	200	195	

Answer:

Budget variances for The Wok Express

	Budgeted figure ($'000)	Actual figure ($'000)	Variance (%) (answer 1)	Variance (%) (answer 2)
Sales	500	495	5 (A)	1% (A)
Cost of sales	200	210	10 (A)	5% (A)
Gross profit	300	285	15 (A)	5% (A)
Expenses	100	90	10 (F)	10% (F)
Net profit	200	195	5 (A)	2.5% (A)

Question 3.9.4   Laptops R Us

(a) Complete the table below for Laptops R Us and identify variances as adverse or favourable.   *[5 marks]*

Variable	Budget	Actual	Variance
Sales of laptop A (units)	250	180	
Sales of laptop B (units)	250	260	
Production costs ($'000)	120	150	
Output per worker (units)	20	22	
Labour costs ($'000)	100	115	

(b) Use your answers from the table to explain why variances are referred to as favourable or adverse variances rather than as positive or negative.   *[4 marks]*

(c) Calculate the variance, in financial terms, for each of the cases below. Show your working.

(i) Laptops R Us had budgeted for $6,000 operating costs in 100 machine hours. However, actual operating costs totalled $5,850 in 100 machine hours.   *[2 marks]*

(ii) Laptops R Us had budgeted production of 250 units of Laptop A in 10 machine hours. Variable costs are $100 per machine hour. In fact, 250 units are produced in 8 machine hours.   *[3 marks]*

Question 3.9.5   Quay's Hair Salon Inc.

Dianna Quay runs a hair salon in Florida, USA. Details of the firm's latest budget are shown below:

Variable	Budgeted ($)	Actual Outcome ($)	Variance ($)	Variance (F/A)
Wages	4,000	4,200		
Salaries	4,500	4,500		
Stock	1,800	1,850		
Revenue	15,700		290	Favourable
Direct costs		2,950	250	Favourable

(a) State **two** examples of 'stock' that are likely to be held by *Quay's Hair Salon Inc.*   *[2 marks]*

(b) State **two** specific examples of direct costs likely to be incurred by *Quay's Hair Salon Inc.*   *[2 marks]*

(c) Complete the missing figures for *Quay's Hair Salon Inc.*   *[5 marks]*

Exam tip !

Adverse variances do not necessarily represent a 'bad' situation for a business. For example, an adverse production (costs) or staff budget might simply have been caused by an increase in output to meet an unplanned surge in demand.

Common mistake

Many candidates state that variance analysis is a useful planning tool. It is important to remember that variance analysis refers only to past data as variances cannot be calculated until the end of the budgeting period. Hence, it raises questions that can aid business planning, but it is not a planning tool in itself.

Budgets and the CUEGIS concepts

Budgeting helps to ensure that managers plan ahead by anticipating the costs and revenues of different business activities. It also involves managers agreeing on priorities and targets. Hence, budgeting has a central role in strategic planning and strategic decision-making. Budgeting is a process, as summarised in Figure 3.9.c.

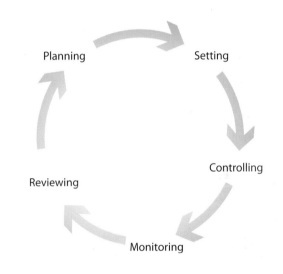

Figure 3.9.c The budgeting process

The way in which budgets are used largely depends on the firm's organizational culture. Organizations that adopt an authoritarian culture tend to be arranged by a tightly controlled budgetary system, such as a zero budgeting arrangement. Targets might also be imposed upon budget holders without any discussion or negotiation. Budget holders are likely to be held accountable for all variance, no matter how minor these might be. By contrast, organizations that have an open and entrusting culture tend to use budgets as a form of empowerment and motivation. Budget holders are likely to be held accountable for all variance, no matter how minor these might be.

Since budgets are financial plans used to achieve strategic goals of the organization, **SMART budgeting** requires budgets to be:

- *Specific* – Budgets should be set in line with the strategic vision of an organization.

- *Measurable* – Any budgeting system should ensure that budget holders are held accountable for their successes or shortcomings. Variance analysis can help in this case.

- *Agreed* – For budgeting to work properly, the budgets should be set through a process of negotiations and discussions to ensure that appropriate budgets are set.

- *Realistic* – Only realistically set budgets can motivate people to reach the set targets. Under-funding will hinder output, whilst over-funding is likely to lead to complacency and wastage.

- *Timed constrained* – Since budgets are financial plans for the foreseeable future, there must be a time constraint. Some businesses allow budget holders to carry forward any unspent funds, whilst other organizations do not encourage this.

During times of change, budgets need to be adjusted to account for strategic and tactical changes. However, unless budgets are adjusted accordingly, the plans and targets become unrealistic or irrelevant. For instance, if the budgeting process is too rigid, the business will not be in a position to respond to changes in the external environment (see Unit 1.5). Therefore, variances have to be examined in context of what has been happening within the business.

Ethical decision-making should also be considered. For example, highly experienced budget holders might be able to negotiate higher budgets so do not have to control costs compared to other budget holders. As organizations become larger, it becomes increasingly difficult for the master budget holders to fully understand all items of business expenditure, so they become reliant on professional or ethical conduct of all budget holders. Also, budgets can lose their purpose if they are unfairly or inappropriately set. In the wrong hands, access to large budgets could lead to unethical use of the funds.

Case study

Enron was once the seventh largest American company and had been voted by Fortune magazine as the "most innovative company" for six consecutive years. However, in 2001, the company went bankrupt due to accounting fraud, which left its investors and 20,600 employees with absolutely nothing.

Case study

In 1995, Barings Bank (established in 1762) collapsed due to illegal insider trading from one of the bank's employees, Nick Leeson, who lost £827 m ($1.4 bn) on the stocks and futures exchange. The bank was subsequently acquired by Dutch financial services provider ING Group for a nominal fee of just £1 ($1.45).

Innovation could be hampered if managers become unwilling to take risks that could lead to adverse variances in their budgets. However, budgets are integral to any growth strategy. Not only are financial plans needed to fund the innovation and growth, budgeting also enables a business to have better cost control as it grows, because costs will clearly increase.

However, budgeting does not come without its problems for business strategy. For example, sales forecasting (see Unit 4.3), which is a prerequisite to setting the sales budget, is only as accurate as the quality of the data used to make the sales predictions.

Nevertheless, used ethically and correctly, budgets can motivate and empower budget holders, foster responsibility and accountability, and aid financial control. Ultimately, effective budgeting avoids inefficient expenditure, thus helping to enhance the organization's competitive strength and supporting its strategic vision.

Theory of knowledge

Do budgets hinder or foster innovation in businesses?

CUEGIS Essay

With reference to an organization of your choice, examine how budgeting influences **innovation** and **strategy**.   *[20 marks]*

REVIEW QUESTIONS

1. What is meant by a budget?

2. Outline four types of budgets.

3. State four reasons for producing budgets.

4. What are the main considerations when setting budgets?

5. What is budgetary control and why is it important to an organization?

6. What are the main limitations of budgeting?

7. Distinguish between cost and profit centres.

8. What are the advantages and disadvantages of businesses using cost and profit centres?

9. What is variance analysis and why is it an important management tool?

10. Distinguish between favourable and adverse variances.

KEY TERMS

Adverse variances are discrepancies between actual outcomes and budgeted outcomes that are detrimental to an organization, such as production costs being higher than expected.

A **budget** is a financial plan of expected revenue and expenditure for a department or an organization, for a given period of time.

Budgetary control refers to the use of corrective measures taken to ensure that actual outcomes equal the budgeted outcomes, by systematic monitoring of budgets and investigating the reasons for any variances.

Contingency fund is a reserve budget that is set aside for emergency and back-up use.

A **cost centre** is a department or unit of a business that incurs costs but is not involved in making any profit. These costs are clearly attributed to the activities of that department, e.g. salaries, wages, lighting, components and capital expenditure.

Favourable variances are discrepancies between actual outcomes and budgeted outcomes that benefit an organization, such as sales revenues being higher than expected.

The **master budget** is the overall or consolidated budget, comprised of all separate budgets. The Chief Financial Officer (CFO) has general control and management of the master budget.

A **profit centre** is a department or unit of a business that incurs both costs and revenues. Profit centres tend to be used by large diversified businesses that have a broad product mix.

SMART budgets are specific, measurable, agreed, realistic and time constrained. This helps to ensure that budgets are appropriately set in order to facilitate budgetary control.

Variance refers to any discrepancy between actual outcomes and budgeted outcomes.

Variance analysis is the management process of comparing planned and actual costs and revenues, in order to measure and compare the degree of budgetary success.

4.1 The role of marketing

"The greatest pleasure in life is doing what people say you cannot do." - Walter Bagehot (1826–1877), British journalist

SL/HL content	Assessment objective
Marketing and its relationship with other business functions	AO1
The differences between marketing of goods and marketing of services	AO2
Market orientation versus product orientation	AO2
The difference between commercial marketing and social marketing	AO2
Characteristics of the market in which an organization operates	AO1
Market share	AO4
The importance of market share and market leadership	AO3
The marketing objectives of for-profit organizations and non-profit organizations	AO3
How marketing strategies evolve as a response to changes in customer preferences	AO3
How innovation, ethical considerations and cultural differences may influence marketing practices and strategies in an organization	AO3

© IBO, 2017

Definition and nature of marketing

Marketing and its relationship with other business functions. AO1

© IBO, 2017

People have different needs and wants. **Needs** are the essential necessities that all humans must have to survive: food, shelter, warmth and water. **Wants** are human desires, i.e. things that people would like to have. Irrespective of personal income or wealth, humans have infinite wants. **Marketing** exists to address people's needs and wants. It is about making customers want to buy the products of a particular business. It therefore looks at the reasons behind people's decisions, such as the price and the product's features (e.g. colour, size, quality or special features of a product). Meeting the needs and wants of customers is particularly important for businesses aiming to make a profit.

Legendary reggae songwriter and singer Bob Marley (1945–1981) famously said that he did not need a BMW (what he described as an expensive car) as he already had an alternative 'BMW' (Bob Marley and the Wailers). This sums up the challenge facing marketers who must tempt customers to buy their products. Management guru Peter F. Drucker famously said, *"Business has only two functions - marketing and innovation"*.

The marketing department of an organization tends to have four main or generic objectives:

- Ensure that the right **products** are supplied to fulfill the needs and wants of customers.

- Set the correct **price** so that customers can afford to buy the product (and to ensure that they do not buy from a rival business).

- Distribute (or **place**) the products conveniently for customers to buy the product.

- Ensure that there is adequate and effective **promotion** to convince customers to buy the firm's products.

There is no single universally accepted definition of the term 'marketing' because it is a complex process and differs from one type of organization to another. For example, the marketing objectives and strategies of charitable and non-

351

profit organizations differ from those of large multinational companies. A widely used and accepted definition is provided by the Chartered Institute of Marketing which defines marketing as:

"The management process involved in identifying, anticipating and satisfying consumer requirements profitably".

This definition is commonly used as it covers the various roles of marketing:

- Marketing is a management process, so it requires people to take responsibility for decision-making.

- Marketing involves identifying the needs and wants of customers. This can be done through market research (see Unit 4.4) and data analysis.

- Marketing involves anticipating or predicting what customers might want in the future. For example, market research and new product development have created markets for laptops, smartphones, hybrid cars and smart TVs. The movie industry is constantly trying to produce films that audiences might want to see.

- Price, availability and quality are essential factors that customers consider when assessing value for money. Satisfied customers are more likely to become loyal customers.

- Marketing is about earning profit profit (or a financial surplus for non-profit organizations). Prices must therefore cover the costs of production. Car manufacturers would not use promotions such as 'buy one get one free' as part of their marketing. All organizations must ensure that the benefits of their marketing outweigh the costs.

Marketing is fundamental to the success of a business as it affects the sales and profits of the organization. However, marketing alone does not ensure success. Its relationship with other business functions should also be considered:

- **Operations management**   The production department works closely with the marketers in using sales forecasts (from market research) to prepare their production schedules. These departments also work directly with each other to research, develop and launch products to meet the changing needs of customers. There may, however, be some conflict between the two departments as production managers may prefer a longer time period

in which to test and develop products whereas marketing managers may urge for a quick launch to maximise sales revenues. Delays in launching a product not only means lost sales but can also be damaging to the organization's corporate image.

- **Finance and accounts**   The marketing department works closely with the finance department to set appropriate budgets. Again, there can be conflict between these departments. For example, marketers might wish to exceed their budget to get maximum marketing exposure. However, the finance team wants all departments to work within their allocated budgets. The finance department would want prices to cover costs of production to generate a profit for the organization. However, marketers might feel that low prices (that do not necessarily cover all costs) are necessary for some products in the short term to get established in the market. Marketers might also use extended credit facilities (such as interest-free repayment plans) to entice customers. However, the finance department will be aware that extended credit can lead to liquidity problems (see Unit 3.7). Hence, both departments need to work collaboratively to strike a balance between their potentially conflicting interests.

- **Human resources (HR)**   Marketing data can help the HR department to identify staffing needs. For example, the introduction of a new product might require hiring extra production staff and sales personnel. The HR department's role is to ensure the business has the right quantity and quality of workers through effective workforce planning (see Unit 2.1) to meet the wants and needs of its customers.

Figure 4.1.a Marketing alone does not ensure success

Marketing goods and services

The differences between marketing of goods and marketing of services. AO2

© IBO, 2017

There are similarities and differences in the marketing of goods and services. For example, both use promotion to build brand recognition, brand awareness and trust. The differences between the marketing of goods and services include the following characteristics:

- **Intangibility** Whilst goods are tangible (physical), services are intangible. Marketers face a challenge to communicate the benefits of the service, e.g. why should customers use a particular hair salon? The choice is based largely on trust. By contrast, marketers tend to have less challenges selling a physical product with tangible attributes that customers can inspect before buying.

- **Inseparability** Services are consumed at the time of purchase, e.g. bus ride, watching a movie at the cinema, or having a massage at a health spa. Inseparability means it is not possible to separate the production and consumption of a service. Marketers strive to ensure the staff are well trained at providing outstanding and consistent customer services.

- **Heterogeneity** It is common to mass produce standardised (homogeneous) goods such as smartphones, books or soft drinks. However, services are heterogeneous because the experience is different for different customers. If customers experience poor customer service, they are likely to opt to use the services provided by other providers.

- **Perishability** Unlike goods, services cannot be stored. For example, each bus, cinema or airline seat that is empty means a loss in potential revenues to the businesses. By contrast, most goods are durable to some extent. For example, Coca-Cola is mass produced and stored in warehouses before distribution to wholesalers and retailers so can be marketed using international marketing strategies (see Unit 4.7).

- **Product strategy** Many businesses provide value-added services to attract customers, e.g. supermarkets and fast food restaurants in many parts of the world offer a free delivery service. Coffee shops, banks and hotels often offer free Wi-Fi. Service companies also have to decide on whether their offerings will be standardised or customised.

Figure 4.1.b Most coffee shops provide wi-fi services

- **Price strategy** As people are a fundamental aspect of marketing services, the cost and hence the price can to be quite high. A challenge for marketers is to get the right pricing strategy for a service that appeals to customers, covers costs of production and generates profit for the business. The pricing decision depends on the source of value to customers, e.g. lawyers, accountants and surgeons provide highly specialised services that would be reflected in the price. Some service providers base their pricing strategy on time spent on providing the service whilst others base it on the level of skills required to provide the service.

- **Promotional strategy** Promoting a service can be a challenge for marketers as it is intangible. Businesses often use the physical environment to promote their services, (such as hotels, gyms and schools) so that customers can visualise the quality of the service being provided. Other common promotional strategies include the use of branding, slogans, logos and celebrity endorsements (see Unit 4.5).

- **Place strategy** The location decision is vital for the marketing of services - customers are unlikely to visit restaurants, hotels, theatres, banks and retailers in highly inconvenient or remote locations. By contrast, most goods can be ordered online (such as books, music, DVDs, clothes or even food products), so the location decision is less important provided there are effective distribution channels to deliver the products to customers. Some retailers, such as petrol stations or supermarkets, often have ATM cash machines, providing added convenience for their customers.

CORE

Marketing

Further information about the marketing of goods is covered in Unit 4.5 (the marketing mix). The marketing of services is covered in more detail in Unit 4.6 (the extended marketing mix) for Higher Level students.

Theory of knowledge

How can we know if it is more difficult to market a good or a service?

Market and product orientation

Market orientation versus product orientation. AO2

© IBO, 2017

Market orientation is a marketing approach used by businesses that are outward looking. They focus on making products that they can sell, rather than selling products that they can make. Market orientation focuses on the customer in order to identify, design, develop and supply products that meet their needs and wants. Such information can be gathered from market research (see Unit 4.4), e.g. the pricing decision is taken after considering information about customers, such as their level of income. Market research and analyses are therefore central to a market orientation approach.

If the needs and wants of customers are ignored, businesses are likely to become uncompetitive, with devastating results in the long term. Market orientation means that businesses do not worry about the costs of doing things for the customer; instead, they consider the costs of not doing these things. For example, home furniture retailer IKEA provides added-value facilities to meet the needs of their customers, such as restaurants, adult-supervised play areas for young children (whilst their parents are shopping), changing rooms and free car parking.

The two main advantages to a business in being market orientated are:

- **Greater flexibility** Businesses can respond quickly to changes in the market as they have access to relevant data and information about customers. Market orientated businesses are also more able to anticipate changing market trends and hence prepare for such changes.

- **Lower risk** Market orientated businesses can be more confident that their products will sell and be more

successful. Without proper market research and analysis, the cost of marketing a product is much more likely to be a gamble.

The main disadvantage of market orientation is that market research (needed to found out what customers want) can be very expensive. In addition, given the dynamic nature of the business environment and the uncertainty of the future, there is no guarantee that this approach will work.

Whether a business adopts a product orientated or market orientated approach depends on several factors, including:

- The market – Producers of hi-tech products, such as smartphones, tend to start off as product orientated businesses. In mass consumer markets, a more market orientated approach tends to be adopted.

- Organizational culture – Businesses that believe customers are the key stakeholder (i.e. that customers are always right) are more likely to be market orientated.

- Barriers to entry – Businesses without much competition tend to be less customer-focused. Such organizations have market power in pricing and distribution decisions so can be more product-orientated.

Product orientation is a marketing approach adopted by businesses that are *inward* looking. They focus on selling products that they make, rather than making products that they can sell. As Steve Jobs said, *"A lot of times, people don't know what they want until you show it to them."* Many hi-tech products that are used in daily life were created using product orientation. Innovative products such as the automobile, television, mobile phone, the Internet and digital media players were all 'unknown' to the mass market during their initial launch. Even Henry Ford did not originally realise that the automobile would become a mass market product.

Economists use Say's law ('*supply creates its own demand*') to describe how product orientation might be successful. The idea is that creative and innovative products are launched onto the market and customers will be tempted to buy these. For example, Microsoft's Kinect sold 10 million units within 3 months of its launch. Sony sold one million PlayStation 4 games consoles in the USA and Canada – within the first 24 hours of its launch. Of course, not all products are successful. The usual result is that product orientation is rather hit-and-miss, i.e. producers are not really sure if the products will sell.

Many product oriented businesses today concentrate on producing high quality products. The belief is that customers are willing to pay a higher price for exclusivity and luxury products. Product orientated businesses generally supply products that they specialise in, such as Ferrari producing sports cars or Airbus producing aircraft. The main advantages of product orientation are that quality can be assured and the business has more control over its operations. Also, by being innovative, product orientation can give organizations a competitive advantage or a unique selling point (USP). For example, Apple gained a USP for its iconic iPhone's 'slide to unlock' technology.

Figure 4.1.c Aircraft manufacturers are product-orientated

However, since the needs of the market are ignored (because product orientated organizations assume they know what the market wants), there is a high failure rate of businesses that use this marketing approach. Hence, the strategy tends to be of high risk, especially due to frequent changes in fashion and tastes. The money spent on research and development of products without taking the customer into consideration, often proves costly.

Commercial marketing and social marketing

The difference between commercial marketing and social marketing. AO2

© IBO, 2017

Commercial marketing is the use of marketing strategies to meet the needs and wants of customers in a profitable way. Unlike social marketing, commercial marketing is largely value free, i.e. ethics play a small role, if any at all. Commercial marketing is about providing what customers want, when they want it and where they want it. There may be controversies with the marketing of fast food, soft drinks, tobacco or alcohol but commercial marketing aims to reap the private benefits of marketing such products, i.e. to earn increased sales revenues and profits. The vast majority of marketing activities is commercial marketing. For instance, the traditional marketing mix (see Unit 4.5) focuses mainly on commercial marketing, i.e. getting the right products to the right customers, in the right place and at the right price.

CORE

Question 4.1.1   Sony

Sony Corporation, formerly the market leader in consumer electronics, had built up a reputation of innovation since its beginnings in 1946. However, its complacency during the late 1990s meant that the Japanese company had to play catch-up. In 2003, *Sony* launched its luxury line of gadgets under the Qualia brand name. This included a ¥380,000 ($25,700) digital camera and a ¥1.5 m ($101,500) audio system.

The big problem, however, was that *Sony* seemed to be more obsessed about the pricey technology than what their **customers** wanted. The Qualia line of products was not well received by customers, especially with the growing competition from the likes of Samsung and Apple. For example, Apple's iPod was outselling *Sony's* digital music players by a ratio of 5 to 1. Critics argued that *Sony* had lost touch with its consumers.

(a) Define the term **customers**.   *[2 marks]*

(b) Outline why *Sony* might be described as a 'product-orientated' business.   *[2 marks]*

(c) Explain **two** disadvantages of product-orientated marketing to businesses such as *Sony*.   *[4 marks]*

Marketing

The Social Marketing Institute defines **social marketing** as *"the planning and implementation of programs designed to bring about social change using concepts from commercial marketing".* Social marketing is therefore the use of mainstream marketing methods to achieve the benefits of social change, such as informing the public about the dangers of under-age drinking. Commercial marketing might support the tobacco industry by arguing that smoking can help people to relax, that it is people's choice to smoke and that it creates jobs. Social marketing focuses on benefits from a different stance, e.g. smoking bans in public areas help to reduce air pollution and create less litter for the benefit of everyone. Social marketing is similar to commercial marketing in that all forms of marketing aim to influence action. Essentially, the marketing process in social marketing is largely the same as commercial marketing but the aim or priority is different.

Figure 4.1.d Smoking is increasingly viewed as antisocial behaviour

Professor Philip Kotler (1971) is credited as the founder of social marketing. He defined social marketing as any activity that seeks to influence social behaviour to benefit the target audience and society as a whole. Aids awareness, anti-smoking, anti-drink-driving, and unwanted teenage pregnancies are examples of social marketing campaigns. This differs markedly from commercial marketing, which focuses on benefits for customers and the business.

The challenge facing social marketers is getting people to change their customary behaviour. Nicotine in tobacco is addictive so getting smokers to change can be difficult. The same applies to drivers who claim they 'need' to drive rather than use public transport.

The clients of social marketing agencies tend to be non-profit organizations (such as charities) and government organizations. However, companies that believe in corporate social responsibility (see Unit 1.3) also use social marketing such as sponsoring events in the local community. This could help to enhance their corporate image. NPOs will also strive to increase their distribution channels (see Unit 4.5) just like any private sector organization. For example, the Red Cross has donation boxes in retail outlets such as supermarkets. NPOs tend to focus more on promoting the image or cause (rather than the product) of the organization for its long-term survival.

Market research (see Unit 4.4) has an important role in social marketing. For example, in order to change people's behaviour, marketers must discover people's perceptions of the issue or problem in question. This helps to determine the actions that might be taken to deal with the social problem. For example, if people do not feel that recycling is a convenient option, then this problem must be corrected by taking appropriate action such as lobbying governments to educate people about the benefits of recycling.

Process is also an important part of social marketing. For example, it must be convenient for people to donate money to charity, perhaps by credit card or online payments. Charities and pressure groups in many countries have also managed to persuade governments to give tax benefits to those who donate money to charitable organizations.

When considering pricing decisions in social marketing, marketers tend to refer to the net benefits, i.e. the difference between the benefits and the costs of taking action. If people believe that the benefits are greater than the costs, then social marketers are more likely to achieve their objectives. In countries where littering is heavily fined, such as Singapore and Hong Kong, people are more likely to refrain from doing so as the cost of littering far outweighs any benefit.

Case study

The "Dumb Ways to Die" social marketing campaign by *Metro Trains Melbourne, Australia* was a huge hit that promoted safety around trains. The catchy song and accompanying music video (www.metrotrains.com.au/) went viral, with over 167 million hits on YouTube (the tagline appears at the end of the video).
Metro Trains Melbourne reported a 21% decline in the number of accidents following the release of its "Dumb Ways to Die campaign". Watch the original video clip here: https://goo.gl/mWYQxR.

Question 4.1.2 Singapore's littering policy

Singapore is considered to be one of the cleanest countries in the world. However, clean cities do not simply come about by chance. Singapore imposes strict laws against littering of any kind. First-time offenders are fined up to S$1,000 ($650). Repeat offenders can be fined up to S$50,00 ($3,265) and face imprisonment. They may be placed under the Corrective Work Order (CWO), which requires litterbugs to spend up to 12 hours of community service cleaning a public place, wearing bright coloured jackets to draw public attention. The government also 'names and shames' offenders by inviting the media to cover the spectacle. Litter laws are taught in schools and promoted by the government to ingrain Singapore's culture of cleanliness.

(a) Define the meaning of **social marketing**. *[2 marks]*

(b) Examine the role of social marketing for the success of the Singaporean government in dealing with litter problems. *[6 marks]*

The main differences between social marketing and commercial marketing include:

- Purpose – The intention of commercial marketing is selling physical goods and intangible services for a profit. Social marketing aims to influence or persuade a desired change in social behaviour or attitudes.

- Benefits – Commercial marketing exists to satisfy individual needs and wants, and thus reaps profit for the business. Social marketing, if successful, satisfies the needs and desires of the general public, and thus reaps benefits for communities.

- Main users – Commercial marketing is used mainly by private sector businesses (although many social marketing campaigns use aspects of commercial marketing strategies). Social marketing is used mainly by the government and non-governmental organizations (NGOs).

The market

Characteristics of the market in which an organization operates.
AO1
© IBO, 2017

A **market** is a place or process whereby customers and suppliers trade. A market exists where there is demand for a particular product (such as textbooks, flowers, laptops or taxi services) and where there is a willingness from businesses to supply these products. Customers can be private individuals, other businesses or the government. Markets that cater for private individuals (i.e. the general public) are known as **consumer markets**, whilst those that cater for organizations (businesses and governments) are known as **industrial markets** or **producer markets**.

Within any particular market, there is likely to be a number of substitute products and suppliers that can be used to satisfy the needs and wants of the consumer. For example, in the luxury clothing industry, the market consists of competitors such as Gucci, Armani, Ralph Lauren and Dior.

Managers are interested in the characteristics of the market in which their business operates. These characteristics include:

- **Market size**   Markets differ in their size as measured by sales revenue. The market for fast food is huge and there is room for growth, especially in overseas markets. The market for horse saddles is much smaller. International trade and globalization have meant that the size of a market is not confined to the domestic market.

- **Customer base**   As an alternative measure of market size, this refers to the total potential number of customers in a particular market. Multinational companies have been expanding into China and India partly because they account for a third of the world's population. The Internet has also broadened the customer base for many businesses around the world.

CORE

Marketing

357

Figure 4.1.e International trade has been a major driver of globalization

- **Barriers to entry** These are obstacles that determine the number of suppliers in the market. In markets such as oil and aircraft manufacturing, the entry barriers are extremely high as there are huge set-up costs and existing businesses already dominate with their market power and huge economies of scale. In other markets where entry barriers are relatively low, there are a lot more businesses that operate on a much smaller scale.

- **Competition** This refers to the degree of rivalry within a particular market. The market for soft drinks, sports apparel or aircraft manufacturing is dominated by only a small number of producers. As the businesses have significant market power, the intensity of competition can be very high in such markets.

- **Geographic characteristics** Some markets focus on a particular area, country or region. For example, Adidas is the market leader in the supply of equipment for Taekwondo (a popular form of martial arts) with around four-fifths of the world's black belt holders residing in Korea. Another example is the one billion vegetarians who reside in India. Other markets, such as motor vehicles or smartphones, target a global audience.

- **Demographic characteristics** Characteristics of consumers include differences in gender, age, ethnicity and religion. For example, the market for Porsche sports cars comprises mainly of males aged 35 and above who earn higher than average incomes. The majority of the customer base for Hot Wheel toy cars is parents who have children aged twelve and below. Marketers can then target their promotional strategies towards these demographic groups.

- **Market growth rate** Market growth refers to an increase in the size of a market per period of time, usually a year. It can be measured by an increase in the value or volume of sales in the market. It is usually expressed as a percentage change to indicate the extent of market growth. For example, if the sales revenue in a particular market rises from $100 million to $110 million, then the market has experienced 10% growth. Market growth is likely to lead to more suppliers entering the market as they are attracted by the potential profits. The number of mobile phone apps has grown immensely following the huge growth in the global market for smartphones in recent years.

- **Seasonal and cyclical characteristics** Some markets are constrained by seasonal factors, e.g. the market for IB textbooks is dependent on the cycle of the academic year in different parts of the world. The weather in a particular area can also affect the market in which businesses operate, e.g. tourists travel to the Swiss Alps, Niseko in Hokkaido (Japan) or Aspen in Colorado (USA) for skiing holidays.

Figure 4.1.f Marketing is affected by seasonal factors

Market share

Market share. AO4

The importance of market share and market leadership. AO3

© IBO, 2017

Market share refers to an organization's portion of the total value of sale revenue within a specific industry. It is measured by expressing the organization's sale revenue as a percentage of the total sales revenue in the industry, per time period:

$$\text{Market Share} = \frac{\text{Firm's sales revenue}}{\text{Industry's sales revenue}} \times 100$$

For example, if an organization's annual sales revenues amount to $100 million in an industry with annual sales of $400 million, then its market share is 25%. In 2018, Google had 36.2% market share in the smart speakers industry that was worth $9 million.

There is a positive relationship between market share and profits, although the business with the largest market share is not necessarily the most profitable. High market share has other benefits such as the status enjoyed from being a dominant market player and the ability to gain a range of economies of scale. Such businesses are known as market leaders (see Table

4.1.a). For example, Nike and Adidas are market leaders in the global sports apparel industry.

Table 4.1.a The world's top 10 global brands (2017

1.	Apple ($184 billion)
2.	Google ($141.7 billion)
3.	Microsoft ($80 billion)
4.	Coca-Cola ($69.7 billion)
5.	Amazon ($64.8 billion)
6.	Samsung ($56.2 billion)
7.	Toyota ($50.3 billion)
8.	Facebook ($48.2 billion)
9.	Mercedes-Benz ($47.8 billion)
10.	IBM ($46.8 billion)

Source: Interbrand, annual survey

In general, businesses with high market share (market leaders) have better price-setting ability and are less threatened by competition. Hence, a common objective of established businesses is to increase their market share by:

- Promotion of their brands (see Unit 4.5)

- Product development, improvements and innovation (see Unit 5.6)

- Motivation and training of the workforce (see Units 2.4 and 2.1) to deliver better customer services

- Establishing property rights, i.e. the use of trademarks, copyrights and patents (see Unit 3.4)

- Use of more efficient channels of distribution (see Unit 4.5).

Market concentration measures the degree of competition that exists within a market by calculating the market share of the largest few firms in the industry, i.e. those with market leadership. The sum of these market shares is known as the **concentration ratio**. For example, an industry with a 3-firm concentration ratio of 98% means that the top three firms have a combined market share of 98%. Hence, this would not be a very competitive industry, as all other businesses would account for just 2% of the total sales revenue of the industry.

CORE

Marketing

359

In reality, most industries within a country are dominated by a few large businesses with market leadership (high market share). Each dominant firm accounts for a large proportion of the industry's overall sales revenues. Some businesses grow so large that they are able to maintain market leadership on a global scale. For example, the markets for smartphones and tablet computers are dominated by Samsung and Apple.

However, calculating market share is not necessarily a straightforward task. For example, it is not always easy to define the industry - when calculating market share in the transport industry, which markets should be included: road, rail, sea and/or air? Sales data are often out-of-date, so any market share information will represent a historical situation and not necessarily signify the current position.

Box 4.1.a Market domination

Many markets are dominated by a few large firms. How many other companies can you think of, apart from the ones listed, for each of the following consumer markets?
- Sports apparel: Nike, Adidas, Puma, and Reebok
- Fast food: McDonald's, Burger King, KFC, Pizza Hut, and
- Subway
- Japanese cars: Toyota, Honda, Nissan, and Mazda
- Smartphones: Samsung, Apples, LG, Huawei, and Lenovo
- Games consoles: Ninendo Wii U, PlayStation 4, and Xbox One
- Televisions: Samsung Sony, Panasonic, LG, and Philips
- Search engines: Google, Yahoo!, and Microsoft
- Web browsers: Chrome, Explorer and Firefox.

Figure 4.1.g What should be included as part of the public transportation industry?

Question 4.1.3   Samsung

Samsung is the world's largest smartphone producer. The South Korean company's global **market share** is greater than 31% whilst that of Apple (its nearest rival) is around 15%. *Samsung's* market dominance has been helped by rising demand for its innovative products. Its market share of the tablet computer industry is approximately 16%, second only to Apple the market leader with greater than 46% market share. *Samsung's* market research showed that customers wanted technology to help them keep fit. In 2014, *Samsung* introduced its wearable smartwatch and fitness band products that link to mobile devices, in an attempt to shift the innovation of smartphones from the hand to the wrist for added consumer convenience.

(a) Calculate the approximate two-firm concentration ratio in the smartphone industry.   *[2 marks]*

(b) Outline what is meant by **market share** and describe how it is calculated.   *[4 marks]*

(c) Examine the importance of market leadership to businesses such as *Samsung*.   *[6 marks]*

Marketing objectives

The marketing objectives of for-profit organizations and non-profit organizations. AO3

© IBO, 2017

Marketing objectives are the specific marketing goals of an organization. The marketing objectives of for-profit (profit-seeking) organizations include:

- Increased sales revenue – By increasing the customer base and/or persuading existing customers to buy more, the business can generate greater sales revenue.

- Higher market share – Higher market share suggests the business is more competitive than its rivals, who might also have generated higher sales revenue but at a slower rate of growth.

- Increased market leadership – Whilst market share might be higher, market leadership means the business enjoys the benefits of having the largest market share in the industry.

- Improved product and brand awareness – Marketing can help a business to promote its products and brands in order to gain brand awareness and customer loyalty.

- Developing new products – Innovation and new products can give businesses a competitive edge over their rivals.

- Enhanced brand perception (product positioning) – Existing and potential customers have a positive perception (opinion or judgement) about the business.

Most definitions of marketing apply to activities that aim to generate profit for a business. This does not necessarily apply to **non-profit organizations** (NPOs) such as charities, educational establishments, religious organizations and government departments. The government, for example, might use television advertisements for reminding citizens to complete their income tax returns on time or to persuade drivers not to drink and drive.

The objectives of social marketing is not primarily profit related, but include:

- To build membership (support) and to connect with new donors

- To generate awareness of the NPO's cause

- To improve brand recognition of the NPO

- To create positive attention to the NPO's operations

- To demonstrate the value of the NPO to the local community or society in general.

It may seem clear that for-profit organizations must market their products successfully. Without market research to create a desirable product, at the right price, promoted effectively and available in the right places, a business is unlikely to survive for long. However, this is also true for NPOs. Marketing remains an integral part of their strategy to communicate and raise awareness of their social cause. Nevertheless, marketing in NPOs is somewhat different from the commonly used definitions of commercial marketing as it tends to be more informative (so does not necessarily aim to increase sale revenues) rather than being persuasive.

IB Learner Profile – Be an inquirer

In an industry once dominated by Motorola, Nokia and then Apple, investigate how Samsung become the world's largest mobile phone maker. A good starting point is this article from *Bloomberg Businessweek*: http://goo.gl/gdTr9Z

Question 4.1.4   FC Barcelona

Spanish football giants *FC Barcelona* have won the UEFA Champions League trophy on five occasions (1992, 2006, 2009, 2011, and 2015). The UEFA Champions League is the second most lucrative football (soccer) competition after the FIFA World Cup. *FC Barcelona*, which is well known for its moral values and not just its football, donates 0.7% of its annual revenue to UNICEF (the world's largest children's charity, set up by the United Nations). The Qatar Foundation, a **non-profit organization** that focuses on education, scientific research and community development, became the Club's first ever shirt **sponsor** in 2011. Both agreements with UNICEF and the Qatar Foundation are symbolic with the Club's social values and motto that it is "more than just a club".

Source: FC Barcelona.com

(a) (i) Define the term **non-profit organization**.   [2 marks]

(a) (ii) Define the terms **sponsorship**.   [2 marks]

(b) Most football clubs are sponsored by commercial supporters. Explain why *FC Barcelona* might have decided to sponsor UNICEF, a non-profit organization.   [4 marks]

(c) Compare and contrast the marketing objectives of *FC Barcelona* with a non-profit organization (NPO) that you have studied.   [10 marks]

CORE

Marketing strategies and changes in customer preferences

How marketing strategies evolve as a response to changes in customer preferences. AO3

© IBO, 2017

The most successful global businesses evolve their organization and marketing strategies to suit changes in customer preferences. Market trends often change rapidly with some in decline and others enjoying high growth rates. Even if market research reveals certain customer preferences, they can change without warning. Nevertheless, having insight into their customers' preferences and buying habits, and how those preferences and habits might change over time, is essential to remain competitive in the market.

There are many variables that cause businesses to change their marketing strategies. Some of the changes are implemented due to ineffective marketing strategies that don't appeal to changing customer preferences whilst others are caused by changes in the external business environment (see Unit 1.5). Reasons why marketing strategies evolve include the following:

- Changing consumer tastes – As consumer tastes are constantly subject to change, marketers must constantly evolve their marketing strategies to remain competitive. For example, the traditional Bollywood movie had three key components: it had to be long (Indians want value for money), there had to be songs and dancing, and there had to be a happy ending. However, due to globalization, Bollywood movie producers have changed this formula to cater for their international customer base. Another example is the growing demand in many parts of the world for organic fruits and vegetables.

Marketing

Figure 4.1.h There is growing demand for organic food products

- Shorter product life cycles – Traditionally, marketers use different strategies at different stages of a product's life cycle. If successful, sales are strong during the introduction and growth stages. Extension strategies (see Unit 4.5) may be used to prevent sales from declining when the market becomes saturated. However, the pace of change and the intensity of competition in many markets means that the product life cycle of products has shortened, e.g. Apple's iPhones are superseded within two years of being launched. Hence, it becomes more difficult for businesses to maintain sales growth so marketing strategies are constantly evolving in these markets.

- Internet and mobile technologies – The e-commerce revolution has also meant that consumers have far more choice than ever before. Mobile devices such as smartphones, laptops and tablet computers has revolutionized the gaming industry. For example, Rovio's Angry Birds turned a small Finnish company into one of the world's best known video games developer. Businesses that have an online presence are better positioned to meet the needs and wants of their customers.

- Competitive rivalry – The intensity of competition in many markets across the world has forced marketers to adapt and evolve their strategies. Competitors may initiate marketing strategies that threaten the profitability or survival of their rivals. For example, a major competitor may challenge the small company's status as the quality leader in the industry. For example, Apple and Samsung's innovative products and aggressive marketing strategies

led to the eventual collapse of Motorola, Nokia and Sony–Ericsson in the mobile phone industry. Evolving the organization's marketing strategies can therefore be seen as a defensive strategy against competitors that pose a threat to the organization's market share and market position.

- Globalization – The globalization phenomenon has made businesses and countries more interdependent with consumer tastes more integrated. This has forced marketers to act globally (see Unit 4.7) but to adapt their strategies to suit varying local preferences and cultural norms. For example, China has become the world's largest consumer market for many products, including televisions, cars, refrigerators and air conditioners. This has meant that marketers evolve their strategies to match the local needs and wants of Chinese consumers.

Case study

Rovio (established in 2003) launched its 52nd game, *Angry Birds* in 2009. Within 3 years, the slingshot puzzle game had reached its one billionth download and secured its status as the world's most downloaded app of all time. Rovio describes itself as "an industry-changing entertainment media company" in response to changing consumer demand for mobile gaming. *Angry Birds* has become a television series and feature film, with *Angry Birds Movie 2* released in 2019.

CORE

Exam tip !

In preparation for Section C of Paper 2, compare and contrast the marketing strategies of two different businesses in a country of your choice. For example, take a look at this comprehensive report on how global businesses market to Chinese consumers based on new findings from Forbes: http://goo.gl/PDowbz

Marketing

Case study

Yum! Brands Inc. is an American company that owns a chain of restaurants including KFC and Pizza Hut. KFC opened its first restaurant in China in 1987 and now operates more than 2,500 restaurants in the country (about half of the restaurants it has in the USA). KFC plans to have more than 20,000 restaurants in China where local customers prefer chicken products over beef burgers.

The role of marketing and the CUEGIS concepts

How innovation, ethical considerations and cultural differences may influence marketing practices and strategies in an organization. AO3

© IBO, 2017

Marketing ethics are the moral aspects of an organization's marketing strategies. Unethical marketing exists when moral codes of practice are not adhered to and when such activities cause offense to members of the general public. For example, *bait and switch* marketing techniques (see Box 4.1.b) are considered to be unethical in many parts of the world. This is a controversial marketing method used to entice customers by advertising deals that are simply too good to be true. Once customers are hooked onto the deal (the bait), they discover that it is no longer available and change to purchasing another more pricey alternative (the switch) from the business. High-pressure sales tactics are used to ensure that targeted customers make the switch. Other examples of misleading, deceptive or unethical marketing techniques include:

- Health fraud – using untested scientific claims or unsubstantiated promises of overnight medical cures.

- Travel fraud – giving misleading information to travellers, e.g. inaccurate descriptions of hotel facilities with 'sea view' rooms.

- 'Get rich quick' schemes that offer people the opportunity to get rich quick with minimal effort.

- Product misrepresentation – using brand names similar to well-known trademarks, e.g. China's Rasonic and JNC (both variations of Japan's Panasonic and JVC).

- Exploitation of weaknesses – using fear tactics that prey on people's vulnerability or pre-empting urgency such as 'limited stocks only'.

- Unsubstantiated claims – marketing claims that cannot be proved, e.g. 'nine out of 10 tests prove …' or '4 out of 5 people prefer …'

- Pester power – using children to harass their parents into buying certain products, e.g. toys, fast food, family cars and holiday destinations.

- Confusion marketing – involves businesses swamping customers with excessive price information, e.g. mobile phone subscription plans or bank mortgage deals. Being inundated with such confusing information prevents customers from making informed choices, so that customers aren't bothered switching to rival products.

Box 4.1.b   Bait & switch – unethical business practices?

- Airlines advertise cheap flights from $10, when in fact only several seats are available at this price. Once these are sold, and quite often to their own staff, the promotion is continued although there are no more seats left at the advertised price. Customers therefore end up paying higher prices.
- Mobile phone retailers advertise a new product, but it is limited in supply or out of stock. Customers end up buying higher priced phones.
- Real estate firms launch new developments using claims such as 'Apartments from just $349,950' when actually only one apartment is being sold at that price. In fact, it is likely to have already been sold before the advertisement even got to the printers.

Whether marketers act ethically will depend on the moral principles that are held by the management, the organizational culture and the values of society as a whole. However, determining whether a specific marketing campaign is ethical can often be rather subjective. This is because what is offensive to one person or group of people might not be to another (see Box 4.1.c below).

Box 4.1.c   Ethical marketing?

Would you consider the following marketing campaigns as unethical and/or offensive acts? Why/not?

- In 2002, advertising producers 2DTV had two adverts banned. One showed President George W. Bush putting a video cassette into a toaster and the other featured football celebrity David Beckham asking his wife how to spell 'DVD'.
- China recently relaxed rules on nudity in magazines and newspapers.
- It is still legal to use TV and radio advertising of cigarettes and tobacco products in some countries.
- Nestlé used the slogan "It's not for girls" on their Yorkie chocolate bar. The company managed to use reverse psychology to its advantage as many females subsequently bought the chocolate bar.
- When Daimler Chrysler released its luxury motor vehicle in 2005, the $2.6m armoured Maybach, the Hong Kong marketing campaign featured mock kidnappers shooting at the bullet proof car.
- In 2011, Italian clothes retailer Benetton launched its global 'Unhate' campaign that features world leaders, such as US President Barack Obama kissing Chinese Premier Hu Jintao.

IB Learner Profile – Be reflective and Be a thinker

In groups of 2 or 3, discuss the following questions. Be prepared to share your responses with others.

- Should marketers be banned from advertising high-sugar and high-energy drinks (such as Coca-Cola, Red Bull and Lucozade) at school-age children?
- Is it acceptable for cinemas and theatres to raise their prices (by using surge pricing) during school holidays?
- Is it acceptable for businesses to use computer games to advertise directly to children?
- Should ambiguous and/or unproven advertising claims be banned?
- Should marketers be allowed to advertise alcohol and tobacco products?

The use of unethical marketing, whether deliberate or otherwise, is a high-risk strategy. Misleading or offensive marketing strategies can backfire and make customers boycott the products of a business. Also, governments have been pressured to ensure that the general public is protected from immoral business practices, e.g. advertising activity is carefully monitored by numerous government organizations. Therefore, most businesses abide by certain guidelines and rules for ethical marketing (known as an **ethical code of practice**), which help to serve three main functions:

- To identify acceptable business practices (from society's point of view).

- To foster internal management and control.

- To avoid confusion regarding what is and what is not acceptable.

Case study

In 2013, pharmaceutical giant Johnson & Johnson was fined more than $2.2bn due to its unethical marketing practices. The US justice department found Johnson & Johnson guilt of paying incentives to doctors and pharmacies who promoted three of the company's medicines. The fine is one of the biggest healthcare fraud settlements in US history.

Theory of knowledge
Given the diverse nature of international cultures and etiquette, can marketers ever know what is ethically right and what is ethically wrong?

CORE

Marketing

Question 4.1.5   Banning pester power

Pester power is a marketing strategy that aims to put pressure on parents by targeting advertisements directly at children. Pester power techniques have been banned in the European Union (EU) since 2007. The EU also prohibits businesses in all member countries from using bait and switch marketing, which it claims is misleading and can upset members of the public.

Children are also being increasingly exposed to marketing due to technological advances and a change in lifestyles. For example, an increasing number of children have access to satellite or cable TV at home, and have their own smartphones with direct access to the Internet (both are potential advertising channels that can be exploited by marketers). The rationale behind the EU's consumer protection laws is to force businesses to operate more ethically.

(a) Examine whether it is ethical to market products directly at children.   *[6 marks]*

(b) Discuss the effectiveness of marketing campaigns designed to deliberately shock, and possibly offend members of the general public.   *[10 marks]*

Question 4.1.6   Nestlé's offensive advertising: a strategy?

Is unethical marketing a business mishap or an intentional strategy? A business might provoke a calculated 'reverse reaction' from customers through deliberately offending a particular **market segment**. For example, Nestlé's Yorkie chocolate bar adopted the slogans "*It's not for girls*" and "*It's not for handbags*". This could have offended many females, but the resulting increase in the sales of Yorkie bars suggests that, if carried out effectively, offensive marketing might not only increase brand awareness but also actually increase demand for the product.

(a) Define the term **market segment**.   *[2 marks]*

(b) Discuss whether businesses should act ethically in their marketing campaigns or whether offensive advertising is simply an effective marketing strategy.   *[10 marks]*

CORE

Marketing

Innovations in Internet technologies are being increasingly used by non-profit organizations as part of their marketing strategy. NPOs use the Internet to promote their cause (mission) in a highly cost-effective way. For example, newsletters are published online and there could be facilities to make online donations. Most for-profit organizations have also adopted the use of online technologies as part of their marketing strategies. For example, luxury car maker Maserati uses its website for customers to design their own specification. Each car is made to order, with customers selecting (online) the colour, the type of leather, the type of wood, the preferred audio and entertainment system, the choice of wheels and so forth.

The emergence of e-commerce (see Unit 4.8) has meant that the location decision for some service providers, such as banks, is no longer such a difficult one. Even so, marketing strategy must ensure that the overall package meets the needs of customers, such as the convenience and reliability of online transactions.

The principles of marketing are equally important to the business strategy of small and non-profit organizations. Professor Philip Kotler argues that almost any business can use informal and low-cost methods of marketing. This is especially the case with developments in Internet technologies. Marketing is about informing, reminding and persuading, whether the purpose is to sell more products to earn more profit or to promote a cause, such as donating money to charities or to reduce under-age drinking.

Cultural differences can have a huge impact on marketing practices and strategies. Marketing is often associated with the strategies of large companies like McDonald's, Coca-Cola, Microsoft and Toyota. They have the financial resources and expertise to carry out effective marketing planning. However, their marketing strategies and marketing mixes do not necessarily work in overseas markets (see Unit 4.8). For example, a television advert that shows a left-hand drive sports car in the USA or Germany would not be so effective

in countries where the driver sits on the right-hand side, such as in Australia and the UK. Cultural knowledge can have a large impact when making consumer choices. For a marketing message to be effective, marketers need to understand how to tailor the message to a particular culture by being aware of cultural values. Multinational companies (MNC) also need to compete with local businesses that have vast local knowledge about how the market works. Hence, MNCs have to ensure their marketing strategies are sensitive to the local and cultural values of people, in order to establish brand awareness and to leave a good impression of their brands.

Figure 4.1.i Culture can have an enormous impact on marketing

The role of marketing is about understanding the market(s) in which a business operates in order to develop appropriate business strategies to influence the action of others. Marketing allows a business to be forward looking as it involves investigating potential opportunities in the marketplace, customer needs and requirements, pricing possibilities, and suitable promotional activities. Different businesses approach marketing strategy in different ways. Those that are market orientated give customers top priority. This strategy may well suit the marketing of services although it is not necessarily the best approach for the marketing of hi-tech goods that require extensive product research and development. Nevertheless, most businesses adopt a market orientation strategy, especially as customers are increasingly more knowledgeable and have greater access to alternative suppliers. . These organizations are more perceptive of their customers' needs and wants, so stand a better chance to survive in an ever-changing business world.

NPOs tend to use social marketing strategies rather than the commercial strategies used by for-profit organizations. The main aim of social marketing campaigns is not to make a profit but for the public to change their social behaviour, such as donating money to a specific charity or providing their support in recycling household products. For many NPOs, the marketing is not about selling a physical product but a mission, vision or cause. In his book *Principles of Marketing*, Professor Philip Kotler suggests that many charities have moved away from traditional ways of collecting funds, opting to use some fairly sophisticated marketing techniques. Government agencies and departments such as the Army and Police Force in many countries use marketing to enhance their image and to attract new recruits. Governments also use social marketing strategies to encourage protection of the environment and safe motoring campaigns.

Figure 4.1.j Motorcyclists in Vietnam using their mobile phones

Marketing strategy often fails due to a lack of proper planning. For example, managers might not have considered the intensity of competition in the marketplace or changes in market conditions. The role of marketing helps give a sense of direction to the business and ensures that marketing is properly coordinated and managed. However, a dilemma faced by marketers is that the nature of business is dynamic and always exposed to the forces of change. This means that marketers need to build in some flexibility so their marketing strategies can be changed spontaneously. In their book *Uncommon Practice*, A. Milligan and S. Smith (2002) argued that the fastest way to build a name in business is to command attention to an organization's products or services. In essence, this is the role and challenge of any marketing strategy.

Theory of knowledge

If there are genuine benefits of ethical business behaviour, why do so many marketers continue to use unethical advertising techniques?

CUEGIS Essay

With reference to an organization of your choice, examine how **innovation** has influenced its marketing **strategy**.

[20 marks]

CUEGIS Essay

With reference to an organization you have studied, discuss how **change** and **ethics** have influenced the role of marketing.

[20 marks]

CUEGIS Essay

With reference to an organization of your choice, examine how differences in **culture** have influenced its marketing **strategy**.

[20 marks]

REVIEW QUESTIONS

1. Distinguish between consumer needs and wants.

2. What does marketing mean?

3. How does marketing relate to the other functions of a business: finance, human resources and operations management?

4. What are the various roles of marketing?

5. How does the marketing of goods differ from the marketing of services?

6. What are the differences between market orientation and product orientation?

7. What are the differences between commercial marketing and social marketing?

8. How do consumer markets differ from industrial (producer) markets?

9. What might the characteristics of a market include?

10. What is market share, and how is it calculated?

11. What is market leadership?

12. Outline the marketing objectives of for-profit organizations.

13. Outline the marketing objectives of non-profit organizations.

14. Why and how do marketing strategies evolve in response to changes in customer preferences?

15. How do the concepts of innovation, ethics and culture influence marketing practices and strategies?

KEY TERMS

Commercial marketing is the use of marketing strategies to meet the needs and wants of customers in a profitable way.

Goods are tangible (physical) products, e.g. televisions, furniture, biscuits and shoes.

Ethical code of practice refers to guidelines that help businesses to act in a moral way by considering what is ethically right or wrong (from society's point of view).

A **market** is a place or process whereby customers and suppliers trade. A market exists where there is demand for a particular product and where there is a willingness from businesses to supply these products.

Market concentration measures the degree of competition that exists within a market by calculating the market share of the largest few firms in the industry.

Market growth refers to the increase in the size of a market (or industry). It is typically expressed as the percentage increase in the market size of an industry per year.

Market leadership refers to businesses with the largest market share in a particular market.

Market orientation is a marketing approach adopted by businesses that are outward looking by focusing on making products that they can sell, rather than selling products that they can make.

Market share measures the value of a firm's sales revenues as a percentage of the total sales revenue in the industry.

Market size refers to the magnitude of an industry, usually measured in terms of the value of sales revenue from all the businesses in a particular market, per time period.

Marketing is the management process of predicting, identifying and meeting the needs and wants of customers in a profitable manner.

Marketing objectives are the specific marketing goals of an organization. The marketing objectives of for-profit (profit-seeking) organizations include increased sales revenue, market leadership and greater market share.

CORE

Marketing

Marketing strategies are the medium to long term plan to achieve an organization's marketing objectives.

Needs are the essentials or necessities that humans *must have* to survive, e.g. food, shelter, warmth and water. Marketers strive to meet the needs of their customers.

Product orientation is a marketing approach used by businesses that are inward looking as they focus on selling products that they can make, rather than making products that they can sell.

Services are intangible (non-physical) products, e.g. transportation services, public utilities (gas, electricity and water), and telecommunications services.

Social marketing refers to any activity that seeks to influence social behaviour to benefit the target audience and society as a whole.

Wants are human desires, i.e. things that people *would like* to have. Irrespective of a person's income or wealth, all people have infinite wants. Meeting people's wants is an integral aspect of marketing.

Luxuries are examples of human desires

4.2 Marketing planning

"You generally hear that what a man doesn't know doesn't hurt him, but in business what a man doesn't know does hurt." - E. St. Elmo Lewis (1872–1948), US author

SL/HL content	Assessment objective
The elements of a marketing plan	AO1, AO2
The role of marketing planning	AO2
The four Ps of the marketing mix	AO2
An appropriate marketing mix for a particular product or business	AO2, AO4
The effectiveness of a marketing mix in achieving marketing objectives	AO3
The difference between target markets and market segments	AO2
Possible target markets and market segments in a given situation	AO4
The difference between niche market and mass market	AO2
How organizations target and segment their market and create consumer profiles	AO2
A product position map / perception map	AO2, AO4
The importance of having a unique selling point/proposition (USP)	AO2
How organizations can differentiate themselves and their products from competitors	AO3

© IBO, 2017

Elements of a marketing plan

The elements of a marketing plan. AO1

The role of marketing planning. AO2

© IBO, 2017

A **marketing plan** is a document outlining an organization's marketing objectives (see Unit 4.1) and the marketing strategies to be used to achieve these objectives. Successful marketers advocate planning marketing objectives and strategies, rather than adopting an ad hoc and uncoordinated approach. A marketing plan is usually preceded by a *marketing audit* – a review of the current position of an organization's marketing mix in terms of its strengths, weaknesses, opportunities and threats. The review may address questions and issues such as the intensity of competition in the market, the firm's product portfolio (see Unit 4.5) and an assessment of the effectiveness of its marketing. From the marketing audit, managers can then produce a marketing plan that is likely to include details of the following elements:

- Marketing objectives that are SMART (specific, measurable, agreed, realistic and time bound), e.g. the expected market share or sales turnover within a specified time frame.

- Methods of market research to be used to identify target markets.

- An assessment of the strengths and weaknesses of competitors in the market.

- Outline of the marketing mix, e.g. the product design, channels of distribution to be used, anticipated price(s) and promotional strategies to employ.

- Details of the marketing budget.

- Outline of the anticipated difficulties and strategies to deal with these anticipated problems.

It is also common to include SWOT and STEEPLE analyses in a marketing plan (see Units 1.3 and 1.5 respectively). These help the organization to assess the internal and external factors affecting the business and its marketing objectives.

Marketing planning is the systematic process of devising marketing objectives and appropriate marketing strategies to achieve these goals. It requires the collection and analysis of information about a particular market, such as market research data on existing and potential customers. The typical marketing planning process involves:

- Marketing audit – an examination of the current climate in which the business operates. Market research is integral to this investigation.

- Marketing objectives – the marketing audit enables the business to set marketing goals and targets, e.g. improved price competitiveness or increased market share.

- Marketing strategies – the plan and use of the marketing mix to achieve marketing objectives.

- Monitoring and review – a continual process of checking and monitoring that targets are being met. Hence, marketing strategies might need to be adjusted accordingly.

- Evaluation – an examination of the extent to which the business has succeeded in achieving its marketing objectives. This aids decision-making and subsequent rounds of marketing planning.

The main advantage of marketing planning is that it improves an organization's chances of success. Of course, the plan does not guarantee success but it can help managers to identify and deal with likely problems. The various functional areas of a business will also have a clearer idea of the organization's objectives and the constraints in which they are to operate. Thus, a key role of marketing planning is to allow marketing managers to have better control of the organization.

However, marketing planning has its limitations. For example, many small businesses do not have the time, resources or expertise to plan their marketing in such a systematic way. They react to (rather than anticipate) changes in the marketplace. Even for large organizations, managers need to devote appropriate resources (time, people and money) to marketing planning. Marketing plans can be inflexible and become outdated quite quickly as they do not allow for sudden changes

in market conditions. This is especially the case in high-tech and fast-paced industries.

The 4 Ps of the marketing mix

The four Ps of the marketing mix. AO2
An appropriate marketing mix for a particular product or business. AO2, AO4
© IBO, 2017

The **marketing mix** is the combination of various elements needed to successfully market a product. It is used to review and develop marketing strategies and is at the heart of marketing planning. The traditional marketing mix is known as the **four Ps**, a term coined by marketing professor Edmund Jerome McCarthy in 1960:

- Product – the good or service being marketed to meet the needs and wants of customers.

- Price – how much customers have to pay to buy the product.

- Promotion – methods of informing, reminding and persuading customers to buy the product.

- Place – the distribution channels used to get the product to customers.

Marketing plans cannot work effectively without all four elements of the marketing mix. This is because the four Ps are interdependent. A high price for a low quality product without any promotion and with limited distribution networks is a recipe for failure.

Product

A **product** is a physical good or an intangible service, such as motor vehicles or motor insurance. In the eyes of customers, products serve one purpose – to fulfil their needs or wants (desires). What differentiates one product from another is the collective and relative customer benefits of that product, such as the brand image, functions, packaging, value for money and after-sales care. The marketing strategy used by a business will depend on the type of product in question:

- **Producer products** are industrial products sold to other businesses to further the production process, such as raw materials, components and machinery. For example, ArcelorMittal (the world's largest steel producer) sells its products to rail and motor companies.

- **Consumer products** are sold to the end user, i.e. private individuals. These products can be further classified as convenience products (or 'fast-moving consumer goods') such as food products, *consumer durables* (long lasting) such as furniture, or *speciality products* (highly expensive items) such as diamonds.

Figure 4.2.a Food containers are consumer durable products

Some products, such as laptop computers and motor vehicles, are sold to both industrial and private customers. The *purpose* of the purchase determines whether the product is classified as a producer or consumer product, i.e. whether it is used for commercial or private use.

To increase its customer base and to maximise profits, a business tends to sell a range of related products. For example, Audi produces a range of cars from its best-selling Audi A4 to its R8–GT supercar. The product mix of Samsung, South Korea's largest company, includes smartphones, TVs, home entertainment systems and laptops.

Price

Price refers to the amount that customers pay for a particular good or service. Pricing can be one of the most difficult decisions to make in the marketing mix. If a product is over-priced, customers may not buy the product, no matter how good it might be. However, if products are priced too low, they can be perceived to lack quality. Customers want a price to reflect value for money and businesses want a price that exceeds their costs to earn sufficient profit. The pricing decision depends on a 'DRASTIC'© number of factors:

- **D**emand – The greater the ability and willingness of customers to pay, the higher the price can be. For example, airline ticket prices soar in the summer due to higher demand.

- **R**ivalry – The higher the degree of competition, the more price-competitive firms tend to be (prices being similar to those set by rivals).

- **A**ims – Charities and non-profit organizations (see Unit 1.2) will price differently from firms seeking to maximise profit due to their dissimilar business objectives.

- **S**upply – The lower the supply of a certain product, the higher its price tends to be. Oil suppliers can charge higher prices than suppliers of tea due to the relative scarcity of oil.

- **T**ime – The price of some products, such as consumer electronics, fall over time as newer versions become available. Other products, such as precious antiques and classic cars, rise in price over time due to their scarcity.

- **I**mage – Businesses with a prestigious and exclusive image can charge higher prices for their products, such as Lamborghini cars or Hyatt hotels.

- **C**osts of production – The higher the costs of production, the higher the price tends to be.

Theory of knowledge

Why is the market price of diamonds so much higher than that of water, when diamonds are not necessary for human survival?

CORE

Marketing

Place (or distribution)

Place describes the methods of distributing products to customers. For example, Coca-Cola uses a range of methods to get its drinks to the customers, e.g. wholesalers, retailers and vending machines. Traditionally, the distribution channel starts at the factory of the manufacturer, which sells the product to wholesalers. Wholesalers such as Costco buy in bulk to reduce the unit cost of the product. They then break the bulk into smaller units and sell these onto retailers. The final distribution channel is then from the retailer to the consumers. Each intermediary in the distribution chain adds a profit margin to the costs paid to its supplier.

The changing demands of customers, such as the need for prompt deliveries, mean that the traditional channels of distribution are less popular today, especially with the increased popularity of e-commerce (see Unit 4.8). The fewer the intermediaries there are in a transaction, the lower the price tends to be. For example, buying directly from the seller is cheaper than going through distributors or agents who charge for their services.

Promotion

Promotion refers to the strategies used to attract customers to buy a firm's products. Branding, for example, helps to differentiate a product from its rivals. Promotion is usually classified as being either above the line (ATL) or below the line (BTL). ATL promotion uses paid-for mass media, e.g. television, radio and newspapers. BTL promotion refers to all other promotion, e.g. packaging, sponsorship and viral marketing. Most businesses use a combination of both ATL and BTL promotion. Examples of promotional activities include:

- **Advertising** – ATL advertising tends to be the most expensive form of promotion. Adverts are commonly carried out via television, radio, newspapers, magazines, posters and the Internet.

- **Sales promotion** – These are temporary methods of boosting sales, e.g. price reductions, gift vouchers and free gifts.

- **Sponsorship** – This refers to financial gifts, donations or payments in support of an event or a business venture in return for a prominent display of the sponsor's name. For example, Coca-Cola is a major sponsor of the Olympic Games.

- **Publicity** – This is the marketing process of getting good press (media) coverage, including the use of famous celebrities to endorse a firm's products.

Theory of knowledge

How can we know how important brand loyalty is as a source of competitive advantage? Does the answer depend of the industry in question?

Figure 4.2.b The traditional four Ps of the marketing mix

Exam tip !

Exam questions may require students to design an appropriate marketing mix for a particular product or business. These types of questions are open-ended and students are expected to use relevant theory that is applicable to the product or business in question. These might include: the traditional marketing mix for goods, the extended marketing mix for services, Ansoff's Matrix, the Boston Matrix, position mapping, or application of the CUEGIS concepts.

Question 4.2.1 Lego

Founded in 1949, *Lego's* plastic interlocking bricks have captured the imagination of all ages and across generations. However, slowing growth in the sales of its toys caused the Danish company to look beyond building blocks as a **revenue stream**. For example, the company developed computer games and themed amusement parks. In 2012, the company launched *Lego* Friends, aimed specifically at girls. In 2014, *Lego* released *The Lego Movie*, which earned over $31.5m in its first three weeks, and worldwide sales in excess of $469 million. Its huge success encouraged producers to make *The Lego Batman Movie* and *The Lego Ninjago Movie* in 2017, and *The Lego Movie 2* in 2019.

(a) Define the term **revenue stream**. [2 marks]

(b) Prepare an appropriate marketing mix for *Lego*. [6 marks]

The marketing mix and marketing objectives

The effectiveness of a marketing mix in achieving marketing objectives. AO3

© IBO, 2017

Marketing objectives are the targets that the marketing department wishes to achieve. These objectives should be compatible with the organization's overall objectives (see Unit 1.3). For example, if growth is an organizational objective, then the marketing department might consider launching new products and/or selling existing products in overseas markets. As with all organizational objectives, marketing objectives should be SMART (specific, measurable, agreed, realistic, and time bound).

Marketing guru Philip Kotler suggested that the fundamental objective of marketing is to create customer satisfaction in a profitable way. Hence, setting marketing objectives is important because the targets can:

- Provide a sense of purpose, direction and motivation for the marketing department.

- Allow progress to be monitored and success to be measured.

- Help in the planning and development of an appropriate marketing mix and marketing strategies.

Marketing objectives include the following:

- **Market share** – This can be achieved through *market penetration* strategies (see Unit 1.3) that allow the business to increase sales revenue and profits.

- **Market leadership** – The business strives for the greatest market share in the industry.

- **Product positioning** – The business attempts to improve the corporate image and perceptions held by consumers (see section on *position maps* in this Unit).

- **Consumer satisfaction** – This can be achieved by ensuring consumers are satisfied with the price, product quality, and the level of customer service.

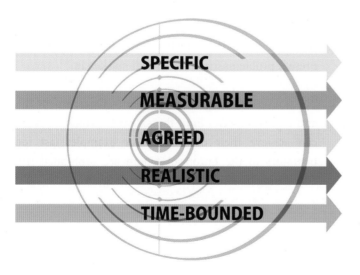

Figure 4.2.c SMART objectives

- **High market standing** – Market standing refers to the extent to which a business has a presence in the marketplace. It is largely based on an organization's image and reputation, which can be maintained or enhanced by effective marketing strategies.

Aspects of the marketing mix form the marketing strategies used to achieve the firm's marketing objectives. Examples of such strategies include:

- **Market development** – involves selling existing products in new markets, such as through the use of international marketing (see Unit 4.7) or e-commerce (see Unit 4.8).

- **Product development** – involves selling new products in existing markets. It is a common marketing strategy for businesses operating in high-tech industries.

- **Diversification** – involves marketing new products in new markets. This high-risk strategy only tends to be used by financially stable businesses pursuing growth and evolution.

- **Product innovation** – refers to the objective of launching an original or new product onto the market. It can help a firm to gain a *first-mover advantage* in establishing itself in the market.

For the marketing of services, three additional Ps are required in the marketing mix:

- **People** – refers to the personnel used in the provision of services, e.g. managers, cleaners, concierge, porters, cashiers, security guards, chefs and waiters.

- **Physical environment** – refers to the tangible aspects of a service, e.g. a clean lobby, nice décor and good quality facilities.

- **Process** – refers to the way in which a service is provided or delivered, e.g. payment methods, waiting (queuing) times and after-sales care.

The effectiveness of any marketing strategy is constrained by numerous constraints (limitations) faced by organizations trying to achieve their marketing objectives. These include both internal constraints (those within the control of the business) and external constraints (those beyond the organization's control), such as:

- Finance – The size of the organization's marketing budget determines the marketing activities that can be undertaken to achieve its objectives.

- Costs of production – The organization's costs (and the ability to exploit economies of scale) determine its capacity to compete on price and/or quality.

- The size and status of the firm – Businesses that do not have high market standing might be unable to achieve their marketing objectives as they are relatively unknown.

- Social factors – The attitude of those in society can also dictate the level of success of any marketing strategy. For example, it might not be socially acceptable to market certain products such as cigarettes or children's war toys. A shift in consumer fashion and tastes also affects the effectiveness of marketing strategies.

- Time lags – There is a delay between an organization's marketing activities (and hence its expenditure) and any impact on customers. This means that time lags can cause short-term liquidity problems (see Unit 3.3) for the business.

- Actions and reactions of competitors – Rivals might launch new or improved products which hinder the success of their competitors' marketing strategies. In addition, businesses are likely to respond to the marketing strategies of their competitors, perhaps by engaging in a price war (see Unit 4.5).

- The state of the economy – It is much harder for a business to achieve its marketing objectives during a global recession as consumers and businesses are more careful about their spending. Fluctuating exchange rates can also present problems for international marketers.

- The political and legal environment – Government rules and regulations can limit the extent to which marketers can achieve their objectives. For example, fast food operators in the European Union are prohibited from advertising on children's television programmes.

Question 4.2.2   Del Monte

Del Monte is an American foods company headquartered in San Francisco. Its products, which include canned fruits and vegetables, fruit snacks, fruit sorbets, tuna, and pet foods, are sold all over the world. According to *Del Monte*, over 55% of American families have a dog and/or cat so the business has been keen to capitalise on this market, trading under the name of Big Heart Pet Brands since 2014. Its **vision statement** is "To be one of the fastest growing global branded food and beverage companies."

Source: adapted from www.delmonte.com/about.aspx

(a) Define the term **vision statement**. [2 marks]

(b) Evaluate how the effectiveness of *Del Monte's* marketing mix helps the company to achieve its marketing objectives. [10 marks]

Target markets and market segments

The difference between target markets and market segments. AO2
© IBO, 2017

A market for a particular good or service consists of different types of customers, subdivided into market segments (distinct subgroups). For instance, there are many markets that exist to meet the needs and wants of children, e.g. education, toys, food, clothing and entertainment. A **market segment** refers to a distinct group of customers with similar characteristics (such as age or gender) and similar wants or needs. By dividing the market into different segments, it is easier for a business to analyse which groups of customers buy the product and then to target these customers more distinctively.

Targeting refers to each distinctive market segment having its own specific marketing mix. For example, business and first-class air travellers are targeted in a very different way from those who travel by economy class. Teaching vacancies are advertised weekly in the *Times Educational Supplement* (www.tes.co.uk), a specialist newspaper publication targeted at teachers.

Consumer profiles are the demographic and psychographic characteristics of consumers in different markets, e.g. their age, gender, occupation, income level, religion, marital status and purchasing habits. For example, the typical pensioner might be described as someone who is older than 60 years of age on a fixed income (pension) and has no mortgage. The consumer profile for Suzuki motorbikes might be males aged between 20–45 years. Knowledge of consumer profiles helps a business to identify the needs and wants of its customers and to identify any segments that might be overlooked. For example, Coca-Cola realised that health-conscious male customers were reluctant to purchase Diet Coke or Coke Light as these products tended to be associated with female customers. This gap in the market led to the launch of Coke Zero, nicknamed 'Bloke Coke', in 2005.

Case study

Eighty-seven per cent of those who read *The Economist* are male; 46% are in senior management positions; and 69% of readers admit to being ambitious. The average reader's net household wealth is $1.688 million.

Source: *The Economist* (http://goo.gl/YQIxMp)

Targeting, segmentation and consumer profiles

How organizations target and segment their market and create consumer profiles. AO2
Possible target markets and market segments in a given situation. AO4
© IBO, 2017

Organizations segment their market in order to create distinct consumer profiles in several ways based on demographic, geographic and/or psychographic factors. Recall that market segmentation is the process of splitting the market into distinct consumer groups to better meet their needs. Businesses segment their markets for several reasons:

- Better understanding of customers – Market segmentation can allow a business to better understand the needs and wants of its various customer groups. A clearer marketing strategy therefore reduces the chances of wasting

CORE

Marketing

resources on marketing products in the wrong places and to the wrong people.

- Higher sales – Being able to cater for a wider range of customers can help a business sell more products, and hence earn more profit.

- Growth opportunities – Effective market segmentation can help businesses identify new opportunities at home and abroad.

- Support for product differentiation – Having a better understanding of different market segments allows a business to effectively differentiate its products and spread its risks.

Segmentation by demographics

Demography is the study of the characteristics of the human population within a certain area, country or region. It looks at a range of variables including:

- *Age* – Each age group (such as teenagers) tends to have similar wants and some (such as retired pensioners) are in similar financial circumstances. Teenagers, middle-aged adults and the retired have different spending patterns.

- *Gender* – Male and females can have very different wants and spending habits. For instance, there is a huge market for women's fashion in comparison to men's fashion (just take a look at the floor space devoted to female clothing compared with that allocated to male customers in a typical shopping mall).

Case study

LEGO's profits jumped 35% in less than a year following its introduction of LEGO Friends™ in 2012, targeted at girls. The Danish toymaker, founded in 1932, had previously targeted their toy products mainly at boys. By 2013, LEGO had overtaken Mattel to become the world's most valuable toy company.

- *Race and ethnicity* – Different races of people have different cultures, which affect their demand for different products. Chinese people eat rice as part of their staple diet whereas the Irish may prefer potatoes. Due to globalization there have been many opportunities for businesses to sell

cultural exports to reach a wider customer base (see Unit 4.7).

- *Marital status* – In many parts of the world, an increasing number of people are delaying marriage, partly due to the soaring costs of weddings and the career aspirations of women. Divorce rates in many Western societies have also been increasing. Such trends can present both opportunities and threats to marketers.

- *Religion* – Jewish people buy kosher foods whereas Muslims eat halal. McDonald's has had to alter its menu in countries such as India where beef is not consumed for religious reasons.

- *Language* – Businesses may cater for different customers based on their mother-tongue language. For example, IB programmes and examinations exist in three main languages: English, Spanish and French. Many famous tourist destinations, such as Stonehenge in the UK and Tokyo Disneyland, cater for international visitors.

Figure 4.2.d Stonehenge is a popular attraction for tourists in the UK

- *Income and socio-economic class* – Very wealthy people tend to have different spending patterns from the rest of the population. For example, the American 'upper-middle class' refers to people who earn in excess of $65,000 per year or have an annual household income of at least $100,000. The UK uses a similar model (see Box 4.2.a). The level of income for different consumer groups can affect the pricing policy of a business. For example, cinemas and theme parks charge different prices to adults, children, students, families and pensioners.

Case study

The Emirates Palace in Abu Dhabi is a 7-star 'super luxury' hotel, which cost $6 billion to build – the world's most expensive hotel ever to be built at the time (2005). It has its own private beach, private cricket ground and a rugby pitch. Suites cost from $10,000 per night, whilst its Valentine's Day package is $1 million per night. Guests staying at the hotel also have the privilege of being able to use the world's first gold vending machine.

Box 4.2.a   Demographic groups (UK model)

Social group	Social status	Description and examples of occupation
A	Upper-middle class	Senior managerial, administrative or professional workers, e.g. company directors, diplomats, barristers and surgeons.
B	Middle class	Middle managerial, administrative or professional workers who tend to be highly educated and salaried staff, e.g. teachers, nurses and accountants.
C1	Lower middle	Skilled non-manual workers, e.g. supervisory (junior managerial), administrative or clerical professionals.
C2	Skilled working class	Skilled manual workers, e.g. self-employed plumbers and electricians.
D	Working class	Semi-skilled and unskilled manual workers, e.g. assembly line factory workers and cleaners.
E	Subsistence	Unskilled and casual workers, pensioners and the unemployed.

Source: http://www.abc1demographic.co.uk/

Box 4.2.b   Creative demographic segmentation

Marketers have invented many creative acronyms and names for various demographic groupings. Examples include:

- *DINKY* – double income, no kids yet
- *DINKER* – double income, no kids, early retirement
- *NILK* – no income, lots of kids
- *OINK* – one income, no kids
- *GLAM* – greying, leisured, affluent, middle-aged
- *ORCHID* – One recent child, hugely in debt
- *OPAL* – older people with active lifestyles
- *WOOF* – Well-off older folk
- *RAP* – Retired affluent people
- *Kidults* – adults who purchase products aimed at children, e.g. certain toys or computer games
- *Tweenagers* – children aged 7– 12
- *SITCOM* – Single income, two children, outrageous mortgage
- *SINBAD* – Single income, no boyfriend and desperate!

In reality, different combinations of these demographic factors are used for marketing purposes. For example, greetings cards are produced for numerous occasions such as birthday cards specifically for girls, boys, teenagers, parents and grandparents, and different cards for Thanksgiving, Christmas, Hanukkah, Diwali and Chinese New Year.

Segmentation by geographic factors

The geographic location of customers can have implications for segmentation because demographic factors can be largely influenced by geographic issues. Race, language and religion are some examples. Geographical factors affecting market segmentation fall into two broad categories:

- *Location* – Different geographical areas and regions may have different cultures and social attitudes. Singapore and Malaysia, for example, are very multicultural and most businesses cater for the three main cultures – Chinese, Malay (or Singaporean) and Indian.

- *Climate* – The typical weather in a geographical area can have a large impact on business activity. Warm clothing product lines such as scarves and hats are unlikely to meet the needs of people living in areas with a tropical climate, or hikers climbing mountains. Hence, many businesses are likely to adjust the products they sell in different parts of the world.

CORE

Marketing

Figure 4.2.e British Columbia, Canada, has plenty of trails for mountain hikers

Segmentation by psychographic factors

Psychographic factors are those that consider the emotions and lifestyle of customers, such as their hobbies, interests and values.

- *Hobbies and interests* – An understanding of the different hobbies and interests of customers can provide plenty of marketing opportunities for a business. For example, the sports industry is huge, catering for customers that actively participate in and/or watch sports.

- *Values* – This refers to people's beliefs, morals and principles. Ethically responsible businesses such as The Body Shop appeal to people who are against the use of animal testing. Advocacy groups (or pressure groups) such as Greenpeace and Amnesty International aim to win the backing of people to support their cause.

- *Religion* – Religious beliefs provide many business opportunities. For example, it is estimated that there are

over 2 billion Christians in the world; a figure that is not overlooked by marketers.

- *Status* – Some people are very conscious of social and economic status, such as the Filipinos, Chinese and the Japanese. A feeling of status can come about by the *feel-good factor* of owning certain assets, such as designer outfits, luxury jewellery or sports cars.

- *Culture* – The culture and buying habits of different ethnic groups can provide immense opportunities for marketers, such as the increased trade in cultural exports.

- *Hobbies and interests* – An understanding of the different hobbies and interests of customers can provide plenty of marketing opportunities for a business. For example, the sports industry is huge, catering for customers that actively participate in and/or watch sports.

Figure 4.2.f Sporting interests provide many marketing opportunities

Case study

Segmentation is about anticipating the needs of different customers. As part of its business strategy, BMW has used segmentation and consumer profiling to increase its sales revenue. BMW's range of cars come in all sorts of sizes (from the entry level 1-Series to its X-Series SUV models) and styling to suit different customers (BMW cars appeal to both men and women of different nationalities earning varying levels of income).

In 2011, BMW launched its i-model plug-in electric vehicles. In less than 5 years, the company had sold over 50,000 units of the BMW i3 and i8 models. Today, the i3 is one of the world's best-selling all-electric cars.

Question 4.2.3   Oasis Hong Kong Airlines

Oasis Hong Kong Airlines (*Oasis*) was the first airline to adopt the budget airline model for long haul flights since the collapse of Laker Airways in 1982. *Oasis's* maiden flight from Hong Kong to London in October 2006 attracted negative media coverage as the flight was delayed by 24 hours due to airspace clearance problems from Russia. The return flight was also delayed by more than two hours due to a damaged emergency exit door.

Faced with intense competition from stronger and more established rivals, such as Cathay Pacific and Singapore Airlines, and with only two aircraft in its fleet, customers were not keen to jump at *Oasis's* low prices. Nevertheless, by June 2007 *Oasis* had launched its second flight route from Hong Kong to Vancouver, Canada.

(a) Outline why *Oasis's* business approach might be considered as being innovative.   *[2 marks]*

(b) Comment on why customers were not overly keen to fly with *Oasis*, despite the airline's low prices.   *[2 marks]*

(c) Examine the key differences in the marketing strategies that *Oasis* could use to attract different market segments.   *[6 marks]*

Question 4.2.4   The business of international students

International students provide many opportunities for businesses. In addition to their direct costs of education, these students help to improve domestic tourism, especially with visiting friends and relatives. World Bank figures show that international students account for a significant proportion of service export earnings in countries such as Australia, New Zealand and the United States.

The international mobility of students is being fuelled by three main factors: the phenomenon of **globalization**; **innovations** that are making education more accessible to people from around the world; and the intensity of competition between universities to attract foreign students.

University of Oxford, England

(a) (i) Outline what is meant by **globalization**.   *[2 marks]*

(a) (ii) Outline what is meant by **innovations**.   *[2 marks]*

(b) Examine how knowledge of market segmentation might help universities to have more cost-effective marketing activities to attract foreign students.   *[6 marks]*

It might not always be possible for a business to effectively carry out market segmentation. Marketers often use the acronym DAMAS as a set of criteria for assessing successful market segmentation:

- **D**ifferential – Segments must be unique and respond to different marketing mixes.

- **A**ctionable – Businesses must be able to provide suitable products to cater for each market segment.

- **M**easurable – The size and purchasing power of each market segment must be quantifiable.

- **A**ccessible – The business and/or its products must be able to reach customers in a cost-effective way.

- **S**ubstantial – Each market segment must be large enough to generate profits.

Once a market has been segmented, **targeting** becomes the next stage in marketing planning. Targeting refers to the market segment(s) that a business wishes to sell to. Appropriate marketing strategies are then developed for these target markets. There are two broad targeting strategies that a business can use: *niche marketing* or *mass marketing*.

Figure 4.2.g Horse riding is a minority sport

Photgraph courtesy of Victor Chine

Case study   Lefty's – The Left Hand Store

Lefty's – The Left Hand Store is a business founded in San Francisco, USA. Founded in 1978, it was the very first business in the USA to specialize in products for left-handed people. Lefty's also has a kiosk at Walt Disney World Resorts in Orlando, Florida.

Visit the company's website to read more about the business and view its product range: http://www.leftyslefthanded.com

Niche and mass markets

The difference between niche market and mass market. AO2

© IBO, 2017

Niche marketing targets a specific and well-defined market segment. An example is businesses that provide high-end speciality goods (such as Louis Vuitton handbags, Bugatti cars and Cartier watches) in niche markets, catering for consumers interested in exclusive luxury goods. Businesses that cater for minority sports, such as horse riding, Ultimate Frisbee and Tae Kwon Do also operate in niche markets.

Case study   The IB's niche market subjects

Did you know that the IBO offers a range of subjects that can be considered as niche market subjects? These subjects follow what is called the 'school based syllabus' (SBS), available at Standard Level only.

SBS subjects include: Asian Arts, Astronomy, Brazilian Social Studies, Drama, Electronics, Fijian Studies, Food Science & Technology, Human Rights, Marine Science, Nature of Science, Turkey in the 20th Century, World Arts & Cultures and World Religions.

CORE

Marketing

Table 4.2.a   Advantages and disadvantages of niche marketing

Advantages	Disadvantages
There is better marketing focus as a specific market segment is targeted. By contrast, mass marketing has little focus and targets products to the 'average' customer.	Niche markets are small which limits the number of potential customers in the market. By contrast, mass markets cater for a much wider customer base.
As there is less competition, businesses can charge higher prices for their unique or exclusive products. This helps the business to gain higher profit margins on its products.	Due to the limited market size, businesses operating in niche markets have few opportunities to exploit economies of scale. Thus, average costs tend to be higher.
Businesses become highly specialized in meeting the needs and wants of their niche target market. This can help to deliver first-rate customer service and encourages customer loyalty.	Successful and profitable niche markets attract new entrants into the industry. The threat of larger firms entering the market might endanger the survival of businesses operating in niche markets.

Question 4.2.5   Pink Ladies

Pink Ladies is a members club for women only, including a unique private car hire service - driven by women for women. The business was established in 2005 by Tina Dutton and Andrea Winders, who had concerns for lone women travellers, and worries about the dangers of the many unlicensed taxi drivers in London, UK. The firm's taxis, which of course are all pink, come with satellite navigation devices and female drivers trained in self-defence. To bolster security even further, the firm has a 'no cash in the car' policy. **Market research** showed that women generally feel happier with a female driver.

(a) Outline what is meant by **market research**, in the context of the case study.

[2 marks]

(b) Explain **two** other market research techniques that *Pink Ladies* were likely to have used.

[4 marks]

(c) Explain **two** advantages for *Pink Ladies* operating in a niche market.

[4 marks]

Photo courtesy of Andrea Winders and Tina Dutton (pictured), www.pinkladiesmembers.co.uk

Mass marketing refers to undifferentiated marketing, i.e. a strategy that ignores targeting individual market segments. Instead, different market segments are targeted to maximise sales volume. Coca-Cola, Samsung, Nike, Toyota and Lenovo all use this strategy to target various market segments. Governments also use this strategy, as a form of *social marketing* (see Unit 4.1), to communicate public announcements such as anti-drink driving campaigns.

In reality, many businesses have operations that use various targeting strategies. For example, French multinational company Kering, which owns luxury brands Gucci and Saint Laurent Paris, developed its product portfolio by taking over sports brand Puma to spread its risks. Kering also owns FNAC, the largest French consumer electronics retailer that operates throughout Europe.

Table 4.2.b   Advantages and disadvantages of mass marketing

Advantages	Disadvantages
Businesses can gain from huge potential economies of scale by supplying products in mass markets.	Mass marketing is not suitable for all businesses as there are high entry barriers for mass production (see Unit 5.2).
There is no need to modify marketing strategies for different segments as the whole market can be targeted with a single marketing campaign. This saves time and resources.	Competition can become quite fierce as customers must be persuaded to buy the firm's products rather than to buy from a rival business. Thus, marketing budgets must be substantial to remain competitive.
Catering for larger (mass) markets means that the business can establish a bigger customer base, thereby earning more profits.	As there is a lack of focus, mass marketing can be quite wasteful, as specific customers are not being directly targeted.

Position (perception) maps

A product position map / perception map. AO2, AO4

© IBO, 2017

A **product position map** (or **perception map**) is a visual tool that reveals customer perceptions of a product or brand in relation to others in the market. The term was coined by marketing guru Jack Trout in 1969. The two-dimensional diagram plots customer perceptions using variables (or criteria) such as price and quality, as shown in Figure 4.2.h:

		Quality	
		High	*Low*
Price	*High*	Premium products	Cowboy products
	Low	Bargain products	Economy products

Figure 4.2.h Perception map (customer perceptions based on price and quality)

- **Premium products** are of high quality and high price, e.g. Lexus and Mercedes–Benz cars.

- **Economy products** are of low quality but at appropriate prices, e.g. supermarkets often supply 'no-frills' own-label branded products to lure price-sensitive customers.

- **Bargain products** are of high quality but with low prices. This strategy is not sustainable and the approach is only used as a short-term tactic to boost sales.

- **Cowboy products** are of poor quality yet highly priced. These products are positioned to deceive customers and are therefore only used as a short-term tactic to gain revenue.

An example of a perception map for motor vehicles is shown in Figure 4.2.i

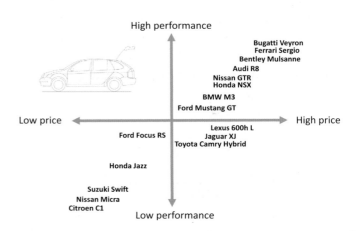

Figure 4.2.i Perception map for the motorcar industry

Position maps allow a business to identify any gaps in its product portfolio (see Unit 4.5). For example, Mercedes–Benz introduced its A Class cars in 1997 after market research revealed there was a market for smaller cars that featured its luxury brand name. Similarly, BMW identified a gap in the market for luxury 4x4 sports utility vehicles so subsequently introduced its X-Class line of cars in 2000. Information in a perception map can also help businesses to refine their marketing strategies. For example, if customers perceive a particular brand to be of high price and high quality, then appropriate market segments can be targeted.

Figure 4.2.j The BMW X6

For example, in the cosmetics industry, Chanel is regarded to be of higher quality and price compared with Rimmel. Similarly, most customers perceive Evian and Perrier as superior brands of bottled water.

Figure 4.2.k Evian is perceived as a premium brand

A major advantage of perception mapping is its simplicity in presenting potentially complex market research findings. The maps are quick and easy to interpret. They can inform management about market opportunities and threats, e.g. if undesired perceptions exist, the business will need to **reposition** its products. For example, British Airways revamped its image to appeal to younger and less affluent customers after market research findings revealed the airline was associated with wealthy and elderly travellers only.

There are three stages to positioning:

- Identify the competitive advantages of the product in question.

- Decide on which aspects of these strengths should be marketed.

- Implement the desired positioning by using an appropriate marketing mix.

Professor Michael Porter proposed three generic (or basic) competitive strategies for businesses to achieve market positioning success:

- Cost leadership – aiming to excel as low-cost suppliers of particular economy products.

- Differentiation – producing distinct products to differentiate products from those supplied by competitors. Having a distinctive selling point can give the organization competitive advantages.

- Focus – paying close attention to a particular market segment, such as high-end premium products or specific niche markets.

Porter argued that it is unrealistic for a business to be good at everything in all market segments, and such an approach would result in the business not being good at anything in particular. He suggested that an organization cannot logically and simultaneously provide cost leadership and high quality.

Box 4.2.c   USA's most admired companies (1983 and 2018)

	2018	1983
1	Apple	IBM
2.	Amazon	Hewlett-Packard
3.	Alphabet	Johnson & Johnson
4.	Berkshire Hathaway	Eastman Kodak
5.	Starbucks	Merck
6.	Walt Disney Company	AT&T
7.	Microsoft	Digital Equipment
8.	Southwest Airlines	SmithKline Beckman
9.	FedEx	General Electric
10.	JP Morgan Chase	General Mills

Source: adapted from *Fortune* magazine's annual survey of 'America's Most Admired Companies', first compiled in 1983 (http://fortune.com/worlds-most-admired-companies/)

CORE

Marketing

Question 4.2.6   The hotel industry, London (UK)

The data below shows customer perceptions of some hotels in London:

Hotel	Price	Quality of service	Desirability of location
Britannia International	High	High	Medium
Holiday Inn	Medium	Medium	Low
Peckham Hotel	Medium	Low	Low
Premier Travel Inn	Medium	Medium	Medium
Raddison	High	Medium	High
Savoy Hotel	High	High	High
Shaftsbury Hyde Park	Medium	Medium	High
Travelodge	Low	Low	Low

(a)   Construct a position map for the hotel industry in London based on the information above.   *[5 marks]*

(b)   Explain the benefits of position maps to the operators of both *Savoy Hotel* and *Peckham Hotel*.   *[6 marks]*

Perception affects the corporate image of a business. Corporate image plays a vital part in the success of a business. In 2007, Pakistan International Airlines was banned from flying to the European Union due to safety concerns. In the same year, USA raised concerns over Indonesian airline carriers due to their poor safety record. A poor image not only drives customers away, but can also cause irrevocable damage (see Box 4.2.d).

Theory of knowledge

To what extent do we rely on sense perception as a Way of Knowing in our study of Business Management?

Case study

One of the most famous corporate bloopers in business history was made by Gerald Ratner in 1991. His company, Ratners, was once the UK's largest mass market jeweller with 80% market share. However, in a speech to over 6,000 members of the Institute of Directors back in 1991, Gerald Ratner joked that his company's earrings were "total crap" and added that a prawn sandwich from Marks & Spencer would cost more and last longer! Subsequent media coverage effectively ended the company after its market value dropped by around £500 million ($725m).

Common mistake

Where students use perception maps as a form of primary research in the Internal Assessment, they often create the position map using their own perceptions of brands and products. However, the tool is used to gauge the perceptions of the target market (customers as a whole, rather than opinions of a single person).

Box 4.2.d Corporate blunders ... how to get the wrong image

- July 2001 – David Shepherd, marketing director of Topman, a British mass market clothes retailer, called his customers "hooligans or whatever", joking that they bought suits either for a job interview or to attend court.
- March 2003 – EMI's chief executive, Alain Levy, said that there were not many people from Finland who could sing; it was his justification for cutting the number of Finnish recording artists.
- Oct 2003 – Matt Barrett, chief executive of Barclays, owner of the UK's largest credit card company, criticised Barclaycard, stating that he would never use it because it was just too expensive.
- April 2006 – Italy's Alitalia Airlines mispriced business-class flights from Toronto to Cyprus for CAD$39 instead of CAD$3,900! Some 2,000 customers booked flights at this price. The airline honoured the mistake, which cost it more than $7m.
- July 2009 – United Airlines baggage handlers broke musician Dave Carroll's bespoke $3,500 guitar and refused to compensate him. Carroll's subsequent song 'United Breaks Guitars' became one of YouTube's greatest viral hits. Watch the music video here: https://goo.gl/NW4uj4
- Jan 2010 – Sweden's H&M was reported in the New York Times to have disposed of bags of new garments, which had been deliberately cut and destroyed rather than donating them to charity.
- Dec 2013 – US discount retailer Target faced major criticisms following a breach of credit card data of up to 40 million customers by hackers.
- Sept 2016 – Samsung's Galaxy Note 7 kept catching fire, and there were reported cases of the batteries on the smartphone exploding. This led to airlines banning the phone on their flights, and a product recall of 2.5 million phones. According to Reuters, the mishap ended costing Samsung $17 billion.
- April 2017 – United Airlines in trouble again, this time for getting police to physically drag a passenger off a plane as he refused to give up his seat to 4 employees of a partner airline. Videos of the incident went viral, as Dr. David Dao was dragged off his seat, knocked unconscious and with blood around his mouth.

Unique selling point (USP)

The importance of having a unique selling point/proposition (USP). AO2

© IBO, 2014

There are many possibilities for a business to improve its corporate image, such as the pursuit of ethical objectives and *corporate social responsibility* (see Unit 1.3). Alternatively, businesses might seek to market their **unique selling point** (USP). A unique selling point, or **unique selling proposition**, is any aspect of a business, product or brand that makes it stand out from those offered by competitors. Consider a USP in the same way as a student applying for a university course or an applicant for a job – both need something unique, or special, to distinguish them from rivals in the market. The USP explains *why* customers buy the product over rival ones, such as its distinctive features or appealing packaging. Products with a USP are often promoted by word of mouth and social media (see Unit 4.5), which also saves the business on its marketing budget. A USP can be a major source of competitive advantage and therefore businesses want to emphasise their USP to attract customers, such as Pink Ladies which offers a females-only taxi service in the UK (see Question 4.2.5). Other, more generic examples of a USP include:

- Being the only firm in a local area to supply a certain good or service.
- Being the first business to provide a certain product (known as a **first mover advantage**).
- Having a reputation for being the 'best' in the market, e.g. Apple, Samsung and Toyota are market leaders.
- Having a reputation for being the lowest cost provider, e.g. Walmart's claim of 'Always Low Prices' or Tata Motor's $2,000 Nano – the world's cheapest car.
- Having a highly popular business slogan, such as 'Just Do It', 'Happy Meal' or 'Because You're Worth It'.

Although having a USP can be advantageous, it can be extremely difficult to find a USP. In reality, once a business establishes a successful USP in a market, others enter the market to compete. Businesses exploit their USP by including it in their marketing strategies.

Case study IBID Press

IBID Press was the first publisher to launch a dedicated textbook for the IB Business Management course, back in 2007 - our USP remains being the most comprehensive textbook available for the IB BM course. Additional resources for the BM course can be found here: http://www.ibid.com.au/business-management/

Case study

De Beers is a group of companies that dominates the market for diamonds. In 2000, *Advertising Age* magazine named 'A diamond is forever' (the corporate slogan of De Beers since 1948) as the best advertising slogan of the twentieth century, having used it successfully to market diamonds as a symbol of enduring love and commitment.

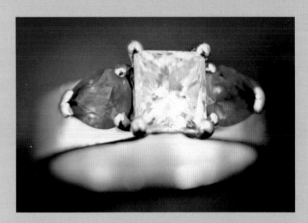

Photograph courtesy of Laura Brown

Case study

Not all distinctive selling points are good ideas. For example, McDonald's launched a 'Buy One Get One Free' offer on its best-selling burger in the USA - the Big Mac. The popularity of the campaign caused many customers to be upset as McDonald's could not supply enough Big Macs to meet the demand. In 2003, *Blockbuster*, the market leader in video-rentals at the time, launched a 'No Late Fees' policy - a disaster as customers wanted the latest movies available but didn't face any penalties for not returning their DVDs!

Common mistake

Do not confuse unique selling propositions with business slogans (catchphrases) or mission statements, even though they may be linked. What a business intends to achieve (through slogans or mission statements) does not necessarily give it a USP.

Case study Coca-Cola and Christmas

Coca-Cola, one of the most recognised brands on the planet, claims to have created the red and white outfit worn by Santa Claus – the same colours as its iconic logo and packaging. To date, no one has been able to successfully dispute Coca-Cola's claim.

Question 4.2.7 J.D. Power and Associates

J.D. Power and Associates is the motor industry's benchmark for judging the quality of new motor vehicles. Lexus and Porsche lead the luxury brands, while Toyota, Honda and Hyundai dominate among the **mass market** brands. These companies tend to use the *J.D. Power and Associates* ratings in their marketing.

(a) Define the term **mass market**.   [2 marks]

(b) Explain how quality awards and ratings, such as those awarded by *J.D. Power and Associates,* can provide car manufacturers with a unique selling point.   [4 marks]

(c) To what extent does having a unique selling point in a highly competitive market, such as the motor industry, help an organization to achieve its objectives?   [10 marks]

Differentiation

How organizations can differentiate themselves and their products from competitors. AO3

© IBO, 2017

Differentiation is the act of distinguishing a business or its products from rivals in the industry. Product differentiation tries to create the perception among customers that the organization's product is different (unique or special), so adds value compared with the substitute products from rival businesses. Hence, a differentiation strategy involves making a product stand out from others. By having a unique or distinctive element to the product, it could help the business to withstand competition. Common methods of differentiation revolve around the 8Ps in the marketing mix:

- **Product** – Distinctive features of a product could include its design, functions, build quality or performance. For example, businesses can differentiate the quality of their products by using better quality raw materials and components or by achieving international quality accreditation. This gives the business a competitive advantage and enables the organization to charge premium prices for its products.

- **Price** – Different pricing strategies (see Unit 4.5) enables a business to sell a range of products, from economy brands to luxury versions. Businesses can also offer discounts for multiple (bulk) purchases. In the service sector, many businesses charge different fees for different levels of service, e.g. business and first-class air travel.

- **Promotion** – Businesses can differentiate themselves or their products from others through various promotional methods (see Unit 4.5) such as logos, slogans and branding. Nike's swoosh or the triple stripes of Adidas allow customers to instantly identify their products. Successful differentiation requires marketing support to promote a business and its products.

- **Place** – Differentiated marketing enables retailers, distributors and wholesalers to reach a wider range of customers. The Internet, for example, continues to grow as a sales channel for many businesses around the world. Having an online presence is a form of differentiation.

- **People** – Businesses can differentiate themselves by the quality of their customer service, especially when customers need a high degree of support, advice and after-sales care. The quality of people in an organization can help to develop a reputation that rivals find hard to match. Unique or special skills and expertise can make the business a more attractive choice.

- **Processes** – The ways things are done and how efficiently these things are done can also be a differentiator for service providers. Providing convenience, such as free home deliver or online payment facilities, can set a business apart from its competitors. In the digital age where people always seem to be in a hurry, convenience is a vital source of competitiveness.

- **Physical environment** – For many businesses, the observable aesthetics and tangible appearance of the business can be an important differentiator. Hotels, schools, theme parks, gyms and jewellers are all examples. The physical location can also make it easier (convenient) for customers, giving the business a competitive benefits.

- **Packaging** – Businesses use packaging in a variety of ways to differentiate their products, such as the use of colours and different packaging materials. Coca-Cola's iconic glass bottle, Red Bull's distinctive can design, Toblerone's triangular shape packing, Pringle's cylinder container and McDonald's Happy Meal boxes are examples of products that can be distinguished by their packaging and design. Some businesses, such as jewellers, use packaging as an added-value service whilst others use it as a form of promotion.

The possibilities for differentiation are almost endless; creativity and imagination are the only obstacles. As Albert Einstein famously said, "Imagination is more important than knowledge. For knowledge is limited."

Figure 4.2.l Luxury handbags can be differentiated by brand, colour, size, material and design

Table 4.2.c   Advantages and disadvantages of differentiation

Advantages	Disadvantages
Price advantages Firms can only charge a relatively low price for standardized products as customers have other substitute suppliers to choose from. By contrast, differentiation can add value to a firm's goods and services, thus allows it to charge higher prices.	**Expensive** Differentiation can be very expensive, e.g. special sales promotions cost the business money. Only large companies have the financial resources to differentiate their products and services in order to target a larger number of customers in different market segments.
Brand recognition and loyalty These can be a source of competitive advantage. High brand awareness creates more opportunities for products to be sold, perhaps due to customer loyalty or simply because customers feel more comfortable buying a familiar product.	**Economies of scale** Savings cannot be fully exploited compared with mass production of a single, standardised product. Differentiation requires additional marketing costs, especially if the business caters for different customers in different markets.
Distribution advantages Retail space is limited so vendors such as supermarkets only stock the best-selling brands. Therefore, successful product differentiation improves placement (distribution) of a firm's products.	**Excessive differentiation** This can drain a firm's resources and confuse customers. Consider, as examples, the pricing packages used by mobile phone service providers or different levels of coverage provided by insurance companies.

Theory of knowledge

Albert Einstein (1879–1955) claimed, *"Imagination is more important than knowledge. For knowledge is limited".* To what extent does this apply to the study of Business Management?

Theory of knowledge

How can managers know whether it is best for the organization to opt for an undifferentiated or differentiated approach to marketing?

IB Learner Profile – Be an inquirer

Investigate examples of differentiation in one of the following industries: airline, fast food, hotels, higher education, or any other industry of your choice. Share your findings with the rest of the class.

Marketing planning and the CUEGIS concepts

Change is an important concept for marketing planning. For example, having a unique selling point can give a business a competitive advantage in the short term, but it is unlikely to last as rivals will respond accordingly. Competition can mean that businesses continually strive to differentiate themselves and their products from their rivals. Changes occur for many reasons beyond the control of an organization, such as changes in technology, fashion and economic conditions. Hence, all aspects of marketing planning (such as marketing plans, the marketing mix and targeting) are exposed to the forces of change. Marketing planning ensures that managers monitor and respond to these changes. It also helps to reduce risks as marketing planning can help managers to make more informed decisions.

Ethical marketing is a growing part of strategic marketing planning. It refers to the social and moral responsibilities of marketers. Ethical marketing can present a moral dilemma for businesses - if they sell products aimed at children that are perfectly legal, such as war toys or fast food products, why shouldn't businesses be allowed to market these? Marketers would argue that advertising can be informative, not just persuasive or pressurising. Marketing can also help customers to make better and more informed decisions. Arguably, using inappropriate and unethical marketing strategies can damage an organization's brand image, so ethics shouldn't be an issue (in theory).

Technological advances have made market research more innovative and cost-effective, e.g. For example, online surveys

CORE

Marketing

can help to capture a large sample, with the software being able to compute the results from the survey.

Strategically, the use of marketing research (see Unit 4.4), customer profiles and perception maps can help to reveal the reasons why customers buy certain brands or are loyal to certain businesses. Strategic marketing planning involves segmentation, targeting and positioning. However, it is unlikely that smaller businesses will have the financial and human resources to target all segments. Essentially, effective marketing planning is an essential part of an organization's strategy, and can help to ensure the firm's longevity. A summary of marketing planning is shown in Figure 4.2.m.

> ## Theory of knowledge
>
> Is it ethical to block online advertisements?

Figure 4.2.m Aspects of strategic marketing planning

In developing a business strategy, marketing managers can choose from an array of tools, such as:

- Perception mapping – Product positioning and repositioning strategies

- Ansoff's matrix – Marketing strategies for growth (see Unit 1.6)

- Boston matrix – Developing of a firm's product portfolio (see Unit 4.5)

- SWOT analysis – Identifying a firm's marketing strengths, weaknesses, opportunities and threats (see Unit 1.3)

- STEEPLE analysis – Identifying restraining and driving forces in the external business environment (see Unit 1.5)

- Force field analysis – Implementing and managing organizational change (see Unit 1.7).

Successful marketing strategies are carefully planned out to achieve the organization's marketing objectives. Professor Robert Lauterborn (1990) argues that successful marketing strategy requires an examination of the marketing mix from the perspective of consumers. He called this the **4 Cs of marketing**: Customer solution (product), Cost to the customer (price), Communication (promotion) and Convenience (place). The marketing strategy should be executed in a cost effective way without the organization having to overspend on its budget.

Marketing planning is essentially a prerequisite to marketing strategy (the ways in which the business intends to achieve its marketing objectives). Strategic decisions will affect the direction of the organization and determine its future prosperity.

> ## CUEGIS Essay
>
> With reference to an organization of your choice, examine how **innovation** and **ethics** have influenced its marketing mix.   *[20 marks]*

> ## CUEGIS Essay
>
> With reference to an organization of your choice, discuss how **change** and **culture** have influenced its marketing planning.   *[20 marks]*

CORE

Marketing

REVIEW QUESTIONS

1. What is a marketing plan?

2. What does the typical marketing planning process involve?

3. What are the benefits and limitations of marketing planning?

4. What is the marketing mix?

5. Differentiate between producer and consumer products.

6. What are the factors that influence the pricing decision? *Hint*: think DRASTIC.

7. Why is distribution (place) important in the marketing mix?

8. Distinguish between above the line and below the line promotion.

9. Outline the relationship between the marketing mix and marketing objectives?

10. What is the difference between target markets and market segments?

11. What is meant by consumer profiles?

12. Differentiate between segmentation by demographics, geographic and psychographic factors.

13. Distinguish between niche markets and mass markets.

14. What is a position (perception) map?

15. Why might it be important for some businesses to have a unique selling point (USP)?

16. How can organizations differentiate themselves and their products from competitors?

KEY TERMS

Consumer profiles are the demographic and psychographic characteristics of consumers in different markets, e.g. their age,

gender, occupation, income level, religion, marital status and purchasing habits.

Differentiation is the act of distinguishing a business or its products from rivals in the industry. It tries to create the perception among customers that the organization's product is different (unique or special) compared with substitute products from rival businesses.

Ethical marketing refers to the moral aspects of an organization's marketing strategies. It can be encouraged by the use of moral codes of practice.

Market segmentation is the process of categorising customers into distinct groups with similar characteristics (such as age or gender) and similar wants or needs.

The **marketing mix** is the combination of various elements needed to successfully market a product. It is used to review and develop marketing strategies and is at the heart of marketing planning. Traditionally, it consists of the 4 Ps: product, price, promotion and place.

Marketing objectives are the targets that the marketing department wishes to achieve, e.g. sales growth or increased market share. Marketing objectives should derive from the organization's overall objectives.

A **marketing plan** refers to the document outlining an organization's marketing objectives and strategies for a specified time period.

Marketing planning is the systematic process of devising marketing objectives and appropriate marketing strategies to achieve these goals. It requires the collection and analysis of information about a particular market, e.g. market research data on existing and potential customers.

Market segments are the various sub-groups of a large market, consisting of customers who share common or similar characteristics, e.g. lifestyle, age, gender, marital status, occupation, educational attainment, and income level.

Marketing strategies are the various long-term actions taken by a business to achieve its marketing goals.

Mass marketing refers to undifferentiated marketing. This is a strategy that ignores targeting individual market segments.

CORE

Marketing

Niche marketing targets a specific and well-defined market segment, e.g. some businesses provide high-end speciality goods (such as Louis Vuitton handbags, Bugatti cars and Cartier watches) in niche markets.

Packaging is a form of non-price competition that focuses on the ways in which a product is presented to the consumer. Psychologists argue that people's moods are affected by aspects of packaging such as colour and texture.

Physical evidence refers to the image portrayed by a business (or perceived by customers) regarding its observable and tangible features, e.g. the cleanliness and physical attributes of an organization.

Place describes the methods of distributing products to customers, e.g. Coca-Cola distributes its drinks to customers via wholesalers, retailers and vending machines.

Position map (or **perception map**) is a visual aid that shows customer perceptions of a product or brand in relation to others in the market, often by comparing perceptions about price and quality.

Price refers to the amount that customers pay for a particular good or service.

Process is part of the extended marketing mix which refers to the methods and procedures used to give clients the best possible experience.

A **product** is a physical good or an intangible service, such as a computer or a haircut. Businesses sell products to fulfil the needs and wants (desires) of their customers.

Promotion refers to the strategies used to attract customers to buy a firm's products. Branding, for example, helps to differentiate a product from its competitors.

Repositioning is a marketing strategy that involves changing the market's perception of a firm's product or brand in comparison to rival businesses.

Segmentation is the process of categorising customers into distinct groups of people with similar characteristics (such as age or gender) and similar buying habits for market research and targeting purposes.

A **target market** refers to a clearly identifiable group of customers, thus enabling marketers to focus their efforts on particular market segments, such as children, adults, men or women.

Targeting refers to each distinctive market segment having its own specific marketing mix. Different markets can be targeted, depending on whether the business operates in niche or mass markets.

Unique selling point (or **unique selling proposition**) refers to any aspect of a product that makes it stand out (in a positive way) from those offered by rival businesses.

Having a USP can help firms to sell their products

CORE

Marketing

4.3 Sales forecasting

"Doubt is the key to knowledge." - Persian proverb

HL content	Assessment objective
Up to four-part moving average, sales trends and forecast (including seasonal, cyclical and random variation) using given data	AO4
The benefits and limitations of sales forecasting	AO3

© IBO, 2017

Sales, trends and forecasting

Up to four-part moving average, sales trends and forecast (including seasonal, cyclical and random variation) using given data. AO4

© IBO, 2017

Sales forecasting is a quantitative management technique used to predict a firm's level of sales over a given time period. It is important because sales forecasts can help a business to identify problems and opportunities in advance. However, trying to predict what will happen in the future is difficult because there are so many variables that are subject to change. Hence, the forecasts may turn out to be completely inaccurate.

Figure 4.3.a Holiday destinations such as Nha Trang, Vietnam are subject to seasonal fluctuations

To make realistic and accurate forecasts, managers use several sales forecasting techniques, such as:

• **Extrapolation** – This forecasting technique identifies the trend by using past data and extending this trend to predict future sales. For example, if a firm's sale revenues have increased by an average of 5% each year for the past several years, then it might be expected that this trend continues in the near future. Graphically, the trend can be shown by a line of best fit, and extrapolation simply extends this line to make predictions (see Figure 4.3.b). Extrapolation works well if there is a clear correlation (relationship) between two sets of numbers, such as sales revenue over a period of time or the correlation between marketing expenditure and sales growth.

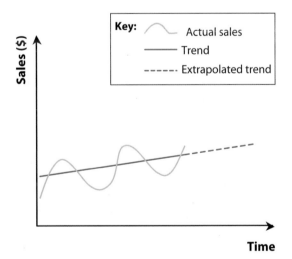

Figure 4.3.b Extrapolation of sales trend

• **Market research** – Identifying and forecasting the buying habits of consumers can be vital to a firm's prosperity and survival. For example, despite being the top global producer of cars for 76 years, General Motors grew complacent and overproduced cars failing to recognise the changing demands of customers. With soaring oil prices and greater concerns for the environment, Toyota

395

took over as the top motor manufacturer, with its highly successful fuel-efficient and hybrid vehicles.

- **Time series analysis** – This technique attempts to predict sales levels by identifying the underlying trend from a sequence of actual sales figures recorded at regular intervals in the past. There are three main elements to time series analysis:

  - *Seasonal variations* – periodic fluctuations in sales revenues over a specified time period (see Box 4.3.a), such as months or quarters of the year.

  - *Cyclical variations* – recurrent fluctuations in sales linked to the economic cycle of booms and slumps. Unlike seasonal variations, cyclical variations can last longer than a year.

  - *Random variations* – unpredictable fluctuations in sales revenues caused by erratic and irregular factors that cannot be practically anticipated. (see Box 4.3.b).

Box 4.3.a   Examples of seasonal demand

Seasonal fluctuations in demand are caused by variations in the demand for certain goods and services during different time periods. For example, they can be caused by changing seasons in the year or religious festivals such as Christmas, Easter, Diwali, Ramadan and Chinese New Year. Examples of seasonal demand include:

- Clothing (winter and summer)
- Easter egg
- Fireworks
- Flights (for holidays)
- Gift cards, e.g. Mothers' Day cards or Valentine's cards
- Sun lotion
- Sunglasses
- Textbooks.

Figure 4.3.c Sales forecasting is useful for predicting demand for seasonal goods such as Christmas crackers

Box 4.3.b   Examples of random variations

- Labour unrest, such as strike action
- Mass-scale product recalls due to safety concerns
- Natural disasters, such as hurricanes, flooding and earthquakes
- Outbreak of a war
- Outbreak of infectious diseases
- Political turmoil and public disorder
- Public relations disaster
- Unexpected, adverse weather conditions.

In practice, businesses are likely to use a combination of sales forecasting methods. The choice depends on several factors, such as:

- Accuracy (how accurate the forecasts need to be) - The greater the degree of certainty needed, the more thorough the methods of sales forecasting need to be. For example, it is more meaningful to use monthly or quarterly data to forecast the sales of ice cream; using annual figures would not reveal seasonal fluctuations in demand. However, this involves more time so incurs higher costs.

- Time (how far ahead forecasts need to be) - It is relatively easy to forecast sales for the next day, week or month. However, to predict sales levels over the next several years is much more ambitious. Extrapolation is only useful if predictions apply to the near future.

- Cost (the availability and cost of data and information collection) - If there is widespread access to a wealth of information at no or very little cost, then this can make forecasting more accurate. However, if it proves difficult to find appropriate and up-to-date information, or if access to information is highly expensive, this will affect the choice of forecasting methods.

- The stage in a product's life cycle - Market research rather than time series analysis will be used during both the 'Research and Development' and 'Launch' stages (see Unit 4.5). More data and information become available during the growth and maturity stages.

Statistical techniques in sales forecasting

There are several statistical techniques that can be used to analyse sales forecasting data:

- *Mean* – The arithmetic mean is the sum of all items divided by the number of items in a data set.

- *Median* – When all numbers are ranked in numerical order, the median is the middle number in the data set.

- *Mode* – This is the number that occurs more frequently than any other value in the data set.

- *Range* – This is the numerical difference between the highest and the lowest numbers in a data set.

- *Standard deviation* – This measures the difference (or digression) of a variable from the mean value in a data set.

Exam tip !

Given that most new products fail to get established on the market, this implies that businesses often over-predict their sales, i.e. sales forecasting is not an exact science, and you need to be aware of the limitations.

Moving averages

The most frequently used method of calculating averages is the arithmetic mean. However, **moving averages** are a more accurate method of identifying trends, so they are a more useful tool for sales forecasting. A moving average is used to establish underlying trends by smoothing out variations in the data set that are caused by seasonal, cyclical and random variations. To illustrate this point, consider the data in Table 4.3.a for Devendar Rawat Clothing Ltd.

The arithmetic mean is the sum of the sales figures ($555,000) divided by the number of items in the data set (in this case, there are five). Hence, the arithmetic mean is $111,000 for the period.

The moving average helps to identify the trend that exists within a data set (as above) by smoothing out fluctuations that might exist. There are a few ways to calculate moving averages with the most common being three-part (quarterly) and four-part moving averages. For example, to calculate a 'three-year moving average' for Devendar Rawat Clothing Ltd, average out three consecutive numbers in the data series:

- Work out the mean for the first three data items, i.e. ($100,000 + $110,000 + $120,000) ÷ 3 = $110,000

- Repeat this for the next three data items, i.e. months 2, 3 and 4. This gives a mean of ($110,000 + $120,000 + $95,000) ÷ 3 = $108,333

- Continue this process for the final 3-month period in the data set (i.e. years 3, 4 and 5). This gives ($120,000 + $95,000 + $130,000) ÷ 3 = $115,000

Whilst more time consuming to calculate than the simple arithmetic mean, moving averages show how the underlying trend changes over the 5-month period, by smoothing out irregular fluctuations in the series of data. Although a four-part moving average smooths out the trend more so than a three-part moving average, the latter method is easier and quicker to calculate. The moving average can also be used to measure variations (seasonal, cyclical or random) from the trend, as shown in Table 4.3.b.

Table 4.3.a   Devendar Rawat Clothing Ltd.

	Month 1	Month 2	Month 3	Month 4	Month 5	Total
Sales ($)	100,000	110,000	120,000	95,000	130,000	555,000

Table 4.3.b   Devender Rawat Clothing Ltd. – variation from the trend

	Month 1	Month 2	Month 3	Month 4	Month 5
Sales ($)	100,000	110,000	120,000	95,000	130,000
3-point moving average		110,000	108,333	115,000	
Variation (Actual –Trend)		0	+ 11,667	– 20,000	

Marketing

Exam tip!
Worked example

Alric Chong, a sole trader, sells organic farm products. Based on historical data, Alric has forecast his sales for the next 6 days as follows:

	Mon	Tues	Wed	Thurs	Fri	Sat
Sales revenue ($)	1,200	870	1,179	1,281	2,202	2,511

Question: Calculate the three-part moving average and comment on your findings.

[5 marks]

Answer:

Mon to Wed	=	(1,200 + 870 + 1,179) ÷ 3	= $1,083
Tues to Thur	=	(870 + 1,179 + 1,281) ÷ 3	= $1110
Wed to Fri	=	(1,179 + 1,281 + 2,202) ÷ 3	= $1,554
Thur to Sat	=	(1,281 + 2,202 + 2,511) ÷ 3	= $1,998

The calculations show a clear trend in rising sales throughout the week, despite the dip on Tuesday. Without using moving averages, it is difficult to identify the underlying trend in Alric Chong's sales due to the variations within the data. For example, it is less busy on Tuesday but far busier towards the weekend. By calculating moving averages, it is possible to remove some of these variations.

To calculate a four-point moving average, the same technique is used, although 'centreing' is used to average two moving averages (see Table 4.3.c):

- The first 4-point moving average is found by the sum of the sales in the first 4 months ($425,000) divided by 4 months = $106,250.

- The next data set (months 2 to 5) gives an average of $455,000 ÷ 4 = $113,750

- The centred trend is found by average these two numbers, i.e. ($106,250 + $113,750) ÷ 2 = $110,000. From this centred figure, it is possible to work out the variation in month 3, i.e. $120,000 – $110,000 = + $10,000.

Table 4.3.c   Calculating a four-point moving average

Month	Sales ($)	4-point moving average (trend)	Centred trend ($)	Variation ($)
1	100,000			
2	110,000			
		106,250		
3	120,000		110,000	+ 10,000
		113,750		
4	95,000		115,625	– 20,625
		117,500		
5	130,000		118,500	+ 11,500
		119,500		
6	125,000			
7	128,000			

Exam tip!

When analysing sales forecasts, make sure you can calculate percentage changes to show what has happened to sales revenue during the time period given. This can help to improve your argument. To calculate percentage changes, work out the numerical difference, divide this by the original number, and express as a percentage, i.e. (New figure – Old figure) ÷ Old figure × 100.

Case study
The McBig Mistake

In 1998, *McDonald's* celebrated its 25th anniversary in the UK by offering a 'Buy One, Get One Free' (BOGOF) deal on its best-selling product – the Big Mac. *McDonald's* doubled their supply of Big Macs for the special offer, but failed to forecast the additional demand that the BOGOF deal would bring. Many *McDonald's* restaurants had sold out of Big Macs by 11am on the first day, upsetting customers across the country. The special promotion went on to become one of the biggest marketing mistakes in UK business history.

Theory of knowledge

Which way of knowing is of most significance when making sales forecasts – faith, intuition, memory or reasoning?

Question 4.3.1   Esswood Campers

Nicola Esswood owns and runs her own camping site in New Plymouth, New Zealand. Located near the waterfront, *Esswood Campers* thrives in the summer season but suffers from a lack of tourists in the winter months.

Her sales forecasts for the next twelve months, based on past data, are shown below:

	Mar	Apr	May	Jun	Jul	Aug	Sep	Oct	Nov	Dec	Jan	Feb
Sales ($)	3500	3000	3000	2500	2800	2600	2900	3000	3600	4500	4200	4000

(a) Calculate the (i) mean, (ii) median, and (iii) modal averages from the sales data above.   *[3 marks]*

(b) Calculate the range and comment on your findings.   *[2 marks]*

(c) Calculate the four-point moving average for *Esswood Campers*.   *[4 marks]*

(d) Using the four-point moving average method, calculate the variation from the trend.   *[4 marks]*

(e) Examine how the above sales forecasting calculations might be of use to *Esswood Campers*.   *[6 marks]*

Marketing

Question 4.3.2   Chatterjee Travel Ltd.

Chatterjee Travel Ltd. is a London-based company that specialises in travel services for wealthy Finnish customers from around the world who are fanatics of The English Premier League (the world's most watched and lucrative sports league). Ira Chatterjee, the CEO, has built a wide customer base of wealthy clients who mainly fly from Finland, Holland and Italy. Sales figures for the latter part of the football (soccer) season are shown below:

Sales (£'000)	Jan	Feb	Mar	Apr	May	Jun
	30	28	32	35	30	0

(a) Outline why *Chatterjee Travel Ltd.* might be described as operating in a niche market.   *[2 marks]*

(b) Calculate the three-part moving averages for *Chatterjee Travel Ltd.* for the period shown.   *[4 marks]*

(c) Construct an appropriate graph to show the actual sales figures and the moving averages.   *[5 marks]*

(d) Comment on the trend and seasonal fluctuations from your graph and outline how such fluctuations might affect *ChatterjeeTravel Ltd.*   *[6 marks]*

Benefits of sales forecasting

The benefits of sales forecasting. AO3

© IBO, 2017

- *Improved working capital and cash flow* (see Unit 3.7) – Sales forecasting can help a business to identify seasonal fluctuations in the demand for its products, and hence the implications for the organization's liquidity position. If managers have a clear idea of expected costs and revenues, they are more likely to have better cash flow management in the coming months.

- *Improved stock control* – Accurate sales forecasts help to ensure that the correct levels of stocks are available for use in production at different times of the year. Holding excessive or insufficient inventory can create problems (see Unit 5.5). Sales forecasting helps managers to optimize their purchasing plans.

- *Improved productive efficiency* (see Unit 5.3) – The ability to plan for the correct level of production means better use of an organization's resources. For example, many retailers temporarily hire part-time staff during peak holiday trading periods due to the high seasonal demand. Accurate sales forecasting therefore allows managers to devote time to strategic planning to develop the business, rather than deal with operational problems caused by a lack of production planning (see Unit 5.5).

- *Helps to secure external sources of finance* – Accurate and realistic sales forecasting can help a business to obtain external financing from investors and lenders. This is especially important for new businesses as sales forecasts are a common requirement in business plans (see Unit 1.1).

- *Improved budgeting* – Accurate sales forecasting helps managers to anticipate changes in the economy and therefore to adjust budgets accordingly. For example, changes in sales trends (the buying habits of customers) make it easier for production managers to know how much inventory to hold and for marketing managers to know how many sales staff to hire at different times of the year.

Figure 4.3.d Sales forecasting can help firms to predict peak trading times

Essentially, the benefits of sales forecasting should help managers to have better control by giving them an informed idea of what to expect in the near future, thereby optimising their marketing plans. This enables the business to operate more efficiently and more profitably.

Theory of knowledge

To what extent can we know something if the knowledge claim is based on predictions?

Question 4.3.3   Acosta Adventures

Jeffrey Acosta runs a cultural tourism business in the Maekok River Resort in Northern Thailand. His company, *Acosta Adventures*, operates a range of activities for tourists, including elephant trekking, river rafting, boat trips, mountain biking and hikes in the beautiful rural surroundings. Most of his customers come from the Asia Pacific region including China, Taiwan, Japan, Australia and New Zealand. The Indian Ocean tsunami (2004) and political unrest (2014) caused fluctuations in the number of tourists in Thailand. Sales data in Thai baht (THB) are shown below.

Year	Quarter	Sales (THB million)	3-part moving average (trend)	Variation (THB million)
Last year	1	7.89		
	2	7.56		
	3	9.55		
	4	6.57		
This year	1	7.69		
	2	7.55		
	3	9.98		
	4	6.47		
Next year	1	7.92		
	2	7.67		
	3	10.32		

(a) Complete the table above for *Acosta Adventures,* showing the three-part moving average and the variation from the trend. *[4 marks]*

(b) Extrapolate the trend for Quarter 4 of next year. *[2 marks]*

(c) Explain how the sales forecasting data above can help the operations of *Acosta Adventures.* *[4 marks]*

Limitations of sales forecasting

The limitations of sales forecasting. AO3

© IBO, 2017

- *Limited information* – Sales forecasting is a prediction based on past data and trends. Sales forecasting does not reveal the whole picture (as the tool is based on assumptions), without any consideration of qualitative factors. As sociologist William B. Cameron (1963) said, *"Not everything that can be counted counts, and not everything that counts can be counted".* Forecasts are only as good as the information and data that are available at the time the forecasts are made.

- *Inaccuracy of predictions* – Critics argue that sales forecasting is part fact and part guesswork. There can be an element of bias or subjectivity in sales forecasting. Even accurate sales forecasts are based on assumptions. Whilst change might be inevitable, sales forecasts can be wrong for many reasons, e.g. figures used might be overly optimistic. Past trends are not indicative of the future. Having no or very limited historical data (because the product is new, for example) can make sales forecasting extremely difficult or inaccurate.

- *Garbage in garbage out (GIGO)* – If the data and information used to predict sales forecasts are outdated, irrelevant or biased, then the forecasts are unrealistic. For example, some managers might deliberately underestimate sales forecasts so that it is easier to reach their targets.

- *External influences* – The external business environment (see Unit 1.5) causes change that may not be predictable, e.g. natural disasters, oil price hikes, fierce competition from abroad, unexpected fluctuations in the business cycle or adverse weather conditions. Such factors can significantly distort sales forecasts.

Theory of knowledge

Is sales forecasting an art or a science?

Common mistake

Some students are often quick to condemn the skills of sales forecasters, stating that the data collected is either biased or unrepresentative. Sales forecasting techniques can be extremely sophisticated (beyond the scope of your IB exams) and give reliable data for marketers. Of course, if actual sales figures vary significantly from the forecasts then questions should be asked; but don't assume that sales forecasts are unreliable simply because they don't match the predicted figures.

Theory of knowledge

Is the ability to predict essentially the same as the ability to know? Does knowing allow us to predict?

Theory of knowledge

To what extent can history, as an area of knowledge, help managers to know about the future?

Figure 4.3.e Unexpected adverse weather conditions will affect sales forecasts

Question 4.3.4   Bhave Bakery

Shobha Bhave runs *Bhave Bakery*, a small bakery in Pune, India. She has recently introduced cookies to her product portfolio to cater for a wider customer base. However, she is having difficulties in forecasting sales of her cookies. Shobha's bank manager has suggested that she calculates the 4-weekly average to **extrapolate the trend**. *Bhave Bakery's* sales data for the first 10 weeks of selling cookies is shown below; figures are in Indian rupees (INR or ₹).

Week	1	2	3	4	5	6	7	8	9	10
Sales (INR ₹)	7,347	6,123	6,735	7,347	7,041	7,531	7,837	6,061	6,000	6,368

(a) Explain what it means to **extrapolate the trend**.   *[2 marks]*

(b) Use the data for *Bhave Bakery* to calculate the four-weekly moving average.   *[4 marks]*

(c) Explain how random fluctuations make sales forecasting difficult for *Bhave Bakery*.   *[4 marks]*

Sales forecasting and the CUEGIS concepts

Changes in the external business environment can quite easily affect the results of sales forecasting. For example, the political unrest in Thailand in 2014 was estimated to cost the economy over $2.7 billion in lost tourism revenue. An economic downturn would have an adverse impact on sales forecasts. Multinational companies are also exposed to fluctuations in exchange rates which also have an impact on sales forecasts. Technological progress that helps reduce average production costs can boost sales if average prices fall.

The culture of the organization or the subculture of the sales department will have an impact on 'how things are done' within the business. Organizational culture has a direct impact on the motivation level of staff (see Unit 2.4), which clearly affects sales forecasting. Risk adverse cultures will tend to be more pessimistic with their forecasts, whereas innovative cultures might be more optimistic, albeit somewhat unrealistic perhaps in their forecasts.

Ethical considerations also play a key role in sales forecasting. If predictions are made on subjective grounds, using unreliable data, then there are clearly ethical questions to be asked.

Managers may overestimate sales forecasts in an attempt to sway decision making. For example, over-predicting sales forecasts may be used to secure financial backing from investors. However, there are ethical implications of such practices; any strategy that depends too heavily on sales forecasts has added risks.

Innovations can positively affect sales forecasts. For example, product innovations such as smartphones have ensured Samsung and Apple enjoy the benefits of market leadership. in particular, the Internet has enabled many small businesses in particular to reach markets they were unable to access in the past. Whilst this change boosts sales revenue, it can make sales forecasting less accurate, at least in the short term. Similarly, the globalization of markets can improve future sales but make sales forecasting less precise.

Marketers can use sales forecast data to make decisions about expanding to overseas markets. The most common basis for forecasting sales of new products is to rely on quantitative primary research data (see Unit 4.4). This is usually combined with test marketing before launching a product to the market.

Test marketing is a strategy that complements sales forecasting as a decision-making tool. This strategy involves launching a new product to a selected panel of customers, often in a particular geographical location to gauge customer acceptance and responses to the new product. The data from test marketing can be used to forecast sales prior to the product being launched nationally or internationally. Although this strategy can be rather expensive and produce unrepresentative results, it tends to provide more reliable sales forecasts, thus reduces the risks of product launches.

IB Learner Profile – Be a thinker

Alibaba, the world's largest online retailer and B2B operator, floated its shares in the USA in an attempt to make the organization more global. Consider how such a move might make sales forecasting more difficult to existing businesses that adopt Alibaba's B2B platform.

CUEGIS Essay

With reference to an organization of your choice, examine how **innovation** affects its ability to **change** and evolve.   *[20 marks]*

REVIEW QUESTIONS

1. What is meant by sales forecasting?

2. What are correlation and extrapolation?

3. How can market research assist sales forecasting?

4. Distinguish between seasonal and cyclical variations.

5. What are random variations?

6. What are moving averages?

7. What is meant by a three-part moving average?

8. How are four-part moving averages calculated?

9. Outline the benefits of sales forecasting.

10. Explain the limitations of sales forecasting.

KEY TERMS

Correlation shows the degree to which two sets of numbers or variables are related, e.g. sales revenue over a period of time. Marketers are interested in establishing a strong correlation between marketing expenditure and sales growth.

Cyclical variations are recurrent fluctuations in sales linked to the economic cycle of booms and slumps. Unlike seasonal variations, cyclical variations can last longer than a year.

Extrapolation is a forecasting technique used to identify the trend by using past data and extending this trend to predict future sales.

Moving averages are used to find underlying trends by smoothing out variations in a data set caused by seasonal, cyclical and random variations. It is common to use up to four-part moving averages, i.e. averaging sales figures for four consecutive time periods.

Sales forecasting is a quantitative management technique used to predict a firm's level of sales over a given time period.

Seasonal variations are periodic fluctuations in sales revenues over a specified time period, such as certain months or quarters of the year.

Random variations are unpredictable fluctuations in sales revenues caused by erratic and irregular factors that cannot be practically anticipated.

Time series analysis is a sales forecasting technique that attempts to predict sales levels by identifying the underlying trend from a sequence of actual sales figures.

4.4 Market research

"Those who have knowledge don't predict. Those who predict don't have knowledge." - Lao Tzu (604–531 BCE), Chinese philosopher

SL/HL content	Assessment objective
Why and how organizations carry out market research	AO2
The following methods/techniques of primary market research: • surveys • interviews • focus groups • observations	AO2
The following methods/techniques of secondary market research: • market analyses • academic journals • government publications • media articles	AO2
Ethical considerations of market research	AO3
The difference between qualitative and quantitative research	AO2
The following methods of sampling: • quota • random • stratified • cluster • snowballing • convenience	AO2
Results from data collection	AO2

© IBO, 2017

The role of market research

Why and how organizations carry out market research. AO2

© IBO, 2017

Market research refers to marketing activities designed to discover the opinions, beliefs and preferences of potential and existing customers, i.e. it serves to identify and anticipate the wants and needs of customers. Market research can involve collecting data and information on competitors and market trends to gain insight into a specific market. Market research can be ad hoc or continuous:

- **Ad hoc research** takes place on an 'as and when necessary' basis. The focus of the research is on specific marketing problems or issues, and tends to be on a one-off basis.

- **Continuous research** takes place on a regular and ongoing basis. For example, governments usually calculate the cost of living based on the price data of a representative sample of products bought by the average household. Market research firms report annual league tables containing information such as the most popular brands in a certain country, region or the world. The movie and music industries also compile weekly 'Top 10' lists based on sales figures.

The role of market research serves several purposes:

- Gives businesses up-to-date information. This is particularly important in fast-paced industries that are always changing, e.g. the fashion and consumer electronics industries.

405

- Enables businesses to improve their marketing strategies by using a distinct marketing mix for each customer target market.

- Assesses customer reactions to a new product by testing it on a small group of customers. This can prevent huge losses had it been unsuccessfully launched on a large scale.

- Gives businesses an understanding of the activities and strategies used by their rivals.

- Helps businesses to predict what is likely to happen in the future. Understanding the likely trends will enable businesses to react accordingly in order to maximise future opportunities.

Effective market research helps to reduce the risk of failure, by investigating the needs and wants of customers. If the research findings show that customers react negatively to the product, then the business can either make necessary adjustments or scrap the project altogether (without having spent huge amounts of money on a national launch). Market research can therefore be used to answer questions such as:

- Are customers likely to buy the product?

- Which market segments are interested in the product?

- How much are customers willing to pay?

- How often are they likely to purchase the product?

- Which brands do customers see as being rivals to the marketed product?

- What are the preferred (most effective) methods of promotion?

- Where and how should the products be sold?

Ultimately, as a strategic planning tool, market research helps businesses to reduce risks. Being able to accurately forecast future market trends gives businesses a greater chance of success, despite the limitations of market research.

Exam tip !

Read this unit before embarking on your Internal Assessment (IA). Market research is a vital part of the IA process in Business Management. Higher Level students are required to conduct primary market research for a real-life organization that faces a specific problem or issue. Standard Level students need to use secondary market research, using three to five supporting documents to focus on a particular aspect of the SL syllabus.

Market research can be conducted in two broad ways: primary and secondary research.

Primary market research

The following methods/techniques of primary market research: surveys, interviews, focus groups and observations. AO2
© IBO, 2017

Primary research is market research that involves gathering new data first-hand for a specific purpose. For example, if an organization wants to know how staff feel about the working environment then it would use primary market research. Primary research (also known as **field research** or **bespoke research**) is often used to gather data and information from customers to identify their buying patterns and to anticipate changes in market trends. There are several methods of conducting primary research, including: surveys (questionnaires), interviews, focus groups and observations.

Common mistake

Students often assume that primary research is always conducted by the business itself. However, many businesses hire specialist research agencies to conduct the market research on their behalf.

CORE

Marketing

Table 4.4.a   Advantages and disadvantages of primary research

Advantages	Disadvantages
Relevance Primary research is carried out for a specific purpose, so directly addresses the questions that need to be answered. By contrast, secondary data is not always in a format that can be easily used by a firm.	**Time consuming** It can be a very tedious and lengthy task to collect primary data that is accurate and representative. This can delay decision-making and could lead to lost market opportunities in the short term.
Up to date Secondary market research data tends to be more dated and therefore often less reliable than primary research findings.	**Costly** Collecting primary data is often costly, due to the time involved to collect quality data or because the data is difficult to collect.
Confidential and unique Since the research is done first-hand, no one else (including rivals) has access to the information.	**Validity** Faults in market research (e.g. poor questionnaire design or sampling errors) will lead to misleading or biased results.

Surveys (or questionnaires)

A **survey** or questionnaire is a document that contains a series of questions used to collect data for a specific purpose. They are the most common method of primary research. There are several types of surveys, such as:

- *Self-completed surveys* are completed by a sample of people, e.g. many hotels and restaurants use these questionnaires to gather views from their customers. The information can help to identify problems, trends and suggestions for improvement.

- *Personal surveys* are conducted face-to-face, rather like an interview. The interviewer can address any questions that might arise from the questionnaire (such as clarifying what certain questions mean). It is also quicker for the interviewer to complete the survey due to familiarity with the questions.

- *Telephone surveys* are similar to personal surveys but use telecommunications technology. The benefit of this is that a larger number of people in a wider geographical spread can be covered. The main drawbacks are the relatively higher costs and the low response rate as a large number of people are not willing to take part in telephone surveys.

- *Online surveys* such as Zoomerang.com or Google Forms are an increasingly popular way of gathering primary data. For example, many schools use online surveys to find out the views of staff and students on a range of issues, such as getting feedback on school uniform and staff training programmes. They are much cheaper than other forms of primary research such as paper-based surveys or telephone surveys. Computer software can also help researchers to collate quantitative research data, thereby saving a lot of time and resources.

- *Postal surveys* are sent to people's home or office address for them to complete in their own time. A drawback is that people might simply treat the surveys as junk mail, so ignore them. To create an incentive for people to return postal surveys, businesses often provide free postage (the business pays for this) or offer prizes and gifts (but this clearly adds to the costs).

Figure 4.4.a Time lags with the post means postal surveys are less popular than online surveys

Due to the potential benefits of using surveys and the potentially high costs, effective survey design is of real importance. Therefore, surveys should:

- Avoid *bias* in order to collect meaningful and useful data. The wording of questions should not distort answers from respondents, e.g. asking people how much they like Coca-Cola is not as good a question as asking them which brand of cola they prefer.

- Avoid *jargon* (technical language) so that respondents understand the questions. This minimises potentially misrepresentative answers.

- Include both *closed* and *open-ended questions*. Closed questions (such as 'yes or no' questions or multiple choice options) make it easier and quicker to complete a survey. They also aid quantitative analysis. Open-ended questions allow the researcher to obtain qualitative answers, such as the reasons why respondents prefer a particular brand. They can also provide ideas or suggestions that enable the business to make better decisions.

- Be *tried* and *tested*. Before using a survey for market research, it is common for it to be trialled (tested) with a small group of people. This can help to identify any errors or omissions in the initial survey so that the results from the final research better serve the needs of the researcher.

- Allow the *objectives* of the survey to be met by gathering only relevant data, e.g. unnecessary questions should be avoided and the length of the survey should be limited as far as possible.

Exam tip !

Consider the above factors when designing your own survey (if used) for your Internal Assessment. Quite often, students produce poorly designed questionnaires that result in superficial findings and impractical recommendations or conclusions.

Question 4.4.1   Questioning questionnaires

Study the survey below and answer the questions that follow.

Survey Research

Is it feasible to open another branch of Pawlyn Greetings Cards in Kennedy Town Centre?

1. Name . . . .

2. Age: Under 10 ☐   10–15 ☐   15–25 ☐

   26–35 ☐   36–64 ☐   65+ ☐

3. Gender:

4. Where do you live? . . . .

5. Do you shop in Kennedy Town Centre? . . . .   **6.** How often? . . . .

7. Do you shop in Pawlyn Greetings Cards? . . . .   **8.** Why? . . . .

9. What item(s) do you buy there? . . . .

10. If a new Pawlyn Greetings Cards store were to open in Kennedy Town Centre, would you use it?   Yes ☐

Thank you!

(a) Use examples from the questionnaire to distinguish between quantitative and qualitative primary market research.

[4 marks]

(b) Describe any **three** mistakes in the questionnaire.

[6 marks]

A major benefit of surveys is the ability to generate quantitative and qualitative answers specific to the needs of the researcher. If designed properly, they can also be very simple to complete thereby making the process easier to gather market research data. However, using surveys for market research can be very costly and time-consuming as it is necessary to use a large sample to get statistically representative findings. There might also be reservations about the results due to bias or dishonest answers from respondents.

Theory of knowledge

Given the complications of survey designs and sample size, can primary market research data ever be truly reliable?

Interviews

Interviews involve one-to-one discussions between an interviewer and interviewees, such as individual customers, to investigate their personal circumstances and opinions. Beliefs, attitudes and feelings can also be examined in detail. Interviews are usually carried out in person (face-to-face) although telephone interviews can also be used. The findings from all interviews are analysed to identify the views that respondents share. Identifying the differences can also be important as it can help a business to refine its marketing strategies. In-depth interviews are often used when a business is planning to introduce change and new initiatives as they can be used to investigate the views of respondents to a new proposal.

However, interviews often provide a range of non-quantifiable information that might prove to be difficult to analyse or to make any extrapolations from. In addition, such interviews tend to be very time consuming. There is also huge scope for interviewer bias which can have an impact on the way in which respondents answer.

Focus groups

Focus groups involve forming small discussion groups to gain insight into the opinions, attitudes and behaviour of respondents. The group is typically made up of participants who share a similar customer profile, such as teenage boys who like to play online computer games. They can provide important information to help a business to devise and refine its marketing strategies. For example, they are often used when a business plans to launch a new product. The focus group might be asked to discuss the merits of alternative adverts or

to give feedback on the prototypes of a product. By using a focus group, detailed questions can be asked and participants are more likely to engage in discussions to generate insightful information. To aid market research analysis, audio-visual recordings of the discussions and observations of the behaviour of the participants are often used.

One drawback of using focus groups is that only extroverts tend to take part; those who shy from group discussions and debates are unlikely to participate and therefore their views are unregistered. In an open forum, there might also be some pressure for group members to conform to the majority view rather than to express their own opinions. Another potential limitation is that focus group participants often have to be paid, either in cash or in lieu (such as a meal voucher) for their time and input. This expense raises the overall costs of market research.

A variation of focus groups is the use of **consumer panels** – small groups of consumers within a business's target market who are used for regular market research. By using the same group, it saves the business from having to find new respondents (as in the case of focus groups). Also, as panellists are usually specialists, such as food critics (food tasters), they are particularly useful for conducting market research that requires specialist knowledge rather than using a random sample. For example, prior to launching new models, car manufacturers often use consumer panels formed by a group of loyal and knowledgeable customers.

Observations

This method of primary research involves watching *how* people behave and respond in different situations. It can be done under controlled conditions (rather like a laboratory test) or as real-life situations (where people do not know that they are being observed). Observations can be carried out using surveillance filming, photographic evidence or in person (by using a checklist or tally charts). Traffic audits, for example, use all of these methods to measure the flow of traffic on certain roads or in certain areas. Observations are often used by businesses such as restaurants, theme parks, health clinics, call centres and the post office in order to measure the average time it takes to serve a customer (queuing times).

A benefit of using observations is that they record people's actual behaviour rather than what people say they would do (as in the case of interviews and surveys). However, observations do not necessarily reveal *why* a person behaves or responds in the way they do. The only way to establish the reasons behind a person's motivation is to ask them, either directly or indirectly.

Question 4.4.2   Zaffran Craftphoria

Wahida Mostafa runs a small business in Dhaka, Bangladesh, where she sells craft products such as table mats, coasters, table runners and embroidered pencil cases. These products are handmade by Wahida. She is keen to get customer feedback on the appeal and quality of her products by using **primary market research**. Her business, *Zaffran Craftphoria*, has recently launched a Facebook website (www.facebook.com/zcraftphoria).

(a) Define the term **primary market research**.   *[2 marks]*

(b) Explain the value of primary market research to small businesses such as *Zaffran Craftphoria*.   *[4 marks]*

Photo courtesy of Sudhamsu Rao

Secondary research

The following methods/techniques of secondary market research: market analyses, academic journals, government publications, and media articles. AO2

© IBO, 2017

Secondary research (or **desk research**) involves the collection of second-hand data and information that already exists. This means that the data and information have previously been gathered by others, such as government publications or news articles.

Secondary research can be collected from internal and external sources. **Internal sources** are those that have already been gathered by the organization itself, such as company annual reports and sales records. **External sources** come from outside the business, e.g. market analyses, academic journals, government publications, and media articles (including the Internet).

Table 4.4.b   Advantages and disadvantages of secondary research

Advantages	Disadvantages
Data or information that is already available is generally cheaper and faster to collect and analyse rather than primary research that has to be collected.	Secondary data is second-hand data, so the results might be outdated or can become obsolete quite quickly.
Secondary research often provides an insight to changes or trends in an industry, such as whether customers are spending more money on household goods, jewellery and tourism. This allows a business to develop strategies in response to these market changes.	The data or information might be in an inappropriate format for the researcher as it has been collected for another purpose. Hence, the research needs to be further adapted or manipulated to suit the specific needs of the business.
There is a huge range of sources that market researchers can use, especially with online sources, making secondary data usually more accessible than primary data.	Secondary research might only provide partial information as it was produced for a different purpose, i.e. it does not address all the questions sought by the researcher.
Findings are often based on large sample sizes, so the results are statistically valid.	Unlike primary research, secondary data and information are widely available to competitors.

CORE

Marketing

Market analyses

A market analysis reveals the characteristics and the outlook (trends) for a particular product or industry, e.g. market size, market share and market growth rates. It can help to measure how well a business is doing compared with its rivals. New businesses often rely on market analyses to formulate their business plans (see Unit 1.1) and strategies. Market analysis data and information can be found in commercial sources and public information sources, such as:

- Market research firms - Specialist market research firms supply a huge range of market analyses, usually only accessible to subscribing clients. Examples include Nielsen, Mintel, Euromonitor and J.D. Power & Associates (see Question 4.2.7).

- Competitors – Company annual reports and websites of competitors are easily accessible, and could contain a wealth of data and information.

- Trade publications – These are specialist magazines targeted at a specific industry, e.g. *The Grocer* is a popular trade publication used in the supermarket industry. Many Business Management teachers around the world subscribe to the Economics, Business and Enterprise Association (EBEA), which publishes the latest trends and thinking in these subjects.

Figure 4.4.b The EBEA magazine (www.ebea.org.uk) is an example of a trade publication

The main advantage of using market analyses is that they enable businesses to access up-to-date and detailed market data and trends. However, it can be very expensive to use market analyses, as they usually have to be paid for. For example, most of the data and analyses on Statista are only available to subscribers who have paid for the service. In addition, data and information from market analyses can become outdated quickly, unless the source provides regular and ongoing updates.

Academic journals

Academic journals are periodical publications from educational and research institutions. Data and information relating to a particular academic discipline are published in these journals. For example, the *Harvard Business Review* is a globally recognised business management magazine from Harvard University. Academic journals publish educational, peer-reviewed articles and findings written by industry experts and academics. The purpose is to distribute and share theoretical work and market research findings, rather than to sell the information for profit.

Figure 4.4.c IB Review is an academic journal for IB educators and Diploma students

Box 4.4.a   Business Management theories and academic journals

Examples of Business Management theories that first appeared in academic journals include the following:
- Adams' equity theory, Journal of Abnormal Psychology (1963)
- Ansoff Matrix, Harvard Business Review (1957)
- Herzberg's two-factor theory of motivation, Harvard Business Review (1968)
- Lewin's force field analysis, Psychological Review (1943)
- Maslow's hierarchy of needs, Psychological Review, Princeton University (1943).

CORE

Marketing

An advantage of using academic journals is that the articles contain the most up-to-date research in an academic discipline. The source is likely to be reliable as it has been authored by academic scholars in a rigorous way (the articles will have been proofread and checked by academic peers and editors.

However, disadvantages include the fact that information or data are not always relevant to the researcher and can become outdated quickly. The findings are often contestable (see TOK question below). Also, universities and academic establishments tend to charge users to access academic journals.

Theory of knowledge

When does academic research become accepted as knowledge?

Government publications

Governments publish a broad range of data, such as: population census, social trends, labour market developments, trade statistics, unemployment figures, inflation rates and so on. Government websites (such as www.statistics.gov.uk and www.usa.gov) are popular sources of secondary market research data.

The main advantage of using government publications is that the data and statistics are usually comprehensive, reliable and up-to-date. In addition, government publications cover a wide range of topics, thus providing researchers with a wealth of data, statistics and information. Also, many government publications are available free of charge.

However, the main disadvantage of government publications is the challenge in identifying and locating the information required, due to the vast amount of information available. There is often a fee for researchers to obtain specialist and detailed information from government publications.

Media articles

The general media can contain valuable data and information as part of secondary market research. Media articles are widely available online, making them a useful source of secondary market research.

Examples of media articles include:

- Newspapers, e.g. *The Financial Times* and *The Wall Street Journal.*

- Business-related journals, e.g. *The Economist, Forbes* and *Bloomberg Businessweek.*

- Television documentaries, e.g. *Super-Size Me, An Inconvenient Truth* and *Food, Inc.*

- Books, e.g. biographies, autobiographies, and texts about specific companies, entrepreneurs or business management themes (such as corporate social responsibility).

- The World Wide Web, e.g. company websites, blogs and social media.

As media articles are released very frequently, a major advantage for researchers is that the data and information are up to date. With advances in digital and mobile technologies, many media sources do not require people to take out a subscription in order to access their resources (a lot of this is funded by advertising revenues). So, media articles enable researchers to have easy access to a wide range of up-to-date information, without necessarily paying for this.

However, a disadvantage is the potential bias from the reporters, journalists and authors of the media articles. Also, the articles can become out of date, and therefore irrelevant, rather quickly. Finally, many media articles require users to subscribe in order to access the information. This can therefore be a costly source of market research data and information.

The Internet

All of the above methods of secondary market research (market analyses, academic journals, government publications and media articles) can be conducted via the Internet. Many people start their secondary research by 'Googling' the topic or using other websites such as Wikipedia. The Internet can provide a range of invaluable information, if not a good starting point to find other sources of secondary market research data and information. Online providers of secondary market research data and information often charge for their services, although careful and tactful use of the Internet can reap plenty of useful information without cost to the researcher.

A major advantage of the internet is that online sources and articles are readily available, 24 hours a day, every day. With advances in internet technologies, researchers have access to websites and apps of countless businesses, large newspaper companies, and news broadcasters from across the world. In addition, the growing popularity of social media and social media marketing (SMM) allow news to be easily spread and shared via social networks (such as Facebook, Instagram, LinkedIn, Twitter and WhatsApp).

In reality, it is common for market researchers to use both primary and secondary data and information. This is because neither method is necessarily better than the other as it depends on what data or information a business needs to collect. Secondary research is generally quicker and cheaper to gather, but might be out of date or might not be sufficiently appropriate. Primary research findings could contain bias or errors, but can provide information not available through secondary data sources.

Ethical considerations of market research

Ethical considerations of market research. AO3
© IBO, 2017

In most countries, marketers need to consider the ethical issues of conducting market research, such as not to access confidential data for personal gain. The use of photography or visual recordings for primary market research can be perceived as an invasion of privacy, especially if used inappropriately. With advances in Internet technologies, it is easier than ever before for businesses to connect directly with their customers and to collect research information for future marketing purposes. Businesses may need to face public criticism if their market research practices are perceived to be unethical.

Market research needs to be systematic, consistent and unbiased. It must be conducted honestly, as must the presentation of the findings. For example, it would be unethical for a market researcher to manipulate the findings in favour of personal preferences. Indeed, many countries impose laws to ensure market researchers adhere to relevant guidelines and regulations.

Ethical market research requires investigators to be reasonable, objective and accurate in the process of planning, collecting, processing and reporting research information. Unethical market research can be remembered by the 5Ds©. These form the guiding principles to avoid when carrying out market research.

- **Damage** – Market researchers must protect the people in their samples by ensuring the information collected is never used in such a way to harm them. The contents of an interview, for example, should be kept for research purposes only and not shared with other parties, which could damage relationships and trust. Acting ethically in the research process is a key way to encourage trust, e.g. being open and transparent about how the research data will be used and not sharing personal information, unless the research subjects have given their prior approval.

CORE

Marketing

413

- **Dishonesty** – Market researchers need to be trustworthy in their attempt to obtain usable data for marketing purposes. Distorting market research findings to misrepresent numerical data is an example. Plagiarism and the lack of referencing for secondary market research is also regarded as dishonest and unethical. In some countries, deceitful acts such as those above are not only unethical but are regarded as fraudulent and unlawful.

- **Deception** – Deceptive practices and misleading methods to access and gather data about customers is an ethical problem. Examples include not telling customers that their telephone interview is being recorded, that surveillance (hidden) cameras are being used for market research purposes, or that information is being collected when customers visit the company's website (such as LinkedIn, Amazon, Facebook and Google's Gmail).

- **Disclosure** – A major ethical issue involved in market research is the potential invasion of privacy and the breach of confidentiality. Researchers have the ability to collect, store, match and share (or sell) customer information that can infringe a customer's privacy rights. Third parties might use this information to target customers with direct marketing materials (such as spam email or junk mail). Any unauthorised disclosure of customer information is unethical.

- **Detachment** – Market researchers need to be detached from personal biases and be objective in their work. Marketing activities can have a huge impact on public perceptions. Bias and prejudgments skew the conduct of market research, thus cause distorted results. For example, deliberately asking misleading questions in a survey will mean misleading and unrepresentative data are collected.

It is equally important to remember that people are not always honest in their own responses to certain market research questions (such as their age, income level, or their ability to pay certain prices for a product). Cultural differences and people's suspicions of the intention of the researcher might also affect the responses given.

Theory of knowledge

Is it ethical for a Head of Department in an IB World School to carry out market research of the best subject resources, resulting in a 'recommendation' to all students to buy the resources personally authored by that Head of Department?

Qualitative and quantitative market research

The difference between qualitative and quantitative research. AO2
© IBO, 2017

In addition to classifying market research as primary or secondary methods, qualitative or quantitative market research can also be used.

Qualitative market research involves getting non-numerical answers and opinions from respondents. It is commonly used as part of primary research. The main purpose of using qualitative data is to understand the behaviour, attitudes and perceptions of customers, employees or other respondents. 'Soft' answers (people's views/opinions rather than hard facts/figures) are sought by the researcher. This might be done by using in-depth interviews or by asking open-ended questions. The two main types of qualitative research methods are focus groups and in-depth interviews.

Theory of knowledge

How important are the opinions of market researchers in the search for knowledge?

Table 4.4.c Advantages and disadvantages of qualitative research

Advantages	Disadvantages
It is better than quantitative research for exploring the driving forces (motivators) and restraining forces (demotivators) concerning the behaviour and attitudes of respondents.	Due to the small sample size typically used in qualitative research, the findings might not be representative of the whole population. Further research might therefore be necessary.
Information gathered from qualitative research can be very rich. Unlike a questionnaire, there is flexibility in the process so extra and useful information from interviews can be gathered.	It can be very time consuming to conduct and to interpret the findings. Quantitative responses are easier and quicker to collate than qualitative responses. Hence, analysis of the results can be somewhat limited.
Due to the low number of respondents involved in qualitative market research, it can be inexpensive yet provide detailed information to the market researchers.	A high level of interviewing expertise is required to engage and encourage respondents. The costs of hiring skilled interviewers can therefore be high.

Quantitative market research relies on a much larger number of responses to get 'hard' answers (factual and measurable information rather than people's opinions). Like qualitative market research, it involves using a representative sample to gauge the views of the population. Two quantitative techniques found in primary research (such as surveys and questionnaires) are:

- *Closed questions*, which allow respondents to choose from a given list of options, e.g. gender, age group, income level, true or false questions, and multiple choice questions.

- *Ranking or sliding scales,* which are used to ask respondents to rank options, e.g. the extent to which they agree with a given statement (using a scale from 'strongly agree' to 'strongly disagree').

Secondary research methods can also supply a wealth of quantitative data, such as market share, sales trends and profitability, or forecast changes in consumer income levels.

The advantages and disadvantages of quantitative market research are the opposite of those for qualitative methods, as outlined above. For example, quantitative market research methods do not have the flexibility of qualitative methods because pre-set questions are used. However, since the findings can be collated and represented numerically, the results are easier to analyse.

Question 4.4.3 Toys 'Я' Us

Prior to its bankruptcy in 2018, *Toys 'Я' Us* was the world's largest retailer of toys, with over 1,640 stores with global annual sales of $14bn. It sold toys that based on the latest and classic trends, such as *Barbie* dolls, *Star Wars* products and *Disney* merchandise. The toy industry is massive, but the high cost of rent and the move to online retailers such as Amazon, caused *Toys 'Я' Us* to collapse. Only a few franchised *Toys 'Я' Us* remain open today.

A recent CNN report showed that Americans spend around $250bn a year on toys - and that's just the figure for children aged between 8 to 12 years (known as preteens or 'tweens'). Toy manufacturers and retailers are often keen to research the television programmes and movies watched by children and the magazines that they read.

(a) Explain why toy retailers might be interested in the television programmes or magazines viewed by children.

[4 marks]

(b) Examine how market research can allow businesses, such as toy retailers, to differentiate themselves. [6 marks]

Figure 4.4.d Surveys can provide both quantitative and qualitative responses

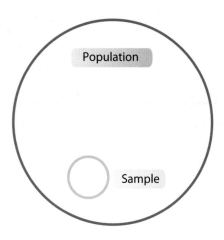

Figure 4.4.e Samples from the population are used for market research

Theory of knowledge

When does market research generate *new* knowledge, if at all?

Exam tip !

All sampling methods have their limitations. Sampling errors occur if the sample is not representative of the population.

Sampling methods

The following methods of sampling: quota, random, stratified, cluster, snowballing and convenience. AO2

© IBO, 2017

All the potential customers of a particular market make up what researchers call the **population**. Since a market can comprise thousands or even millions of potential customers (such as the market for laptop computers), businesses lack the time and resources to conduct market research on every person in the population. Besides, this would be unnecessary to get statistically valid results. Instead, a sample of the population is selected for market research. **Sampling** is the practice of selecting a small group (or sample) of the population for a particular market for primary research purposes.

The key questions to ask when deciding on the type of sampling method to use are: who needs to be asked, what needs to be asked and whether the costs of the market research can be justified. The 'best' sampling method will entail research from a large enough sample to generate representative responses. The six main methods of sampling are: quota, random, stratified, cluster, snowballing and convenience.

Quota sampling

Quota sampling is the most commonly used sampling method, whereby a certain number of people (known as the quota) from different market segments is selected. The sample is grouped according to shared characteristics such as age, gender or occupation. For example, in a business with 1,000 people, a researcher might want to interview 50 middle managers and five senior managers about specific work-related issues.

An advantage of using quota sampling is that a relatively representative sample can be obtained quickly. Also, the findings are more reliable than simply asking anyone on a random basis to participate in the market research.

The disadvantage of quota sampling is that the number of people interviewed in each segment and how randomly they are chosen for interview, are not always representative of the population. For example, if a researcher had a quota of 100 female customers to interview, then the first 100 women might be asked to take part in the market research, without considering whether these respondents are representative of the population. Sampling errors are therefore likely to occur since not everyone gets an equal chance to be sampled.

Random sampling

Random sampling involves giving everyone in the population an equal chance of being selected for the sample. The respondents are often randomly chosen by a computer using information from a database. Random sampling is useful when all members of a population have the same or very similar characteristics, e.g. airlines might use this method to get feedback from their passengers travelling on business and first-class. Parents of children in a school may be randomly selected to get their views on school uniform and other school-related issues.

An advantage of random sampling is that it is quite easy to get a sample. Also, everyone has an equal chance of being selected so this might help to minimise bias or unrepresentative samples being judgmentally selected (as in the case of quota samples).

The main drawback of random sampling is that it is indiscriminate, i.e. it might select people who are not part of the target group due to the randomness of selection. Therefore, sample sizes need to be large enough to get representative and meaningful results.

Stratified sampling

Stratified sampling is similar to quota sampling in that it involves segmentation. The population is likely to be heterogeneous so needs to be subdivided into segments (known as strata) that share homogeneous or very similar characteristics. The difference is that stratified sampling chooses a number of respondents from each stratum that is proportional to the population and then randomly selects them as the sample. For example, if the retired population of a country accounted for 20% of the overall population, then one in five chosen for the sample would be a retired person.

This method benefits from using samples that are more representative of a particular market segment as it involves only using those with key characteristics required for the sample. Sampling is usually random (known as stratified random sampling) but with clearer focus so the findings will be more relevant and with less sampling errors.

One disadvantage of stratified sampling is that it can be difficult to select relevant strata, especially if the subgroups of a population are largely homogeneous. It can also be an expensive task to generate accurate information about the population and then to further subdivide this into representative subgroups.

Cluster

Cluster sampling is used when getting feedback from respondents involves too much time, travelling or money. For example, it would be too time consuming and costly for a multinational company to randomly interview people across all the countries that it operates in. Instead, it is more cost-effective to select several geographical areas (known as clusters) and then to randomly interview people within each of the chosen clusters. For example, a business selling travel insurance might choose to survey people living in towns near airports. The opinions from the selected clusters are used to represent the views of the population.

The main advantages of using cluster sampling are that it is quicker, easier and cheaper than other methods of sampling if the population is widely dispersed over different geographical areas. In particular, where characteristics of customers are homogeneous, then it is not necessary to sample people from every location.

The main potential drawbacks of using cluster sampling are bias and sampling error. By selecting and using just a few locations, the results might be biased as people living in the same area are likely to share similar views or characteristics, such as lifestyle and social status. Increasing the number of clusters in the sample would reduce bias and sampling errors but will clearly add to costs and prolong data analysis.

Snowballing

Snowballing refers to market research carried out with individuals who then suggest other friends, family members or colleagues to increase the sample size. Businesses use snowballing when they are unable to get hold of appropriate respondents as the population is not clear. Snowballing is common in the financial services sector (such as health insurance, life assurance and personal financial planning). Businesses can gain access to a huge number of people for market research purposes from an individual's acquaintances. Essentially, snowballing uses 'word of mouth' to enlarge the sample size.

The main advantage of snowballing is that it can be cheap and quick to get hold of relevant contacts for enlarging the sample. However, due to the nature of such respondent-driven sampling, it is often difficult to determine unbiased findings from the sample. For example, a wealthy person's acquaintances are likely to have similar lifestyles and attitudes thereby enlarging potential bias in the sample.

Exam tip !
Worked example

Assume the management team at a school is proposing to change the timings of the school day. This will involve an earlier start to the day, but an earlier finish too. The management team is seeking the views of teaching staff and wishes to use a stratified sample of 30 from a total of 100 teachers. The demographics of the staff are as follows:

- Full-time teachers: 40 male and 30 female staff
- Part-time teachers: 10 male and 20 female staff

Question: In order to get their stratified sample, calculate how many people should be sampled from each segment according to the above information. *[4 marks]*

Answer:

Apply the formula for stratified sampling:

$$\frac{\text{Group Size}}{\text{Total Size}} \times \text{sample size}$$

Step 1: Calculate the percentage of staff in each stratum group

Step 2: Stratify each group according to the percentages found in Step 1 (see below)

Stratum group		Percentage (per stratum)	Straified sample size
Full-time	Males	(40/100) = 40%	40% of 30 = 12
	Females	(30/100) = 30%	30% of 30 = 9
Part-time	Males	(10/100) = 10%	10% of 30 = 3
	Females	(20/100) = 20%	20% of 30 = 6
Total		100%	30 staff

The above calculations tell the management team to select (for the sample of 30) the following from each stratum group:

- 12 male full-time teachers to represent 40% of the teaching population
- 9 female full-time teachers to represent 30% of the population
- 3 male part-time teachers to represent 10% of the teaching staff
- 6 female part-time teachers to represent 20% of the teachers.

Convenience sampling

Convenience sampling uses subjects that are easy (convenient) to reach. For example, students often use their classmates and friends in a research study. A news reporter might conveniently interview passers-by in a shopping mall or on the street. Convenience sampling relies on ease of reach and volunteers because of their availability.

The main advantages of convenience sampling is the ease (availability and the quickness) of data collection. It is particularly useful when time or cost is a factor for market researchers or if they want to quickly determine whether further market research is necessary.

Figure 4.4.f Busy shopping areas are ideal for convenience sampling

However, the main disadvantage is that market researchers inadvertently exclude a large proportion of the population, thus the findings are often highly skewed and unrepresentative of the population. For example, a study conducted during a weekday afternoon to determine the average amount that customers spend at a restaurant is unlikely to give the same results as if the study was conducted during a Saturday evening.

Exam tip!

So which sampling method is the best method? Each technique has its own strengths and weaknesses. There is always the risk that a sample does not truly represent the population, whichever sampling method is chosen. Sampling errors (such as bias or an inadequate sample size) will hinder the validity of the findings. The 'best' method of sampling for a business depends on its size, financial resources, the purpose of its market research and the extent to which customers have homogeneous or heterogeneous tastes. It is important, as always, to write your answers in the context of the business.

Results from data collection

Results from data collection. AO2

© IBO, 2017

Market research is not a perfect science so the results from data collection might not be absolutely reliable. For example, there is always the chance that respondents do not give representative or truthful answers. Sampling errors occur when findings from the sample differ from the actual population. The larger the sample size, the more statistically reliable answers are in reflecting the views of the population, but the more expensive this becomes. Careful sample design (the process of sample selection, sample structure and the plans for interpreting the results) can also help to reduce sampling errors. There are two types of potential errors in the results from data collection: sampling errors and non-sampling errors.

- **Non-sampling errors** are caused by human error or human behaviour. They arise from the researcher's mistakes in recording, processing or analysing data. They can also occur because respondents do not always give truthful and honest answers. Such errors distort the final results of the research. Statisticians use confidence levels to allow for a margin of error. This measures the extent to which certainty can be attached to market research findings. Most statisticians accept nothing less than 95%

confidence levels, i.e. only a 5% chance (2.5% either way of the predictions) that the results are inaccurate.

- **Sampling errors** are caused by mistakes made in the sample design, such as:

  - The sample size is too small to get statistically valid answers within desired confidence levels (margins of error). Hence, there will be large sampling discrepancies (differences in the views of the actual population and the selected sample).

  - The sample selected is not representative of the population, perhaps due to poor sample design. Asking only smokers about their views on banning smoking in public places will produce highly biased results!

  - An inappropriate sampling method is used. Random sampling will, in theory, have little bias since everyone has an equal chance of being selected, but snowballing is less likely to generate such results.

  - There is bias in the research. This usually comes from bad sample design, but bias can also arise from misleading questions in an interview or survey.

The results from data collection can be presented in several different ways, depending on the purpose. For example:

- *Bar charts* are useful for showing frequencies and for ease of comparison

- *Pie charts* are used for expressing percentage figures, such as data on market share

- *Line graphs* show time-series data, such as sales figures during the past twelve months

- *Histograms* are useful for showing trends over time

- *Scatter diagrams* are used to show possible correlations, such as household income and expenditure.

- *Tables* are used to present numerical data in various formats (see Table 4.4.d for an example).

CORE

Marketing

Table 4.4.d - The world's 10 most expensive and cheapest cities (2017)

	Expensive		Cheapest
1	Singapore	1	Almaty, Russia
2	Hong Kong	2	Lagos, Nigeria
3	Zurich, Switzerland	3	Bangalore, India
4	Tokyo, Japan	4	Karachi, Pakistan
5	Osaka, Japan	5	Algiers, Algeria
6	Seoul, South Korea	6	Chennai, India
7	Geneva, Switzerland	7	Mumbai, India
8	Paris, France	8	Kiev, Ukraine
9	New York, USA	9	Bucharest, Romania
10	Copenhagen, Denmark	10	New Delhi, India

Source: The Economist Intelligence Unit (EIU)

The results from market research should be treated with some caution due to the limitations, which include the following:

- Findings are only as good as the research methodology used. This concept of **garbage-in-garbage-out** (GIGO) applies, whereby unreliable or inaccurate input data generates poor quality output of information. For example, pointless results will be generated if customers are asked whether they are willing to pay higher prices or if smokers are asked if smoking should be banned from public areas.

- Data and information can also be inaccurate or unreliable due to bias. For example, company annual reports or company websites will understandably report on the more positive aspects of business performance. Interviewer bias can also distort the results of market research.

- The cost of good market research is often very high. For instance, postal and telephone questionnaires can be expensive. Data analysts also need time and money to generate and analyse the results from market research.

Market research and the CUEGIS concepts

The pace of change in many industries has fuelled the need for more effective market research. The dynamic nature of change means marketers have to rethink the way they conduct research. Even established brands have to adapt to change - think about the decline of Blockbuster (video rentals) Motorola and Nokia (mobile phones), Kodak (camera film), Toys 'Я' Us (toys), and MySpace (social media). These were all brand leaders that ruled their markets but have been challenged by new entrants and business models that have changed the corporate landscape. Hence, in a world of continual yet erratic change, market research must adapt in order to allow businesses to know what and how things are changing.

Culture also influences market research. With globalization and the spread of international marketing (see Unit 4.8), marketers are spending an increasing amount of time and resources trying to understand cultural differences. Regional cultures will have an impact on how marketers conduct their research. For example, in some cultures, people feel uncomfortable being frank (direct) or confrontational, so will refrain from saying 'no' even if they want to. Disagreeing is regarded as being rude, yet in other cultures this generates discussion and negotiated outcomes.

Cultural sensitivity should also be considered when conducting interviews and questionnaires. What is culturally acceptable in one country is not necessarily so in others. For example, in some cultures, it is rude to ask for a person's age or their income level, but this is absolutely fine in other cultures. International marketers must also be aware of possible errors in the translation of questions.

There are potentially huge ethical issues surrounding the practice of market research. Marketers may be questioned about whether their research methods comply with an ethical code of conduct within the organization. In compliance with corporate social responsibility (CSR), the collection, processing and management of personal data needs to done in an ethical manner. Passing on personal data to third parties (often by selling the data) without consent is generally regarded as unethical business practice. Apple, Barclays, Facebook and Google have all be sued in recent years for allegations of selling personal data without consent.

Globalization causes market research to be integral to business strategy in overseas markets. Differences in language, culture and etiquette can create both opportunities and threats for businesses. For example, Durex is a highly popular brand of condoms in many parts of the world. However, Durex is also a registered brand in Brazil for adhesive tape; in Mexico it is a brand of socks; in Canada, it is the name of a steel company; and in the USA it is also a brand name of badminton racquets! Hence, careful strategic planning is important in communicating the correct marketing message to the correct target audience in different regions of the world.

Box 4.4.b   Culture and brand names

- In Quebec, Canada's French-speaking province, KFC is known as PFK (Poulet Frit Kentucky).
- Burger King is known as Hungry Jack's in Australia, as an existing business had already registered the BK brand name.
- Diet Coke is branded as Coca-Cola Light in many parts of the world.
- Lay's crisps, owned by PepsiCo, is known as Walkers in the UK, Smith's in Australia, Sabritas in Mexico, and Chipsy in Egypt, and Elma Chips in Brazil.
- The best-selling Mars chocolate bar is called Mars in the UK, but MilkyWay in the USA. Confusingly, the MilkyWay bar in the UK is called 3Musketeers in the USA.
- Poland's candy brand Fart Bar translates to 'lucky bar'.
- Ghana's popular Pee Cola translates to 'very good cola'.
- Nokia's Lumia smartphone is slang for 'call girl' or 'prostitute' in Spanish.
- Norwegian meat processing company Gilde produces a brand of canned meat called Bog (which, in other cultures, means a wet, decaying swamp or is slang for 'toilet').
- Looza is a brand of soft drink found in Luxembourg.

Innovation can influence and be influenced by market research. For example, observations are a common method for gaining an understanding of how to refine products for different market segments in different parts of the world. Car manufacturers such as Honda, Toyota and Audi observed that women in the USA with long fingernails carrying their handbags often had difficulties finding their keys, opening the door and starting the engine. Hence, the introduction of remote control locks and keyless engine starters by these car manufacturers helped to better meet the needs of their customers.

Figure 4.4.g Keyless engine starters enable drivers to start their engines without inserting a key

Technological innovations have also changed how researchers conduct their work. For example, many businesses have switched to using social media to gain market research data from the likes of SurveyMonkey, Zoomerang, Instagram, WhatsApp, Facebook, Google+, LinkedIn and Twitter. There is also an array of dedicated software to collect, process and present data. Ultimately, technological innovations have enabled businesses to gain a better understanding of their customers and to formulate their business strategy.

Theory of knowledge

How does the language used in market research influence our knowledge?

CORE

Marketing

CUEGIS Essay

With reference to an organization of your choice, discuss how market research influences **change** and **strategy**.   *[20 marks]*

CUEGIS Essay

With reference to an organization of your choice, examine how **innovation** and **ethics** have affected market research.   *[20 marks]*

REVIEW QUESTIONS

1. What is market research?

2. Distinguish between field research and desk research.

3. Distinguish between the main methods of primary market research.

4. Outline the advantages and disadvantages of using surveys for market research.

5. Outline the main methods of conducting secondary market research.

6. What are the ethical issues that market researchers should take into consideration?

7. Distinguish between quantitative and qualitative market research.

8. What is sampling and why do market researchers use it?

9. Distinguish between quota, random, stratified, snowballing, convenience and cluster sampling methods.

10. Distinguish between sampling and non-sampling errors in market research.

KEY TERMS

Academic journals are periodical publications from educational and research institutions that publish data and information relating to a particular academic discipline.

Ad-hoc market research is market research that is conducted as and when required by an organization in order to deal with a specific problem or issue.

Bar graphs are a visual method of presenting market research data, such as sales figures during different periods of time.

Cluster sampling is used when getting feedback from respondents involves too much time, travelling or money. For example, it would be too time consuming and costly for a company to randomly interview people across all the countries that it operates in.

Continuous market research is a method of market research that is conducted on an ongoing basis, rather than a one-off (ad-hoc) basis.

Convenience sampling uses subjects that are easy (convenient) to reach, e.g. students often use their classmates and friends in a research study. It relies on ease of reach and volunteers because of their availability.

Focus groups involve forming small discussion groups to gain insight into the attitudes and behaviour of respondents. The group is typically made up of participants who share a similar customer profile, such as teenage boys who like to play online computer games.

Government publications are a type of secondary market research, referring to official documents and publications released by government entities and agencies.

Histograms are a visual method of presenting market research data by using a type of bar graph to show frequency and the range within a data set.

Interviews are a type of primary research that involve discussions between an interviewer and interviewees to investigate their personal circumstances and opinions. Beliefs, attitudes and feelings can be examined in detail.

Line graphs are a method of visual presentation of market research data, used to show time-series information, such as changes in profit figures over time.

A **market analysis** reveals the characteristics and the outlook (trends) for a particular product or industry, e.g. market size, market share and market growth rate.

Market research refers to marketing activities designed to discover the opinions, beliefs and preferences of potential and existing customers in order to identify and anticipate their wants and needs.

Media articles are a type of secondary market research referring to the documents (articles) in print or online media. They are written by trained journalists and authors.

Non-sampling errors are caused by human error or human behaviour. They arise from the researcher's mistakes in recording, processing or analysing data, or because respondents do not always give truthful and honest answers.

Observations are a method of primary research that involves watching how people behave or respond in different situations. It can be done under controlled conditions (like a laboratory test) or as real-life situations (where people do not know that they are being watched).

Pie charts are a method of visual presentation of market research data, used to show percentages, e.g. market share figures.

The **population**, in marketing terms, refers to all potential customers of a particular market.

Primary research (also known as **field research** or **bespoke research**) is market research that involves gathering new data first-hand for a specific purpose. Methods of primary research include: surveys (questionnaires), interviews, focus groups and observations.

Qualitative market research involves getting non-numerical answers and opinions from respondents. The main purpose is to understand the behaviour, attitudes and perceptions of customers, employees or other respondents.

Quantitative market research is about collecting and using factual and measurable information rather than opinions.

Quota sampling is the most common sampling method, involving a certain number of people (known as the quota) from different market segments being used for research.

Random sampling gives everyone in the population an equal chance of being selected for the sample.

A **sample** is a selected proportion of the population used for primary market research purposes.

Sampling errors are caused by mistakes made in the sample design, such as an unrepresentative sample being used or the sample size being too small.

Scatter diagrams are a visual method of presenting market research data, used to show possible correlations between two variables, e.g. the relationship between levels of household income and their expenditure.

Secondary research (or **desk research**) involves the collection of second-hand data and information that already exists, previously gathered by others. Examples include government publications and news articles.

Snowballing refers to market research carried out with individuals who then suggest other friends, family members or colleagues thereby increasing the sample size. It is used when businesses are unable to get hold of appropriate respondents, as the population is not clear.

Stratified sampling involves subdividing the market into segments (known as strata) that share homogeneous or very similar characteristics. A number of respondents from each stratum that is proportional to the population is then randomly selected for the sample.

A **survey** (or **questionnaire**) is a document that contains a series of questions used to collect data for a specific purpose. It is the most common method of primary research.

Surveys are a common method of collecting market research data

4.5 The four Ps (produ...

place)

"It is not the employer who pays wages – he only handles the money. It is ...
(1863–1947), founder of the Ford Moto...

SL/HL content	A...
Product The product life cycle The relationship between the product life cycle and the marketing mix Extension strategies The relationship between the product life cycle, investment, profit and cash flow	
Boston Consulting Group (BCG) matrix on an organization's products	AO3, AO...
The following aspects of branding: awareness, development, loyalty and value	AO2
The importance of branding	AO3
The importance of packaging	AO3
Price The appropriateness of the following pricing strategies: cost-plus (mark-up), penetration, skimming, psychological, loss leader, price discrimination, price leadership and predatory	AO3
Promotion The following aspects of promotion: above the line promotion, below the line promotion and promotional mix	AO2
The impact of changing technology on promotional strategies (such as viral marketing, social media marketing and social networking)	AO3
Guerrilla marketing and its effectiveness as a promotional method	AO3
Place The importance of place in the marketing mix	AO2
The effectiveness of different types of distribution channels	AO3

© IBO, 2017

CORE

...ning the product all the way from the soil to the table." - Henry John Heinz
...–1919), American businessman and founder of Heinz Foods

...tent	Assessment objective
...uct	
The product life cycle	AO4
The relationship between the product life cycle and the marketing mix	AO2
Extension strategies	AO3
The relationship between the product life cycle, investment, profit and cash flow	AO2
Boston Consulting Group (BCG) matrix on an organization's products	AO3, AO4
The following aspects of branding: awareness, development, loyalty and value	AO2
The importance of branding	AO3
The importance of packaging	AO3

© IBO, 2017

Product in the marketing mix

A **product** is any good or service that serves to satisfy the needs or wants of customers. Products can be **tangible** (physical products such as computers) or **intangible** (services such as education). They can be sold to private individuals, to other businesses or to governments.

Each year, there are countless new products launched in both consumer and producer markets. Most new products fail but a special few may succeed to become global successes. Before customers part with their money, they ask themselves whether the product offers value for money, i.e. whether the price justifies the benefits of consumption. Products must have added value in order to stand any chance of success. Marketing has a large role in adding value to a product, perhaps through the use of product differentiation such as quality, packaging and/or branding.

Products can be classified as consumer or producer goods. **Consumer products** are those purchased by private individuals for their own personal use (see Box 4.5.a). **Producer products** are goods purchased for commercial use, rather than for private use. They are used in the production process to help the running of a business, e.g. raw materials and components (used to make other products) and the purchase of **fixed assets** (see Unit 3.1) such as land, machinery, tools and vehicles. In reality, many products (such as stationery, furniture and computers) cater for both private individuals and businesses.

Their classification is different based only on who buys the product, rather than the physical attributes of the product.

Box 4.5.a   Classification of products

- **Fast-moving consumer goods** (FMCGs) are everyday convenience products sold in retail outlets such as supermarkets, e.g. personal health care products, groceries, newspapers and confectionery.
- **Consumer perishables** are products that do not last very long, e.g. fresh flowers, fresh fruits and vegetables, or fresh seafood. They are different to FMCGs in that purchases are not necessarily as frequent or stable and that they may carry high profit margins.
- **Consumer durables** are products that last for a relatively long time. They can take up a rather large proportion of consumers' incomes so are purchased irregularly, e.g. cars, furniture, sports equipment and electronic appliances.
- **Speciality products** are exclusive and highly expensive products that take up a significant proportion of the average consumer's income. Hence, such purchases often require a large amount of commitment (money and time), e.g. designer jewellery, residential property and exclusive sports cars. Businesses can earn huge profit margins by charging premium prices for such prestigious products.

Figure 4.5.a Fresh fruits and vegetables are perishable products

Theory of knowledge

What is beauty? Are businesses that promote beauty products ultimately acting unethically?

Theory of knowledge

Is it ethical business practice to significantly raise the price of fresh flowers on Mothers' Day and Valentine's Day? Are there any socially acceptable reasons for businesses exploiting the ability and willingness of consumers to pay higher prices?

Product life cycle

The product life cycle. AO4
The relationship between the product life cycle and the marketing mix. AO2
The relationship between the product life cycle, investment, profit and cash flow. AO2
© IBO, 2017

The product life cycle shows the different stages that a product is likely to go through from its initial design and launch to its decline (and eventual withdrawal in most cases). Its life cycle is measured over time in terms of sales revenue. The use of a product life cycle (PLC) allows managers to identify any

necessary changes and to take appropriate action as part of an improved marketing strategy.

Some products have a relatively short PLC whilst other products have very long life cycles. For example, Levi's, Nokia and Colgate were established more than 150 years ago. Moët & Chandon (a well-known brand of champagne) has existed since 1743. Other products may have a much shorter life cycle, e.g. textbooks, movies, fashion (clothing) products, pop music bands or mobile phones. According to *Newsweek* magazine, mobile phones have a life cycle of 18 months in the USA before consumers replace them because newer and better-designed models are readily available on the market, even though they are made to last for around five years.

For most products, there are generally five stages to their life cycle: research and development, launch (introduction), growth, maturity, and decline (see Figure 4.5.b). Each stage is likely to have a different marketing mix and affect cash flows and profits in different ways.

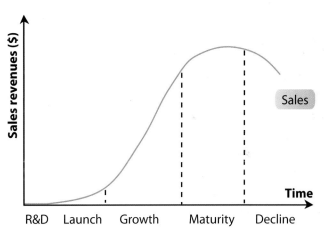

Figure 4.5.b The product life cycle

1. Research and development stage

The **research and development (R&D)** stage of a product's life cycle involves designing and testing the product. This tends to be a time-consuming task. A **prototype** (trial product) is often produced along with detailed market research to assess the potential success of the product. **Test marketing** will usually take place. This involves trialling a new product with a sample of customers, perhaps in a limited geographical area, to determine the reactions of customers and to gather valuable feedback. Advertising guru David Ogilvy suggests that the most important aspect of R&D is testing. He argues that if a business pre-tests its product with consumers and pre-tests its advertising, then it will have a much higher chance of success. This helps to minimise costs (and embarrassment) if the product is unsuccessful. If the product is unsuccessful at this stage, the business can either make changes based on the feedback of customers or discontinue the product. However, test marketing can be expensive and competitors might find out about the product before its launch. Studies have shown that most ideas at this stage do not proceed to the commercial launch stage, i.e. there is a high failure rate. Products that are commercialised must be priced competitively yet high enough to recover the R&D costs of both the successfully launched product and all those products that failed.

2. Launch (introduction) stage

The launch stage of the PLC requires careful marketing planning. Sales will be relatively low as customers are not fully aware of the product's existence. However, costs are very high due to the expenses involved in the launch (such as the costs of publicity, promotion and distribution). Hence, the product is unprofitable at this stage of its PLC, and the business may face cash flow issues. Therefore, marketing managers aim to get the product to the next stage as soon as possible. This will be easier to achieve for some products (such as blockbuster Hollywood movies) but harder for others (such as new books by unknown authors). Customers who tend to buy products during their launch are referred to as **innovators**, i.e. those who like to be the first to own a certain product, perhaps due to prestige or because they are fanatics of the product, brand or company. Innovators were observed queuing days before the launch of the *Star Wars* movies, *Harry Potter* books, Apple smartphones and Sony games consoles in order to be one of the first customers to purchase these products.

3. Growth stage

The growth stage of a product's life cycle sees sales revenue increasing. Growth is partly due to the business using wider channels of distribution to get the product to different customers in numerous locations. Brand awareness and the influx of customers at this stage of the PLC, known as the **early adopters**, also help to boost sales and cash flow (see Figure 4.5.c). Profits may materialise due to sales revenue rising and the possibility of lower unit costs from economies of scale in production. Businesses strive to prolong this stage as far as possible. However, profits will attract rivals to the industry. Hence, to remain competitive, the marketing mix of the business may need to be reviewed.

Figure 4.5.c Early adopters of Apple's iPod helped establish its market dominance

4. Maturity stage

During the **maturity** stage of a product's life cycle, sales revenues continue to rise but at a much slower rate. The business may have obtained significant market share as sales revenues are at their peak. Cash flow and profits will be favourable. Economies of scale will give the organization a competitive advantage, although there are likely to be many rivals in the market at this stage. **Saturation** occurs when there are too many competitors in the market and sales have peaked or have started to fall. The marketing mix will therefore focus on promotional activities to remind customers, rather than to persuade them, in an attempt to emphasise brand loyalty and repeat purchases. Marketing managers might also look to exploit new market segments for the product. Coca-Cola is an example of a product at its maturity stage – but it has been there for a very long time now!

5. Decline stage

Decline is the final stage of the PLC (before its withdrawal or 'death' happens). During decline, sales and profit of the product fall and cash flow is less favourable. This could be due to lower customer demand, caused by changing fashion and tastes or new replacement models being available on the market, thus making the existing product obsolete. Investment for the product, including promotional expenditure, is cut and the price plummets. In reality, new products are likely to be launched before the previous product enters decline as this helps a business to maintain its cash flow and profitability.

The life cycle of a product will therefore have varying effects on an organization's level of investment, profits and cash flow, outlined in Table 4.5.a on the following page.

Table 4.5.a   The PLC and its relationship with investment, profit and cash flow

PLC stage	Investment level	Profit	Cash flow
R&D	Very high (research and development)	None	Highly negative
Launch	Very high (marketing)	Little, if any	Negative
Growth	High (persuasive)	Yes, rising	Positive
Maturity	Less (mainly reminding)	High, but little or no growth	Positive
Decline	Little, if any (extension strategies)	Yes, but falling	Positive, but falling

Question 4.5.1   Sony PlayStation 4

Sony launched its eighth-generation games console, the PlayStation 4, in late 2013, seven years after its predecessor the PS3 was launched. It was quick to win positive reviews. The PS4 offers online connections to the Internet, 3D Blu-ray player, 500 GB storage space and an optional PlayStation Camera. However, many existing customers became rather annoyed that the PS4 is not backward compatible with PlayStation 3 games. Nevertheless, *Sony's* **first mover advantage** in the next-generation games console market led to sales of one million units and gross profit of $18 million in the US and Canada – all within the first 24 hours. Microsoft was unable to launch its more expensive Xbox One games console until a week later. During its **product life cycle**, the PS3 consoles had sales of 10.5 million units worldwide each year. *Sony* reported annual sales of 18.4 million units of the PS4 during the first 4 years. In September 2016, *Sony* launched the PlayStation 4 Pro, a high-end version of the games console.

(a) (i) Define the term **first mover advantage**.   *[2 marks]*

(a) (ii) Define the term **product life cycle**.   *[2 marks]*

(b) In the context of the case study, examine the relationship between a product's cash flow position and its life cycle.   *[6 marks]*

Extension strategies and the product life cycle

Extension strategies. AO3

© IBO, 2017

For products that reach saturation in their life cycle, various extension strategies can be implemented to prolong their sales revenue. Extension strategies are any means of lengthening the product's life cycle and delaying its decline. Apple's highly successful iPod was launched in 2001. To prolong the iPod's life cycle, Apple introduced a range of iPod accessories and variations of the original product (such as the iPod Nano and iPod Shuffle). The effects of extension strategies on a product's sales and life cycle are shown in Figure 4.5.d.

Common extension strategies include:

- **Price reductions** to increase demand for a product. Businesses also use price cuts to get rid of excess stocks before they become obsolete.

- **Redesigning** involves introducing special features or 'limited editions' to a current product. This adds value to the product to entice more customers to buy it.

429

- **Repackaging** involves changing the packaging of a product to help revive demand, perhaps by using more attractive colours or materials. The appearance of a product, including its packaging, can have a large effect on demand.

- **New markets** for a current product can also extend its life cycle, e.g. trying to sell the product in new retail outlets, different regions or overseas.

- **Brand extension** refers to the use of an existing and successful brand name to launch a new or modified version of the product, thus prolonging its life cycle.

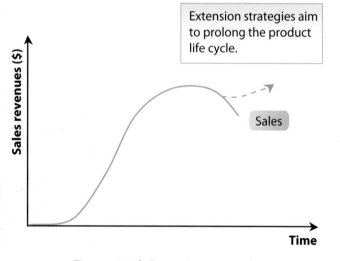

Extension strategies aim to prolong the product life cycle.

Sales

Figure 4.5.d Extension strategies

Product differentiation can also help to prolong a product's life cycle (see Box 4.5.b). This is any marketing strategy that involves making a product stand out from others offered by rival businesses. By having a unique or distinctive element to the products offered by a firm, it could help the business to withstand competition. Successful product differentiation requires marketing support such as sales promotion.

Box 4.5.b Methods of product differentiation

- **Colour** The different flavoured crisps (potato chips) can be distinguished by their colour. IKEA's infamous yellow and blue combination is symbolic of the Swedish flag. Red and white combinations are used by many firms, such as Colgate, KFC, Virgin and Coca-Cola.
- **Size** The physical size of a product can make it stand out. Large sized TVs come at a premium price. By contrast, miniaturization is preferred for other products such as mobile services.
- **Quality** Car manufacturers such as BMW and Audi use the high performance and build quality of their cars to differentiate themselves from competitors.
- **Design** The design of Apple's iPhone or Sony's PS4 helps to attract customers. Design has a vital role in the purchase of expensive products.
- **After-sales care** Customers who purchase consumer durables tend to receive some form of after-sales services, e.g. warranties, installation or servicing. Firms that offer after-sales care are more likely to satisfy their customers' needs, thereby gaining customer loyalty.
- **Packaging** Presentation plays an important part in the marketing of most products, such as adding value to the product. Japanese consumers are very particular about packaging.
- **Purchase terms** Many businesses offer special purchase terms to attract customers, e.g. 0% financing, hire purchase, part-exchange and 'buy now, pay later' plans.
- **Customer relations management** The level of customer care is very important, especially in the service sector. Hotels, airlines, banks and retailers rely on their staff to deliver a first-rate customer experience in order to maintain their market share.

Box 4.5.c   Ten e-commerce brands with longevity

1. WhatApp (2010)
2. Twitter (2006)
3. YouTube (2005)
4. Facebook (2004)
5. LinkedIn (2003)
6. Wikipedia (2001)
7. Google (1998)
8. Netflix (1997)
9. eBay (1995)
10. Amazon (1994)

Case study

Unilever is an Anglo-Dutch multinational company, founded in 1929. Its product portfolio is vast, including food, beverages, personal care and cleaning products. Unilever owns over 400 brands, which include: Axe/Lynx, Ben & Jerry's, Cif, Dove, Flora, Lipton, Magnum, Marmite, Persil, PG Tips, Pot Noodle, Slim Fast, Tony & Guy and Vaseline.

Boston Consulting Group (BCG) matrix

> Boston Consulting Group (BCG) matrix on an organization's products. AO3 and AO4
>
> © IBO, 2017

The **Boston Consulting Group matrix** (or the **Boston matrix** for short) was devised by Bruce D. Henderson (1970). The BCG matrix is a marketing planning tool that helps managers to plan for a balanced **product portfolio**, i.e. the variety of products owned by a business. For example, Japanese conglomerate Hitachi has a product portfolio that includes products as diverse as consumer electronics, car parts and high-speed trains. A product portfolio can also contain the various **strategic business units (SBUs)** of an organization – divisions of an organization, such as Gatorade, 7-Up, Lay's, Doritos, Taco Bell, Pizza Hut and KFC, which are owned by PepsiCo.

The Boston matrix looks at two dimensions: market share and market growth in order to assess new and existing products in terms of their market potential (see Figure 4.5.e). Henderson said that successful businesses have a portfolio of products with different market growth rates and different rates of market share. Product portfolio analysis allows a business to decide which products should receive more (or less) investment. Products that do not have high market share may be withdrawn or remarketed, for example. The analysis also allows a business to develop growth strategies (see Unit 1.6) by adding new products to an existing or new product range.

A business would place each individual product or brand in its product portfolio onto one of the quadrants based on the product's relative market share and the product's market growth in the industry. There are four possible outcomes:

Question 4.5.2   Mattel

Mattel is one of the world's largest manufacturer of toys. Established in 1945, the American company has profited from products such as Barbie dolls and Elmo cuddly toys (of Sesame Street). *Mattel's* brands include Fisher-Price, Hot Wheels, Matchbox, Tyco, UNO, Pictionary and Scrabble. *Mattel's* market leadership is backed by other products in its **product portfolio,** such as strong sales of toys based on Pixar's animated films *Cars* and *Toy Story*.

(a) Define the term **product portfolio**. *[2 marks]*

(b) Examine the importance of a broad product portfolio for a business such as *Mattel*. *[6 marks]*

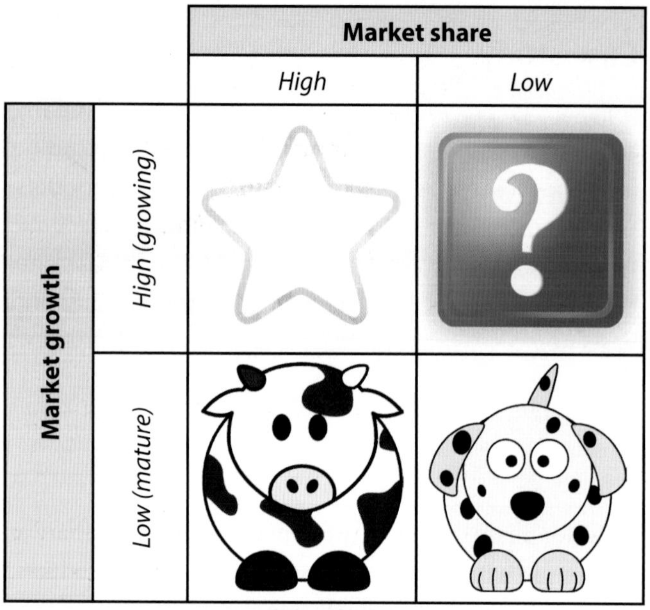

Figure 4.5.e The Boston matrix

- **Dogs** are products with low market share operating in a low growth market. Dogs do not generate much cash for the business as the market tends to be stagnant or declining, so businesses may use product extension strategies or try to dispose of the dogs. Businesses that have too many dogs may face liquidity problems.

- **Question marks** (or **problem children**) are products that operate in a high market growth sector, but have low market share. This can be a concern as this may suggest inferior marketing or product quality. The business should analyse reasons for its low market share and then develop strategies to gain a higher share of the growing market. This means problem children are the main users of cash in the BCG matrix. Question marks are also known as **wild cards** as it is not always clear whether a business should invest more in these products.

- **Stars** are products that operate in high growth markets and have high market share. Therefore, stars are successful products that tend to generate high amounts of cash for a business. Therefore, businesses tend to invest money to develop and promote their stars. The cash generated from stars can be used in an attempt to turn some of the question marks into stars. It is hoped that stars will eventually turn into cash cows.

- **Cash cows** are products with high market share operating in a low-growth market. Such markets tend to be mature and the products are very well established (such as Coca-Cola in the soft drinks industry), thereby generating superb net cash flow. Cash cows generate large amounts of

profits. However, some cash cows run the risk of becoming dogs, so businesses tend to use extension strategies to prolong their high earning potential.

The BCG matrix shows that the ideal product portfolio for a business is to have a balanced portfolio, which might include some stars, a few question marks and several cash cows. It is important to note that the BCG matrix is not a static model. The money generated from cash cows is used to turn the question marks into stars, otherwise they may quickly become dogs. The term **rising star** is often used to describe problem children turning into stars. Similarly, stars may ultimately become cash cows. Appropriate marketing strategies need to be devised to foster these changes. Managers also need to decide whether to spend money on reviving demand for dogs or to withdraw all investments in them, thereby releasing cash for other products. Hence, it is important that a business has a balanced range of products in its portfolio.

A diverse product portfolio is important for an organization's cash flow because only selling to a single market limits the revenues of the business. For example, French designer company Agnès b has a broad product portfolio that spans beyond clothing to also include: confectionary, flowers, food (cafés and restaurants), shoes, and fashion accessories (handbags, sunglasses, wallets, travel bags, belts and watches). A diverse product portfolio also helps to spread risks because a decline in sales for one product may be offset by favourable sales of other products in the portfolio.

A criticism of this model is the assumption that higher profits come from higher sales or market share. This is not necessarily the case. For example, Disneyland Paris made huge losses between 2002-2006 despite receiving large amounts of revenue and having a high market share in the theme parks industry. The company even had to raise a further $350m through share issues in 2005 to prevent it going into liquidation. The attractiveness of its brand meant the Walt Disney Company gained high market share quickly, but still faced the problem of recouping its high redevelopment costs. The theme park was burdened with debt, equal to around 15 times its gross earnings. In 2017, the Walt Disney Company needed to invest an additional €1.5 billion ($1.75bn) to strengthen the Park.

In addition, whilst the BCG Matrix can provide a quick synopsis of a firm's product portfolio, it fails to explain the position of the products in the grid. Hence, the Boston Matrix (as with any other business model) should be used in conjunction with other planning tools such as Ansoff's Growth Matrix (see Unit 1.3).

Question 4.5.3 Virgin Group

Virgin Group was set up in the early 1970s by British **entrepreneur** Sir Richard Branson. His entrepreneurial skills have led to the *Virgin Group* consisting of more than 200 companies. The core areas of the business are travel, entertainment and lifestyle. Its product portfolio includes Virgin Atlantic Airways, Virgin Trains, Virgin Cola, Virgin Mobile, Virgin Flowers and Virgin Spa.

(a) Define the term **entrepreneur**. [2 marks]

(b) Examine the reasons why *Virgin Group* needs a different marketing mix for each of its distinct products and services. [6 marks]

Branding

The importance of branding. AO3

© IBO, 2017

Branding is a form of differentiating an organization's products from those of its competitors. A brand refers to a name that is identifiable with a product of a particular business (although the term can also refer to a sign, symbol, colour scheme, font or design). For example, Microsoft's brands include: Windows, Hotmail, Explorer, MS Word, MS Excel and PowerPoint. Interbrand, the internationally renowned branding consultants, defines a brand as "a mixture of tangible and intangible attributes symbolised in a trademark". A trademark gives legal protection to the owner to have exclusive use of the brand name.

FRENCH CONNECTION

Figure 4.5.f British brand French Connection is a recognised brand around the world

Research has shown that the world's most well-known brand, Coca-Cola, can be so influential that it actually alters the consumer's feelings and/or their perception of the product's taste. It is important for marketers and managers to realise the importance of branding:

- *Branding is a legal instrument.* Brand names create a legal identity for a product by giving it a unique and recognisable name and image to differentiate it from other products (see Box 4.5.d). For example, some businesses use branding to create an upmarket image for their products, such as Gucci, Versace and Rolls–Royce. As a legal instrument, branding gives lawful ownership to the business and protects it from imitations.

- *Branding is a risk reducer.* Brands can give new products a better chance of survival. They can create a sense of value for money and encourage brand awareness. There is plenty of research to show that customers remain devoted to the purchase of well-known brands. Brands also help to prolong the life cycle of a product. However, this requires the business to invest money in promoting and sustaining the loyalty to the brand.

- *Branding is an image enhancer.* Successful brands allow a business to charge a premium price because customers are often willing to pay a substantially higher price for a 'good' brand. This allows the business to earn higher profit margins. Lexus, the luxury division of Toyota, is able to charge premium prices due to the high-class image of its brand of cars. Psychologists and marketers have shown that purchasing decisions are not simply based on the price or functions of a product but also the 'feel good factor' associated with owning a particular brand.

- *Branding is a revenue earner.* Branding can encourage brand loyalty. This means that customers have a preference over other brands. Customers might also perceive the brand as superior to others so will not tend to buy substitutes. Thus, the demand for the firm's product is less sensitive to changes in prices. Being able to charge a proportionately higher price without losing customers means that the business earns higher sales revenues. Brand loyalty also makes brand extension strategies much easier to accomplish.

Ultimately, these interlinked factors mean that branding is important to a business as it enables the firm to earn more profits. For example, the strength of sports club brands such as 'Manchester United', 'Real Madrid', 'Houston Rockets', and 'New York Yankees' has enabled such businesses to extend their merchandising in overseas markets, to provide financial services and to have their own digital TV channels. Businesses that use branding effectively gain from improved profitability. However, developing a brand is very expensive and can take many years. Most brands fail to ever become established in the marketplace, whilst many existing brands need regular investment or must evolve to survive.

Advocates of branding as a marketing strategy go as far as to argue that a brand is more important than the product itself, because they differ in several ways:

- *Intangibility* – Brands represent the intangible value that customers place on the actual physical product. Marketers argue that it is the brand that sells a product, not the other way round.

- *Uniqueness* – Brands are unique, whereas a product is quite easily copied.

- *Timeless* – Successful brands are timeless, whereas products can become obsolete (i.e. they reach the end of their life cycle). Sony's Walkman personal stereos and first generation PlayStation games consoles were withdrawn in the late 1990s, but both brand names live on.

Case study

The name 'Nike' was chosen by Phil Knight, the company's founder and Chairman, because Nike was the Greek Goddess of Victory. It is also a short name, so is easier to spell and remember. Good brand names can stimulate positive associations with the product or business.

Box 4.5.d Behind the names of the famous brands

- 7-Eleven – Founded in 1927, the opening times of 7-Eleven convenience stores were originally from 7am to 11pm.
- Adidas – The sports apparel giant got its name from the founder of the company, Adi Dassler.
- Amstrad – The electronics company gets its name from the initials of its founder – British entrpreneur Sir Alan Michael Sugar – and the first three letters of Trading.
- Duracell – The world's top selling AA and AAA sized battery brand takes its name by blending the words 'Durable Cell'.
- Hotmail – Microsoft's email service (HoTMaiL) was created using the Internet-based computer language called HTML by two ex-employees of Apple who worked on the project.
- IKEA – The world's largest home furnishing business, established in 1943 by Ingvar Kamprad, gets its name from the initials of the founder and Elmtaryd Agunnaryd, the farm and village where he grew up.
- Intel – The world's leading producer of microprocessors and semiconductors was founded in 1968 as Integrated Electronics Corporation.
- Mattel – The toy producer, with brands such as Fisher–Price, Tyco, Barbie, Matchbox, and Hot Wheels, gets its name from the company's founders – Harold 'Matt' Matson and Elliot Handler.
- Spam – A registered trademark of Hormel Foods Corporation, 'Hormel Spiced Ham' (luncheon meat), didn't really catch on, so was changed to Spam, derived from 'SPiced hAM'.

Question 4.5.4 Lexus

Lexus, the luxury division of *Toyota*, is a relatively young brand, having been introduced in 1989. However, its success has been incredible. Since 2000, *Lexus* has sold more luxury vehicles in the USA than any of its foreign and domestic rivals, such as *Mercedes-Benz, Jaguar, Audi, BMW, Lincoln* and *Cadillac*. *Lexus* has also secured significant market share in many countries, including Singapore, Taiwan, South Korea, Thailand and Brunei. Time after time, *Lexus* has been voted by drivers as the most reliable car brand on the planet. Today, the *Lexus* brand is sold in over 70 countries, and is one of Japan's largest global brands by market value.

(a) Explain why *Toyota* might have chosen to label its luxury cars as 'Lexus' rather than 'Toyota', a much more globally recognised brand at the time. *[4 marks]*

(b) Discuss the role and importance of branding to a multinational company such as *Toyota*. *[10 marks]*

CORE

Marketing

Question 4.5.5   Coca-Cola

Coca-Cola is one of the biggest brands in the world. The company claims that its brand name is the second most-understood word in the English language (after 'OK'). *Coca-Cola* (also referred to by its trademark name 'Coke') is synonymous with American culture. The company preserves the position of its brand by devoting a huge amount of money (in the region of $2 billion) to its marketing each year. For example, *Coca-Cola* is one of the largest sponsors of sporting events, such as the NBA (basketball), the NHL (hockey), the Olympic Games and the FIFA World Cup (football).

Source: www.cocacola.com

(a) Explain why a brand name is of huge importance to a business such as *Coca-Cola*. [4 marks]

(b) Examine whether organizations, such as *Coca-Cola*, should devote time and resources to brand development. [6 marks]

Box 4.5.e   Famous brands named after their founder

- Ferdinand Porsche
- Michael Dell
- Coco Chanel
- Enzo Ferrari
- J.P. Morgan
- Ann Summers
- William Fox
- William Boeing
- William Colgate
- William Wrigley Jr
- Will Keith Kellogg
- James L. Kraft
- Ferruccio Lamborghini
- Levi Strauss
- Louis Vuitton
- Frank C. Mars
- Henry Ford
- Henri Nestlé
- Alfred Nobel
- Walt Disney

Theory of knowledge

Scientists and business analysts have shown that branding can be so remarkable that it affects the human brain. For example, the Coca-Cola brand stimulates parts of the human brain associated with cultural knowledge, memory and self-image. What role do scientific knowledge claims have in our acquisition of knowledge in Business Management?

There are several advantages of successful branding:

- *Price advantages* – Businesses that sell homogeneous products, such as bananas from a fruit market, can only charge low prices as there are plenty of substitutes. By contrast, branding can add value to a product, so allows a business to charge higher prices.

- *Recognition and loyalty* – Brand recognition can be a source of competitive advantage as there is a greater chance of the products being sold. This could be due to brand loyalty or simply because customers feel more comfortable buying a brand that they are familiar with (see Box 4.5.d on page 434).

- *Distribution advantages* – Retail space is limited so vendors only stock the best-selling brands. Hence, successful branding improves placement (distribution) of a firm's products.

CORE

Aspects of branding

The following aspects of branding: awareness, development, loyalty and value. AO2
© IBO, 2017

Brand awareness

Brand awareness measures the extent to which potential customers or the general public recognise a particular brand. It is usually expressed as a percentage of the sample surveyed, e.g. 98% of respondents might recognise the Coca-Cola brand. Creating brand awareness is a key part of promoting a product or business. For example, in the bottled mineral water industry, there is very little separating the many suppliers in terms of

Marketing

taste. However, there is high brand awareness of Evian, Perrier, Dasani and Aquafina.

Theory of knowledge

Did you know that *Evian* spelt backwards is 'Naïve'? Did you know that Dasani is produced by Coca-Cola and that Aquafina is made by Pepsi Co.? Perrier claims that there are 50 million bubbles in its bottled water – does it matter that such a knowledge claim is made or should this statement be proved as 'fact'?

Brand awareness plays a major part in the buying decision of consumers. For example, the Apple brand has huge brand awareness and is often the first brand that people associate with smartphones and tablet computers. In general, the higher the level of brand awareness, the higher sales revenues are likely to be. In addition, brand awareness gives the business a competitive edge over its rivals, resulting in greater market share. It can also encourage repeat purchases if customers like and trust the brand. Raising brand awareness is also of particular importance during the launch stage of a product's life cycle.

IB Learner Profile – Be knowledgeable and be reflective

Try the many online logos quizzes (such as www. guessthelogo.com) or download the free logos quiz apps on your smartphone. How many of the brands do you recognize?

Brand development

Brand awareness is a prerequisite to **brand development**. This refers to the marketing process of improving and enlarging the brand name in order to boost sales revenue and market share. Both brand awareness and brand development help a business to stand out from the others in the market. Whilst brand awareness can occur quite quickly, especially with an effective marketing strategy, it takes a lot longer to develop a brand and the desired image.

Successful brand development helps to extend a product's life cycle. For example, Coca-Cola and Johnson & Johnson products were first launched in 1886, but remain highly successful brands today. However, the costs of brand development can be extremely high. Nevertheless, brand owners generally strive to maximise the popularity of their trademarks. Some brands have become so famous (or 'genericised') that they are often mistaken for the name of the product itself (see Box 4.5.f). Such brands are known as **generic brands**. There is a danger, however, that the generic use of a brand name leads to problems of enforcing copyright protection of the trademark.

Brand loyalty

Brand loyalty occurs when customers buy the same brand of a product time and time again. They are devoted to the brand since they have brand preference over other brand names. Brand loyalty is important to businesses for several reasons:

- It helps businesses to maintain or improve their market share.

- It allows businesses with brand loyalty to charge premium prices for their products, which improves their profit margins.

- It acts as a barrier to entry in highly competitive markets such as the fashion and clothing industry. This is because brand loyalty reduces the likelihood of brand switching.

- It plays a major role in the future success of a business, helping to prolong the product and brand's life cycles.

The opposite of brand loyalty is *brand switching*, i.e. consumers turn to alternative brands mainly because the original brand has lost some of its former appeal. For example, customers might switch to rival brands that are more competitively priced or because the competing product might offer better functions and services. To prevent brand switching, businesses often use **customer loyalty schemes**. These are a form of sales promotion used to entice customers to stick to the brand by rewarding devoted customers, e.g. the Air Miles loyalty scheme used by many airlines.

Box 4.5.f   Brand or product?

Brand name	Product	Company
Aspirin	Acetylsalicylic acid (drug)	Bayer AG, Germany
Astro Turf	Artificial lawn (or grass)	Textiles Management Associates
Band-Aid	Adhesive bandage	Johnson & Johnson
Biro	Ballpoint pen	Invented by Laszlo Biro in 1938
Blu-Tack	Reusable putty adhesive	Bostik Findley, Australia
Bubble Wrap	Air cellular cushioning material	Sealed Air Corporation, USA
Coke	Cola	Coca-Cola
Frisbee	Flying disc	Wham-O, USA
Hoover	Vacuum cleaner	The Hoover Company,
Hula hoop	Toy hoop	Wham-O, USA
iPod	Portable media player	Apple Inc., USA
Jacuzzi	Whirlpool bathtub	Jacuzzi, USA
Kleenex	Tissue paper	Kimberley-Clark, USA
Rollerblade	Inline skates	Tecnica Group, Italy
Tipp-Ex	Correction fluid	BIC Corporation, France
Wyteboard Marker	Board marker pen	Pilot, Japan

Brand value

Brand value refers to the premium that customers are willing to pay for a brand name over and above the value of the product itself. This means that customers are willing to pay more for a reputable brand, such as a Starbucks coffee, than for the product itself, such as coffee from a low-cost fast food restaurant. This is because consumers believe that a well-known brand has better value for money than products that are less well-known. Brand awareness, brand development and brand loyalty all have a role in improving an organization's brand value. There are numerous advantages for businesses that try to boost their brand value:

- **Higher market share** – Market share is an indicator of the level of brand development and brand loyalty. There is a strong and positive relationship between a firm's market share and its brand value. Marketers try to improve this by investing money in brand development, e.g. by using persuasive advertising.

- **Premium prices** – Having brand value allows a business to charge higher prices for its products because customers feel that they are paying for the added value that the brand carries, such as the reputation of the brand. This gives customers reassurance that the product is genuine, reliable and of good quality. Market leaders are also able to set their own prices whereas rivals could be forced into charging prices determined by the brand leader.

- **Higher barriers to entry** – Brand value makes it more difficult for new businesses to enter the market because customers are loyal to the existing brand. The dominance of brands such as Adidas, Coca-Cola, McDonald's and Samsung has created huge problems for rival brands. Products with high brand value can then enjoy the status of being cash cows for the business.

CORE

Question 4.5.6   The top brands in the world

Interbrand, the world's largest branding consultancy firm, conducts annual rankings of the world's top brands. These brands must have a global presence with at least 20% of sales coming from outside their home country. Interbrand assesses each brand based on its future earning potential. Some of the most valuable global brands include: Apple, Coca-Cola, GE, Google, IBM, Intel, McDonald's, Microsoft and Toyota.

Source: www.interbrand.com

(a) Explain why globally recognised brands such as Coca-Cola, Microsoft and Toyota continue to spend huge amounts of money on brand development. *[4 marks]*

(b) Examine how the brand name might determine the future success of a business. *[6 marks]*

Marketing

Question 4.5.7   French Connection, UK

British clothes retailer *French Connection (FCUK)* sells its clothing products and accessories throughout the world. *FCUK* reported that 2005 was one of its most difficult years, after announcing that profits had fallen by a huge 53%. Customers, it seemed, were growing tired of the *FCUK* brand which lost its **brand loyalty** and shock factor over time. In response, *FCUK* launched several more potentially offensive marketing campaigns including one that featured two women kung fu fighting before embracing one another. Unsurprisingly, a number of their advertisements were banned in the UK and USA.

(a) Define the term **brand loyalty**.   *[2 marks]*

(b) Explain why brand loyalty is important to a business such as *FCUK*.   *[4 marks]*

Packaging

The importance of packaging. AO3

© IBO, 2017

Packaging refers to the ways in which a product is presented to the consumer. For example, most jewellers offer a special wrapping service. Packaging is a form of product differentiation. It can be important if a product's design, functions or features cannot be easily differentiated from others on the market. Psychologists have shown that people's moods are affected by things such as colour, texture and appearances. Businesses have therefore used packaging to entice customers by using different colours, shapes, sizes and material. Packaging can be very important in the marketing mix due to its varied functions:

- Packaging has a profound impact on customer perceptions of a product or brand, e.g. imagine buying jewellery from Tiffany & Co., a handbag from Chanel or perfume from Christian Dior and receiving the contents in a bland plastic carrier bag! Customers perceive quality packaging with a quality product.

- It acts as a form of product differentiation, e.g. free gift wrapping services offered by retailers during the Christmas trading period might be enough to sway customers away from rivals that do not offer such a service.

- Packaging protects a product against damage during transportation and distribution of the product. Imagine buying a large high-definition television or a crystal chandelier without any form of protective packaging!

- Labelling can be used to provide information. This might be to meet legal obligations (such as health warnings on cigarette packs or nutritional information on packaged food products) or for promotional purposes (such as competitions on cereal boxes).

- Packaging makes the distribution of products easier. Boxes can be stacked on top of each other, thereby making distribution safer and faster.

- Packaging can be used to encourage *impulse buying* (unplanned purchases). Confectionery and other food items sold in supermarkets often have eye-catching packaging to entice customers to buy the product.

- It is used to promote the brand or the business. For example, shopping bags usually incorporate the name of the business, some businesses use their own brand label wrapping paper, and coffee shops use disposable cups advertising their brand name.

One drawback of packaging is its cost. Customers are the ones who ultimately pay for the privilege of attractive packaging. Environmentalists argue that marketing creates excess packaging, at the cost of environmental damage. Some marketers argue that packaging should not be seen as a separate element of the marketing mix because, essentially, it is a form of promotion. Nevertheless, there is little doubt that packaging does affect costs, prices, customer perceptions and consumer demand.

Figure 4.5.g Packaging toilet tissue is an art form in Japan

Product and the CUEGIS concepts

Successful products provide customers with added value. *Functional value* refers to what the product actually does for customers, e.g. Coca-Cola helps to quench people's thirst, whilst Apple's iPod lets consumers listen to music. *Emotional value* refers to the psychology and feel-good factor behind the purchase of a product, e.g. designs that suit personal style and taste or feeling proud of owning a particular brand or product. This means that product strategy, such as design and branding, is vital in adding value to a product. This will depend, of course, on cultural differences and regional preferences.

Successful products also foster brand loyalty, which helps a business to develop and launch new products under the same brand name (known as **brand extension strategies**). Cadbury's, Virgin and Samsung are examples of successful businesses that have used their brand names to enlarge their product portfolios, thereby strengthening their competitive position in a globalized world.

Globalization has provided many opportunities for multinational businesses, although product strategy becomes more difficult when operating on an international basis. Some products have become so popular on an international scale that they are called **global brands**, i.e. the same product is sold using exactly the same (or very similar) marketing strategies in overseas markets. Examples of global brands include: Coca-Cola, Disney, HSBC, McDonald's, Microsoft, Rolex and Mercedes–Benz. Their image, physical make-up and appearance are almost identical wherever they are marketed on the planet, i.e. there is consistency in the marketing of these products. The key driving forces for global branding strategies are brand exposure and the cost savings gained from using a single marketing approach.

Nevertheless, cultural and ethical considerations have led to a greater focus on the local needs of overseas consumers. Thus, global brands have been **glocalized** to cater for local preferences whilst retaining the core elements of the global brand. For example, the core food menu at McDonald's is almost the same throughout the world, but additional products are included to cater for local tastes and preferences.

In an ever-changing business world, the products of a business are vital to its success. Microsoft, Apple, Boeing and Nike are all examples of market leaders that have managed to successfully market their products. Technology, fashion, tastes and trends are constantly subject to change and it is the businesses that are able to adapt their product portfolios that stand a chance of doing well. For example, Nokia started as a wood manufacturing business in 1865; Nintendo made playing cards back in 1889; Wrigley produced soap powder in 1891 before specialising in chewing gum; and Motorola initially produced car radios in 1928. The dynamic nature of business activity means that complacency is potentially disastrous. Theodore Levitt (1960) pointed this out when he wrote about **marketing myopia**. This exists when businesses become complacent about their product strategy, thereby failing to keep up with market changes.

Innovation has also intensified competition in many industries, and in particular consumer electronics. For example, when cameras were first invented only the rich few could afford them. The introduction of portable cameras that used 35 mm camera film brought the product to the masses. This resulted in businesses such as Kodak, Fujitsu and Konica, competing on a regional basis and focusing their strategy on continuous improvement (see Figure 4.5.h). However, the mass adoption of digital technologies and mobile devices in the globalized business world resulted in global competition and business strategy focusing on continuous innovation.

Limited competition	Regional competition	Global competition
Stability	Continuous improvement	Continuous innovation

Figure 4.5.h Innovation and product strategy

CORE

Marketing

Although 'product' is often said to be the most important part of the marketing mix, a product strategy cannot succeed without integrating the other elements of the marketing mix and marketing planning. For example, to fully understand and cater for different customer needs, market segmentation and consumer profiling (see Unit 4.2) might be necessary. The use of position mapping (see Unit 4.2) can give managers insightful information regarding consumers' perceptions of a product. Understanding these perceptions can help managers to devise and implement better product strategies.

However, producing the 'right' product to the right people at the right price is difficult due to the costs and other complexities involved. Different products require different strategies. Fiat Group, Italy's largest car manufacturer, does not market Fiat cars in the same way it markets its Alfa Romeo, Maserati and Ferrari marques (brands). For a business to remain competitive, it has to carefully plan its product strategy whilst managing a diverse portfolio of products. Many large companies, such as Fiat, have benefited from developing a **multi-brand strategy**. This involves a business developing two or more brands in the same product category. For example, Coca-Cola uses brands such as Fanta and Sprite to gain a greater share of the soft drinks market. However, **product cannibalisation** is a potential problem of a multi-brand strategy – when brands from the same business directly compete with each other.

Brand management has become an increasingly important management task, especially as technological innovations continue to shorten product life cycles of many types of products. Product and brand strategies can be aided by tools such as SWOT analysis (see Unit 1.3). Managers can analyse the strengths to be developed, such as brand extension strategies to launch new products. The SWOT analysis will also highlight weaknesses that need to be addressed. Managers can also identify potential market opportunities or threats before deciding on the best strategy to respond to these.

A common strategy is to increase the product mix, enabling the business to generate more revenue and to spread its risks. For example, Starbucks sells and distributes music and film (soundtracks, movies and DVDs) in addition to its coffee business. In the USA, Starbucks managed to secure exclusive deals for the release of new albums by Alanis Morissette, Bob Dylan and Sir Paul McCartney. In 2018, Starbucks expanded into Italy to spread its risks even further. Product portfolio analysis can help managers to determine their product strategy. The Boston Matrix suggests four different strategies to deal with stars, dogs, problem children and cash cows (see Figure 4.5.i).

		Market share	
		High	Low
Market growth	High (growing)	Harvest	Build
	Low (mature)	Hold	Divest

Figure 4.5.i The Boston matrix and product strategy

- **Build** This strategy is used to turn question marks into stars by investing necessary resources to gain market share. If nothing is done to increase their market share, then they will simply drain cash from the business.

- **Harvest** This strategy involves reaping the benefits (profits) of a product. The purpose is to turn stars into cash cows. This might require huge amounts of advertising to turn the product into a cash cow.

- **Hold** This strategy involves investing enough resources to keep cash cows in their current position in the BCG matrix. Investment is likely to be minimal as market growth for cash cows will be low.

- **Divest** This strategy involves phasing out or selling off dogs. This frees up resources to be used elsewhere, such as investing in certain problem children. Some question marks might also face divestment, especially those that are unlikely to turn into stars.

Within the BCG matrix, the problem children are the main users of cash whilst the cash cows are the main generators of cash. The optimal product portfolio strategy is one that takes advantage of the firm's strengths (stars and cash cows) to develop other attractive opportunities (problem children and rising stars).

IB Learner Profile – Be an inquirer

How do multinationals market their products to different cultures? As a starting point, you can watch this short video on the comparative marketing approaches of McDonald's in China and the USA: http://goo.gl/WFivUI.

CORE

Marketing

Theory of knowledge

When does the life of a product actually begin? What determines whether marketers consider to be the first stage of the product life cycle: launch or R&D (research and development)?

CUEGIS Essay

With reference to an organization of your choice, discuss how **change** and **innovation** have influenced the product life cycle of the organization or its brand.

[20 marks]

REVIEW QUESTIONS

1. What is a product?

2. Distinguish between consumer durables, consumer perishable products, and fast-moving consumer goods.

3. What are the stages in a typical product life cycle?

4. Explain how the life cycle of a product has varying effects on a firm's level of investment, profits and cash flow.

5. Use examples to explain the meaning of extension strategies.

6. Distinguish between the four quadrants in the Boston Consulting Group matrix.

7. Why is it important for a business to have a balanced product portfolio?

8. What is branding and why is it important for businesses?

9. What is the difference between 'brand loyalty' and 'brand development'?

10. Explain how brand value depends of brand awareness, brand development and brand loyalty.

KEY TERMS

The **Boston matrix** (or Boston Consulting Group matrix) is a marketing tool for analysing the product portfolio of a business. It shows whether products have high or low market share and operate in high or low market growth industries.

Brand awareness measures the extent to which potential customers or the general public recognise a particular brand. It is usually expressed as a percentage of the sample surveyed.

Brand development is a long-term product strategy that involves strengthening the name and image of a brand to boost its appeal and sales.

Brand loyalty occurs when customers buy the same brand of a product time and time again. They are devoted to the brand since they have brand preference over other brand names.

Brand value refers to the premium that customers are willing to pay for a brand over and above the value of the product itself, i.e. customers are willing to pay more for a reputable brand.

Branding refers to the use of an exclusive name, symbol or design to identify a specific product or organization. It differentiates a product from similar ones offered by competitors.

Cash cow is a term used by the Boston Consulting Group to refer to any product that generates significant money due to its large market share in a mature market.

Consumer goods are products bought for personal consumption, such as *consumer durables* (e.g. furniture, computers and cars) and *perishables* (e.g. food and flowers).

Dogs are products in the BCG matrix that have low market share and operate in low growth or stagnant markets. Hence, dogs do not generate much cash or profit for a business.

An **extension strategy** is an attempt by marketers to lengthen the life cycle of a particular product, typically used during the maturity or early decline stages of the product's life cycle.

Global brands are highly popular products sold with exactly the same (or very similar) marketing strategies in overseas markets, using the same brand name in different countries.

Marketing myopia exists when a business becomes complacent about its product strategy, thereby failing to keep up with market changes.

CORE

Marketing

441

Fast-moving consumer goods (FMCGs) are everyday convenience products sold in retail outlets such as supermarkets, e.g. personal health care products and groceries.

Packaging is the art of presenting products in an advantageous way in order to improve sales.

Producer goods are products purchased for commercial use, rather than for private use, such as machinery, vehicles and land.

Product refers to any physical or non-physical item (good or service) that is purchased by commercial or private customers.

Product differentiation refers to any strategy used to make a product appear to be distinct from others, such as quality, branding and packaging.

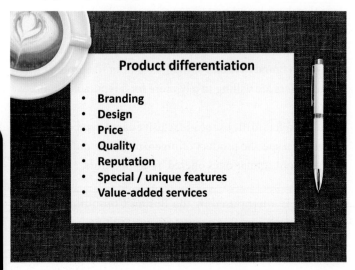

The **product life cycle** (PLC) is the typical process that products go through from their initial design and launch to their decline and eventual withdrawal. Different products undergo each of the five stages (research, launch, growth, maturity and decline) at varying speeds.

Product portfolio refers to the range of products or strategic business units owned and developed by an organization at any one point in time.

Question marks (or **problem children**) are products in a BCG matrix that compete in high market growth industries, but have low market share. They consume lots of cash but do not generate much profit, if any.

Rising stars (or **stars**) are products in the BCG matrix that have high or rising market share in a high growth market.

Price

"The higher the price you have to pay, the more you will cherish it." - Lloyd C. Douglas (1877–1951), American minister of religion and author

SL/HL content	Assessment objective
Price The appropriateness of the following pricing strategies: • cost-plus (mark-up) • penetration • skimming • psychological • loss leader • price discrimination • price leadership and • predatory	AO3

© IBO, 2017

Price

The appropriateness of the following pricing strategies: cost-plus (mark-up), penetration, skimming, psychological, loss leader, price discrimination, price leadership and predatory. AO3

© IBO, 2014

Price refers to the amount paid by a customer to purchase a good or service. The pricing decision is a crucial part of any marketing strategy. Many products fail due to poor pricing decisions (see Question 4.1.1). The dilemma facing businesses is to set a price that is competitive yet also profitable as the pricing decision has a direct impact on the level of sales revenues. Setting too high a price deters customers, whilst setting too low a price could lead to a lack of stock and hence dissatisfied customers.

Price can also affect the corporate image of a business or its products. Producers and suppliers of luxury brands, such as Versace or Gucci, might benefit from some price cuts in the short term but sustaining lower prices in the long term will damage their reputation, perhaps irrevocably. Hence, businesses need to have a clear understanding of the link between the price and the demand for their products. The main pricing strategies are: cost-plus (mark-up), penetration, skimming, psychological, loss leader, price discrimination, price leadership and predatory pricing.

Cost-plus (mark-up) pricing

Cost-plus (mark-up) pricing involves adding a percentage or predetermined amount of profit to the cost per unit of output to determine the selling price. The percentage or specified amount is known as the **mark-up** (or **profit margin**). For example, if a coffee shop estimates the average cost of its products to be $4 and wants to have a 50% mark-up, the price is set at $6. Alternatively, if the firm wanted to earn $2.50 profit on each cup of coffee sold, the selling price would be $6.50. The main advantage of cost-plus pricing is its simplicity and ease of calculation. However, cost-plus pricing often relies too much on intuitive decision-making rather than on the needs of customers.

Figure 4.5.j Not all price discounts are what they first seem

Question 4.5.8   Tulgestke Trampolines Co.

The average cost of production for *Tulgestke Trampolines Co.'s* best-selling trampolines is $150. The company uses a **mark-up** of 90%.

(a) Define the term **mark-up**.   *[2 marks]*

(b) Calculate the selling price of *Tulgestke Trampolines Co.'s* best-selling trampolines.   *[2 marks]*

Tulgestke Trampolines Co. sells a cheaper trampoline for $105, for which the production costs are $65.

(c) Calculate the percentage profit margin (mark-up) on these cheaper trampolines.   *[2 marks]*

Figure 4.5.k Mark-up pricing is commonly used for cups of coffee

Price skimming

Price skimming is used for technologically advanced and innovative products. Since new product development (NPD) can be very expensive, a high price is initially set to recoup the costs of research and development. As there are unlikely to be any substitutes, the business can charge a premium price to maximise profits. A high initial price can also create a unique and prestigious image for the product. Games consoles, smartphones and flat-screen televisions have all been priced using this strategy.

Due to the large potential profits that can be earned, other businesses `will eventually be attracted to enter the industry. When this happens, the original firm will skim (gradually reduce) its price. When Apple launched the iPhone 4S, it was priced at $399, but the launch of the iPhone 5 caused the price of the iPhone 4S to drop to just $99. However, marketing by its very nature is integrated. Price skimming can only be successful if it is supported by other elements of the marketing mix.

Psychological pricing

Psychological pricing involves rounding down numbers, such as $9.99 or $14,995, to make prices seem lower (than $10.00 or $15,000). Hence, customers psychologically feel that they are getting a bargain (better price) for the product. This method is widely used and can work for almost any product, from groceries sold in a supermarket to expensive motor vehicles or residential property. It also works well when selling the same product in larger quantities. For example, supermarkets might sell a product at $4.99 for one or $14.97 for three (the price is exactly the same per unit but it can be deceiving). Psychological pricing does not work well for some businesses, such as taxi firms, as rounded or whole numbers are more suitable for the customer and the service provider.

Penetration pricing

Penetration pricing sets a relatively low price (or a 'special introductory price') to help establish a new product in the industry, i.e. to gain brand recognition and market share. For example, in 2007 China's Brilliance Automobiles launched its cars in Europe at around 15% lower than the prices of rival Korean carmakers such as Hyundai and Kia. As the product becomes established over time, the price can be raised. This strategy is suitable for mass market products sold in large enough quantities to sustain low profit margins, *e.g. fast moving consumer goods (FMCG)*. A potential problem is that setting prices too low can cause customers to perceive the product as inferior and of poor quality.

Table 4.5.b   Loss leader pricing in the gaming industry

	Cost to make (p/unit) level	Selling price (p/unit)
Sony PS3 60GB	$840	$600
Microsoft Xbox 360	$525	$399
Sony PS4	$381	$400
Microsoft Xbox One	$471	$500

Menu *Fabio's Pizza Home*

Any large family pizza

1.5l bottled soft drink

Garlic bread

Spaghetti Bolognese

Self-collect @ $28.90
Delivered @ $3390

Figure 4.5.l The importance of the decimal place in pricing!

Loss leader

Loss leader pricing involves selling a product below its cost value. Retailers such as supermarkets often use this strategy by heavily marketing the loss leader (such as toilet tissue or carbonated soft drinks) in the hope of attracting customers. It is unlikely for customers to purchase only the loss leader when visiting a supermarket, yet the existence of loss leaders can attract many customers. Loss leaders can also be used to encourage brand switching, which in the long term can make up for losses incurred whilst the product was priced at a loss. Games console makers such as Sony, Nintendo and Microsoft often sell their hardware at a loss to attract buyers (see Table 4.5.b). The aim is to recoup the loss by sales of complementary goods such as gaming software and accessories, and collecting royalty payments from games manufacturers.

Price discrimination

Price discrimination occurs when the same product, usually a service, is sold at different prices to different customers. For example, children and adults pay different prices for entering the same cinema, theme park or hair salon. The product they pay for is essentially the same but the prices are different. Three conditions must be met for successful price discrimination:

- The business must have some degree of market power to set prices.

- Customers must have different degrees of willingness to pay, otherwise the business cannot charge different prices to different segments of the market.

- Markets must be kept separate to prevent resale, e.g. a child cannot sell his or her theatre or train ticket to an adult.

Businesses are likely to raise prices during peak periods. For example, airlines hike their prices during the school holiday season. This is partly because there is increased demand and largely because firms know that the degree of sensitivity of demand to changes in price during peak periods is lower, i.e. customers are willing to pay higher prices and are less responsive to price variations.

CORE

Marketing

Figure 4.5.m Price discrimination is common in the tourism industry

Price discrimination is not only about setting higher prices to customers who can afford to pay. Statistically, restaurants and cinemas throughout the world face their quietest trading day of the week on a Tuesday, which is why many of these businesses offer discounted prices to diners and cinema-goers on Tuesdays.

Price leadership

Price leadership is a strategy often used for the best-selling products or brands in a particular market. Customers perceive there to be few substitutes for such products, so the dominant business can set its own prices. Competitors then 'follow the leader' by setting their prices based on the price of the market (or price) leader.

If the market leader sets a relatively high price, businesses in the industry will enjoy higher profit margins. However, if the dominant firms sets a low price, this can create problems for other businesses that are unable to match the price as they do not have the same economies of scale as the market leader.

Question 4.5.9 Price discrimination at theme parks

Theme parks (amusement parks) such as Disneyland, Universal Studios and SeaWorld use **price discrimination** to increase their sales revenue. An example of such a pricing strategy is shown below:

	Child (age 3–11)	Adult (12 and older)
1 Day Pass	$78	$88
Family (2 adults, 2 children) 1 Day Pass	$305	
Family (1 adult, 2 children) 1 Day Pass	$230	
Annual Pass (Mon–Fri entry)	$275	$308
Annual Pass (Mon–Sun entry)	$390	$440
Free admission for children under 3-years-old and local senior residents aged 65 years old or above, with proof of identity and age.		

(a) Define the term **price discrimination**.   [2 marks]

(b) With reference to the above data, examine how theme parks use price discrimination to increase their revenue.   [6 marks]

Question 4.5.10 The price of price wars

The world's largest supermarket chains (such as Walmart, Carrefour and Tesco) have huge market power to reduce prices. Price reductions, including the use of **loss leader pricing**, are a key technique used by supermarkets to improve their competitiveness. For example, British consumers have grown accustomed to supermarket **price wars**, with more than £1 billion ($1.45bn) of price reductions each year.

(a) (i) Define the term **loss leader pricing**.   [2 marks]

(a) (ii) Define the term **price wars**.   [2 marks]

(b) Examine the winners and losers of a price war in the short run and the long run.   [6 marks]

(c) Justify **two** forms of non-price competition that supermarkets might use to increase their competitiveness.   [10 marks]

CORE

Marketing

Question 4.5.11 Virgin Australia Airlines

Virgin Australia Airlines was the creation of Sir Richard Branson, founder and CEO of the Virgin Group (see Question 4.5.3). Branson and the airline's CEO, Brett Godfrey, launched the airline carrier in 2000 to enter the Australian market. Initially set up as a low fare carrier, the company only flew between Brisbane and Sydney. Since then, it has become Australia's second largest airline, covering all major cities in Australia. To cut **direct costs**, customers pay for their in-flight meals and drinks and *Virgin Australia Airlines* uses a system of e-ticketing (a telephone and internet-based ticketing system).

(a) Define the term **direct costs**.   *[2 marks]*

(b) Describe **two** potential pricing strategies that airline companies can adopt when entering a new market.   *[4 marks]*

(c) Evaluate **two** possible pricing strategies that airline carriers such as *Virgin Australia Airlines* could use to increase their sales revenue.   *[10 marks]*

Exam tip !

Classifying pricing strategies is not necessarily straightforward. A business selling a product at $9.95 might be perceived to be using psychological pricing, but this could equally be any other pricing strategy, such as mark-up, penetration, loss leader, or predatory pricing. For other products, it might even be a premium price.

What pricing strategy is this (USD191.4 for a bunch of Japanese Shine Muscat grapes)?!

Predatory pricing

Predatory pricing involves temporarily reducing price in an attempt to force competitors out of the industry as they cannot compete profitably. Due to the aggressive nature of this strategy, it is sometimes referred to as **destroyer pricing**. The strategy often stems from a **price war**, whereby businesses compete by a series of continuous and/or intensive price cuts. This might even mean selling products at below cost value. Price wars are common in the supermarket, airline and mobile phone industries. If the strategy is successful, the firm will benefit from being in a more dominant position, and can therefore raise its prices to recoup any losses previously incurred. Although price wars can bring some benefits to customers in the short term, predatory pricing itself is illegal in many parts of the world (such as in the USA and EU) since it is regarded as an anti-competitive trade practice.

Price and the CUEGIS concepts

In reality, an organization's pricing strategy will consist of a combination of various pricing methods. It is vital that the pricing strategy adopted by a business provides adequate profit for all products in its portfolio. It is also important that the pricing of a new product does not destroy profit margins on more established products. However, the pricing decision must be consistent with the organization's marketing objectives, e.g. penetration pricing might be used to establish or gain market share. Strategically, the pricing decision must be consistent with all other aspects of marketing, such as:

CORE

Marketing

- *Marketing planning* – Pricing decisions need to consider the nature of the targeted market. Segmentation data such as income levels and demographics (including cultural issues) can prove useful in setting suitable prices.

- *Place* – The distribution methods used will also affect prices, e.g. cosmetics sold through mail order catalogues are priced differently from those sold at exclusive cosmetic boutiques. The more intermediaries that are used, the greater the costs and hence the higher the price tends to be.

- *Product* – Features of a product such as the quality and design also affect the price charged. Innovative products can demand a high price, whereas 'me-too' products can only command lower prices.

- *Promotion* – The type of promotional methods used to market a product affects the costs, which in turn influences the price. For example, mass media television advertising or expensive celebrity endorsements ultimately result in higher prices being charged to customers.

In addition to marketing issues, there are other factors that can affect pricing strategy:

- *The nature of the business* – Profit maximising businesses with significant market share are likely to use pricing strategies with high profit margins, such as price discrimination. By contrast, cost-based methods may be more appropriate for non-profit organizations.

- *The nature of barriers to entry* – This refers to the degree of competition within the industry, i.e. high entry barriers limit competition in an industry, but allow existing businesses to charge higher prices. By contrast, businesses operating in highly competitive markets take more notice of the prices being charged by their rivals.

- *Business image* – Organizations with a reputable and prestigious corporate image can charge higher prices. By contrast, firms with inferior products or brands will charge lower prices.

- *Business costs* – Whatever strategy is chosen, a business must cover its costs of production in the long run. For example, the high production costs of making handmade silk rugs mean that relatively high prices need to be charged.

- *The state of the economy* – Like any good business strategy, flexibility allows pricing strategies to change in line with the state of the economy. For example, a common strategy is that most businesses tend to reduce prices during an economic recession, especially those that make luxury products.

Figure 4.5.n An innovative pricing strategy?

Despite the huge importance placed on pricing strategies, businesses are also likely to use non-pricing strategies to market their products. These can take the form of promotional strategies such as advertising, branding, gift vouchers and packaging. Note that price and marketing are integrated as part of the overall business strategy; no amount of price discounts can sell a product that does not meet the needs or wants of the consumer.

Theory of knowledge

Can we ever know if the prices charged by businesses are ethical? Does it matter?

Exam tip !

Exam questions often require candidates to suggest and justify suitable pricing strategies that can be used by a business to enter new markets. Rather than simply explaining the various types of pricing methods in the syllabus, it is more important to put these into the context of the organization. It might be appropriate to consider several issues first, before advising suitable pricing strategies, such as:

- Although the market is 'new' for the organization in question, there might be other established businesses already in the market. However, price skimming might be appropriate if the firm is the first entrant to a market.
- Unless the product is original and innovative, customers will already have perceptions about what the correct prices ought to be.
- For some products, price discrimination is highly suitable whilst loss leaders work better for other products.
- What sort of image does the business want to portray? Clearly, the pricing strategy used for high quality and specialist products will be different from that used for mass market products with plenty of substitutes.
- Finally, it is important to consider the likely reaction of competitors to the pricing strategies used by a business. If low prices are used and this sparks off a price war, then most businesses will tend to lose out.

Theory of knowledge

To what extent can we know the true value of a product from its price?

CUEGIS Essay

With reference to an organization of your choice, examine how **change** has affected its pricing **strategies**.
[20 marks]

CUEGIS Essay

With reference to an organization of your choice, discuss how **ethics** have influence **pricing strategies**.
[20 marks]

REVIEW QUESTIONS

1. What is meant by 'price'?

2. Explain why the price decision (deciding on the 'right' price) is such a difficult task.

3. Explain the link between the price of a product and its perceived quality.

4. What is 'mark-up'?

5. Why do some businesses use 'loss leaders'?

6. What is price leadership?

7. What is the difference between penetration pricing and skimming pricing?

8. Why might customers not necessarily benefit from predatory pricing, such as price wars?

9. Why do some businesses use psychological pricing

10. What is meant by non-pricing strategies?

KEY TERMS

Cost-plus pricing (or **mark-up pricing**) involves adding a percentage or predetermined amount of profit to the cost per unit of output to determine the selling price.

Loss leader pricing involves setting the price of a product below its costs of production. The purpose is to entice customers to buy other products with high profit margins in addition to purchasing the loss leader product.

Mark-up refers to the extra amount charged by a business on top of its unit costs of production in order to earn a profit margin. This can be expressed as an absolute amount (e.g. $10 per bottle) or as a percentage of the cost (e.g. 25% per bottle).

CORE

Marketing

Non-pricing strategies refer to the methods used by a business to market its products other than by focusing on price. Examples include advertising, branding, packaging and customer loyalty schemes.

Penetration pricing involves setting low prices to gain entry into a new market. Once the product has established market share, prices can be raised.

Predatory pricing involves temporarily setting prices so low that rivals, especially smaller businesses, cannot compete at a profitable level.

Price refers to the amount paid by a customer to purchase a good or service.

Price discrimination involves charging different prices to different groups of customers for the same product, e.g. adult and child airline tickets.

Price leadership is used for best-selling products or brands in a particular market. Customers perceive there to be few substitutes for such products so the dominant firm can set its own prices. Competitors set their prices based on the price of the market (or price) leader.

Price skimming involves initially charging high prices for innovative or high-tech products. Price is reduced as the novelty wears off and as substitute products appear.

Pricing strategies are the various methods of setting the amount that customers pay for certain goods and services, e.g. mark-up, penetration, skimming, psychological, loss leader, price discrimination, price leadership and predatory pricing.

Price wars involve businesses competing by a series of continuous and/or intensive price cuts to threaten the competitiveness of rival firms.

Psychological pricing involves rounding down numbers such as $990 or $14,995 to make prices seem lower (than $1,000 or $15,000).

Supermarkets are experts at pricing strategies

CORE

Marketing

Promotion

"Advertising is the art of convincing people to spend money they don't have for something they don't need." - Will Rogers (1879–1935), American comedian and actor

SL/HL content	Assessment objective
Promotion The following aspects of promotion: above the line promotion, below the line promotion and promotional mix	AO2
The impact of changing technology on promotional strategies (such as viral marketing, social media marketing and social networking)	AO3
Guerrilla marketing and its effectiveness as a promotional method	AO3

© IBO, 2017

Promotion

Promotion refers to methods of communicating messages to the market, usually with the intention of selling a firm's products. Examples include advertising and raising publicity (awareness). Some types of promotion are paid for (e.g. mass media advertising) whilst some are not (e.g. word of mouth). Although promotional activities are important, especially during the early stages of a product's life cycle, they can also be extremely expensive. Determining the optimum promotional budget and forecasting its probable impact on sales is by no means an easy task. Nevertheless, effective promotion can certainly improve the financial health and sustainability of a business.

There are three key objectives to any promotional strategy: to *inform*, to *persuade* and to *remind* the market about the firm's product(s).

- *Informative promotion* aims to alert the market about a firm's products, especially new or updated products. Promotion might include information such as product functions and price. It is often based on providing facts and figures about a business or its products. The aim is to give customers sufficient information to influence their purchasing decisions.

- *Persuasive promotion* aims to encourage customers to make a purchase, to switch from rival products and to create brand loyalty. To entice customers to buy their products, businesses might adopt product differentiation techniques such as branding to create a unique identity or to enhance the product's image. Successful persuasion can also generate impulse buying - when customers make

a purchase without having planned to do so, i.e. there is a subconscious urge to buy the product.

- *Reminder promotion* are techniques used to retain customer awareness of, and interest in an established product. Reminder promotion is suitable for products that are in the maturity or saturation stages of their product life cycle. Leading brands such as McDonald's and Coca-Cola often use this form of promotion.

The vast majority of promotions are of the persuasive kind. However, most promotional campaigns contain an element of both persuasion and information. Governments and non-profit organizations account for the majority of informative promotional campaigns.

Case study

The producers of the first *Spider-Man* movie spent $50 million on its promotional campaign in 2002. This spending has to be justified and its success (or otherwise) has to be measured. *Spider-Man 3* was a huge success, costing $258 million to make, but returning $890.8 million.

Above the line promotion

The following aspects of promotion: above the line promotion.

AO2

© IBO, 2017

Above the line (ATL) promotion is any form of paid-for promotional method through independent mass media sources (such as television, magazines and radio) to promote a business, its brands or its products. The main methods of ATL promotion include the following:

Television advertising

The first American TV advertisement appeared in 1941. UK television advertisements first appeared in 1955 and had a profound impact on the marketing industry. According to the Broadcasters Audience Research Board (www.barb.co.uk), the UK TV advertising industry is worth more than £5 billion ($8 billion) per year. The fact that expenditure on TV advertising is such big business, and that it exceeds spending on all other forms of promotion, suggests it has huge advantages. Advertising on TV exploits the power of combining sound and moving images to convey very powerful messages to viewers. TV advertisements can also be designed to meet specific needs, such as advertisements aimed at children being aired during children's television programmes. With advances in technology, such as high definition digital television, it is possible to broadcast TV advertisements to a global audience.

However, the major drawback is the huge costs of producing and broadcasting television advertisements. Media specialist and author Frank Dane explained this by stating, "Time is money, especially when you are talking to a lawyer or buying a commercial". Television companies sell 'advertising slots' to businesses based on the level of demand (peak-time slots will obviously sell for a higher price). Hence, marketers must try to get their message across in a very short time frame, usually within 30 seconds. In fact, the cost of a 30-second weekend TV advertising spot during peak time in Hong Kong and the UK starts from approximately $60,000.

Case study

The annual Super Bowl (American Football), with 93 million viewers, is the USA's most watched sporting event. This creates huge promotional opportunities for businesses with large advertising budgets. In 2013, the average cost of a 30-second advertisement during the Super Bowl was $4m! The best advertisements during the Super Bowl earn a place in history, being broadcast on television and the Internet for years to come.

Radio advertising

As with television advertising, radio time slots are sold to businesses, with peak listening times in the morning and evening rush hour periods. Commercial radio stations require a licence to broadcast. Their activities are monitored and regulated by a government agency. The content of radio advertisements in most countries must be legal, decent, honest and truthful.

Radio advertising is able to reach a very large audience yet it is significantly cheaper than TV advertising. Unlike TV advertising, radio commercials do not rely on viewers having to be immobile in front of a TV screen. Instead, radio listeners are exposed to the promotions whilst they continue to do other things, such as driving, eating a meal or getting changed for school or work. Advances in technology, such as wireless broadband, mean that radio commercials can be broadcast to almost anyone around the world (see Figure 4.5.o).

The main drawback of radio advertising is that it can only communicate audio messages, i.e. there is no visual impact. Research has shown that people can retain oral messages better when there is a visual stimulus. Another related disadvantage is that audiences have lower attention levels compared with TV advertisements, which exploit the dynamics of moving images.

IB Learner Profile – Be an inquirer

Visit www.veryfunnyads.com for some good humoured television adverts. As a tip, browse the 'most watched' or 'top rated'. You can also get some insight into cultural differences by viewing the adverts from different countries.

Figure 4.5.o Radio advertising is a form of ATL promotion

Cinema

Statistics show growing visitor numbers at cinemas around the world, which has attracted more marketers to use the cinema as an advertising medium. For example, data from the UN Institute for Statistics shows that China's box office revenues increased by 731% in the first five years following the global financial crisis of 2008.

A key advantage of using cinema advertising is that audiences can be directly targeted. Promotion can be tailored to the specific market segments (such as the genre of film and age groups of the cinemagoers). The size of cinema screens can exert more impact compared to other forms of promotion, especially with the increased popularity of 3D movies. Furthermore, unlike television or radio commercials, marketers have a captured audience as it is much harder for viewers to ignore or switch off the advertisements (especially as most cinemagoers perceive the advertisements as part of the overall cinema experience). The main drawback is its limited audience size compared with that of radio listeners and television viewers.

Newspaper advertising

Newspaper advertising has the advantage of potentially reaching a wide audience yet is much cheaper than using TV advertising. Unlike radio advertisements, newspaper advertisements can be referred to at a later date meaning that important information can be included. Although television advertisements today can be targeted at specific market segments (at least to some extent), newspaper advertisements can target different markets better (see Figure 4.5.p). For example, teaching jobs are advertised in *The Times Educational Supplement*, a specialist newspaper for educators, and on its website (www.tes.co.uk). As newspaper firms have their own dedicated websites, they can have a much wider reach, which makes newspaper advertising more attractive.

The main constraint of newspaper advertising is the high cost, particularly for small businesses. Newspaper firms charge higher prices for colour advertisements, images or photos. Some firms base their charges on the size of an advert whilst others charge on the basis of the number of words, letters or characters used in the advert. For a newspaper advert to stand out from the many others that appear, businesses may need to spend a lot more money than their rivals to ensure that readers are attracted to their advert. Unlike other print media, such as magazines or outdoor posters, newspapers have a very short shelf life; people will not usually read yesterday's "news", so many adverts are simply left unseen and unnoticed.

Figure 4.5.p Newspapers are a popular medium in which to advertise jobs

Magazines

Promotion in magazines has the advantage of being able to use high photo-quality colour images to attract the attention of readers. Targeting the right market segment is possible through the use of specialist magazines such as *Car, Brides, PC Gamer* and *Vogue*. Advertisements in magazines can be referred back to at a later date. Magazines also have a longer shelf-life than newspapers.

One downside to using magazine promotion is that it is static. Hence, it is quite usual for a business to place several different advertisements in the same magazine (think of all the various advertisements used by fashion designers in clothing magazines for example). Also, readers are bombarded with advertisements (known as **advertising clutter**) so may unintentionally miss, or deliberately ignore, the advertisements. A third disadvantage is that there can be a long lead-time between submitting an advertisement and its actual publication in a magazine, i.e. there is a period when sales are potentially lost unless other forms of promotion are used.

CORE

Marketing

Outdoor advertising

Outdoor advertising refers to the use of commercial billboards, banners and posters to promote a business, its brands or its products. These can often be seen at sporting events, in shopping malls, at the roadside and on vehicles (such as buses, trains and taxis). Outdoor advertising is often used by car manufacturers, food producers, clothing firms and businesses involved in leisure and tourism.

With advances in technology, ordinary outdoor advertisements have been transformed into billboards that automatically rotate (thereby increasing the number of advertisements that can be shown on each billboard) and digital billboards that can combine moving images and sound. This has given outdoor advertising a dynamic dimension. Another advantage is that they have high exposure, especially if businesses use the same advertisement in many different locations.

However, a disadvantage of outdoor advertising is the difficulty in monitoring its effectiveness because targeting is very difficult (making it only suitable for promoting mass market products). Traditional billboards are also prone to damage caused by bad weather, vandalism and graffiti. Furthermore, there can be high levels of competition in terms of advertising clutter – central business districts such as New York, Shanghai and London are swamped with billboard advertisements. In Sao Paolo, Brazil, outdoor advertising has been outlawed because it had become so overused that critics argued it created 'advertising pollution', i.e. the billboards became too much of an eyesore for the city's 20 million inhabitants.

Figure 4.5.q Advertising clutter can be an eyesore

In summary, the main advantage of ATL promotion is that it reaches a potentially large number of customers. Research has shown that customers tend to take more notice of ATL promotion as they are more interesting and appealing. However, ATL promotion is very expensive and might not appeal to the audience. For example, many outdoor billboard advertisements go unnoticed because they do not specifically target a market segment. Many advertisements are ignored because people switch channels during television and radio commercial breaks; readers often take no notice of advertisements in magazines; and people complain about the number of pop-up advertisements on the Internet.

Question 4.5.12   The entertainment industry

The entertainment industry is a huge business - just consider the immense popularity of reality TV shows. The movie and music industries are constantly using **above the line** promotional strategies to market their latest products. Trailers (previews) for the latest movies and music albums are frequently aired on television, whilst posters for these latest releases appear all over glossy magazines, in newspapers and on billboards. There are even dedicated Internet websites set up to promote the launch of a movie or music album. Most albums and movies tend to have a short life span, whilst a special few, such as *The Beatles* albums and the *Star Wars* movies, have entertained people since the 1960s and 1970s respectively.

(a) Define the term **above the line** (ATL) promotional strategies.   [2 marks]

(b) Examine **two** reasons for using ATL methods to promote the entertainment industry.   [6 marks]

IB Learner Profile – Be knowlegdeable and be an inquirer

São Paulo, Brazil's largest city, banned outdoor advertising in 2006. Read this New York Times article to investigate the reasons behind the decision: http://goo.gl/EQPkuS and take a look at some before and after photos here: http://goo.gl/0fYp4c.

Theory of knowledge

To what extent does the mass media drive society's perceptions of beauty?

Common mistake

It seems that many students think of marketing as promotion or advertising. In fact, all three are different topics, albeit interrelated. Advertising is a form of promotion, but certainly not the only one, whilst promotion is just one element of the marketing mix.

Below the line promotion

The following aspects of promotion: below the line promotion.
AO2
© IBO, 2017

Below the line (BTL) promotion refers to the use of non-mass media promotional activities, allowing the business to have direct control. Unlike ATL promotion, this means that no commission has been paid to external media agencies. These methods tend to be relatively cheap in relation to methods of ATL promotion. The main BTL promotional strategies are outlined below.

Branding

A huge amount of money is spent each year on promoting brands. Coca-Cola, the world's most recognised brand, has a promotional budget of $2 billion a year. Successful brands are instantly recognisable. Companies such as Apple, Virgin,

Microsoft and Sony use branding to promote their company and their products. They also use brand extension strategies to launch and promote new products under the company brand name.

Slogans

Slogans are memorable catchphrases used to gain and retain the attention of customers. A slogan is a concise message designed to represent the essence of a business or its products in a memorable set of words. Skeptics argue that customers are not so easily fooled by the use of a few words that promise to deliver. The product itself, they argue, is of more importance to make businesses stand out from their rivals. However, some slogans have become so well known that they are synonymous with the brand. Heinz, for example, launched their 'Beanz Meanz Heinz' slogan in 1967 and although it was dropped for ten years, the slogan was relaunched due to public demand. Box 4.5.g shows other examples of highly successful corporate slogans.

Box 4.5.g   Popular business slogans

- *Impossible is nothing* – Adidas
- *The ultimate driving machine* – BMW
- *The world's local bank* – HSBC
- *Finger lickin' good* – KFC
- *Because I'm worth it* – L'Oreal
- *I'm Lovin' It* – McDonald's
- *Just do it* – Nike
- *Gives you wings* – Red Bull
- *Low prices. Every day. On everything.* – Walmart

Effective slogans can help to give a business a competitive advantage over its rivals. In order to judge the effectiveness of a slogan, marketers may look at the following 'MAID' criteria:

- Simplicity, so that the slogan is **memorable**, perhaps through the use of mnemonics, music and catchy tunes.

- Outlines or hints at the **advantages** of the product or the brand.

- Portrays an upbeat **image** for the business and/or its products.

- Creates a sense of **desire** or need for the product.

CORE

Marketing

Theory of knowledge

Are knowledge claims actually being made when businesses use slogans such as 'Probably the best beer in the world' (Carlsberg) and 'A Mars a day helps you work, rest and play' (Mars)? Does truth matter in the use of business slogans?

Logos

Logos are essentially a form of branding that uses a visual symbol to represent a business, its brands or its products. The golden arches (the 'M') of McDonald's and the three stripes of Adidas are two examples of globally recognised logos. Businesses can spend millions of dollars coming up with suitable logos that are distinctive, eye-catching and appealing. Logos can also create a monetary value for businesses, e.g. BMW bought the Rolls–Royce 'RR' logo and brand for £40 million ($65 million) in 1998. Many non-profit organizations, such as The International Red Cross and the World Wild Fund for Nature (WWF), also use logos as part of their promotional strategy.

Figure 4.5.r The WWF logo is widely recognised

Packaging

Packaging can be a powerful component of the marketing mix. Almost every manufacturer and retailer uses protective packaging or carrier bags for their products, displaying the name of the business. Customers who reuse these bags are in effect helping to promote a business after a purchase has been made. The art of using shopping bags to promote a business, its products or its brand has been jargonised as 'Bagvertising' by marketers.

Word-of-mouth promotion

Word-of-mouth (WOM) promotion refers to the spread of information from one person to another through oral communication. A. Milligan and S. Smith (2002) argue in their book *Uncommon Practice*, that the fastest way to build a brand is through word-of-mouth. Their research suggests that conventional ATL advertising expenditure can therefore be very wasteful. Similarly, US artist Ray Johnson said that ordinary people can spread news faster than marketers. WOM is possibly the most effective form of promotion because messages about a product are passed on to friends and family without any direct costs to the business. Jeff Bezos, the world's richest man and the founder of Amazon, said, *"If you do build a great experience, customers tell each other about that. Word of mouth is very powerful."* However, it can be potentially damaging if the word spreads that a business or its products are sub-standard.

Direct marketing

Direct marketing refers to promotional activities that aim to sell a product straight to a customer rather than using an intermediary. For example, property developers might use their database containing information of previous clients (who may be interested in purchasing another property), rather than paying real estate agents to find customers. Direct marketing techniques include making telephone calls (known as **telemarketing**), sending email advertisements, and distributing direct mail to clients. Some businesses, such as insurance and financial planning firms, use brokers (agents) who visit clients in person.

An advantage of direct marketing is that the business keeps a larger share of any profits as there are no intermediaries to pay. In addition, the business is free to market its products in a way that it sees fit, rather than passing on control of marketing to an external agency.

A major drawback of direct marketing is the cost of producing and distributing promotional material such as leaflets, menus, brochures and catalogues. Research also shows that most people ignore and dispose of 'junk' (unsolicited) mail and that they do not welcome unwarranted telephone calls from telesales personnel.

Direct mail

Direct mail is a type of direct marketing that involves mailing promotional material to customers in an attempt to persuade them to buy an organization's products. Mail order businesses tend to rely heavily on this BTL method of promotion. Locally run restaurants also tend to distribute menus to local residents and offer a delivery service to entice customers. Due to the large volume of direct mail, a major drawback of this method is that people often regard most promotional material sent through the post as junk mail. Furthermore, direct mail does not always target the right audience, and hence represents a waste of resources. An example would be people who do not have young children but still receive mailed materials promoting schools, toys, children's books and clothes.

Sales promotions

Sales promotions are temporary ways to boost sales and attract new buyers, such as:

- BOGOF (buy one, get one free) deals, which are often used to get rid of excess stock or sometimes used as loss leaders.

- Money-off coupons (discount vouchers) offering customers a discounted price on a product. These often appear as cut-out coupons in magazines and newspapers.

- Free samples of products, e.g. shampoo sachets, or food and wine taster sessions.

- Competitions that give buyers the chance to win a prize, such as a holiday or a car.

- 'Free' gifts to customers making a purchase, such as a free spare battery when buying a digital camera or free 3D glasses when purchasing a smart TV.

- Customer loyalty schemes where repeat purchasers are rewarded. Points collected on loyalty schemes can be redeemed for special discounts or gifts. Some of these schemes have been so successful that they have become a long-term strategy to promote an organization's brands or products, such as the airline frequent flyer programmes.

Essentially, they are short term promotional tactics used to entice customers to buy a certain product. Sales promotions can be beneficial to a business because they boost sales (at least in the short run). They can also sway customers away from rival brands. More importantly, sales promotion encourages 'action' (the desire to make a purchase), rather than only informing or reminding customers about a product.

However, free samples, gifts, price discounts, competitions and so forth all add to the marketing costs of a business. Hence, sales promotion can reduce the profit margin on each product – the greater the cost of the promotion, the lower the profit margin tends to be. In addition, sales promotions are only short term and might not be sustainable in the long term, so other BTL strategies still need to be devised for the future.

Point of sales promotion

The term **point of sales** refers to the promotion of a product at the place or location where the customer buys the product. Supermarkets use this method extensively – whilst customers are queuing at the checkouts, they are exposed to the promotion and sales of batteries, confectionary items and magazines. Large in-store displays, stands and posters can encourage **impulse buying** by attracting customers to buy products that they had not intended to.

Publicity

Publicity is the process of promoting a business and its products by getting media coverage without directly paying for it. Famous celebrities are often snapped wearing designer labels, which gives those brands free publicity in the media. Ferrari, for instance, found that it was cheaper to give away a car to football celebrity David Beckham than to advertise its vehicles on television. The subsequent media publicity that was generated was much more favourable than Ferrari could have hoped for from any commercial advertisement.

Sponsorship

Sponsorship involves a business providing financial funds and resources to support an event or another organization in return for publicity and prime advertising space. For example, Arsenal Football Club received a €132 million ($178 million) sponsorship deal in 2006 with Emirates Airline. In return, Arsenal named its new stadium *The Emirates Stadium* (see Question 5.5.5). In 2012, Emirates Airline agreed a further £150m ($245m) sponsorship deal. Then in 2018, this was extended until 2024 as part of a sponsorship deal worth over £200m ($290m). Emirates Airline also sponsor Real Madrid, AC Milan and Paris Saint-Germain. Other airlines that sponsor top football (soccer) clubs include Etihad Airways (Manchester City), Qatar Airways (FC Barcelona) and South African Airways (Sunderland).

CORE

Marketing

Question 4.5.13   Sponsoring the FIFA World Cup

According to SouthAfrica.info, the 2010 FIFA World Cup created an estimated 695,000 jobs and increased host nation South Africa's GDP by 93 billion rand ($13.4bn). The world's largest sporting event, as measured by global viewers and **revenue**, attracts a phenomenal amount of **sponsorship** money. Official sponsors such as Gillette, Yahoo! and Philips benefit most from having paid tens of billions of dollars to sponsor the World Cup because their products are sold all around the world. The cumulative television audience for the tournament was forecast by *Forbes* to be in excess of 40 billion viewers in more than 200 countries. The benefits were so encouraging that some of the larger sponsors (such as Adidas, Sony, Coca-Cola, Hyundai and Emirates Airlines) had already secured sponsorship deals for the 2014 event in Brazil before the start of the World Cup in Germany in 2006. Adidas, Coca-Cola and Hyundai continued their sponsorship of the FIFA World Cup in 2018 in Russia. Qatar Airlines also announced in 2018 that it would become the official airline sponsor in the 2022 FIFA World Cup, to be held in Qatar.

Source: adapted from www.southafrica.info and The World Cup and Economics 2010, Goldman Sachs

(a) (i) Define the term **revenue**.   *[2 marks]*

(a) (ii) Define the term **sponsorship**.   *[2 marks]*

(b) Examine **two** benefits to multinational companies that sponsor events such as the World Cup.   *[6 marks]*

Box 4.5.h   Differences between ATL and BTL promotion

- ATL promotion is targeted at mass market audiences; BTL promotion is at aimed individuals
- ATL promotion helps to establish brand awareness; BTL promotion aims to secure actual sales
- The success of ATL promotion is relatively difficult to measure
- ATL methods use external agencies and hence incur professional fees
- Marketers have more control over BTL promotional methods.

Exam tip !

Writing your answers in context is important in the examination. Promotion on the Internet can be a form of BTL if the business has its own website and uses it as a form of promotion. It can also be a form of ATL promotion if the business pays for advertisements on popular websites such as Google and Facebook.

Promotional mix

The UK Chartered Institute of Marketing defines the promotional mix as "the set of tools that a business can use to communicate effectively the benefits of its products or services to its customers". In essence, the promotional mix is the range of ATL and BTL methods used to market a product as part of the larger marketing mix. In deciding on a promotional mix, marketers often consider the marketing acronym AIDA:

- **A**ttention – The promotional mix should raise the awareness of the product by getting the attention of existing and potential customers.

- **I**nterest – The promotional mix should stimulate and keep customers interested, perhaps by using sales promotion or a memorable and interesting slogan.

- **D**esire – The mix should generate a desire or feeling of 'need' for the product, perhaps through the use of free samples to lure customers.

- **A**ction – It is vital that the promotional mix encourages customers to take action, i.e. to buy the product, perhaps through the use of discount vouchers or other promotional methods.

An alternative approach to AIDA is to use the abbreviation FAB (Features, Advantages and Benefits) when devising a promotional mix. FAB promotional campaigns do not focus on what a product *is*, but what the product actually *does* for the customer. For example, FAB can be used as a framework for promoting and selling cars, such as the Ford Mustang GT350.

- **Features** refer to the facts or characteristics about the product. For example, features of a Ford Mustang include a 2-door, 5.2 litre V8 engine, 526 horsepower, 10-speed automatic transmission and rear-wheel drive.

- **Advantages** outline what the features do for the customer. For example, the Ford Mustang GT's new transmission system transmission automatically adjusts to the owner's preferred driving style, with high performance and quicker acceleration.

- **Benefits** refer to how customers gain from buying the product. It connects the facts about the product with the needs or desires of the customer. For example, the Ford Mustang GT offers high levels of safety for a sports car, with its high-performance breaks, adaptive cruise control and lane change monitoring system.

Trade fairs, exhibitions and demonstrations are also suitable for marketing textbooks. Book publishers and distributors are likely to use a FAB promotional mix framework at trade fairs and exhibitions. For example, IBID Press attend IB Global Conferences to promote their textbooks dedicated to the IB Diploma

Figure 4.5.s IBID Press representative at a trade fair in Dubai

Each method of promotion has its advantages and limitations. The important thing is to select the mixture of promotional activities that best suits the organization's particular needs. In devising a promotional mix, marketers consider a combination of factors, including:

- *Cost* – TV advertising has the highest potential reach but it is also the most expensive. Promotion on the Internet is relatively cheap – a key reason why it has grown in popularity. Businesses often consider the cost per head (cost of promotion divided by the potential audience size) when selecting the most appropriate methods of promotion.

- *Product* – Certain products are suited to a particular type of promotion. For example, personal selling is highly suitable for insurance services and financial planning whereas women's magazines are relevant media for beauty and cosmetic products. An advertisement for new movies or new cars could appear on television and/or in specialist magazines.

- *Product life cycle* – The promotion mix used is dependent on the product's position in its life cycle. During the launch stage, there will be extensive promotion to get the product noticed and established in the market. During the decline stage, promotion may be withdrawn as the business focuses on marketing new products instead.

CORE

Marketing

Legislation – Rules and regulations can prevent certain products (such as tobacco or alcohol) from being advertised in certain media such as on television. This means that other forms of promotion are required in the promotional mix.

For most products, a combination of ATL and BTL methods is used as part of the firm's promotional mix. Using a promotional technique in isolation is unlikely to be effective. Different methods can be used to deliver a slightly different but reinforcing message about the product. When promoting a new movie, for example, the promotional mix might include the use of:

- Television – to show trailers of the movie.

- Radio – to raise awareness and excitement and to inform people about release dates.

- Outdoor advertising – using large outdoor posters (billboards) to promote the movie.

- Newspapers – to support the above methods and to show screening times at local cinemas.

- Internet - website to provide detailed information about the movie, the cast, director and producer.

- Cinema – trailers of the new movie are shown at the cinema (point of sale).

The Chartered Institute of Marketing suggests four key elements to a promotional mix. These consist of: advertising, personal selling, public relations and sales promotion.

1. Advertising

Canadian economist Stephen Butler Leacock (1869–1944) defined advertising as "the science of arresting the human intelligence long enough to get money from it". Thus, advertising is used to shape and develop awareness, perceptions, knowledge and attitudes. Advertising is a form of promotion that communicates marketing messages in a persuasive and/or informative way.

The general public is bombarded with advertisements on a daily basis. There are advertisements on the Internet, on buses and trains, on the street, in shops, on shopping bags, and even in schools and offices. A successful advertising campaign must therefore be distinctive, rather than being relegated to *advertising clutter*, so that the advertisements are not simply ignored by the average person (see Figure 4.5.t on following page).

Question 4.5.14   The Paris Motor Show

The Paris Motor Show is one of the top auto shows in the world. Established as the world's first motor show back in 1898, it is a public exhibition of current, debut and concept cars. The biannual event attracts all the major motor manufacturers who see the show as a vital **publicity** exercise, for promoting their cars. Television and press coverage of the event ensures that the major exhibitors get maximum publicity.

(a) In the context of marketing, define the term **publicity**.   *[2 marks]*

(b) Explain why trade shows are important for businesses such as car manufacturers.   *[4 marks]*

(c) Comment on the reasons for car manufacturers using motor shows to exhibit debut (new) products rather than through the use of direct marketing.   *[4 marks]*

Figure 4.5.t Advertising clutter in Taipei, Taiwan

In marketing, *what* is said and *how* it is said are of equal importance when trying to stand out from the competition. Marketing experts focus their creativity on devising original and outstanding advertising messages. Frequently used techniques are outlined in Box 4.5.i.

Most businesses hire an advertising agency to design and produce advertisements on their behalf. Advertising agencies are businesses that specialise in the planning, organization and production of advertising campaigns for their clients (other businesses). They produce television advertisements, radio commercials, billboard posters and so forth based on the requests and demands of their customers. The advantage of using an agency is that they are experts in their field so have the experience, know-how and resources to produce a relatively successful campaign. Agencies are also more aware of legislation affecting advertising, such as legal considerations and copyright laws.

Box 4.5.i Common advertising techniques

- **Bargain appeals** – good deals and give-away schemes that encourage customers to buy a product by offering preferential terms, such as a reduced price or interest-free credit for a limited time period.
- **Celebrity endorsement** (or **hero endorsement**) – the use of famous celebrities (such as movie stars or sports personalities) to advertise a brand.
- **Comparative advertising** – comparing a product or brand with substitutes on the market. This method must be used with caution as claims may be legally disputed by competitors.
- **Direct response advertising** – the use of contact details (such as providing a phone number, email address or mailing address) to encourage customers to directly respond to an advert.
- **Feel good factor** – advertisements that focus on the morale and image boosting benefits of buying a particular product, such as health care products.
- **Guarantees** – the use of promises, such as 'guaranteed to work or your money back' schemes, to entice and reassure customers.
- **Numerical or scientific claims** – using alleged statistics to promote products or brands, such as '9 out of 10 drivers prefer X', '3 in 4 doctors recommend Y' or 'research shows that Z can help with weight loss'.
- **Sex appeal** – methods that portray the sexual attraction of certain products, such as perfume, aftershave, lingerie, chocolate, ice cream and clothing.
- **Slogans** – the use of catchphrases, tunes and music that stick in the minds of customers.

CORE

Marketing

Theory of knowledge

To what extent do you agree with the view that all advertisements lie?

Common mistake

Advertising is not synonomous with promotion. Indeed, advertising is a form of promotion. Promotion, however, is far more than just advertising.

Question 4.5.15 Tiger Woods

Legendary golfer Tiger Woods was the first sports person to earn more than $1 billion from sponsorship deals and **endorsements**. From humble beginnings, Tiger Woods went on to secure sponsorship deals with businesses that sought to use him as part of their **promotional mix**. Perhaps the most prolific of these companies was Nike. Tiger Woods is credited for increasing the popularity of golf as a sport since winning his first major competition (the Masters Tournament) in 1997. In 2009, Tiger Woods was named 'Athlete of the Decade' by the Associated Press.

However, in late 2009 following his admission of marital infidelity and the negative media publicity that followed, sponsors including Gillette, Accenture, AT&T, Tag Heuer and Gatorade decided to cut ties with Tiger Woods, despite him being the greatest golfer of all time.

(a) (i) Define the term **endorsements**.   [2 marks]

(a) (ii) Define the term **promotional mix**.   [2 marks]

(b) Examine the advantages and disadvantages of using celebrity endorsement as part of an organization's promotional strategy.   [6 marks]

Case study - Celebrity endorsement fails

- Brazilian soccer star Ronaldinho appeared at a press conference drinking Pepsi despite a $750,000 endorsement deal with Coca-Cola.
- Britney Spears made the reverse mistake of drinking Coca-Cola, instead of Pepsi despite their endorsement deal of $50 million!
- David Beckham's agreement to be the face of Motorola's Aura phone ended when the mass media exposed him using his iPhone.
- Infidelity cost legendary golfer Tiger Woods millions of dollars in lost endorsement deals (from brands such as Tag Heuer, Gatorade and Accenture), after more than a dozen women came forward about their relationship with him.

presence, knowledge, assistance and enthusiasm. Customers might have many questions and/or concerns about a particular product so specialist sales people are used to address these issues.

One benefit of using personal selling is that it can be tailored to the individual needs of the customer. The salesperson and the customer engage in dialogue to establish the customer's views and preferences, to answer any questions and to promote the organization's products to suit the needs of the customer. Personal selling can also help the business to build a positive, trusting and long-term relationship with customers.

A disadvantage of using personal selling is that sales agents can be very expensive to hire. For example, sales representatives at health and beauty counters in large department stores are skilled in their product knowledge and application, so are therefore rewarded accordingly. They also earn good rates of commission on the sale of each item.

2. Personal selling

Personal selling refers to promotional techniques that rely on sales representatives directly helping and persuading customers to buy. Examples include sales presentations, face-to-face meetings with clients, telemarketing and door-to-door sales. It is a common technique used in the provision of financial services such as health insurance, life assurance and investment planning. It is also used by real estate agencies in the sale and letting (rental) of commercial and residential property. Sales people promote the products of a business through their

3. Public relations (PR)

Public relations refers to business activities aimed at establishing and protecting the desired image of an organization. PR is concerned with getting good media coverage, usually without directly paying for it (otherwise it would be considered as ATL advertising). PR experts get the media to report events in a positive way and from the business's point of view. Examples of PR include:

- having a launch party for a new product

- organizing press conferences

- radio or television interviews, or appearances on talk shows

- book signing events

- publicity events

- endorsements by celebrities or famous people

- social media, such as using Facebook, Twitter, Instagram, LinkedIn and online blogs

- making prominent donations to charities, and

- strategic distribution of company literature (such as brochures, company annual reports and newsletters to selected stakeholder groups).

PR is, however, a long term and on-going marketing strategy. PR experts are relied upon heavily when a business faces a crisis (see Unit 5.7). They try to get the press to cover the story in a sympathetic and reassuring way.

4. Sales promotion

Sales promotions provide short-term incentives designed to stimulate demand for a product, e.g. discount coupons, special offers, prize draws, and free product samples. Research has shown that people are more likely to take notice of paper-based adverts if they feature discounts or special offers. Sales promotion can help businesses to gain a short-term competitive edge, to get rid of excess or old stock, and to encourage customer loyalty. However, sales promotions (such as free installation and a period of complimentary viewing when customers subscribe to satellite television) can be highly expensive, so marketing managers carefully monitor the progress of the campaigns to ensure that costs are kept under control.

Technology and promotion

The impact of changing technology on promotional strategies (such as viral marketing, social media marketing and social networking). AO3

© IBO, 2017

The impact of new technologies including Internet technologies have significantly broadened the opportunities available to businesses to extend their promotional strategies. For example, businesses are increasingly using web banners and online search engines to promote their brands. The main trends include viral marketing, social media marketing and social networking.

CORE

Question 4.5.16   Kim Do Yi Limited

Kim Do Yi Ltd. (*KDY*) is a martial arts organization based in Hong Kong and New York. It was established in 1995 by Master Instructor Rickie Chan Ka Ching. The organization specialises in the Korean martial arts of Taekwondo and Hapkido. It is affiliated to the World Taekwondo Federation (the governing body of Olympic-style Taekwondo).

KDY's core **target market** is children of primary and secondary school age. *KDY* does not have its own kwans (training studios), preferring instead to hire venues in numerous locations throughout Hong Kong and New York City. *KDY* believes this approach makes access easier and cheaper for its customers.

Sources: Ricky Chan Ka Ching and www.kimdoyikwan.com

Marketing

(a) Define the term **target market**.   *[2 marks]*

(b) Explain why promotion is important to an organization such as *KDY*.   *[4 marks]*

(c) Recommend a a suitable promotional mix for *KDY*.   *[10 marks]*

Viral marketing (also known as **peer-to-peer (P2P)** marketing) is similar to word-of-mouth marketing except P2P relies on the electronic transfer and spread of promotional messages. Hence, it is sometimes referred to as 'word of mouse'. It is an increasingly powerful form of promotion. American artist Ray Johnson (1927-1995) said *"Ordinary people can spread good and bad information about brands faster than marketers."*

Viral marketing is usually done through the Internet via emails and social networking services that often spread exponentially. For example, Hotmail, Gmail, LinkedIn and Dropbox use viral marketing to promote their services. Each time a user emails someone, an embedded advertisement entices the recipient to sign up for an account. Movie (film) producers upload their trailers to platforms such as YouTube in order to target a wide, global audience. The movie producers hope that online viewers will share and spread the promotion of the movie to their friends, families and followers of like-minded people.

Social media marketing

Social media marketing (SMM) refers to the practice of gaining Internet traffic through social media websites such as Facebook, Twitter, YouTube and Google. The strategy focuses on creating marketing content that attracts attention and encourages people to share this using their own electronic methods, such as social networks, web sites, blogs, instant messaging and news feeds. Information is presented on specific topics, usually on a regular basis, e.g. weekly film reviews.

Like WOM marketing, social media marketing about an event, product, brand or business spreads from person to person. It helps to build trust as the marketing message come from a trusted, third-party source rather than from a commercial marketer. However, the potential reach is much greater and faster due to internet technologies, and remains highly cost-effective to the business. SMM is a relatively inexpensive way to gain promotional exposure and the contents can be easily shared. For example, celebrities are often 'followed' on social media by their fans (and customers).

Social media marketing has become increasingly popular as the global number of internet users continues to grow. Facebook, for example, has over 1 billion users so provides a major promotional platform for many businesses around the world. SMM is also a relatively inexpensive promotional strategy for businesses. However, the key drawback is that businesses have no control over what is written or shared about their brand, products or service, i.e. negative publicity. Hackers also present a threat as they could deliberately spread false information about the business that can go viral, creating a public relations problem.

Social networking

Social networking refers to any platform used mainly by individuals to build social relationships between people, often because they are friends or share things in common. Social network services such as Twitter, LinkedIn, Pinterest, Google+, Instagram and Facebook can be individual-centred or group-centred (as an online community). Social networking websites allow members to share information with people in their online network. For example, LinkedIn allows professionals and businesses to network online by sharing their professional profiles and discussion forums. Very few social network service providers charge for membership to attract a large number of users, i.e. pricing their service would be counterproductive. Instead, providers, such as Facebook, sell online advertising space on their website to businesses that want to reach out to the billions of people around the world who use social networking. According to Facebook, the most talked about brand on its social network is Coca-Cola.

Exam tip !
The distinction between social media and social networking is not always made clear. Social media is the tool (e.g. video) while social networking is the human interaction that the tool encourages. Social media (e.g. YouTube) is one directional – something that pushes media out to people while social networking (e.g. LinkedIn) is multi-directional. Confusingly, Facebook and Google+ are a combination of both.

Other changing Internet technologies include the increased use of **web banners** for promotion. Web banners embed advertisements onto a web page (such as YouTube) to attract and redirect online traffic to the advertiser's website. In many cases, the advertising business pays the host on a *cost per click* (CPC) basis. This also makes it easier for the business to monitor the results and effectiveness of its web banners. Businesses can also pay for a sponsored link on popular **search engines** such as Google and Yahoo! This appears at the top of a list of results when customers enter a particular word or phrase in the search engine. Businesses pay the host on a *pay per click* (PPC) basis, i.e. the advertiser only pays the host if their online advertisement is clicked.

CORE

Marketing

Question 4.5.17   YouTube

YouTube, the world's largest Internet video-sharing website, was launched at the start of 2006 by Steve Chen, Chad Hurley and Jawed Karim, all in their late twenties at the time. Just ten months later, *YouTube* had grown so immensely throughout the world due to **viral marketing** that Google acquired the business for a staggering $1.65 billion. In the same year, *TIME* magazine named *YouTube* as Invention of the Year.

According to *YouTube*, there are over 6 billion hours of video clips accessed every day, and 100 hours of video uploaded per minute on its website. Google's goal is to use *YouTube* to earn money, mainly through advertising. It also strives to convince television, movie and music executives that *YouTube* is a huge revenue opportunity.

(a) Define the term **viral marketing.**   *[2 marks]*

(b) Examine the benefits to businesses that choose to advertise on Internet video sharing websites such as *YouTube*.   *[6 marks]*

Case study

In 2004, Mozilla Corporation's web browser, Firefox, was unknown until the company used guerrilla marketing and some clever public relations. The company used a fan base of volunteers who managed to generate 13 million downloads in just 45 days! The use of peer persuasion and recommendation was far more effective than any other form of promotion. By the end of the first year, there had been over 100 million downloads. Ten years later, in 2014, Firefox had 500 million users around the world.

Theory of knowledge

Promotion aims to change perceptions. Perception is reality. To what extent do you agree with this statement?

Guerrilla marketing

Guerrilla marketing and its effectiveness as a promotional method.

AO3

© IBO, 2017

Guerrilla marketing was coined by Jay Conrad Levinson in 1984, who described the concept as "achieving conventional goals, such as profit and joy, with unconventional methods, such as investing energy instead of money". Levinson argued that a business should not simply invest money into promotion but focus instead on time, energy, and imagination. As a promotional strategy, it is highly suitable for businesses that operate on a tight budget.

Guerrilla marketing, sometimes known as **stealth marketing**, uses untraditional, unconventional and perhaps unruly but creative and original methods of promotion, on a relatively low budget. It is often designed to make the target audience unaware that they are being targeted and is favoured by small businesses since they cannot afford mainstream ATL promotional methods such as television or newspaper advertising. Nevertheless, the shrewd tactics used by guerrilla marketers can achieve big results. It aims to ambush or catch the attention of customers through unusual and/or shocking techniques (see Box 4.5.j). Advances in technology such as the Internet have made guerrilla marketing more accessible to businesses.

CORE

Marketing

Table 4.5.c   Advantages and disadvantages of guerilla marketing

Advantages	Disadvantages
The Pareto Principle (or the 80:20 rule) suggests that 20% of marketing activities generate 80% of the firm's revenues, i.e. it is not always necessary to spend huge amounts of money on ATL methods to make a promotional campaign successful.	Guerrilla marketing does not always reach the right target market. Quite often, guerrilla marketing campaigns use a scattershot approach, aiming at every person and any market segment within reach, but this does not necessarily generate much business.
It can lead to viral marketing, i.e. word of mouth marketing that facilitates and encourages people to spread a marketing message (rather like a virus) to family, friends and other acquaintances. This helps the business to gain reputable and free publicity.	Guerrilla marketing techniques can be rather intrusive (in your face). People are already bombarded with advertisements from the moment they wake up. The invasive nature of unsolicited guerrilla marketing techniques may simply add to everyday advertising clutter.
Guerrilla marketing can be very inexpensive and is often free. Levinson suggested that the main measure of promotional success is profits and not sales, i.e. traditional ATL promotional methods might bring in more sales but the huge costs involved ultimately yield lower levels of profit.	Controversial and unethical methods are sometimes used. Many guerrilla techniques have been accused of being deceptive, confusing, distasteful or offensive. This can actually create negative publicity for the business.
In ever-competitive markets, guerrilla marketing can promote creativity and healthy competition. Guerrilla marketing can be an innovative way to promote and sell a product. As playwright Oscar Wilde once said, "The worst sin that one can commit is to be dull".	There can be a large opportunity cost in terms of the time and resources spent in devising an original campaign. Spending lots of time and money to raise publicity does not necessarily bring in more customers for the business.
Guerrilla tactics can help a business to better understand the needs of its customers by coming up with creative ways to communicate its products. Traditional market research methods used to expand a firm's customer base can be both costly and fruitless. Instead, it might be more effective to target the right people and to build a relationship with customers to gain their loyalty.	Guerrilla marketing does not always work, e.g. IBM was fined $120,000 for spray-painting the streets of San Francisco in 2001. In 2002, Microsoft blanketed Manhattan, New York with thousands of their iconic but extremely difficult to remove butterfly stickers. Microsoft was fined for littering, made to apologise to the people of New York and ordered to help in the clean-up of the city.

Box 4.5.j   Examples of guerrilla marketing techniques

- Automobiles – using signs and adverts on vehicles such as trucks and vans to promote a firm's products or brands
- 'Bagvertising' – the art of using carrier bags and luggage to advertise a brand or product of a business
- 'Bra-vertising' – using models (usually females) dressed only in underwear to promote a brand
- Buzz marketing – the use of word-of-mouth techniques to create a buzz or craze for a firm's products
- Fancy dress – dressing up in extravagant outfits to catch the attention of passers-by

(continued) …

(continued) …

- Graffiti – painting or spraying the name of the brand in public areas, such as bridges and railway stations.
- Lavatories – advertising found in washrooms, such as in urinals or on the mirrors
- Shock tactics – Unconventional and often offensive methods (deliberate or otherwise) used to gain maximum publicity
- Stickers – covering large areas of a city with stickers displaying the organization's logo or brand
- Even escalators and elevators (lifts) have not managed to escape the guerrilla marketers!

The most effective guerrilla marketing strategies are simple, flexible, inexpensive and target specific market segments. Successful promotion relies on the creativity of marketers. Guerrilla marketing is based on human psychology rather than guesswork or inferences. Given that competitors will have similar marketing tactics and resources, the originality and creativeness of a guerrilla marketing campaign can give a business the competitive edge that it seeks. Although Levinson suggested that it is more suitable for small businesses, large companies have increasingly used it, including businesses such as Microsoft, Nike, Citigroup, Vodafone and BMW.

Case study

According to *gmarketing.com*, Levinson's concept of guerrilla marketing (1984) is required reading for many MBA courses throughout the world. His book is available in 62 different languages. Jay Conrad Levinson (1933 - 2013) was credited as one of the most prolific and respected marketers in the world.

Promotion and the CUEGIS concepts

As it often takes many attempts for a promotional message to be noticed or acted upon, promotion can be a highly expensive business strategy. In addition, some types of promotion are considered to be socially irresponsible (see Box 4.5.k) Critics argue that much of the expenditure on promotion is wasteful and could have been better spent on researching and developing better products. The ethical question is whether it is a justifiable strategy to spend millions of dollars on a logo or slogan rather than using the money to benefit customers (lower prices) or employees (higher wages and benefits).

Whilst marketers need to be creative in their strategic planning, laws must be obeyed. Legal constraints exist, such as cigarette advertising being banned from TV or radio broadcasts in many countries. If promotional activities are considered to be unethical (socially unacceptable), the authorities may withdraw the campaign (see Box 4.5.k). For example, with obesity being a growing problem in Europe, there are time restrictions on television commercials featuring fast food to prevent children from being exposed to such advertisements in the European Union.

Box 4.5.k Unethical promotional techniques

- **Pester power** – the controversial influence (which stems from advertising) that children have over purchases made by adults. Children frequently nag parents to buy them the latest toys, electronic devices, movies and computer games. Marketers have exploited parental weakness by targeting 'must have' purchases at children.

- **Confusion marketing** – the use of tactics that deliberately confuse the customer so that it is easier to guide (or mislead) them into making a purchase. This controversial strategy is often used by providers of financial services, supermarkets and mobile telephone network companies, where pricing options are so varied with complicated choices, thus making price comparisons literally impossible.

- **Ambush marketing** – the planned attempt by a business to associate itself with an event without incurring the costs of being an official sponsor. Nike, for example, deliberately chose advertising slots during TV coverage of the football World Cup (Adidas being the official sponsor for the 2006, 2010, 2014 and 2018 FIFA World Cup events). It gains maximum exposure at the cost of the official sponsors. Viewers are often confused about who the official sponsors are.

- **Infiltration marketing** – marketers contributing to blogs, tweets and online chat rooms by acting as ordinary customers. They might write about receiving excellent customer service or being highly satisfied with the purchase of a company's products, when in fact they are actually marketing their own products as personal endorsements.

- **Pop-up advertisements** – Internet advertisements that are randomly and automatically launched in a small window on top of another webpage. Market research has suggested that these advertisements are highly annoying but not easy to ignore or avoid. Marketers have extended this strategy to children's websites and online games where advertisements appear before users are able to access the website or progress to the next stage of the game.

CORE

Marketing

Unethical and controversial promotional marketing strategies, including guerilla marketing (see Box 4.5.j on page 466), have prompted governments and pressure groups to introduce legislation and ethical codes of practice. For example, SCAMP (Stop Crude Advertising Material in Public) is a pressure group against offensive advertising in the UK. Consumer protection laws exist to prevent consumers from being deceived by misleading or dishonest advertising. In some countries, advertising activities are monitored and regulated by government agencies, which deal with customer complaints about advertisements. Penalties and other sanctions can be imposed on businesses that break the law or do not abide with ethical codes of practice.

IB Learner Profile – Be knowlegdeable and be an inquirer

Investigate the importance of business ethics and business etiquette for international marketers in a country of your choice.

As a strategy, public relations campaigns and a devotion to corporate social responsibility (such as donating money to charities or sponsoring local community projects) can be costly. Nevertheless, there can be major benefits for the business: it can gain media publicity since PR can promote the brand and improve community relations. Change and innovation have also provided new opportunities for publicity and promotion, through the use of viral marketing, social media and social networking.

The strategic implementation of a promotional mix is dependent on the creativity of marketers and the product in question. The promotional mix for a single product also changes over its product life cycle. Promotion then is a complex but vital component of any marketing strategy. It is important to remember that promotion must be used in relation to other aspects of business strategy; no amount of money spent on promotion will generate sustainable sales growth if the other elements of the marketing mix are ignored.

Theory of knowledge

Are anti-slimming advertisements banned in your country? Should they be? What are the roles of ethics and culture in addressing this question?

Innovation and advances in technology have directly affected guerrilla marketing and other forms of promotion, e.g. smartphones, blogs and social media mean that guerrilla marketing has become accessible to businesses of all sizes in all locations throughout the world. Indeed, companies such as Amazon, eBay, Yahoo! and Google grew into huge businesses without the initial use of traditional advertising methods.

Nevertheless, as with any effective business strategy, promotion is unlikely to work if used in isolation. Other marketing strategies are likely to be used to complement and foster the benefits of using a promotional mix and guerrilla marketing.

Theory of knowledge

British author Norman Douglas (1868-1952) said that "You can tell the ideals of a nation by its advertisements." To what extent do you agree with this statement?

CUEGIS Essay

With reference to an organization of your choice, examine the role of **culture** on its promotional **strategy**.

[20 marks]

CUEGIS Essay

With reference to an organization of your choice, examine the role of **ethics** on its promotional **strategy**.

[20 marks]

CORE

Marketing

CUEGIS Essay

With reference to an organization of your choice, examine the role of **globalization** on its above-the-line promotional **strategies**.   *[20 marks]*

REVIEW QUESTIONS

1. What is promotion and what are its main objectives?

2. Using examples, differentiate between above the line and below the line promotion.

3. What is meant by promotional mix?

4. What are the advantages and disadvantages of sales promotion?

5. What does AIDA stand for?

6. Explain the difference between advertising and promotion.

7. Briefly explain how technology affects promotional strategies.

8. Distinguish between viral marketing, social networking and social media.

9. What is meant by guerrilla marketing?

10. Use examples to outline unethical and socially irresponsible promotional techniques.

KEY TERMS

Above the line (ATL) promotion is any form of paid-for promotion through the mass media (such as television and radio) to reach a wide audience.

Advertising is a method of informative and/or persuasive promotion that is usually paid for. The aim of commercial advertising is to raise the level of demand for a firm's products.

Advertising clutter refers to the huge volume of advertisements that the public is bombarded with.

Below the line (BTL) promotion does not use paid-for mass media sources, e.g. free samples (toiletries, food, drinks, etc), discount vouchers (to entice customers to buy the product) and added-value promotions (e.g. special introductory deals).

Celebrity endorsement is the use of famous people (such as movie stars, music stars and sports stars) to promote a particular brand or organization.

Customer loyalty schemes are reward systems used to encourage customers to make repurchases, such as the use of price discounts or free gifts for members of these schemes.

Direct mail is the use of postal correspondence for promoting an organization's goods and/or services.

Direct marketing refers to promotional activities that aim to sell a product straight to a customer rather than by using an intermediary.

Guerrilla marketing is a promotional strategy that aims to ambush or catch the attention of customers through unusual, innovative, unconventional and/or shocking techniques, on a relatively low budget.

Impulse buying refers to unplanned or unintentional purchases due to the lure of eye-catching point of sales promotions.

Logos are a form of product differentiation that use a visual symbol to represent a business, its brands or its products, e.g. Nike's Swoosh, Rolex's golden crown, or the globe of Wikipedia.

Merchandise is a retailer's range of goods that are available for sale.

Personal selling is the use of sales staff to promote and sell goods and/or services to customers, on a face-to-face basis.

Point of sale (POS) is the promotion of goods in retail stores at the place where customers can buy the goods, e.g. displays at supermarket counters.

Promotion is a component of the marketing mix. It refers to the methods used to inform, persuade and/or remind people about a firm's products or brands.

CORE

Marketing

Promotional mix refers to the combination of individual ATL and BTL promotional methods used by a business, such as advertising, direct marketing, packaging and sales promotion.

Public relations (PR) refers to business activities aimed at establishing and protecting the desired image of an organization. PR is concerned with getting good media coverage, usually without directly paying for it.

Publicity is the process of promoting a business and its products by getting positive media exposure without directly paying for it.

Sales promotions are short-term incentives designed to stimulate demand for a product, e.g. discount coupons, prize draws, price cuts and trade fairs.

Social media marketing (SMM) refers to the marketing practice of gaining Internet traffic through social media websites such as Facebook, Twitter, YouTube and Google.

SMM is being increasingly used by marketers

Social networking refers to any platform used mainly by individuals to build social relationships between people, often because they are friends or share things in common. Social network services include Google+, Instagram and Facebook.

Slogans are catchphrases designed to represent the essence of a business or its products using a memorable set of words.

Sponsorship is a promotional technique that involves funding, supporting or donating resources for an event or business venture in return for prominent publicity.

Telemarketing is a form of direct marketing that involves marketers making telephone calls to existing and potential customers.

Trade fairs are promotional events where firms exhibit and showcase their products for sale to potential customers.

Viral marketing is a promotional strategy that combines online technologies with word of mouth (WOM) techniques.

It is usually done through the Internet via emails and social networks.

Word of mouth (WOM) is the spreading of marketing messages about an organization and the quality of its products or its customer service. It is perhaps the most cost-effective form of promotion.

Place

"When you have completed 95 per cent of your journey, you are only halfway there." - Japanese proverb

SL/HL content	Assessment objective
Place The importance of place in the marketing mix	AO2
The effectiveness of different types of distribution channels	AO3

© IBO, 2017

Place (distribution)

The importance of place in the marketing mix. AO2

© IBO, 2017

Place refers to the distribution of products, i.e. how products get from the producer to the consumer. For instance, products could be available at large warehouses, at retail outlets, through agents or via the Internet. The Chartered Institute of Management defines place (or **distribution**) as "getting the right products to the right customers at the right price in the right place and at the right time."

For example, consumers can use banking services at a branch or via the Internet. They can purchase clothes at a retail outlet or via mail order. Most products are not sold directly from the manufacturer to the final consumer (the end-user of the product). Coca-Cola, for instance, does not sell its mass produced products to the general public. This is partly because individual consumers would never purchase enough cans of cola directly from the manufacturer to make it worthwhile for the producer. Instead, Coca-Cola's customers are the supermarkets and other retailers that buy from the manufacturer and then split the bulk to sell to consumers in much smaller units.

The distribution decision requires management skills in persuading retailers to stock a firm's products. Retailers such as supermarkets have limited shelf and floor space so will only want to hold supplies of products that sell well. Cinemas have a limited number of screens so only purchase and show movies that will generate high sales. Window displays in estate agencies are very limited so the advertisements they choose to show need to get quick sales. In essence, marketing managers need to convince distributors and other intermediaries to sell their products over those of their rivals. Place also addresses the geographical distribution (local, national or international) of products.

Channels of distribution

The effectiveness of different types of distribution channels. AO3

© IBO, 2017

The **channel of distribution** refers to the means used to get a product to the consumer (Figures 4.5.u - 4.5.w). **Intermediation** is the process used to facilitate this. **Intermediaries** are agents or businesses that act as a middle person in the channel of distribution between the manufacturer and consumers of a product. The traditional channel of distribution consists of manufacturers, wholesalers and retailers. A long channel of distribution tends to raise prices for the consumer as each intermediary adds a profit margin to their price. Furthermore, a longer channel of distribution lengthens the distribution process, meaning that such processes are not appropriate for perishable products. Marketing guru Dr. Philip Kotler referred to distributional channels as 'levels':

- A **zero-level channel** does not have any intermediaries, i.e. the producer sells directly to the consumer (see Figure 4.5u). Examples include the use of mail order, e-commerce and telesales. Direct distribution is common in the service industry, e.g. customers can book their rooms at a hotel or make restaurant reservations without using an intermediary.

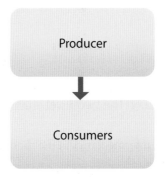

Figure 4.5.u The zero-level channel chain

CORE

Marketing

- A one-level channel has one intermediary, such as retailers, agents or distributors being used to sell products to consumers (see Figure 4.5.v). For example, estate agents are used to sell residential and commercial property on behalf of their clients.

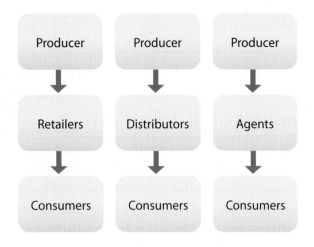

Figure 4.5.v The one-level channel chain

- A two-level channel has two intermediaries, such as the use of wholesalers and retailers to get products to consumers (see Figure 4.5.w).

Figure 4.5.w The two-level channel chain

The main types of intermediaries in the channel of distribution are considered next.

Wholesalers

Wholesalers are businesses that purchase large quantities of products from a manufacturer and then separate or 'break' the bulk-purchases into smaller units for resale, mainly to retailers. They act as the intermediary between producers and retailers. Examples of wholesalers include Costco, Sam's Club (owned by Walmart) and Makro. Using wholesalers has many benefits for producers and retailers such as:

- Wholesalers bear the costs of storage, thereby freeing up space for retailers and manufacturers.

- By breaking bulk, wholesalers sell smaller batches of products to retailers thus eliminating their need to purchase huge quantities directly from a manufacturer.

- There are lower transactions costs (such as invoicing and transportation) for the producer, as wholesalers are the customers, not the countless smaller individual retailers.

- Frees up time for manufacturers to focus on production, as wholesalers deal with distribution issues and problems.

However, a key limitation of using wholesalers is that the producer takes a risk in passing on the responsibility of marketing its products. Wholesalers might not promote the manufacturer's products in a way that it might want, thereby ruining the producer's efforts. Also, some retailers (such as hypermarkets) do not use wholesalers, choosing instead to order directly from manufacturers. This cuts out the costs of using an intermediary to the detriment of the wholesaler.

Figure 4.5.x Wholesalers are an important intermediary

Question 4.5.18 Costco

Costco is the world's largest wholesale chain and the second largest retailer after *Walmart*. Its product range is huge, including items such as: electronic appliances, beauty products, books, music and DVDs, clothing, flowers, fresh fruits and vegetables, groceries, beverages, home and office furniture, jewellery, sports equipment, toys, power tools, baby products, photo processing, and automobile accessories - all under one roof!

The company was founded in 1983 and has grown to more than 750 outlets throughout North and South America, Europe and Asia Pacific. *Costco* boasts annual sales revenues in excess of $129 billion. The **wholesaler** focuses on selling products at low prices by selling in small bulks to boost sales volume. Its clients are mainly small businesses and families. *Costco* does not usually carry multiple brands of the same product, thus resulting in high volume sales for a single producer or supplier.

Source: adapted from www.costco.com (Investor Relations)

(a) Define the term **wholesaler**. [2 marks]

(b) Examine the benefits to both businesses and consumers in using wholesalers such as *Costco*. [6 marks]

Distributors and agents

Distributors are independent and specialist businesses that trade in the products of only a few manufacturers. For example, car distributors typically sell the products of one manufacturer, (such as Honda or BMW) to the consumer.

Agents (or brokers) are negotiators who act on behalf of buyers and vendors (sellers) of a product. They are not usually employed by the producer but are used as an intermediary to help sell the vendor's products. They are experts in their particular markets and charge commission (a fee based on the level or percentage of the sales made) for their services. For instance, estate agents earn commission on each sale of real estate (property) made on behalf of their clients, whilst travel agents earn commission on the holidays and other leisure packages that they sell.

Agents usually offer a range of products for the consumer to choose from, perhaps from several different suppliers. For example, insurance brokers often try to find the 'best deal' for their clients from the various insurance companies that they have access to. Financial advisors also have a range of products, from savings accounts to high-risk stock market investments that their clients can apply for.

Agents tend to rely on personal selling techniques, such as door-to-door sales, telesales, trade fairs and exhibitions. Personal selling allows the sales agents to demonstrate how the product

actually works and enables the customer to ask questions relating to the product.

Figure 4.5.y Trade fairs and exhibitions can be used to promote and distribute products

Retailers

Retailers are the sellers of products to the final consumer. They are often referred to as 'shops' in everyday language. Retailers play an important role in the distribution of most products as retailers have the ability to reach large numbers of consumers, especially those that have a global reach. There are several types of retailers:

CORE

Marketing

473

- **Independent retailers** are small local vendors often owned by a sole proprietor. They usually sell a small range of products or are specialist outlets such as hair salons.

- **Multiple retailers** (or **chain stores**) are retailers that have numerous outlets, such as H&M, Toys R Us and Mothercare. They can benefit from brand recognition and brand loyalty.

- **Supermarkets** are retailers that sell mainly foodstuffs and groceries. Examples include Tesco, Lidl, Aldi, Target and Walmart. Due to their scale of operation, supermarkets tend to buy their produce and other products directly from manufacturers, thereby cutting out wholesalers.

- **Hypermarkets** (or **superstores**) are huge outlets that stock a broad range of products, such as foodstuffs and consumer durables. Due to their enormous size, they tend to be located in out of town areas where the space is available and the cost of land is relatively low. Examples of hypermarkets include Carrefour and Walmart. Some supermarkets such as Tesco also operate superstores.

- **Department stores** are retail outlets that sell a large range of products to the general public, such as furniture, jewellery, kitchen equipment, clothing, toys and cosmetics. It is quite common that franchisors run different parts of the store (hence the name 'department' stores). Unlike hypermarkets that are built on one floor (storey), department stores are built over several floors and are located in busy retail districts. Examples include Harrods (London), Macy's (New York City), Le Bon Marché (Paris) and Sogo (Tokyo).

Figure 4.5.z Superstores sell a very large range of products

Most retailers rely on stocking well-known brands to attract customers. They base this decision on sales (or profits) per square metre. For example, if Coca-Cola products generate more sales or profits than rival brands, then retailers will devote more shelf space to Coca-Cola goods. Similarly, prime space, such as the entrance to a store or other busier areas of an outlet tend to be reserved for the best-selling products or for the client that can offer the highest rental price in the store.

Most businesses use a range of channels to distribute their products. This is known as a **multi-channel distribution strategy**. For example, an airline company might use travel agencies, the Internet and airport outlets to sell its tickets. This enables the business to reach a wider range of customers, located in different areas and in different market segments.

Question 4.5.19   7-Eleven

In November 2005, Japanese conglomerate *Seven & I Holdings Co.* completed the purchase of *7-Eleven Inc.* (originally an American company, founded in 1927). Today, *7-Eleven* is the world's largest chain of convenience stores, with over 65,000 outlets in many parts of the world. The **retailer** operates most of its stores as international franchises.

Source: www.7-eleven.com

(a) Define the term **retailer**. *[2 marks]*

(b) Outline the type of organization that *7-Eleven* might be classified as. *[2 marks]*

(c) In the context of place in the marketing mix, examine the reasons for conglomerates such as *Seven & I Holdings Co.* operating international franchises. *[6 marks]*

Speciality channels of distribution

A speciality channel of distribution is any indirect way to distribute products that does not involve retailers, i.e. distribution without the use of intermediaries. Examples include: telemarketing, e-commerce, vending machines and mail order. There are several advantages of speciality distribution channels:

- As there are no intermediaries, the business does not have to share out so much of its profits.

- Businesses can have direct control over their distribution, rather than relying on retailers or wholesalers.

- The growing popularity of e-commerce means that customers are more willing to use the Internet as a distribution channel, especially with improved online payment security.

- Speciality distribution channels can reach potential customers who do not have easy access to retail outlets.

Telemarketing

Telemarketing is the use of telephone systems to sell products directly to potential customers. This can be done through automated voice or text messages that promote a firm's goods and services or by using sales people to call customers. Telemarketing is commonly used by businesses that have a database of existing clients, such as a satellite TV company that calls customers about a new special package. Insurance companies also call clients to remind them about renewing their insurance premiums.

A disadvantage of using telemarketing is that mass telephone calls can be very costly, especially if employees are paid to make these calls. In addition, most customers do not like 'cold calls' where they are bombarded with text and voice messages from marketers trying to make a sale.

E-commerce

E-commerce is trading via the Internet (see Unit 4.8). The Internet has had a profound impact on marketing for businesses, and is an increasingly suitable distribution channel for marketing many products. More and more businesses now use dedicated websites to provide product information and payment options to entice customers from around the world to buy their products, from the convenience of their home or office. It is also an effective way to reduce the costs and risks of international marketing (see Unit 4.7).

CORE

Question 4.5.20   Sacha Cosmetics

Sacha Cosmetics, founded in 1979 in Trinidad and Tobago, was the world's first supplier of makeup products that are Haalal certified, with its products distributed in 23 countries. It has used the internet as an effective **channel of distribution** for propelling its business. The family-owned company has enjoyed the status of being the official cosmetics sponsor of the Miss Universe, Miss USA, Miss Panama, Miss Bahamas, and Miss Jamaica Pageants, and this which has helped it to become a global brand. In 2015, *Sacha Cosmetics* was the winner of the inaugural Caribbean Exporter of the Year Awards. Furthermore, due to the company's **online presence**, American retail giant Walmart now carries full displays of the Trinidadian make-up line in many of its stores and on Amazon.com.

(a) (i) Define the term **channel of distribution**. *[2 marks]*

(a) (ii) Define the term **online presence**. *[2 marks]*

(b) Discuss the view that the Internet is an effective distribution channel for propelling businesses, such as *Sacha Cosmetics*. *[10 marks]*

Marketing

However, not all products are suitable for online distribution. Customers buying cars, glasses (spectacles), or jewellery will probably want to have direct contact with sales people who can give a more personalised service. For most retailers, such as supermarkets or motor vehicle dealers, the Internet is not a replacement for traditional distribution activities, but complements and supports the marketing strategies of these businesses.

Nevertheless, e-commerce continues to be an increasingly important distribution channel as more and more people have access to the Internet. The growth in the number of credit cards issued around the world has also propelled distributors and businesses that have an online presence.

Vending machines

Vending machines are specialist machines that stock products for sale, e.g. cigarettes, drinks, snacks, toys, umbrellas and even hot meals. Due to their compact size, they can be placed almost anywhere (such as an office, recreation centre, shopping mall, public car park, school or airport). Modern vending machines allow customers to pay by a range of smartcard methods, including credit cards and debit cards, thereby enhancing their convenience.

A key advantage of vending machines is that running and maintenance costs are minimal. For example, sales people are not needed to sell the products. In addition, if the manufacturer owns the vending machines, it will stock only its own products which can help to reduce competition. However, vending machines can be prone to vandalism and mechanical failures which will halt sales. Due to the low capacity of any single vending machine, only a small range of products can be sold via this distribution channel.

Figure 4.5.ai Umbrellas are available through vending machines

Question 4.5.21   Dell and Walmart

Dell Inc. was founded in 1984 by Michael Dell, the company's Chief Executive Officer. In 2007, the computer company announced plans to sell its personal computers through *Walmart*. Retail giant *Walmart*, renowned for its low prices, started selling *Dell* computers in its *Walmart* and *Sam's Club* stores in the USA, Canada and Puerto Rico.

The move was a major shift for *Dell*, which had traditionally sold its products directly to the consumer, cutting out the need for **intermediaries**. The company hoped the strategy would boost *Dell's* competitiveness and market share against rivals such as Lenovo and Hewlett-Packard.

(a) Define the term **intermediaries**.   [2 marks]

(b) Explain **two** advantages to *Walmart* in establishing a deal with *Dell Inc.*   [4 marks]

(c) Evaluate *Dell's* decision to use intermediation to broaden its channel of distribution.   [10 marks]

Mail order and direct mail

Mail order involves a business sending promotional material, such as a catalogue, via the postal system to entice customers to buy a firm's products. Businesses that have a customer database tend to use this channel of distribution. However, the costs of producing comprehensive and up-to-date catalogues in colour are high, yet the shelf-life is relatively short due to changing prices and new products being added to the market.

Mail order is often associated with direct mail – the use of unsolicited advertising materials sent to prospective clients via the mail. Detailed information aimed at different market segments can also be used in an attempt to boost sales. However, a major limitation of direct mail is that people tend to regard much of the correspondence as junk mail so there is a low response rate, i.e. people do not bother reading the mail. In addition, the information in a database often goes out of date. For example, when people move home they do not necessarily inform the business of this, resulting in a large amount of direct mail being sent to the wrong (old) address.

Place and the CUEGIS concepts

Place is concerned with how businesses ensure that their products reach both current and potential consumers. Strategic planning and analysis requires marketing managers to deal with two key placement issues: the most suitable channels of distribution to use to get the firm's products to the consumer and how it will ensure that intermediaries stock the firm's products. An efficient and cost effective distribution strategy enables a business to make its products conveniently available to consumers. This raises the likelihood of customers purchasing the firm's products. There are several factors that can affect the distribution strategy, including:

- *The product* – Perishables cannot be distributed through long chains of distribution, e.g. fresh flowers and fresh meat. Hence, shorter distribution channels will be necessary. By contrast, fast-moving consumer goods need to be sold in large volumes, so the use of wholesalers and retailers would be appropriate. Innovations in technology have meant that many products are sold directly through the Internet, e.g. books, music, movies, clothes, toys, theatre tickets and bookings for overseas holidays.

- *The market* – Local niche markets can be catered for by a supplier without the use of intermediaries. By contrast, large and dispersed markets usually require the use of intermediaries as part of the channels of distribution.

- *Time* – Whilst e-commerce can be a convenient channel of distribution, there is a time lag between customers paying for a product and receiving it. Hence, this method is unsuitable for buying items that require urgent delivery. Instead, the most direct channel of distribution would be more suitable.

- *Legal constraints* – Government rules and regulations can prohibit the distribution of certain products, e.g. restaurants need special licenses to sell alcohol on their premises. Macau is renowned for being a casino magnet as many neighbouring countries such as Hong Kong and Malaysia have strict gambling laws. Hence, legal dimensions affect the distribution decision.

- *Cost and benefits* – Direct selling, without the use of intermediaries, reduces the costs of distribution. However, retailers and distributors may have better access to customers, especially in foreign markets where local knowledge of cultural norms can be an advantage. Hence, businesses need to weigh up the costs and benefits of using intermediaries. Firms also need to consider the relative merits of different transportation methods (road, rail, air or sea) as part of their distribution strategy.

Figure 4.5.aii Air freight (cargo) at Hong Kong International Airport

For some businesses, such as Heinz and Coca-Cola, the distribution strategy focuses on maximising the number of outlets that sell their products. This helps to increase their sales and profits. A straightforward but relatively expensive way to ensure that retailers stock a firm's products is to open its own retail store, an approach used by Nike and Adidas.

477

Alternatively, the firm can use franchise agreements (see Unit 1.6)) to allow other certified firms and people to run the stores under the name of the business. However, the marketers at other businesses, such as Tiffany & Co and Rolls Royce, do not aim to have their products distributed in the same way; to do so would remove the exclusivity of their products and brands.

Alternatively, **vertical integration** (see Unit 1.6) can be used as a growth strategy to unify the supplier, producer, wholesalers and retailers. This strategy enables a manufacturer to have its own retail outlets (forward vertical integration) and/or owns its suppliers (backward vertical integration). Being vertically integrated allows a business to have more direct control over its distribution channels. Hence, the business is able to retain better control of all its marketing activities. However, vertical integration is not a realistic strategy for most businesses due to the high costs involved. This means that the majority of firms need to compete for floor or shelf space in retail outlets. The producer needs to convince retailers to stock its products rather than giving preference to its rivals. This is usually based on a pre-determined criterion such as sales or profits per square foot of retail space. Hence, place can act as a major barrier to entry for new and smaller firms. Retailers need an incentive to stock less established products and brands, such as those with a unique selling point or products that are truly innovative.

Globalization of markets has been fuelled by the increasing number of businesses that sell their products in overseas markets via exporting. However, an export strategy presents further complications to a firm's distribution strategy due to various external constraints, such as:

- Fluctuating exchanges rates – The changing nature of exchange rates can make products cheaper (in which case export sales are likely to rise) but can also lead to higher export prices (in which case, demand will most probably fall).

- Government intervention – Overseas governments may place trade barriers and legal constraints on exported products. Such intervention makes it more difficult and/ or more costly to distribute the product.

- Language barriers – These constraints can cause communication problems with overseas intermediaries and customers.

- Cultural differences – Similarly, diversity in cultural norms might mean that some products are not suited to certain regions or countries, such as pork products in Muslim countries.

Change, globalization and innovation result in a need for an integrated distribution strategy. For example, large supermarkets can no longer rely on customers revisiting their outlets to maintain market share. Internet technolgy now allows supermarkets to offer customers the added choice of online shopping. The largest supermarket chains have exploited Internet technologies as a channel of distribution and have seen their costs fall significantly. Changing lifestyles have also led to supermarkets adopting longer opening hours and delivery services to attract customers. This has made distribution and logistics increasingly important for retailers, such as supermarkets.

Figure 4.5.aiii Retailers rely on efficient delivery and transportation services

Innovations have also influenced distribution strategies. For example, the growing use of digital and mobile technologies has created many business opportunities. Many businesses use downloadable apps for distributing video games, music, movies, travel, taxi services, and social media.

Theory of knowledge

Are reasoning and emotions mutually exclusive when marketing goods and services to customers?

Theory of knowledge

Which of the 4Ps does the Internet best fit under? How does the Internet change our knowledge and understanding of the traditional marketing mix for business organizations?

CUEGIS Essay

With reference to a multinational company of your choice, examine how **globalization** has influenced its distribution **strategy**.   *[20 marks]*

CUEGIS Essay

With reference to an organization of your choice, examine how **change** has influenced distribution **strategy**.   *[20 marks]*

REVIEW QUESTIONS

1. What is meant by 'place' in the marketing mix?

2. What are distribution channels?

3. What are intermediaries?

4. What role do intermediaries have in the distribution of goods and services?

5. Differentiate between wholesalers, retailers, agents and speciality channels of distribution.

6. What is a multi-channel distribution strategy?

7. Explain the meaning of telemarketing.

8. How has e-commerce benefited some businesses in terms of their placement decision?

9. State two advantages and two disadvantages of using direct mail.

10. What are the factors that affect the overall choice of distribution channels?

KEY TERMS

Agents (or **brokers**) are negotiators who help to sell a vendor's products, such as real estate agents selling residential and commercial property for their clients.

Channels of distribution are the ways that a product gets from the manufacturer to the consumer. Examples include wholesalers, agents, retailers, e-commerce and vending machines.

Direct mail refers to promotional material sent directly to people's homes or places of work, often with personal details gathered from a database containing information about known customers.

Direct marketing refers to any promotional activity that involves making direct contact with customers, such as personal selling and direct mail.

CORE

Marketing

479

Distribution (or **place**) refers to the process of getting the right products to the right customers at the right time and place in the most cost-effective way.

Distributors are independent businesses that act as intermediaries by specialising in the trade of products made by certain manufacturers.

Intermediaries are agents or other businesses that act as a middle person in the chain of distribution.

Intermediation is the process of using intermediaries in the chain of distribution between the manufacturers and consumers of a product.

A **one-channel distribution network** is a method of distribution that involves the use of a single intermediary, such as an agent or retailer.

Place refers to the distribution of products, i.e. how products get from the producer to the consumer. For example, products could be available at large warehouses, at retail outlets, through agents or via the Internet (e-commerce).

Retailers are the sellers of products to the general public (i.e. consumers) that operate in outlets (or 'shops' in everyday language).

Speciality channel of distribution is any indirect way to distribute products that does not involve retailers, i.e. distribution without the use of intermediaries such as e-commerce, vending machines and mail order.

Telemarketing refers to the use of telephone systems (audio and text messaging) to sell products directly to potential customers.

A **three-channel distribution network** is a type of distribution channel that uses three intermediaries. It typically involves an agent, wholesalers and retailers.

A **two-channel distribution network** is a method of distribution that involves the use of two intermediaries. These are typically wholesalers and retailers.

Wholesalers are businesses that purchase large quantities of products from a manufacturer and then separate or 'break' the bulk-purchases into smaller units for resale, mainly to retailers.

A **zero-level distribution channel** (also known as **direct distribution**) skips any intermediaries, i.e. the producer sells directly to the consumer.

Farmers often use direct distribution to sell to customers

CORE

Marketing

480

4.6 The extended marketing mix

"A business absolutely devoted to service will have only one worry about profits; they will be embarrassingly large." -
Henry Ford (1863–1947), founder of the Ford Motor Company

HL content	Assessment objective
The seven Ps model in a service-based market	AO2
People The importance of employee–customer relationships in marketing a service and cultural variation in these relationships	AO3
Processes The importance of delivery processes in marketing a service and changes in these processes	AO3
Physical evidence The importance of tangible physical evidence in marketing a service	AO3

© IBO, 2017

The marketing of services

The seven Ps model in a service-based market. AO2

© IBO, 2017

A service is an intangible product such as a bus ride, a visit to the library, a trip to the theatre or a haircut. Unlike physical goods, buyers of services do not actually take anything away with them after payment is made, i.e. there is no ownership of the product. The product is also perishable (as it cannot be kept). Services are heterogeneous, i.e. customers get a different experience each time and, unlike mass market goods, the quality is therefore varied. Businesses can also provide services to other organizations, such as transportation (freight), insurance, legal, consultancy, security and distribution services.

Customers pay for services to fulfill their wants and needs, such as to gain advice or support, e.g. banking, counseling and tutoring services. Product differentiation is therefore important for the marketing of services. For example, banks offer a range of different services such as savings accounts, overdrafts and mortgages. They use marketing tools to entice customers to these different services. However, in addition to the traditional marketing mix for physical goods (price, product, promotion and place), the marketing of services includes three additional elements: people, processes and physical evidence. Together these form the **7Ps model** in the marketing of services, first suggested by Bernard Booms and Mary Bitner in 1981.

Figure 4.6.a The 7Ps model of marketing

People

The importance of employee–customer relationships in marketing a service and cultural variation in these relationships. AO3
© IBO, 2017

The provision of services relies on the goodwill of all employees. Schools require teachers who are passionate about their subjects to deliver engaging and purposeful lessons to students. Hotel staff are crucial in helping holiday makers enjoy their vacation. The cabin crew are vital in making a flight a pleasant experience for travellers. It is important for service-orientated businesses to build good relationships and trust with their customers.

The effectiveness of people in marketing or delivering a service can be measured in a number of ways:

- **Appearance and body language** of the staff – Uniforms and formal clothing are worn in many occupations to portray a more professional appearance. For example, newsreaders on television dress conservatively to portray a formal and serious image. McDonald's operates a 'Smiles are free' policy to ensure that their customers are greeted with a friendly smile.

- **Aptitudes and attitudes** – Managers will ask a range of questions concerning the capability and behaviour of their staff, such as: whether staff have sufficient product knowledge; whether they are proactive (whether they are attentive to the needs of their clients); and whether they are caring, courteous and confident. If the answers to these questions are positive, then it is highly likely that customers will be happy with the service being delivered. This can have profound effects on the business through positive word of mouth marketing (see Unit 4.5).

- **Feedback** – Comments made by various stakeholder groups can also provide useful information regarding the effectiveness of people in delivering good customer service. Schemes such as 'Employee of the month',

suggestion schemes, and records of customer complaints can also provide useful feedback to further improve the marketing of services.

- **Efficiency** – Staff who do not keep customers waiting and who do not make careless mistakes will help the business to gain a better reputation and corporate image. For example, restaurants, cinemas, theatres, concerts and airlines often have staff to assist customers to their seats. Training is therefore important to ensure employees are efficient in their jobs. By contrast, late deliveries and long waiting times (before customers are served) are signs of poor customer care and inefficiencies. Such inadequacies make it more difficult for the business to market its products and services.

Figure 4.6.b Training people is vital for the successful marketing of services

However, people are not consistent and numerous factors affect their motivation (see Unit 2.4), which can change from day to day In addition, cultural variations have a direct impact on how people interact with customers. For example, Indian and Japanese cultures are averse to critical disagreements, so saying 'no' is regarded as being rather rude. Instead, any disagreements should be expressed with the use of diplomatic language. The Chinese consider staring to be rude and a lack of respect, so any interaction with customers may involve minimal eye contact to give customers space (or privacy). Due to the pace of doing business in Hong Kong, people prefer to serve customers quickly rather than paying attention to the quality of customer care. In the USA, supermarket staff help customers to pack their bags, whereas in Germany customers prefer to pack their own. It is common in the UK for customer service to be formal and conservative, whereas the French, Italian and Spanish are rather more laid back (relaxed) in their approach.

Case study

Singapore Airlines is the world's most awarded airline. These include: Best Corporate Social Responsibility, Best In-flight Service, Best Cabin Staff, Best First Class, Best Business Class, and Best Economy Class. The airline is well-known for its outstanding level of customer service, delivered from its female flight crew. Its marketing slogan 'Singapore Girls' has been part of its highly successful promotional campaigns. Its most prestigious award is winning the *Best Airline* for over 20 consecutive years.

Processes

The importance of delivery processes in marketing a service and changes in these processes. AO3
© IBO, 2017

Process refers to the way in which a service is provided or delivered. It can be difficult for a business to demonstrate the benefits of services to its customers. Insurance brokers, for example, often have a challenging task in convincing clients to buy life assurance policies as the process is complex. Businesses selling physical goods, however, tend to have a relatively easier task in demonstrating and convincing customers of the benefits.

Processes in the marketing of services include:

- **Payment methods** – Businesses may offer their customers the convenience of different methods of payment, e.g. cash, cheque, bank transfer, hire purchase (see Unit 3.1) or credit card. This makes the process of paying for a service more convenient for customers, but some businesses add a surcharge for the use of credit cards or bank transfers.

Figure 4.6.c Different payment systems add convenience for customers

- **Waiting (queuing) time** – There can be negative consequences if businesses do not manage the waiting time of their customers. These consequences include a poorer corporate image, customer complaints, and disgruntled customers. Many pizza companies offer a discount or do not charge the customer if the product is delivered late. Similarly, diners might switch to another restaurant if they have to wait too long for a table.

- **Customer services** – This refers to the degree of attentiveness, care and politeness of staff towards their customers. Feedback on the quality of customer service can be obtained from customer service satisfaction surveys, suggestion schemes, or comment cards.

- **After-sales care** – A business can gain a competitive edge if it provides after-sales services. These are services that are offered following the sale of the product, e.g. installation, maintenance, technical support and warranties (guarantees).

- **Delivery processes** – Businesses can enhance the buying process of services (and goods) by providing various delivery options (see Figure 4.6.d). Providing a delivery service, whether it is free of charge or not, can give a business a competitive edge. For example, in many parts

Marketing

of the world, McDonald's, Pizza Hut and KFC offer a free delivery service. Retailers that sell bulky items, such as washing machines or furniture, often offer a delivery service, which improves the buying process for customers.

Figure 4.6.d Delivery processes are part of the marketing mix for services

Processes are important as they can determine whether customers will make repeat purchases. For example, if customers experience excellent standards of customer care at a spa or hair salon, they are likely to tell their friends and family, perhaps spreading the message on their social networks. This can provide the business with vital word of mouth promotion and viral marketing (see Unit 4.5).

Theory of knowledge

IKEA, the world's largest retailer of home furniture, sells most of its products in flat packs so that they are easy for customers to take home. IKEA claims that there is no such thing as free delivery; it charges customers for each delivery. However, many businesses do offer free delivery as part of their service. Can firms genuinely claim that they offer free delivery?

Physical evidence

The importance of tangible physical evidence in marketing a service. AO3

© IBO, 2017

Physical evidence refers to the tangible aspects of a service. In a 5-star hotel, for example, we might expect to see a clean lobby with nice décor and well-groomed hotel staff. The restaurants and hotel facilities (such as hi-speed Wi-Fi, spas, gyms and swimming pools) should also be of high quality (see Figure 4.6.e). The rooms should be clean with fresh towels and bed sheets. This all helps the customer to feel happy with the overall service provided by the hotel. Similarly, students will be interested in the physical environment when choosing a university for higher education, rather than just the quality of the courses on offer. For example, students (the customers) will be interested in the quality of the accommodation and learning environment (such as learning spaces on campus and other on-site facilities).

Figure 4.6.e Top hotels have outstanding facilities such as modern swimming pools

Physical evidence is important for service businesses in most industries. Examples include tourist attractions (such as theme parks and hotels), large multinational companies (the physical building of their head office), cinemas (the size of the screens), football matches (the stadium), museums (the exhibits) and schools. The physical environment is designed to make customers feel welcome, safe, and comfortable in order to ensure visitors (customers) have a memorable time.

Many businesses use peripheral products in delivering their services. These are additional products, such as drinks or magazines offered to clients in a hair salon, used to enhance the overall service provided to customers.

Question 4.6.1   Wallington High School for Girls

Wallington High School for Girls (WHSG), located in Surrey (UK) and founded in 1888, is a selective grammar school for girls. Selection is based on an academic entrance exam. There are several other selective and private fee-paying schools in the proximity. Surrey has a reputation for having the 'best' schools in the UK. Like all schools, *WHSG* is involved in the marketing of its service. Each year, the school management team deliberately runs events to market the organization. These events include: parents' information evenings, charity events, celebration evenings, music concerts and drama productions. *WHSG* has Engineering Status, which gives it extra funding from the government, and it proudly markets this achievement. The school also communicates its outstanding examination results to all key stakeholders.

Source: www.wallingtongirls.sutton.sch.uk

(a) Explain **two** reasons why marketing is important to *WHSG*.   *[4 marks]*

(b) Examine how people, process and physical evidence are vital elements of the marketing mix for *WHSG*.   *[6 marks]*

The extended marketing mix and the CUEGIS concepts

In modern societies, it is common for the majority of the country's workforce to be engaged in the services (or tertiary) sector of the economy (see Unit 1.1). This heightens the importance of marketing services (the use of the three extra Ps in the marketing mix) as part of any business strategy. Managing the provision of services can be very challenging compared with managing the marketing of physical goods. These challenges include:

- Correcting mistakes – It can be relatively easy to correct mistakes made during the manufacturing of physical goods, albeit costly perhaps. However, with the provision of services it can be very difficult to correct any mistakes made. A poor image caused by substandard customer service might be irreversible.

- Measuring productivity – How can we measure the output of teachers, newsreaders, doctors and actors? They all provide a service although it can be difficult to measure their productivity in the same way as measuring the output of workers in the manufacturing of physical products. As it is difficult to measure the output of intangible products, devising strategies to reward staff who are most productive can be very difficult.

- People management – The provision of services tends to be labour-intensive, which can be costly to an organization. Lawyers, architects and accountants, for example, are paid well for their skills and expertise. In service industries that require a large workforce, such as supermarkets and fast-food restaurants, it might be difficult for managers to ensure that all staff are consistent in their delivery of customer service. The lack of motivation from just one worker, for example, could be enough to tarnish the reputation of the business. Managing people in such professions requires effective leadership.

Therefore, the extended marketing mix can only be effective if a service culture is built within the organization. Human resource managers, for example, must pay attention to hiring the right people, retaining the best people, and developing people to deliver quality customer service. Operations managers must ensure processes are convenient and efficient for customers. This, along with attention to physical evidence, gives the organization a competitive edge in a changing business environment.

Innovation creates challenges, changes and opportunities for marketing managers. For example, QR codes enable businesses to market their services by interacting with customers using their mobile devices. Innovations in internet technologies, such as social media, means that customers are more empowered than ever before. Poor customer service, such as long queuing times or a bad experience, will quickly air

Marketing

their complaints via the internet using media such as Twitter, Facebook, WhatsApp and a host of customer review websites. Emails have regained some popularity with the widespread use of smartphones and tablet mobile devices, such as the iPad. This also creates many opportunities for firms to market their services to a global audience. Marketing strategies increasingly include the use of social networking, social media, blogs, microblogging and viral marketing.

Figure 4.6.f QR codes are used to promote goods and services

Exam tip !

In the examination, you will be asked to apply the CUEGIS concepts to a number of topics. For example, you could be required to examine how any two of the CUEGIS concepts influenced the extended marketing mix for a company that you have studied.

CUEGIS Essay

With reference to an organization of your choice (such as a hotel, theme park, or restaurant), examine how **culture** and **change** have influenced the extended marketing mix.   *[20 marks]*

CUEGIS Essay

With reference to an organization of your choice, examine how **globalization** and **ethics** have affected the extended marketing mix.   *[20 marks]*

REVIEW QUESTIONS

1. What is meant by a service?

2. Why are people considered important for the marketing mix of services?

3. How might cultural differences affect the importance of employee–customer relationships?

4. In the context of the marketing of services, what are processes?

5. Why is physical evidence important to the marketing of services?

KEY TERMS

Goods are physical products, e.g. smartphones, toys, books and clothes.

People are the employees who interact with customers, thereby delivering the service to customers. The reputation of a business largely depends on the training, motivation and communication skills of employees.

Physical evidence refers to the tangible aspects of a service, e.g. a luxury hotel with a welcoming lobby, nice décor, well-groomed hotel staff, spas, gyms and swimming pools.

Processes are the ways in which a service is provided or delivered, including payment systems, queuing times, customer services, after-sales care and delivery services.

A **service** is an intangible product supplied by a business, e.g. bus rides, library facilities, theatre shows, insurance deals and haircuts.

The **seven Ps model** refers to the marketing of services which includes three additional Ps (people, processes and physical evidence) in addition to the traditional 4Ps in the marketing mix (product, price, promotion and place).

4.7 International marketing

"Advertising is the mother of trade." - Japanese proverb

HL content	Assessment objective
Methods of entry into international markets	AO2
The opportunities and threats posed by entry into international markets	AO3
The strategic and operational implications of international marketing	AO3
The role of cultural differences in international marketing	AO3
The implications of globalization on international marketing	AO3

© IBO, 2017

Entry into international markets

Methods of entry into international markets. AO2

© IBO, 2017

Rovio Entertainment, the creators of the world's most downloaded app *Angry Birds*, generates more than 95% of its sales revenues from outside Finland, its home country. **International marketing** is the marketing of a firm's products in foreign countries. International marketing can be challenging for businesses because they need to deal with external factors and constraints such as differences in political systems, legislation, language and cultures. Hence, international marketing usually requires an amended marketing mix to suit the local market. A lack of understanding of different cultures can prove troublesome for even large businesses. For example, Walmart, the world's largest retailer, had to sell its stores in Germany to local rival Metro when it discovered that its American practises (such as helping customers to pack their bags at the supermarket) were unsuccessful and did not suit the German culture.

There are various methods that a business can use to enter international markets. These include internal methods (e.g. exporting, direct investment and e-commerce) and external methods (e.g. joint ventures, strategic alliances, franchising, mergers and acquisitions).

- **Exporting** – Here, the business operating in the domestic country sells its products directly to overseas buyers. The main advantage of exporting is that it eliminates the need to set up a business abroad (with the associated costs and risks). However, exporters can be exposed to the uncertainties of fluctuations in exchange rates.

- **Direct investment** – This refers to a business setting up overseas production and/or distribution facilities. Having a wider distribution channel overcomes the problem of exporting (which limits the potential number of foreign buyers). For example, Honda, Toyota and Nissan all have manufacturing plants in France and the UK, enabling the Japanese car producers to gain access to the huge market in Europe. BMW's manufacturing plant in Chennai (India's fourth largest city) helps the German company to avoid a 60% import tax on its cars. However, the main drawback of this method is the high costs of the investment, such as the need to rent or buy premises for production.

- **E-commerce** – This is conducting business via the internet (see Unit 4.8). E-commerce is an effective way to reduce the costs and risks of international marketing. Many online retailers, such as Amazon and eBay, have gained access to foreign markets without having to physically set up production facilities and retail stores.

Figure 4.7.a E-commerce enables businesses to access international markets

487

- **Joint ventures** – These occur when two or more companies invest in a shared business project, pooling their resources to form a separate business. The companies retain their separate legal identities but share the risks and returns from the joint venture. Many foreign businesses have formed joint ventures with Chinese and Indian companies to gain access to these large and growing markets.

Case study

In 2007, Exxon formed a $5 billion joint venture with China's Sinopec and Saudi Aramco (the largest supplier of oil to China). The project involves the three organizations being engaged in oil supply, refinery and retail in China. Sinopec is the world's largest oil refining, gas and petrochemicals company. Saudi Aramco is the world's largest oil exporter.

- **Strategic alliances** – These are similar to joint ventures except the partners do not form a new business with a separate legal identity. For example, the *Star Alliance*, which was established in 1997, has 27 member airlines that share marketing and branding to facilitate passengers making inter-airline connections on their flights. Again, strategic alliances with foreign firms can allow a business to gain access to overseas markets.

Case study

Nissan (Japan's second largest car manufacturer) and Renault (a major French vehicles producer) formed an alliance in 1999, giving both businesses access to each other's markets. The alliance places the companies fifth in global sales of cars (after Toyota, Volkswagen, Hyundai, GM and Ford) with an approximate 10% of the world market share.

- **Franchising** – This involves a business allowing others to trade under its name, in return for a fee and a royalty payment based on a predetermined share of the sales revenues. McDonald's, Subway, KFC, Pizza Hut, Hertz, 7-Eleven and Burger King all use this growth strategy to enter overseas markets.

Case study

In 2014, McDonald's opened its first restaurant in Vietnam, owned by Henry Nguyen, son-in-law of Vietnam's communist-ruled leader. International marketing has led to heavy foreign direct investment (FDI) in Vietnam, and more local people buying global consumer brands. Four decades after the Vietnam War with America ended, McDonald's followed US rivals Burger King, KFC and coffee shop chain Starbucks into Vietnam.

- **Licensing** occurs when another organization (licensee) buys the right to produce the goods of the licensor. Nike licenses the production of its sports shoes and sportswear to businesses in Indonesia; Disney licenses the production of its soft toys and other merchandise to businesses in Vietnam; Disney also licenses it characters such as Mickey Mouse and Donald Duck in India. Licensing patents can apply to trademarks, copyrights, designs and other forms of intellectual property rights for which the licensor also earns money from royalty payments paid by the licensees.

- **Mergers** – These take place when two businesses agree to integrate into a single organization. Merging with a foreign company can help businesses gain access to overseas markets. For example, India's Mittal Steel Company and Luxembourg's Arcelor merged in 2006 to form Arcelor–Mittal, the world's largest steelmaking company.

- **Acquisitions** (or **takeovers**) – These occur when one business buys out another by purchasing a majority stake in the target company. UK mobile phone giant Vodafone's acquisition of India's mobile operator Essar meant that it gained access to the huge potential market in the world's second most populous country. Microsoft's cash purchase of Skype for $8.56 billion gave the software giant access to over 660 million worldwide users at the time.

Question 4.7.1   Colgate–Palmolive

Colgate-Palmolive is an American multinational company that produces personal hygiene products (such as toothpaste and soaps) and cleaning products (such as detergents). The company has a global marketing presence, with operations in countries as diverse as the USA and Vietnam. The company's growth has been driven by strong **sales revenue** of its internationally recognized brands of toothpaste, soap and other household products.

Source: www.colgatepalmolive.com/en-us

(a) Define the term **sales revenue**.   *[2 marks]*

(b) Describe the type of product *Colgate* toothpaste might be classified as.   *[2 marks]*

(c) To what extent is the brand name of a product, such as *Colgate* or *Palmolive*, important for successful international marketing?   *[10 marks]*

Opportunities and threats of international marketing

The opportunities and threats posed by entry into international markets. AO3

© IBO, 2017

Opportunities of entry into international markets

- **Increased customer base** – The size of a market can be enlarged by marketing products to overseas buyers. This should lead to greater sales revenue and possibly higher market share for the business.

- **Economies of scale** – By operating on a larger scale, a business is likely to benefit from cost savings known as *economies of scale* (see Unit 1.6). These cost-reducing benefits of larger scale operations can enable growing businesses to gain higher profit margins or to reduce their prices (thereby giving them a price advantage over their rivals). Businesses can benefit from lower production costs by operating in overseas markets, such as cheaper labour costs.

Figure 4.7.b Many businesses have benefited from offshoring production to China

- **Increased brand recognition** – Having a standardized marketing strategy across the world (such as using identical packaging and advertising) not only reduces average costs of production, but can also lead to greater international recognition of a brand. This can lead to improved brand loyalty and increased sales revenues.

- **Spread risks** – By operating in various international markets, a business is less exposed to the risks in one particular country (such as a recession or changes in fashion and tastes).

Marketing

489

- **Extend the product life cycle** – A business might find that the domestic market for its product is saturated or in decline. By marketing the product overseas, the business can expand its life cycle to generate higher sales revenues. Mobile phone companies use this strategy when selling older models of their phones in less affluent countries.

- **Gain more profit** – Ultimately, all the reasons above for international marketing can help to generate more profits for the business. Overseas markets provide an extra source of revenue and can be financially lucrative.

Case study

Jaguar Land Rover (JLR) is a luxury brand owned by Indian conglomerate Tata Group. Over 80% of JLR's sales are to overseas markets. Originally British brands, China is the largest market for Jaguar and Land Rover cars, as JLR exploits the opportunities of international marketing.

Threats of entry into international markets

The legal, political, social and economic issues surrounding international marketing can pose both opportunities and threats to businesses.

Legal issues

Entry into international markets can also be a problem due to different **legal systems**, e.g. advertising cigarettes on television has been banned in the USA since 1971. Advertising in general prohibited in Cuba and in São Paulo, Brazil, so even for large multinational companies this would present a major barrier to international marketing. Governments can set up other international trade barriers to protect their domestic industries (see Box 4.7.a).

Case study

In 2014, China lifted its embargo (ban) on foreign video games consoles in the Shanghai free trade zone. Japan's Nintendo, the makers of the popular Wii U console, saw its share price jump 11% following the announcement. China had banned gaming consoles in 2000.

Box 4.7.a   International trade barriers

- **Quotas** – quantitative restrictions on imported goods, thus limiting the number of foreign products entering the country.
- **Tariffs** – import taxes increase the price of imports and raise government tax revenues.
- **Embargoes** – bans on certain products entering a country due to major health and safety threats or political conflict.
- **Administrative barriers** – such as safety regulations, licenses and employment visas (thereby making entry much more difficult).
- **Subsidies** – financial assistance given to domestic businesses to reduce their costs of production (hence giving them a cost advantage over foreign rivals).

Copyright, **trademark** and **patent** legislation must also be adhered to. This covers issues such as brand names, slogans, inventions, works of art, and processes already legally assigned to other businesses. Marketers need to take this legal factor into consideration when devising their international marketing campaigns.

Differences in **consumer protection laws** must also be observed by international marketers. Many countries have their own code of conduct on advertising and packaging information, so these must be respected. The British Advertising Standards Authority, for example, states that all advertisements must be "decent, truthful and accurate". In most EU countries, there are legally binding controls over the use of advertisements aimed directly at children, e.g. in Sweden it is illegal to advertise products on television to children under the age of twelve.

Political issues

Businesses that market their products overseas need to consider the different political systems abroad. Countries that have a stable political climate tend to be less risky and more receptive to foreign businesses selling products in their territory. In Singapore and Hong Kong, there are few political barriers. By contrast, there are huge political hurdles to deal with if businesses wish to market their products in countries such as Afghanistan or North Korea.

Figure 4.7.c Singapore is consistently ranked by the World Bank as the best place to do business

Figure 4.7.d Malaysia is a highly multicultural country

Social and demographic issues

Different **socioeconomic** and **demographic conditions** mean that businesses may need to reconsider their international marketing. When exporting to less affluent countries, the product and price may differ from that sold in more prosperous nations. Overseas customers in Japan (expatriates and tourists) are not very well catered for as only about 1% of the population are foreigners. By contrast, in highly multicultural societies such as Malaysia (see Figure 4.7.d), marketing caters for a much wider audience with the same advertisements in Malay, Chinese and Indian languages.

With growing prosperity and income in some parts of the world, international marketers can target different customers with different products. In 2006, supercar manufacturer Lamborghini opened its first showroom in China due to the country's phenomenal economic growth rate. Japan and Italy have the world's oldest populations (as measured by the average age of the population) so marketers take a different approach to pricing, product, place and promotion when targeting these countries than if they were marketing to nations with younger populations such as Kenya or Vietnam.

Organizations also need to consider societal norms regarding **business etiquette.** This refers to the mannerisms and customs by which business is conducted in different parts of the world. Having local knowledge and a good level of understanding of differences in business etiquette can help international marketers to succeed in overseas markets.

Pressure groups concerned about the impacts of business activity on society can also create problems for marketers hoping to gain a foothold in foreign markets. Hong Kong Disneyland faced many problems from animal activist groups when it opened, including protests about sharks fin soup being on the food menu. People for the Ethical Treatment of Animals (PETA), the world's largest animal rights group, has caused many problems for companies operating in overseas markets, such as McDonald's, KFC and Procter & Gamble.

Economic issues

A key argument for more and freer **international trade** is that it enables people to have a greater choice of products at more competitive prices. International trade also allows citizens to have access to products that would otherwise be unavailable in their own country because domestic producers cannot supply such products in a cost effective manner, such as tropical fruits being grown in cold countries. These arguments can present major international marketing opportunities for large businesses.

However, international marketing of products also increases the degree of competition in the marketplace. Transportation costs, exchange rate fluctuations, interest rates and communication costs are further economic issues that need to be considered when marketing products overseas.

Marketing

Question 4.7.2 Tesco

Tesco is the UK's largest retailer, with annual sales in excess of £60 billion ($88bn). Although the company has entered several international markets such as France, Poland and China, the vast majority of its sales still come from within the UK. *Tesco* set up its first supermarket in the USA in 2007, although the American market remained rather untouched with *Walmart* being the dominant **market leader**. By 2013, *Tesco* had pulled out of the USA.

(a) Define the term **market leader**.   *[2 marks]*

(b) Explain how customers in overseas markets might benefit from the presence of *Tesco* in their country.   *[4 marks]*

(c) Evaluate the opportunities and threats to *Tesco* of their overseas expansion plans.   *[10 marks]*

The implications of international marketing

The strategic and operational implications of international marketing. AO3

© IBO, 2017

International marketing has operational and strategic implications for businesses marketing their products overseas. It is not as simple as extending domestic marketing strategies abroad, but applying these to meet the different market segments, demographics and cultures of customers in overseas markets. Operational implications affect businesses on a daily basis (such as language issues and the distribution of products) whilst strategic implications are broader and longer term (such as establishing a strategic alliance or joint venture in overseas markets). Strategically, international marketing through diversification (see Unit 1.6) helps to spread risks. For example, the impacts of economic and political problems in one country can be minimized if the business markets its products in other countries.

Operational and strategic implications of international marketing may include:

- Language and cultural differences – International marketing managers need to be aware of potential differences in language and cultures and how these impact upon their marketing strategies (see Box 4.7.b). For example, frozen food products such as microwave-ready meals are popular in some European countries but are not in many Southeast Asian nations.

- Legal differences – Different countries have different legal systems and laws, which will impact upon strategic and operational decisions of marketers. Even the same law (e.g. packaging and labelling of food products) may have different standards. This means it might be more difficult (and hence more expensive) to sell the same products in overseas markets. Tax laws will also differ from country to country.

- Political environment – The degree of political stability within a country can have a major impact on whether international marketers succeed in overseas markets. For example, trade protection (see Box 1.5.c) such as tariffs, quotas and subsidies for domestic businesses create major obstacles for international marketing. Political unrest, such as the violent protests and attacks in Kenya (2013), Egypt (2014) and Turkey (2016), and corruption will destabilize operational and strategic decisions for multinational companies operating in these countries.

- Economic environment – The state of the economy directly affects the degree of success of international marketing. During a global financial crisis, for example, most businesses will struggle irrespective of their marketing strategies and budgets. The World Bank ranks Singapore, Hong Kong and Denmark as countries where doing business is open and straightforward, whereas it is far more bureaucratic and difficult for multinational companies operating in China, India and Brazil. Exchange rate fluctuations (see Unit 1.5) can also have an impact on the success of international marketing.

- Infrastructure – The state of a country's transportation networks and communications technologies can have an impact on international marketing. For example, channels of distribution rely heavily on transportation networks (such as rail, air and sea) whilst Internet technologies affect how well marketers can use viral marketing and social media. For example, Google and Facebook are banned or have restricted access in a few countries.

Figure 4.7.e International marketing relies on effective transportation networks

Exam tip !

When examining the strategic and operational implications of international marketing, you can use a PEST analysis framework (looking at political, economic, social and technological factors) or the CUEGIS concepts to structure your answers.

Case study

In 2013, Starbucks was heavily criticised in China for charging locals higher prices for its coffee than in other major markets. The world's largest coffee retail chain claimed the higher prices were due to higher costs of food and logistics in China.

Cultural differences in international marketing

The role of cultural differences in international marketing. AO3
© IBO, 2017

It is important that marketers do not assume that people overseas behave in the same way that they themselves are personally accustomed to. David Ogilvy, a world renowned advertising executive, argues that businesses trying to market their products to different people should use local language, i.e. the language in which these people think. International business etiquette is particularly important when doing business in other people's territory. To facilitate a more successful international marketing strategy, the key point is an awareness and understanding of the local business context, the people involved and the different cultures.

Cultural exports are the commercial transfer of ideas and values from one country to another, e.g. American fast food, Hollywood movies, drive-through outlets (first introduced in the USA in 1975), satellite (cable) television and sports apparel. Even the sales of Harry Potter books have proven to be one of Britain's most successful exports, helping to make J.K. Rowling the world's first author to earn over $1 billion. Other British cultural exports include fish and chips, the Royal Family, the James Bond franchise, and The Beatles. These products originate from the UK and are associated with British culture, but are consumed around the world. Western traditions of celebrating events such as St. Valentine's Day and Halloween have also spread throughout the world, bringing huge commercial opportunities for businesses. Another example of cultural exports is Japanese lean production methods, such as Kaizen, Kanban, Andon and just-in-time (see Unit 5.3). Due to freer international trade and the growth in globalization, trade in cultural exports has grown exponentially.

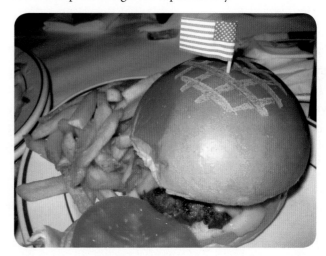

Figure 4.7.f The beef burger is an American cultural export

However, in their pursuit of exporting more, a business must consider the cultural differences between different countries and regions of the world. For instance, marketers need to consider local preferences when formulating their international marketing strategies. In China, the menus in McDonald's restaurants rely more heavily on chicken than in other international markets, reflecting the local preference for poultry products rather than hamburgers. The cultural difference has also meant that KFC, which specialises in chicken fast-food products, has far more branches than McDonald's in China.

Language is embedded in culture. Although English is the official language of business in many parts of the world, ignorance of local cultures and languages can have detrimental effects on a business. Many marketing mistakes have been made due to such ignorance (see Figure 4.7.g and Box 4.7.b).

Figure 4.7.g Offensive, or just a type of French lavender?

Box 4.7.b Language, cultural and marketing misjudgements

- Charlottetown Sewer and Water Department (Nova Scotia, Canada) repositioned their brand as *AquaPoo*.
- An American beverage producer, Monarch Beverage Company, sells a brand of soft drink called *Kickapoo*.
- In Sweden, *Plopp* and *Skum* are popular brands of candy bars; the French have the brand Crap's; in China, Swine is a well-known brand of chocolate.
- Would you want to eat in the *Liar Café Bar* in Istanbul, Turkey?
- A popular British meal is called *Toad in the hole* - it's actually a Yorkshire pudding with sausages.
- Rolls–Royce produced the Silver Mist but in Germany the word 'mist' means dung. Toyota's *MR2*, pronounced "Em-Air-De" in French, sounds like 'merde' which also means dung. Ford had problems selling its *Pinto* in Brazil, where pinto is slang for 'small male genitals'. Vauxhall (Opel) faced cultural problems with its small car, the Nova - Spanish for "does not go". Shanghai Auto's 'Roewe' cars symbolise power and honour; but the English pronunciation is 'rong wei' or 'wrong way'.
- In Southeast Asia, a top selling consumer electronics brand is Japan's *Top Con*.
- Would you try these drinks: *Pipi* (Yugoslavian orangeade), *Pocari Sweat* (Japanese sports drink), *Zit* (Greek soft drink) or *Pee Cola* (Ghanaian soft drink)?
- Manchester United Football Club fans in Malaysia were ordered not to wear the famous *Red Devils* football jersey as the logo depicts a demon, which is regarded as sinful in the Islamic country.
- KFC's global slogan *'We do chicken right'* is literally translated as "It is good for us to be a prostitute" in Chinese Cantonese.

Question 4.7.3 Viya Crab Products Company

Viya Crab Products Co. is a Thai producer of several varieties of ready-to-eat canned crab meat products. Founded in 2005, the company has a well-established local market, with steady export earnings from various countries in Southeast Asia. However, the business has bigger plans to sell its products in the USA and European markets.

Source: www.viyacrabproducts.co.th/

(a) Outline why ready-to-eat canned crab meat might be classed as a **cultural export**. *[2 marks]*

(b) Examine the role of international marketing to a business such as *Viya Crab Products Co.* *[6 marks]*

Ethics are another cultural issue that can present problems for international marketing. What is acceptable in one country might not be acceptable in others. For example, in modern societies, the employment of children is illegal whilst in other countries the use of child labour is seen as vital to their economic development. Pester power marketing (high-pressured marketing aimed at young children) is banned in the European Union but not in many other parts of the world. Smoking is allowed to be heavily advertised in some parts of the world whilst it is banned in other parts - is this ethical? To whom?

A final cultural issue that businesses must consider when marketing overseas is the differences in **international business etiquette** – the mannerism and customs by which business is conducted in different countries. An awareness and understanding of differences in business etiquette and cultural factors have become crucial elements of international marketing. A lack of awareness of the different ways in which business is conducted throughout different parts of the world (see Box 4.7.c) could mean that the organization fails to secure deals or contracts with foreign businesses.

IB Learner Profile – Be an inquirer and be knowledgeable

McDonald's is sensitive to the needs of customers in markets where pork and beef products are not consumed, due to religious reasons. Research other examples where culture and religious believes directly impact on international marketing.

Theory of knowledge

Discuss the role of language in marketing a product in international markets.

Box 4.7.c International business etiquette

- **Numbers** – In most cultures, there is some association of luck (or bad luck) with numbers, e.g. the number 13 is unlucky in some western societies, whereas 4 is unlucky in many Asian countries, such as China, Taiwan and Japan. Many multinational hotels are aware of this and do not have a 13th floor or a 4th floor (although they physically exist of course!)
- **Spoken language** – Although English is the most widely spoken business language in the world, there are still subtle differences which can lead to communication problems, e.g. Australians use 'Sand shoes' whereas the British use 'trainers'; they use 'thongs' whereas Brits use 'flip flops'. The British certainly wouldn't expect to walk out on the beach with thongs on their feet! The Japanese prefer not to use the word 'no'. Confusingly for many, they may simply respond with a 'yes' but in fact clearly mean 'no'! Understanding this can be crucial in a business negotiation.
- **Greetings** – First impressions count. This does not just refer to physical appearance but also how you greet your employees, suppliers, clients and other key stakeholders. It is the norm in many cultures to offer a firm handshake upon greeting and leaving a business meeting, but physical contact is avoided in other cultures. The Chinese do not have an actual word for "Hello", so it may seem odd that they might not greet you in the same way as expected in other cultures. Instead, they often greet others by asking if they have eaten (a meal) recently.
- **Physical contact** – It is not generally accepted that a man should shake the hands of Jewish women. This is a religious observation that should be respected. Many Europeans kiss each other on the cheek – once in some countries, twice in others or three times for others still! Japanese and Koreans frown on open displays of affection as physical contact with the opposite sex in public as highly inappropriate.

continued ...

Marketing

Box 4.7.c ... *continued*

- **Dress code** – In countries such as Hong Kong, Singapore and Malaysia, the weather can be incredibly hot and humidity levels go above 90%. Hence, business attire in these countries is often relatively casual. Suit jackets are not required. In Portugal, long-sleeved shirts and blouses are important; only expatriates in Portugal wear short-sleeved shirts. Women in Japan should not wear trousers in a business situation as the locals generally find this offensive.

- **Body language** – What you do is often more important than what you say. Research has shown that words account for only 7% of the messages communicated by a person whereas the remaining 93% is non-verbal. In India, for example, placing your hands on your hips is seen as an angry and aggressive posture; whistling is rude; and winking may be taken as either an insult or a sexual proposition. The Japanese do not talk using their hands as this is distracting. Pointing at people is also unacceptable.

Ultimately, international marketers must understand the culture, language and business etiquette of their clients; otherwise, it can be a particularly expensive oversight. Such mistake or ignorance can mean the business is disadvantaged unintentionally.

Globalization and international marketing

The implications of globalization on international marketing. AO3
© IBO, 2017

Globalization is the integration and interdependence of the world's economies. For international marketers, this means an attempt to efficiently produce and sell the same products in different countries. The outcome of globalization is that markets, cultures and tastes have converged at an accelerating pace (see Box 4.7.d).

Some businesses simply export their products to benefit from a larger customer base and to reap the cost savings from larger scale operations (economies of scale). For example, Heineken, the Dutch brewery, exports its beer to 170 different countries. Other companies, such as McDonald's and Pizza Hut, have "gone global" by establishing overseas franchises. Alternatively, organizations such as Honda and Toyota have gone global by establishing overseas manufacturing facilities.

Figure 4.7.h The globalization of cultural foods is big business

Global marketing is an extension of international marketing. It involves selling the same product using the same marketing approach throughout the world, as used by global brand leaders such as McDonald's, Nike and Coca-Cola. These multinational companies design and market their products to a world audience. Consumers around the world easily recognize and have similar tastes for their products. In the case of McDonald's, even the production processes are largely the same throughout the world; burgers and fries are cooked in exactly the same way irrespective of where the McDonald's restaurant is located in the world. The Coca-Cola brand is one of the most recognized in the world. Thus, these businesses are able to exploit global marketing and production economies of scale (see Unit 1.6). By contrast, international marketing refers to differentiated marketing that is tailored to suit different countries.

Globalization and the aggressive growth strategies of some large multinational companies have promoted the increased use of international marketing strategies. Due to the growing presence of foreign competitors, businesses are finding it increasingly important to consider the opportunities and threats of international marketing.

Today's business environment is more global than ever before. Communication can take place from anywhere on the planet, whether via video-conferencing, telephones, social networking or face-to-face meetings. With developments in ICT there are huge opportunities to interact with clients on an international level. As the world continues to globalize at an increasing pace, perhaps the most important element of success for marketers with an international outlook may be the appreciation and respect for cultural differences and cultural diversity. It is useful to remember the saying, "*When in Rome, do as the Romans do*", which is used to advise people to adapt to different cultures and etiquette when visiting other countries. Hence, the strategic use of joint ventures and strategic alliances may prove highly practical for international marketers. An understanding and awareness of international business etiquette can ultimately give an organization a competitive advantage in an ever-competitive and changing business world.

Box 4.7.d   Indicators of globalization

- Higher value of international trade over time
- Higher levels of foreign direct investment (FDI), e.g. Japanese car manufacturers setting up production facilities in the USA and the European Union
- Multinational companies accounting for a greater share of Gross Domestic Product (national output)
- Greater cultural awareness and exchange, e.g. the export of cultural foods and other cultural exports
- Spreading of multiculturalism, such as Hollywood and Bollywood movies, and popular music
- Higher spending on international travel and tourism
- Internet technologies throughout the world, e.g. increased usage of social networking and e-commerce
- Greater cultural awareness and exchange, e.g. the export of cultural foods and other cultural exports.

Case study

In 2013, Starbucks joined forces with Tata Group (which owns Jaguar and Land Rover) to set up coffee shops in India. The partnership created 34 stores within the first year, although Café Coffee Day, India's largest shop chain, has over 1,500 outlets, serving more than 1.8 billion cups of coffee each year.

Theory of knowledge

Does the value of an artwork (as used in international marketing) depend of its economic value?

Question 4.7.4   Ford Motor Company

Ford Motor Company launched its *Pinto* model in 1971. This was a compact sized family car that came in several different engine sizes with slight variations such as 2-door and 4-door versions. The *Pinto* brand didn't work well in Brazil as 'pinto' is slang for 'small male genitals'. Ford eventually became aware of this and renamed the car *Corcel,* which means horse. In America, the *Pinto* was named *Mercury Bobcat*. By 1981, the *Pinto* name had been replaced by *Escort*. In 1998, the *Escort* brand was finally replaced by a single global name: the *Focus.*

The Ford Focus

(a) Explain **two** benefits to *Ford Motor Company* in using 'Focus' as a single brand name on an international level.

[4 marks]

(b) Examine whether there are any justifications for *Ford Motor Company* using different brand names in different parts of the world.

[6 marks]

International marketing and the CUEGIS concepts

Changes in the global business environment mean that businesses which are able to adopt international marketing strategies benefit from being able to market their products throughout the world. After all, having to change products to suit local preferences or cultures can be costly. The dilemma facing managers is trying to gain marketing economies of scale by using a single global strategy yet still cater for local or regional preferences and tastes. While it is possible for large multinational companies such as Coca-Cola and McDonald's to make the odd costly mistake, smaller companies cannot afford to do so. Smaller businesses therefore need to ensure that their international marketing strategies are very carefully researched and planned since failure overseas can be disastrous to the organization.

In today's ever-globalized world, ethical principles have extended across cultures and nationalities. Nevertheless, cultural differences are still widespread so what is acceptable in one country may not be in others. For example, the European Union bans the use of pester power marketing (see Unit 4.5), yet child labour is socially acceptable in other cultures. Businesses have to be sensitive to the beliefs and values of local and global communities; exporting cultural norms and values is not always an ethical practice. It is therefore important for international marketers to understand the countries and cultures in which they operate, such as societal norms and values.

Case study

Foxconn, the world's largest electronics contract producer, makes the iPhone, iPad, Kindle, Xbox One, PlayStation 4 and Wii U. However, the Taiwanese manufacturer has been involved in several controversies relating to how it treats its workers who are subjected to poor working conditions and long working hours. News media reported cases of accidents in the factory, riots at work and even 14 workplace suicides in 2010.

Branding (see Unit 4.5) is integral to any international marketing strategy. Scientists, economists, psychologists and marketers have all produced evidence to show that branding can have a huge impact on the buying decisions made by consumers. It is very common that consumers make their purchasing decisions based on the perception of a brand rather than the qualities of the actual product. Careful market research and planning

are required to extend the success overseas. Matt Haig, author of Brand Failures, found that highly successful brands can lose their value overnight because customer perception of products and brands can be fragile. A successful branding strategy in one part of the world does not mean that the same formula will work in other places. Branding also becomes a more complicated issue when operating overseas. Language and cultural considerations become important to the success of international brands. Box 4.7.e shows some brands that are unlikely to excel on a global scale.

Box 4.7.e International branding mishaps

- Brazilian fruit candy: Suks
- Czech health drink: Urinal
- French food and beverages: Kraps & Co.
- Jamaican citrus fruit: Ugli
- Taiwanese biscuits: Only Puke
- Chinese chocolate candy: Swine
- Chinese tailors: The Chinese Arrogant Men's Clothing Brand
- Ghanaian cola: Pee Cola
- Japanese driving school: Terra Bal
- Japanese sports drink: Pocari Sweat
- Korean bank: Woori Bank
- Swedish confectionery: Plopp and Skum
- Swedish toilet tissue: Edet Krapp
- Thai restaurant: Cabbages & Condoms
- US clothing company: BUM Equipment
- UK air conditioning service: Stiff Nipples

Globalization and international marketing strategy come with their critics. Pressure groups and the media have provided another perspective on the impacts of globalization. For instance, in his book *Fast Food Nation*, Eric Schlosser discusses how globalization of the fast-food industry has led to increased obesity in China and Japan. The documentary movie *Supersize Me* and the film adaptation of Schlosser's book have highlighted some of the drawbacks from the marketing of US fast-food culture throughout the world.

Despite the uniformity and opportunities brought by globalization, countries still have their national identities through language, culture and other unique characteristics. Hence, marketing strategies are likely to need businesses to adapt products and services to meet the varying needs of their international clients.

Question 4.7.5   McDonald's

McDonald's, the world's largest fast-food chain, has global sales revenue in excess of $28 billlion. With more than 37,000 restaurants worldwide and a workforce of more than 1.9 million people, *McDonald's* is an expert in **international marketing**. For example, to revamp its global business, the company added salads, fruits and other healthy options to its traditional menu. The company marketed this change for its product portfolio by publicising nutritional facts on its food products. Critics have argued that *McDonald's* foods and drinks remain unhealthy and high in calories. Their marketing strategies aimed at children, such as their trademark Happy Meals™, have been attacked due to soaring obesity levels in children. Equal opportunities groups have also complained that Happy Meal™ toys cater predominantly for boys.

(a) Define the term **international marketing**.   *[2 marks]*

(b) Outline one possible problem created by the critics of *McDonald's* for the business.   *[2 marks]*

(c) Examine **two** reasons for the growth in *McDonald's* global sales revenue.   *[6 marks]*

(d) Discuss the extent to which the fast food industry is a globalized industry.   *[10 marks]*

IB Learner Profile – Be an inquirer

Use Google images to search for photos of the brands in Box 4.7.e. Try to find other examples of branding mishaps from around the world and consider how businesses might learn from these mistakes.

CUEGIS Essay

With reference to an organization of your choice, examine how **ethics** have impacted its international marketing **strategies**.   *[20 marks]*

CUEGIS Essay

With reference to an organization of your choice, examine how **change** has influenced its international marketing **strategies**.   *[20 marks]*

Theory of knowledge

To what extent does cultural tourism respect local cultures and promote societal norms and values?

Tourists in Morocco

CUEGIS Essay

With reference to an organization of your choice, examine how **culture** has influenced its international marketing **strategies**.   *[20 marks]*

CUEGIS Essay

With reference to an organization of your choice, examine how **globalization** has influenced its international marketing **strategies**.   *[20 marks]*

Marketing

REVIEW QUESTIONS

1. What is meant by international marketing?

2. Explain the advantages of international marketing to businesses.

3. Distinguish between strategic alliance, joint ventures and franchising as methods of entering international markets.

4. What are the opportunities and threats posed by entry into international markets?

5. What are the strategic and operational implications of international marketing?

6. How do cultural differences affect international marketing?

7. What are cultural exports?

8. What is meant by business etiquette?

9. How does globalization affect international marketing?

10. What is global marketing and how does it differ from international marketing?

KEY TERMS

Business etiquette refers to the mannerism and customs (traditions) by which business is conducted in different countries.

Cultural exports are the commercial transfer of ideas and values from one country to another, e.g. US fast-food, Hollywood movies and drive-through outlets.

Direct investment refers to a business setting up production and/or distribution facilities in overseas markets.

E-commerce is the buying and selling of goods and services via electronic means. Most international marketers rely on e-commerce via the Internet to reach a global audience.

Exporting is the practice of selling domestically produced goods and/or services to overseas buyers in order to gain access to larger international markets.

Global marketing is the marketing of a product by using the same marketing strategy in numerous countries to gain from marketing economies of scale.

Globalization is the integration and interdependence of the world's economies, resulting in cultures and tastes converging at an accelerating pace.

Glocalization is the use of a differentiated international marketing mix in order to meet local tastes and cultures.

International marketing is the marketing of an organization's products in foreign countries.

Legal constraints are the lawful rules and regulations of a country that set the parameters for how businesses operate, including what international marketers can and cannot do.

Licensing occurs when a third party organization (licensee) buys the right to produce the goods of another business (the licensor).

Pizza is an Italian cultural exports, enjoyed by people around the world

4.8 E-commerce

"Unless in communicating with it one says exactly what one means, trouble is bound to result." - Alan Turing (1912–1954), British mathematician and computer scientist

SL/HL content	Assessment objective
Features of e-commerce	AO1
The effects of changing technology and e-commerce on the marketing mix	AO2
The difference between the following types of e-commerce: • business to business (B2B) • business to consumer (B2C) • consumer to consumer (C2C)	AO2
The costs and benefits of e-commerce to firms and consumers	AO3

© IBO, 2017

Features of e-commerce

Features of e-commerce. AO1

© IBO, 2017

E-commerce (or **electronic commerce**) is the trading of goods and services via the Internet, electronic systems and computer networks. It has come a very long way since its humble beginnings back in August 1991. The Internet has since become an increasingly important method of business activity as e-commerce allows businesses to operate 24 hours a day, with an international reach. E-commerce mainly takes place via the use of a computer linked to the Internet. The growth in the use of mobile devices has presented further opportunities for online trading.

Figure 4.8.a E-commerce creates many business opportunities

Examples of e-markets include:

- Financial services – banking, foreign exchange and share trading can all be done online.

- Gaming – the Internet has intensified competition in the sale of online gaming.

- Retailing – groceries, clothing, books, DVDs and toys can all be traded on the Internet.

Common features of e-commerce include:

- **Global reach** – Unlike traditional retailers, e-commerce breaks geographical barriers, allowing businesses to sell their products to customers in almost any part of the world.

- **24/7 accessibility** – Whilst most retailers have 'opening hours', e-commerce is accessible at all times, allowing customers to buy products from the comfort of their home, whilst mobile or at the office. Thus, e-commerce provides added convenience for customers.

- **Access to information** – Businesses use the internet to provide detailed and accurate product information, which ultimately helps customers to make more informed buying decisions.

- **Consumer reviews** – Customers have been empowered by e-commerce, which allows them to post online consumer reviews, which can have a direct impact on the buying decisions of other customers (not all products get positive reviews). Many e-commerce businesses also use "share" and "like" buttons, which allow users to post and share information about a product via their social networks such as Facebook and Twitter.

- **Impersonal interaction** – Business to consumer (B2C) organizations are very reliant on e-commerce technologies to reach their customers. Unlike retailers, the nature of the interaction with consumers under a system of e-commerce is impersonal.

- **Barrier to entry** – Technology has helped e-commerce businesses break traditional entry barriers as set-up costs for an e-tailer are usually far less than the costs for a physical retailer. However, cultural differences still exist, such as many customers in India not trusting the use of online payments to e-tailers, which also creates entry barriers.

Figure 4.8.b E-commerce can act as a barrier to entry

Case study

PayPal is one of the world's largest suppliers of e-commerce payment systems, providing consumers and businesses with a securely encrypted payment system. Over 20 million customers use PayPal's C2C platform each year, with another 7 million businesses that use its B2C platform. It processes around 8 million online transactions each day, across 193 markets using 26 different currencies. PayPal is also available as an online app for use on smartphones and mobile devices.

E-commerce and the marketing mix

The effects of changing technology and e-commerce on the marketing mix. AO2

© IBO, 2017

The pace of change in technology and the growing use of e-commerce have major effects on the marketing mix of businesses.

Price

The Internet increases **price transparency** to the advantage of the customer who is able to gain a better knowledge of price comparisons in an instant. For example, they can use price comparison websites to compare the prices of books, toys,

Question 4.8.1   Aggregators: Price-comparison websites

Knowledgeable shoppers know that the best deals can often be found online. They also know better than to surf from one e-tailer to the next in search of the lowest prices. Instead, these savvy shoppers turn to price-comparison websites, known as aggregators, which show the prices from a number of online vendors. This helps to secure the best deal and saves the customer a huge amount of time - all within a few seconds of inputting the search.

Aggregators were originally devised for comparing the prices of computers and electronics, such as iPods, DVD players and televisions. However, there are plenty of other products catered for by aggregators, such as motor vehicles, golf clubs, flights, holiday packages and kitchen utensils. More sophisticated aggregators allow customers to narrow their searches based on various criteria, such as price, brand and functions. However, it is difficult for aggregators to link to every single online merchant. Hence, the lowest price found on one website might not be the lowest price available elsewhere. So it may still pay to shop around.

(a) Explain **two** benefits of aggregators (price comparison websites) to customers.   [4 marks]

(b) Examine the view that aggregators pose a threat to e-commerce businesses.   [6 marks]

clothes and holidays. This forces organizations to be ever more competitive in terms of pricing strategies in order to maintain their market share. Many businesses have also exploited the ability to adjust and update pricing strategies instantaneously according to the level of demand. For example, a Picasso painting (*Dora Maar au Chat*) was was sold on eBay in mid-2006 for a staggering $95 million! The Apple iTunes music store allows people to purchase and download individual tracks without having to pay the price of an entire CD album.

Figure 4.8.c Traditional price lists can be time consuming to update

The Internet also allows businesses to cut out intermediaries such as wholesalers and retailers. Instead, they can sell directly to the consumer. Thus, prices may be reduced as there are lower costs; with each intermediary there is a percentage mark-up in order to make a profit. However, e-commerce businesses (known as **e-tailers**) will usually add postage and shipping costs to the price of their products, which may then make their prices less competitive. Furthermore, e-tailers need to be aware of international trading standards and regulations that may also add to their costs, e.g. customs declarations and import taxes.

Some businesses are less vulnerable to price competition than others, such as those selling products with few, if any, substitutes and those that enjoy being a regional monopoly (the only supplier of a product in a particular geographical area). These businesses face a new threat from the emergence of e-commerce as there is no longer the same degree of privilege or autonomy in being able to set premium prices.

Finally, it is important to remember (as with all aspects of the marketing mix) that price should not be looked at in isolation. Consumers do not necessarily base their purchasing decisions

on price alone; they will tend to go for products that offer the best overall value for money.

Theory of knowledge

Can customers ever truly 'know' that they have received value for money when buying goods or services?

Case study

Trivago is a German technology company that operates a hotel price comparison website. It was founded in 2005 with €1 million from investors. In 2013, American travel company Expedia bought a 61.6% stake in *Trivago* for $632 million. *Trivago* is the world's largest online hotel search site, with over 120 million visitors per month. The company earns money from advertising using a cost-per-click (CPC) business model. Customers, such as hoteliers and other providers, pay *Trivago* for the clicks received from *Trivago* users.

Place (distribution)

Distribution is an integral part of any marketing strategy. E-commerce enables many businesses to reach a global audience at a fraction of the cost. Nevertheless, there are the logistics of ensuring that products sold online can reach the customer. The rise of e-commerce has therefore provided many opportunities for courier companies such as DHL, UPS and FedEx. In addition, the Internet has fuelled competition as countless other businesses start to realise the potential of e-commerce to reach a potentially enormous customer base.

As fewer intermediaries are used, e-commerce shortens the *channel of distribution* (see Unit 4.5). This means that businesses can benefit from enormous savings on their operating costs. Amazon is an example of a business that has benefited from being able to use the Internet as a means of distribution. Established in 1995, Amazon became the world's largest book retailer in just six years, partly due to its relatively low costs resulting from not having to use intermediaries to sell its products.

CORE

Marketing

Figure 4.8.d Books are widely available for purchase via e-commerce

E-commerce is also often more convenient for customers, e.g. there is no need to visit retail outlets as purchases can be done online. Many supermarkets have a dedicated website as an alternative distribution channel, offering online purchases, in addition to their traditional retail stores. This gives customers the added convenience of being able to shop at any time, irrespective of whether the actual supermarket is open or closed. Not-for-profit organizations, such as universities, have also used the Internet to enhance place in the marketing mix. For example, it is common for universities to have millions of e-books available to staff and students.

E-commerce offers a further advantage as a distribution channel in that different languages can be used to capture an even larger audience. Language translation is a relatively small operational cost, especially when compared to the potential benefits of being able to capture the attention of customers from around the world. Websites that have options in Chinese, English, Hindi and Spanish will cover the languages understood by most people in the world.

However, customers may not be willing to purchase certain products online, perhaps because they cannot examine or test the product, such as jewellery, pets, glasses (spectacle) or second hand cars. Cautious or more reserved customers might feel that online descriptions may not be very accurate and that it is too much of a gamble to buy products online. Instead, such customers may feel a sense of security in dealing with people directly in a physical retail outlet. They can ask questions and get immediate feedback. By contrast, online businesses offer a relatively impersonal service.

Product

The products being sold by a business can be promoted online, making it more convenient for customers to access the information at any time they choose. It also benefits the business as there is no need to stock or display all of its products, thereby reducing storage costs. Physical retail outlets face the problem of limited stocks as space is constrained. Hence, they tend to stock only the best selling products. Jeff Bezos, the founder of Amazon, started his e-commerce business by storing books in his own home. Having a book shop would have meant he needed to buy or rent premises to store all the books.

Businesses need sufficient demand before they can offer a variety of products. For example, the market for Ferrari cars limits production levels and variations; original colours only come in red, black or yellow. With the introduction of the Internet, businesses are able to sell their products to an enlarged customer base. For example, BMW uses an interactive website where customers can customise design features, such as changing the colour of a car and the styling of the alloy wheels. This not only gives customers a more interactive online shopping experience, but allows them to visualise the product in ways that may not be possible at a physical car showroom. BMW stores the information on a database to determine the most popular customer designs. This information can then be used to develop its marketing strategy, such as which cars to display in their showrooms. Dell is an example of a successful e-tailer, employing over 103,000 people and earning annual sales revenues of around $55 billion. The company sells personal computers direct to customers, who select their own specifications and add-on features, e.g. a DVD-RW drive, surround sound speakers or a wireless keyboard. Internet technologies allow businesses, such as Dell, to sell an increasingly wide range of products.

Packaging may also be less of an issue for e-tailers because they do not have to rely so much on packaging to appeal to online customers. Therefore e-tailers may be able to reduce their overall costs. This can then transform into higher profit margins for the business or reduced prices for its customers. For society, e-commerce can also mean reduced wastage as there is no need for excess packaging.

A further benefit of using e-commerce as a marketing strategy is that additional detailed information and product updates can be placed on the organization's website. Product specifications can be very detailed without causing environmental damage created by printing lots of colourful and expensive brochures. For example, instruction manuals are typically translated into several different languages, and placed inside the packaging

of products such as laptops, televisions, and games consoles. Instead, with e-commerce, customers can download the manuals in the language of their choice.

Nevertheless, certain products remain largely unaffected by the growth in e-commerce. These include perishable products (such as fresh seafood), specialist products (such as medicine) and highly expensive luxury products (such as diamonds or sports cars).

Theory of knowledge

What role do faith, intuition and reasoning have in ecommerce?

Figure 4.8.e Fresh seafood is sold in wet markets rather than via e-commerce

Question 4.8.2 Amazon.com Inc

Amazon is perhaps the most widely recognised e-commerce business in the world today, with operations in 220 countries and with annual **sales turnover** in excess of $89 billion. Founded in 1994, it was not until 2003 that the company started to make profit. From starting out as an online book store, *Amazon* has gone on to extend its product portfolio to include: CDs, DVDs, computer software, toys and games, food, jewellery, clothing, furniture, auctioneering and much more.

The success of *Amazon* is a combination of maximising market share and forming customer loyalty. This has been created by offering an unparalleled online shopping experience, with great choice, value for money and **after-sales service**. This has led to customers having trust and assurance in the brand. Jeff Bezos, founder of *Amazon*, said that branding is more important in the virtual (online) world than it is in the physical world.

(a) (i) Define the term **sales turnover**. [2 marks]

(a) (ii) Define the term **after-sales service**. [2 marks]

(b) Explain the strategies used by *Amazon* to achieve success in e-commerce. [4 marks]

(c) Evaluate the view that *Amazon* can be equally successful in selling its much broader product range as it has been with selling books online. [10 marks]

CORE

Marketing

505

Promotion

Businesses spend a huge amount of money every year to promote their products. With the growing importance of globalization, which has been fuelled by Internet technologies, many organizations have cut costs by using online marketing strategies that appeal to a global audience. For example, more detailed information can be communicated via online advertisements; customers can take their time browsing information about products which may not be possible with above-the-line promotional techniques. Marketers can also use embedded video clips, audio and images to promote their goods or services. Estate agents, for example, use the Internet to showcase homes for sale and rental; some use 360 degree digital camera technology so that clients can have a 'virtual tour' of the properties from the comfort of their home or office.

E-commerce has also enabled businesses to implement **viral marketing** as a promotional strategy (see Unit 4.5). This is similar to word-of-mouth marketing but focuses on using social networks (including emails and banner advertisements) on the Internet, allowing such promotions to be seen by potential customers around the world. Mass emails can also be sent to potential and existing clients, especially as email can be a very cost-effective form of promotion. However, unlike WOM (word of mouth) promotion, the use of viral marketing has been questioned, e.g. email spam has been criticised as an unethical and undesirable form of promotion. Similarly, many people have become accustomed to online banners and pop-up advertisements, so they tend to ignore these advertisements.

Nevertheless, online technologies can be an effective part of the marketing mix. For example, car manufacturers use the Internet to promote their corporate mission as well as promoting their product range. E-commerce allows marketing managers to create an online sales channel that supports the needs of the international community, e.g. by allowing users to select their preferred language option from the company's home page. Many organizations have set up a 'frequently asked questions' (FAQs) section on their website to pass on important information to clients. Information can be easily updated at a relatively low cost. This would not be possible with other forms of promotional media such as posters, radio announcements or TV advertisements.

Essentially, e-commerce provides an additional medium of promotion for businesses to reach their customers. As more people go online and as e-commerce continues to prosper, further opportunities present themselves for marketers using Internet technologies as a promotional tool.

Theory of knowledge

Does a framework, such as the 4Ps in the marketing mix of goods, hinder the search for knowledge in Business Management?

Question 4.8.3   Apple iTunes

The popularity of *iTunes* has never been greater. The largest *iTunes* customer, The Open University, has over 20 million *iTunes* downloads. According to research consultants Nielsen Media Research, teenagers are twice as likely to visit the *iTunes* site compared with other age groups. Like many other rival websites that have followed, *iTunes* allows customers to purchase hand-picked songs for downloading. This saves customers money as they do not need to purchase a whole music album. Founded in 2001, *iTunes* has added other **products** to its online store, including music videos, TV shows, iPhone apps, audio books, e-books and movies. These products can be purchased at a fraction of the price compared with CDs, DVDs or hardback books.

(a) Define the **products**.   *[2 marks]*

(b) Describe **two** possible reasons for the huge increase in demand for *iTunes* products.   *[4 marks]*

(c) To what extent has e-commerce saved the music and movie industries from copyright violation and piracy?
                                                                                                                          [10 marks]

Types of e-commerce

The difference between the following types of e-commerce: business to business (B2B), business to consumer (B2C) and consumer to consumer (C2C). AO2
© IBO, 2017

E-commerce can be classified as business to business (B2B), business to consumer (B2C) or consumer to consumer (C2C).

Business to business (B2B)

B2B refers to e-commerce catered for the needs of other businesses. Examples of B2B services include: corporate banking, suppliers of equipment and spare parts, insurance, general maintenance and advertising agency services. Note that B2B technically exists both online and off-line, although the term is usually used in the context of e-commerce. China's Alibaba.com, owned by Alibaba Group, is the world's largest B2B e-commerce provider, with operations in more than 200 countries.

Specialists in the B2B field often argue that consumer marketing strategies (used by B2C businesses) are not suitable or sufficient for marketing B2B products and services. This is because B2B involves professional buyers, who have a totally different agenda. For instance, look at how the B2C telecom operators approach their marketing – targeting teenagers, who cannot really afford the services, and totally neglecting the business community. It is the latter segment of the market that really need mobile telephones with Internet access and who could afford to pay for it. Hence, the focus of marketing campaigns from mobile phone operators becomes somewhat questionable.

Case study

Alibaba Group was founded in 1999 by Jack Ma, who had previously taught English in China. The company's revenue exceeds that of Amazon and eBay, combined! Jack Ma started the e-commerce business with just $60,000 and turned it into a multi-billion dollar business in less than 10 years. Today, more than 60% of the parcels delivered in China are attributed to *Alibaba Group*. By 2015, Jack Ma had become the richest man in China.

Theory of knowledge

In 2013, *The Economist* magazine reported that *Alibaba Group* had a market valuation of between $55 billion to $120 billion. Is there any value in a claim of such large variation?

Business to consumer (B2C)

B2C refers to e-commerce directly catered for the end-user, i.e. the consumer. For example, consumers can download music and learning materials (such as e-books and revision apps). Some of the most prominent English language B2C businesses are outlined in Box 4.8.a.

Box 4.8.a   Top 10 visited English language websites

1. Google - world's most popular search engine
2. YouTube - world's top video sharing site
3. Facebook - world's most popular social networking site
4. Baidu - China's top search engine
5. Wikipedia - world's largest online collaborative encyclopaedia
6. Reddit - user-generated social news links and discussions website
7. Yahoo! - internet portal offering search results, news, chatrooms and email
8. QQ - China's largest and most used Internet service portal
9. Taobao - China and the world's largest C2C online shopping platform
10. Amazon - probably the most well-known online retailer.

Source: adapted from http://www.alexa.com/topsites

Many businesses are engaged in both B2B and B2C. Google and Yahoo! not only allow customers to carry out searches on their websites but also sell advertising slots to other businesses. They operate a 'pay-per-click' scheme, where the advertisers pay Google and Yahoo! each time a person clicks on the advertising banner.

Question 4.8.4   HMV

In 2006, *HMV* announced that sales at its music stores and *Waterstone*'s bookshops fell due to customers switching to *Amazon* and supermarkets. An increasing number of people download music or buy CDs, DVDs and books online and/or in supermarkets. Not surprisingly then, *HMV* declared that it would end its partnership with *Amazon* Instead, *HMV* chose to set up its own website. *HMV* also chose to reduce prices in response to these threats. Established in 1899, *HMV* continued to struggle and in 2014 its flagship store in Oxford Street, London – the largest music store in the world – closed down.

(a) Outline why *HMV* may be classed as a B2C business.   *[2 marks]*

(b) Explain why there has been an increasing trend to buy music and books online.   *[4 marks]*

(c) Suggest one other strategy, apart from reduced prices, that *HMV* could have used to prevent its sales from declining further.   *[4 marks]*

Figure 4.8.f Most e-commerce transactions are completed using credit card

Case study

In late 2013, the last remaining 300 *Blockbuster* video film rental stores closed down in the USA, due to unrelenting competition from online digital video. This resulted in around 2800 people losing their jobs in early 2014. *Blockbuster*'s bankruptcy was blamed on the huge success of *Netflix,* the TV and film online streaming service. In 2014, *Netflix* reported that global subscriber numbers exceeded 50 million. By 2018, *Netflix* had more than 125 million subscribers worldwide.

Consumer to consumer (C2C)

Consumer to consumer is an e-commerce platform, such as eBay, that enables customers to trade with each other. C2C marketing has gained immense popularity following the arrival of the Internet, enabling customers to have greater interaction with each other. C2C websites earn their money from charging fees to the sellers who list their items for sale, e.g. second-hand goods (such as cars, music equipment and furniture) or private tuition services. Taoboa.com (owned by Alibaba Group) is the world's largest C2C business and is one of the ten most visited websites globally. Taoboa features over a billion products on its website.

C2C is forecast to continue its growth in the future because it is highly cost-effective. It minimises the advertising cost to consumers as third party providers are not involved. However, C2C suffers from a lack of quality control for the buyer and lacks payment guarantees from the buyer. For example, consumers may lack the confidence to pay other people, preferring to buy from an online business instead (B2C). Nevertheless, the increased use of secure online payment providers, such as PayPal and Alipay, has made C2C much more accessible and efficient.

The benefits of e-commerce

The benefits of e-commerce to firms and consumers. AO3

© IBO, 2017

- E-commerce provides another **source of revenue** for many organizations. For example, Google and Facebook earn revenues from selling advertising space ('sponsored links') on their web pages. In late 2013, Facebook reported its first quarterly profits in excess of $2 billion. In addition to traditional 'walk-in' stores, customers can now shop online from the comfort of their own home or office. E-commerce can therefore help a firm to increase its customer base.

- The Internet gives businesses another **channel of distribution**. It allows organizations to sell to anyone in any part of the world at any time of the day. E-commerce is set to grow as more people and businesses are able to access broadband technologies and because of improved confidence in Internet security.

- E-commerce provides greater **flexibility** for organizations to respond more quickly to competitors. For example, a company can publicise revisions to its services and products (such as price changes) much faster via its website than through printing updated hardcopy materials. IKEA, the home furnishing giant, prints and distributes a colossal 208 million copies of its catalogue each year; without their huge product range being available on the Internet, this figure would be much higher.

- **Reduced packaging**. Many businesses require their customers to use the Internet to download or view manuals (instructional guides), rather than the traditional method of printing these guides in several different languages. This not only reduces waste and excess packaging, but also cuts production costs. Furthermore, updating technical information for innovative products such as an Apple iPhone or an Amazon Kindle can be done easier online.

- Retail outlets have higher **overheads** due to costs such as rent, storage, insurance and staffing. These costs can be reduced by operating online. Hence, businesses are able to pass on some of these savings to customers. Customers can also save on associated transactions costs (such as travel time and transportation costs) as there is no need for face-to-face trading.

- **Operating costs** can be reduced by e-commerce. For example, newspaper firms such as Singapore's *Straits Times* or the USA's *Wall Street Journal* run their subscription online editions for a tiny fraction of the costs of their paper-based publications. The *New York Times* sells single articles as well as offering bundle packages for those wishing to purchase a larger number of archived articles. The marginal cost of supplying extra online editions to new customers is close to zero – the use of the Internet means that there is no significant difference in the firm's total costs if it sells 1,000 or 100,000 online subscriptions. Banks and utility companies (such as gas, electricity and water providers) use online bills and statements to save costs and to protect the environment.

- Customers have more **choice** and **convenience** because e-commerce reduces many barriers to entry, thereby allowing unknown firms to set up and compete with established businesses. For example, Amazon revolutionised the way that books are sold. Customers can book tickets for the cinema, theatre, concert, theme park or overseas holiday at any time of the day from the comfort of their home or office (see Figure 4.8.g). Search functions on company websites also make it quicker to find products and for orders to be placed with relative ease.

Figure 4.8.g Customers can book concert tickets online

In summary, e-commerce has essentially cut costs and intensified competition. Hence, businesses can reduce prices yet offer a wider choice to customers.

Question 4.8.5   Christmas online shopping

Retailers looking forward to a bumper Christmas have turned to online sales. With so much competition during the festive season, a greater number of online retailers have lured customers with promises of free postage and delivery in order to take the hassle out of Christmas shopping. Popular items bought on the Internet during the world's busiest trading season include consumer electronics, children's toys and clothing.

(a)   Describe **two** opportunities that e-commerce presents for businesses.   *[4 marks]*

(b)   Explain the benefits to consumers using the Internet as a channel of distribution.   *[4 marks]*

Case study

In December 2013, the British Bankers Association reported that the number of robberies on British bank branches had dropped by 90% in the past decade. This was largely due to a number of innovative technologies making it extremely difficult to rob a bank, e.g. CCTV, protective screens that rise in less than a second, and special disorientating fog designed to disperse criminals.

The costs of e-commerce

The costs of e-commerce to firms and consumers. AO3

© IBO, 2014

- **Set-up costs** can be high. Many businesses hire specialists to set up and market their website and e-commerce operations. For example, arranging electronic payment systems can be very costly. Additional **running costs** also need to be considered, e.g. the costs of postage, packaging and distribution.

- Credit card companies impose **finance charges** for using their services (for online payments). These charges may be passed onto the customers in the form of higher prices or absorbed by the business by accepting lower profit margins.

- **Fraudulent trade** takes place. For example, there is no way that a buyer can authenticate items being sold on eBay or other C2C websites. The increase in online fraud and identity theft (when criminals use other people's personal details to gain access to bank accounts and credit cards) also costs businesses billions of dollars each year.

- **Spam** and unethical marketing opportunities. For example, email hoaxes are widespread, with the intention of geting hold of personal email accounts for sending on advertising spam (inappropriate and unsolicited online publicity and Internet marketing messages). Pop-up advertisements on websites can also be annoying and waste the customer's time. According to InsideSpam.com, around 40% of daily emails are considered to be spam.

- E-commerce is **unsuitable** for some businesses and customers. Although e-commerce can be cost-effective, customers may find browsing online quite time consuming and onerous. It is okay to use the Internet to search for more information about a motor car before making a purchase, but the customer will still want to visit a showroom to see the physical product and to take a test drive. Moreover, customers cannot simply take the online-purchased products home as there is a time lag between purchase and delivery of the products. Many supermarkets deliver fresh fruits and vegetables, but most customers still prefer to select their own from a retail outlet. It may also prove difficult or inconvenient to return faulty products that were purchased online.

- E-commerce is reliant on advanced technology that is not necessarily available to all businesses or in all countries. In addition, websites and web pages need to be regularly updated, yet remain easy for viewers to browse and follow. The maintenance costs must therefore be considered by online retailers.

- There are far more Internet web pages than there are people in the world. To deal with this, search engines such as Google, Bing, Baidu and Yahoo! have become very popular. Nevertheless, many websites and web pages

Question 4.8.6   Online banking fraud

The UK's finance watchdog, the Financial Services Authority (FSA), has revealed that half of Internet users are either 'extremely' or 'very concerned' about the risks of online fraud, especially as the number of cases is on the rise. For example, bogus online banking websites have been set up to capture people's personal banking details.

In response, banks such as HSBC have tightened up online security. They claim to never ask for personal details and passwords in an email. HSBC customers are issued with a keychain security gadget that generates a random six-digit password based on a highly complex mathematical logarithm. The security code is used in addition to online usernames and passwords.

(a) Outline **two** limitations of e-commerce to organizations such as banks.   *[4 marks]*

(b) To what extent does e-commerce benefit customers of banking services?   *[10 marks]*

---

have too much information or too many high resolution graphics and photos, so loading time is slow. Information overload can also mean that people prefer to visit a physical retail outlet and engage in human interaction to purchase their goods and services.

- The Internet is volatile as it is prone to hackers and breakdowns. Maintenance and upgrades will further add to the costs of e-commerce. For example, an earthquake on Boxing Day 2006 in Southeast Asia severely disrupted Internet services for more than two weeks in Taiwan, Singapore, Hong Kong, Vietnam, South Korea and Japan. In 2018, Visa faced huge problems as retailers throughout Europe were unable to accept credit card payments from its customers, due to hardware problems.

- International e-commerce can cause major problems for a country's currency flows. When paying for foreign goods and services via e-commerce, domestic currencies flow out of the country causing problems such as a fall in the value of its exchange rate and a fall in the country's currency reserves.

- A shift to e-commerce from traditional methods of retailing may result in job losses. Businesses need to devise strategies to deal with redundancies (see Unit 2.1). Moreover, job losses can harm industrial relations at work (see Unit 2.6) and give the organization a poor corporate image.

E-commerce and the CUEGIS concepts

E-commerce has made a huge impact on the way in which business is conducted throughout the world. It has accelerated the growth in world trade, with wider market opportunities and improved efficiency. As a business strategy, it presents many opportunities for businesses to grow, whatever their size. Businesses are selling more products and services online, in more markets and in more languages than ever before. In the UK, B2C e-commerce exceeded £100bn ($160bn) for the first time in 2010. Global e-commerce trade surpassed $1 trillion for the first time in 2012. In the USA, the value of e-commerce exceeds $1 billion per day! According to Business.com, China's annual online sales are around $672 billion (approximately the same as Switzerland's GDP, and larger than the GDP of Saudi Arabia, Argentina and Taiwan). The benefits also mean that businesses can provide much more information about their products and services than would otherwise be the case. Hence, having an online presence has become much more of a strategic priority for managers.

In her book *e.Volve!*, Rosabeth Moss Kanter (2001) suggested that the Internet could connect everyone throughout the world; a clear opportunity for businesses with a global perspective. Having conducted thousands of interviews with businesses throughout the world, she suggests that the best managers in the digital era will be those with curiosity, imagination and good communication skills in a globalized context.

Change through e-commerce has also empowered consumers through price transparency, convenience and more choice. For example, websites such as tripadvisor.com allow customers to type in the name of hotel or resort that they are planning to stay at, and to read comments by customers who have stayed at those hotels. Businesses therefore have to place an even greater emphasis on their global marketing strategies because customers are able to access information easily, from any part of the world. E-commerce is also likely to reduce the influence and importance of people, physical evidence, and packaging in the marketing mix. These cannot, of course, be ignored but their relative importance for many e-tailers is likely to decline.

However, managers need to be aware of the legal, social and cultural implications of e-commerce. Generic responsibilities include the careful treatment of personal data (Data Protection Acts impose limits on how businesses can use their clients' personal details), compliance with copyright legislation, and consideration of online security for customers. Online businesses trading overseas need to consider the external environment (see Unit 1.5) such as fluctuating exchange rates and different tax systems. Furthermore, the threat of job losses due to the escalating reliance on e-commerce means that businesses are expected to manage this process in an ethical and socially responsible way.

Furthermore, having an online presence does not guarantee success. Almost all large companies have a dedicated e-commerce platform, and the resources to maintain it, so this creates another form of competition. One of the biggest mistakes made by many businesses is to over-complicate their homepage. According to consultancy firm Business Bricks Ltd., the average attention span of people browsing the Internet is only 9 seconds. Another study by the BBC showed that most online shoppers wait up to just 4 seconds for a webpage to load before abandoning it. These issues mean that any business strategy needs to consider:

- Prioritising information that goes on the homepage of a company's website

- Marketing only the most unique or interesting benefits of the business, its products or services.

The vast amount of information on the Internet means that businesses have perhaps 10–15 seconds at best to captivate the minds of customers browsing the web. This idea is known as the **elevator pitch**, which refers to the short time span available to hold the interest of customers. The concept doesn't just apply to e-commerce; think about why most TV advertisements rarely

go beyond 30 seconds. There is no point in telling customers all the reasons why they should buy your products – it is more effective to keep the message simple and to focus on the key benefits on offer. Essentially, businesses have to ask what they want potential online customers to do when visiting their websites.

Figure 4.8.h The elevator pitch: E-commerce firms have only a few seconds to impress customers

Following the strategic implementation of e-commerce, managers need to review the effectiveness of their e-commerce strategies. Methods that can be used to judge the success of an e-commerce strategy include:

- Increased sales revenue following the launch (or relaunch) of a firm's website and e-commerce operations.

- Larger proportion of sales revenue coming from the e-commerce section of the business.

- Higher market share following the implementation of an e-commerce strategy.

- Greater brand exposure and awareness (although this may be difficult to measure).

Despite the benefits of e-commerce, many analysts argue that businesses have yet to exploit the Internet's true potential to reach a global audience and to reduce costs. Business strategy that successfully integrates e-commerce in a globalized world, with effective organizational change (see Unit 2.2), can lead to improved efficiency and productivity. Thus, it can give organizations a competitive advantage in today's dynamic and ever-changing business environment. Nevertheless, the advantages of e-commerce depend largely on the extent to which an organization uses and relies on e-commerce. Hence, e-commerce should be used alongside other strategies. Most commentators believe that the rapid growth in e-commerce since the late 1990s is set to continue and significantly change the way in which business is conducted.

IB Learner Profile – Be an inquirer and be knowledgeable

Investigate the e-commerce strategy for a company of your choice. A good starting point, if you are interested in the online strategy of USA clothing company Gap, is here: http://goo.gl/7j0rcp.

Exam tip !

Airbnb is an American C2C business, established in 2008. It helps people to lease or rent short-term accommodation, such as apartments in city centres, holiday homes , homestays (with a spare bedroom), or hotel rooms. Customers can rent out their spare accommodation (such as a spare room or an entire home). Airbnb facilitates the booking and payment processes for its users, and charges a commission (fee) for its services. It operates in over 190 countries, employs over 3,100 people and earns over $2.6 in annual revenues, but does not own any real estate.

Case study

Alibaba Group was founded in 1999 by Jack Ma, who had previously taught English in China. The company's revenue exceeds that of Amazon and eBay, combined! Jack Ma started the e-commerce business with just $60,000 and turned it into a multi-billion dollar business in less than 10 years. Today, more than 60% of the parcels delivered in China are attributed to *Alibaba Group*. By 2015, Jack Ma had become the richest man in China.

Exam tip !

Follow the author on Twitter for more revision tips and exam advice prior to the Business Management examinations: paulhoang88

Theory of knowledge

Is it possible for social media websites, such as Facebook, Twitter and LinkedIn, to know you better than you know yourself?

CUEGIS Essay

With reference to a business of your choice, examine how **change** has influenced the organization's e-commerce **strategy**.   *[20 marks]*

REVIEW QUESTIONS

1. What is meant by e-commerce?

2. What are the main features of e-commerce?

3. Distinguish between B2B, B2C and C2C.

4. Outline the advantages and disadvantages of e-commerce to businesses.

5. Outline the advantages and disadvantages of e-commerce to customers.

6. Explain how product in the marketing mix is affected by e-commerce.

7. Explain how price in the marketing mix is affected by e-commerce.

8. Explain how promotion in the marketing mix is affected by e-commerce.

CORE

Marketing

9. Explain how place in the marketing mix is affected by e-commerce.

10. Distinguish between spam and viral marketing.

KEY TERMS

B2B (business to business) refers to e-commerce conducted directly for business customers rather than the end user (consumers), e.g. Amazon supplies books to retailers such as Barnes & Noble.

B2C (business to consumer) refers to e-commerce business conducted directly for the end-user (the consumer), e.g. Amazon selling books directly to private individuals.

C2C (consumer to consumer) is an e-commerce platform, such as eBay and Taobao, that enables customers to trade with each other.

E-commerce (electronic commerce) is the trading of goods and services via the Internet, electronic systems and computer networks.

E-tailers are businesses that operate predominantly online, such as Alibaba.com, eBay, Facebook and Google. They are different from retailers that operate physical stores and outlets.

The **elevator pitch** refers to the idea that marketers only have a short time span available to hold the interest of customers. It is an important consideration for e-marketers when designing their websites.

Price transparency refers to the openness in communication about prices being charged by businesses. E-commerce allows customers to access price comparisons quite easily.

Spam refers to unsolicited and superfluous marketing messages via email or pop-up advertisements. The common purpose of 'spamming' is to advertise a firm's products, such as financial services or computer software.

Spam refers to unsolicited marketing messages

Viral marketing is a promotional technique that relies on the use of online social networks, such as email, blogs, Twitter and YouTube.

5.1 The role of operations management

"You can have any colour you want … as long as it's black." - Henry Ford (1863–1947), founder of the Ford Motor Company

SL/HL content	Assessment objective
Operations management and its relationship with other business functions	AO1
Operations management in organizations producing goods and/or services	AO2
Operations management strategies and practices for ecological, social (human resource) and economic sustainability	AO3

© IBO, 2017

Operations management and business functions

Operations management and its relationship with other business functions. AO1

© IBO, 2017

Operations management, often referred to as production, is concerned with providing the right goods and services in the right quantities and at the right quality level in a cost-effective and timely manner. The role of operations management impacts on all functional areas of a business. For example, a change in production methods (see Unit 5.2) can be caused by numerous reasons, including attempts to achieve greater efficiency (see Unit 5.3), the use of just in time production (see Unit 5.5) or simply because of the growth of the business. These changes, whatever the reasons, have a direct impact on the other functional areas of the organization.

- **Marketing implications** The production method used will affect both the quality and the individuality of the product. The output of an exclusive product means that it can be marketed at a high price due to its uniqueness and high quality. Packaging, physical evidence and people also play an important part in the overall marketing mix. For example, customers of Bugatti are invited to have a meeting with a sales manager to discuss their personal requirements for the supercar. By contrast, mass produced goods are standardised. There are likely to be plenty of substitutes available on the market, so prices are much more competitive. Promotional strategies are also more impersonal and aggressive in order to gain market share from rival firms. Businesses that rely on high volume sales to gain high profits (such as supermarkets), aim to increase the number of distribution channels to ensure maximum sales.

- **HRM implications** The role of operations management has a direct impact on human resource management. For example, a change in production methods can either reduce or increase the size of the workforce. Many multinational companies managed to enter China (prior to its membership of the World Trade Organization) by setting up labour-intensive operations. For instance, Black & Decker (the power tools manufacturer) hires a large number of workers in its Shenzhen plant even though many of the operations could easily be automated. Alternatively, mass production uses capital-intensive technologies so tends to deskill the workforce. Motivation can also be affected by aspects of operations management. Whilst flow production suffers from a lack of teamwork and group dynamics, cell production (see Unit 5.2) benefits from using the individual skills of people working within a team. There are also training implications. Job production techniques require more training whereas mass production requires minimal instructional training only. It is relatively easy to hire workers for mass production whereas attractive remuneration packages may be needed to entice specialist workers for job production. Crisis management (see Unit 5.7) can be highly disruptive and unsettling for people, so effective contingency plans are needed.

515

- **Finance implications** Capital intensity (see Unit 5.2) and lean production (see Unit 5.3) require heavy investment in machinery and equipment. This is expensive, although with mass production the fixed investment costs can be spread over time. Capital-intensive organizations are likely to use *investment appraisal* techniques to assess whether the risks are worthwhile (see Unit 3.8). They are also likely to need external sources of finance (see Unit 3.1) to fund the investment projects. A *contingency fund* (finance kept for emergency use) may also be reserved in case of machinery breakdowns or late deliveries from a supplier, which would delay production. By contrast, labour-intensive production requires a greater proportion of a firm's cost to go into remunerating workers with wages, salaries and other financial benefits.

Figure 5.1.a The role of operations management has a direct impact on a firm's finances

Operations management and the provision of goods and services

Operations management in organizations producing goods and/or services. AO2

© IBO, 2017

Operations management does not only apply to manufacturing because production is concerned with all four sectors of the economy:

- **Primary sector** – extracting raw materials, harvesting crops and rearing animals, e.g. mining, agriculture and fishing (see Figure 5.1.b).

- **Secondary sector** – turning natural resources into processed or finished goods, e.g. steel production and car manufacturing.

- **Tertiary sector** – the provision of services, e.g. finance, insurance, travel and tourism, transportation, and healthcare.

- **Quaternary sector** – the provision of intellectual, knowledge-based activities that generate and share information, e.g. ICT, R&D, consultancy services, and scientific research.

Figure 5.1.b Fishing is part of primary sector production

Essentially, the role of production is to turn factors of production into the output of goods and services cost-effectively.

The factors of production (land, labour, capital and enterprise) are commonly known to marketing and production managers as the *Five Ms* – materials, manpower, money, machines and management, i.e. the available resources to a business. The 5 Ms can be a useful tool in devising both marketing and production plans. They are combined in a cost-effective way to ensure that there is **value-added** during the 'production' stage of the transformation process, i.e. the value of the output is greater than the costs of production, thereby earning a profit for the business (see Figure 5.1.c).

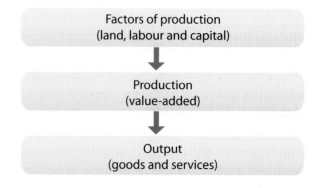

Figure 5.1.c The transformation (production) process

To ensure that output can be sold for more than the input costs, production managers need to deal with several key aspects of operations management, including:

- Methods of production (see Unit 5.2 and see Figure 5.1.d)

- Size, scope and timing of production (see Units 1.6 and 1.7)

- Production planning, e.g. stock control (see Unit 5.5)

- Quality control systems (see Unit 5.3)

- Research & development and innovation (see Unit 5.6).

Figure 5.1.d Bottled water is mass produced using computerised systems and quality controllers

The role of operations management looks at the need for businesses to decide how production should take place. For example, the type of product (such as a haircut or a commercial building) will affect the production method chosen. Even the same kind of product can be produced using different methods, such as Casio calculators and Rolex watches.

Operations management strategies and practices

Operations management strategies and practices for ecological, social (human resource) and economic sustainability. AO3

© IBO, 2017

Operations management has an important role in ensuring sustainability by creating a balance between the ecological, social and economic needs of people today and those of future generations. This might include the use of green technologies and recycling, for example. **Sustainability** is a concept that

promotes intergenerational equity, i.e. production enables consumption of goods and services for the people of today without compromising the consumption for the people of tomorrow. It is about meeting the needs of the current generation in such a way that it does not jeopardise the needs of future generations.

There has been growing interest in the reporting of **the triple bottom line** (TBL or 3BL) for-profit, non-profit and government organizations. The triple bottom line provides a framework for sustainable business operations, founded on three "pillars" (see Figure 5.1.e). Increasingly, businesses report more than profits (the traditional 'bottom' line), and choose to also report on their impact on the planet (ecological sustainability) and people (social sustainability). TBL was coined by John Elkington in 1994, a British and internationally renowned author of sustainability.

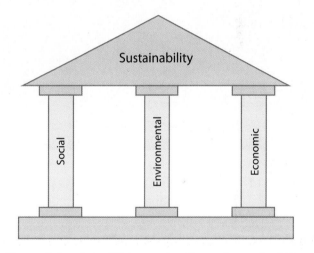

Figure 5.1.e John Elkington's pillars of sustainability (1994)

Ecological sustainability

Ecological sustainability refers to the capacity of the natural environment to meet the needs of the current generation without jeopardising the ability of future generations to meet their needs. For example, overfishing or the continual destruction of rain forests are not ecologically sustainable. A lack of ecological sustainability means that production can exhaust (deplete) the earth's natural resources for future generations. Ecological sustainability requires efficient and sensible use of the world's scarce resources so that they do not become exhausted or over polluted.

Figure 5.1.f Ecological sustainability involves efficient waste management

The world's population reached one billion people in 1804. It reached 2 billion by 1930 (some 126 years later). However, with improved standards of living, the global population reached 3 billion just 30 years later in 1960. It has since more than doubled to over 7 billion (this milestone was reached in 2011). The UN estimates the world's population will rise to 8 billion by 2030, although other estimates put this as early as 2023 (see Box 5.1.b). Clearly, such exponential population growth puts huge pressure on the world's scarce resources. This makes ecological sustainability a key priority for many production managers and business executives. Hence, ecological sustainability requires production (operations management) to consider more environmentally friendly practices, such as those in Box 5.1.a.

Box 5.1.a Ecologically sustainable practices

- **Green technologies** Environmentally friendly innovations that consider the long-term impact on the environment, e.g. renewable energy sources such as solar panels and wind turbines.
- **Recycling** Turning waste products (such as bottles) into reusable materials. It is the process of making new products from those that have already been used for another purpose. It ensures that used products are disposed of in an appropriate and environmentally friendly way.
- **Ecological footprint** This measures the impact of resource consumption and waste production on the natural environment. It assesses whether people are living beyond the capacity of the planet, e.g. how many people drive, or whether executives really need to fly (in business or first class).
- **Cradle to cradle production** Putting an end to traditional single-use manufactured products ('cradle to grave') by creating products that can be easily recycled and re-used.
- **Conservation** Using Earth's finite resources in a sustainable way by using renewable resources (such as trees and fish) at a rate that enables these resources to self-replenish. It is also about reducing the reliance and use of non-renewable resources, such as coal and oil.
- **Preservation** Protecting Earth's resources by reducing the human impact on the physical environment (e.g. national parks), the natural environment (e.g. rainforests) and the cultural environment (e.g. ancient civilization and heritage sites).

Figure 5.1.g Preservation of heritage sites is an important aspect of ecological sustainability

Social sustainability

The social aspect of sustainability examines social interactions and structures that are necessary for sustainable development, i.e. it is the ability of the society to develop in such a way that it meets the social well-being needs of the current and future generations. For example, the world's population continues to grow at an increasing rate (see Box 5.1.b), resulting in greater levels of consumption and depletion of the planet's natural resources. Social sustainability enables society to optimize the quality of life for people and their descendants. By contrast, social barriers prevent a community from advancing, e.g. poverty, unemployment and social exclusion (including racism and gender inequalities).

Male business leaders need to accept women as equals if there is to be social sustainability and development. Former South African President Nelson Mandela (1994–1999) said, "*For every moment we remain silent, we conspire against our women*". Indeed, embracing social justice can bring many business opportunities in terms of recruitment, retention and reputation. Gender discrimination (see Box 5.1.c) represents an inefficient allocation of resources for society as a whole. Gender equality is fundamental to both economic and human development. From a humanitarian viewpoint, removing social inequalities gives communities a better chance of achieving sustainable development.

Box 5.1.b	World population milestones:
• 8 billion:	2023 (est)
• 7 billion:	2011
• 6 billion:	1999
• 5 billion:	1987
• 4 billion:	1974
• 3 billion:	1960
• 2 billion:	1930
• 1 billion:	1804
Source: http://www.worldometers.info/world-population/	

A key social role of businesses is job creation, thus directly helping to foster economic and social prosperity and reducing poverty. In addition to creating jobs and paying taxes, many countries expect businesses to fulfil their corporate social responsibilities (see Unit 1.3). Not doing so can attract unwanted media publicity. Hence, an increasing number of businesses apply corporate social responsibility (CSR) in operations management practices.

Being socially responsible means the business consults with internal stakeholders (e.g. employees and shareholders) and external stakeholders (e.g. customers, suppliers, the local community and the government) to determine their social priorities.

Box 5.1.c   Gender inequalities

- According to the UN, discrimination against women and girls is the most persistent form of inequality.
- According to the Australian government, two-thirds of the 800 million people in the world who lack basic literacy skills are female.
- Estimates from the UN Development Programme show that in South Asian countries like India and Pakistan, fewer than 35% of women do paid work.
- Cambodia, China, and Vietnam do much better with nearly 70% of women in paid work – well above the global average of 53%.

Theory of knowledge

If there is no universally agreed definition of 'human rights', can this ever be achieved globally for social sustainability?

Theory of knowledge

Can gender equality and morality ever be mutually exclusive? Are the concepts of equity and diversity incompatible in society?

Economic sustainability

Economic sustainability refers to development that meets the economic needs of the present generation using existing available resources without compromising the ability of future generations to meet their needs. It requires production managers to consider which resources (land, labour, capital and enterprise) are not used efficiently in order to correct the situation.

More of a threat to economic wellbeing is the overuse of resources that makes it ever more difficult to sustain output of goods and services over time. For example, the use of fossil fuels as energy sources (e.g. coal, oil and natural gas) has huge repercussions on the natural environment, including climate change. The rapid economic development in China and India, for example, has resulted in high levels of pollution and environmental damage. Globally, economic activity has led to the rapid depletion of the world's finite resources, especially non-renewable resources. With the continual rise in world population growth, the question for businesses is whether economic growth and its associated impact on the natural environment is sustainable.

Case study

In 2014, Panasonic introduced a wage premium to expatriate workers in China. The Japanese electronics company became the world's first company to introduce a higher pay scheme to compensate employees sent to China due to the country's hazardous air pollution. According to the US embassy in Beijing, air pollution in the capital is more than 16 times the World Health Organization's (WHO) safety guideline.

Common mistake

Some students comment that achieving zero pollution is the solution to economic and social sustainability. This is incorrect as the only way to ensure zero pollution is to have no output! Sustainability is about managing operations in such a way that businesses can still thrive in the future.

Economic sustainability encourages businesses to be more responsible in their use of resources, such as selecting raw materials that are more environmentally friendly and designing products that are easier to recycle or that are biodegradable (see Figure 5.1.h). Paying attention to sustainability improves the chances of business operations in the long run. However, in striving to maximise profits, the potentially higher costs of operating in a sustainable way mean that businesses often do not make efficient use of available resources. Resistance to change or to embrace the ethos of sustainability creates further obstacles for economic sustainability.

Figure 5.1.h Recycling is vital for sustainability

Nevertheless, most analysts believe that economic sustainability is vital for any business striving to establish profitability over the long term. This will enable the business to continue operating year after year. From this perspective, economic sustainability as an operations management strategy helps a business to survive, thrive and contribute to the economic wellbeing of others via the creation of jobs and wealth.

Question 5.1.1   Plastic carrier bag levy

Prior to July 2009, Hong Kong used an average of 30 million non-biodegradable plastic carrier bags every day! For a relatively small population of 7 million people, this meant the average person in Hong Kong was using more than four plastic carrier bags every day, often on a single-use basis. This staggering figure meant that the country's landfills struggled to cope with the volume of plastic carrier bags being thrown away. Hong Kong's introduction of a HK$0.50 tax (6.5 US cents) on the use of each carrier bag has encouraged people to use eco-friendly reusable shopping bags and be aware of **environmental sustainability**. Demand for plastic carrier bags fell by 85% within the first two days of the tax being introduced. The decision by lawmakers followed similar moves made in other countries such as China (in 2009) and Ireland (in 2002).

Source: adapted from *South China Morning Post*

(a) Define the term **environmental sustainability**.   *[2 marks]*

(b) Justify the use of taxes to achieve environmental sustainability.   *[10 marks]*

The role of operations management and the CUEGIS concepts

In an ever changing business environment, organizations are constantly trying to improve their efficiency. In its simplest sense, efficiency occurs when a business operates at its maximum output with minimum costs per unit of output. Efficiency is, therefore, a measure of how well a business uses its resources in the production process. An inefficient business can have high unit costs due to its idle resources (human and capital resources that are not used effectively, yet contribute towards the firm's costs). Hence, such organizations become uncompetitive and might not survive in the long-term. Many businesses have collapsed or been taken over due to their inefficiencies in production. For example, Concorde proved highly unprofitable despite its unique selling point (supersonic air travel), and ceased operation in 2003. Changes in the industry, such as the introduction of low-cost airlines, caused major problems for Concorde.

Technological progress and innovations have meant that productivity can often be improved by using modern equipment and machinery. **Productivity** is the rate at which inputs are transformed into outputs and are a good measure of a firm's efficiency level. For example, the productivity of Post Office staff can be measured by the number of customers that are served per period of time. Alternatively, managers can also use financial and non-financial methods of motivation (see Unit 2.4) to raise labour productivity. However, achieving higher levels of productivity and efficiency is not straightforward. In theory, increased capital intensity can increase both productivity and efficiency. However, in reality, businesses may not be able to afford such technologies. There is also likely to be resistance to change from the workforce due to the uncertainty of new working practices and the threat of redundancies. Businesses will strive to stay competitive by looking at the various aspects of their operations and how they can raise productivity levels.

Modern management thinking has led to strategies to consider more efficient and sustainable production, such as the use of total quality management in the workplace (see Unit 5.3) and just-in-time stock management (see Unit 5.5). Business strategy cannot simultaneously and sustainably aim for high quality products at low prices. Instead, strategy must focus on either earning high profit margins by selling unique products of outstanding quality, or on selling mass market products that earn low profit margins but sell in large volumes. There is a potential trade-off between quality and productivity; businesses cannot simply speed up production of goods without sacrificing quality standards. The decision of operations managers will therefore have an implication on the type of production method used (see Unit 5.2). This decision is further complicated with the globalization of many products and markets.

Cultural attitudes also have a direct impact on the role of operations management and sustainability. Elkington argues that organizations need to embrace social justices, such as the fair treatment of women in the workplace. Such a cultural shift can result in many business opportunities, such as productivity gains, improved staff morale, and a more positive corporate image. Ethically, greater gender equality is part of the United Nations Development Programme (UNDP)'s Sustainable Development Goals. Hence, a change in the culture of empowering women is vital to both economic and social sustainability in the long term.

CUEGIS Essay

With reference to an organization that you have studied, examine how **change** has impacted on its sustainable business **strategy**. *[20 marks]*

REVIEW QUESTIONS

1. What is meant by operations management?

2. What is the relationship between operations management and the other functions of a business (finance, human resources and marketing)?

3. What are the four sectors of an economy?

4. How does operations management apply to all production sectors of the economy?

5. What is the production (or transformation) process?

6. How does the production process 'add value' to output of goods and services?

7. What is meant by sustainability?

8. What is meant by ecological sustainability?

9. What is meant by social sustainability?

10. What is meant by economic sustainability?

KEY TERMS

Capital intensive means that the manufacturing or provision of a product relies heavily on machinery and equipment, e.g. automated production systems. Hence, capital costs account for most of a capital-intensive firm's overall production costs.

Ecological footprint measures the impact of resource consumption and waste production on the natural environment. It assesses whether people are living beyond the capacity of the planet, such as how many people drive cars or whether managers really need to fly overseas for a meeting.

Ecological sustainability refers to the capacity of the natural environment to meet the needs of the current generation without jeopardising the ability of future generations to meet their needs.

Economic sustainability refers to development that meets the economic needs of the present generation using existing available resources without compromising the ability of future generations to meet their needs.

Factors of production are the resources needed to produce a good or service, namely land, labour, capital and enterprise.

Green technologies are environmentally friendly innovations that consider the long-term impact on the environment, e.g. renewable energy sources such as solar panels and wind turbines.

Solar power are a type of green technologies.

Labour intensive means that the manufacturing or provision of a product relies heavily on labour, e.g. teaching and legal services. Hence, labour accounts for the most significant proportion of a labour-intensive firm's overall costs of production.

Operations management (or **production**) is concerned with providing the right goods and services in the right quantities and at the right quality level in a cost-effective and timely manner.

Preservation of resources is about protecting Earth's scarce resources by reducing the human impact on the physical environment (e.g. public beaches), the natural environment (e.g. rainforests) and the cultural environment (e.g. heritage sites).

Production process (or the **transformation process**) refers to the method of turning factor inputs into outputs by adding value in a cost-effective way.

Productivity is a measure of a firm's efficiency level, calculating the rate at which inputs (factors of production) are transformed into outputs (good and services).

Social sustainability examines social interactions and structures that are necessary for sustainable development, i.e. it is the ability of the society to develop in such a way that it meets the social wellbeing needs of the current and future generations.

Sustainability promotes intergenerational equity, i.e. production enables consumption of goods and services for the people of today without compromising consumption for future generations.

The **triple bottom line** refers to John Elkington's notion of three pillars (aspects) of sustainability that businesses must consider: social, ecological and economic sustainability (or people, planet and profits).

Value-added occurs during the production of a good or service because the value of the output is greater than the costs of production. Businesses cannot earn a profit if value-adding does not occur in the production process.

5.2 Production methods

SL/HL content	Assessment objective
The following production methods: • job/customized production • batch production • mass production • flow/process production • cellular manufacturing	AO2
The most appropriate method of production for a given situation	AO3

© IBO, 2017

Job production

The following production methods: job/customized production.

AO2

The most appropriate method of production for a given situation.

AO3

© IBO, 2017

Job production involves customizing an individual product from start to finish, tailor made to meet the specific requirements of the client. Typically, these products are one-off, unique items such as an office building, a wedding dress, a Hollywood movie, music composition, portait painting, private dance lesson or a haircut. A single worker (such as a tailor) or a group of workers (such as a team of painters and decorators) handle the complete job.

Job production (or **customized production**) covers a whole range of tasks from those that are small scale involving little or no technology (e.g. a private tutor or a hairdresser) to complex jobs that cannot be completed without high technology (e.g. the construction of a hotel, theme park or bridge).

The advantages and disadvantages of job production are shown in Table 5.2.a. on the following page.

Figure 5.2.a Tower Bridge in London, UK was built between 1886 and 1894 using job production

Case study

Italian luxury shoe brand *Aquazzura* makes its shoes in a small factory in Florence, Italy. *Aquazzura* shoes can take up to 10 months to produce. Up to 120 skilled labourers are used to produce a single high heel shoe. Much of the work is completed by hand, but machines are used to help finish certain aspects of each shoe. The workers some techniques that are over 100 years old.

523

Table 5.2.a   Advantages and disadvantages of job production

Advantages	Disadvantages
Quality of production (and service delivery) because highly skilled labour is used, e.g. a wedding planner will give customers more personal attention than a supermarket cashier would to individual customers.	The production process is relatively **time consuming** due to the varying and specific requirements of customers. It is usually difficult and impractical to speed up production as quality standards may fall.
Motivation of workers is also likely to be very high. Workers can feel proud of the finished project, e.g. a tailor-made pair of shoes or a prestigious hand-made sports car. Team spirit can also be a motivating factor (see Unit 2.4).	It tends to be **labour-intensive** and is therefore a relatively expensive production method. As labour accounts for the largest share of costs in most firms, the final price charged reflects the high costs of production.
Flexibility during the planning stages is possible as each product's design and specifications can be altered according to the customer's requests such as the type of car and flowers for a wedding. It is often possible to change the specifications of a job even when the work has already begun. This flexibility can provide major marketing benefits for a business.	There is likely to be a relatively **long working capital cycle** due to the length of time involved in producing a product (via job production) and then selling it. Ferrari has a 9 to 12 months waiting list for its cars, so clients do not fully pay for their purchases until the cars are delivered. However, during this time, Ferrari still needs cash to pay for its costs.
Uniqueness of the product not only helps to maintain staff motivation, but adds value to the production process. The exclusivity can also act as a unique selling point (USP) for the business and helps to secure a premium price for the finished product.	**Few economies of scale** can be enjoyed as each good or service is likely to be very unique rather than produced in batches. A tailor might enjoy some economies of scale from buying materials in bulk, but then faces storage and insurance costs.
The **customization of job production** creates a variety of **choice** for the customer that cannot be met by other methods of production.	The **irregularity of orders** means that production is unpredictable, so can cause cash flow problems (see Unit 3.7) for the business.

Question 5.2.1   Bristol Cars Ltd.

Bristol Cars Ltd. is a producer of luxury cars, founded in 1945 in Bristol, UK. Only around 100 cars are made per year. Each car is uniquely produced, allowing the firm to claim that the *Bristol Car* is *"Great Britain's most exclusive luxury car."* Bristol Cars Ltd. has no distributors or dealerships. Every part of the car is given the necessary time and attention to detail to satisfy both the client and the company. Only when each task is done to perfection can the highly skilled workers move onto the next task. The cost of perfection means it can take a long time to produce each car, but *Bristol Cars Ltd.* claims that *"the car is produced for those who can afford and appreciate the best"*. A designated sales person ensures that each customer receives a highly personalised service, even after the sale of the car.

Source: www.bristolcars.co.uk

(a) Outline what is meant by 'Ltd', as in *Bristol Cars Ltd.*   *[2 marks]*

(b) Explain the method of production used by *Bristol Cars Ltd.*   *[4 marks]*

(c) Examine the impact of this production method for *Bristol Cars Ltd.*, its employees and its customers.   *[10 marks]*

Batch production

The following production methods: batch production. AO2

The most appropriate method of production for a given situation. AO3

© IBO, 2017

Batch production involves simultaneously producing a number of identical products (known as a **batch**). Work on each batch is fully completed before production switches to another batch, using the same staff and machinery. For example, a small bakery might produce 12 loaves of bread before changing production systems to bake 24 blueberry muffins. It is highly suited to businesses that make a range of products, unlike with job production. Clothing retailers such as H&M and Gap have their garments produced in batches of different sizes and colours. Hotels that offer buffet dinners prepare and cook food in batches. Package holidays sold through travel agents are also a form of batch production.

Figure 5.2.b Batch produced glass ornaments from Italy

Batch production tends to be used when the level of demand for a product is not clear. Instead, estimates of sales volumes are made and carefully monitored. Output can then be adjusted accordingly. Production of one product line can be stopped if necessary, perhaps to work on another more urgent batch.

The advantages and disadvantages of batch production are shown in Table 5.2.b.

Common mistake

Students often comment that batch production is only suitable when small quantities are being produced. Whilst this is true to some extent, batch production can be used to produce large quantities of output too. However, production is not continuous as in the case of mass production and flow production.

Mass production

The following production methods: mass production. AO2

The most appropriate method of production for a given situation. AO3

© IBO, 2017

Mass production is the manufacturing of large amounts of a standardized product. It often involves the assembly of individual components, with parts (components) bought from other companies. It tends to be capital-intensive, with many tasks relying on automation. Therefore, unit costs of production are relatively low.

Operations management

CORE

Table 5.2.b Advantages and disadvantages of batch production

Advantages	Disadvantages
Economies of scale can be enjoyed as machinery can be used to produce larger quantities (*technical economies*). Raw materials and components can also be bought in bulk (*purchasing economies*).	**Storage** is important as batch production can result in a high amount of stock (inventory). However, this will increase production costs, e.g. storage costs and insurance against damage or loss of stock.
Specialization in the various production processes is likely to lead to increased *productivity* (output per worker) and better quality products.	As with all systems of division of labour, jobs get repetitive and this can lead to **boredom**. This might, therefore, reduce motivation and productive efficiency.
As a **variety** of products can be made, customers have more choice, e.g. birthday cakes produced in batches can still be tailored to the needs of individual customers at a relatively low cost.	A degree of **inflexibility** exists because once the production run for a batch has started, it is difficult to switch to or work on another batch. This can therefore cause delays to the overall production process.
Variety can **reduce risks** of producing just a single product with limited sales potential.	**High production costs** due to the reliance on sophisticated machinery and equipment.

An essential part of mass production is **specialization** – specialized capital equipment and people are used at each workstation to carry out a different function essential to the overall production process, resulting in high levels of productivity. Mass production was first commercialised by Henry Ford in the USA. Ford, who was heavily influenced by the work of F.W. Taylor (see Unit 2.4), introduced the world's first automated production line in the 1920s for the production of his 'Model T' cars. Instead of the workers moving from one work station to another (which is rather inefficient), he used an automated production line to boost the firm's productivity.

Unlike batch production, the standardized products made using mass production (such as mobile phones and DVD players) are produced or assembled on a large scale. Examples of mass produced goods include: buttons, ball bearings, computer microprocessors, motor vehicles, LEGO toys and office supplies.

Figure 5.2.c Mass production helps to lower average costs

Flow production

The following production methods: flow/process production. AO2
The most appropriate method of production for a given situation. AO3

© IBO, 2017

Flow production (or **process production**) focuses on a continuous production process of manufacturing products that are standardized (or homogeneous) in large quantities, e.g. printing millions of identical copies of a particular daily newspaper on a production line. Flow production differs from mass production in that production occurs on a much larger scale, with production assembly lines often kept running 24 hours a day, seven days a week to maximise output and to eliminate waste (the extra costs of starting and stopping

the production process). Flow production relies entirely on automated systems with very few workers required. For example, the Coca-Cola company uses flow production processes to make 10,000 bottles of water in a single factory every minute of the day!

Figure 5.2.d Flow production relies heavily on automation

Common mistake

Many students treat mass production and flow production as the same method of production. Whilst there are similarities, be sure you can explain the differences.

Theory of knowledge

How might we determine the true costs of production for goods such as 'blood diamonds' or cheap (genetically modified) food products?

Oil refineries and producers of bottled water, beer, toothpicks, screws, and nails and use a system similar to the one shown in Figure 5.2.e. on the following page.

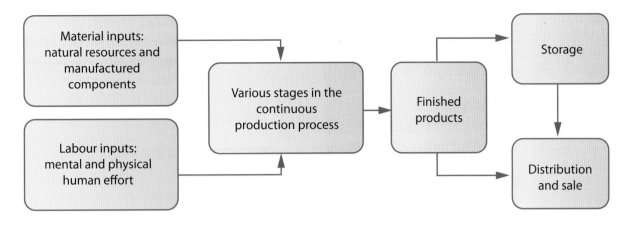

Figure 5.2.e Basic flow production process

Table 5.2.c   Advantages and disadvantages of mass and flow production

Advantages	Disadvantages
As these production methods are capital-intensive, output is on a large scale. For example, Coca-Cola produces 2,000 cans of Coke per minute when operating at full capacity at its bottling plant.	The work is likely to be monotonous and therefore boring, e.g. designated workers at Coca-Cola check every glass bottle to ensure that there are no cracks or defects before any beverage is poured into the bottles.
These methods are the most cost-effective methods of production as costs can be spread over the high volume of output, thereby reducing average fixed costs through *technical economies of scale*. Machines can work continuously if necessary. Machines may break down from time to time, but they do not require wages, rest breaks or motivating, which helps to reduce costs of production in the long run.	There is inflexibility because once the production process begins there is little chance of altering the design or specifications. Products must be standardized so cannot be made to the customer's individual needs. There can be some variety in the finishing touches towards the end of the assembly line, such as colour, although these are also produced on a relatively large scale.
The use of dedicated machinery and equipment means that products are of a standardized quality. Workers also specialize so become experts in their area of the production process. This enables the business to achieve a low *defect rate* (see Unit 5.3) and to maintain quality standards.	The methods are capital intensive and thus involve huge *set-up costs* (e.g. purchase and installation), *running costs* (e.g. servicing and maintenance) and *replacement costs* (when equipment becomes obsolete). The reliance on assembly lines means any breakdowns will cause major problems for the business.
Labour costs are low, as relatively unskilled workers are required to operate machinery, e.g. workers in the Black & Decker factory in Shenzhen, China work 10-hour shifts, earning the minimum wage. They can be hired easily and trained to work on the assembly line within a couple of hours.	The systems are inflexible. Unlike job or batch production, it is not possible to rework products that are substandard as production is continuous. Any reworking will bring other operations to a halt. Large-scale output also means the need for an effective storage system due to the large volume of stock.

Question 5.2.2   Choosing the appropriate method of production

Describe the most appropriate method of production for each product below:

(a) Navy battleships   *[2 marks]*
(b) Wedding cakes   *[2 marks]*
(c) Cookies (biscuits)   *[2 marks]*
(d) Samsung smartphones   *[2 marks]*
(e) Evian bottled mineral water. *[2 marks]*

Operations management

CORE

Exam tip !

In reality, it is not always so straightforward to classify output as job, batch, flow or mass production. Many goods are made using a combination of production methods. For example, a tailor-made suit uses job production and labour intensive techniques. Even though the suit is made to the individual requirements of the customer, the materials (such as the cloth, thread and buttons) are bought in batches.

Cellular manufacturing

The following production methods: cellular manufacturing. AO2
The most appropriate method of production for a given situation.
AO3
© IBO, 2017

A key drawback of traditional mass and flow production methods is that people working in isolation become bored, so this negatively affects their levels of motivation and productivity. **Cellular manufacturing** (or **cell production**) is a modern adaptation of assembly line production whereby sets of tasks are completed by teams (or 'cells') by splitting the production process into a number of self-contained units. Each cell, with its specialized grouping of machines, materials and manpower, is given responsibility for completing a part of the overall production process. Complete units of work are then passed on to another cell in the production process. Work is arranged so that each person can do all the tasks within their assigned group, thus creating opportunities for job rotation as the team is multiskilled.

Whilst cellular manufacturing promotes teamwork, cells are independent of one another but rely on each other to ensure that final production targets are met. Typically, each cell has its own responsibility for organizing the team's work schedules, including covering for team members who may be absent due to sickness, maternity leave or holidays. Cell production is often combined with *just-in-time* production with each cell responsible for quality assurance (see Unit 5.3).

Table 5.2.d shows the advantages and disadvantages of cell production.

The appropriateness of different production methods

The most appropriate method of production for a given situation.
AO3
© IBO, 2017

Some methods of production are **labour-intensive** whilst others are **capital-intensive**. Production methods that use a greater proportion of labour than any other factor input (in terms of their cost) are known as *labour-intensive*. Examples range from rural farming in economically developing countries to management consultancy services in advanced countries. Job production and the service sector tend to be labour-intensive, e.g. tailor made suits and wedding gowns. By contrast, *capital-intensive* industries are those that have a relatively high proportion of capital costs in comparison with labour costs. Capital intensity is typically found in batch, mass and flow production. It is, of course, possible to have job production that is capital-intensive, such as the construction of roller coasters.

Table 5.2.d Advantages and disadvantages of cell production

Advantages	Disadvantages
There is some autonomy in decision-making, e.g. the team selects its own leader and arranges rest breaks for each member. In effect, each team operates as a small and cohesive industrial unit.	Cellular manufacturing usually results in lower output compared with traditional mass and flow production methods; production cells work on completing sets of output. Cells (teams) are not equally productive or efficient.
Team members have collective responsibility for their production targets and are held accountable for the quality of the items that they pass to the next group in the production process. Responsibility and accountability can lead to an improvement in quality standards.	Cell production is rather capital-intensive so the business still has to spend a lot of money buying, installing and servicing new machinery and equipment for each cell. Therefore, purchase, maintenance and replacement costs can be high.
There are positive impacts on motivation from team working and autonomy in decision making. Each team is likely to see a finished product (which is passed on in the production process), creating a sense of achievement.	Conflict within teams can cause production problems, especially if the team leader is ineffective. It can also exist between different cells, especially if there are production delays (no one likes to be left waiting).
Specialization, coupled with team dynamics and team spirit within each cell, can lead to higher levels of productivity.	Capacity utilization of machinery is lower than mass and flow production, so average fixed costs tend to be higher.

Increasing capital investment expenditure (i.e. becoming more capital-intensive) often leads to improved levels of output and productivity, especially if the business can mass produce its products. Machinery can be made to work efficiently without any rest breaks or financial compensation, thus reducing average costs of production in the medium to long term as costs are spread over a larger volume of output. However, for this to happen there must be sufficient demand for the product to justify its mass production.

Figure 5.2.g Production of Bristol Fighter cars is labour-intensive

Figure 5.2.f The construction of roller coasters is capital-intensive

A limitation of capital intensity is that products tend to be highly homogeneous, i.e. there is no unique selling point (USP). Standardization results in a lower selling price for the product, with lower profit margins being made. In addition, capital-intensive businesses tend to have high fixed costs of production because the costs of machinery, equipment and automation can be extremely high. By contrast, a labour-intensive industry has a higher proportion of costs attributed to its workforce than its capital structure. For example, around 80% of a school's budget typically goes towards the payment of staff salaries. This means only around 20% is available for spending on other items, such as textbooks, stationery and capital equipment. Labour intensity can be found in highly skilled professions, such as lawyers and financial consultants.

A key benefit of labour intensity is the ability to offer a personalized service. Labour-intensive car manufacturers that hand-build their vehicles, such as Bristol Cars (see Question 5.2.1), can benefit from having a USP since customers can create their own specifications, so it would be appropriate to charge higher prices. Teachers and health care professionals also offer a human touch, which would not be as effective if these services were capital-intensive (imagine being taught exclusively by computers!)

Whether it is more appropriate for a business to adopt more capital or labour intensive methods of production depends on several factors, including:

- The relative cost of labour and capital – Assuming that substitution of resources is feasible, relatively higher labour costs mean that the business will choose to use more capital-intensive production methods.

- The size of the market – Larger markets tend to use capital-intensive technologies (and hence mass and flow production methods), whereas small firms are likely to be more labour-intensive.

- The aims and objectives of the organization – If profit is the main objective, then businesses are more likely to want to operate in mass markets, thereby choosing to use more capital-intensive technologies to minimise unit costs of production. Businesses that are risk-averse and worried about survival during a recession may prefer to be more labour-intensive as cost reduction and cost control are relatively easier.

In reality, businesses are likely to combine different methods of production. For example, Burger King generally uses batch production. However, it also uses job production to a lesser extent – its corporate slogan 'Have it your way' is based on the notion that customers can customize their burgers as long as the ingredients are available. Combining different methods of production allows a business to gain from the benefits of each method used. The highly successful BMW Mini, for example, is produced according to the exact number of orders. Customers can customize their cars from BMW's predetermined options list. This is possible due to BMW's use of advanced automation technologies. The result is that Mini customers get a personalised product with the added benefit of lower production costs from the use of mass production processes.

Operations management

CORE

Figure 5.2.h The Mini is made using a combination of production methods

Case study

The Boeing 787 Dreamliner is an American commercial aircraft. Boeing's production target is ten 787 Dreamliner aircraft per month. Whilst each plane is worked on individually (job production), the vast majority of parts and components are mass produced. The 787 Dreamliner is priced between $146m to $200m, depending on the specifications. Boeing reported that it had spent over $32 billion on the 787 Dreamliner program.

Question 5.2.3   Appropriate methods of production

Explain why it might not be easy to categorise the production method used to make the following products:

(a) Dell personal computers that are 'made to order', i.e. customers set their own specifications.   *[4 marks]*

(b) Birthday cakes sold at large supermarkets such as Carrefour, Tesco and Walmart.   *[4 marks]*

The role of production methods and the CUEGIS concepts

The CUEGIS concepts can be applied to all aspects of production methods. For example, favourable market changes can mean that a business switches from batch production to mass production. For example, Apple's entry into China, a country with over 750 million mobile phone users, meant that its quarterly sales exceeded $40 million for the first time in 2014. The iPad has been Apple's fastest growing product in the company's history with over 360 million units sold at the time of writing. Over 3 million units of the iPad 3 were sold in the first 3 days of its launch.

Organizational culture also has a large impact on the choice of production methods (see the example of Bristol Cars Ltd. in Question 5.2.1).

Ethics can influence the choice of suppliers or outsourced providers. Apple had to intervene with Foxconn, its outsourced producer of iPads and iPhones, due to media exposure of unethical business practices in Foxconn's production plants in China. Nevertheless, the pressures of globalization have led to many large multinational companies using outsourced and offshored suppliers (see Unit 5.4), despite ethical issues such as poor working conditions and the use of child labour.

Innovations in the production process and production methods have given businesses more opportunities. For example, e-commerce has given small businesses a platform to compete with larger companies. They are able to source suppliers from anywhere on the planet through the use of B2B operators (see Unit 4.8) such as Alibaba. Such technological advances and innovations have meant that productivity can be improved without incurring high costs of buying modern equipment and machinery.

Different production methods have varying implications on the other strategic functions of a business (human resources, finances and marketing). The choice of production method will also affect other aspects of operations management, such as stock control systems (see Unit 5.5) and quality control (see Unit 5.3). With flow production, for example, it is important that businesses use suppliers that delivery standardized raw materials and components on time to prevent bottlenecks in the production process. Modern management thinking has led to business strategy that involves a combination of production methods and a total quality culture in the workplace (see Unit 5.3).

Theory of knowledge

Can it ever be ethically correct for an innovative business to make people redundant in the process of adopting a capital-intensive business strategy?

IB Learner Profile

Visit the Standford University website to see "how everyday things are made": http://manufacturing. stanford.edu/hetm.html

You can choose any one of the products from the left side of the screen, such as: airplanes, motorcycles, jelly beans, chocolate plastic bottles, or denim. Make notes on the different methods of production used, and be prepared to discuss your findings with the rest of the class.

CUEGIS Essay

With reference to an organization of your choice, examine how **change** and **ethics** have influenced its production methods.   *[20 marks]*

REVIEW QUESTIONS

1. What is job production?

2. What are the advantages and disadvantages of job production?

3. What is batch production and how does it differ from job production?

4. What are the advantages of batch production compared to job production?

5. What is mass production?

6. What is flow production and how does it differ from mass production?

7. What are the advantages and disadvantages of mass and flow production methods?

8. Why might a business choose to use cellular manufacturing?

9. Using examples, distinguish between capital-intensive and labour-intensive industries.

10. Why do many businesses choose to use a combination of various methods of production?

KEY TERMS

Batch production involves producing a set of identical products. Work on each batch is fully completed before production switches to another batch. It is used where the demand for a product is frequent and steady.

Capital intensive means that the manufacturing or provision of a product relies heavily on machinery and equipment, such as automated production systems. Hence, the cost of capital accounts for the largest proportion of a capital-intensive firm's overall production costs.

Cellular manufacturing (or **cell production**) organizes workers into independent 'cells' with each team comprising of multiskilled staff with responsibility and autonomy for completing a whole unit of work in the production process.

Operations management

CORE

531

Flow production (or **process production**) uses continuous and progressive processes, carried out in sequence. When one task is completed, the next stage of production starts immediately.

Mass production is the large-scale manufacturing of a homogeneous (standardised) product. Unit costs of production are relatively low when using mass production methods.

Job production involves the manufacturing of a unique or one-off job. The job can be completed by one person (such as a tailor) or by a team of people (such as architects and engineers).

Labour intensive means that production relies heavily on labour input, so the cost of labour accounts for the largest proportion of a firm's overall production costs. It is most apparent in the provision of personalized services, e.g. private tutors, hair dressers, masseurs and artists.

Productivity measures the level of labour and/or capital efficiency of a business by comparing its level of inputs with the level of its output.

Specialization means the division of a large task or project into smaller tasks, allowing individuals to concentrate on an area of expertise. It is an essential part of mass and flow production.

Standardization means producing an identical or homogeneous product in large quantities, such as printing a particular magazine, book or newspaper.

Fig 5.2.i Textbooks are produced in a standardised format

5.3 Lean production and quality management

"I'm a slow walker, but I never walk back." - Abraham Lincoln (1809–1865), 16th president of the USA

HL content	Assessment objective
The following features of lean production: • less waste • greater efficiency	AO1
The following methods of lean production: • continuous improvement (*kaizen*) • just-in-time (JIT) • *kanban* • *andon*	AO2
Features of cradle to cradle design and manufacturing	AO2
Features of quality control and quality assurance	AO1
The following methods of managing quality: • quality circle • benchmarking • total quality management (TQM)	AO2
The impact of lean production and TQM on an organization	AO3
The importance of national and international quality standards	AO2

© IBO, 2017

Features of lean production

The following features of lean production: less waste and greater efficiency. AO1

© IBO, 2017

Lean production is the process of streamlining operations and processes to reduce all forms of waste and to achieve greater efficiency. Thus, lean production should lead to improved quality and reduced costs. It was first used in Japan during the 1950s. Businesses are increasingly trying to reduce wastage (or **muda**, the Japanese term for 'waste') in the production process. "OTHER"© examples of muda include:

• **O**ver-processing - This means a business adds more features or functions to a product than is necessary to meet the needs of customers. Over-processing does not add much value for the customer, but increases the organization's production costs. Consider the many functions and features on your smartphone or computer that you do not use (or are even aware of).

• **T**ime - Delays in the production process (perhaps due to inefficient machinery or poor training) or the delivery process have a large negative impact on productivity and perceptions of quality. Delays can also occur due to excess movement of employees between workstations, which wastes time and reduces labour productivity.

• **H**uman effort - Tasks may need to be reworked (done again) due to waste from substandard and defective output.

• **E**nergy - Leaving on lights, heating or air conditioning when not needed is a huge and unnecessary drain on financial resources.

• **R**esources and materials - There can be wastage of materials and resources that have not been used efficiently, such as floor space. Wastage also occurs if there is underproduction (resulting in shortages and causing a

533

HIGHER LEVEL

Operations management

loss of potential customers) or overproduction (producing more than necessary, which leads to stockpiling).

Figure 5.3.a Overstocking is a source of muda (waste)

In adopting lean production, several principles are followed:

- Waste minimisation – This requires the business to remove any operation or process that does not add value to the product. It involves making more efficient use of a firm's scarce resources (its land, labour and capital resources).

- 'Right first time' approach - Businesses aim for zero defects by identifying and resolving all problems at source. It is more efficient to use resources to prevent mistakes rather than trying to correct them as this eliminates the need for quality controllers to spend time checking the quality of the output.

- Flexibility - Resources must be adaptable to the changing needs of the business, e.g. firms might use multi-skilled workers who can work on several projects simultaneously.

- Continuous improvement - Lean production requires the continual strive to improve quality and efficiency, thereby reducing average costs of production.

- Supply Chain Management - Businesses must develop and maintain good professional working relationships with their suppliers and intermediaries to help streamline the supply chain process (see Unit 5.5).

Question 5.3.1   Subway

Subway is a private limited company, founded in 1965, that specialises in the sale of fresh 'submarine sandwiches'. Operating on a global scale, it is the world's largest **franchise** restaurant operator. The secret to its success has been the focus on promoting an image of being a health-conscious restaurant chain. With over 45,000 restaurants in around 105 countries, **quality management** is a critical aspect of *Subway's* operations and its growth strategy. Its homepage (www.subway.com) has a dedicated section for customers to comment on their experiences at *Subway*, which helps the company to gain customer feedback to further improve its quality standards.

(a) (i) Define the term **franchise**.   *[2 marks]*

(a) (ii) Define the term **quality management**.   *[2 marks]*

(b) Explain why quality management is important to a global franchise business such as *Subway*.   *[4 marks]*

(c) Examine the potential problems of quality management as *Subway* continues its rapid expansion plans.   *[6 marks]*

Methods of lean production

The following methods of lean production: continuous improvement (*kaizen*), just-in-time (JIT), *kanban* and *andon*. AO2

© IBO, 2017

Kaizen (continuous improvement)

Dutch artist Vincent Van Gogh (1853–1890) said, "*Great things are not done by impulse, but by a series of small things brought together*". **Kaizen** is the Japanese word for a philosophy of **continuous improvement**. Kaizen is made up of two words – 'Kai' meaning *change* and 'Zen' meaning *better*. Hence, kaizen comes about by changing for the better. It has become a widespread approach in the workplace where workers and managers constantly try to find ways to improve work processes and efficiency.

The concept of kaizen is therefore a process of productivity and efficiency gains that come from *small and continuous improvements* being made, rather than a large one-off improvement. The Turkish have a saying, '*Stairs are climbed step by step*'. Confucius, the Chinese philosopher, said, "*It does not matter how slowly you go so long as you do not stop*". These sayings are similar to the famous children's fable about the hare and the tortoise (see Box 5.3.a).

Figure 5.3.b Kaizen is about making small steps to continually improve

Box 5.3.a   The hare and the tortoise (a case of continuous improvement)

A hare and a tortoise were in a race together. The hare thought that its natural superiority would mean winning the race would be simple. The hare leapt ahead and after a short while the tortoise was nowhere in sight. Complacent, the hare decided to take a rest and fell asleep. This allowed the tortoise, with its small but continuous steps, to eventually overtake the hare and win the race.

The kaizen process involves forming small groups of employees whose role is to identify changes and improvements to the organization's products, processes and procedures. The aim is to establish a steady flow of small improvements rather than one-off and/or radical changes. This is partly because people tend to be resistant to change, especially change that is large scale and disruptive to the organization. Change is easier to manage when there are small and continuous improvements. Kaizen groups do not tend to directly look at cost cutting; the focus remains on continual improvements in quality. However, by doing so, kaizen often brings about cost savings.

Kaizen also aims to eliminate waste by looking at ways to improve the productivity and efficiency of the firm's operations. For example, if a worker is late to work for just one minute each day, then that equates to 5 minutes per week or over 4 hours per year. If this was the norm for a workforce of 50 people, then the lost production time would be more than 200 hours each year (or around 25 days of lost output). Kaizen is therefore an integral part of quality management. The philosophy behind kaizen is that *anyone* in the organization, irrespective of their rank, can make a contribution. The best suggestions often come from employees who have direct contact with customers. They are the ones best positioned to understand the benefits of changes to certain operations. This has the added benefit of motivating staff as they are able to use their initiative and have some input in the decision-making process.

Just-in-time (JIT)

Just-in-time (JIT) is an inventory management system based on stocks being delivered as and when they are needed in the production process. As stocks are delivered just before they are used, there is no need to have a stock control system as buffer stocks are not required (see Unit 5.5). Finished goods are dispatched as soon as they have been produced, thereby eliminating the need for storage. JIT, a Japanese philosophy first advocated by former Toyota Executive Taiichi Ohno, is a method of lean production because inventory is costly and wasteful.

JIT is common in car manufacturing. For example, the BMW Mini is assembled using a JIT system. A customer places a specific order before the vehicle is made. Each component is ordered to be available when needed for production. The use of bar codes for these components helps to ensure the right parts are supplied at the right time. Unlike traditional assembly lines used in mass production (see Unit 5.2), JIT allows a series of Mini cars, all of different colours and engine sizes, to be produced on the same production line. The JIT system relies on automation, bar codes and the use of highly skilled and motivated workers. The advantages and disadvantages of JIT are covered in Unit 5.5.

Case study

How's this for an example of lean production? On 17th November 2017, the Metropolitan Intercity Railway Company, a Japanese rail operator, formally apologised after one of its trains left 20 seconds too early. A spokesperson for the rail company said the train conductor had not checked the train's timetable properly, and added that employees were instructed to follow procedures strictly to prevent a recurrence. For passengers who missed the train, the next scheduled one arrived (on time) four minutes later.

Kanban

Kanban is a method of lean production developed by Taiichi Ohno, a Toyota executive, to ensure that inventory is based on actual customer orders rather than sales forecasts. At its simplest level, kanban uses a card system with an inventory number attached to each component in the production process. Kanban is Japanese for visual card. The system starts when a customer places an order – a part (component) is only used (or ordered) if there is a kanban card for it. A kanban must accompany each item or component at all times in the production process and

no item is used or moved on without a kanban card. Any defects are identified to prevent it being moved on to the next process.

A typical kanban card shows operatives *what* is to be produced, *how much* of that item is to be produced and by *when* it needs to be made. Traditional sushi restaurants use kanbans, with customers placing their orders using a card system, i.e. what dishes they want and how many of each. Although orders can be placed using computers in modern restaurants, the process is still based on a (computerised) kanban system. Examples of other businesses that have used kanban include Xerox, Expedia, Rovio and Groupon.

Figure 5.3.c Kanban is commonly used in Japanese restaurants

As a visual tool to monitor and manage workflow, kanban boards are created using named columns to show where each task is in the production process (see Figure 5.3.d). The visual nature of the kanban board makes it easier for operatives to see what tasks have been completed, which ones are works in progress (WIP) and which ones are yet to be started. Each stage in the workflow process has a limited (or maximum) number of tasks that can be worked on at any point in time (shown in brackets). Having these WIP limits helps to ensure that production keeps flowing at a steady pace, workers complete tasks before they take on any more work, and reduce waste as workers do not have to spend too much time switching between tasks. Kanban allows workers to see if there are any bottlenecks in the production process so that teams can work together to solve the problem, thus ensuring workflow continues.

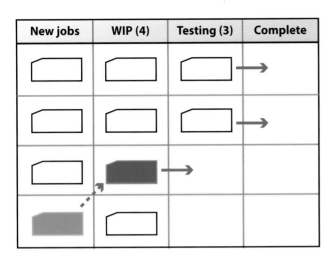

Figure 5.3.d Kanban board

In Figure 5.3.d, it can be seen that there are four new jobs to be started. However, as the WIP limit is four and there are currently four tasks in progress, none of the new tasks can be started. The aim of the team is to complete one of the WIP tasks (represented by the red kanban card) so it can be moved to the 'Testing' column. This would then allow a new task (shown by the green kanban) to be started. There are currently only two products being tested before they are completed, so there is capacity to test one more. Any items in the 'Complete' column must be delivered promptly to customers (such as sushi being served to diners in the restaurant).

Common mistake

Kanban is not a stock control system. Instead, it is a lean production method used to control the logistical (supply) chain. It is one way to achieve JIT production.

Andon

Andon is a Japanese visual control system used to indicate the status of an aspect of the production process, e.g. machinery, production line or work process. Andon is often supplemented with audible sound systems (alarms) to alert supervisors of a change in status. The combination of visual-audio notification systems is an effective way to alert workers who must attend to several manufacturing processes at the same time or those who work in multiple parts of the production floor. Andon systems are typically color-coded using a traffic light system:

- Green = normal operations in progress
- Yellow = attention will be needed soon
- Red = immediate attention is required.

An everyday example of andon is the warning system in a car. When the petrol tank is almost empty, the andon system uses a red warning sign on the dashboard to warn the driver that fuel is running low. The empty fuel sign flashes to indicate to the driver to fill up at the petrol (gas) station. Many local governments also use an andon system to alert motorists of their driving speed (see http://goo.gl/asQjLu for an example).

Figure 5.3.e Andons are used in car systems

In a factory setting with mass production, an andon system provides visual feedback to workers and supervisors on the production floor. Using the traffic light system, and on systems indicate to workers the status of the production line, alert supervisors to where assistance is needed and empowers factory operatives to halt the production process if there are difficulties such as emergencies, malfunctions and quality control issues (thus preventing product defects in the process). Signal boards, lights and audio systems are combined to indicate which workstation has a problem. Depending on the business operation, andon alert systems can be activated manually by pressing a button or pulling a cord at the workstation, or can be activated automatically by the machinery and equipment itself, e.g. bottlenecks in the production process. Manufacturing is stopped until a solution has been found. It is common practice, and sometimes a legal requirement, for any red alerts to be logged (recorded) so that these can be monitored as part of the firm's lean production programme.

Andon is an important method of lean production due to its benefits, which include:

- Bringing instant attention to production problems as they arise in the manufacturing process.

- Providing a consistent and simple communication tool for all factory floor workers and supervisors.

- Encouraging workers and supervisors to take immediate action to deal with production, quality and safety problems.

- Improving the ability of supervisors to identify and resolve production issues in an efficient and cost-effective way.

Common mistake

Students often comment that lean production gives a business a significant competitive advantage over its rivals. Whilst this can be true, make sure you substantiate your comment. This competitive advantage will not exist if, for example, competitors have access to the same lean production technologies, or if the firm has to use lean production technologies just to keep pace with market leaders.

Exam tip !

Lean production is a philosophical vision for businesses. In reality, it can never truly be achieved. However, this does not stop organizations trying to make lean production become the norm (in terms of employee attitudes and operational procedures), due to the benefits of reduced waste (such as cutting unnecessary costs), reduced defects, and improved efficiency.

Cradle to cradle design and manufacturing

Features of cradle to cradle design and manufacturing. AO2
© IBO, 2017

Cradle to cradle (C2C) refers to a sustainable model of production based on natural processes, thus benefiting the environment. The underlying principle of C2C is that there is no waste in nature, making it sustainable. This implies that C2C manufacturing is designed in such a way that production is efficient and generates minimal or no waste, so is sustainable for future generations. By contrast, **cradle to grave** refers to one-time use, which is the most common form of manufacturing. Have you ever noticed the amount of waste products from a single Happy Meal or Extra Value Meal at McDonald's? The waste from each meal includes: the paper mat, food wrapping,

straw, paper cup, plastic paper cup lid, tissues, sauce wrappers, and even uneaten food.

Walter R. Stahel (born 1946), a Swiss architect, is credited for coining the term 'cradle to cradle' in 1971. C2C provides a framework for operations managers to design production techniques that are efficient (free of waste) and sustainable, e.g. glass bottles used in the production of beverages such as beer, soft drinks, water and wine. Glass bottles are quite easy to reuse and/or recycle. **Recycling** enables old materials to be reprocessed into new products, with the aim of preventing waste. **Reuse** is different from recycling as the product is not made into a new material or product. Reusing resources also prevents waste. Designing products or materials to be reused and/or recycled allows for sustainability. Another example is coffee cups made out of cornstarch – a biodegradable component. These cups can be used, reused and eventually composted, supplying nutrients to plants or crops.

Figure 5.3.f Most glass products are C2C but some are easier to recycle than others

Buildings (such as homes and offices) are increasingly being made using C2C processes. Technical components of the building ensure materials are not toxic, but the building is designed and created in an environmentally friendly way. The C2C approach also minimises the environmental impact of disposal in order to promote sustainability. Hence, the C2C philosophy is an important component of a firm's corporate social responsibility (CSR).

Businesses that adopt the C2C philosophy design and manufacture products that are ecologically and environmentally friendly. C2C practices enable businesses to repeatedly use the same components rather than disposing of them because products can be either reused in the production process or broken down organically as food for the natural environment.

Critics of the C2C philosophy argue that such practices can restrict the ability of businesses to operate in a cost-effective and therefore efficient way.

Figure 5.3.g Eco-friendly businesses use C2C practices

IB Learner Profile – Be an inquirer and be knowledgeable

The Aeron chair, made by Herman Miller, is a C2C product. Investigate what makes this product a good example of C2C design and manufacturing. What other products are also good examples of C2C?

Quality control and quality assurance

Features of quality control and quality assurance. AO1
© IBO, 2017

Quality means that a product fulfils its purpose and meets the expectations of the consumer. Hence, quality is not exclusive to expensive products. A Honda or Ford motor car can be of good quality as long as the vehicles meet the standards desired by the customer. Likewise, the quality of teaching and learning in a government funded school is not necessarily inferior to that offered at an expensive fee-paying private school. Products that do not meet the needs or expectations of customers, producers or governments are said to be **substandard** and such products can be very costly to a business (see Box 5.3.b). Customers perceive quality by observing and comparing several interrelated factors, including:

- Physical appearance and design – Are the look, design and features of the product appealing to customers?

- Image and reputation of manufacturer or seller – A widely known and reputable brand will tend to be associated with higher quality.

- Reliability – Good quality products are of high quality, e.g. Lexus is renowned for building the world's most reliable cars and hence are of good quality.

- Durability – This is the extent to which a product will last. Products that need to be replaced or are in regular need of maintenance are perceived to be of poor quality.

- Fit for purpose – How well does the product fulfill its purpose? For example, how accurate is the watch; how tasty is the meal; and how waterproof and wind resistant is the rain coat?

- Safety features – Products that are safe to use are considered to be of good quality. By contrast, products that need to be recalled due to safety problems are of substandard quality.

- Customer service – High quality firms provide outstanding customer service, e.g. courteous and knowledgeable staff.

- After-sales services – These might include guarantees, warranties, technical support, a prompt delivery service and ensuring that spare parts are available and at reasonable prices.

In essence, quality is determined by the perceived value for money. Customers assess what they get for their money by comparing the benefits of consumption with the price of the product.

Common mistake

Quality does not mean that a product has to be expensive, prestigious or exclusive. Many students incorrectly define quality as products that are the 'best' in their industry, such as Rolex watches. There are plenty of good quality watches that are relatively inexpensive.

The quality of an organization's products is important for two main reasons: its reputation and its ability to control costs. **Quality management** is the function concerned with controlling business activities to ensure that products are fit for their purpose. Advocates of quality management argue that the quality of a product should be seen as an overall package, from the production and purchase of the product to its use and beyond. Four driving forces have led to quality being a paramount priority for many businesses:

- *Increasing consumer awareness* – Today's consumers have easier access to information, such as through consumer protection organizations, the media and the Internet. Any mistake made by large multinational companies is likely to be reported in various sources very quickly all over the world.

- *Increasing competition* – Rivalry has meant that firms which provide higher quality products may be able to establish brand loyalty and a larger customer base. Quality, as a form of product differentiation, can give a firm a competitive advantage, i.e. a unique selling point.

- *Government legislation* – Changes and developments to competition laws have forced businesses to improve their quality standards.

- *Increasing consumer incomes* – With greater disposable income, consumers are more able and willing to buy higher quality products, such as high-end smart TVs and luxury motor vehicles.

There are two main categories of quality management: quality control and quality assurance:

- **Quality control** (QC) is the traditional way of quality management that involves inspecting, testing and sampling the quality of work. Products must be made to the required specification. This approach to managing quality is mainly based on detecting faulty or poor quality output, from the delivery of raw materials to the output of finished products. It helps to identify problems such as substandard quality before products are sold to consumers.

- **Quality assurance** (QA) is the management process of guaranteeing (assuring) the consumer of a product's quality by ensuring that everything is done 'right first time', i.e. there are no defects. It informs customers that products have been made to the required specification and that certain quality standards have been met. QA can be an important source of competitive advantage. It is more concerned about preventing poor quality output than rectifying the problems (see Box 5.3.b). As American poet Henry Wadsworth Longfellow (1807–1882) said, "*It takes less time to do a thing right than to explain why you did it wrong*".

In 1997 Mercedes–Benz launched its first small car – the A Class. They had spent close to $2 billion on the research and development of the product but found very shortly after the launch that there were major safety problems and had to recall all the cars sold. The German carmaker spent another $280 million to fix the problems and, to their credit, the car has been a huge success ever since. Similarly, in 2010 Tata suffered an 85% drop in its sales of the Nano, the world's cheapest car, following incidents of its cars catching fire, which were exposed in the media.

Table 5.3.a Advantages and disadvantages of quality control

Advantages	Disadvantages
QC is used to prevent faulty products reaching the customer, thereby safeguarding the firm's reputation.	QC does not prevent mistakes being made yet can be expensive. Hence, quality assurance might be a better alternative.
It is cheaper to have trained QC inspectors than to have every individual being trained to be responsible for quality assurance.	The root cause of the problem is not dealt with as there is a lack of a quality culture, i.e. substandard output is rejected or reworked.
QC inspectors can find widespread issues and problems across the organization.	Individuals are not accountable for the quality of their work, so slack is encouraged.

Box 5.3.b   The costs of poor quality

- Substandard quality will adversely affect the reputation of a business, perhaps irrevocably.
- Poor product design may lead to problems with the finished product, thereby affecting its demand. Customer complaints will rise and therefore customers are unlikely to purchase such products again.
- It costs time and money to rework the substandard products.
- Unsafe products can cause physical harm to customers.
- Equipment and machinery that regularly break down will need to be repaired. Hence, this adds to the costs of the business.
- Poor labour productivity will raise average costs of production.
- Late deliveries can result in compensation claims being made and/or harm the firm's reputation.

Ultimately, poor quality harms the organization's competitiveness by affecting its reputation and costs in an unfavourable manner.

Advantages of quality assurance include:

- QA programmes involve employee participation as workers have more ownership and recognition for their work, thereby improving staff morale as they feel more valued.
- Employee participation can also help to generate new ideas for improving the quality of products, operations and processes.
- QA can help break down a 'them and us' culture (see Unit 2.5) between employees and managers because there is no formal inspection of the work by quality controllers.
- There is less wastage and reworking as products and processes are checked at every stage of output. This helps to reduce production costs.

In today's business environment, QA is seen as being superior to traditional quality control as prevention of poor quality is far better than conventional methods of detecting defects and imperfections. The main drawback of QA is the time, energy and training needed to nurture a total quality culture within the organization.

Question 5.3.2   Nissan

In May 2013, *Nissan* recalled 841,000 cars worldwide due to **quality control** issues caused by faulty steering wheels, although no accidents were recorded. *Nissan* stated that each car would take 15 minutes to repair. Car manufacturers are continually striving to reduce their costs by using the same components across a range of models. This can help firms such as *Nissan* to gain from **economies of scale**, but it has also increased the number of product recalls (defects).

Earlier in 2013, *Nissan* recalled 500,000 vehicles due to faulty passenger airbags. *Nissan's* larger rival, Toyota, also recalled 885,000 vehicles in October 2013 due to an airbag defect and 1.9 million of its top-selling Prius hybrid cars in February 2014 due to a software fault. However, in 2017, *Nissan* recalled 1.2 million passenger vehicles in Japan after discovering final vehicle inspections were not made. The cost of *Nissan's* product recall was around 25 billion yen ($222 million).

(a) (i) Define the term **quality control**. [2 marks]

(a) (ii) Define the term **economies of scale**. [2 marks]

(b) Examine how a major product recall can be costly to businesses such as *Nissan*. [6 marks]

Professor W. Edwards Deming (1900–1993), considered by many as the father of quality management, argued that QC methods are ineffective and costly. He suggested that quality comes from a system that improves, rather than inspects, the production process. Deming's philosophy for quality improvement is based around four key phases:

- *Plan* – Improve quality by designing or revising operations and processes.

- *Do* – Execute the plan.

- *Check* – Monitor and measure the performance, and assess the results.

- *Act* – Decide on any necessary changes that are needed to further improve the process.

Quality assurance, as a major feature of **total quality management** (see section below), is an ongoing process. Once a business has achieved a certain quality standard, its processes are regularly inspected by the respective awarding body to ensure that the standards are being maintained. For example, a school can only offer the IB programme if it is fully authorised by the International Baccalaureate (IB) as an 'IB World School'. This status is in recognition of the school having met the quality standards set by the IB. If quality standards are subsequently found to have dropped below the expected standards, then the business will be stripped of its QA award.

Whilst quality management can be costly to implement, it is important to recognize that it can be profitable in the long run. There are no shortcuts to QA and businesses must spend some money (on quality management) in order to earn money.

Box 5.3.c   CAD and CAM

Firms such as IKEA use CAD and CAM technology to help achieve zero defects. **Computer aided design (CAD)** is the process of using dedicated computer hardware and software in the design process, such as three-dimensional designs of a product. CAD software enables a wider range of designs to be completed and in a much quicker timeframe. **Computer aided manufacturing (CAM)** uses sophisticated automation and machinery in the production process. CAM is far more superior to human input in terms of both speed and accuracy of output.

Question 5.3.3   McDonald's "100% Quality Food"

As part of its **quality assurance**, *McDonald's* 100% Quality Food" campaign informs customers that it believes in great tasting food, based on only the best quality ingredients. In-store displays and literature support this claim by stating that:

- Only 100% beef is used without additives.
- Only prime white fish is used.
- Only chicken approved by the national authority responsible for ensuring food safety is used.
- Only the freshest eggs are used. Eggs are washed and sanitised to remove dirt from the shells.
- Only Russet Burbank potatoes are used to make French fries that are fluffy inside and crispy outside.

Source: McDonald's in-store literature

(a) Define the term **quality assurance**.   *[2 marks]*

(b) Examine the importance of quality management for multinational companies such as *McDonald's*.   *[6 marks]*

Case study

In late 2013, Europe's largest carmaker Volkswagen recalled a staggering 2.6 million cars worldwide due to lighting engine oil problems. Around 25% of the cars were recalled from China, a crucial growth market for the German carmaker. In 2017, Volkswagen recalled more than 600,000 vehicles in the USA due to defects that could result in fires or airbag malfunctions.

Case study

In 2014, Walmart recalled a donkey meat snack product (a popular item in some parts of China) after the Shandong Food and Drug Administration found traces of fox meat. In an attempt to reassure customers of its reputation for food safety, Walmart took legal action against its supplier of the tainted donkey meat.

Case study

In 2014, Kraft Foods recalled 96,000 lb (43,545kg) of its Oscar Mayer hot dogs in the USA because they had been wrong packaged as the company's Classic Cheese Dogs. Kraft's cheese sausages contain dairy products, which can cause allergic reactions. Earlier in the same year, Kraft also recalled more than 1,000,000 lb of its Velveeta Cheesy Skillets because of improper labelling.

Given the importance that organizations attach to achieving a desired level of quality, it is essential to understand how businesses can measure quality. The most common methods are:

- Reject rates – The higher the reject rate, the lower quality assurance tends to be.

- Level of product returns – Faulty and substandard products are far more likely to be returned by disgruntled customers.

- Product recalls – Faulty products may need to be recalled (brought back for corrections) by the firm to prevent a major public relations disaster (see Question 5.3.2).

- Level of customer satisfaction – Dissatisfied customers are more likely to complain about the quality of a product or a

firm's services. By contrast, good quality leads to enhanced customer relations (determined by customer satisfaction surveys).

- Degree of customer loyalty – Good quality is likely to encourage repeat purchases. This can be measured by customer retention levels.

- Market share – Good quality is likely to earn a business greater market share as sales revenues and brand loyalty (see Unit 4.5) both improve.

Exam tip !

The concept of quality can be somewhat subjective, i.e. what constitutes as 'quality' will depend on the product in question, and personal opinions will vary from one individual to another. Furthermore, not all aspects of quality are easily measureable, such as the value of a brand or a firm's reputation. It is important to note that quality is always evolving and is expensive to implement. Hence, whilst quality is important to all businesses, it is necessary to ensure the benefits of quality assurance outweigh the costs in the long run.

Methods of managing quality

The following methods of managing quality: quality circle, benchmarking and total quality management (TQM). AO2
The impact of lean production and TQM on an organization. AO3
© IBO, 2017

Quality circles

Quality circles are small groups of people who meet regularly to examine issues relating to the quality of output and make recommendations for improvement. The term was coined by Professor Kaoru Ishikawa in 1962. Members of a quality circle consist of volunteers from various departments, although it is common for a senior manager to chair the meetings. It is believed that such arrangements encourage communication and teamwork in order to solve problems that have a negative effect on quality. Like kaizen groups, quality circles are a vital part of quality management, emphasising improvements through the involvement of staff. However, unlike kaizen, members of quality circles are also directly involved in the execution and management of the recommendations or solutions.

Advocates of quality circles emphasise the importance of team cohesiveness in managing and improving quality. Businesses that fail to acknowledge the contributions of their staff often find a drop in the level of motivation and standards of work. Furthermore, such corporate cultures result in employees being only motivated by self-interest rather than feeling a sense of responsibility for the success of the organization. By contrast, businesses that adopt quality circles believe that there is always room for improvement, in all aspects of their operation, and not just the production process. This includes investigating ways to improve marketing, human resource management and financial control. The ultimate impacts on the organization are increased efficiency, productivity and profitability.

A limitation to quality circles is that some individuals remain unmotivated by teamworking, extra responsibility or empowerment (see Unit 2.4). These people prefer to be told what to do and see work as a means to an end, i.e. they perceive no loyalty to the organization and work only for pay.

Benchmarking

Benchmarking, or **Best Practice Benchmarking** (BPB), refers to a business comparing its products, operations and processes with others in the same industry, especially market leaders. BPB then becomes a point of reference for the business to target. The purpose is to allow the business to emulate best practice (excellence) in order to improve its own operational efficiency, e.g. luxury car manufacturers might benchmark their products and processes against market leaders such as Mercedes–Benz and BMW. Box 5.3.d outlines the various types of BPB.

Figure 5.3.h Benchmarking is intended to help improve performance

Box 5.3.d Types of benchmarking

- *Performance benchmarking* is used to benchmark the key performance indicators of a business, e.g. productivity and labour turnover rates.
- *Process benchmarking* is used to benchmark the processes and operations of a business, e.g. queuing times at restaurants, hotels or theme parks.
- *Internal benchmarking* involves benchmarking different operations or functions within the same organization, e.g. output or sales revenue per worker in different departments.
- *External benchmarking* involves benchmarking against products or organizations that are classed as the best in the industry.
- *International benchmarking* is BPB against the performance of organizations in overseas markets.

Box 5.3.e Stages in the benchmarking process

1. Identify the performance indicator to be benchmarked.
2. Measure the internal performance against a set of criteria.
3. Identify the most appropriate competitors to measure against (those with best practice).
4. Measure the external performance (of rivals).
5. Use the comparative data to determine the main weaknesses of the firm.
6. Set the standards for quality improvements.
7. Implement changes to achieve the required benchmarked standards.
8. Evaluate outcome of implementation to check for measured improvements.

There are two methods of benchmarking:

- *Historical benchmarking* involves comparing the same performance data over time, e.g. sales turnover, market share, profits and staff turnover. This is used for internal benchmarking whereby the performance of the organization can be measured.
- *Inter-firm benchmarking* involves comparing the same performance data of different businesses. For example, Citibank might compare its staff turnover rate with other financial institutions such as HSBC, Standard Chartered or Bank of America.

Table 5.3.b   Benefits and limitations of benchmarking

Benefits	Limitations
Benchmarking allows a business to reduce the performance gap with its rivals if BPB is successfully implemented.	The costs and time implications of collecting relevant and up-to-date information for BPB can be a major issue.
Dealing with problems of quality by using external benchmarking is more effective than simple guesswork.	Replicating the ideas and best practice of other firms is perhaps second best, without any distinctive selling points.
It looks at comparisons from the perception of customers and therefore BPB should help the business to take appropriate action to meet its customers' needs and wants.	The costs of implementing best practice can be very high. Sufficient time and finance must be made available to implement the findings from the benchmarking exercise.
The successful implementation of BPB can help a business to improve its competitiveness and *lower* production costs simultaneously.	Relying on BPB and ideas from others can discourage initiative and constrain creative and innovative thinking (see Unit 5.6).

Question 5.3.4   Mercedes–Benz

Mercedes–Benz is one of the most recognized brand names in the world. Rivals such as BMW and Audi often **benchmark** against the quality standards set by *Mercedes–Benz*. All new *Mercedes–Benz* cars come with a 1- to 3-year warranty, with the manufacturer undertaking any necessary work arising from any **defects** in the product, free of charge. Top of the range high-performance engines carry the 'AMG' badge as a sign of their superior build quality and performance.

(a) (i) Define the term **benchmark**.   *[2 marks]*

(a) (ii) Define the term **defects**.   *[2 marks]*

(b) Discuss the extent to which benchmarking can help businesses such as *Mercedes–Benz* to achieve quality assurance.   *[10 marks]*

Like the concept of kaizen, benchmarking cannot be a one-off exercise if the organization is to achieve quality assurance. As Greek philosopher Aristotle put it *"Quality is not an act, it is a habit"*.

To be effective, BPB has to be a continuous process that involves the commitment and involvement of every employee. This allows the firm to gain lasting improvements in quality.

IB Learner Profile – Be an inquirer

J.D. Power and Associates is a market research firm that provides global marketing information services. Founded in 1968, the American firm is best known for its customer satisfaction surveys. Visit www.jdpower.com to find out which car manufacturer has topped this year's chart for producing the best quality cars.

HIGHER LEVEL

Operations management

Total quality management (TQM)

Total Quality Management (TQM) is a process that requires the dedication of everyone in the organization to commit to achieving quality standards. Quality is seen from the perspective of the consumer rather than the producer. TQM removes wastage and inefficiencies in all forms of business activity (production, marketing, finance and personnel). However, this requires all employees to be properly trained to check and correct their own work.

A **total quality culture (TQC)** is a philosophy that embeds quality in every business operation and process. It places quality as the core focus in all functional areas, i.e. every employee is responsible for quality assurance, rather than it being the traditional role of the quality control department. TQC is a prerequisite to achieving TQM.

TQM empowers every employee to take corrective measures if quality is unacceptable (substandard). The purpose is to achieve **zero defects** in the organization. This means that all products, operations and processes are monitored and managed to ensure that they meet the required quality standards without any faults. If achieved, this will eliminate waste and the need to rectify mistakes. Ultimately, the impacts are positive, leading to improved customer satisfaction.

National and international quality standards

The importance of national and international quality standards.
AO2

© IBO, 2017

National and international quality awards are used to show that certain quality standards have been met. Businesses that meet or exceed these standards can include the quality award symbols or logos on their products and in their promotional campaigns. This helps to assure customers that the products are of high quality. National and international quality standards are important because they help businesses to:

- promote quality awareness within the organization

- improve organizational performance

- recognize quality achievements

- motivate the workforce

- help attract high calibre employees

- strengthen the firm's competitiveness.

Table 5.3.c Benefits and limitations of total quality management

Benefits	Limitations
Staff motivation is likely to improve since workers are empowered and involved in decision-making.	There are costs in establishing and maintaining a TQM system, e.g. on-going costs of market research into customer satisfaction levels.
Reduces or eliminates wastage (defective goods and re-working) as things are done right first time, thereby lowering production costs.	TQM can become quite bureaucratic as procedures and processes must be properly audited and administered.
Having a reputation for TQM improves the organization's corporate image.	Improving quality standards requires sufficient funding for staff training and development.
Customer needs (of quality assurance) are a central focus of the production process, so TQM can help to give a business a competitive advantage.	TQM only works if every member of the organization, irrespective of their rank, is fully committed. This also means that managers must set an example for others to follow.
TQM improves the chances of business survival; poor quality is not sustainable.	There is a time lag (sometimes lasting several years) before the benefits of TQM surface.

Question 5.3.5   Durex

Durex is the world's most popular brand of condoms. Reckitt Benckiser, the British multinational that produces *Durex* condoms, has around 25% of the world market share, with output of 1 billion units each year. The *Durex* brand name is short for Durable, Reliable and Excellence. Each *Durex* condom can hold up to 40 litres of air, or 9 gallons of water, before bursting. Samples, including condoms that have been artificially aged, are tested to destruction for physical strength. The *Durex* factory in Bangkok, Thailand reports a greater than 97% pass rate. Thailand is the world's leading exporter of condoms, with an annual output of over 300 million units from the *Durex* factory alone.

Source: adapted from www.durex.com

(a) Calculate the approximate quantity of defective *Durex* condoms produced each year at the Bangkok factory.   [2 marks]

(b) Explain why quality assurance is crucial to firms such as Reckitt Benckiser.   [4 marks]

(c) Comment on how Total Quality Management might help Reckitt Benckiser to reduce its defect rate of *Durex* condoms.   [4 marks]

There are numerous organizations that promote and regulate product and service quality. They usually operate as autonomous bodies (independent of any government) to promote and recognise the quality performance of organizations. Examples of national and international quality standards include:

- *The CE Mark* – This is the European Union's award for products that meet mandatory health and safety standards. 'CE' stands for Conformité Européenne, French for European Conformity.

- *The ASQ Award* – The American Society for Quality (ASQ) is an organization dedicated to the promotion and advancement of quality in the USA. It administers the prestigious Malcolm Baldrige National Quality Award which recognises businesses that have achieved performance excellence. It is one of only two US Presidential awards given to businesses.

- *The BSI Kitemark* – The British Standards Institution (BSI) is the official organization responsible for setting quality standards in the UK. Products that carry the BSI Kitemark help to inform customers that they have been manufactured to a high level of quality.

- *The Lion Mark* – This is awarded by the British Toy and Hobby Association (BTHA) for products that meet a strict code of practice on toy safety. It also assures customers that the product is genuine and not a counterfeit.

IB Learner Profile – Be an inquirer

Visit the websites of the Council of International Schools (www.cois.org) and Western Association of Schools and Colleges (www.wascweb.org) to investigate the benefits to schools and colleges that gain CIS-WASC accreditation.

IB Learner Profile – Be an inquirer and be a thinker

Investigate the national quality standards in your own country – or a country of your choice. Find out about the work of the organization(s) that is (are) in charge of regulating quality standards in this country.

In order to obtain quality standard awards, products tend to undergo stringent and regular testing by independent agents. Only if a business has proved that its products meet or exceed these standards is it given the quality award in recognition of its achievements.

The most prominent global organization for quality assurance is the **International Organization for Standardization (ISO)**, founded in 1947 and based in Geneva, Switzerland. It is made up of representatives from 163 national quality standards bodies, such as the ASQ and the BSI. The ISO's goal is to facilitate international trade by providing a single set of quality standards that consumers and businesses throughout the world would recognise and respect. The ISO is one of the most powerful non-governmental organizations (NGO) in the world as it is influential in affecting government legislation.

The most widely recognized ISO Standard for quality management is the ISO 9000. It is awarded by independent auditors who certify that the ISO Standards have been met. The ISO then endorses that the business has:

- Monitored operations and processes to ensure that quality goods are being produced.

- Checked products for defects before they are distributed, having carried out corrective measures where necessary.

- Regularly reviewed its operations and processes to sustain or improve its efficiency.

- Proper record keeping.

Businesses that meet the ISO Standards can publicise their achievement by stating themselves to be 'ISO 9000 certified' or 'ISO 9000 registered'. The ISO Standards apply to both manufactured goods and the provision of services.

Lean production, quality management and the CUEGIS concepts

To achieve a culture within the organization that is committed to quality, all managers and employees must constantly strive to improve their working practices. Modern business strategy focuses on quality management being an on-going process that involves the continual updating and improvement of an organization's products, functions and processes. Every aspect of business activity can be improved. Today's ever-changing and competitive business environment leaves no room for error. Hence, quality management requires all internal stakeholders to be dedicated to this total quality culture and philosophy. Businesses can do this through motivational methods (see Unit 2.4), developing multi-skilled workers, and using flexible working structures (see Unit 2.1). A business with a highly trained, flexible and motivated workforce is more likely to achieve total quality management. TQM might also require flatter and/or more flexible organizational structures (see Unit 2.2). Strategically, this should enable the organization to be more effective in responding to market changes. In addition, organizational change is easier to manage when there are small and continuous improvements, rather than one-off and radical changes made.

Traditionally, consumers had to make a choice between the price and the quality of a product. Quality used to come at a high price. Today, technological innovations and globalization (growing national and international competitive pressures)

Question 5.3.6   The BSI Kitemark

The British Standards Institution (BSI) is the organization responsible for setting quality standards in the UK. Products that carry the BSI Kitemark show customers that they have been independently tested for quality and safety so are fit for their purpose. According to the BSI, around 82% of British adults recognise the Kitemark as a sign of quality and safety. It also claims that a staggering 88% of the public believe that a Kitemark shows that the product comes from a reputable company, so they would be prepared to pay higher prices for such products.

Source: : www.bsigroup.com

(a) Explain the role of a regulatory body, such as the BSI, in ensuring quality standards. *[4 marks]*

(b) Examine the advantages to organizations that hold an external quality assurance certificate such as the BSI Kitemark. *[6 marks]*

have meant that quality is an integral part of business strategy. Quality management is crucial for retaining customer loyalty. It also affects the reputation of an organization. This is particularly true for service sector organizations such as air travel, health care providers and theme parks where customer safety has to be given top priority. For instance, Hong Kong Disneyland has a specialist team of over 120 technicians who inspect, repair and maintain all the rides at the theme park on a daily basis. Hence, QA plays a vital role in business strategy as quality management can determine the success and profitability of a business.

Many businesses pursue a *six sigma* lean production strategy to increase quality by striving to limit defects to no more than 3.4 imperfections per million units of output (the statistical value of six sigma), i.e. a success rate of 99.73%. In essence, it is a systematic approach to achieving near perfection or zero defects. Companies that have used this strategy include Motorola, Boeing, General Electric, Ford, Apple and Bank of America. Motorola announced a saving of over $17 billion during the first 20 years of using the six sigma strategy. Similarly, General Electric estimated a saving of $10 billion during its first 5 years of using the strategy.

Quality management must be considered at all stages in the production process, from the initial design of a product to its sale and beyond (after-sales services). Although the costs of meeting quality management might be very high, perhaps the costs of *not* meeting these standards are even greater to a business, particularly in the long run. There is also the argument that businesses are ethically or morally obliged to ensure products are safe to use, so must meet minimum quality standards. The slogan of Italian luxury brand Gucci sums this up very well: "*Quality is remembered long after the price is forgotten.*"

Theory of knowledge

Does the meaning of 'quality' apply across different cultures?

Theory of knowledge

Does our understanding and knowledge of 'quality' stand the test of time?

CUEGIS Essay

With reference to an organization of your choice, examine the impacts of **change** and **culture** on its quality management. *[20 marks]*

CUEGIS Essay

With reference to an organization of your choice, examine how quality management is influenced by **innovation** and **ethics**. *[20 marks]*

REVIEW QUESTIONS

1. What is meant by lean production?

2. What principles are important in the pursuit of lean production?

3. What is meant by kaizen?

4. How is just-in-time a method of lean production?

5. What is kanban?

6. Why is andon an important method of lean production?

7. What is cradle to cradle design and manufacturing?

8. What is meant by the term 'quality'?

9. Why is quality important to both consumers and producers?

10. How does quality assurance differ from quality control?

11. What is quality management?

12. What are quality circles?

13. What are the costs and benefits of best practice benchmarking (BPB)?

14. What is total quality management (TQM)?

HIGHER LEVEL

Operations management

15. What is the purpose of national and international quality standards?

KEY TERMS

Andon is a lean production method that uses visual control systems to indicate the status of an aspect of the production process, e.g. machinery, production line or work process.

Benchmarking is the process of identifying best practice in an industry, in relation to products, processes and operations. It sets the standards for other firms to emulate.

Cradle to cradle (C2C) is a sustainable model of production based on natural processes. The underlying principle of C2C is that there is no waste in nature, making production sustainable for future generations.

Efficiency means using resources more productively, in order to generate more output.

ISO 9000 is the world's most widely recognised standard for quality management. It is endorsed by the ISO to firms that use quality management systems to meet the needs of customers.

Just-in-time (JIT) is an inventory management system based on stocks being delivered as and when they are needed in the production process. As stocks are delivered just before they are used, there is no need to have buffer stocks.

Kaizen is the Japanese term for 'continuous improvement', a lean production philosophy where workers and managers continually try to find ways to improve work processes and efficiency.

Kanban is a method of lean production used to ensure that inventory is based on actual customer orders using a card system with an inventory number attached to each component in the production process.

Lean production refers to the approach used to eliminate waste (muda) in an organization. As a result, lean organizations benefit from higher productivity and lower costs.

Quality means that a good or service must be fit for its purpose by meeting or exceeding the expectations of consumers.

Quality assurance refers to the methods used by a business to reassure customers that its products meet certain quality standards, such as the ISO 9000.

Quality circles are groups of workers that meet on a regular basis to identify problems related to quality assurance, to consider alternative solutions to the identified problems, and to make feasible recommendations for improvement.

Quality control is the traditional way of quality management that involves checking and reviewing work processes. This is usually carried out by quality controllers and inspectors.

Quality management is the function concerned with controlling business activities to ensure that products are fit for their purpose. The quality of a product is seen as an overall package, from the production and purchase of the product to its use and beyond (after-sales care).

Quality standards refer to national and/or international benchmarks that enable certification of quality assurance. These certify that the product has met certain minimum quality standards to meet the needs of customers.

Total Quality Management (TQM) is the process that attempts to encourage all employees to make quality assurance paramount in the various functions (production, finance, marketing and HRM) of an organization.

Waste refers to anything that prevents an organization from being efficient or lean, e.g. product defects, stockpiling and overproduction.

Zero defects is the goal of producing each and every product without any mistakes or imperfections, thereby eliminating waste and reworking time (the time taken to correct faults).

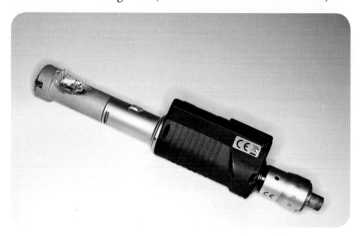

Zero defects aims to eliminate waste

5.4 Location

SL/HL content	Assessment objective
The reasons for a specific location of production	AO2
The following ways of reorganizing production, both nationally and internationally: • outsourcing/subcontracting • offshoring • insourcing	AO3

© IBO, 2017

Operations management

Factors affecting location decisions

The reasons for a specific location of production. AO2

© IBO, 2017

All businesses need to be located somewhere. Sole traders might operate from a room in their own home. Amazon.com operates from huge warehouses in out-of-town areas. Large multinational companies are located throughout the world. Online businesses still need a physical location where they operate. Managers have a crucial role in weighing up the costs and benefits of a specific location. In the property (real estate) industry, the three rules to business success are simply location, location and location! Although somewhat of an over-generalisation, there is a large degree of accuracy in this saying.

Location refers to the geographical position of a business, i.e. where it is sited. The location decision depends on many factors such as the nature of the business (e.g. retail outlet or oil extraction), the nature of the product (e.g. agricultural products or tourism) and the nature of human resources (e.g. unskilled or skilled). Location decisions will occur in different situations. New businesses need to consider the location of their first premises. Businesses planning to expand, domestically and internationally, also have to choose between different locations. The **relocation** decision occurs when managers consider moving to alternative premises, perhaps because of uncompetitive or unaffordable rents.

The location decision is one of the most important that senior managers have to make, especially as it is often an irreversible decision, i.e. they cannot simply afford to relocate if things do not work out as planned. Even if relocation is possible, the costs of doing so can be extremely high. For many new businesses, the location decision incurs a highly significant proportion of their costs. It is unlikely that most of these costs can be recovered (known as *sunk costs*) if the business is unsuccessful. Hence, the location decision can have profound implications on the profitability and survival of the business. The decision is so important that it is classed as a long-term strategic goal and the decision is only made by entrepreneurs or the senior leadership team.

Figure 5.4.a Location is a major decision for all businesses

CORE

551

Quantitative reasons for a specific location of production

Quantitative reasons are those that can be numerically calculated, such as the cost of purchasing or renting premises. The finance department and senior managers will be keen to look at the financial costs and benefits of locating or relocating the organization. Quantitative factors include the following:

Availability, suitability and cost of land

The quantity, quality and cost of land are important factors when choosing a location. Decision makers consider the cost of land with earning potential; the busier the area, the higher the earning potential but the greater the cost of land. As rent forms a large proportion of fixed costs for most businesses, the high cost of land may reduce corporate profits. However, the cheapest location is not necessarily ideal as it is 'cheap' for a reason – perhaps the location lacks passing trade or the premises are in need of attention.

There are two main reasons why the cost of land is higher in city centres than elsewhere. First, there is more *demand* for land in city centres, largely due to the convenience such centres provide for customers, suppliers and employees. Second, the *supply of land* is very limited in these areas. The combination of high demand and low supply means that property prices and rents are higher in popular cities. It is no wonder then that the 38 million people who reside in Tokyo (the most populated city on the planet) make it one of the world's most expensive locations.

Figure 5.4.b Property prices and rents are higher in popular cities such as London

For some businesses, the suitability of land must also be considered. Agricultural businesses need to locate in areas with arable land and suitable climate. Businesses engaged in the production of dangerous products or harmful by-products need to locate away from highly populated areas.

Some organizations, such as hypermarkets or vehicle manufacturers need to buy cheap land simply because they need so much of it. Hence, they tend to be located away from central business districts where land is both scarce and expensive. Provided that there is adequate infrastructure, such as communication and road networks, this should not be a problem as such businesses do not need to locate near their customers. Motor vehicles are distributed to showrooms and franchised dealerships that sell the vehicles. Hypermarket customers tend to drive out of town to do their shopping.

The availability, suitability and cost of land also apply on a global scale. The opportunities found in lower cost locations abroad have led to many businesses moving their operations overseas. Audi, Phillips and Coca-Cola are just some examples of manufacturers that have relocated to less affluent countries, largely due to the lower cost of land – a highly important consideration for firms that require a vast amount of space.

Availability, quality and cost of labour

The availability and quality of labour affect the level of wages paid to workers, so are therefore critical to any location decision. Tenneco, an American manufacturer of exhaust pipes for General Motors, Volkswagen and Peugeot, chose to locate in Shanghai (China) largely due to the high supply and low cost of labour. A study carried out by *Fortune* magazine found that labour accounted for just 1% of production costs in China's Tenneco plant. By contrast, other manufacturers such as Ferrari or Boeing need highly skilled workers , who are well remunerated.

The supply and quality of labour varies even within a country, affected by factors such as the reputation of local schools and colleges, socioeconomic demographics and regional unemployment rates. The inequality is much greater on an international scale. Firms requiring highly skilled engineers might locate in Germany where there is a readily available supply of skilled labour. Likewise, businesses wanting to locate in Norway, Japan, Denmark and Finland should consider the high cost of living when remunerating their workforce in these countries. By contrast, mass market manufacturers such as Nike can locate in highly populated countries, such as Indonesia, where there is an abundance of labour at a relatively low cost.

Question 5.4.1 The cost of a good location

Growing demand from financial institutions and other businesses has raised land and property prices in central business districts throughout the world. The world's most expensive places to rent office spaces include London, San Francisco, New York City, Tokyo and Hong Kong. Prime office rents have also been surging in Moscow, Paris, Wellington, Dublin and Abu Dhabi.

(a) Outline how rising demand for land can push up its price.

[2 marks]

Manhattan, New York City, USA

(b) Examine the advantages and disadvantages for businesses considering to relocate overseas. [6 marks]

Proximity to the market (customers)

Certain products such as bottled water or alcohol will increase in weight during the production process. These are known as **bulk-increasing** or **weight-gaining industries**, commonly found in businesses that assemble components. If they were to locate near the source of the raw materials, such as lakes and hop farms (for alcohol), this would increase their transportation costs when the final, heavier and bulkier product needs to be delivered. Hence, it makes more sense for these businesses to locate nearer to their markets.

In the manufacturing sector, firms that rely on *just-in-time production* (see Unit 5.3) need to locate near their suppliers. This reduces transportation costs and time, thereby minimising delays in the delivery of products to customers. In the tertiary sector, proximity to the market can also be vital. In retailing and service industries, customers demand convenience so it is important for businesses such as hotels, restaurants and hair salons to be suitably located near their markets.

Case study

In 2006, Audi halted investments of over 1 billion euros ($1.45bn) in Hungary, where it makes the Audi TT sports car. This was because the Hungarian government had decided to raise taxes to reduce its huge budget deficit (when the government's spending exceeds its tax revenues).

Figure 5.4.c Sole traders generally need to be located near their customers

Proximity and access to raw materials

The nearness to and availability of raw materials is a major determinant of location for firms operating in primary and manufacturing industries. **Bulk-reducing businesses** (or **weight-losing industries**) locate near the source of raw materials that are heavier and costlier to transport than the final product, i.e. the weight or size of the finished product is less than that of the raw materials used to produce it. For example, it is cheaper to extract steel, iron, sugar and oil at source than to transport these to other manufacturing sites because of the sheer weight and the high amount of waste products from the raw materials.

Government incentives and limitations

Governments often try to attract businesses to locate in or relocate to a certain area by offering financial incentives, such as grants and subsidies to help reduce their costs of production. Low or interest-free loans may also be offered by the government to encourage businesses to invest in a particular location. Such financial incentives are more likely to be approved if businesses locate in *assisted areas* or *enterprise zones* (areas suffering from high unemployment, low incomes and/or undergoing economic regeneration).

On the other hand, the government can also impose limitations that affect business location. For example, a business might find it more difficult to obtain a license to trade overseas than within the domestic country. Planning permission for extensions or modifications to a site might be a further problem and therefore affects the choice of business location. Corporation tax rates can also have large implications for the international location decision. For example, Cameroon has a corporate tax rate of 38.5% whereas the United Arab Emirates, the British Virgin Islands and the Cayman Islands have a zero rate corporate tax.

Feasibility of e-commerce

E-commerce can have a huge effect on reducing the financial costs of location. Many businesses no longer need to be located near their customers as they are now able to sell products via the Internet (see Unit 4.8). For example, insurance companies, book retailers and music distributors can be located anywhere in the world yet still reach a global audience.

However, having a virtual business (e-business) rather than a physical presence (retailer) is not feasible for all organizations. For example, Airbus aircraft would not be purchased online. Instead, Airbus can use its website to market the company and its products, but the actual purchase is done through other means.

Similarly, convenience stores such as 7-Eleven, Circle K, FamilyMart and Tesco Express all need to be located near their markets. These businesses often locate in busy commercial and residential districts.

Question 5.4.2   Doing business in Singapore

Singapore has been consistently rated very highly in the World Bank's annual "Ease of Doing Business" report. The report ranks 178 economies in terms of regulations that either enhance or constrain business activity. Such regulations include: starting a business, obtaining licences, employing workers, registering property and investor protection.

Singapore is often ranked the top country in the world to do business due to its simplistic business procedures. For example, it only takes six days to start a business in Singapore, whereas it takes 97 days in Indonesia, 141 days in Venezuela and 694 days in Suriname! Singapore is also a global manufacturing hub and a regional financial centre. However, Singapore is also the world's most expensive city to live in, according to the Economist Intelligence Unit.

Source: adapted from The World Bank (www.doingbusiness.org) and Economist Intelligence Unit (www.eiu.com)

(a) Explain how government rules and regulations can constrain or enhance business activity.   *[4 marks]*

(b) Examine the quantitative factors that businesses may need to consider before deciding whether to locate in highly rated countries such as Singapore.   *[6 marks]*

Qualitative reasons for a specific location of production

Qualitative factors deal with the psychological and emotional aspects of location or relocation, such as familiarity with a particular area or consideration for the welfare of workers in the local community. Qualitative factors are not easy to measure, if measurable at all, but they can be just as important as quantitative factors when deciding where to locate a business.

Management preferences

Managers may prefer a certain location due to personal reasons, familiarity, gut feeling (instinct) or because they feel that the location will serve workers and the local community better. The headquarters of the Body Shop is in Littlehampton (UK) simply because its founder, Anita Roddick, was born and grew up there. For Roddick, there was an emotional attachment to the area rather than basing her location decision on financial reasoning. Managers may also prefer a certain location because of its history. Hollywood movie director Oliver Stone had little to think about when choosing New York as the location for filming *The World Trade Center*, which recalled the tragic events of the 11 September 2001 attacks on the USA.

Theory of knowledge

How useful is intuition as a way of knowing in Business Management?

Local knowledge

Similarly, businesses may locate in a certain area because they know the location and its culture. This inside information makes it easier and less risky for a business to establish itself, thereby giving it a potential competitive advantage. HSBC's highly successful global slogan, '*HSBC – the world's local bank*' suggests that multinational companies must consider the cultural differences that exist throughout the world. A lack of local knowledge can prove disastrous. For example, the launch of *OK!* magazine in the USA was, at that time, the world's largest magazine launch (as measured by advertising and publishing expenditure) but sales were a disaster because the UK firm did not realise that US supermarket shelf sizes were too small to hold the oversized magazine! Similarly, the Sock Shop opted for a large scale launch in Florida (nicknamed the 'Sunshine State') and found sales were disappointing as the hotter climate limited the sale of socks.

Infrastructure

This is perhaps the most common qualitative factor affecting the location decision. Infrastructure is the term used to describe transportation, communication and support networks:

- *Transportation networks* include links to roads, rail, sea and air. The most appropriate transportation network for a business depends on its size and the products that it sells, e.g. courier companies such as UPS, DHL and FedEx will want to be located in areas with good road and air networks.

- *Communication networks* cover access to telephone lines (for telecommunications coverage and Internet services) and postal services.

- *Support networks* refer to the back-up (maintenance) and complementary services that are essential for running a business, e.g. utilities companies provide fuel, water, power and waste management.

The government is responsible for the economy's infrastructure. Not only does the infrastructure affect the location of businesses, it also affects a country's international competitiveness. For example, some large multinational companies have been reluctant to locate in India due to its outdated infrastructure. Businesses want to locate in areas with good infrastructure so that they can supply goods and services more efficiently and more cost effectively. This helps to increase national output and reduce costs of production, thereby improving the country's international competitiveness. Manufacturers and distributors need easy access to rail, port and road networks. Although e-commerce firms such as Taobao, Amazon.com and eBay can be located almost anywhere, they still need easy access to transportation networks to ensure that deliveries are swift.

Infrastructure is also important to ensure that employees can get to and from work without too much hassle. Location can therefore have an impact on recruitment, retention and motivation of staff. For example, people who work at out-of-town theme parks or at the airport often have their travel expenses subsidised. This helps to compensate for the cost and time involved in travelling to these places of work. However, this also means an increase in the organization's costs.

Operations management

CORE

Figure 5.4.d Poor infrastructure limits incentives to locate in a particular location

Political stability

Even if monetary-related factors are favourable in a particular location, managers may still need to consider the political stability of the country that they wish to locate in. A stable political environment helps a business to trade effectively, thereby reducing the risks of operating overseas. Countries that can offer political harmony, free from corruption, a good law and order system, a stable exchange rate system and low rates of taxation will tend to be more attractive to businesses. Reports by the World Bank show that Congo is one of the worst places to conduct business. This is largely attributed to corrupt government activities, huge rates of taxes and poor infrastructure. In 2014, anti-government protesters and rioters caused major disruptions to Thailand's economy.

Government restrictions and regulations

Businesses need to consider government policies and regulations that constrain business activity as administrative and bureaucratic processes vary from country to country. For example, it takes just 2 days to register a company in Canada and Australia, whereas it takes an average of 8 days in France, 152 days in Brazil and a tedious 203 days in Haiti. The difficulty in obtaining licenses, permits, copyrights and planning permission may lead to businesses looking to locate in alternative countries.

The Heritage Foundation, a research organization based in the USA, publishes an annual 'Index of Economic Freedom' which ranks the attractiveness of countries based on how government intervention can restrict or aid economic relations and business activity. The annual survey ranks the freedom (or ease) to do business in different countries based on criteria such as economic freedom, political freedom, measures of anti-corruption, and fiscal freedom (tax rates). Hong Kong, Singapore, Australia, New Zealand and Switzerland tend to rank very highly in the Heritage Foundation's league tables.

Question 5.4.3 Doing business in India

Deregulation of markets in India has allowed foreign retailers to own their own stores in the country. Before the liberalisation of trade, foreign business activity was heavily regulated as a way of protecting domestic jobs and businesses. The change presents many investment opportunities for multinational companies such as Nike, Reebok, PepsiCo and Marks & Spencer.

India is opening up to Western cultures and has huge market potential for businesses. Foreign firms will have a larger role in supporting the rapid development of the country's retail, tourism and aviation industries.

However, India's bureaucratic procedures mean that doing business in India has its problems. Corruption is also an ongoing problem in India. Transparency International, a global non-governmental organization, claims that there is a strong correlation between corruption, poverty and competitiveness, i.e. higher levels of corruption in a country jeopardise the nation's ability to alleviate poverty and to be competitive on an international scale.

(a) Explain the risks involved for multinational companies, such as Nike, Reebok, PepsiCo and Marks & Spencer, wishing to invest in economically developing countries like India.   *[4 marks]*

(b) Examine the opportunities that might exist for businesses that plan to invest in a country such as India.   *[6 marks]*

Figure 5.4.e Australia ranks high in The Heritage Foundation's Index of Economic Freedom

and famous. According to *Business Week*, the average suit takes 12 weeks to make and is priced at £3,755 ($5,450) and more from any of the various tailors on the street.

Figure 5.4.f Bespoke ties from London's Savile Row

Ethical issues

Decisions regarding the international location or relocation of a business often include an ethical dimension. For example, a business that exerts lots of waste, noise and pollution might choose to locate in out-of-town and remote areas to avoid complaints from the local community. It may also be seen as unethical for a business to relocate if this will cause major job losses in a certain area, thereby potentially damaging the firm's reputation, sales and profits.

Comparative shopping (clustering)

Clustering means that firms locate near other businesses that cater for similar or complementary markets. For example, London's Savile Row is internationally renowned for its bespoke (custom made-to-measure) suits for men and women. The main clientele of businesses located on Savile Row are the rich

Similarly, retailers of computer hardware and mobile phones tend to locate near one another to make the most of the passing trade. Fast food chains locate in busy shopping malls to take advantage of people who need to eat and drink whilst at the mall. Accountancy and law firms also locate close to each other whilst shoes and clothes retailers locate near one another.

Exam tip!

In reality, organizations consider a combination of quantitative and qualitative factors when considering the attractiveness of business locations. This applies to domestic and overseas locations and relocations. As always, it is vital to consider these factors in the context of the business, e.g. different stakeholders may have different views about the best choice of location.

Question 5.4.4 Fifth Avenue, New York

Retail space in New York's Fifth Avenue has one of the highest rental values on earth and is known by locals as the 'most expensive street in the world'. The high price of leasing land has been accelerated by the world's top brands competing to secure a key spot in this prime location. Other highly sought after retail locations include Causeway Bay in Hong Kong, Ginza in Tokyo, Oxford Street in London, and Avenue des Champs Elysees in Paris.

(a) Explain why location is an important management decision for retail businesses. *[4 marks]*

(b) Examine why retail businesses might be prepared to pay exceptionally high rents in prime locations such as Fifth Avenue. *[6 marks]*

Operations management

CORE

Reorganizing production

The following ways of re-organizing production, both nationally and internationally: outsourcing/subcontracting, offshoring and insourcing. AO3

© IBO, 2017

Outsourcing (or subcontracting)

Outsourcing (or **subcontracting**) is the practice of transferring internal business activities to an external organization to reduce costs and increase productivity. Subcontractors can carry out the outsourced work more cost-effectively without compromising quality. Typical operations that are outsourced include recruitment, office cleaning, accounting, property management, call centres, customer support, security systems and ICT maintenance.

Figure 5.4.g Security services are often outsourced

The main advantages of outsourcing are:

- Activities that are not core to the functions of the business can be outsourced to third parties. This allows the business to concentrate on its core activities, i.e. what it is best at doing.

- Quality output can occur despite the business lacking specific skills such as ICT management systems, security services and accountancy.

- It helps to cut production costs for the contractor. Outsourcing is used if it leads to productivity gains and cost advantages, perhaps by subcontracting operations abroad to benefit from lower labour costs.

However, there are four interrelated limitations or concerns regarding outsourcing:

- There must be mutual trust between the business and the subcontractor. Any conflict can therefore be potentially damaging to the functioning of the business.

- The quality of the outsourced service is passed onto an external party. Hence, there can be concerns regarding whether the expected standards will be met. Allowing subcontractors to have such a large influence on the reputation of a firm can be potentially disastrous.

- Outsourcing still requires effective two-way communication and careful coordination.

- It can cause uncertainty among the workforce due to restructuring and staff redundancies.

Offshoring

Offshoring is an extension of outsourcing, which involves relocating business functions and processes overseas. This means that offshored functions can remain within the business (operating overseas) or outsourced to an overseas organization. In the latter case, this is known as **offshore outsourcing**. For example, Blackberry, Sony, Xiaomi and Apple use offshore outsourcing for the production of their smartphones, using Taiwan's Foxconn as the subcontractor. Nintendo, Sony and Microsoft also outsource the production of their games consoles to Foxconn. In addition to manufacturing, other typically offshored functions or services include telesales, call centres, research and development (R&D) and accounting services.

The advantages of outsourcing also apply to offshoring. Findings from Forrester Research Inc. show the number of US jobs offshored rose from 0.5 million people in 2004 to over 3 million in 2014. Businesses chooses to outsource largely because of the lower labour costs in overseas markets. For example, the minimum wages per hour in Luxembourg ($11.55) and New Zealand ($9.45) are significantly higher than in Vietnam ($1.57) and Indonesia ($1.30). Offshore outsourcing can also help businesses to avoid trade protectionist measures used by governments (see Box 1.5.c). For example, Nissan, Honda and Toyota have offshore production facilities in the UK. This helps the Japanese carmakers to avoid protectionist measures used by the European Union, such as tariffs (import taxes) imposed on the sale of cars imported from outside the EU.

However, offshoring has often been associated with unethical practices, e.g. the exploitation of labour in low income countries such as poor working conditions, low pay, the use of child labour and poor health and safety policies. Quality assurance therefore becomes more difficult. Offshoring can also be vulnerable to external influences such as economic and political instability. For example, Venezuela, Ukraine and Thailand faced major political unrest in 2014, with negative impacts on businesses with offshored activities in these countries. The unemployment rate in Greece exceeded 20% in 2017, with the youth unemployment rate (for those aged under 25 without a job) reaching 47.4%. This would clearly have major consequences for businesses operating in Greece.

There are two categories of offshoring: *production offshoring* (manufacturing) and *services offshoring* (such as call centres). These often take place in low income countries where labour costs are low. Offshoring has brought about many benefits for host countries, such as job creation and relatively higher wages compared with wages paid by local firms. China and Vietnam have proved to be popular locations for production offshoring whilst India has emerged as a magnet for services offshoring.

Exam tip !

Be sure you can explain the differences between outsourcing, offshoring and offshore outsourcing:

- Outsourcing refers to the use of a third-party subcontractor paid to carry out specific work.
- Offshoring refers to getting business activities or functions done in a different country, usually due to cost advantages of locating overseas.
- Offshore outsourcing is the hiring of a subcontractor to do the work overseas, usually to lower costs and to take advantage of the vendor's local expertise.

Figure 5.4.h Vietnam is a popular choice for offshore outsourcing

Operations management

CORE

Question 5.4.5   Volkswagen

Volkswagen, the German car manufacturer and owner of **brands** such as Audi, Bentley and Beetle, were given permission in 2006 to build a car plant in Punjab, India. Despite India's underdeveloped **infrastructure**, Volkswagen announced that it was to invest about 15 billion rupees ($340 million) in the plant, creating 5,000 jobs. In addition, there would be around 50,000 jobs created indirectly. Other car manufacturers also have a presence in India, such as Mercedes–Benz (since 1983) and BMW (since 2007). Analysts expect car sales in India to carry on booming as the world's second most populated country continues to enjoy high rates of economic growth.

(a) (i) Define the term **brands**.   *[2 marks]*

(a) (ii) Define the term **infrastructure**.   *[2 marks]*

(b) Evaluate the decision of Volkswagen to locate its business in India.   *[10 marks]*

Question 5.4.6   Offshore outsourcing: a risky business?

Mattel, one of the world's largest toy makers, recalled more than 18 million faulty toys in 2007. The die-cast toys were produced by an outsourced firm called *Hong Li Da* in China. It was discovered that *Hong Li Da* had used contaminated materials from unauthorised suppliers. The product recall seriously damaged the 'Made in China' brand image throughout Europe and the USA.

Similarly, media coverage in 2010 revealed that factory workers at *Foxconn* were being mistreated and forced to work at **full capacity** to make the iPhone, leading to a series of suicides. Taiwan's *Foxconn* is the world's largest maker of electronic components with clients such as Apple, Dell, Sony, Nintendo, Microsoft and HP.

In 2013, French food giant *Danone* announced it would cancel its supply contract with New Zealand's *Fonterra* after the botulism scare. Food safety tests found botulism-causing bacteria in the dairy products made by *Fonterra*, causing a recall of about 1,000 tons of consumer products.

(a) Explain **two** drawbacks of *Foxconn* workers operating at **full capacity**.   *[4 marks]*

(b) Discuss the arguments for and against multinational companies such as *Mattel, Apple* and *Danone* outsourcing some of their operations overseas.   *[10 marks]*

Question 5.4.7   Offshoring in India

Indian software firms have benefited from the influx of European and US companies that have been **offshoring** their operations in order to cut costs. For instance, Bangalore-based Wipro offers services in ICT, software development and call centre services to foreign customers such as Cisco Systems and Nortel. Foreign companies are attracted by the relatively low wage costs and the abundant supply of skilled labour in India. British and American companies are also attracted by India's large English-speaking workforce.

(a) Define the term **offshoring**.   *[2 marks]*

(b) Evaluate the reasons for and against multinational companies choosing to offshore some of their functions to external organizations located overseas.   *[10 marks]*

Insourcing

Insourcing is the use of an organization's own people and resources to accomplish a certain function or task, which would otherwise have been outsourced. There are two main reasons for insourcing to occur:

- The business had previously outsourced a particular function or task but is no longer satisfied with the quality of work being done. The task is then assigned to someone in-house in the hope of an improved result.

- There are no longer cost-saving benefits from using a subcontractor and the function or task can be assigned to people in-house to cut costs.

Although outsourcing is commonly used by multinational companies to cut costs, it is sometimes more cost effective to use insourcing if the work can be done better in-house. At times, businesses may also need to consider re-shoring (bringing back operations from overseas). This might be due to rising labour costs abroad and/or higher rents being demanded. However, there are problems with relocation (see Box 5.4.a) so there is often a reluctance to relocate. This concept is known as **industrial inertia**. The term was coined by Allan Rogers (1952) who found that American steel producers tended to continue to invest and reinvest in an existing location, even when the competitive advantages for such location no longer existed.

Ultimately, the location decision is likely to affect all functional areas and aspects of business activity. The scope of these impacts depends on the type and size of the business, the products it sells and the features of the location itself. Considering these factors in the context of the business and its objectives allows better judgements to be made.

Location and the CUEGIS concepts

The location decision is one of the most important and most difficult strategic decisions for any business. Good location decisions require significant planning and quantitative analysis of the costs and benefits of alternative options. Two commonly used quantitative methods are *investment appraisal* (see Unit 3.8) and *break-even analysis* (see Unit 3.3). Investment appraisal methods are used to calculate the location with the quickest and/or highest financial return. Break-even analysis can help a business to identify which location is most likely to break even first after which the firm will start to earn profit. However, these methods must be used with caution since the calculations are based on forecasts. Therefore, most managers will also use qualitative factors in their strategic assessment of the location decision.

Globalization has meant that an increasing number of organizations have to consider both domestic and international location decisions. This undoubtedly makes decision-making more difficult as there are external factors to consider (such as language and cultural issues, or the political stability of the country). For example, globalization has been fuelled by the removal of trade restrictions (see Unit 1.5) by national governments.

International location decisions are further complicated by differences in exchange rates, which makes financial comparisons rather more difficult. Globalization has also meant that businesses have to increasingly consider qualitative factors when locating overseas. For example, McDonald's, KFC, Nike and Walmart have all been heavily criticised in the past for allegedly paying low wages to staff. Hence, international location decisions have increasingly been influenced by ethical factors. Other issues also need some consideration, such as differences in language, culture, etiquette and the political environment. Some of these factors present opportunities, such as:

- **Production costs** – The costs of labour, materials and transportation can be significantly lower in overseas markets. However, these benefits will need to be considered in relation to potentially higher distribution costs from the new location.

- **Government rules and regulations** – Direct investment in overseas locations can help a business to get around government bureaucracy, such as import restrictions and duties (taxes). However, this may need to be weighed up against the costs of relocation.

- **Economies of scale** – Large multinational companies (MNCs) can gain huge cost savings by operating on a global scale, especially in countries with good infrastructure (such as transportation links and telecommunications networks). These economies of scale (see Unit 1.6) can therefore help the business to be more competitive.

Figure 5.4.i Singapore's infrastructure helps to attract MNCs

Operations management

CORE

However, the international location decision can also bring about its potential limitations, including:

- **Regulations and legalities** – As different countries have different laws, it can be costly to get proper legal advice about consumer protection, employment rights and health and safety laws.

- **Social responsibilities** – Ethical and moral issues may need to be considered. Coca-Cola, symbolic of American culture, controversially opened a bottling plant in Afghanistan during the 'war against terrorism' under the presidency of George W. Bush.

- **Political environment and stability** – The political stability of a country will affect the profitability of firms, e.g. corrupt governments hinder business growth whereas financial incentives and tax concessions ease the burden associated with international location decisions.

- **Economic environment** – The economic prosperity of a country will also determine the profitability of businesses. Controlling inflation, unemployment, interest rates and exchange rates (see Unit 1.5) will all help a country to attract foreign direct investment.

- **Communications** – Time zone differences and longer chains of command (see Unit 2.2) may create barriers to effective communication within the organization.

- **Culture** – Societal norms and business etiquette will vary from country to country and region to region. A lack of cultural awareness can get a business into all sorts of trouble (see Unit 4.7).

- **Language** – Communications can be an issue if there are insufficient resources to deal with problems, e.g. the costs of hiring linguists and translators can be quite considerable (see Box 5.4.b).

Innovations, especially with the spread of technology and developments in e-commerce, have made international location decisions somewhat easier for many businesses. For example, many retailers have relocated their call centres to India where there is readily available and suitably skilled labour. The spread of e-commerce means that banks can provide the convenience of e-banking facilities (such as electronic bill payments, funds transfer, stock exchange dealings, foreign exchange transactions and travel insurance) which reduces the need for many customers to physically visit a bank. Such innovative changes

have enabled more businesses to be **footloose organizations** because there are no cost advantages of any particular location. Jeff Bezos, founder of Amazon.com, started off by selling books from his own home. Dell computers are mainly ordered online without the need to visit a conveniently located retail store.

Changes in workforce planning (see Unit 2.1) have meant a larger pool of flexible staff that work from their own home. This has helped in the relocation decision of many firms as they no longer need such large premises in expensive locations. It may also be possible to relocate to less expensive areas if staff do not have an issue with access and transportation to the new site.

Box 5.4.b 'Interesting' international locations

- Boring - Oregon, USA
- Cape Disappointment - Kentucky, USA
- Condom - Midi-Pyrénées, France
- Dull - Perth and Kinross, Scotland
- Great Snoring - North Norfolk, England
- Hell - Cayman Islands
- Kickapoo Drive - Texas, USA
- Middelfart - Funen, Denmark
- Nasty - Hertfordshire, England
- Pratt's Bottom - Bromley, England
- Roskilde Badfart - Copenhagen, Denmark
- Santa Claus - Indiana, USA
- Slaughter - Los Angeles, USA
- Skive - Denmark
- Slack - West Yorkshire, England
- Thong - Kent, England
- Ugley - Uttlesford, Essex, England

Common mistake

Some students seem to think that it does not matter where a footloose business locates. Whilst footloose businesses have a greater degree of choice of where they locate, the location decision is still important for business success. Even businesses that operate from home need to consider the logistics of delivering their products to customers.

Question 5.4.8   KFC, Vietnam

US fast-food **multinational company** *KFC* opened its first store in Hanoi, Vietnam in 2006. *KFC* was the first high-profile fast-food chain to locate in the former communist country. Economic and political reforms have transformed the country with its relatively untapped retail potential. Vietnam has a large and youthful population and a fast-growing economy. Its entry into the World Trade Organization in 2007 has undoubtedly led to a significant increase in foreign direct investment. It has been earmarked to become a developed country by 2020. It is no surprise then, that *KFC* opened its 100th store in 2010. In 2014, *McDonald's* followed *KFC's* move by opening its first restaurant in Hanoi, the country's capital city.

(a) Define the term **multinational company**.   *[2 marks]*

(b) Outline one benefit to *KFC* in being the first high-profile (well-known) fast-food chain to locate in Vietnam.   *[2 marks]*

(c) Examine the factors that make Vietnam an attractive location for global giants such as *KFC* and *McDonald's*.   *[6 marks]*

Box 5.4.c   Did you know that…?

- Badminton was named after the place where the sport was invented – in Badminton, UK
- Brussels Sprouts were first farmed in Brussels, Belgium in the 13th Century
- Buffalo Wings were invented in 1964 in Buffalo, New York
- Champagne is named after the place where the sparkling wine was invented, in France
- Cheddar Cheese got its name from the town of origin in Cheddar, England
- Denim is named after de Nîmes, in France
- 'Geysers' comes from Geysir, Iceland
- Hamburgers got their inspiration from Hamburg, Germany where meat from Hamburg cows were minced to create beef patties
- 'Italic' means 'Of Italy', as the style of handwriting was invented by Italian printer Aldus Manutius in 1501.

Geysers are a natural spectacle, caused by the shooting of hot spring water through a vent in the earth

Theory of knowledge

To what extent do you think that a country's ability to develop depends on its willingness and ability to embrace globalization?

Theory of knowledge

To what extent do language and culture influence international location decisions?

CUEGIS Essay

With reference to an organization of your choice, examine how **culture** and **globalization** have influenced its location decision.   *[20 marks]*

REVIEW QUESTIONS

1. What is meant by the location decision?

2. Why might a location decision be said to be 'irreversible'?

3. Outline four quantitative factors that affect the location decision.

4. Distinguish between bulk-increasing and bulk-reducing industries.

5. How might e-commerce affect the location decision?

6. Outline four qualitative factors that affect the location decision.

7. How might government incentives help to boost assisted areas (enterprise zones)?

8. What is meant by outsourcing?

9. What is the difference between outsourcing and offshoring?

10. What is meant by insourcing?

KEY TERMS

Assisted areas (or **enterprise zones**) are regions identified by the government to be suffering from relatively high unemployment and low incomes, so are in need of regeneration through financial assistance.

Bulk-increasing businesses are involved with products that increase in weight during the production process, so need to be located near their customers in order to reduce costs.

Bulk-reducing businesses are those that need to locate near the source of raw materials because they are heavier, and hence more costly, to transport than the final product.

Clustering means that a business locates near other organizations that operate in similar or complementary markets.

A **footloose organization** is a business that does not gain any cost reducing advantages from locating in a particular location. Hence, the firm can locate in almost any location.

Government incentives are financial enticements offered by the state to businesses to locate in a particular area or region, perhaps due to high unemployment. Examples include government grants, subsidies, tax allowances and interest-free loans.

Industrial inertia describes the reluctance to relocate due to the inconvenience of moving. Managers may feel that the potential inconveniences and costs of relocation outweigh the benefits.

Infrastructure is the term used to describe the transportation, communication and support networks in a certain area.

Insourcing is the use of an organization's own people and resources to accomplish a certain function or task which would otherwise have been outsourced.

Location refers to the geographical position of a business. The location is a crucial one, and depends on both quantitative and qualitative factors.

Offshoring involves relocating business functions and processes overseas. The offshored functions can remain within the business (with overseas operations) or outsourced to an overseas organization (known as offshore outsourcing).

Outsourcing (or **subcontracting**) is the practice of transferring internal business activities to an external organization to reduce costs and increase productivity.

Subcontractors are outsourced firms that undertake non-core activities for an organization. They are used for their expertise and the cost advantages they bring.

Mining is a bulk-reducing industry

5.5 Production planning

"It's a bad plan that cannot be changed." - Italian proverb

The supply chain process

The **supply chain** (or **logistics**) refers to the sequence of activities from the production of a good or service to it being delivered to the end customer. **Supply chain management** (SCM) is the art of managing and controlling these logistics, which must be efficient and cost effective for a business to be profitable. SCM will usually involve several key functions:

- Stock control – Managers must plan, implement and monitor the movement and storage of all stocks (which are categorised as raw materials, work-in-progress or finished goods).

- Quality control – All stages in the supply chain must add value in order to attract customers to buy quality products, thereby generating profit for all firms in the supply chain.

- Supplier networks – The decision will need to be made regarding which suppliers or intermediaries to use. Collaboration between the partners in the supply chain can facilitate improvements in logistics, thereby helping to reduce costs without compromising quality.

- Transportation – The most cost-effective methods of distributing products to customers must be investigated. This will depend on factors such as the frequency, speed, reliability and the costs of different transportation systems (see Figure 5.5.a). Large businesses such as supermarket chains are able to provide their own distribution networks, whereas smaller organizations may need to use subcontractors and couriers.

Figure 5.5.a Rail networks are fundamental to a country's transportation system

Reasons for using supply chain management include:

- Long supply chains increase the chances of things going wrong. Hence, effective SCM can prevent mistakes that would otherwise adversely affect the business.

- SCM helps to ensure that an appropriate supply of stocks is used to meet the level of demand. Too much supply causes stockpiling, with its associated costs, whilst a lack of stock causes delays to the rest of the supply chain. SCM helps to identify and prevent such bottlenecks.

- SCM is a tool for achieving *lean production* (a system based on minimal input for maximum output) by helping an organization to identify areas of wastage and inefficiency.

All suppliers in the supply chain are *interdependent*. For example, the retailer is dependent on the manufacturer, who in turn depends on suppliers of components and raw materials. However, suppliers of raw materials rely on retailers who sell the final product to consumers in the tertiary sector. For example, there is little need to harvest cocoa if there is low consumer demand for chocolates. Hence, it is in the best interest of all firms in the supply chain to work collaboratively for their mutual benefits.

However, SCM has its potential problems:

- With increased globalization, international sourcing becomes more complex. There are more partners in the supply chain to deal with, perhaps from various parts of the world, dealing in different languages and time zones. Time lags and potential cultural conflicts can delay getting the right products to the right customers in a cost-effective way.

- Greater interdependence also means that a single problem in the supply chain can cause major disruptions. The greater need for partners to share information and to collaborate requires building trust among the partners. This requires sufficient time and resources.

Just in time (JIT) and Just in case (JIC)

The difference between JIT and just-in-case (JIC). AO2

© IBO, 2017

One of the key aims of production planning is to minimize the costs of holding stocks whilst ensuring that there are sufficient resources for production to be able to meet customer demand in a timely manner. This is complicated by seasonal fluctuations in demand, e.g. high demand for fresh flowers on Valentine's Day and Mother's Day whilst there may be little demand for flowers at other times of the year. Stock control examines the need for businesses to identify their optimum stock levels in order to remain competitive. This requires careful production planning and flexible processes, such as spare capacity to operate during peak trading periods and multiskilled staff who are able to perform different jobs at short notice. Just-in-time (JIT) and just-in-case (JIC) are two types of stock control methods.

Just-in-time (JIT)

Just-in-time (JIT) is a stock control system based on stocks being delivered as and when they are needed in the production process. This means that a **buffer stock** (the predetermined minimum level of stock) is not required. Finished goods are dispatched as soon as they have been produced, thus eliminating the need for storage (see Table 5.5.a). JIT, a Japanese philosophy first advocated by former Toyota executive Taiichi Ohno, is seen as a prerequisite to lean production (see Unit 5.3) because inventory is regarded as costly and wasteful. The JIT system

---

Question 5.5.1 Carrefour

Carrefour is a French hypermarket chain that operates on a global scale. It is one of the largest retailers in the world, with annual sales in the region of €80 billion ($95bn). The vast amount of products sold in its retail stores (over 12,300 of them) means that the company must have an effective **supply chain process**. *Carrefour's* brand strategy is simple: it places emphasis on price, complemented by its constant pursuit of improvement in services for customers.

Source: adapted from Carrefour website (www.carrefour.com)

(a) Define what is meant by the **supply chain process**. *[2 marks]*

(b) Examine how *Carrefour* can improve the efficiency of its supply chain process. *[6 marks]*

relies on automation, barcodes and the use of highly skilled and motivated workers. JIT is covered in greater detail in Unit 5.3.

Figure 5.5.b JIT relies on reliable suppliers to deliver stocks on time

Case study

The BMW Mini is assembled using a JIT system. Customers place specific orders before the cars are made. Each component is ordered to be available when needed for production. The use of bar codes for these components ensures the right parts are supplied at the right time. JIT allows a series of Minis, all of different colours and engine sizes, to be made on the same production line.

Case study

FedEx Corporation is an American multinational company that specialises in courier delivery services. Established in 1971, FedEx earns annual revenues in excess of $60 billion and employs over 400,000 workers around the world. FedEx gained a first mover advantage by pioneering a tracking system with real-time updates on package location. This enables the company to monitor the delivery process and locate lost any packages that may be delayed or lost. Customers are also able to the estimated time of delivery. Today, this feature is also used by most of FedEx's competitors.

Table 5.5.a Advantages and disadvantages of just-in-time stock control

Advantages	Disadvantages
JIT eliminates the costs of holding stock, e.g. rent (of storage space), insurance, stockpiling and the costs of theft or spoilage of inventories.	JIT relies on sophisticated technologies to ensure that the correct stocks are ordered and delivered at the right time and place. Errors or malfunctions could bring production to a halt.
As cash is not tied up in stocks, working capital can be better used elsewhere, thus improving the firm's cash flow position (see Unit 3.7).	Administration and transactions costs are higher as JIT requires frequent re-ordering of stock.
JIT can help firms to reduce their break-even (see Unit 3.3), e.g. Rolls-Royce claimed that its annual break-even halved following its use of JIT.	Stocks must be of good quality in order to prevent bottlenecks in the production process. Hence, quality control (see Unit 5.3) can become an issue.
JIT allows firms to be more flexible and responsive to the needs of their customers, such as seasonal changes in demand.	There is a huge reliance on efficient and dependable suppliers. Major problems arise if stocks are not delivered on time.
The JIT system can improve motivation by encouraging employee participation and teamwork (both important elements of JIT).	As stocks are only ordered when needed, there are fewer opportunities to exploit economies of scale (see Unit 1.6), such as bulk discounts.
JIT reduces wastage; inventory does not perish or go out of date, as there is no buffer stock.	JIT systems prove to be inflexible in trying to cope with a sudden increase in demand.
JIT can help to strengthen a firm's professional relationship with its suppliers, thereby helping to reduce lead times in the production process.	Minimal stock levels mean that there is little scope for mistakes. The need for 'right first time' production can bring added pressures to staff.
The need for zero defects means that time is not needed to rework substandard output, i.e. JIT promotes a 'right first time' approach to production.	Since JIT is a philosophy, it must be embedded into the organization's culture. JIT requires the belief, support and commitment of all workers.

Just-in-case (JIC)

Just-in-case (JIC) is the traditional stock control system that maintains large amounts of stock in case there are supply or demand fluctuations. A buffer stock (or reserve stock) of raw materials, semi-finished goods and finished goods is used just in case there are any issues, such as late delivery of stocks from a supplier or a sudden increase in demand for output. JIC ensures that there is always sufficient stock available to meet customer demands (see Table 5.5.b).

However, JIC might mean that a business holds too much stock, i.e. overestimates the level of demand for its products. This can cause serious problems for the business. In the 1980s and 1990s, Rover tried desperately to compete with BMW but the lack of demand led to huge stockpiling of Rover cars and its eventual downfall. This led to BMW buying out the Mini brand from Rover, which it has used successfully since 2000, having rebranded it as the BMW Mini.

Figure 5.5.c JIT rely on an effective stock control management system

Table 5.5.b Advantages and disadvantages of just-in-case stock control

Advantages	Disadvantages
JIC allows a business to meet a sudden increase in demand as there is a buffer stock to rely on.	JIC imposes high costs of storage, including insurance and maintenance costs.
JIC allows a business to take advantage of purchasing economies of scale (from bulk buying raw materials and components for production).	Some stocks are perishable (so buffer stocks are not feasible) whilst other inventories are subject to damage or theft.
It reduces downtime (inactivity) caused by a stock-out as there is no need to wait for delivery of stocks from suppliers.	There is also an opportunity cost of money being tied up in stocks, i.e. the money might have been used more profitably elsewhere in the business.

Question 5.5.2   DS Café

DS Café is run by Dave Stevens as a **sole trader** in Brisbane, Australia. Sales revenue has been falling and the high level of stocks held at the business is causing cash flow problems. Dave feels that he is too busy to place orders based on sales forecasts produced by his assistant manager. A further complication is that *DS Café's* main supplier has suddenly gone out of business, so he will now need to search for a new supplier.

(a) Define the term **sole trader**. *[2 marks]*

(b) Explain how introducing Just-In-Time might be suitable for *DS Café*. *[4 marks]*

(c) Comment on why it might be advisable to base inventory orders on sales forecasts. *[4 marks]*

Stock control

Stock control charts based on the following: lead time, buffer stock, re-order level and re-order quantity. AO2, AO4

© IBO, 2017

Stocks (or **inventories**) are the materials, components and products used in the production process. There are three categories of stocks:

- **Raw materials** – These are the natural resources used for production, e.g. crude oil, metal ores, soil, wheat and timber.

- **Work-in-progress** – These are semi-finished (unfinished) products, e.g. parts and components to be used in the production process.

- **Finished goods** – These are complete units of output that are ready for sale, e.g. furniture, books, bread and cars.

Managing stock levels is an important task for all businesses. Without sufficient stock, production and sales will be interrupted. Stock control involves careful planning and control to ensure that sufficient stocks are available and at the right time. Businesses have to decide on the optimal level of stock because there are costs and drawbacks to poor stock control. Both **stockpiling** (holding too much stock) and **stock-outs** (holding insufficient stocks) create problems for a business.

Stockpiling can be caused by overproduction and/or falling demand. Alternatively, stockpiling can be deliberate as retail businesses prepare for seasonal peaks in demand, such as on Black Friday and during Christmas trading periods. Whatever the cause or purpose, stockpiling incurs higher costs which can possibly cause liquidity problems (see Unit 3.7).

Table 5.5.c   The costs of poor stock control

Costs of stockpiling	Costs of stock-outs
Storage costs (rent, insurance, maintenance and security costs) can be expensive, especially for firms that produce large, bulky and valuable products such as motor vehicles or aircraft.	Damaged corporate image and reputation due to disgruntled customers (caused by late deliveries or inconvenience). This can also damage customer loyalty and goodwill.
Some types of stock may perish or deteriorate, e.g. fresh flowers or food products. Hence holding large volumes of stock can be wasteful and expensive.	Higher administration costs, as the firm needs to place more orders more often. Also, smaller orders do not attract discounts compared to bulk purchases.
Stocks, such as semi-finished goods, can be illiquid yet they consume working capital that could have been better used elsewhere.	Lost sales since stocks are not available to meet customer orders. Worse still, customers might choose to buy from a rival business that has stock.
Changing fashions and tastes will mean that excess and obsolete stocks need to be heavily discounted in order to offload the products.	Inefficiencies as production comes to a standstill, i.e. machinery and other resources are left idle. Still, staffing costs and overheads need to be paid.

Figure 5.5.d Changing fashion and trends mean that stockpiling can be costly

Question 5.5.3   Ford's stockpiling nightmare

At the turn of the millennium, *Ford Motor Company* had struggled to remain profitable with huge **stockpiles** of its cars. *Ford's* continued efforts to cut costs saw the company reduce production by 21% in North America in 2006. By 2008, despite producing over 5.5 million automobiles, *Ford* had sold off its majority stake in *Mazda* and luxury brands *Aston Martin, Jaguar* and *Land Rover*. Troubles continued for the American automaker and in 2010, *Ford* had also sold *Volvo* to China's *Geely Group*.

Ford claimed that the cuts were necessary to remove excess and unprofitable production, despite the negative effects on employees and suppliers. The strategy helped *Ford* to record a net profit of $6.6 billion in 2010, although its net debts stood at $14.5 billion. In response to growing competition and the need for better cost control, *Ford* announced in 2018 that it would discontinue the production of almost all of its car models in North America within two years. Instead, the company chose to focus production on vehicles that its customers prefer, such as Sports Utility Vehicles (SUVs) and the timeless Ford Mustang.

(a) (i) Define the term **stockpiles**. [2 marks]

(a) (ii) Define the term **net profit**. [2 marks]

(b) Examine the costs of poor stock control to *Ford Motor Company*. [6 marks]

Stock control charts (see Figures 5.5.e and 5.5.f) are used to graphically illustrate a simplistic system of stock control. For ease of illustration, stock control charts are usually drawn on the assumption that sales (and hence stock usage) are constant, although they can be easily adjusted to suit the needs of a business.

Case study

In 2018, a warehouse at a whiskey distillery in Kentucky, USA collapsed causing around 9,000 of the 20,000 barrels of whiskey to be damaged. Each cask contained about 53 gallons of whiskey. The cost of the damage for Barton 1792 Distillery went beyond the loss of expensive stock, as the spillage caused polluted a nearby river, destroying natural habitats and killing hundreds of fish.

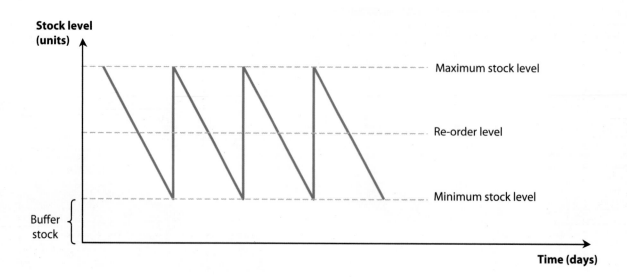

Figure 5.5.e Traditional stock control

There are several key concepts of stock control charts (refer to Figure 5.5.e):

- **Maximum stock level** – This is the upper limit of stock that a business wishes to hold, determined partly by the physical storage space that is available and the level of demand for output, per period of time.

- **Re-order level** – There is a time lag between a firm placing an order for stocks and it being delivered. Hence, when inventories fall to the re-order level, an order is placed. This helps to ensure that the order arrives just before stocks fall below the pre-set minimum level.

- **Minimum stock level** (or **buffer stock**) – This is the lowest amount of inventory that a business wishes to hold. Buffer stocks are held as a precautionary measure against any unexpected events, such as late deliveries or a sudden increase in demand. The more efficient the firm, the lower buffer stocks tend to be.

Stock control charts can also help businesses with their management of stocks. With reference to Figure 5.5.f, several other features can be seen:

- **Re-order quantity** – This is the amount of new stock ordered. In Figure 5.5.f, the re-order quantity is equal to 20,000 units (i.e. 30,000 minus 10,000). This order is placed whenever stock levels hit the *re-order level* (15,000 units in this case).

- **Lead time** – This measures the time lag between placing an order and receiving the stocks. The greater the lead time, the higher the buffer stock level needs to be. Delays can prolong lead times so stock levels go below the desired minimum level, so it is important to have sufficient buffer stocks to deal with unforeseen situations.

- Also, notice from the chart that the level of stocks goes up vertically whenever there is a delivery of stocks. If the correct amount of stocks is delivered on the right day, the increase should bring stocks back to their maximum level.

- In reality, the chart might not be so predictable due to miscalculations, such as late deliveries or the incorrect amount of stocks being delivered. The **usage rate** (the speed at which stocks are depleted) might also be different from originally predicted, resulting in either a stock shortage or stockpiling.

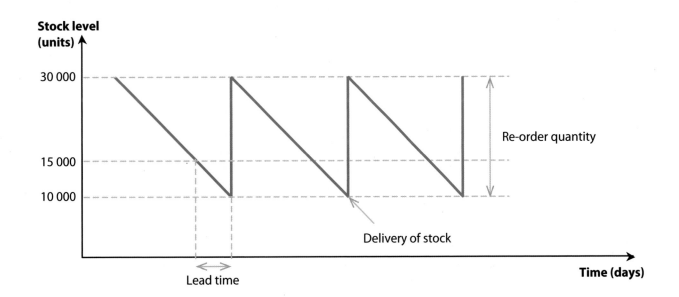

Figure 5.5.f Re-order quantity and lead times

Optimum level of stocks

The best possible level of stocks for a business varies from one business or industry to another, e.g. the optimal stock level for a supermarket is quite different from that of a small florist or restaurant. Firms face a dilemma when they order stocks: larger orders generate cost savings through economies of scale but increase storage and maintenance costs. Striking a balance relies on the expertise of managers to establish the **economic order quantity**. This is the optimum stock level that ensures there are sufficient stocks for uninterrupted production, but also minimises inventory costs.

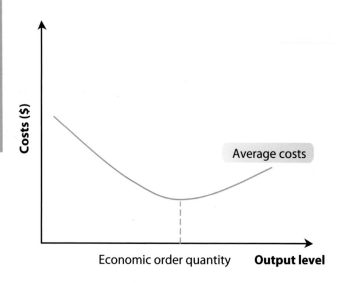

Figure 5.5.g Economic order quantity

Several factors influence the amount of stock a business holds and orders:

- Type of product – *Fast-moving consumer goods* (FMCGs), such as soft drinks and personal hygiene products sold in supermarkets, are re-ordered in large quantities. This is because by the time that new stocks are delivered, the firm would have sold many more units of the FMCGs. Conversely, *consumer durables* such motor vehicles, furniture or consumer electronics, have a slower stock usage rate so will be re-ordered in much smaller quantities. Unlike FMCGs, stockpiles of *perishable* products (such as fresh flowers and seafood) would be disastrous for a business.

- Expected level of demand – The higher the level of demand, the greater the amount of stock needed. A supermarket will stock more of the better selling brands on its shelves. Car showrooms will stock more of their relatively cheaper,

better selling models. Stock levels rise during peak trading periods, such as barbeque products during the summer, and decline again during off peak seasons.

- Lead times – Suppliers that can guarantee short lead times allow a business to have minimal buffer stocks. Conversely, larger volumes of stock need to be re-ordered if there are long lead times, such as shipment of heavy and bulky products from an overseas supplier.

- Costs of holding stock – The higher the opportunity cost of stockpiling, the lower the optimal stock level tends to be. It can be costly for a luxury car producer or jeweller to hold excess stock of its most expensive brands and products (due to the limited demand for these and the risks of theft or damage). By contrast, the pace at which low-cost FMCGs are sold allows retailers to hold large volumes of stock.

Figure 5.5.h Stockholding of perishable products such as fresh flowers can be very costly

Large businesses use computerised stock control systems that enable them to manage stocks from hundreds of product lines without workers having to manually count the inventory (which would be a horrendous task for large retailers such as Walmart, Costco, Tesco, and Carrefour). For example, each time a barcode on a product is scanned at the checkouts, the computerised system updates the level of stocks. When the stock level reaches the re-order level, the computer system automatically places an order. It is common for the more popular product lines in supermarkets to be replenished several times a week.

With more sophisticated systems, it is possible to input data such as public holidays and festivals to determine the optimal stock level at different times of the year, e.g. Christmas, New Year, Valentine's Day, Mothers' Day, Diwali, Fathers' Day, summer holidays, 'Back to School' season, Halloween and so forth. Being able to stock the right products at the time when consumers want them can certainly help to give the business a competitive advantage. It is also useful to know which of the less popular products should be discontinued (since they take up shelf space without the expected sales revenues).

Figure 5.5.i How do retailers work out how many 'Happy Anniversary' cards to keep in stock?

Question 5.5.4   QE Bakery

QE Bakery is a profitable business that produces bread and cakes for several large supermarket chains in the local area. However, the production manager, Bill Harshbarger, thinks that *QE Bakery* holds too much stock and this has limited its growth and profits. Bill Harshbarger has produced the following stock control chart to present at a board meeting, alongside his proposals for introducing a **just-in-time** stock system.

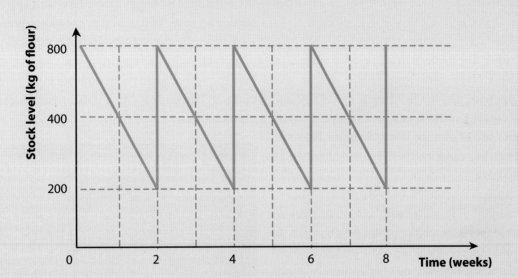

(a) Define the term **just-in-time**.   *[2 marks]*

(b) Use the stock control chart prepared by Bill Harshbarger to identify *QE Bakery's*:

  (i)   Re-order level   (iii) Buffer stock

  (ii) Re-order quantity   (iv) Lead time.   *[4 marks]*

(c) Explain why a supermarket is likely to have a higher re-order quantity than *QE Bakery*.   *[4 marks]*

(d) Examine the advantages and disadvantages for *QE Bakery* of using just-in-time production rather than the traditional just-in-case system.   *[6 marks]*

Capacity utilization

Capacity utilization rate. AO2, AO4

© IBO, 2017

Capacity utilization measures a firm's existing level of output as a proportion of its potential output. For instance, if a firm's maximum possible output is 10,000 units per month, but it actually produces 8,500 units, then its capacity utilization is 85%. High capacity utilization means that the level of output is close to its maximum (known as the **productive capacity**). Hence, capacity utilization is a measure of a firm's efficiency as it reveals the extent to which there are idle (unused) resources in the organization. High capacity utilization is financially important as it spreads out fixed and indirect costs of production over a large level of output (see Unit 3.2).

Capacity utilization is calculated by using the following formula

$$\text{Capacity utilization} = \frac{\text{Actual output}}{\text{Productive capacity}} \times 100$$

High capacity utilization is likely to be relatively more important to firms that have:

- High fixed costs – The higher a firm's capacity utilization, the lower the average fixed costs (AFC) will be. For example, suppose a firm has fixed costs of $10,000 and a productive capacity of 2,000 units per month. It would have AFC equal to $10 if output was 1,000 units. However, if it operates at full capacity, the AFC would fall to $5 ($10,000/2,000 units).

- Low profit margins – Products with low profit margins contribute little (per unit) to the profits of a business so need to be sold in large quantities to be profitable. Mass market products such as fast-moving consumer goods (FMCG) have low profit margins, but the high volume of sales can generate plenty of profit.

- High levels of break-even – Similarly, high capacity utilization is needed if a firm has a high break-even quantity (see Unit 3.3). This might be due to exceptionally high production costs (such as in aircraft manufacturing) or because products have low profit margins (thus limiting the unit contribution and raising the break-even level of output).

- Low marginal costs – If the extra cost of providing a particular good or service to an additional customer is close to zero, then high capacity utilization will be

important for profitability. Airlines, schools, theme parks, cinemas, hotels, coffee shops and downloadable apps all fall into this category.

Figure 5.5.i High capacity utilization is important for airlines

Costs are incurred 24 hours a day. For example, a restaurateur needs to pay rent, insurance and salaries, no matter how busy the restaurant is. Empty tables represent spare capacity and a burden on costs. Idle resources not only represent wastage and inefficiency, but are also a drain on finances. Hence, schools often rent out their facilities in the evening, at weekends and over the school holidays to generate extra revenues. Box 5.5.a outlines various ways that a firm can increase its capacity utilization.

Box 5.5.a   Methods to increase capacity utilization

- Improved marketing strategies – Increased sales automatically lead to higher capacity utilization. Of course, spending more on marketing does not necessarily generate more sales, as there are many other factors that influence the level of demand for a product. These include income levels and the price of substitutes.

- Subcontract work – This involves using external firms to help supply the firm's products. The main drawback is that profit margins are likely to be lower (if prices are kept constant) or prices need to be raised (to maintain profit margins, but this can reduce the demand for a firm's products).

- Reduce capacity – Spare capacity might exist because of excess capacity. General Motors, Ford and Dell have closed down operations in the past to reduce excess capacity. Whilst this causes job losses, it is often necessary for the firm's profitability.

Drawbacks of high capacity utilization

Although there are significant benefits of working near or at full capacity, there are also potential drawbacks. As the English proverb says, "*A full cup must be carried steadily*", i.e. operating at full capacity brings its own burdens and potential drawbacks:

- High capacity utilization requires equipment and machinery to be used constantly, without there being any time for routine servicing and maintenance. This is likely to lead to future breakdowns, which will delay output.

- Operating at full capacity can burden workers with stress. This can be counter-productive, especially if staff are constantly required to work overtime. Thus, quality is also likely to suffer.

- For services such as theme parks, restaurants or hair salons, operating at or near full capacity can lead to all sorts of problems, such as longer waiting times and lower standards of customer service. There might also be health and safety concerns, such as overcrowding.

- High capacity utilization is not a substitute for organizational growth. For a business to take on more orders to meet rising levels of demand, it needs to expand the scale of production, i.e. raise its productive capacity.

Figure 5.5.k Low capacity utilization is costly for businesses such as car park operators

Question 5.5.5   The Emirates Stadium, London

The seating capacity at Arsenal Football Club's *Emirates Stadium* is 59,867 making it the third largest stadium in England, after Wembley Stadium (the national football stadium with 90,000 seats) and Old Trafford (home of Manchester United, with a capacity of 74,994). On a typical home fixture at *The Emirates Stadium*, the North London football club sells 59,846 tickets. However, the highest attendance recorded was 60,161 (selling 294 more tickets than the stadium capacity) in a match against Manchester United.

(a) Calculate the average capacity utilization rate at *The Emirates Stadium*.
[2 marks]

(b) Explain how it is possible for Arsenal Football Club to temporarily operate at more than 100% capacity by "selling 294 more tickets than the stadium capacity".
[4 marks]

Question 5.5.6 Sherman Skyline Inc.

Use the following data from *Sherman Skyline Inc. (SSI)* to answer the questions that follow:
- Total fixed cost = $10,000 a month
- Productive capacity = 30,000 units
- Demand = 20,100 units
- Average variable costs = $5
- Price = $15

(a) Calculate *SSI's* capacity utilization. *[2 marks]*

(b) Calculate *SSI's* average costs of production at 20,100 units and 30,000 units. *[3 marks]*

(c) Calculate the profit margin for *SSI* at its current output and at its full capacity. *[3 marks]*

(d) Calculate the percentage change in *SSI's* total profit if it increases sales from its current level to its productive capacity. *[4 marks]*

Common mistake

Do not confuse the drawbacks of higher capacity utilization with diseconomies of scale. The above disadvantages can apply when a business operates near or at its productive capacity. Diseconomies of scale can only happen if the business operates on a larger scale, i.e. if its productive capacity has increased.

Exam tip !

It is important to consider the *context* of the business when deciding whether it should increase or decrease its capacity utilization. For example, a product in its launch phase of the product life cycle is likely to have low capacity utilization. Only if demand for the product surges will the firm increase its capacity utilization.

Question 5.5.7 AMC Theatres

AMC Theatres (or *AMC Cinemas*, as it is known in some parts of the world) is the USA's second largest chain of cinemas. *AMC Theatres* was the first US cinema chain to expand operations into foreign countries. When movies are being screened, the marginal cost of an extra customer is close to zero. Hence, cinemas rely heavily on high **capacity utilization**. However, overcapacity might bring even greater problems for *AMC Theatres* if it has to turn away some customers.

(a) Define the term **capacity utilization**. *[2 marks]*

(b) Outline why the "marginal cost of an extra customer [at the cinema] is close to zero". *[2 marks]*

(c) Examine the importance of high capacity utilization for *AMC Theatres*. *[6 marks]*

Productivity

Productivity rate. AO2, AO4

© IBO, 2017

The **productivity rate** measures how well resources are used in the production process. For example, **labour productivity** is a measure of the efficiency of the workers by calculating the output per worker (see Figure 5.5.l). The higher the labour productivity rate, the more productive (or efficient) the workers are. The formula for calculating labour productivity is:

$$\text{Labour productivity} = \frac{\text{Actual output}}{\text{Number of workers}} \times 100$$

Figure 5.5.l The factors of labour productivity

Higher productivity rates are important to businesses for several reasons, which can be remembered using the '4 Es':

- **Economies of scale** – Higher levels of output help to reduce the average costs of production. The cost savings can be passed onto customers by reducing prices, e.g. the mass production of smartphones, tablet computers and flat-screen televisions (see Figure 5.5.m) has made these goods much more affordable to customers around the world. Cost savings from the higher productivity rate can also help businesses to gain a greater profit margin on each product sold.

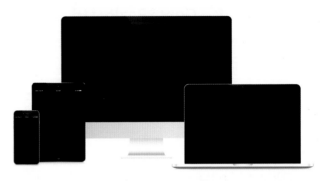

Figure 5.5.m Consumer electronics are mass produced and shipped worldwide

- **Earnings (higher profits and wages)** – Higher productivity rates are a source of cost savings and higher profits for businesses. Higher profitability enables firms to pay higher wages to their workers who are more productive. Competitive wages can also help to attract higher calibre employees. Higher profits can be reinvested back into the business to fund research and development or used to expand its operations.

- **Efficiency (improved competitiveness)** – Highly productive businesses can gain advantages beyond economies of scale. As they are more productive, they can compete more effectively on an international scale. For example, Samsung's productivity gains during the late 2000s meant the company overtook Apple and Nokia to become the market leader of smartphones.

- **Evolution (growth)** – The combined benefits of these factors mean that a higher productivity rate is a source of growth for businesses because it increases their productive capacity. For example, huge productivity gains at Google have made the company one of the world's largest businesses.

Section 5 Operations management

Question 5.5.8 Gupta Realty Ltd and Jenkins Realty Co.

The figures below relate to two real estate firms that sell residential property.

Firm	Sales revenue ($)	Units sold (per week)	Sales staff
Gupta Realty Ltd.	15,450,372	54	18
Jenkins Realty Co.	13,075,560	60	16

(a) Calculate the the labour productivity rate using sales revenue per worker for both *Gupta Realty Ltd.* and *Jenkins Realty Co.* [3 marks]

b) Using the above figures, explain why it might be difficult to conclude whether *Gupta Realty Ltd.* or *Jenkins Realty Co.* is the more productive firm. [4 marks]

Determinants of productivity rates

The five key determinants of productivity rates can be remembered using the acronym 'TRIES':

- **Technology** In general, investment in the latest technologies helps workers to be more productive, i.e. to produce more output that is of better quality. Information communication technology has also enabled firms to operate globally, irrespective of time zone differences.

- **Rivalry** Competition creates an incentive for businesses to be more productive in order to remain competitive. Without rivalry, firms might lack the incentive to be efficient or innovative.

- **Innovation** This is the commercialization of new ideas and products. Innovative products such as tablet computers and smartphones have changed the way many people work as they are able to work whilst mobile rather than at the office, thereby increasing productivity.

Figure 5.5.n Innovation is changing the way we work

- **Entrepreneurship** Entrepreneurs take business risks in the pursuit of profit. A firm's productivity rate is largely dependent on the leadership and personal motivation of entrepreneurs, such as their willingness and ability to exploit new business opportunities.

- **Skills and experience** The labour productivity rate is determined by the quantity and quality of labour. Education, training and development can increase a firm's human capital (the skills and experiences of the workforce), thereby improving labour productivity.

Exam tip !

Remember that Business Management is an interrelated discipline. For example, non-financial rewards, such as recognition of workers' achievements, can have a positive effect on the productivity rate. Consider how genuine praise from your teachers or parents can influence your attitude to learning!

However, in the pursuit of achieving a high productivity rate, there can be unnecessary stress imposed on workers, which can cause a decrease in quality. Thus, there comes a point when reaching a high productivity rate actually costs a business more money.

Question 5.5.9   Social media and productivity

The Associated Chambers of Commerce and Industry recently found that employees in India spend an average of one hour a day (during office hours) on social network websites such as Facebook and Twitter, causing a 12.5% decline in **labour productivity**. In total, 4,000 employees were surveyed across 60 cities in India with over 40% of respondents admitting to building their entire social network profile at work. Similar findings were reported in the *Daily Telegraph*, which highlighted that **social networking** websites cost the British economy a staggering £14 billion ($20.3bn) a year in lost work time. More than 2 million workers admitted to wasting over an hour each day at work adding friends, uploading photos and videos, and sending tweets.

(a) (i) Define the term **labour productivity**. *[2 marks]*

(a) (ii) Define the term **social networking**. *[2 marks]*

(b) With reference to the case study, examine the costs of low productivity for businesses. *[6 marks]*

IB Learner Profile – Be reflective

How can students improve their productivity rate in the IB Diploma Programme? Share your suggestions with the rest of the class and determine which ideas best suit your own preferred learning style.

Case study

Kodak was once the world's largest supplier of photographic camera film, but was too slow to switch to digital technology in the late 1990s. Founded in 1888, Kodak dominated throughout most of the twentieth century, with its market share peaking at 90% in 1976. However, Kodak's inability to make profit for five consecutive years meant the company stopped production of digital cameras and filed for bankruptcy in 2012.

Cost to buy (CTB) and Cost to make (CTM)

Cost to buy (CTB) and Cost to make (CTM). AO2, AO4
© IBO, 2017

A business faces a **make-or-buy decision** when it has a choice between manufacturing a product or purchasing it from an external supplier. There are several quantitative methods that can aid this decision. Examples include break-even analysis (see Unit 3.3) and investment appraisal (see Unit 3.8). The main quantitative method is to consider the relative costs of manufacturing the product (known as the **cost-to-make**) and the costs to purchase the product (**cost-to-buy**) from a third-party supplier. If the cost of producing the product is lower than the supplier's price, it makes financial sense to make the product rather than to buy it, and vice versa. For example, Apple considered its cost-to-make (CTM) the iPhone to be higher than to use Foxconn in China to manufacture the product, i.e. the cost-to-buy (CTB) from Foxconn is lower than Apple's CTM.

The make-or-buy decision involves an assessment of both quantitative and qualitative factors. The 'buy' decision should go ahead if a business does not have the expertise, equipment or productive capacity to efficiently manufacture a product. As with outsourcing (see Unit 5.4), non-core functions and products can be contracted to outside suppliers. If the firm is financially better off by making the product then the 'make' decision is pursued, i.e. these activities are part of the organization's core competencies. When deciding whether to make or buy, four key variables must be known:

- The expected sales volume or quantity (Q).

- The fixed costs (FC) associated with making the product, e.g. tools, equipment and machinery.

- The average variable costs (AVC) of making the product, e.g. wages and material costs.

- The price per unit (P) charged by the supplier.

To decide whether to make or to buy, a firm needs to work out the values of both:

The cost-to-buy: **CTB = P × Q**

The cost-to-make: **CTM = FC + (AVC × Q)**

If CTM is greater than CTB, then it is more financially desirable to 'buy'. Conversely, if CTB is greater than CTM, it makes financial sense to 'make'. Hence:

- If the CTB < CTM, the organization will use outsource the work to subcontractors.

- If the CTM < CTB, the organization will use insourcing (in-house production).

Qualitative factors are also usually considered with make-or-buy decisions, such as:

- The relative product quality if produced in-house compared with an external supplier.

- The timeframe in which the products can be produced in-house compared with buying them from an external vendor (seller).

- Whether the business has spare capacity to meet extra orders.

- The reliability of suppliers, e.g. their track record and reputation for delivering products on time.

- An assessment of the firm's core competencies and its non-core activities and functions, e.g. suppliers might have greater design flexibility and access to better technological innovations.

- Whether the decision is irreversible, i.e. the terms and conditions of the contract.

Case study

Foxconn is the global market leader in the electronics contract industry. The Taiwanese company makes some of the world's best-known electronic products for its clients, including Apple (iPad, iPod and iPhone), Amazon (Kindle), Sony (PlayStation), Microsoft (Xbox One), and Nintendo (Wii U). Other clients include Acer, Cisco, Dell, Google, HP, Microsoft, Nokia, Sony and Toshiba. Foxconn has factories in China, Brazil, Mexico, India, Japan, Malaysia, Hungary, Slovakia and the Czech Republic.

Question 5.5.10   To Make or to Buy?

Brothers Luke and Jake are about to celebrate their 4th and 6th birthdays next month. They have asked for a train table for their collection of wooden trains. Their father, Ned, has found only one retailer in the town that sells the product, made from high quality solid wood at a cost of $155. However, the design is very bland and rather simplistic, so Ned feels that his boys might not like the design. If he were to make a similar product, he could personalise the train table for his sons. Ned has estimated that if he chooses to make the train table, the cost would be approximately $80 for all materials plus about fifteen hours of his time. He has yet to calculate the **cost-to-make** and the **cost-to-buy**.

(a) (i) Define the term **cost-to-make**. [2 marks]

(a) (ii) Define the term **cost-to-buy**. [2 marks]

(b) Recommend to Ned whether he should make or buy the train table. Use both quantitative and qualitative considerations in your answer. [10 marks]

Production planning and CUEGIS concepts

Production planning is a vital strategy for a business in order to improve its operational efficiency and cost control. Thus, it can give the firm a competitive advantage, especially if it is able to pass on some of the cost savings to customers in the form of lower prices. Effective stock control also helps to ensure production can meet the demand of customers, thereby contributing towards customer satisfaction and brand loyalty (see Unit 4.5).

Managers need to establish the optimum stock level for their organization. Insufficient stocks will lead to production problems, which will disappoint customers. However, overstocking (stockpiling) can lead to cash flow problems due to storage and other related costs (see Unit 3.7). Establishing the optimal level of stock is not an easy task, especially for businesses facing change, and often relies on trial and error. Effective stock control also requires various departments of a firm to work collaboratively, e.g. the marketing department might provide sales forecast data (see Unit 4.3) to inform the operations department about the right stock levels needed for production. Whether this happens will depend partly on the organizational culture of the business.

Most firms find it difficult to know the exact amount of stock to hold at any one point in time, so will often hold a buffer stock as part of their strategy. This acts as a safety net, just in case there are unforeseen problematic changes such as a sudden surge in demand or late delivery of stocks. How firms decide on what their minimum stock level should be is another matter. The decision will depend on several factors such as the type and size of the business, its organizational culture, the level of demand, lead times with suppliers, and the costs of holding stock.

Domestic and international competitive pressures in a globalized world have led many firms to focus their strategy on cost competitiveness, often by outsourcing and offshoring strategies (see Unit 2.1). For example, many large multinational companies have to make 'make-or-buy' decisions, i.e. deciding whether to make the products themselves or to purchase these from a lower cost supplier. Globalization has created more choice for firms in making such decisions. Outsourcing provides many opportunities for businesses in terms of cost control, access to stocks and productive efficiency gains. For example, a business working at full capacity or experiencing rapid growth can continue to expand its operations by subcontracting. However, a successful outsourcing strategy requires proactive involvement and commitment from both parties given the dynamic and changing nature of the business environment.

Effective production planning is based on the notion that higher levels of productivity lead to improved competitiveness. However, stock control is just one of many ways that a firm can achieve greater productivity and lean production (see Unit 5.3). Other methods to achieve productivity gains include: staff training and development (see Unit 2.1), improved staff motivation (see Unit 2.4), enhanced quality management, and reduced wastage (see Unit 5.3). These points highlight the integrated nature of Business Management. Nevertheless, careful production planning and control are vital to the competitiveness of a business. As US Army General George S. Patton (1885–1945) said, "*A good plan today is better than a perfect plan tomorrow.*" In today's fast-paced, frequently changing business world, a so-called perfect strategic plan that is poorly timed will often prove too little too late.

Theory of knowledge

Is sales forecasting an art or science? To what extent can effective production planning take place without sales forecasting?

Theory of knowledge

How can knowledge of change in the external business environment create both opportunities and threats for production planning?

CUEGIS Essay

With reference to an organization of your choice, discuss the role of **change** and **innovation** in production planning. *[20 marks]*

REVIEW QUESTIONS

1. What is meant by the supply chain process?

2. Why are all businesses in the supply chain said to be interdependent?

3. What is just-in-time stock control?

4. Outline the meaning of just-in-case stock control.

5. What are the advantages and drawbacks of using a JIT stock control system?

6. What are the advantages and drawbacks of using a JIC stock control system?

7. What are the three categories (types) of inventories?

8. What are the costs of holding stock or stockpiling?

9. What is a stock-out?

10. Why can a stock-out be costly to a business?

11. What is a stock control chart?

12. Why do businesses hold a maximum and a minimum stock level (buffer stock)?

13. Distinguish between the re-order level and the re-order quantity.

14. What is meant by an optimal stock level?

15. Distinguish between a firm's productive capacity and its capacity utilization.

16. Outline three methods that businesses can use to increase their capacity utilization.

17. Explain how cost benefit analysis might be used in 'make or buy' decisions.

18. What is meant by productivity?

19. Explain how productivity is calculated.

20. Distinguish between the cost to buy (CTB) and the cost to make (CTM).

KEY TERMS

Buffer stock refers to the minimum stock level held by a business in case there are unexpected events, e.g. late deliveries of components or a sudden increase in demand for the firm's product.

Capacity utilization measures a firm's existing level of output as a proportion of its potential output. High capacity utilization means that the firm is producing close to its productive capacity.

Finished goods are a category of stocks (inventory), referring to complete units of output that are ready for sale to customers and consumers, e.g. furniture, books, bread and cars.

Just-in-case (JIC) is the traditional stock management system that maintains buffer stocks in case there are unexpected fluctuations in supply (such as delayed delivery of stocks) or sudden changes in demand.

Just-in-time (JIT) is a stock control system whereby materials and components are scheduled to arrive precisely when they are needed in the production process.

Labour productivity is a measure of the efficiency of a firm's workers by calculating the output per worker. It is an indicator of the current level of skills and motivation of the workforce.

Lead time measures the duration between placing an order and receiving it. The longer the lead time, the higher buffer stocks tend to be.

Make-or-buy decisions refer to situations where a firm has to decide between manufacturing a product and purchasing it from a supplier, based on comparing the cost to make (CTM) with the cost to buy (CTB).

Maximum stock level refers to the upper limit of inventories that a firm wishes to hold at any point in time.

Minimum stock level refers to the smallest amount of inventories that a business wishes to hold. For many businesses, this minimum is above zero as a precautionary measure.

The **optimum stock level** (or the **economic order quantity**) refers to the best inventory level for a firm, which ensures that there are sufficient stocks for production whilst incurring minimal costs.

Productive capacity refers to a firm's maximum (potential) output if all its resources are used fully and efficiently.

The **productivity rate** measures the degree of efficiency in the use of resources in the production process. It uses an average measure, e.g. output per worker, revenue per sales person or output per machine hour.

Raw materials are a category of stocks (inventory), referring to the natural resources used for production, e.g. crude oil, metal ores, soil, wheat and timber.

Re-order level refers to the level of stock when a new order is placed. Lead times mean that the re-order level helps to prevent production problems arising from a lack of stock.

Re-order quantity refers to the amount of new stock ordered. It can be seen from a stock control chart by calculating the difference between the maximum and minimum stock levels.

A **stock-out** occurs if a business does not hold enough stocks to meet orders for production.

Stockpiling occurs when a business over-produces so holds too much stock. This is detrimental to the firm's cash flow position.

Stocks (or **inventories**) are the materials, components and products used in the production process, i.e. raw materials, semi-finished goods and finished goods.

The **supply chain** is the sequence of activities from the production of a good or service to it being delivered to the end customer.

The **usage rate** refers to the speed at which stocks are depleted. The higher the usage rate, the more frequent re-ordering of stocks needs to be.

Work-in-progress is a category of stocks (inventory), referring to semi-finished (unfinished) products, e.g. parts and components to be used in the production process.

5.6 Research and development

"Anyone who has never made a mistake has never tried anything new." - Albert Einstein (1879–1955),
Nobel Prize for Physics, 1921

HL content	Assessment objective
The importance of research and development for a business	AO3
The importance of developing goods and services that address customers' unmet needs (of which the customers may or may not be aware)	AO2
The following types of innovation: • product • process • positioning • paradigm	AO2
The difference between adaptive creativity (adapting something that exists) and innovative creativity (creating something new)	AO2
How pace of change in an industry, organizational culture and ethical considerations may influence research and development practices and strategies in an organization	AO3

© IBO, 2017

Research and development (R&D)

The importance of research and development for a business.
AO3

© IBO, 2017

Research refers to investigating the unknown, such as new products or processes. **Development** involves using research findings to create products that can be commercialised. Development can also mean improving existing processes or products, i.e. improvements in *process innovation* and *cost-reducing innovations*. The purpose of **research and development (R&D)** is to provide continual advancement (e.g. modifications or improvements to existing products) and to launch new products to satisfy customer needs in a profitable way.

R&D involves conducting extensive research into new products, their designs, testing, and development of **prototypes** (trial or test products). Only the most promising ones are considered for commercialisation. However, the R&D process can be extremely lengthy and drain the resources of a business. For example, pharmaceuticals spend hundreds of millions of dollars each year on R&D and it can take more than a decade to commercialise a drug or medicine.

Figure 5.6.a Prototypes are used as part of the R&D process

R&D can be vital to an organization's long-term survival and success. Kodak, for instance, went bankrupt after falling behind the times as customers switched from using camera film (see Figure 5.6.b) to digital camera technology. R&D can also improve the efficiency and performance of an organization, thereby adding value in the production process. For example, Apple and Microsoft have thrived on R&D as a source of higher sales growth and increased market value. Japanese carmaker Honda allocates 5% of its annual budget for R&D.

R&D is often beneficial for businesses that operate in **sunrise industries** (those that have rapid growth potential, such as high-tech industries). In addition, R&D can generate a *first-mover advantage*. This refers to the benefits of being the first business to launch a new and innovative product, such as Tesla's electric car (2012), Apple iPod (October 2001) or Pfizer's Viagra impotence drug (March 1998). Such benefits include the ability to charge a high price, to develop a favourable corporate image and to establish strong market share. Hence, having a first-mover advantage better prepares a business to contend with the likely competition that follows.

By contrast, R&D expenditure in **sunset industries** (where there is negative or deteriorating growth potential) is likely to be unprofitable. Furthermore, studies have consistently shown that for every ten products that are developed and test-marketed, only one product reaches commercialisation. Hence, the successful product that is launched must recoup the high costs of R&D, even if this takes several years.

R&D is a continual process. American inventor Thomas Edison (1847–1931) said, "*I have not failed. I've just found 10,000 ways that won't work*". Firms that continue to invest in R&D, even if everyone else is cutting back, perhaps due to a recession, are the ones most likely to thrive. Successful R&D can give businesses a competitive edge in terms of cost advantages and/or quality improvements in the long term.

Despite the importance of R&D to businesses, there are limitations:

- High costs – Investment in Research and Development is highly expensive and requires sufficient labour and financial resources.

- High failure rate – Most new ideas fail to materialise. Even for the few ideas that might work, most are not commercially feasible. Failure not only leads to a loss of investment funds, it also demoralises the workforce.

- Budgetary constraints – R&D is often held back by funding problems. Even if an innovative idea is realistically achievable, budget constraints can prevent the project from being undertaken.

Box 5.6.a   Benefits and goals of innovation

- **Growth opportunities** Innovation can be a source of business growth and evolution. Nintendo (games consoles) originally sold playing cards, whilst Nokia (mobile phones) started business in the pulp mill industry.
- **Productivity gains** Process innovation can help a business to increase its productivity levels.
- **International competitiveness** Innovation can give a business or country a competitive edge over its (foreign) competitors.
- **Brand switching** This occurs when consumers turn away from rival products for a more appealing or innovative product. Consumer electronics firms constantly try to get customers to switch to their brands and products.
- **Job creation** Product innovation can create plenty of employment opportunities.
- **Social benefits** Innovation can often improve the quality of life for many people, e.g. developments in laser technology for correcting eyesight has meant that many people no longer need to rely on glasses or contact lenses.

Theory of knowledge

At the turn of the decade, the iPhone was voted by the British public as the World's Best Product. *The Economist* voted the modern flush toilet as the most useful invention in history. How do people determine what is the 'best' product? How can we 'know' whether technology has truly improved our quality of life?

Theory of knowledge

The 2008 global financial crisis caused banks around the world to be bailed out. For example, the UK government spent over £139.5 billion ($203 billion), or about 20% of its GDP, on rescuing banks. Should businesses, irrespective of their size, be allowed to fail?

Question 5.6.1   Johnson & Johnson

Johnson & Johnson is one of the world's largest health care and pharmaceutical companies. Founded in 1886, the company sells its products in more than 175 countries, with annual sales revenues in excess of $76 billion. Its brands include Johnson's Baby products, Acuvue contact lenses, Neutrogena skin and beauty products and Band-Aid bandages.

Its subsidiary, *Johnson & Johnson Pharmaceutical Research and Development* (J&JPRD), is responsible for discovering and developing pharmaceutical drugs, with research facilities in the USA, Belgium and Spain. *Johnson & Johnson's* website has a section dedicated to innovation, which invites the general public to submit their ideas for the company's consideration.

Source: Company website (www.jnj.com/student_resources)

(a) Define the term **innovation**.   *[2 marks]*

(b) Explain the importance of Research and Development (R&D) to *Johnson & Johnson*.   *[4 marks]*

(c) Given that most new products fail to reach the market, discuss the extent to which R&D expenditure can be justified.   *[10 marks]*

R&D and customers' unmet needs

The importance of developing goods and services that address customers' unmet needs (of which the customers may or may not be aware). AO2

© 2017

Innovation is the process of commercially pioneering new ideas and creations in the production process. It stems from successful R&D in order to meet the needs of customers. These unmet needs may be known to customers (perhaps from market research), whereas some of these unmet needs will be unknown to customers. For example, Apple's co-founder Steve Jobs famously said that he would create products that customers don't even know they need yet. Examples of innovations include:

- Discovery of new production processes – Henry Ford, for example, discovered and applied the benefits of mass production and mechanisation to the automobile industry. Online banking in the early twenty-first century transformed the finance industry. Marketing strategies have also evolved with developments in social media, viral marketing and guerrilla marketing (see Unit 4.5).

- Successful exploitation of creative ideas – Sir James Dyson is credited for inventing the bag-less vacuum cleaner, helping to turn Dyson into a multi-billion dollar business. Sabeer Bhatia, inventor of Hotmail, sold his email idea to Microsoft for $400 million in 1997 (see Question 5.6.3).

YouTube was sold to Google for $1.65bn in 2006, less than 2 years after it was set up by three ex-employees of PayPal.

- Introduction of new products – Coco Chanel popularised the 'little black dress' (simple but stylish black evening dress) in 1928, which is still as popular today. The Apple iPod revolutionised the way in which music is delivered to customers (the global decline in music CD sales is largely due to Apple iTunes as customers switch to buying music online). The multimedia Apple iPhone also transformed the mobile phone market. Australia was the first country to issue polymer plastic bank notes, with more than 20 countries following its lead. The Bank of England used cotton paper notes for over 100 years, but converted to polymer bank notes in 2016.

Figure 5.6.b Kodak failed to keep up with customers' changing needs

HIGHER LEVEL

Operations management

- Entering new markets – Ferrari has long faced the dilemma of wanting to sell more cars without damaging its image of exclusivity. Ferrari recently expanded into China, allowing it to exceed its quota of 5,000 cars produced each year since the Chinese market does not affect the elitism enjoyed by Ferrari customers in Europe and North America.

Management guru Peter Drucker said that all successful businesses at some point required a manager to make courageous decisions. He argued that businesses cannot grow through cost cutting alone, but required R&D and innovation to sustain or increase their profitability. For instance, Apple's revolutionary iPod was introduced in October 2001 and in just 5 years had sold over 60 million units worldwide. By early 2007, Apple had sold its 100 millionth iPod, significantly boosting the company's earnings. As Ken Loh, Regional Director of Kalmar (a multinational B2B manufacturer of heavy industry products and vehicles) said, "*The future success of a company is dependent on whether it will invest to meet customers' expectations in order to increase competitiveness.*" A list of famous inventors is given in Box 5.6.b.

IB Learner Profile – Be knowledgeable

Did you know about a secret button at pedestrian crossings that is installed to help blind people to cross the road? Read this BBC article to find out more: http://goo.gl/ogxJl.

IB Learner Profile – Be an inquirer

In 2014, Mozilla launched a prototype $25 smartphone aimed at customers in less economically developed countries. Investigate the motives behind this for Mozilla, which is more famous for its Firefox Internet browser. How do such innovations address unmet customer needs yet disrupt the market? A good starting point is this BBC article: http://goo.gl/LNJQG8.

Theory of knowledge

The *International Business Times* reported that a Ferrari 458 Italia is priced at about $230,000 in the USA, but the same car is priced at $724,000 in China. What role, if any, do ethics have in commercialised innovations?

Box 5.6.b   Famous inventors and inventions

Although there are technical differences between innovation and inventions, the terms are often used interchangeably. Examples of famous inventors and inventions include:

- **Levi Strauss** and business partner Jacob Davis (1873) secured a patent for trousers, strengthened with metal rivets to make work wear more durable. They later modified this for their famous blue denim jeans.
- **Coca-Cola** (1886) was invented by John Pemberton, a US pharmacist. He sold the product as a remedy for depression, hysteria and anxiety.
- **Band-Aid** (1920), the adhesive bandage, was invented by Johnson & Johnson employee Earle Dickson. Dickson went on to become vice president of the company.
- **Laszlo Biro** (1938) was a Hungarian journalist who invented the ballpoint pen.
- **Bubble Wrap** (1957) was invented by Alfred Fielding and Marc Chavasnnes, founders of the Sealed Air Corporation. Bubble Wrap is a registered trademark of the US packaging materials company.
- **Roy Jacuzzi** (1968) invented the first autonomous bath with fitted water jets.
- **Post-it notes** (1968) were accidentally invented by Arthur Fry and Dr. Spencer Silver, employees of 3M. The company's slogan is a single word – 'Innovation'.
- **Microsoft** (1983) announced the introduction of its new operating system – 'Windows' (although it was originally called Interface Manager).
- **Facebook** (2004), the world's largest social networking site, reached 1 billion users in just eight years. CEO Mark Zukerberg became the world's youngest billionaire, aged just 26 at the time.
- **WhatsApp** (2009) is the world's most used instant messaging service for smartphone devices, with over 450 million registered users within its first 5 years. It was bought by Facebook in 2014 for $19 billion.

Question 5.6.2   Nintendo Company

The Nintendo Company (*Nintendo*) is a Japanese multinational company that specialises in the games console market. Established in 1889, the company originally produced playing cards. *Nintendo* introduced its first video games in the late 1970s. Since then, games such as *Donkey Kong* and *Mario Bros* and products such as *Game Boy, Super Nintendo* and *Nintendo GameCube* have made the company a household name throughout the world. In December 2006, the company launched its seventh generation games console, the *Nintendo Wii* which used wireless and Bluetooth technology. *Nintendo* allocated over $200 million for the launch of the *Wii* to ensure its success. This is important for the company's **brand loyalty** as *Nintendo* launched its eighth generation console, the *Wii U* in late 2012.

(a) Define the term **brand loyalty**.   *[2 marks]*

(b) Comment on the importance of innovation for businesses operating in a rapidly changing market, such as the games console industry.   *[4 marks]*

(c) Examine the factors that affect the degree of Research and Development in a business such as *Nintendo*.
                                                                                                                                  [6 marks]

Types of innovation

The following types of innovation: product, process, positioning and paradigm. AO2

© IBO, 2017

There are several classifications of innovation: product, process, positioning and paradigm innovation. The **4Ps of innovation** was developed by Professors John Bessant and Joe Tidd, who hypothesised that successful innovation is essentially about positive change. The model suggest four types of innovation where positive change can take place:

Product innovation – This refers to new creations or development of existing products. Examples include the introduction of new products, better functionality, improved ease of use and better reliability or performance. For example, toothpaste was originally made and sold in jars until Colgate introduced toothpaste in tubes in 1908. Product innovation is common in industries with high research and development (R&D) expenditure, such as pharmaceuticals, consumer electronics, car manufacturing, telecommunications and movies. The iPhone is an example of a product innovation from Apple, which has benefited from a range of incremental innovations since its launch in 2007.

Theory of knowledge

Do marketers make people happier? Is it possible to know through the various ways of knowing whether marketers really care?

Figure 5.6.c Steve Jobs , visionary innovator and co-founder of Apple Inc.

Case study

Tesla is a US multinational company known for its well-designed and high-quality electric vehicles, although the business also specialises in lithium-ion battery energy storage and solar panel manufacturing. Founded in 2003, the first all-electric Model S car was sold in 2012. Sales of Tesla's electric cars passed the 300,000 vehicles milestone in early 2018.

Process innovation – This refers to changes in the way production or delivery takes place, i.e. *how* something is done. Process innovation aims to improve the method of production and the logistics of getting the product from the factory floor to the consumer. For instance, many businesses have used 3D modelling software in the process of developing new products. Delivery systems may include bar codes, scanning equipment and computerised tracking systems.

Positioning innovation – Bessant and Tidd define position innovation as changing the context of a product. The focus of this type of innovation is to reposition the perception of an established product. For example, Levi-Strauss jeans were originally developed for manual workers, but repositioned as fashionable casual wear. Lucozade was originally sold as a health drink for the unwell, but was repositioned for the mass market. Lucozade's sales revenues increased from $115,000 to more than $8 million in the first seven years after the change. Other examples are shown in Box 5.6.c. Positioning is vital in today's globalized and competitive world, as brand perception is often more important to customers than how good the actual good or service is.

Paradigm innovation – This refers to innovative change, often quite radical, that changes the nature of certain markets. Henry Ford's introduction of an assembly line to mass produce motor cars is an example. The microchip revolution helped to reduce costs across all industries. The entry of low-cost (no-frills) airlines such as AirAsia, easyJet and Ryanair has reduced prices charged by other mainstream airline carriers. E-commerce has revolutionised buying and selling, creating greater choice and convenience for consumers (see Unit 4.8). Steve Jobs predicted, prior to the official launch, that the iPhone would change the world. Jobs was right, and the iPhone went on to become a huge global success (and cash cow) for Apple. Paradigm innovations often contribute to a changing corporate culture (see Unit 2.5).

Box 5.6.c Examples of positioning innovation

Product	Original purpose	Repositioned product
7-Up	Mood-stabilizing drug	Carbonated soft drink
Bubble Wrap	Wallpaper	Protective packaging material
Coca-Cola	Headache and fatigue medication	Carbonated soft drink
Frisbee	Containers for the Frisbie Pie Company	Frisbee, flying disc toy
Kleenex	Make-up remover	Tissue
Listerine	Floor wash	Mouthwash
Play-Doh	Wallpaper cleaner	Toy modeling clay
Vans	Skateboard shoes	Fashion and casual footwear
Wrigley's	Washing powder	Chewing gum

Question 5.6.3 Hotmail

Hotmail, the free email service, was started in 1996 by Sabeer Bhatia and Jack Smith, both ex-employees of Apple. Their vision was to give people access to email from any computer in the world. Bhatia and Smith had attracted their one millionth subscriber within the first six months of *Hotmail's* launch. By its 18th month, on Bhatia's 29th birthday, *Hotmail* had been bought by Microsoft for $400 million.

Hotmail has moved on since its early days. For example, MSN Messenger was launched in 1999 and allowed *Hotmail* subscribers to use instant messaging services. Webcam technology also allowed MSN Messenger customers to use audio and visual features. This has since been replaced by the upgraded Windows Live Messenger. In 2007, *Hotmail* was revamped and rebranded as *Windows Live Hotmail*.

(a) Explain why *Hotmail* was seen as an innovative product.   *[4 marks]*

(b) Examine the importance of innovation to high-tech businesses such as Microsoft.   *[6 marks]*

Innovation can also be classed as either incremental or radical:

- **Incremental innovation** refers to minor improvements to products or work processes, e.g. car manufacturers might work on developing safer and more energy efficient vehicles. Most innovations are incremental in nature and are less disruptive to organizations.

- **Radical innovation** refers to major and disruptive innovations that tend to involve high risks. They can be a major source of competitive advantage. For example, vinyl and cassette tapes were replaced by CD technology (which has succumbed to the growing use of Internet downloads); VHS videos were replaced by DVD technology, and digital photography replaced film photography.

Figure 5.6.d VHS videos were replaced by DVD technology

Theory of knowledge

To what extent is research and development (R&D) limited by ethical considerations?

Adaptive creativity and innovative creativity

The difference between adaptive creativity (adapting something that exists) and innovative creativity (creating something new).
AO2
© IBO, 2017

Creativity is a vital prerequisite to innovation. It is the process of generating new ideas, often stemming from divergent thinking. It is the ability to create new ideas (see Figure 5.6.e). According to psychologist Dr. Michael Kirton (1976), there are two categories of creativity: adaptive and innovative.

Adaptive creativity is a category of incremental innovation that adjusts or develops something that already exists. It is common across most industries, where new generations or models replace existing products, such as Samsung's latest smartphones, laptops, cameras or smart televisions. **Adaptors** (people with adaptive creativity) tend to accept the embedded paradigm within the organization, such as current policies, perspectives and practices. Adaptors produce several new ideas that build on the continuity of practices and organizational norms (the current way of doing things), but with improved ways of doing so. For example, adaptive creativity is often linked to the product life cycle and extension strategies (see Unit 4.5). In practice, most organizations are adaptive in their orientation (change happens gradually) as it is relatively low risk and cheaper to implement.

Innovative creativity is more radical as it involves creating something that is new. **Innovators** (people with innovative creativity) redefine problems and cultural norms. They create solutions aimed at doing things differently. Unlike those with adaptive creativity who tend to prefer scientific decision-making, people with innovative creativity often have a preference for intuitive decision-making. Innovators often question the status quo (existing perspectives) and are often insensitive to others. Supporters of innovative creativity argue that businesses cannot survive if they are unable to break away from their rivals with new ideas and creations. For example, Steve Jobs, co-founder of Apple, was a visionary who reinvented computing, music and mobile phones. Jobs said, "*Innovation distinguishes between a leader and a follower.*" Nevertheless, innovative creativity is less easily understood and has unpredictable outcomes, so is of high risk.

Most successful organizations adopt both these different creative styles as they each have merits under different circumstances. Kirton argued that people have a preferred style to tackling problems, either by working within the rules of the organization and seeking consensus (adaptors) or by being original and taking calculated risks (innovators).

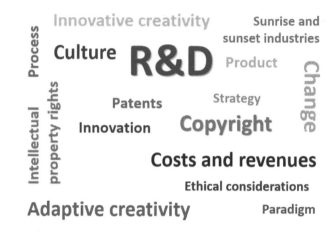

Figure 5.6.e Many factors can influence R&D in an organization

Question 5.6.4   The International Academy School

Mike Trigg was recently appointed as the new Principal of The International Academy School (TIAS). Having reviewed school policies and spoken to all key **internal stakeholders** of TIAS, including teachers, during his first year at the school, Mike Trigg proposed the following changes for the new academic year:

- Change from having 4 lessons a day to 5 lessons a day to create greater flexibility in the timetable. This would require shortening lessons from 75 minutes to 60 minutes.

- Expand the senior leadership team by creating a new post: a Director of Studies to oversee the Extended Essay, TOK and CAS Coordinators.

- Introduce a new House system. This would involve students being rehoused from the current 6 Houses to 4 new Houses to create more House spirit and cohesiveness.

- Introduce a monthly "Open Forum" meeting for all staff to make suggestions on how to improve the quality of teaching and learning at TIAS.

Mike Trigg's predecessor served as Principal for 15 years before her retirement. Mike's proposals were met with concerns from some teachers, including a member of his own senior leadership team.

(a) Define the term **internal stakeholders**.   *[2 marks]*

(b) Suggest **two** reasons why Mike Trigg's proposals might be described as innovative creativity.   *[4 marks]*

Exam tip !

Make sure you understand the difference between creativity and innovation. Creativity is the process of generating new ideas, often stemming from divergent thinking. It is the ability to create. Innovation is the act of commercialising a new idea or concept. In other words, creativity is the generation of new ideas whereas innovation goes one step further by turning these ideas into action.

Theory of knowledge

Using two ways of knowing, discuss why nations desire to innovate.

Research & development and the CUEGIS concepts

How pace of change in an industry, organizational culture and ethical considerations may influence research and development practices and strategies in an organization. AO3

© IBO, 2017

The pace of change in certain industries means that effective R&D expenditure is increasingly important. When cameras were first invented, there was very limited competition so manufacturers enjoyed stability in the industry. Over time, with the invention of 35mm camera film, the market became dominated by market leaders such as Kodak, Minolta and Fuji. Competition led to continuous improvements driving R&D. However, with the introduction of digital cameras and then mobile devices with camera functions, competition has intensified to a global level with R&D focusing on continuous innovation. Stability becomes less certain in an ever-changing business world. R&D can certainly be the catalyst for change. For example, the first edition of the Encyclopaedia Britannica was printed in Edinburgh, Scotland but it finally went out of print in 2012 after 244 years. This was the harsh reality of the digital age, including competition from the Wikipedia. Although Faber-Castell has over 250 years of history in producing pens and pencils, is it simply a matter of time before we no longer need to use pens and pencils? The ability to adapt to and manage changes in the business environment enables organizations to achieve better customer satisfaction, and hence to improve their profitability.

Figure 5.6.f How long will it be before these products become innovations of yesteryear?

In rapidly changing markets, such as the movie industry or the computer games market, R&D and innovation are key factors to business success. Product life cycles in these markets are very short and consumer demand is constantly changing (demanding 'better' and more exciting films and computer games). In addition, production costs tend to be very high, thereby making the risk of failure a real threat. Therefore, innovation is paramount in these industries. Seeking new market opportunities is a crucial source of innovation, e.g. downloading television programmes, movies and computer games onto mobile phones and portable media players.

Essentially, businesses that are able to embrace change are more likely to survive and thrive, especially in industries where the life cycle of many products is short. Hence, any effective strategy is likely to include R&D expenditure to ensure the business copes with changes in the external environment.

The organizational culture (see Unit 2.5) may also influence R&D practices in a business. Innovative organizations such as Apple, Google and 3M have an open and inclusive culture that encourages creativity and risk taking. By contrast, other organizations have a culture of reserving R&D to a team of experts. For example, McDonald's R&D team is responsible for product development, so other employees have no input in this process. In risk-adverse cultures, managers can be put off by the threat of failure, leading to financial losses and reduced staff morale. R&D expenditure is often ignored, limited or postponed in organizations due to budgetary constraints. Organizational culture can also be largely affected by national cultures - some countries are known for devoting a significant proportion of their resources to R&D and innovation, e.g. South Korea, USA, Japan, Sweden and The Netherlands.

Most governments encourage R&D and innovation through the protection of **intellectual property rights** (see Box 5.6.d). Intellectual property rights (IPRs) are the legal rights to exclusive ownership of certain inventions or pieces of work. IPRs have become of greater concern to many businesses due to developments in Internet technologies. Some countries do not have laws governing the use of IPR on the Internet. The common practice of music and video downloads, for example, is still very hard for governments to police. The United Nation's World Intellectual Property Organization (WIPO) has gone some way to encourage and promote the protection of IPRs around the world. However, the existence of non-complying and non-participating countries, such as Taiwan, presents somewhat of a challenge for multinational companies and the WIPO. America's accusations of China's poor governance of IPRs is another example.

Box 5.6.d   Intellectual Property Rights (IPR)

- **Patents** provide legal protection, for a finite period of time, to the registered producer or user of a newly invented product or process.
- **Copyrights** provide legal protection, for a limited period of time, to artists and authors by preventing others from using or plagiarising their published works without permission. This book is copyrighted, and making photocopies is illegal.
- **Trademarks** are signs or logos used to represent a business, its brands and/or its products.

Ethical considerations may also influence R&D practices and strategies. There are huge ethical issues and implications of *how* R&D is conducted. For example, cosmetic firms might test their products on animals. Similarly, R&D can impact on the ethical practices of organizations. For example, many schools around the world have used professional research findings to promote healthy eating, so have banned junk food and high-caffeine, sugary and energy drinks such as coffee, Coca-Cola, Red Bull and Lucozade.

R&D and innovation can help to address the unmet needs of customers. Innovation is at the heart of problem-solving and is a major force of change. Billionaire Stelios Haji-Loannou, founder of the easyGroup, made his fortunes by being innovative. He suggested that entrepreneurs ought to be pioneers not copiers of the ideas of others, so that customers choose their products over those of their competitors. Some industries, such as pharmaceuticals and consumer electronics, rely more on R&D than others. Nevertheless, R&D and innovation can give any business a large competitive advantage, so most businesses devote some time and resources to them.

Case study

In 1998, BMW paid £40 million ($60m) for the Rolls–Royce logo and name, which it has been able to use since 2003. This was considered as a major bargain by most analysts, given the high status and reputation of the Rolls-Royce trademark. The acquisition enabled BMW to take control of Rolls–Royce Motor Cars Ltd., makers of luxury automobiles.

R&D can be an essential component of strategy for a business to maintain competitiveness. Charles H. Duell, Commissioner of the US Office of Patents in 1899 claimed, "*Everything that can be invented has been invented*". How wrong he was! Innovation is an ongoing phenomenon in today's business environment. Bill Gates, co-founder of Microsoft, is alleged to have claimed in 1981 that 640 kilobytes of computer memory was enough for people. Of course, Bill Gates clearly recognises that change and innovation are vital to the long-term survival of a business. He argues that organizations should not become complacent with their successes but continue to innovate as part of their business strategy. Globalization, for example, presents opportunities for product development and product innovation as business strategies. The changing nature of the business environment has meant that R&D has become a continuous process for many industries. Shorter product life cycles and the use of innovation as a source of competitive advantage mean that managers have to place greater emphasis on being innovative.

Finally, whilst R&D provides potentially huge benefits to an organization, the cost implications and the high failure rates often prove too large a barrier. R&D expenditure cannot and does not guarantee success. As Coco Chanel said, "*One cannot be forever innovating. I want to create classics.*" On the other hand, "classics" can only be achieved if businesses are prepared to take risks. After all, it is not possible for businesses to grow without taking some calculated risks. As Charles Darwin (1809-1882) said "*It is not the strongest of the species that survive, not the most intelligent, but the one most responsive to change.*" The challenge for managers is to strike the right balance.

Theory of knowledge

Does innovation determine the wealth of a country?

CUEGIS Essay

With reference to an organization of your choice, discuss how **change** and **culture** have affected research and development (R&D) practices.   *[20 marks]*

REVIEW QUESTIONS

1.   What is meant by Research and Development (R&D)?

2.   What are prototypes?

3.   What are the benefits of R&D?

4.   What are the limitations of R&D?

5.   What is innovation?

6.   How might successful R&D help to address the unmet needs of customers?

7.   Distinguish between the 4 types of innovation (product, process, positing and paradigm).

8.   Using examples, distinguish between radical and incremental innovation.

9.   What is the difference between adaptive creativity and innovative creativity?

10. How do the concepts of change, culture and ethics influence the R&D practices of businesses?

KEY TERMS

Adaptive creativity is a category of incremental innovation that adjusts or develops something that already exists.

Adaptors approach creativity (a prerequisite to innovation) by working within the rules of the organization and seek consensus.

Copyrights are a form of intellectual property right, which provides legal protection for the owner(s) of published works, such as those of authors, artists, composers, journalists, musicians, photographers, and movie (film) directors. Note: this textbook is protected by international copyrights. Reproduction and redistribution in physical or electric format are strictly prohibited.

Creativity is the process of generating new ideas, often stemming from divergent thinking, i.e. it is the ability to create new ideas. Creativity is a vital prerequisite to innovation.

Development is the use of research findings to create products that might be commercialised. It can also mean improving existing processes or products.

Incremental innovation refers to minor improvements to products or work processes.

Innovation is the process of commercially pioneering new ideas and creations in the production process. It stems from successful R&D in order to meet the needs of customers in a profitable way.

Innovative creativity is radical in nature as it involves creating something that is new. Innovators redefine problems and cultural norms.

Innovators approach creativity (a prerequisite to innovation) by being original and taking calculated risks. They create solutions aimed at doing things differently.

Patents are the exclusive intellectual right given to the registered owner to commercialise an invention, for a pre-determined length of time.

Paradigm innovation refers to innovative change, usually of a radical nature. Such innovations change the nature of certain markets and/or organizational cultures, e.g. low-cost airlines and e-commerce.

Positioning innovation refers to changing the context of a product. It focuses on repositioning the perception of an established product by the use of appropriate innovation strategies.

Process innovation refers to changes to the way production or delivery takes place, i.e. how something is done. It aims to improve the method of production and the logistics of getting the product from the factory floor to the consumer.

Product innovation refers to new creations or the development and improvement of existing products, e.g. the introduction of new products, superior functionality, better ease of use and improved reliability or performance.

Prototypes are trial or test products used in the R&D process. Prototypes are designed, tested and developed with the hope of eventual commercialisation, i.e. the product being launched.

Radical innovation refers to major and disruptive innovations that tend to involve high risks. They can be a major source of competitive advantage.

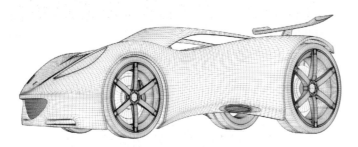

Prototypes are an essential part of the R&D process

Research refers to the commercial investigation of the unknown, such as new products or processes.

Research and development (R&D) is the technological and scientific research that helps to generate a flow of new ideas and processes, e.g. modifications or improvements to existing products and launching new products.

A **sunrise industry** is a growing industry that has significant growth potential, so R&D expenditure is justified.

A **sunset industry** is a declining industry where there is no or even negative growth in the market. This makes R&D expenditure difficult to justify, so it is minimal or withdrawn

Trademarks are the intellectual property rights given to the owner to have exclusive access to a particular sign or symbol that belongs to the organization, e.g. brand names and corporate logo.

5.7 Crisis management and contingency planning

"The pessimist sees the difficulty in every opportunity. An optimist sees the opportunity in every difficulty"-
Sir Winston Churchill, Prime Minister of the UK (1940–1945 and 1951–1955)

HL content	Assessment objective
The difference between crisis management and contingency planning	AO2
• The following factors that affect effective crisis management: • Transparency • Communication • Speed • Control	AO2
The following advantages and disadvantages of contingency planning for a given organization or situation: • Cost • Time • Risks • Safety	AO2

© IBO, 2017

Crisis management

The difference between crisis management and contingency
planning. AO2

© IBO, 2017

A **crisis** is a situation of instability that results in major problems for a business. Crises are usually unexpected and often unpredictable. In the event of an actual crisis, it is probable that costs to the business will be significant in terms of both time and money. At its extreme, a crisis can threaten the survival of a business. All businesses, irrespective of their size, face the risk of experiencing a crisis (see Box 5.7.a). Hence, managers devise plans to minimise the damage that crises can cause to their organizations.

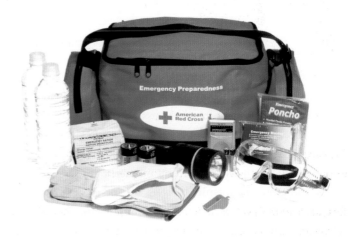

Figure 5.7.a Crises can take many forms

597

Box 5.7.a shows some examples of real crises in the business world. Broader examples of crises include:

- A lack of working capital to pay workers and suppliers (see Unit 3.7)

- Theft and vandalism

- Negative and damaging media publicity, e.g. food poisoning at a restaurant

- Computer hacking or data loss

- Accidents such as fire damage to stock and property

- Soaring levels of staff turnover

- Natural disasters such as floods, storms or earthquakes

- No power due to a blackout or power cut

- Computer failure

- Delayed flights due to computer failure at airports

- Outbreaks of infectious diseases

- Loss or long-term sickness of key personnel

- Terrorist attacks.

Crisis management refers to the response of an organization to a crisis situation. It is about being *reactive* to events that can cause serious harm to a business. The first decade of the twenty-first century saw events such as the terrorist attacks of 11 September 2001 in the USA, the deadly SARS outbreak and a tsunami in Southeast Asia, world oil prices hitting historical highs, and global pandemics of avian flu and swine flu. Crises can also be unique to a business, such as a fire in the building or a sudden announcement of a hostile takeover from a rival company. Most businesses find it extremely difficult (and unnecessarily expensive) to plan for such unpredictable and unquantifiable risks, which can have profound impacts on their operations. Hence, crisis management involves formulating the best response to a crisis. If a business finds itself faced with an emergency, then crisis management is required to minimise the impact on the business. Radical measures, centralised decision making and an autocratic style of leadership are likely to prevail.

Box 5.7.a Corporate crises

- 1985 – Coca-Cola, partly in response to the infamous *Pepsi Challenge*, launched a replacement product for regular Coke called New Coke. With 40,000 written complaints each day about the new product, Coca-Cola was forced to bring back its original-flavoured drink.

- 2004 – Coca-Cola introduced its bottled 'natural still water' called Dasani in England. It was later discovered that the water came from a tap and contained prohibited levels of bromate (a chemical compound that can cause cancer).

- 2006 – Sony recalled almost six million lithium ion laptop batteries from its clients Dell and Apple, which cost Sony up to 20% of its net profits for that year.

- 2006 – Disney oversold tickets for its first Chinese New Year season at the Hong Kong Disneyland theme park. Tourists from China were turned away even though they had valid tickets. The poor public relations that followed meant Disney fell short of its annual attendance target.

- 2006 – Cadbury's suffered a £30 million ($44m) loss when a burst pipe in its Birmingham factory caused salmonella contamination to one million bars of chocolate.

- 2007 – Toys-R-Us, removed all *Thomas The Tank Engine* products from its shelves, following findings that the paint on the wooden toy trains contained traces of toxic lead. More than 1.5 million units were recalled in North America alone.

- 2009 – UK retailers faced calamities during December when snowstorms prevented Christmas shoppers from going home. Customers stranded in John Lewis (a department store) and IKEA were allowed to use the in-store beds.

- 2011 – A 9.0 magnitude earthquake and tsunami caused major damage to Japan – the worst natural disaster in its recorded history. The damage cost the economy 25 trillion yen ($309bn), and would take up to five years to sort out.

- 2013 – Typhoon Haiyan, the deadliest tropical cyclone ever to hit the Philippines, caused more than 6,200 deaths and more than $1.5 billion of damage.

- 2016 – Political and social turmoil in Turkey, caused by military attempts to seize control of several key places including Ankara and Istanbul.

- 2018 – Visa faced huge problems when hardware failure prevented customers throughout Europe from using their credit cards to make payments at retail outlets.

Figure 5.7.b The 2003 SARS outbreak caused schools to close in many parts of Southeast Asia

Successful managers have the ability to respond to significant disruptions to their business by implementing a contingency plan to restore its business operations. Hence, crisis management is sometimes referred to as **disaster recovery**. Effective crisis management requires the crisis management team to deal with crises in a swift manner before they escalate into a terminal problem for the organization.

Contingency planning is about being *proactive* to changes in the business environment. It involves developing a plan before an unwanted or unlikely event occurs, by using "what if?" questions to identify probable threats. Contingency planning helps with crisis management by preparing for a crisis or emergency. Anyone working in the insurance industry will testify that the future is difficult to predict; things are likely to turn out differently from what may have been planned. However, to reduce the risks and impacts of encountering a crisis, businesses carry out contingency planning. Managers examine what might happen, estimate the likelihood of these events happening and assess the probable impacts on the business, e.g. a downturn in the economy, the loss of electricity and power, extreme weather conditions, or strike action by the workforce. Contingency plans help managers to be better prepared if there is a crisis, in order to ensure the continuity of the business.

Most organizations have a contingency plan for the possibility of a fire in the workplace. The plan includes procedures for evacuation of the buildings (including the use of emergency exits) and contacting the emergency services (fire, police and ambulance). It also includes details of the roles and responsibilities of members of the crisis management team. The crisis plan needs to be tested, e.g. fire drills are rehearsed to test the contingency plan. This might include actions such as response rates (how efficiently people evacuate the building) and other tests performed under safe conditions. A review is then conducted and a report submitted to the crisis management team, with recommendations for further improvements to the contingency plan.

Case study

In 2010, BP was far too complacent with its safety checks, which led to an oil rig exploding in the Gulf of Mexico. The fatal blast at Deepwater Horizon took the lives of 11 workers and caused 4.9 million barrels of oil to spill into the ocean. The company's lack of a contingency plan, slow response to the crisis, and poor disaster recovery plan resulted in the company being fined a record $20.8bn by the authorities. The overall cost of the oil spill to BP was around $62bn. The Deepwater Horizon disaster was so colossal that Hollywood made a movie about it.

Question 5.7.1   Meat products recalled in the USA

In 2014, the Department of Agriculture raised concerns that diseased and unfit animals were processed without the required inspections from Rancho Feeding Corporation, suppliers of meat products to retailers including *Nestlé, Walmart* and *Sam's Club*. The public were shocked that diseased beef was processed without consideration for public safety. More than 3.62 million kilograms of meat were recalled. European supermarkets and retailers were hit by a similar crisis the year before when traces of horsemeat were found in frozen beef products.

(a) Describe, in the context of the case study, the meaning of a crisis.   *[2 marks]*

(b) Examine how crisis management can help retailers such as *Walmart* to deal with such a crisis.   *[6 marks]*

The more quantifiable the crisis, the more effective a contingency plan tends to be. For example, the governments of Macau and the Philippines have contingency plans for the onslaught of tropical typhoons and torrential rain. In Hong Kong, warning signs for typhoons and/or heavy rain are broadcast on the radio, Internet and television to inform and warn people In extreme cases, such as a 'Hurricane signal 10' or a 'black rainstorm' warning, businesses and schools are closed, as the severe weather conditions threaten people's safety. Similarly, in Middle Eastern countries such as Dubai and Qatar, severe heat warnings are signalled by governments. Schools and businesses are closed if the heat proves too dangerous for people to be outside for extended periods of time.

✕9	INCREASING GALE OR STORM SIGNAL NO. 9
✚10	HURRICANE SIGNAL NO. 10
Amber 黃	AMBER RAINSTORM WARNING SIGNAL
Red 紅	RED RAINSTORM WARNING SIGNAL
Black 黑	BLACK RAINSTORM WARNING SIGNAL
雷暴 Thunderstorm	THUNDERSTORM WARNING
	SPECIAL ANNOUNCEMENT ON FLOODING IN THE NORTHERN NEW TERRITORIES
	LANDSLIP WARNING
季候風 Monsoons	STRONG MONSOON SIGNAL

Figure 5.7.c Some of Hong Kong's weather warnings

Hence, effective contingency plans enable a business to be better prepared to manage a crisis (by being proactive), rather than being totally unprepared to cope with the crisis when it occurs (by being reactive or passive). This is far easier to do if all risks and crises are identified and quantified.

However, some risks are uninsurable since they are so difficult to quantify. This makes contingency planning challenging and perhaps meaningless. Nevertheless, careful and effective planning can help an organization to become better prepared and resilient to any major catastrophes. Although some people argue that the plans may be unnecessary, given the low probability or unquantifiable nature of crises, most experts believe that businesses would become extremely exposed to the dangers of crises if they have no plan at all to follow. Of course, contingency planning does not eliminate all eventualities of a problem occurring. Nevertheless, careful planning can mean that the number and extent of surprises are reduced. As the saying goes, if we fail to prepare, then we are preparing to fail.

Common mistake

Students often confuse crisis management and contingency planning, using the terms interchangeably. **Crisis management** (or disaster recovery) occurs *during* and *after* an event (such as the outbreak of a fire) whilst **contingency planning** happens *before* (planning a fire drill). The latter asks 'what if?' questions, such as what the firm should do if exchange rates or interest rates rise, whereas crisis management asks 'what now?' questions.

Question 5.7.2 Bausch & Lomb

In April 2006, American eye care company Bausch & Lomb (*B&L*) had $500 million wiped off its stock market value following findings that the company's top-selling 'ReNu' contact lens solutions were linked to an unusual eye infection. Shipments of the contact lens solution from its South Carolina factory were halted by the US Centre for Disease Control and Prevention. According to the Association for Research in Vision and Ophthalmology (ARVO), about half of all contact lens wearers experience contact lens discomfort.

(a) In the context of the case study, describe what is meant by 'crisis planning'. *[2 marks]*

(b) Discuss how far it is possible for a business such as *B&L* to plan for a crisis. *[10 marks]*

Theory of knowledge

Which way of knowing plays the greatest role in contingency planning: emotion, imagination, intuition or reasoning?

IB Learner Profile – Be an inquirer and a thinker

Investigate a case where a celebrity endorsed by a company or brand has severely tarnished its image by inappropriate behaviour. Discuss how far it is possible to plan for such a crisis.

Exam tip !
Worked example

Question: The managers at a production plant have estimated that, in the worst case scenario, a crisis would cost the firm $100 million. To what extent should the firm spend $500,000 today on crisis planning, knowing that the crisis might never happen?   *[10 marks]*

Answer: Remember to start with definitions - in this case, define the terms 'crisis' (a sudden and unexpected threat to the survival of the business) and crisis planning. Then present both sides of the argument:

Arguments for spending the $500,000 might include:

• Limits the damage caused in the event of an actual crisis.
• The $500,000 is only 0.5% of the costs in the worst case scenario, i.e. not spending this money can actually cost the firm much more if there is a crisis.
• It can give managers and workers a sense of security (peace of mind).

Arguments against spending the $500,000 include:

• Spending the money does not prevent a crisis from occurring.
• The $500,000 will diminish the firm's cash flow position today.
• The money might have been better spent on another project that would yield a return for the firm.
• The likelihood of a crisis occurring is too low to justify the expenditure.

As the exam question requires you to address the 'extent' to which the spending is justified, a decision or judgment must be made. This will depend on several factors:

• The probability of the crisis occurring.
• The nature and scale of the crisis.
• The nature of the business and its operations, e.g. the size of the firm and its financial strength.
• Management traits, preferences and experiences.

Answers, as always, must be written in the context of the business and its organizational objectives.

Factors affecting effective crisis management

The following factors that affect effective crisis management: Transparency, Communication, Speed and Control. AO2
© IBO, 2017

The effectiveness of crisis management is dependent on several factors, including:

Transparency – Most experts believe that it is best to be transparent (open and honest) during a time of crisis. Three examples of different decades are outlined below.

• In 1990, for example, authorities in the USA found traces of benzene in Perrier bottled mineral water. The producer tried to hide the truth from the general public but this only served to damage its image. The mass media saw Perrier putting profits before the interest of people, and this led to the recall of 160 million bottles of Perrier.

• China's Sanlu Group was given a bankruptcy order from the government in 2008 for its involvement and attempted cover up in an adulterated baby milk powder scandal. Sanlu was found guilty of contaminating its product with traces of melamine, which caused kidney stones and other complications in almost 300,000 infants, and killing six babies in China. The lesson to be learnt is that in times of such crises, acting in a transparent and socially irresponsible way is more likely to cause a firm long-term damage than if it had acted responsibly and taken necessary corrective measures from the outset.

• In 2015, the US Environmental Protection Agency (EPA) found that Volkswagen, Europe's largest carmaker, had deliberately programmed its diesel engines to cheat laboratory emissions tests, which were about 40 times higher than what is allowed in the USA. The scandal resulted in its share price plummeting and the CEO resigning. The German company had to spend $18.32bn to rectify the emissions issue, and faced a criminal fine of $2.8bn in 2017.

Communication – Effective communication with all key stakeholders is critical in a crisis situation, such as contacting the emergency services and insurers. Effective crisis management also requires leaders to develop a crisis communications plan, including an understanding of how the news media works. In the event of a crisis, leaders need to get a press release out immediately to contain the situation. They need to work with the media and attempt to get the press on their side. With the use of Internet technologies, it is relatively easy to communicate via the organization's website. This was the method used by Apple when announcing the death of Steve Jobs in 2011, the company's CEO at the time. Effective communications help to reassure employees, customers, suppliers, investors and other stakeholder groups.

Speed – In a crisis situation, the speed of response is critical to the effectiveness of crisis management. This is comparable to a person who has had a major accident and needs immediate medical attention; if the critically injured person is treated straight away, the chances of survival increase significantly. The same principle applies to crisis management. The speed of response to the crisis influences the chances of containing or reducing the damages caused. This is far more likely to happen if managers have an effective contingency plan.

Control – A major crisis truly tests the performance of the leadership team within an organization. Leaders need to be able to control the crisis situation. This entails many skills, including the ability to work under extreme pressure, to communicate with all key stakeholders (including the ability to manage the news media) and to make quick and effective decisions. A crisis will require leaders to have instant access to cash funds to control the situation and to continue business as usual (or as much as possible).

Case study

The Fukushima nuclear power plant disaster in 2011 was caused by the tsunami that followed the Tōhoku earthquake. The nuclear disaster caused substantial amounts of radioactive materials to be released. It was the largest nuclear incident since the Chernobyl disaster in 1986. Following a formal investigation into the accident, investigators blamed the catastrophe on a culture of complacency around nuclear safety and poor crisis management.

The advantages and disadvantages of contingency planning

The following advantages and disadvantages of contingency planning for a given organization or situation: Cost, Time, Risks and Safety. AO2

© IBO, 2017

- **Cost** – The public can be quite forgiving, especially if crises are beyond the control of a business. Untruthful and deceitful cover-up stories are frowned upon by the public and the media. Acting in a socially responsible way (see Unit 1.3) can be a source of competitive advantage. Contingency plans can therefore help to minimise negative reactions and hence the costs (financial losses) of crises.

- **Time** – Planning takes time, but can save time in the event of a crisis. Would you know what to do if you were at school when a fire broke out? What about in the event of a lockdown if an intruder were to attack the school? Prompt action is imperative to the disaster recovery process. Delays in responding to a crisis can allow problems to escalate beyond repair.

- **Risks** – Advocates of contingency planning argue that it helps to reduce risks as most risks or eventualities can be accounted for. A well thought-out plan to follow in the event of a disaster therefore helps to reduce overall risks. In the event of a catastrophic loss (such as injury or death to people), then the directors, managers or employees may be held personally or severally liable if guidelines were not followed, such as the non-compliance of health and safety legislation. For example, most schools produce risk assessments for education field trips, sporting activities and other outdoor pursuits. As part of a contingency plan, the risk assessments are produced to keep students and teachers as safe as possible, helping staff to know what to do in the event of an emergency.

- **Safety** – Immediate actions, such as communications with the organization's personnel, can help to alleviate or minimize the concerns of staff and meet their security needs (see Unit 2.4). Contingency plans help in the process of effective handling of staff concerns and anxieties, which is vital for the disaster recovery process.

Figure 5.7.d Health and safety are at the core of contingency planning

Ultimately, the advantages of contingency planning enhance the chances of the organization's survival during a time of crisis. The disadvantages of contingency planning include:

- **Cost** – Crises may never happen, so the time and money invested into contingency planning could have been better used elsewhere. No amount of planning can prevent the totally unexpected, such as natural disasters.

- **Time** – Contingency planning uses up valuable management time and resources, thereby increasing costs. It is also impossible to consider all scenarios; the more 'what if' scenarios that are considered, the more time that is spent on devising the plans. Time and resources are also needed to update these plans.

- **Risks** – If plans are based on outdated or inaccurate data, then inappropriate actions may be taken if a crisis occurs. Contingency plans, no matter how detailed and well thought out, do not guarantee the survival of the business or the safety of its people. There is also the risk that people outside of the contingency planning team do not take things so seriously (perhaps due to ignorance), which severely limits the advantages of producing these plans.

Question 5.7.3   H5N1 bird flu

In 2006, the World Health Organization (WHO) confirmed the outbreak of the deadly avian flu in Turkey, the first case in Europe. Health experts believed that the H5N1 virus could quickly spread from birds to humans, thereby harming the global economy if sick employees were forced to stay away from work. Not surprisingly, Turkey's lucrative tourism industry was badly hit by the news.

Many international businesses, such as HSBC, responded to the threat of a global outbreak by devising **contingency plans** to deal with the potential outbreak. Schools in Japan, Singapore and Hong Kong (all highly densely populated countries) drew up plans to respond to a possible pandemic. Many schools trained their teachers to work from home, using Internet technologies.

(a) Define the term **contingency plan**.   [2 marks]

(b) Examine the costs and benefits to organizations such as banks and schools in devising contingency plans.   [6 marks]

HIGHER LEVEL

Operations management

Common mistake

It is wrong to assume that insurance is the solution to a crisis. Indeed, insurance can help to recover some of the damages caused by a crisis, such as floods or fires. However, some risks are simply unquantifiable, such as financial losses due to terrorist attacks. Hence, not all risks can be covered by insurance.

IB Learner Profile – Be an inquirer and be reflective

Investigate a recent corporate crisis in a country of your choice. How effective was the crisis management team in handling the crisis?

Box 5.7.b   Inventions and War

The following products have been credited to come out of the two World Wars:

- Agricultural fertilisers
- Ballpoint pens
- Daylight saving time
- Jet engines
- Photocopying
- Wristwatches
- Kleenex sanitary tissues
- Plastic surgery
- Canned foods
- Duck tape
- Stainless steel
- Tea bags
- Vegetarian sausages
- Zips

Theory of knowledge

Which ways of knowing do you think business leaders use most when deciding how to deal with crises?

Theory of knowledge

Can anything good come out of a crisis that poses a severe threat to the survival of a business?

Question 5.7.4   Toyota

Toyota faced one of its biggest crises during 2009-2011 with a total of 9 million vehicles being recalled due to various mechanical problems. Analysts calculated the cost of the crisis for *Toyota* was $2.47 billion in the USA alone (or around $2 million a month in revenue per *Toyota* dealership). *Toyota* also suffered from lost sales of new cars, estimated to be in the region of $2 billion. By March 2011, *Toyota* had put the crisis behind itself with sales in the USA rebounding by over 40%. However, in 2014 *Toyota* recalled another 2.1 million of its Prius, RAV4, Tacoma and Lexus models across Europe, North America and Japan, due to a software problem that could cause the cars to stop suddenly. *Toyota's* head of global operations made a public appearance in the USA, to apologise for the safety problems with its cars.

(a) Explain why product recalls can be damaging to a firm's corporate reputation.   *[4 marks]*

(b) Evaluate whether it would be in *Toyota's* best interest to spend money on contingency planning or improving the quality of its cars.   *[10 marks]*

Crisis management, contingency planning and the CUEGIS concepts

A crisis is a threat to business strategy. Crisis management is about dealing with the changes that such threats can bring. Contingency plans can go some way to deal with crises in an open and succinct manner. With any crisis, it is the planned prevention (contingency planning) and the proactive response of managers that minimise the impacts of a crisis. The contingency plans must be properly and regularly tested, reviewed and updated. The crisis coordinator, usually a senior executive, works closely with a crisis management team and external agencies (such as lawyers, the press and the emergency services) to develop an effective crisis management system.

Whatever the strategy, it is important to act fast during the outbreak of a crisis. The mistakes of businesses such as Perrier and Bausch & Lomb have shown that immediate and transparent action can allow managers to take control of the situation. However, such responses require both careful contingency planning and an effective crisis management team. For example, only a properly trained representative should handle the media as the organization's official spokesperson.

Case study

Adverse weather conditions can affect the actual IB examinations! Therefore, it is common for IB World Schools to have contingency plans in place, to prepare for severe weather conditions that result in the IB examinations being postponed. For example, severe snowstorms, hurricanes or flooding in the month of May in some countries mean that students are unable to travel to school to take their IB exams. Hence, schools need to include a detailed communications strategy to inform students and parents about procedures for rescheduling exams during adverse weather conditions, natural disasters and political turmoil.

Snowstorms can cause school closures

Ultimately, the way in which a business responds to a crisis will depend on its corporate culture. For example, contingency planning and crisis management often involve a strong focus on public relations (PR). A crisis could damage the corporate image of a business and reduce stakeholder confidence in the organization. Therefore, an adaptive business culture focuses on rectifying this damage to assure stakeholders that recovery is imminent. The PR strategy will involve marketing activities aimed at establishing and protecting a desired corporate image. It is about getting positive press coverage, usually without directly paying for it.

So just how far should strategic planning cater for a crisis? Crises change the environment in which a business operates so crisis management can be vital for business survival. Yet, it is questionable whether time and resources (and/or how much) should be devoted in any strategy to planning for events that may never happen. Moreover, some risks are simply not quantifiable, so dedicating management time and resources to contingency planning may not be regarded as cost effective. Even if a plan exists, given the unpredictable nature of crises, it is possible that management do not act according to plans once they actually face a crisis. For example, US regulators fined South Korea's Asiana Airlines $500,000 in 2014 for failing to help victims of a flight that crashed at San Francisco airport a year earlier. Hence, how a business acts in a crisis can also raise ethical issues.

Nevertheless, effective crisis management allows the organization to deal with any uncertainties and the dynamics of change. Albert Einstein said, "*Intellectuals solve problems; geniuses prevent them*". Effective managers must be both geniuses (by having contingency plans to prevent or minimise the impact of crises) and intellectuals (by having effective crisis management).

As part of its strategy, businesses need to review how they manage an actual crisis that materialises. The crisis management team will need to investigate the root cause(s) of the crisis. Various tools can be used for this, such as Ishikawa's fishbone model (see Unit 1.7). Although no two crises are exactly the same, there is much to be learnt from one situation that can help the firm to deal with future crises. Contingency planning takes time but can save managers a lot of time if a crisis does materialise. Crisis experts use their plans to create business opportunities out of a threat. John F. Kennedy (1917–1963), the 35th president of the USA, famously pointed out that the Chinese word for 'crisis' is composed of two characters – danger and opportunity. The Chinese characters for crisis are "危機", with the first character meaning danger or threat, and the second character being part

HIGHER LEVEL

Operations management

of the characters that make up the word opportunity or chance "機會". Hence, out of every crisis, an opportunity arises.

The words of US politician and ambassador Benjamin Franklin (1706–1790) sums up the purpose of crisis management and contingency planning as part of an overall business strategy: "*By failing to prepare, you are preparing to fail.*"

Theory of knowledge

To what extent do you think that globalization necessitates a change in values and traditional cultures?

Case study

During World War II, the Germans banned the import of Coca-Cola under a trade embargo. The head of Coca-Cola Deutschland (Germany) decided to produce an alternative drink called Fanta, using domestically sourced ingredients at the time. The name came from 'fantasie', the German word for 'imagination'. Ten years later, Coca-Cola launched Fanta across the world.

Common mistake

Too often, students write about major crises, assuming that crises have to occur on a national or international scale. However, crises can occur on a small scale, affecting a single organization. Examples include an expected power cut, machinery breakdown, or the sudden illness of the CEO or owner of the business.

Question 5.7.5 Chaos at Hong Kong Disneyland

The first year of operations proved problematic for *Hong Kong Disneyland (HKDL)*, with some major **public relations** setbacks in 2005. *HKDL* ran into trouble with **labour unions** after staff complained of being overworked and underpaid. The company also faced complaints from international conservationists who forced *HKDL* caterers to remove shark fin soup from their menus.

The general public were outraged during Chinese New Year when thousands of ticket holders were denied access to *HKDL* due to overcrowding. Despite holding valid prepurchased tickets, many customers who had travelled from China were turned away at the gates. Hong Kong lawmakers said that *HKDL's* decision to refuse ticket holders entry was a breach of contract.

HKDL apologised for the disaster, claiming that it was placing public safety as a priority. It also announced extended opening hours to cater for more visitors. The company admitted to underestimating demand as it had not predicted the huge influx of tourists during the Chinese New Year holiday week.

(a) (i) Define the term **public relations**.   [2 marks]

(a) (ii) Define the term **labour unions**.   [2 marks]

(b) Examine **two** strategies that *HKDL* could have used to deal with the poor public relations that it faced.   [6 marks]

(c) Justify whether *HKDL* could have been better prepared for dealing with the excess number of visitors to its theme park.   [10 marks]

CUEGIS Essay

With reference to a business of your choice, examine how organizational **culture** and **ethics** affect the contingency planning and crisis management.

[20 marks]

REVIEW QUESTIONS

1. What is the meaning of a crisis?

2. What is crisis management and why is it of value to businesses?

3. What is contingency planning?

4. How does crisis management differ from contingency planning?

5. Outline the factors that affect the effectiveness of crisis management.

6. What are the advantages of contingency planning?

7. What are the disadvantages of contingency planning?

8. Why is it important to take immediate action when a crisis occurs?

9. Why is it important to be transparent about issues and concerns during a crisis?

10. Why do some people question the financial value of contingency planning?

KEY TERMS

Communication is one of the factors that affect the effectiveness of crisis management, by informing internal and external stakeholders to help them to know and understand the issue.

Contingency planning is about being *proactive* to changes in the business environment. It involves developing a plan before an unwanted or unlikely event occurs by using "what if?" questions to identify all probable threats.

Control is one of the factors that affect the effectiveness of crisis management, by using a crisis management (or critical incident) team to handle a crisis and ensure there is leadership and governance.

A **crisis** is a situation of instability that results in major problems for a business. Crises are usually unexpected and often unpredictable, e.g. natural disasters, accidents and computer failure.

Crisis management (also known as disaster recover) is about being *reactive* to events and disasters that can cause serious disruptions and harm to a business, i.e. taking action as and when a crisis happens.

Quantifiable risks (or **insurable risks**) are probable and financially measurable threats to a business, such as fire damage.

Speed is one of the factors that affect the effectiveness of crisis management, by making prompt decisions and actions in order to return to normal operations as soon as possible.

Transparency is one of the factors that affect the effectiveness of crisis management, by being open and honest with all stakeholders during a crisis. It is about disclosing the truth, such as the scale or severity of the crisis.

Unquantifiable risks (or **uninsurable risks**) are threats to a business that are impossible or prohibitively expensive to examine and measure.

607

6.1 Concept-based learning: Introducing the CUEGIS concepts

"The world is moving at a tremendous rate. Going no one knows where. We must prepare our children, not for the world of the past. Not for our world. But for their world. The world of the future".
John Dewey (1859–1952), American educational leader, philosopher and psychologist

What is concept-based learning?

Concept-based learning (CBL), as defined by education consultant Dr. H. Lynn Erickson, is a three-dimensional model that frames **facts** (content) and **skills** with **concepts** of the Business Management (BM) course – change, culture, ethics, globalization, innovation and strategy. The rigour of the BM course creates two approaches to teaching and learning: either students can be told what they need to know (based on factual knowledge and skills in BM) or teachers can get their students excited enough to discover and deepen their understanding of BM for themselves.

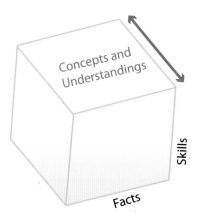

The 21st century learner lives in a mobile and digital world with access to facts and information at their fingertips. As educationalists, we cannot expect our students to learn ever more content in BM. However, we have to help students to connect the factual knowledge to more permanent (timeless) concepts to advance knowledge and understandings (see Table 6.1.a on the following page). In BM, concepts are used to give students the tools necessary to make sense of the world. Supporters of CBL argue that it is through these conceptual lenses (tools) that learning truly begins to make sense for students.

Concept-based learning is *not* about learning facts and figures in isolation. Instead, CBL is about encouraging students to:

- think beyond the factual contets of the BM course
- be active learners rather than passive learners (for example, there is huge scope in BM to use learning technologies to engage our learners)
- be inquiring and curious learners who want to further their understanding and knowledge (perhaps through the use of real-world case studies that would interest our students)
- make connections of knowledge in BM to the CUEGIS concepts (**c**hange, **c**ulture, **e**thics, **g**lobalization, **i**nnovation and **s**trategy), i.e. ideas transferable across BM topics
- apply their knowledge and thinking to solve problems using an organized framework (CUEGIS)
- develop a deeper understanding of BM topics that learners find of personal interest, relevance and meaning
- use multiple sources and media to gain knowledge
- recognise the transferability of knowledge to familiar and unfamiliar situations
- discuss and collaborate with peers to progress in their learning
- organize and make sense of their own learning
- make meaning of their learning
- think critically and creatively to solve problems
- extend knowledge to understanding
- own and drive their own learning in a synergistic way.

Table 6.1.a The difference between knowledge and understanding

Knowledge	Understanding
Factual awareness, connected to a particular time, place or situation. Knowledge changes over time.	Conceptual appreciation of factual knowledge that transfers through time and across situations and cultures. Concepts are timeless.
Example: According to F.W. Taylor (1911), people are motivated by money, so scientific management can be used to create a one 'best way' to increase productivity.	There is no single way to motivate all people all of the time in all situations across all cultures. Change can bring about positive and negative impacts on motivation.
Example 2: Budgets can be used as a control tool to ensure managers are held accountable for their activities.	Budgets can constrain innovation, yet are shaped by the culture of the organization and are vital to its business strategy.

Exam tip !

For definitions and examples of how the six concepts can be used in BM, refer to pages 12 – 14 in the syllabus (Guide).

Exam tip !

Be aware that the CUEGIS essay in Paper 2, Section C, can take one of three generic approaches:

1. the question asks for the impacts of two concepts on content from the BM syllabus, e.g. Paper 2, November 2017, Q8.
2. the question asks for the impact of one concept on another concept, with you choosing your own content from the BM syllabus, e.g. Paper 2, May 2016, Q7.
3. the questions asks for the impact of one concept on another in the context of a specific aspect of the course, e.g. Paper 2, May 2018, Q6.

Concept-based learning in Business Management

The traditional curriculum is designed to be 'topic based' (or content based) rather than 'concept based'. However, critics of content-based curricula argue that the model is outdated (just ask Google!) and does not encourage twenty-first century learners to develop personal intellects. CBL is ideal for the BM course as it promotes a more holistic approach to create a deeper understanding of the subject content. The CUEGIS concepts create six **conceptual lenses** through which students (and teachers) investigate, analyse and evaluate factual content to create a deeper understanding of Business Management.

One of the arguments in favour of a CBL approach to BM is that a content-driven syllabus, which requires students to memorise facts and information, rarely engages learners or challenges their intellects. Motivation experts such as Pink (see Unit 2.4) suggest that being personally engaged drives motivation. The same applies to CBL – students who are personally and intellectually engaged are far more likely to be motivated to learn. Compare the different experiences for learners who face 'chalk and talk' lessons on the following topics (in an abstract and unengaging way) compared to using a CBL approach:

- The 4Ps of Marketing (Unit 4.5) – students can be challenged in their personal learning and application by being involved in an interschool marketing competition (http://goo.gl/dC8Kv5).

- Business organizations (Unit 1.2) – students can gain hands-on experience in setting up and running a business organization by being involved in Young Enterprise (http://goo.gl/neXMCc) or the Junior Achievement Company Programme (http://goo.gl/NuJ7zo).

- Teamworking as a form of non-financial motivation (Unit 2.4) – students can get more engaged in their learning and understanding of how teamworking can work as a form of motivation by taking the Marshmallow Challenge (http://goo.gl/rcp1).

An alternative way to view CBL in Business Management is to use the **triangle model** (see Figure 6.1.b). This consists of the **content** of the syllabus, integrated with business case studies to provide a **context** to the learning, and embedded in **concepts** to transcend understanding of Business Management. An example of a classroom activity that embraces these building blocks is to get students to investigate how marketing strategy is influenced by Change, Culture, Ethics, Globalization and Innovation for an organization of their choice.

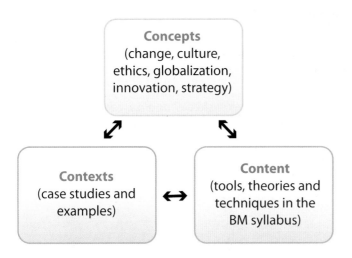

Figure 6.1.a The triangle model (building blocks) of Business Management © IBO, 2017

Theory of knowledge

If it is not possible to teach everything that is important, how do we know what is actually worth teaching?

The CUEGIS concepts in examination questions

Examples of the types of questions in Paper 2 Section C (SL and HL) include:

- With reference to an organization of your choice, examine how **innovation** has brought about a **change** in human resource management.

- With reference to an organization of your choice, examine how **culture** and **ethics** influence promotion (in the marketing mix).

- With reference to an organization of your choice, discuss the importance of **innovation** and **globalization**.

- Examine how the concepts of **globalization** and **ethics** have influenced the extended marketing mix for an organization of your choice.

- With reference to an organization of your choice, compare and contrast the importance of **innovation** and of **culture**.

- Discuss how **ethical** considerations and **cultural** differences influence employer-employee relations in an organization that you have studied.

- With reference to an organization of your choice, examine how **change** may influence marketing **strategy**.

Exam tip !

It is acceptable to conclude that there is a minimal impact (of one concept on another). However, this must be based on a balanced response in the essay, supported by evaluative comments that are substantiated.

Concept-based learning – Give it a go

Decide how you can best move from a traditional content-driven approach of teaching and learning a topic (such as corporate social responsibility) by applying the triangle model, i.e. how would you move from the 'content' (of teaching or learning CSR) to the triangular model of 'content, contexts, concepts'?

How would you integrate the conceptual lenses (of change, culture, ethics, globalization, innovation and strategy) throughout the 37 topics in the Business Management course? As an example, consider the following case for teaching and learning Budgeting (Unit 3.9):

Exam tip !

In preparation for the CUEGIS essay, find out answers to the following questions for the organization of your choice:

1. What is the firm's mission statement?
2. What are key facts about the organization that are worthy of knowing?
3. What do you know about the CEO or a particular individual in the firm?
4. Who are the main rivals?

Budgeting and the CUEGIS concepts

- <u>C</u>hange - the changing business environment may require adjustments to corporate plans and budgets, but does this mean that flexible budgets are better than zero budgeting? How do changes caused by natural disasters impact on the budgeting of businesses?

- <u>C</u>ulture - how do corporate culture and cross-border cultures impact on how budgets are set and managed? How does organizational culture and the impact of the leader influence budgeting?

- <u>E</u>thics - all budget holders are responsible for the money of their organization, yet this responsibility carries ethical considerations. History has shown that budgetary powers have corrupted many business leaders, across all industries.

- <u>G</u>lobalization - the rise in cross-border trade due to globalization has enabled larger scale operations, enabling firms to benefit from economies of scale (see Unit 1.6). Whilst this reduces the average costs of production, exchange rate fluctuations can cause problems for budget holders. How does the drive of globalization and overseas operations impact on the budgets of businesses?

- <u>I</u>nnovation - to what extent does budgeting constrain innovation?

- <u>S</u>trategy - budgets are integral to any business strategy, as finance is needed to fund all business ventures, e.g. a growth strategy entails larger budgets to be allocated to finance larger-scale operations.

Figure 6.1.b Budgets are integral to business strategy

Using the CUEGIS concepts in Business Management

<u>C</u>hange

"When you're finished changing, you're finished." - Benjamin Franklin (1706–1790), one of the Founding Fathers of the United States of America

US novelist, Ellen Glasgow (1873–1945) said, "*All change is not growth, as all movement is not forward*". In other words, change should only be pursued if there is a clear purpose. Figure 6.1.c shows the two different forces of change. **Driving forces** push for change whilst **restraining forces** act against change. Due to the conflicting forces, change must be managed within organizations if they are to move forward and remain competitive. The relative strength of these forces determines whether the change should take place.

Before instigating any organizational change, managers must ask themselves:

- Why is change needed?

- What do we hope to achieve with such change?

- Who is affected by this change and how are they likely to react to the change?

- How will we know that the change has been successfully implemented?

This set of questions is reccurring as businesses constantly face change. A popular management tool to aid this process is **force field analysis** (see Unit 1.7), which acts as a framework for helping managers to understand the pressures for and against any change situation. By identifying these forces, managers are able to assess the effects that the forces may have and to decide on a course of action. Managers can then plan to strengthen the forces supporting a decision for change, and reduce the impacts of opposition to it (see Figure 6.1.c).

Driving forces
(e.g. productivity gains)

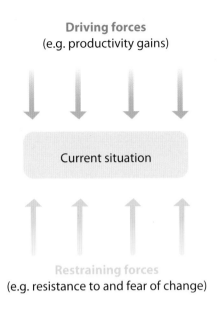

Current situation

Restraining forces
(e.g. resistance to and fear of change)

Figure 6.1.c Forces of change

There are usually four phases of change (FRIA), all of which need to be managed although to varying degrees:

- **F**ear of the unknown

- **R**ejection due to misunderstandings of the need or purpose of change

- **I**nterest (buy-in from the staff)

- **A**cceptance of the need for and purpose of change.

Case study

Businesses that have changed their names include LG Electronics (formerly Lucky and GoldStar Co). Nissan was originally Datsun. AuctionWeb became eBay. Pete's Super Submarines became Subway. Dell Computers was originally called PC's Limited. Relentless.com became Amazon.com. Computing Tabulating Recording Corporation was rebranded as IBM. Pepsi was called Brad's Drink. Nike started off as Blue Ribbon Sports. Firebird became Firefox. Google was originally called BackRub!

Case study

For generations, photography was synonymous with Kodak. Founded in 1889, Kodak was one of the best-known brands of the 20th century. However, with the rapid rise in demand for digital cameras, the market for camera films (dominated by Kodak) died a pretty quick death. At the turn of the millennium, Kodak had clearly ignored the change of times, having expanded its global workforce and increased production of the old technology (camera film). By 2006, Kodak was selling an obsolete product. In 2013, the company filed for bankruptcy protection.

Culture

"A people without the knowledge of their past history, origin and culture is like a tree without roots." - Marcus Garvey (1887–1940) Jamaican political leader and entrepreneur

Culture is about the norms of an organization, a country or other social grouping. Culture shapes the values, beliefs and customs of people (see Unit 2.5). HSBC's global slogan "The World's Local Bank" highlights the importance of cultural awareness when doing business in overseas markets. As the popular proverb goes, *"When in Rome, do as the Romans do"*, i.e. it is advisable for businesses to follow the cultural conventions of the local area in which they operate.

CORE

Supplementary information

Figure 6.1.d Culture: *When in Rome, do as the Romans do*

Take a look at some of their adverts available on YouTube to gain a better understanding of the importance of local knowledge for multinational companies:

- Cultural differences in dining between English and Chinese etiquette: http://goo.gl/eOatfd

- Cultural differences when travelling on the train: http://goo.gl/mjXTtl

- A series of seven HSBC advertisements are available here on YouTube: http://goo.gl/lw7k2x

This short clip from *National Geographic* follows several Sudanese men who travel to the USA and discover some interesting cultural differences: http://goo.gl/umPbt. What lessons can managers learn from the awareness of cultural differences and the role of culture in consumer behaviour?

Other culture-related questions relevant to Business Management include:

- What are the cultural norms in your country regarding work–life balance?

- Do you know about the business etiquette in your country? What about in other countries? See Box 4.7.c for some examples.

- What does 'human rights' mean in your country? How is this translated in the workplace?

- How are equal opportunities interpreted in your country? To what extent do gender inqualities exist in your culture? What does 'inequality' mean? To whom?

- Should all schools abandon their homework policies to allow students (and parents) to take more ownership of their own learning? Wouldn't this better promote the traits of the IB Learner Profile?

Culture has a direct impact on our learning. Take the following theorists as example. Do you know what they all have in common?

- H. Gantt – Gantt charts (Unit 1.7)

- F. Herzberg – Motivation theory (Unit 2.4)

- D. H. Pink – Motivation theory (Unit 2.4)

- Maslow – Motivation theory (Unit 2.4)

- F.W. Taylor – Motivation theory (Unit 2.4)

- J.S. Adams – Motivation theory (Unit 2.4)

- John Paul Kotter – Resistance to change (Unit 2.6)

- Philip Kotler – Social marketing (Unit 4.1)

- Jack Trout – Perception mapping (Unit 4.2)

- E.J. McCarthy – The 4Ps of marketing / the marketing mix (Unit 4.5)

- J.C. Levinson – Guerrilla marketing (Unit 4.5)

- B.H. Booms & M.J. Bitner – The extended marketing mix / the 7Ps (Unit 4.6).

Apart from they all feature in the BM syllabus(!), the theorists are all from the USA. How does cultural bias affect our knowledge and understanding of BM? Does this matter?

Language is an integral part of culture. Even in countries that share a common language (such as Australia, USA and UK), cultural differences are embedded in language (see Table 6.1.b).

CORE

Table 6.1.b   English language and cultural differences

Dummy	Pacifier
Boot	Trunk
Service station	Gas station
Footpath	Sidewalk
Jumper	Sweater
Jam	Jelly
Bill	Check
Lift	Elevator
Sauce	Ketchup
Soft drink	Soda
Biscuit	Cookie
Sweets	Candy
Nappies	Diapers

Anorak	Parka
English person	Pom
Sausages	Snag
Underpants	Jocks
Trainers	Runners
It's fine	She's apples
Excellent	Ace
Chocolate	Chokkie
Flip flops	Thongs

IB Learner Profile – Be balanced and open-minded

Investigate the importance of business etiquette for international marketers for two countries of your choice.

Exam tip !

If the CUEGIS essay asks you to discuss "organizational culture" (such as the impact of change or ethics on organizational culture), make sure you do not discuss *national* culture.

If the question does not refer to organization culture, then you can choose to discuss organizational culture, national cultures, or both.

Ethics

"You cannot make yourself feel something you do not feel, but you can make yourself do right in spite of your feelings." - Pearl S. Buck (1892–1973), US writer and novelist

Ethics are the socially accepted moral principles that guide decision-making, based on the collective belief of what is right and what is wrong. The rather subjective nature of ethics means it is not always clear what is 'right' or 'wrong', especially when looking at different cases from around the world. Consider the examples below and discuss the extent to which you think each case is ethical?

- In 2013, Gareth Bale (aged 24) became the world's most expensive football player having switched from London's Tottenham Hotspur to Spain's Real Madrid, who paid a world record 100 million euros ($137.7 million) for his services until 2019. Bale's weekly wages were reported to be around $413,000, i.e. $59,000 a day or more than $40 every minute, even when asleep! The UK prime minister's daily salary is around $622.

- In 2014, the United Arab Emirates introduced a law for all new mothers to breastfeed their babies for at least two years (if they are physically able to), banning all forms of baby milk powder. The law also allows the husband to sue his wife if she refuses to breastfeed their baby.

- In 2014, a six-year-old schoolboy in the UK made headline news when he was suspended from school for four days – he had brought a cheese snack into school as part of his lunch. The 'Mini Cheddars' were deemed to contravene the school's healthy eating policy.

- *The Education Post* reported that Hong Kong parents send their babies to private tutors at the age of just 15 months.

CORE

Supplementary information

Are Hong Kong people forcing their children to learn too much too fast? Isn't free play more important?

- In 2017, Serena Williams was the only female featured in Forbes' list of the 100 highest paid sports stars. In 2018, for the first time ever, no females made the list, despite global pressures and support to close the gender pay gap.

- In 2018, *The Wall Street Journal* reported that Walmart's CEO was paid a staggering 1,188 times more than the median salary of employee at the American retailer. Can such huge wage differentials be truly justifiable?

- A 2018 journal report in *Medical Education* found that lecturers who gave out biscuits (cookies) in their lessons got higher ratings from their undergraduates medical students.

- It was not until 2018 that women in Saudi Arabia were permitted to attend football (soccer) matches. In the same year, Saudi women were allowed to drive for the first time in the country's history.

Consider these questions based on business ethics. What are your opinions about each of these?

- Is it acceptable for workers to browse the Internet and make personal telephone calls whilst at work?

- Is it possible to ensure equity and equality in the workplace?

- Should the business of beauty pageants (such as Miss World or Mr. Universe) be banned?

- Is it right for a business to fabricate its financial accounts if this prevents job losses?

- Should a business monitor the online activities, including email communications, of employees?

- Can taking the credit for the work of others ever be morally acceptable?

- Can acting unethically ever be 'good' for a business?

- Does acting ethically hinder innovation?

Figure 6.1.e Should businesses use renewable energy, even if it is more costly to do so?

IB Learner Profile – Be balanced and open-minded

Which multinational companies do you think are the most ethical? Have a look at the Ethisphere website, which compiles an annual league table of the world's most ethical businesses: http://www.worldsmostethicalcompanies.com/honorees/. Investigate the criteria used by Ethisphere to compile this list.

Ethics and Theory of knowledge

If ethics are based on a set of beliefs of what is morally right or wrong, can we ever really 'know' what is right or wrong?

Case studies

- Baby milk powder scandal (2008) – Chinese producers of baby milk powder were found guilty of adulterating its products with melamine (a chemical used for paints, plastics and paper). The scandal resulted in the death of six babies and the hospitalisation of 54,000 infants, and resulted in three verdicts of life imprisonments and two cases of execution under Chinese prosecution laws.

- Pfizer (2009) – The US pharmaceutical multinational company was fined an industry-record $2.3 billion for the illegal marketing of the arthritis drug Bextra. Its use had not been approved by the US Food and Drug Administration (FDA).

- Foxconn (2010) – Fourteen people committed suicide at the production plant that made the iPhone, due to poor working conditions including reports of worker abuse and illegal overtime.

- Kaupthing (2013) – Four executives from the largest of the Icelandic banks that went bankrupt in 2008 were found guilty of financial fraud and sentenced to between 3 to 5 years imprisonment.

- Lloyds Bank (2013) – The British bank was fined £28 million ($45.7m) by the Financial Conduct Authority for the unethical selling of products to customers in relation to bonus schemes for staff.

- Horsemeat scandal (2013) – The discovery of horsemeat in processed beef products resulted in large scale product recalls throughout Europe, including UK, Ireland, France, Norway, Austria, Sweden and Germany.

- Baby milk powder price-fixing (2013) – Six Chinese producers of milk powder were fined a record $109 million for price fixing.

- Walmart (2017) - The CEO of Walmart, Doug McMillion, earned $22.8 million, causing outrage with labour unions and workers, as his annual salary was 1,188 times larger than the median employee's pay of $19,177

Note: this textbook is not available in PDF format – so if you are using a soft-copy, not only is this unethical, it is also a breach of international copyrights.

Theory of knowledge

How can we know if there is anything unethical about charitable organizations?

Globalization

"To be yourself in a world that is constantly trying to make you something else is the greatest accomplishment." - Ralph Waldo Emerson (1803–1882), American poet

Some indicators of globalization are outlined in Box 4.7.d. Globalization provides both opportunities and threats for businesses:

- Globalization considerably increases the level of competition, such as Vodafone (UK) competing with mobile operator '3', owned by Hutchison Telecom (Hong Kong). The Internet has also reduced costs for many industries, thereby reducing barriers to entry and attracting global competition.

- Meeting customer expectations and needs becomes increasingly more demanding. Businesses must now meet the ever-greater customer demands for quality, service, price and after-sales care in order to have any competitive advantage.

- Businesses that are able to build a global presence can benefit from economies of scale, such as the advantages of global marketing economies and risk-bearing economies (see Unit 1.6). Self-made billionaire Li Ka-Shing, Asia's second richest man when he retired in 2018, had a reported wealth of over $35.3 billion, mainly accumulated through the sheer diversity of his businesses in the property, food, telecommunications, consumer electronics, utilities and ports industries

- Multinational companies have greater choice of location of their production facilities. Like many other global businesses, Apple has chosen to outsource production to China due to the relatively low costs of labour and rent. Apple products are '*Designed in California, Assembled in China.*' The choice of location can therefore help to reduce the firm's costs of production.

CORE

Supplementary information

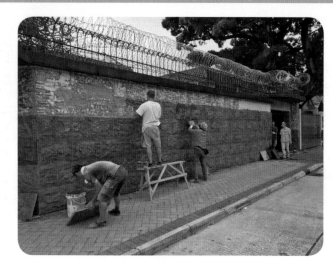

Figure 6.1.f Is it ethical to deliberately hire cheap labour?

- Mergers, acquisitions and joint ventures allow businesses to grow at a faster pace than if they were to expand organically (see Unit 1.6). With globalization, businesses have more opportunities in their expansion plans. For example, BMW's joint venture with Brilliance China Automotive in 2003 gave the German carmaker direct access to the lucrative Chinese market.

- Multinational companies and e-commerce businesses in particular benefit from the increased customer base that globalization brings. With China and India both embracing changes in the global business environment, there are vast opportunities for businesses that trade with the world's two most populated countries (around 35% of the world's population).

Theory of knowledge

How can you know whether globalization brings net benefits or drawbacks, given the multitude of stakeholders that are affected?

Case study

Businesses that want to embrace the opportunities of globalization have to adapt to different market needs, including cultural considerations. This might even include a change of name for the organization, in order to have greater brand appeal. For example, Japan's Nintendo was created in 1889 as Marafuku Company. Panasonic was originally Matsushita Electric Corporation. Tokyo Tsushin Kogyo was rebranded as Sony - and the rest is history.

Innovation

"If you hear a voice within you say, 'You cannot paint,' then by all means paint, and that voice will be silenced."
- Vincent van Gogh (1853–1890), Dutch post-Impressionist painter

Innovations in the corporate world can empower businesses. Many of the most economically successful businesses and countries are the ones that innovate. Innovative entrepreneurs are those who come up with and commercialise a new idea or reinvent (redefine) an old idea. In some cases, they even create new industries, such as smartphones and tablet computers. In today's highly unpredictable business world, innovations can give organizations a competitive edge. Hence, most large multinational companies are financially committed to innovation.

Innovation applies to all aspects of business activities, not just products. Innovation is integral to kaizen (continuous improvements). Innovative entrepreneurs create new sources of revenue based on changing technology and other changes in the market, e.g. changing demographics and changing customer demands (needs and wants). Management guru Michael Porter said that innovation is the central issue for the prospects of a business and for the economic prosperity of a country. Hence, innovation forces managers to think creatively and more holistically about their entire business.

Theory of knowledge

Are all innovations disruptive to corporate culture? Does this matter?

Exam tip !

If the CUEGIS essay asks about the impact of innovation (for example, on the culture or strategy of your chosen organization), make sure you refer to the type(s) of innovation in the syllabus: product, process, positioning, paradigm, adaptive creativity or innovative creativity.

CORE

Supplementary information

Case study

In 1973, Slade recorded *Merry Christmas Everybody*. Over 45 years on, the song remains top of the charts for royalty-earning Christmas songs, with the band receiving an impressive $1.28m each year!

IB Learner Profile – Be an Inquirer and Be Knowledgeable (1)

Place these innovations in chronological order, based on the year of their commercialisation:

- Escalator
- Vacuum cleaner
- Air conditioner
- Crayons
- Teabags
- Einstein's Theory of Relativity
- Cornflakes
- Helicopter

IB Learner Profile – Be an Inquirer and Be Knowledgeable (2)

Place these innovations in chronological order, based on the year of their commercialisation:

- Fortune cookies
- Lie detector
- Radar
- Colour television
- Bar codes
- Soft contact lenses
- Post-It notes
- Digital cell phones

Theory of knowledge

Does outstanding examination success in highly academic schools stifle curriculum innovation?

Theory of knowledge

Watch this short news clip about how e-waste (electronic waste such as old mobile phones and games consoles) is affecting people in parts of China: http://goo.gl/4m0sMx. Whilst e-waste management is a thriving business opportunity, what are the true social costs of innovation? Does innovation ultimately have unethical consequences for society?

Strategy

"If you don't drive your business you will be driven out of business." - B.C. Forbes (1880–1954), Founder of *Forbes* magazine

Strategy is about devising plans to achieve the long-term goals of an organization, i.e. to get to where it wants to be. There are three stages to the strategy process:

1. Strategic analysis
2. Strategic choice
3. Strategic implementation

Stage 1: Strategic analysis – determining the current position of an organization (where are we now?)

The German proverb, '*What's the use of running if you are not on the right road?*' is fitting. Most organizations strive to anticipate the future needs of their stakeholders in order to be successful. Strategic analysis is a thorough review of an organization's current situation. It is concerned with examining an organization's vision, mission, aims and objectives.

Strategic analysis is vital for the prosperity of a business because managers can become too focused on current needs so fail to see the future direction of the organization. It can help to provide a clear framework to aid decision-making. This can therefore help to allocate resources more effectively. It can also help to

CORE

involve, inform and motivate all those involved and affected by the process.

Stage 2: Strategic choice – determining the desired future of the organization (where do we want to be?)

Ancient Chinese philosopher Lao Tzu said that "*A journey of a thousand miles must begin with a single step.*" Strategic choice is concerned with generating strategic options for the organization so it can move on. It requires an assessment of the financial costs and benefits of the available choices and consideration of qualitative factors (the 'PORSCHE©' factors) before selecting the most appropriate strategy:

- **P**redictions (intuition) – strategic choice is often based on the gut feelings of managers and their forecasts of changes in the future.

- **O**bjectives – a profit seeking firm will tend to prefer using quantitative methods in deciding on its business strategy whereas charities may take a different approach.

- **R**isk profile – firms with a low risk profile are less likely to choose strategies that incur high-risk, high-return investments, opting for lower risk projects with more certain returns.

- **S**tate of the economy – in a booming economy, firms are more likely to choose higher-risk strategies.

- **C**orporate image – managers must consider how a particular strategic choice might affect its public relations and corporate image.

- **H**uman relations – managers also need to consider the impact of a particular strategic choice on staff morale and whether there will be training needs (and costs).

- **E**xternal shocks – unquantifiable risks may have to be considered when making strategic choices.

Stage 3: Strategic implementation – determining the path to get the organization to where it wants to be (how do we get there?)

Strategic implementation is about putting the selected plan (strategic choice) into practice and developing the strategy. Implementing strategy usually involves change and change management. Effective leadership is at the heart of successful change management and strategic implementation. Tools, concepts and theories that can aid strategic implementation

include: brand development, external growth strategies (such as joint ventures, strategic alliances and franchising), flexible working practices, outsourcing and subcontracting, quality management, repositioning and workforce planning.

Exam tip !

For HL students, be aware that Section C of the Paper 1 exam will often require candidates to discuss the merits and drawbacks of various strategic options for the organization in the case study. Students are also usually asked to evaluate the strategic implementation and/or the change in the strategic direction of the organization.

Theory of knowledge

To some extent, science offers certainty when organizations face continual change, diversity and evolution. Based on the various management tools, concepts and theories you have studied during the BM course, justify whether you think that management is more of an art or a science?

Limitations of strategy include:

- Strategic plans are devised by senior managers who are not necessarily directly affected by the plans in the same way as the workforce.

- The future is unknown; long-term trends are difficult, if not impossible, to predict.

- There is a large cost in creating detailed strategic plans, both in terms of management time and in resources.

- Strategic plans are often inflexible and are not adaptive to sudden changes in the marketplace.

- Rigid strategic plans limit an organization's ability to be innovative.

As Sir Winston Churchill (1874–1965) said, "*However beautiful the strategy, you should occasionally look at the results*".

CORE

Supplementary information

Theory of knowledge

To what extent does the Persian proverb, *"Doubt is the key to knowledge"* apply to business strategy?

Exam tip !

When faced with an exam question about business strategy (such as 'Discuss the strategic options for …'), remember to write your answers using the three-stage strategy framework:

1. Strategic analysis – where are we now?
2. Strategic choice – where do we want to be?
3. Strategic implementation – how do we get there?

Also make sure you can use the appropriate tools for the different stages, e.g. SWOT analysis for strategic analysis, investment appraisal when examining strategic choice and growth strategies for strategic implementation.

Figure 6.1.g Strategy is complex but essential for all businesses

The challenge facing entrepreneurs and managers in the modern business environment is much greater than it has been in the past. With trends such as e-commerce, flexible working practices and intense competition from emerging markets, entrepreneurs and managers have less control than ever. Strategies that worked in the past may not necessarily work today and new problems may demand new strategies and solutions.

Further resources to help teachers

IB teachers can access further information about concept-based teaching and learning via the Online Curriculum Centre, or via this weblink for Dr. H. Lynn Erickson's IB position paper: http://goo.gl/YEQvop.

- This is also another useful resource on CBL, from Moving Beyond the Page: http://goo.gl/dPjCfT

- Conceptual Learning for a Thinking Classroom: http://goo.gl/31mknG

- 50 Excellent CUEGIS Essays: www.level7education.com

- CUEGIS posters pack: www.level7education.com

Final thoughts on CBL and Business Management

"If we teach today's students as we taught yesterday's, we rob them of tomorrow." - John Dewey (1859–1952), renowned educational reformer

Many teachers will have been using a concept based learning (CBL) approach *before* the launch of the current Business Management course (first exams 2016). Whilst CBL might seem 'new' to some teachers, it is nothing to fear. The CUEGIS concepts provide a useful framework of six conceptual lenses that students (and teachers) can use to provide a more holistic and meaningful way to understand and gain knowledge in Business Management. Students who embrace such an approach in their studies will naturally recognise the links between CBL and TOK (both are interdisciplinary and intradisciplinary, promoting higher-order critical thinking skills). For instance, consider how business activity impacts on climate change and damage to the natural environment. It should be possible to make such considerations through the CUEGIS lenses (or framework):

- Change – What changes are instigated by the organization in response to protection of the environment? Is this part of the firm's corporate social responsibilities (CSR)? What changes are imposed on the business?

- Culture – What is the corporate culture towards the protection of the environment? Is CSR part of the

CORE

Supplementary information

organizational culture? What evidence of this is there? What are the values of society towards climate change and protection of the environment?

- Ethics – Is it ethical to put profits before people and the planet? Are unsustainable business operations ethical? It is ethical to charge customers higher prices due to ethical business practices that are more costly to implement?

- Globalization – What are the impacts on the organization due to increased consumption around the world? How can the organization make the most of the opportunities created by globalization without imposing further damage to the environment?

- Innovation – What innovations should the organization consider to reduce its carbon footprint and the impact of its business activities on climate change?

- Strategy – What sustainable strategies should the organization implement to ensure it does its part for the environment, and to remain relevant and competitive?

Figure 6.1.h The CUEGIS concepts can be applied to the impacts of business activity on climate change

Embracing CBL and the CUEGIS concepts in Business Management can certainly empower students in their Internal Assessment, the Extended Essay, their final IB examinations and, perhaps far more importantly, beyond.

For teachers, CBL is far from revolutionary but certainly requires teacher input. Consider the following questions that you might be asked during a job interview, a performance management meeting or after a lesson observation:

- What makes a lesson 'successful'?

- How do you engage your students in their learning?

- What makes teaching (and/or learning) meaningful?

- How do you know your students are learning?

Quite simply and frankly, doesn't CBL help to address the above questions to a rather large extent?

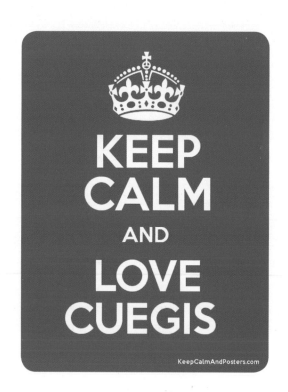

Theory of knowledge

Do you think the CUEGIS concepts provide the foundations for education or indoctrination in the study of Business Management?

6.2 Internal assessment

"The secret of getting ahead is getting started." - Mark Twain (1835–1910), US author

Top tips for the Internal Assessment [HL]

The Internal Assessment (IA) is a compulsory component of the Business Management course. HL students need to choose an organization with a real business decision or issue. Recommendations must be made to the organization to help address the title question being investigated. This should be done through research and application of BM tools, theories and concepts. Before formulating a title question, students should contact the organization to see if it can help to provide the necessary support and information, e.g. interviews, staff surveys or access to financial documentation.

The IA is internally marked by your teacher, but externally moderated by an examiner. The IB recommends 30 hours are spent in total on producing the IA (see page 72 of the subject guide). The IA has a 25% weighting of the overall assessment.

The title question

- Ensure the title question is forward-looking and addresses a real business problem or issue.

- Keep the title question simple and specific. It should have a clear focus, i.e. relate to a specific component of the BM syllabus. Questions about the 'marketing mix' make poor titles (there are 7 Ps in the marketing mix).

- The best IA titles tend to have the word 'should' in them, e.g. Should Matthew MacMillan Inc. invest in the construction of a new multipurpose sports complex?

- Check the suitability of the title question with your teacher(s).

- Before starting the IA, ensure that the information you need is available to you, including access to relevant primary research.

The Research Proposal (RP) and Action Plan (AP): 500 words

- Like much of the real business world, ultimately the key to a successful IA is careful planning.

- Outline *why* you are interested in researching the chosen organization.

- Focus on the collection and application of **primary research** and data. Secondary research can be used if this supports the investigation.

- State the sample size and sampling method to be used, with a brief outline of the reasons.

- For the theoretical framework, identify the appropriate theory to be used to investigate the decision or issue. Cover the relevant areas of the syllabus but remember that BM is a holistic subject.

- Consider anticipated difficulties (problems) in conducting the research and the possible solutions.

- Use a table to construct the Action Plan or a Gantt chart as this helps to make the most of the 500-word limit. Moderators do not read beyond the word limit.

- Be aware of the required format for the RP and AP, which consists of four parts:

  - the research question

  - proposed methodology (rationale for study, areas of the syllabus to be covered (theoretical framework), possible sources of information, organizations and

623

individuals to be contacted, research methodology and rationale, and the sequence of activities/timescale of the IA)

– anticipated difficulties

– action plan.

- The RP and AP should be written in future tense as these form the main planning document.

- It should be reviewed regularly and modified / updated as and when necessary.

The Executive Summary (ES): 200 words

- The ES (an abstract) has a maximum word count of 200 words.

- It should be a succinct summary of the IA and outline the answer to the title question.

- The ES should be written in past tense.

The Written Report: 2,000 words

- Refer back to the RP and AP to guide writing of the Written Report.

- Do not use footnotes for definitions – only use footnotes for referencing.

- Use a standardised and recognised referencing system such as the MLA style (www.mla.org).

- Referencing is not included in the 2,000 word count.

- Do not include a full SWOT analysis or STEEPLE analysis – these will account for a significant number of words. If these tools are to be used, place them in the appendix and reference accordingly within the Written Report. Highlight relevant parts of the SWOT or STEEPLE analysis to show which sections you have used.

- If using an interview for primary research, place the transcript in the appendices and highlight the relevant parts to show use of the information.

- Recommendations must be realistic and applicable to the organization in question.

- Ensure you have a well-argued conclusion that stems from the evidence presented in the Written Report. The conclusion must answer the title question. Acknowledge any limitations and unanswered questions in the Written Report.

- Treat the IA as a professional document; you should be able to send a copy to the organization once the Written Report is completed.

HL IA – the required format

- Title page

- Acknowledgements

- Contents page (with page numbering)

- Executive summary

- Introduction (background)

- Research question

- Methodology used (primary research and, only where relevant, secondary research)

- Main results and findings

- Analysis and discussion

- Conclusion(s) and recommendation(s)

- References and bibliography

- Appendices (supporting data and information).

See pages 81–82 of the subject guide for further details.

HL IA titles (some suitable titles)

1. Should Restaurant X diversify its menu in order to gain higher market share?

2. How should Muller Bookstores differentiate itself from other bookstores in Dusseldorf?

3. How should *The Studio* adjust its promotional strategy to attract a wider target market in Clifton, Bristol?

4. What pricing strategy should *Oasis Airlines* implement to gain market share of the Hong Kong to Vancouver route?

5. Should Hayes Reprographics buy two new photocopiers or opt to lease these machines?

6. What methods of non-financial motivation should Pointwell Ltd. implement to retain staff?

7. How financially viable would investing in reefer trucks be for Integrated Shun Hing (Shenzhen) Co. Ltd.?

8. How should Big Bao improve its cash flow position?

9. Should Ted's Bakers purchase a new delivery truck to cater for customers on Lantau Island?

10. Should JT Taxi Company purchase a new urban taxi licence for HK$3.6 million?

Figure 6.2.a Investment appraisal questions, such as Q10 above, tend to work well

Unsuitable titles …

- How should McDonald's improve its profitability? – This is too broad and rather ambitious; if you could answer this question, you'd be running McDonald's!

- An investigation into the causes of demotivation at Awasthi Motors – This is not phrased as a question (so does not require recommendations to be made) and the report is likely to be highly descriptive.

- How can Laurie & Johnston Co. increase profit by changing its marketing mix? – Avoid titles with 'marketing mix' as the 7Ps cannot be examined in sufficient depth given the 2,000 word limit.

- To what extent did the merger of Murtagh and Sharma increase productivity? – This is not a forward-looking title.

- An investigation into the profitability of 7-Eleven's franchise model in Japan. – This is not phrased as a question, nor does it demand any judgements to be made.

- How can Starbuck's entry into India increase its success? – This title falls short in many areas. "How can" tends to lead to descriptive answers; India is probably too broad; and success is too vague (perhaps market share, profits, or sales revenue could be used instead).

Finally, as the IA is externally moderated, ensure you have a copy of the Assessment Criteria from your teacher (see subject guide, pages 82–86). This set of criteria is used to mark your IA so you should familiarise yourself with how the marks are awarded.

Top tips for the Internal Assessment [SL]

The SL IA is a compulsory component of the course and accounts for 25% of the overall assessment. Students complete a 1,500-word **written commentary**. The title of the IA is phrased as a **question**. The question must be based on a real and contemporary problem or issue of a single business organization and must be related to the BM <u>SL</u> syllabus.

The IA is internally marked by your teacher, but externally moderated by an examiner. The IB recommends 15 hours are spent in total on producing the IA, which has a 25% weighting

CORE

Supplementary information

of the overall assessment. Other important points about the SL IA include:

- The written commentary requires analysis and evaluation of the issue or problem, i.e. the student must form judgements.

- It is based on **secondary** sources for the supporting documents. These must be suitable (relevant to the title question) and provide sufficient breadth and depth. Primary research can be used as support *if* relevant.

- Three to five supporting documents must be included. The supporting documents must be contemporary, i.e. within a maximum of 3 years prior to submission of the written commentary to the IB. They form the majority of the information for producing the commentary.

- One of the documents can be a transcript of a video/audio source, such as a television documentary or radio broadcast. This needs to be authentic so that it can be traced (checked).

- Students must provide a declaration of authenticity (on the coversheet of the IA) to confirm that the work is his or her own original work.

- All supporting documents and any additional sources must be included in a bibliography. The referencing system must enable the moderator to locate the original sources easily.

- Supporting documents, placed in the appendices, must be highlighted to show which parts of each document are used to relate directly to the written commentary. These documents should be clearly labelled, e.g. 'Supporting document 1'.

- If students do not reference their work, issues about the authenticity of the work may be raised. In-text citation/referencing of the supporting documents can be used, although the documents must be included in the bibliography.

- The word limit is 1,500 words – moderators will not read beyond the 1,500th word of the written commentary.

Examples of supporting documents (which should provide a range of views and ideas) include:

- Academic journals / publications

- Business plans

- Company annual reports (final accounts)

- Company website

- Government statistics

- Market research surveys

- Mission statements

- Newspaper articles

- Web-based report.

Textbooks and class notes can be used as additional sources for the SL IA, but do not count as supporting documents. However, if used, these must be referenced and recorded in a bibliography.

Business theories, concepts and tools that could be used in the SL IA include:

- Ansoff's matrix

- Boston matrix

- Economies of scale

- Investment appraisal

- Marketing strategies

- Motivation theory

- Outsourcing

- Position (Perception) mapping

- Product portfolio analysis

- Ratio analysis.

Note: a SWOT/STEEPLE analysis produced by the candidate does not qualify as a supporting document.

Recommended format for the SL IA

- Title page, including the research question

- Contents page

- Introduction (including the methodology)

- Findings (based on the supporting documents)

- Analysis and discussion of the findings

- Conclusion(s)

- Bibliography and references (including page numbers)

- Appendices: the 3–5 supporting documents.

SL IA titles (a sample)

1. Is including a product line for male customers a profitable decision for Dan & Glover?

2. Is an increase in wages an effective way to increase productivity at Happy Valley Inc.?

3. Is Charnley Motor's decision to increase productive capacity by building a new plant a sound financial decision?

4. Can EscobarSolar Corp.'s strategy work to rescue the company's operations in Taiwan?

5. Can the HKJC's current social marketing strategy address the issue of recent declines in revenue?

6. Will PCCW's current promotional strategy be able to overcome the problem of slow market growth in the fixed-line telecoms industry?

7. Should Nathani Tuition College outsource its services to Guangzhou College of Learning?

8. Should Juke Printers buy Cottam Stationers?

9. To what extent will the merger of Continental and United Airlines be a success?

10. Will the introduction of pay per view for Times online be profitable?

11. What impact will the recall of Toyota cars have on the brand in New Zealand?

12. How can British Airways resolve the industrial dispute with its cabin crew?

13. How effective is the zero pricing strategy for 'The Standard' (newspaper)?

14. How effective is Greenpeace's promotional strategy in Hong Kong?

15. How effective is The Body Shop's promotional campaign in raising public awareness of 'safe sex' in Thailand?

To what extent is *South Lakes Solar Inc.'s* decision to increase output in Virginia, USA, a sensible one?

Figure 6.2.b Why is this a good IA title?

Top tips from students [HL and SL]

Finally, these are some top tips from some of my own students:

- Do an IA on something you are confident that you can get information from, e.g. family or friend's business; use a local business instead of an overseas one.   *Joshua Chan*

- Try to use quantitative analysis and tools because these help to give clearer conclusions.   *Keillian Tai*

- If you use interviews or questionnaires make sure your teacher checks over them because if your questions aren't that good, you won't get meaningful data.   *Chris Ting*

- Do your very best on the first draft (complete it) so that the written feedback will really help you to get top marks in the final draft.   *Aska Mertens*

CORE

Supplementary information

- Plan the IA well; not only will this allow you to enjoy this unique experience learning about a real business but it will also save a lot of frustration and stress as the deadline approaches. *JK Park*

- Refer to your title frequently to ensure that you won't stray off topic. *Beverly Nam*

- Remember to save and cite (or footnote) your sources in the bibliography as you work through your IA, or else you will forget where these are from and it is very time consuming to find it all later. *Jacklyn Kwok*

- After writing your draft, check against the marking criteria that you have written only what is necessary, and get rid of anything else – it will only take up your word count! *Shelly Yuen.*

- Only the information you put in the main body of the IA counts towards the overall assessment, so don't put any analysis in the appendices as moderators won't read or credit this. *Nicollette Scrouther*

- Avoid vague or broad IA titles, as this causes a lack of focus, which negatively impacts on your final grade. *Lucas Rothwell*

- For HL students choose a relatively small organization, as it tends to be easier to collect the primary research data, and recommendations are more likely to be realistic and practical for the business. *Regina Wang*

- Make sure your research question is forward-looking and sufficiently focused in order to avoid wide generalisations being made. *Danielle Leung*

- HL students need to aake sure they actually explain their choice of research methods (don't just say you're using random sampling, for example) and the reasons for approaching certain individuals or groups (as part of your primary research). *Letizia Wan*

- For HL students, use a Gantt chart for your action plan, as it is easier to identify the progress made, and also easier to remain within the 500-word limit. *Sean Mitchell*

- It's really hard to do a proper PEST or SWOT analysis within the word, especially for SL students, so it's best to avoid these. Evidence and referencing are required, so that's really difficult given the word limit. *Sayeeda Urbana*

- When you write your conclusion(s), you must address the research question – it is so easy to lose focus and address another question instead. *Maleah Do Cao*

- Ask your teacher for an IA checklist to ensure you meet the assessment criteria – the IB produces these for the IA. *Ashley Lau*

- For SL students, make sure each of the supporting documents chosen are clearly relevant to addressing the research question. *Jakey Solomon*

For both HL and SL students, remember to provide **evidence** to substantiate your points. HL students must use primary market research for their Internal Assessment, whereas SL students need to use secondary sources. Irrespective, it is vital collect and present meaningful evidence. Watch this short but very funny video clip, featuring comedian Joe Lycett's parking ticket story to see why providing evidence is so important: https://goo.gl/M45cYG.

My final tip is to conscientiously make the time to work on your IA. This component of the Business Management course is worth 25% of the final exam (that's the equivalent of two grade boundaries), so by putting in the effort you are essentially working on your final examination score. As German writer Johann Wolfgang von Goethe (1749–1832) said, *"What is not started today is never finished tomorrow".*

Good luck with the IA!

6.3 Theory of knowledge

"Knowledge is justified true belief." - Plato, Ancient Greek philosopher

The aim of Theory of knowledge

Theory of knowledge (TOK) examines what it means to know something. The TOK course aims to promote critical thinking skills by exploring knowledge itself. TOK is at the heart of the IB Diploma Programme with every subject having something to contribute to acquiring, reinforcing and developing knowledge issues. TOK skills can help students develop their ability to think analytically and critically.

What is TOK about?

"To know that we know what we know, and that we do not know what we do not know, that is true knowledge." - Confucius, (551–479 BC), Chinese philosopher

TOK examines the ways of acquiring and transmitting knowledge, such as the use of language, sense perception, emotion and reasoning. The four key questions in TOK are:

- What is knowledge?

- How is knowledge acquired?

- What do we know?

- How do we know what we know?

There are over 155 TOK questions throughout the textbook, plus an extra 45 TOK questions in this chapter, to get students thinking about the above questions about knowledge.

Figure 6.3.a TOK is thinking about and questioning knowledge

How do you know what you know?

"The power to question is the basis of all human progress." - Indira Gandhi (1917–1984), 3rd prime minister of India

A baffling question for those new to TOK is 'How do you know what you know?' Essentially, this question is about the Ways of Knowing (WOK), such as:

- I worked it out (reasoning).

- I saw it (sense perception).

- Someone told me (language).

- I can feel it (emotion).

- I remember/recall it (memory).

- I believe it to be true (faith).

- It is obvious (intuition).

- I visualize it to be so (imagination).

Figure 6.3.b illustrates the balance between Ways of Knowing in the Theory of Knowing.

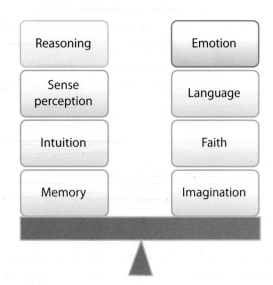

Figure 6.3.b The ways of knowing (WOK)

Examples of how the WOK apply to the study of Business Management include:

- The role of **reasoning** – investment appraisal, break-even analysis, ratio analysis, budgeting and Gantt charts.

- The role of **emotions** – consider the roles of intuition and empathy in marketing; greed in motivation and organizational growth; or pride, anxiety, jealousy, anger, conflict and fear in Human Resource Planning and Management.

- The role of **sense perception** – advertising, promotional offers, branding, stakeholder priorities, pricing strategies, product development, change management, crisis management and conflict resolution.

- The role of **language** – communication, advertising, promotion, appraisal, recruitment and selection, branding strategy, international marketing, globalization and organizational structure all rely on the use of effective language.

- Many people rely on **memory** as a key way of knowing (see Box 6.3.a), e.g. students rely on memory for their examinations. Memory has direct effects on our emotions, sense perception, faith and intuition.

- **Imagination** can be vital for innovation. Successful entrepreneurs such as Steve Jobs and Walt Disney relied on their skills of imagination to lead their companies, not on their academic knowledge acquired at school or university.

IB Learner Profile and Theory of knowledge activity

Using the Internet, find a suitable image for the front cover of a new IB textbook in each of the following subjects:
- Chinese
- History
- Maths
- Chemistry
- Psychology
- Business Management

(a) What role did the Ways of Knowing have in your decision?

(b) Which of the ten IB Learner Profiles did you use to complete this task?

Box 6.3.a   Memory as a WOK in Business Management

Memory is a way of knowing. Test your 'knowledge' of famous business names from the quick quiz below by identifying the correct spelling. You can then use the Internet to check your answers:

1	McDonald's	McDonalds	Mcdonalds
2	*I'm loving it*	*I'm lovin' it*	*I'm luving it*
3	7-Eleven	7 ELEVEN	7-ELEVEn
4	Marks & Spencer	MARKS & SPENCER	Marks and Spencer
5	Coca Cola	Coca-Cola	Coca-cola
6	Appstore	Apps Store	App Store
7	eBay	e-Bay	Ebay
8	Facebook	facebook	Face book
9	Vodafone	vodafone	Vodaphone
10	Ikea	Ikia	IKEA
11	iPhone	iphone	Iphone
12	Ipad	iPad	I-Pad
13	Wal-Mart	Walmart	WalMart
14	Gillette	Gilette	Gillete
15	Krispy Cream	Krispy Kreme	Krispy Kream

TOK and Business Management

"The important thing is not to stop questioning. Curiosity has its own reason for existing" - Albert Einstein (1879–1955), *TIME* person of the century

Consider the following 45 questions about knowledge in the context of Business Management:

1. As theories (such as the motivation theories of Taylor, Maslow, Herzberg and Pink) are culturally biased, should they gain international acceptance?

2. Can theory, such as leadership and motivation, be truly free from cultural bias?

3. To what extent are theories and tools (such as break-even analysis and investment appraisal) applicable in the real corporate world?

4. Is *Wikipedia* an authoritative source for research in Business Management? What are the knowledge claims used to address this question?

5. Is the easy access to information via the Internet an impediment to critical thinking in Business Management?

6. How can the various ways of knowing help managers differentiate what is true from something that is believed to be true?

7. Does emotion or creativity have a larger role in marketing?

8. If Business Management relies heavily on quantitative decision-making, is there any role for faith, imagination or intuition as ways of knowing in the corporate world?

9. How important is the role of mathematics as an area of knowledge in Business Management?

10. Are quantitative knowledge claims or qualitative knowledge claims more important in the discipline of Business Management?

11. What role does 'rationality' have in Business Management?

12. Why do sales assistants in Hong Kong, who must be fluent in three languages (English, Cantonese and Mandarin), get paid significantly less than a Sales Director who speaks only English?

13. Why do women, on average, get paid less than men? How do we know that this matters?

14. Why do men retire later than women, on average, yet women live longer?

15. What roles do the various ways of knowing have in the acquisition of new knowledge in Business Management?

16. How do we test knowledge claims made in Business Management?

17. How do we judge what is fair and what is not fair in the corporate world?

18. What makes a good argument in Business Management?

19. What is considered to be a good explanation in Business Management?

20. Is 'business ethics' an oxymoron?

21. To what extent can businesses be truly altruistic?

22. How do we know if lying in the corporate world is immoral?

23. To what extent are ethics irrational in business management?

24. To what extent do emotions hinder judgement in business management?

25. Are emotions integral to decision-making in business management or do they simply cloud judgement?

26. Is the pursuit of knowledge in business management limited by ethical and religious factors?

27. To what extent should we place limitations on the language we use in the corporate world? (see Box 6.3.b and Box 6.3.c).

28. In the world of business, does language shape reality or does reality shape language?

29. Are there any universal rights or wrongs in the corporate world?

30. Are some truths in business management better left unsaid?

31. Do business analysts and management consultants share any similarities with the natural sciences in their pursuit of knowledge?

32. Chinese philosopher Lao Tzu claimed that "Those who have knowledge don't predict. *Those who predict don't have knowledge.*" Discuss these knowledge claims with reference to the study of Business Management.

33. American philosopher Ralph Waldo Emerson said that "*Knowledge is knowing that we cannot know.*" Is there any point with management decision-making tools such as perception mapping and decision trees or techniques such as market research.

34. Sceptics argue that it is impossible to be certain about anything. To what extent does this apply to the study of Business Management?

35. By what means do we come to know about the real world of business?

36. To what extent can experience in the business world justify what we know about Business Management as a subject?

37. Is a management theory created anew each time it is read (interpreted)?

38. Who creates and who owns the history of the corporate world?

39. Is it possible to determine which one of the Ways of Knowing is of most significance to the study of Business Management? If so, which one?

40. Do emotions hinder or encourage successful business decision-making?

Figure 6.3.c Emotions are a way of knowing

41. Is Business Management invented or discovered? Consider four ways of knowing in your answer.

42. What is the best way to test knowledge claims in Business Management?

43. Can a Business Management theory or model be considered as knowledge if it cannot be tested in reality?

44. Socrates said that "*The more you know, the more you realize you know nothing.*" To what extent does this apply to the study of Business Management?

Taking it one step further:

45. To what extent does the country you come from (or reside in) and its culture affect how you addressed the above TOK questions?

CORE

Supplementary information

Box 6.3.b Language, TOK and BM

Do these BM terms cause havoc in your classrooms?

- Job enlargement
- Natural wastage
- Penetrate (new markets)
- Penetration (pricing)
- Sleeping partners
- Waste management

Box 6.3.c Oxymora and BM language

- Assistant manager
- Budget deficit
- Certain risks
- Constant change
- Crisis management
- Demerit goods (such as alcohol, tobacco and gambling)
- Ethical business practices
- Expect the unexpected (contingency planning)
- Extended deadline
- Flexible budgets
- Free trade
- Friendly competition or friendly rivalry
- Homeworking
- Irregular trends
- Mass customization
- Negative growth (recession)
- Negative profit
- Paid volunteers
- Profit and loss account
- Real potential
- Retired worker
- Safety hazard
- Small fortune
- Unemployed workers
- Unknown risks
- Working holiday
- Working holiday (vacation)
- Working lunch

Box 6.3.d Business Management lingo

1. Al Desko (taking a lunch 'break' at the desk)
2. Bring to the table (contribution being made)
3. Cracking the whip (use of authority to make people work harder)
4. Dot the I's and cross the t's (to pay attention to something)
5. Heads up (giving advanced warning or notification)
6. Hit the ground running (being able to start work quickly)
7. Look under the bonnet (to analyse a situation or an issue)
8. No brainer (it's obvious)
9. On the radar (it's being considered)
10. Out of the loop (to not be involved in a decision)

What does it mean to 'look under the bonnet'?

Watch this TED Talk about how language shapes the way we think: https://goo.gl/JESJef.

The challenge for students …

"The proof that you know something is that you are able to teach it." - Aristotle, Greek philosopher (384 BC–322 BC)

"Man can learn nothing except by going from the known to the unknown." - Claude Bernard, French physiologist (1813–1878)

CORE

Supplementary information

And finally, one of my favourite TOK questions... Given that all students eventually work in business organizations, shouldn't Business Management be a compulsory subject in schools?

Finally, a great resource for teachers and students is IB Review magazine from Hodder Education. All subject-specific articles in the magazine have TOK links, and there are specific TOK articles too.

Download the free Teacher Edition here: goo.gl/NujxBV

CORE

Supplementary information

6.4 Extended Essay

"When something can be read without effort, great effort has gone into its writing." - Enrique Jardiel Poncela
(1901–1952), Spanish playwright and novelist

The Extended Essay (EE)

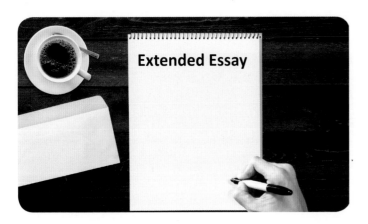

The Extended Essay (EE) provides students with the opportunity to complete an extensive piece of academically rigorous research. The EE is compulsory for all IB Diploma students, and should be based on an area of personal interest to the student. Students who fail to submit an EE are not awarded the IB Diploma. The guidelines (first exams 2018) suggest that students spend approximately 40 hours on the EE, writing up to 4,000 words. For the EE Supervisor, it is suggested that 3 to 5 hours are spent with each student, including time spent on three compulsory reflections sessions, ending with the *viva voce* (an oral interview following final submission of the EE). The essay is externally marked out of 34 points by an examiner.

Note: since May 2015, an 'E' grade in the Extended Essay or TOK constitutes a "failing condition" (see http://goo.gl/wPhX89).

Aims of the Extended Essay

The aims of the EE are to provide students with the opportunity to:

- engage in independent research with intellectual initiative and rigour

- develop research, thinking, self-management and communication skills

- reflect on what has been learned throughout the research and writing process.

© IBO, 2018

Responsibilities of the EE Supervisor

- Read and comment on the <u>first</u> and only draft (version) of the completed EE. Supervisors must not edit any of the draft EE.

- Monitor the progress of the supervisee to ensure that the EE is the student's own work.

- Offer guidance to the student in accordance to the guidelines specified in the EE Guide.

- Read the <u>final</u> draft (version) of the EE to confirm its authenticity.

- Complete the EE Supervisor's comments on the Reflections on Planning Progress Form (RPPF). Students must complete 3 written reflections of no more than 500 words in total on the RPPF sheet.

- Submit a predicted grade for the EE based on the Assessment Criteria.

- Conduct three reflection sessions with the candidate: one early on in the process, an interim meeting and then the final *viva voce*. Other sessions are allowed but do not need to be recorded on the RPPF sheet.

Exam tip !

The EE-RPPF has a word limit of 500 words. It is suggested that you write up to 150 words for each of the first two reflections. Write up to 200 words for the third and final reflection.

The Business Management Extended Essay

- The BM EE must be based on conventional (accepted) BM theory – students are therefore advised to stick to the topics within the current BM syllabus.*

- BM EEs can be backwards looking but must enable students to be evaluative in their work (not simply describing historical events).

- Students must avoid hypothetical questions, based on possible future events.

- The EE requires application of BM theory, tools and techniques.

- The essay should be written in a coherent and structured way.

- The EE should include breadth and depth of analysis and embrace extensive and detailed research.

- The emphasis of BM EEs from 2018 is on the use of **secondary data**. Students can use primary research if this helps to address the research question.

- A wide range of sources should be used including: BM textbooks, general business management texts, industry analyses and company annual reports. After all, undue dependence on one particular source is likely to mean the student writes an unbalanced essay that lacks critical thinking.

- Adding conceptual perspectives (the CUEGIS concepts) can add interest and depth to the EE, e.g. the ethical and cultural impacts of business decisions.

- The EE is marked using the assessment criteria in the EE Guide (see https://goo.gl/2pGFLH). Make sure you get a copy of this and become familiar with the expectations for each criterion.

- Examiners will not read beyond the 4,000th word of the EE (excluding the bibliography and appendices). This clearly means that marks will be lost.

* Note that from 2018, students may also use (appropriate) analytical tools that are not included in the syllabus, such as Michael Porter's *five forces analysis* or Porter's *generic strategies*.

Exam tip !

Ensure that all components of the EE are unmistakably related to the research question. This will help you to maintain focus and not drift off the subject.

Note: the 4,000-word limit does not include the: acknowledgements, contents page, maps, charts, diagrams, annotated illustrations, tables, equations, formulae and calculations, citations/references, footnotes or end notes, the bibliography and appendices. Also, the RPPF is not part of the 4,000 word limit.

© IBO, 2018

Formulating an Extended research question

- The essay should be phrased as a probing question, i.e. one that demands inquiry.

- The research question should allow the student to show and use a variety of analytical tools.

- Make sure the research question has a clear focus that allows the application of BM theory, tools and techniques. This is often supported by statistical data to assist discussion and evaluation.

CORE

Supplementary information

- The essay should also allow the student to engage in broad and detailed research, requiring the selection and use of a range of sources.

Examples of suitable EE research questions:

1. How significant is market positioning in establishing Audi as a premium brand in Hong Kong?

2. How effective has the joint venture between 7-Eleven and Ocean Park been as a growth strategy?

3. How effective have the campaigns of Ronald McDonald House Charities been in raising awareness of McDonald's corporate social responsibility in Bromley, UK?

4. To what extent has the joint venture between Nestle and Haagan Dazs increased its market share in the US ice cream industry in Denver, Colorado?

5. To what extent is cost-plus pricing suitable for Savita Solar?

6. How significant is Maslow's hierarchy of needs in explaining the improved level of motivation at the English Schools Foundation?

7. How effective has the takeover of Cadbury's been as a growth strategy for Kraft Foods in the Chicago, USA?

8. To what extent are ethical objectives relevant to Pamoja in delivering its online courses?

9. Will HTC's release of its latest smartphone save it from insolvency?

10. Should Ford remove its sedans from it product portfolio in order to focus on its SUVs and Mustang models in its Kansas City Assembly Plant?

Should Ford focus on its best-sellers, such as the Mustang?

Format of the Extended Essay

- Title page - include the essay research question, your personal code, and the date of submission.

- Contents page - show all sub-sections of the essay, including page numbers.

- Introduction - this section includes a brief background to the organization and an outline of the methodology used.

- Body - this section includes the findings (results) and analysis. Good essays show evidence of critical thinking within the body of the EE.

- Conclusion - this should stem from the research carried out, with the conclusion backed with evidence presented in the body of the essay.

- References and bibliography - a comprehensive list that references all sources used. Note that the omission of a bibliography is deemed to be unacceptable for Criterion I, so zero marks would be awarded.

- Appendices - supplementary evidence and supporting documentation (such as excerpts of company annual

CORE

Supplementary information

reports and newspaper articles) should be placed in this section.

Analytical tools

It is vital to incorporate the use of analytical tools in the EE – after all, this is a BM essay. Examples of BM tools, concepts and theories that can aid analysis in the EE include:

- Ansoff matrix (Unit 1.3)

- BCG matrix (Unit 4.5)

- Break-even analysis (Unit 3.3)

- *Budgets* (Unit 3.9)

- Cash flow forecasting (Unit 3.7)

- Cost-based pricing strategies (Unit 4.5)

- *Gantt charts* (Unit 1.7)

- *Decision tree analysis* (Unit 1.7)

- Final accounts (Unit 3.4)

- *Force field analysis* (Unit 1.7)

- Motivation theory (Unit 2.4)

- Investment appraisal (Unit 3.8)

- *Ishikawa fishbone analysis* (Unit 1.7)

- Perception maps (Unit 4.2)

- Ratio analysis (Units 3.5 and 3.6)

- Stakeholder mapping (Unit 1.4)

- STEEPLE analysis (Unit 1.5)

- SWOT analysis (Unit 1.3)

Note: analytical tools, techniques and theories in italics are HL Only.

Assessment criteria

The EE is marked out of **34 marks**. All extended essays are marked according to the following set of assessment criteria:

- Criterion A: Focus and method 6 marks

- Criterion B: Knowledge and understanding 6 marks

- Criterion C: Critical thinking 12 marks

- Criterion D: Presentation 4 marks

- Criterion E: Engagement 6 marks.

© IBO, March 2018

As critical thinking accounts for around 35% of the assessment criteria, a critical approach to the Business Management EE, in which students display the skills of analysis and evaluation, is absolutely essential.

Citation and referencing

Although there are no points explicitly for citation and referencing (C&R), it is expected as part of the IB's guidelines on academic honesty. Moreover, C&R forms part of Criterion D (formal presentation), worth 4 marks. Incorrect referencing is viewed as academic malpractice, so can result in a failing condition. Ultimately, it is the student's responsibility to ensure that the EE is authentic, so the works or ideas of others must be acknowledged fully and accurately. Students should use a recognised system of academic referencing, such as the Modern Languages Association (MLA) system.

Examiner Report feedback

The regular EE Subject Reports feature some useful tips for both teachers and students, including the need to:

- Spend adequate time to formulate a research question and framework for the essay.

- Read past essays to gain a better understanding of the requirements of the EE.

- Read and interpret the Assessment Criteria before, during and after the EE has been written.

- Maintain a good working relationship and open communications between the EE supervisor and the student.

Exam tip !

Students should 'mark' a past Extended Essay using the Assessment Criteria. The marks can then be discussed with the supervisor. This should help students gain a better understanding of the Assessment Criteria before they write their own essay.

Getting help

- Teachers should consult with staff at the school who have more EE supervision experience.

- Get help directly from the school's EE Coordinator.

- Students should use their school librarian for resources and/or for suggestions to develop research and referencing skills.

- Teachers should access MyIB for online teacher support materials, including exemplar essays. Your IB Coordinator can help you with setting up an account.

Academic honesty

- Academic honesty can be defined as any act that enables a student to gain an unfair advantage in an assessed piece of work.

- Examples of academic dishonesty include plagiarism, collusion, duplication of work, deliberately missing an assessment deadline, or the fabrication of research data

- It is the student's responsibility to ensure that the EE is his/her own work. The use of ideas or the work of others must be fully acknowledged.

- The IB recommends that students adopt an academic referencing system, such as the Modern Languages Association system (www.mla.org).

- Schools might choose to use computer software, such as www.turnitin.com, to detect plagiarism.

- To help with authenticating the essay, the reflection sessions including the *viva voce* became compulsory for all EEs from 2018.

Note: Each and every EE received by the IB is checked via text matching software for possible academic malpractice.

Final top tips for writing a good Extended Essay

- Choose a topic you are interested in, because the best essays usually stem from a student's genuine interest in a particular topic.

- Ensure your essay is realistically achievable - can you access an appropriate range of different sources, views and perspectives in order to write a sustained argument?

- Get the research question right – this is vital to ensure you meet all the assessment criteria and avoid writing a descriptive essay.

CORE

Supplementary information

- Maintain a good relationship with your supervisor, who can guide you throughout the entire process, including the planning, reflection and writing process of your essay.

- The essay should be written in an objective way (leave out subjective comments and personal preconceptions).

- Focus on the use of secondary data sources for the EE. Primary data can be used if appropriate in supplementing the secondary research.

- The EE is a written (typed) piece of work. Hence, do not include digital and multimedia resources as part of the essay. Instead, cite and reference these resources appropriately.

- The analysis and conclusions should only be derived from the data and evidence presented in the essay.

- Do not introduce anything new in the conclusion, except any unanswered or new questions that may have arisen from the research.

- Make sure there is evidence of critical thinking in the essay. Your EE supervisor can provide some guidance here.

Evidence of critical thinking is vital for a good EE

- Above all, ensure that the essay fulfills the Assessment Criteria.

For further advice about the EE, you may wish to refer to *Extended Essay for the IB Diploma: Skills for Success*, published by Hodder Education. Download a free chapter from the book, and an infographic poster here: https://goo.gl/ECfXNF

Finally, another great resource for teachers and students is IB Review magazine from Hodder Education. There are specific EE articles in each issue, which provide invaluable help for students. Download the free Teacher Edition of *IB Review* here: goo.gl/NujxBV

Good luck to all those undertaking an Extended Essay in Business Management!

6.5 Exam technique

"Proper preparation prevents poor performance." - The five Ps of effective exam preparation

Command words

It is crucial that command words are read properly in the examinations. Each command word in a question indicates to students the depth of answers required (see below). Hence, if asked to **calculate** the break-even point for a business, there is no need to **define** or to **explain** break-even. Note the new syllabus uses Assessment Objectives (AO) rather than Learning Outcomes (as in the previous syllabus).

Define	AO1	**Assessment Objective 1** Demonstrate knowledge and understanding	These command terms require students to learn and comprehend the meaning of information.
Describe	AO1		
Outline	AO1		
State	AO1		

Analyse	AO2	**Assessment Objective 2** Demonstrate application and analysis	These command terms require students to use their knowledge and skills to break down ideas into simpler parts and to see how the parts relate.
Apply	AO2		
Comment	AO2		
Demonstrate	AO2		
Distinguish	AO2		
Explain	AO2		
Suggest	AO2		

Compare	AO3	**Assessment Objective 3** Demonstrate synthesis and evaluation	These command terms require students to rearrange component ideas into a new whole and make judgments based on evidence or a set of criteria.
Compare and contrast	AO3		
Contrast	AO3		
Discuss	AO3		
Evaluate	AO3		
Examine	AO3		
Justify	AO3		
Recommend	AO3		
To what extent	AO3		

Annotate	AO4
Calculate	AO4
Complete	AO4
Construct	AO4
Determine	AO4
Draw	AO4
Identify	AO4
Label	AO4
Plot	AO4
Prepare	AO4

Assessment Objective 4

Demonstrate a variety of appropriate skills

These command terms require students to demonstrate the selection and use of subject-specific skills and techniques.

© IBO, May 2017

Consult the syllabus guide (pages 92–95) for an explanation and example of each of these command words. Note that the command term **'analyse'** has dropped to AO2, to be in line with other Group 3 subjects. Other command terms introduced for exams from 2016 include: annotate, draw and label (all AO4).

Exam tip !

Each and every exam question will contain a command word, so make sure you know what the command term means and the skills level it corresponds to.

Exam tip !

Except for the command terms "State" and "Identify", do not write your answers in bullet point format. This approach tends to encourage students to give vague, unexplained and unsubstantiated responses.

Tackling the exam papers

Due to the intertwining topics in Business Management, the pre-seen Paper 1 case study is useful in promoting a holistic approach to the study of the subject. Paper 1 assesses all five topics of the Business Management syllabus and carries 35% weighting in the examination for HL students and 30% for SL students. It is based on a pre-issued case study about a hypothetical business organization, with the intention of assessing the ability of students to apply relevant Business Management content, concepts and contexts to the given situation.

The Paper 1 examination:

The Paper 1 examination consists of the following structure:

- **Section A** [HL and SL] – answer any *two* out of three structured questions (10 marks each).

- **Section B** [HL and SL] – answer the *one* compulsory structured question, based mainly on the additional unseen material that will be included in the final exam (20 marks).

- **Section C** [HL only] – answer the *one* compulsory extended response question, based mainly on the additional stimulus material. HL topics may be assessed in this section (20 marks).

© IBO, 2017

For **Section C** of Paper 1 [HL only], there are five assessment criteria, each worth 4 marks (see the syllabus Guide for further details, pages 65–68). Use the **KARSI** acronym to remember these:

- Criterion A: **K**nowledge and understanding of tools, techniques and theories

- Criterion B: **A**pplication

- Criterion C: **R**easoned arguments

- Criterion D: **S**tructure

- Criterion E: **I**ndividual and societies

Level	Section	Marks	Total marks	Weighting %	Assessment objectives	Timing (hours)
SL	A	20	40	30	AO1, AO2, AO4	1 hour 15 minutes
	B	20			AO1–AO4	
HL	A	20	60	35	AO1, AO2, AO4	2 hours 15 minutes
	B	20			AO1–AO4	
	C	20			AO3	

Note: Sections A and B can contain common questions for SL and HL examinations.

Paper 1 is 'difficult' in that it seeks extensive **analytical** and **critical thinking** skills. The pre-seen case study paper examines your skills of problem identification, data handling and analysis, critical thinking, judgemental ability, logical reasoning and justified decision-making. The guidelines in this section should enable you to be better prepared to tackle the Paper 1 examination. It is by no means an exhaustive list of ideas and alternative or additional approaches should be used.

Exam tip !

To show evidence of **reasoning**, use the words 'because…' (to explain/justify the reasons why you have presented certain arguments), 'such as…', and 'for example…'.

5 things to do when you get the Paper 1 Case Study

1. Make a copy of the case study – one as an original reference and one to write notes on. You might want to photocopy this on A3 paper so that there is more space for you to make notes in the margins. Key stakeholders, theories, decisions, constraints, opportunities or problems can be written in the margins for future reference.

2. Read through the case study carefully to get an overall feel and idea about the organization, the people involved and the problems it faces. Do this twice!

3. Make sure that you understand all the issues arising from the case study. Use a dictionary to look up key terms or words that you do not understand.

4. HL students should identify and apply the relevant sections of the syllabus exclusive to them, e.g. organizational planning tools (Unit 1.7), corporate culture (Unit 2.5), industrial/employee relations (Unit 2.6) and contingency planning (Unit 5.7).

5. Obtain a soft copy of the case study in PDF format to make searching much easier. You can also convert the PDF file to Word format using free online software (www.pdftoword.comm) to make it easier for you to add notes or references to the case study.

Exam tip !

Whilst tackling the pre-seen case study, it is important to remember the following:

- Avoid copying large chunks of the case study, even if these are in quotation marks, because this wastes time and does not really reveal your level of understanding.
- Support answers with information and quantitative data presented in the case study.
- Refer to the mark allocations for each question when writing your answers.

10 preparation activities for Paper 1

In preparing for the Paper 1 examination, you may want to tackle the following (generic) tasks. It is important to write your answers in the context of the actual case study.

1. Identify and define all **key terms** in the case study (there are usually around 100 key terms in a pre-seen case study and any of these can be asked in the actual exam!)

2. Produce a **time line** of events (read the case study to produce a chronological list of events and the people involved).

3. Produce, as far as possible, an **organization chart** for the business. Alternatively, you could produce a **personnel profile** of all the people mentioned in the case study:

CORE

Supplementary information

643

who they are, their roles, their strengths/weaknesses and so forth.

4. Study the **financial information** of the organization to determine its financial position. If possible, carry out a full **ratio analysis** of the business and comment on your findings. Figures may be given, or ratios can be worked out from the final accounts, often attached in the appendices of the case study.

5. Produce a **stakeholder map** (see Unit 1.4) for the organization. Distinguish between the internal and external stakeholders. Examine the various areas of stakeholder conflict. Determine which stakeholders are the most important.

6. List all the **problems** or **issues** faced by the organization, under headings such as: Finance and Accounts, Human resource management, Marketing and Operations Management. Alternatively, the problems could be classified as internal and external constraints/problems. For HL students, consider the sources of conflict in the organization (Unit 2.6).

7. Produce a fully applied **SWOT analysis** of the business. To test your understanding, you could produce another jumbled up version of the SWOT analysis (Unit 1.3) to see if you can place the points in the correct category (strengths, weaknesses, opportunities or threats).

8. Conduct an overall **STEEPLE analysis** (Unit 1.5) for the business by examining the opportunities and threats outlined in the case study. This will usually involve an analysis of the data in the appendices.

9. Produce a **podcast** of the case study. You can then listen to the case study on your media player; ideal for auditory learners and a great way to learn the case study.

10. Apply relevant **business management theory** to the case study, e.g. you could try to use the Ansoff Matrix (Unit 1.3) to examine the strategic options available to the organization.

When tackling Paper 1 examination questions, consider the following points:

- Use relevant examples from the case study to support your answers (there is no need to reference the line number, as examiners will be familiar with the case study).

- Consider the context of the organization. For example, public sector organizations have different aims and objectives compared with private companies or charitable social enterprises.

- Similarly, remember that all business decisions will affect the personnel of the organization. Hence, when making recommendations, consider the need for training and/or the effect on staff morale (wellbeing).

- Since Business Management is an integrated subject, analogies and examples from other (relevant) case studies that you have studied can be used to help support your answers.

Teachers may also be interested in the annual Case Study Pack distributed by L7E (www.level7education.com), which includes a wide variety of classroom activities and separate SL and HL Paper 1 mock exams, with full mark schemes.

Good luck with all your preparations!

The Paper 2 examination:

The Paper 2 examination is the largest component for SL and HL students, accounting for 45% and 40% of the examination respectively. All assessment objectives (AO1 to AO4) are tested in all three sections, covering all five sections of the syllabus. Paper 2 consists of the following structure:

- **Section A** [HL and SL] – answer *one* of the two quantitative questions. (10 marks)

- **Section B** – SL students answer *one* and HL students answer *two* of the three structured questions from Units 1 to 5 of the syllabus. (20 marks per question)

- **Section C** [HL and SL] – answer *one* of the three conceptual essays with a focus on any two of the CUEGIS concepts that underpin the Business Management course. (20 marks)

© IBO, 2017

Level	Section	Marks	Total marks	Weighting %	Assessment objectives	Timing (hours)
SL	A	10	50	45	AO1, AO2 and AO4	1 hour 45 minutes
	B	20			AO1–AO4	
	C	20			AO3	
HL	A	10	70	40	AO1, AO2 and AO4	2 hours 15 minutes
	B	40			AO1–AO4	
	C	20			AO3	

Note: Paper 2 can contain common questions for SL and HL examinations, although HL students answer more questions.

Section C

- The main focus of the questions will be on *two* of the six concepts – but you need to draw on your knowledge of other relevant content, concepts and contexts to answer the question.

- There is no stimulus material included, so you will need to rely on your ability to apply real-world examples and case studies examined during your course and/or your Internal Assessment.

- You need to address the question in relation to (at least) one real-world business organization. This means you should not refer to the (hypothetical) business organization in Paper 1. You cannot use any of the case studies in Section A and B of Paper 2 either.

- As part of your holistic judgement, you should consider the perspectives of different stakeholder groups (individuals and societies) of the real-world business organization.

- HL students are expected to draw on their knowledge of HL topics in the syllabus.

For **Section C** Paper 2 (SL and HL), there are five assessment criteria, each worth 4 marks. These can be remembered by using the acronym **KARSI** (which also applies to Section C of the HL Paper 1):

- Criterion A: **K**nowledge and conceptual understanding

- Criterion B: **A**pplication

- Criterion C: **R**easoned arguments*

- Criterion D: **S**tructure

- Criterion E: **I**ndividual and societies   © IBO, 2017

Refer to pages 68 – 70 for an explanation of each criterion. Note that it is not necessary for every single part of the level descriptor to be met in order for examiners to award the top marks – examiners will apply the "best fit" level descriptor.

However, if you only address **one** of the two concepts in the essay, the following will apply:

- Up to *3 marks* for Criteria A, B, C and E

- Up to *4 marks* for Criterion D (structure).

This means a student *can* earn up to 16 marks out of 20 marks if only one of the two concepts are addressed. However, this is not something that students should be encouraged to do! The reality is that most candidates will lose up to half the marks in Criteria A, B, C and E.

In particular, for Criterion C, a candidate can be awarded up to *2 marks* if an unbalanced, one-sided argument is presented. Counter-arguments must be provided to be awarded more than *2 marks*. For *3 marks*, some arguments are balanced or justified. For *4 marks*, there is a two-sided argument, with justification provided.

As with all good essays, the structure (Criterion D) requires:

- An introduction

- A body

- A conclusion

- Fit-for-purpose paragraphs.

When writing fit-for-purpose paragraphs (Criterion D), remember to use the PEELS framework. Each paragraph should contain:

- A single point (the idea or argument being presented)

- An explanation of your point

- Examples to help clarify your argument

- A link back to the CUEGIS essay question

- Consideration of different stakeholder perspectives to show evidence of critical thinking.

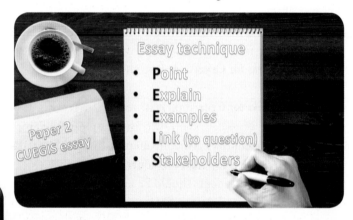

For Criterion E (individuals and societies), it is required to consider the perspectives of an **individual** as well as a stakeholder **group(s)**. An individual could be the CEO, Founder, manager, or even an employee. Stakeholder groups can include consumers, management team, board of directors, employees, suppliers, creditors, the local community, pressure groups, or the government. For 4 marks, the CUEGIS essay must contain a balanced response, with consideration of the perspective of at least one individual and one stakeholder group. The individual and group(s) must be clearly applicable and relevant to the essay question

Exam tip !

Where appropriate, consider a brand ambassador or celebrity as an individual for the organization. These individuals can have a huge impact on the business, especially with the use of social media such as Twitter, Facebook and Instagram.

The 225 exam-style questions in this textbook follow the style of Paper 2 examinations. Also, use past examination papers for

further practise. There are over 125 short case studies featured throughout the textbook to get you engaged in your learning.

The choice of organization

The assessment rubrics clearly state that the organization used in the CUEGIS essay must not be from the Paper 1 case study (a fictitious organization), or any of the organizations that appear in Sections A and B of Paper 2. If a candidate does not comply with this rule, the maximum marks they can be awarded is 6 out of 20 marks:

- Up to *1 mark* for Criterion A, as the student might show some understanding of the concepts, although the fictitious organizations makes both content and context irrelevant.

- Zero marks for Criterion B, as there is no connection made to a real organization.

- Up to *1 mark* for Criterion C, as the arguments and reasoning can only be superficially justified.

- Up to *4 marks* for Criterion D (structure).

- Zero marks for criterion E, as the perspectives of stakeholders (at least one individual and group) is irrelevant (to the fictitious organization).

Top tips for the CUEGIS essay

- Do not try to write a "model" answer from an essay you have previously studied – focus instead on addressing what the actual question is asking.

- All CUEGIS essays refer to two concepts. Too often, students neglect one of these concepts.

- Learn to structure your essay; use fit-for-purpose paragraphs (see PEELS and KARSI frameworks above).

- Learn to integrate stakeholder perspectives throughout the essay; too often, this is done as an afterthought and superficially at the end of the essay.

- For questions that asks for impacts of two concepts on BM content, it is acceptable to explain that one concept may be of more significance to the organization than the other.

- For Criterion C (reasoning), do not allow the examiner to ask "Why?" or "How is this relevant?", i.e. ensure you

CORE

Supplementary information

explain your arguments and provide adequate evidence of logic, information (or data), and reasoning.

Teachers may also be interested in the 50 Excellent CUEGIS Essays Pack distributed by L7E (www.level7education.com). The Pack includes 50 essays for students to read and mark, and teacher versions to show where the examiners have awarded each assessment criterion, along with an overall comment about the quality of each essay.

Top tips for improving evaluation in Business Management

"Do not go where the path may lead; go instead where there is no path and leave a trail." - Ralph Waldo Emerson (1803–1882), US philosopher

The hierarchy of skills

Examination scripts are marked against a set of assessment criteria. These in turn test the student's demonstration of skills, from knowledge of information (which crudely equates to a Level 4) and evaluation (Level 7).

- Evaluation

- Examination

- Application

- Information (Knowledge)

What is 'examination'?

- 'Examine' means the assessment of a business management issue or problem.

- It requires the weighing up of the relative importance of different arguments.

- 'Examine' as a command term considers a balanced, two-sided argument.

- It requires current real-world examples to add substance to your answers.

What is 'evaluation'?

- Evaluation compares different views about a business management issue or problem.

- Views and arguments are substantiated, with examples and evidence provided where possible.

- Evaluation requires a reasoned (justified) conclusion.

- Judgement is made about which argument holds most significance.

- It requires evidence of critical thinking (think TOK!)

Evaluation and Theory of knowledge (TOK)

The skill of evaluation is embedded in TOK (see Unit 6.3). Evaluation is as much about asking questions as answering them. For example, students might question:

- Business Management theories, tools and concepts – are these culturally biased? Do they apply to different organizations across the globe? Are they applicable (realistic) in the real and complex business world?

- Data and statistics – how reliable are the results? Is there a 'hidden agenda' behind the figures, such as the possibility of window dressing (see Unit 3.4)? How up to date are the data?

Evaluation and the integrated nature of Business Management

Remember that BM is an integrated discipline and therefore a single event will have impacts on other aspects of a business. For example, a hostile takeover is likely to affect:

- Organizational structure (Unit 2.2)

- Leadership and management (Unit 2.3)

- Levels of staff motivation (Unit 2.4)

- Organizational and corporate culture (Unit 2.5)

- Cash flow and working capital (Unit 3.7)

- *Budgets (Unit 3.9)*

- *Crisis management and contingency planning (Unit 5.7).*

Useful evaluation phrases

The suggested phrases below might help to focus your answers and incorporate critical thinking to show that you are evaluating Business Management concepts, theories and tools. Remember that the best answers are written in the context of the case study, with application of real-world examples where appropriate.

- However, …

- Nevertheless, …

- On the other hand, …

- Conversely, …

- By contrast, …

- In reality, …

- Other stakeholders of the organization might …

- In the short term … but in the long term …

- Time lags should be considered because …

- This is likely to cause … because …

- The most significant of these factors to the organization is … because …

- Managers might question the feasibility of this option because …

- Hence, this might not be practical because …

- This could cause conflict in the organization because …

- Other factors should be considered by the organization, such as … because …

- It depends on whether …

- The text suggests that … although …

- The data in the case study imply … but …

- Overall, …

- In conclusion …

Evaluation frameworks

It is useful to have a framework when writing your longer-response answers, such as questions about business strategy. This applies to your Internal Assessment as well as the final exams (external assessment). Here are four frameworks that you might find useful.

1. The DEAD and DEADER Principles

Brett Hillman and Fiona Charnley passed on a top tip during an IB Workshop that I was running in Hong Kong: the DEAD and DEADER principles. In order to gain a Level 6, students have to include:

- **D**efinition(s)

- **E**xplanations/examples

- **A**dvantages

- **D**isadvantages

In order to gain a Level 7, students need to demonstrate two more skills:

- **D**efinition(s)

- **E**xplanations/examples

- **A**dvantages

- **D**isadvantages

- **E**valuation

- **R**ecommendation(s)

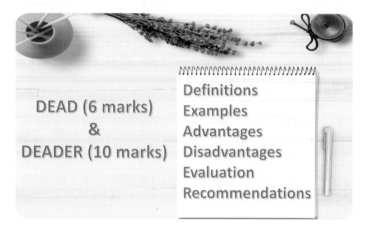

DEAD (6 marks)
&
DEADER (10 marks)

Definitions
Examples
Advantages
Disadvantages
Evaluation
Recommendations

CORE

Supplementary information

The DEADER acronym is particularly useful as 'Recommendations' reminds us that Business Management is ultimately about two things: **problem-solving** and **decision-making** in business organizations.

2. The SSCCOOMM Principle

Barbara Cooper, a former Vice Principal at Victoria Shanghai Academy in Hong Kong, introduced me to the SSCCOOMM framework:

- **S**takeholder influence / perspectives

- **S**hort-term vs long-term impacts

- **C**ost implications

- **C**hange management

- **O**pportunity cost (every decision has an alternative)

- **O**bjectives

- **M**arket trends

- **M**anagement and leadership styles / expertise / preference

3. The DATE SLAP© Principle

My students really like this one – go on a DATE with an examiner to score high marks!

- **D**efinitions

- **A**pplication

- **T**heory

- **E**valuation.

At the end of the date, you don't want to see the examiner again, so make a judgement call – add a SLAP to conclude the end of your date:

- **S**takeholder perspectives

- **L**ong term versus short term impacts

- **A**ssumptions made in the arguments

- **P**rioritise your arguments.

Students are often confused about how best to evaluate, so use any combination of the above SLAP methods to help.

Of course, your DATE doesn't have to end with a SLAP, as you may choose to just be PALS.

4. The LOSERS© Principle

My personal (and favourite) acronym is the **LOSERS©** principle. In evaluating the strategic options and decisions of a business, it is important to consider the:

- **L**ong term – strategic decision-making is about a firm's future direction and competitiveness.

- **O**bjectives – are the strategic decisions in line with the organization's corporate objectives?

- **S**takeholders – who are the key stakeholders? Which ones are most affected by the decision?

- **E**xternal environment – what are the constraining and driving forces that are beyond the firm's control?

- **R**esources – does the business have the financial and human resources to implement the plans (recommendations)?

- **S**ynergies – overall, does the decision or strategy add value (synergy) to the organization?

CORE

Supplementary information

Top five exam preparation tips

Continuous effort – not strength or intelligence – is the key to unlocking our potential. Sir Winston Churchill (1874–1965), UK prime minister 1940–1945 and 1951–1955

Tip #1 – Learn the command terms

It is crucial that command words are read properly in the examinations. Each command word in a question indicates to students the depth of response that is required. Hence, if asked to *calculate* the break-even point for a business, there is no need to *define* or to *explain* the concept of break-even. Refer to the Business Management guide for an explanation and example of each of these command words (pages 92–95).

Do you know what is required of these command terms? If not, find out or ask your teacher!

- Analyse

- Complete

- Explain

- Identify

- Outline

- Annotate

- Construct

- Examine

- Justify

- Recommend

Note: if using past examination questions for your revision, note that 'analyse' is no longer an AO3 command term in the new BM syllabus (first examinations in 2016).

Tip #2 – Learn the structure of the exam papers

There are two externally assessed papers for the BM exams. **Paper 1** assesses all five topics of the syllabus. It is based on a pre-seen case study, usually around 4 pages in length, and based around a hypothetical organization. There will be additional unseen material added to both sections B and C in the final exam. The Paper 1 examination accounts for 30% of the SL exam and 35% of the HL exam. It consists of the following structure:

- **Section A** [HL and SL] – answer *two* of the three structured questions (2 x 20 marks)

- **Section B** [HL and SL] – answer the compulsory structured question* (20 marks)

- **Section C** [HL only] – answer the compulsory question using mainly the additional material* (20 marks).

*Additional material is included in these sections in the actual examination.

The **Paper 2** examination is the largest component of the exam, accounting for 45% of the SL examination and 40% of the HL examination. All assessment objectives (AO1 to AO4) are tested in all three sections. Paper 2 consists of the following structure:

- **Section A** [HL and SL] – answer *one* of the two quantitative questions (10 marks)

- **Section B** – SL students answer *one* and HL students answer *two* of the three structured questions from Units 1 to 5 of the syllabus (20 marks per question)

- **Section C** [HL and SL] – answer *one* of the three conceptual essays with a focus on the CUEGIS concepts that underpin the Business Management course (20 marks).

Tip #3 – Plan your revision carefully

Trying to learn the whole Business Management syllabus without a proper plan is not going to work. A more effective technique is to revise sections of the syllabus in manageable sessions, following a well-structured revision timetable. For example, you might want to revise Finance and Accounts in a particular revision session, perhaps focusing on one or two aspects, such as cash flow forecasting (Unit 3.7) or sources of finance (Unit 3.1).

It is vital to build in revision time to learn your quantitative methods. There are plenty of formulae to learn, especially as not all of these are included in the formulae sheets in the exams, such as:

- Average costs (Unit 3.2)

- Break-even output (Unit 3.3)

- Closing balance (Unit 3.7)

- Margin of safety (Unit 3.3)

- Net profit (Unit 3.4)

- Payback period (Unit 3.8)

- Reducing balance depreciation (Unit 3.4)

- Variance (Unit 3.9).

Whatever you do, don't leave everything until the last minute – you simply cannot revise the entire BM curriculum in a few nights. Without a plan, you don't know where you're going and how you're going to get there. This means valuable revision time is likely to be wasted. Remember the famous saying that failing to plan is planning to fail. Below is a list of some of the things you could try as part of your revision plan:

- Use the BM syllabus (pages 24–49) as a starting point when planning your revision.

- Draw up a revision plan for each week – and stick to it! Some flexibility might be necessary but remain focused and disciplined.

- Take careful note of the Assessment Objectives in the syllabus as examiners use these when setting exam questions!

- Allocate more time to the topics that you find most difficult.

- Build in time for sufficient rest breaks and recreation; a refreshed mind is a more productive one.

- Don't procrastinate – turn off your smartphone, games consoles and the Internet (personally, I think Twitter, Instagram, WhatsApp and YouTube are great, but they must be the world's best procrastination tools!)

Tip #4 – Learn the quantitative methods

The BM syllabus incorporates many quantitative techniques (HL topics shown in italics) such as:

- *Decision trees (Unit 1.7)*

- Investment appraisal (Unit 3.8)

- *Budgeting (Unit 3.9)*

- Cash flow forecasting (Unit 3.7)

- Balance Sheets (Unit 3.4)

- *Depreciation (Unit 3.4)*

- Profit and Loss accounts (Unit 3.4)

- Ratio analysis (Units 3.5 and 3.6)

- *Gantt charts (Unit 1.7)*

- Market share (Unit 4.1)

- Costs and revenue (Unit 3.2)

- Break-even analysis (Unit 3.3)

- *Cost to make (Unit 5.5)*

- *Four-part moving averages (Unit 4.3).*

It is important to learn these quantitative techniques and to be able to use them to aid decision-making. Make sure you know the formula for the following:

- Average cost

- Break-even point

- Capital employed

- Closing balance

- Cost of goods sold

- Gross profit

- Labour turnover

- *Lead time*

- Market share

- Net assets

- Net cash flow

- Net profit

- Payback period

- *Re-order quantity*

- Safety margin

- *Straight line depreciation*

- Total costs

- Unit contribution

- *Variance*

- Working capital.

Again, make sure you learn the definitions and the formulae for the above. Note that the terms in *italics* apply only to HL students.

Tip #5 – Practise, practise, practise

Ask your teacher for some past BM exam papers and have a go at answering the questions under timed conditions – especially the quantitative questions. There's nothing like applying BM to a case study about motivation or leadership to really reinforce your knowledge and understanding.

Revision and Study Tips

Read these ten articles, which provide plenty of revision and study tips in preparation for the exams.

1. Read this article from *The Guardian* with suggestions about how to improve your study habits: https://goo.gl/xm2hes

2. This article discusses wow to pass your exams, with 10 tips and tricks: https://goo.gl/LX8HHD

3. Written for university students in mind, this article from the *Times Higher Education* (THS) gives tips on how to deal with exam stress: https://goo.gl/EUdvTF

4. This article provides five practical tips for revising over the holidays: https://goo.gl/iZhb5c

5. This article from *Teacher Toolkit* gives five top tips to survive the exam season: https://goo.gl/RzxsN5

6. Read this article from *The Telegraph* about how to get a better score in the IB: https://goo.gl/q45gwT

7. This OSC blog provides some very useful advice for IB Diploma students, about how best to revise, review, and remember: https://goo.gl/DmsBJL

8. Here is some top revision tips and advice for your IB exams, provided by an IB alumni: https://goo.gl/b3Xe24

9. Being organized is vital to succeed in your studies. This blog provides some excellent study and exam advice to IB students: https://goo.gl/Ui3nK8

10. Finally, some top tips from a student who achieved 45 points in the IB Diploma: https://goo.gl/nadnKt.

Final message from the author

Dear students,

I hope that you find this fourth edition textbook to be of interest and of use in preparing you for learning the Business Management course. I hope you enjoy reading the book as much as I have enjoyed writing it. Two final pieces of advice come from a couple of my favourite proverbs:

On time management and organization:
"Tomorrow is often the busiest day of the week." Spanish proverb.

On evaluation:
"One-third of what you see is in front of your eyes, the other two-thirds are behind your eyes."
Chinese proverb

Best wishes for your studies and examinations!

Paul Hoang

Email: paulhoang88@gmail.com

Twitter: @paulhoang88 #IBBusinessManagement

Index

Index